Aptitudes and Instructional Methods

APTITUDES AND INSTRUCTIONAL METHODS

A HANDBOOK FOR RESEARCH ON INTERACTIONS

LEE J. CRONBACH

and

RICHARD E. SNOW

STANFORD UNIVERSITY

1977

IRVINGTON PUBLISHERS, INC., NEW YORK
Distributed by HALSTED PRESS, Division of
JOHN WILEY & SONS, INC.
NEW YORK   LONDON   TORONTO   SYDNEY

Copyright © 1977 by IRVINGTON PUBLISHERS, INC.

Distributed by HALSTED PRESS
A division of JOHN WILEY & SONS, Inc., New York

Library of Congress cataloging in publication information:
Cronbach, Lee Joseph, 1916–
  Aptitudes and instructional methods.

  1. Educational tests and measurements. 2. Teaching.
I. Snow, Richard E., joint author. II. Title. LB3051.C76
371.1'02   76-5510
ISBN 0-470-15066-1

Printed in the United States of America

To
HELEN
and
ALEXANDRA

Preface

Our book is addressed to psychologists and educators who are learning to ask a new question about individual differences. The question posed during the past century was, almost invariably, upon whom should society place its bets? Society wants good leaders and invests massive resources to get them. But it tends to forget that what constitutes talent depends on the conditions in which the race is run. On a rainy day the horseplayer bets on a horse he would never choose for a dry track. There are even culprits who wet down the track to capitalize on the talents of the horse who "under standard conditions" would be an also-ran. In education, the time has come to vary the track conditions so that more runners will finish strong. For many, standard conditions are not best conditions.

What lies before us is the task of accumulating knowledge about how a person's characteristics influence his or her response to the alternatives educators can offer or invent. It is unconscionable merely to predict which few will win. Probable losers must be converted into winners. That is the psychological and social enterprise to which this book is a contribution.

Much as we favor adaptation of schooling, we have had to retreat from the simple concept of "placement decisions" out of which our work originated. Instructional decisions must be based on a whole complex of student characteristics and teacher actions. There is no such thing as a homogeneous group of students or a specifiable "method" of instruction. Educational practice over the next decade or two—if not eternally—will have to make its adaptations informally and judiciously, not by an actuarial technology of cutting scores and regression equations. But with greater knowledge the adaptations can profitably be more radical than they have been in the past.

In any applied science the day when one stands atop a problem and sees its contours clearly is far distant from the day the problem first looms on the horizon. The expedition cannot head straight for the summit. At first there will be wandering excursions into the foothills. Some end in culs-de-sac; some capture distant views of promising paths for the ascent. Further preparation—the invention of incisive research methods, and the consolidation of limited substantive findings—comes before even a base camp is established. Only then does the climb toward grander theories and tested applications begin. As yet, research workers have only wandered among the foothills of the problem of differential response to instruction. This book aspires to be a Lewis-and-Clark report, coming at the end of a significant period of exploration. It describes a rich and rewarding territory and provides a handbook for the surveyors and settlers to come.

With few exceptions, we have limited ourselves to research on instruction. Other research on interactions could be drawn from the experimental laboratory and from applied settings other than the school. We have not reviewed the literature in clinical or organizational psychology, where interaction research is also coming to the fore. Our methodological statements are fully pertinent to such fields, however, and some of our substantive conclusions will be suggestive there.

This state-of-the-art report has been more difficult to assemble than anticipated when we began in 1965. One reason is the breadth of the topic. To study scores on conventional ability tests is not sufficient, for the student's response to instruction is, in principle, conditioned by *all* his characteristics, including personality traits. It is necessary also to consider what Glaser calls "the new aptitudes," the specific intellectual-processing skills that are lost from sight in an aggregate mental measure.

We have located more research than anticipated. In the older literature, many interactions were reported incidentally; now, deliberate work on interactions is gaining momentum. Nor did we anticipate the amount of critical review that would be needed before the literature could be collated. We discovered that the words of an investigator's conclusion need not coincide with what the tabled data told us. As we gained insight into the statistical peculiarities of Aptitude x Treatment interactions, we found that conventional notions of elegant design and statistical rigor had misled investigators and had given false impressions to the reader of journals. The predominant techniques evaluate the soundness of one particular hypothesis on the basis of one isolated set of data, often a small set. This is poor strategy for the initial mapping of a field; explorations ought to be cumulative. Our book was originally intended to bring together what has been established by past inquiry. While the book fulfils this function, our main purpose now is to make future studies more enlightening. We believe our survey of the past literature to be sufficiently comprehensive that further search would not appreciably alter our conclusions. We have probably overlooked a few important findings, since our search has had to rely more on serendipity than system. We have excluded studies for which we had only an abstract, since it is impossible to evaluate a purported finding without a full report. The amount of space given to a study is not necessarily proportional to its significance. At times important studies are described succinctly. On the other hand, we have felt a particular obligation to elaborate our reasoning when we did not accept an author's conclusion, so that a person doing similar studies in the future will profit from the example.

As this comment implies, we have done far more than recount the literature. We started with that intent, but found ourselves increasingly forming our own conclusions from the investigators' tables, charts, and appendices, and at times we have borrowed original data for reprocessing. This gives us a large body of original research to report even though the data rarely originated with us.

It is a sign of forward movement and of the interest in our topic that we must now apologize to investigators misled by our unpublished report of 1969. To fulfil a contract obligation, we were forced by the supporting agency to deliver the report prematurely. Its preface warned that our thinking was incomplete and not to be trusted. This was thoroughly demonstrated in the subsequent years, during which we located many sources overlooked earlier, became aware of the critical relevance of statistical power, and consequently changed our interpretations of individual studies and sometimes of whole bodies of literature. We have now had to dismiss some published findings we once trusted, and have occasionally unearthed positive evidence buried beneath an author's original negative conclusion. Even though we distributed only a few copies of the 1969 report, the topic concerned enough psychologists that the report was widely cited and followed. Long after we had changed our views, the initial report was still influencing investigators. We recognize the risk that some of the ideas in the present book may also misdirect efforts since ideas in this field are still forming. But at least the present volume is issued after considerable reflection, and was sent to the publisher at a time of our own choosing.

We are indebted to many colleagues at Stanford and elsewhere who over the years have challenged or encouraged our views, supplied us with unpublished material, and helped us to state our ideas more accurately and clearly. Janet Elashoff, Rosedith Sitgreaves, and Joseph Deken have contributed greatly to our statistical understanding and have corrected many errors in Chapters 2 through 4. Our students have carried out a number of informative investigations and we have learned much in looking over their shoulders. Students and associates have also made literature searches, and processed data for us; these include Katherine Baker, Susan Crockenberg, Mike Friedman, Jennifer Greene, Nancy Hamilton Markle, Akimichi Omura, Pearl Paulsen, Penelope Peterson, Tamarra Pickford, Enoch Sawin, Nicholas Stayrook, and Reenie Webb. Many others have helped through seminar discussions of portions of this book. We especially thank our secretaries, Pat R. Jones and Olga Baca, for meeting exceptional demands. Preparation of a limited amount of material in Chapter 4 and elsewhere, on new analytic methods, was supported by a grant from the Spencer Foundation in 1973-74.

Lee J. Cronbach

Richard E. Snow

Contents

Contents

List of figures

List of tables

Chapter 1 | A perspective on aptitude and instruction

The volume of research on learning, instruction, and individual differences is enormous; but only limited progress has been made toward an integrated understanding of the nature of individual differences in ability to learn. This book assesses the present state of knowledge and proposes directions for further research and development.

The educational context

The educator continually devises and applies new instructional treatments, hoping for improved results. He seeks the best method of instruction for a given purpose. Since learners differ, the search for generally superior methods should be supplemented by a search for ways to fit the instruction to each kind of learner. One can expect interactions between learner characteristics and instructional method. Where these exist, the instructional approach that is best on the average is not best for all persons.

Intuitive adaptations, guided by the teacher's experience and his impressions of each student, take place continually in the classroom. The task for research is to formulate principles by which the adaptation of instruction can be made systematic and productive. Certainly the casual adaptations teachers make are not the most valid adaptations possible. From Binet's earliest study of children whom teachers identified as intellectually superior to the latest studies of judgments by professional clinical psychologists, biases and errors have been found in impressionistic judgments. Unvalidated actuarial rules are no better justified.

Homogeneous grouping is an example of ill-regulated adaptation. The idea that

1

learners with good school records will profit most from one program, and those
who have done badly in school from another, is reasonable enough. But "Should
the school group its students by ability?" is much too limited a question; research cast in this mold has inevitably given conflicting and useless results. What
is done for the "fast" and "slow" groups has to be the focus of attention. Grouping will have negligible consequences for learning unless the treatment is redesigned to fit each kind of student. Streaming plans intended merely to simplify
the teacher's task are properly condemned as perpetuating social stratification.
Stratification in school is even more objectionable when the plans force different *kinds* of educational goals upon students with different abilities. For most
purposes the school needs a plan that directs all learners in the same intellectual
and developmental directions, but using procedures designed to fit each one's
characteristics. Such a plan could hope to *reduce* social stratification.

It is socially indefensible to give some children good education and some poor
education. This is captured in the slogan "equality of educational opportunity."
But simple equalization too easily degenerates into inviting each child to compete for a place in the system. Guaranteeing a fair race, while putting all the
burden on the individual, is a passive policy. In this century, social policy has
turned to an active effort to design social conditions that will help everyone
to run his strongest race. Jensen (1969) offered the appropriate slogan for the
school: "Optimal diversity of educational opportunity." To spell out just what
is optimal presents tasks for the philosopher, the empirical scientist, and the
practical educator.

Most criticisms of the schools return in some way to the theme of individual
differences and to interactions, though this may not be recognized. Thus it is
contended that the schools are designed to serve the middle class and not the
lower class. This view embraces the hypothesis that children of the working class
and the poor fail not merely because they lack preparation and motivation, but
because they are unready for the *particular* program now usual in schools. It is
further implied that with a change in school organization, curricular materials, or
teaching procedures these students could progress much faster. To be sure, some
changes can be imagined that will benefit all children, but the thrust of the criticism is that certain changes will benefit the lower-class child even if they have
no value to children from middle-class homes.

The methodological context

The scientific problem is to locate interactions of individual differences among
learners with instructional treatments, that is, Aptitude x Treatment interactions.
To establish the existence of interactions requires a special style of educational-
psychological research. Two broad lines of behavioral science, the experimental
and the correlational, have been the standard ways of investigating instructional
methods and aptitudes, respectively. Interaction research combines the two
(Cronbach, 1957, 1975).

Experimental research concerns itself with differences among the effects of treatments or policies. Investigators seek to establish significant main effects, of a form such as "Programmed instruction is superior to lecture-discussion" or "Grouping students by mental age works better than grouping by chronological age." Correlational research concerns itself with the association between characteristics of persons. It tests such hypotheses as "In learning stenography, good spellers succeed more often than poor spellers" or "Independent-minded students are more likely than others to drop out of engineering school." Its method is to compare the standing of persons on one variable with their standing on another.

An interaction is said to be present when a situation has one effect on one kind of person and a different effect on another. Interactional ideas are commonplace in science. The possibility of interaction is recognized in the physical scientist's ubiquitous qualifier "other things being equal . . ." and in the social scientist's "Can you generalize to other groups (communities, cultures, etc.)?" Cronbach (1953), while contrasting the method of "correlation between persons" with the conventional correlation of tests (situations), saw the two methods as playing coordinate roles in sorting out interactions. The whole process of seeking order in behavioral and biological science is one of partitioning a grand matrix of organisms and situations into blocks in such a manner that a single generalization applies to all the organisms and all the situations classified within a block. The science of human behavior is built up by identifying a class of persons who respond similarly to some particular range of situations.

Questions about interaction need especially to be asked in connection with instruction. What characteristics make instructional situations "similar," in the sense that the situations all benefit the same kind of learner? And what variables define "similar" learners, i.e., those ready to profit more or less equally from the same kind of instruction? Theories of instruction cannot be developed until instructional procedures are characterized in reasonably general and comparable terms and pertinent categorizations of learners are invented.

While this book arises out of the concerns of the educational psychologist, most other kinds of psychology also have to investigate interactions. Thus, interaction is a fundamental concept in genetics, and students of the genetic bases of behavior have offered impressive evidence that a treatment has different effects on animals with different genotypes.

All of comparative psychology is concerned with species differences in responses to comparable tasks. While main effects are found—"higher" species do better than "lower" species on most tasks—the differences are not at all consistent across tasks and there are many reversals of order. These inconsistencies are interactions. Excellent examples may be seen in Freedman's study (1958) of response of dogs of different breeds to training on various tasks, or in the Cooper-Zubek (1958) work with maze-bright and maze-dull rats in restricted, normal, and enriched environments.

The social psychologist inquires about the performance of a group, considering the leader's personality or style on one hand, and the group composition or structure on the other; the finding that there is no universally best style of leadership (Fiedler, 1973), indicates that there are interactions to be teased out. Virtually all studies of personality also are interactionist. The finding that some persons are generally more adaptable and emotionally stable, and others not, speaks of a main effect or general factor. But any deeper inquiry has to explain why different persons are sensitive to different stressors. A description of personality in terms of the coping styles or roles a person has mastered likewise implies effective response in one kind of situation and ineffective response in another—i.e., it postulates interactions. In experimental psychology, theories have to take into account the cognitive structure or response repertoire the subject brings to the experimental task; these differ from person to person and facilitate one performance while interfering with another. Interaction is implicit, for example, in psycholinguistic research from Whorf down to Cole, Gay, Glick, and Sharp (1971), where it is suggested that the difficulty of a problem depends on the person's possession of coding machinery appropriate for the specific input. In these various examples, the attributes of the subject that give rise to interactions come from many sources; his genes, the culture that shaped him, his specific developmental history, or his recent motivational history, among others.

Modern statistical methods for experimental and correlational studies derive from the work of Karl Pearson and his contemporaries. R. A. Fisher's series of impressive contributions advanced both lines of inquiry, but he also introduced the possibility of systematically testing for interactions. Some technical developments of the 1930's, particularly those arising in Neyman's wing of the statistics department at the University of London, have been neglected in behavioral science even though highly pertinent to the interaction problem; we shall return to them in due course. Fisherian methods of testing interactions (e.g., between species of wheat and effects of fertilizers) were duly relayed to experimental psychologists. Among experimental studies of learning one finds many reports of significant interactions of IQ or sex (these being formally analogous to Fisher's "species"). Experimenters most often regarded these interactions as nuisances rather than as basic discoveries to be interpreted, but at times such a result became the focus of a special line of investigation, as in the Iowa research on anxiety and learning in the 1950's. As for correlational psychologists, they confined themselves to relating one test to another or to a criterion. They overlooked the pertinence of interactions until developments in mathematical decision theory came to their attention.

In attempting to formulate the problems of the tester in decision-theoretic terms, Cronbach and Gleser (1957, revised 1965) considered the use of tests for classification. A classification or placement test cannot be validated simply by correlating the pretest with subsequent outcome, as in the conventional selection study. Rather, one needs to know whether the outcome is bettered when the treatment is chosen for the individual. Classification research was conducted during World War II, but prediction models rather than decision models were used in its evaluation. Each wartime study was seen as one of selection; e.g., there were comments on "pilot selection" or "navigator selection," even though this work was intended to decide *which* of the two an air cadet should become. With the advent of guidance batteries after the war, thought was given to "differential validity," but the validation procedure was restricted to the study of correlations. Psychometric theorists studying the classification problem (e.g.,

Brogden, 1951) came to recognize the importance of regression or payoff functions. The decision-theoretic work showed formally that to validate a classification procedure one must demonstrate an Aptitude x Treatment interaction (ATI). For any treatment there is a payoff function relating outcome from the treatment to aptitude. Functions for alternative treatments are compared to learn what benefit can be obtained by allocating persons among treatments. An ATI exists whenever the regression of outcome from Treatment A, upon some kind of information about the person's pretreatment characteristics, differs in slope from the regression of outcome from Treatment B on the same information. We shall elaborate upon and qualify this statement later.

Substantive interests of the 1950's and 1960's stirred thought about interactions. We have mentioned the studies of anxiety and learning. An experimental psychology of childhood also emerged, wherein it became apparent that treatment variables often interact with sex, age, social class, etc. Personality theorists and social psychologists, following Lewin and Murray, had begun to emphasize that the situation in which one person functions well is not necessarily best for another. Increasingly, psychologists were urged to bring interactions to the center of the stage. Cronbach (1957) chided "the two disciplines of scientific psychology"—the one for regarding individual differences as "sampling error" beclouding experimental effects, and the other for regarding situational variance as "error in the criterion" that beclouds the prediction of individual success. He urged a fusion of correlational and experimental methods into one discipline. Eysenck (1957) insisted that no sound theory of personality *or* of task performance can be developed; a proper theory must be a theory of person *and* situation.

Despite such tentative moves, interactionist research has gained momentum slowly. The studies are relatively expensive, how to conduct them is unclear, and substantive ideas that could guide such research are little better than speculative.

The time is ripe for stocktaking. Many studies have been reported, in diverse contexts. The concern of educators for adaptation to individual differences is mounting. The concern of psychologists is demonstrated by the numerous references to Person x Situation interaction in each *Annual Review of Psychology*. Research is necessarily highly specific: a study of specific persons exposed to a specific treatment and measured in a specific way. But the main contribution of research is not the microscopic findings of single studies. It is rather the conception of nature that is woven in the debate about and extrapolation from specific findings. The conception, rather than the specific findings, guides men in dealing with the world. One of our aims is to extract broad interpretations, if possible, from the numerous specific reports of interactional studies.

A second outgrowth of research effort is that scientists learn how to investigate. The logic of research into interactions has not been clear, and the special statistical requirements of interaction studies have been little recognized. Investigators have often failed to capitalize on their data. Indeed, demonstrably false conclusions have been reported, due to inappropriate methods of analysis. Until such faults are remedied, the mix of trustworthy and untrustworthy findings in the literature provides a crumbly foundation for theory.

This book, then, aims to survey work on ATI (with particular reference to education), to make methodological recommendations and to indicate suitable strategies for future investigation, and to evaluate the substantive findings now in hand. Lest the reader build up false expectations, we should say at once that well-substantiated findings regarding ATI are scarce. Few investigations have been replicated. Many reports (of both positive and negative results) must be discounted because of poor procedure. Occasionally, results of two sound studies on the same point are strangely inconsistent. The available findings are chiefly useful as leads toward future research rather than as guides to educational practice.

To keep the problem as open as possible, "aptitude" is here defined as any characteristic of a person that forecasts his probability of success under a given treatment. We emphatically do not confine our interest to "aptitude tests." Personality as well as ability influences response to a given kind of instruction. Nontest variables (social class, ethnic background, educational history) may serve as proxies for characteristics of the learner that are not directly measurable. Attention ought to go to variables that were neglected in aptitude tests developed under selection models, since tests that predict outcome under a standard treatment may not be *differentially* predictive of success when more than one treatment is considered. New kinds of aptitude probably need to be detected and measured.

Some current writers are substituting "trait-treatment interaction" (TTI) or the like for the phrase we use. The world will be as well served by any label, so long as the research itself goes forward. We have stressed the term "aptitude" for the paradoxical reason that we hope to persuade the world that it is wrong to conceive of "aptitude" in the traditional narrow way. Any aspect of the individual, including some matters untouched by conventional ability and personality measures, can predict response to instruction and hence can be a source of "aptitude."

We also give "treatment" a broad meaning. It covers any manipulable variable. Instructional studies vary the pace, method, or style of instruction. Classroom environments and teacher characteristics are also treatment variables of interest. Even where a characteristic cannot be manipulated (e.g., teacher sex), the student's experience can be manipulated by an assignment policy. Ultimately, findings about ATI in education have to overarch ideas as diverse as work on the "fit" of personalities to occupational roles or college environments (Pace & Stern, 1958; Stern, 1969; Pervin, 1968), Thelen's (1967) emphasis on principles for assembling teachable groups, and the branching rules and strategies of computer-aided instruction.

The social and philosophical context

Darwinian theory is interactionist—selection is said to occur because a certain species thrived in a certain ecology. Even Spencer's phrase "survival of the fittest" was meant to refer to the likelihood of a species' emerging intact from the stresses of a particular time and place. Spencer and the Social Darwinists who followed him thought only of conditions on the grand scale—and thought little about alternative environments that could be established within that society. Mankind was certain to progress, following in the footsteps of the most highly evolved nation and the most highly capable within that nation. For all present purposes, some men were "fitter" than others. It had been almost universally accepted—even by the environmentalist Locke—that some were born with more talent than others, and Galton's *Hereditary Genius* (1869) proclaimed that talent was not a gift of arbitrary gods but a natural, lawful phenomenon.

Also in the 1860's, Civil Service examinations were being forced down the throats of nepotistic British Cabinet Ministers. These examinations purported to appraise intelligence or general adaptability rather than mere book learning. John Stuart Mill was even proposing that, as the suffrage was broadened, tests be given to determine a man's intellectual qualifications so that he could be allowed a proportionate number of votes.

In most of these discussions, merit was seen as a single rank-ordering, and this concept was ultimately embodied in Spearman's general intelligence or g. Selection on merit was consistent with the Darwinists' emphasis on competition among species, within species, and against natural hazards. Selection by test made the elimination less brutal by changing it to a short sharp shock, and prevented places in government offices and in schools from being preempted by dolts with influential patrons.

The first wave of Social Darwinism, which flourished more in America than in Britain, made competition the highest social principle. The insistence on saving democracy from itself is captured in this quotation from William Graham Sumner:

> Let it be understood that we cannot go outside of this alternative: liberty, inequality, survival of the fittest; not-liberty, equality, survival of the un-fittest. The former carries society forward and favors all its best members; the latter carries society downwards and favors all its worst members.

(See Persons, 1950, pp. 76–77.)

In the 1800's education and social status were increasingly available—to the middle class if not to the poor—as goods to be won by competing. Impartial tests could enable all the likely winners to get into the competition. In the context of 1860, it was liberalizing to make merit the basis for preferment in place of hereditary privilege and patronage. This opened up "equality of opportunity," but it was an equality of opportunity to compete. The terms of the competition were firmly fixed. It was assumed that scholastic examinations in traditional subjects were an adequate machinery for deciding who would move ahead.

Selection tests for admission to higher levels of schooling—which in turn prepared one for Civil Service tests and for the professions—came in only gradually. Influential writers such as Huxley opposed entrance examinations even for the university, while insisting on tests of competence to certify completion of training at each level. There were competitive examinations, however, to select students for grants to the better schools; hence the length and quality of a student's training did depend upon his accomplishment at successive levels. And, increasingly, the length of the person's schooling—whether in a regular program or in an institution for adult education—came to determine his vocational options.

Following World War I, psychological testing of aptitude began to play much of the role formerly played by measures of educational accomplishment. American college admissions were based to a significant degree on the test devised by Thurstone for the American Council on Education, and its successor, the College Board Scholastic Aptitude Test. Tests were given at about the ninth grade to identify pupils who should take algebra and foreign languages, and so to embark on a college preparatory program. Those who did not show to advantage on these tests were not encouraged to aspire to higher education and sometimes were actively discouraged. After World War II, the British examinations at Age 11 were allowed to predetermine the child's fortunes in life. While there was little outright selection in either country at earlier ages, mental tests were used to identify especially promising beginners so that the teacher could give them special encouragement. This was intended to give high-scoring pupils a special advantage and no doubt it did. At the other end of the scale, tests were used to remove the "feebleminded" from school and, under a later policy, to segregate the "educationally handicapped" into special programs.

Selecting those best fitted to survive in the schools had, in the end, a conservative influence. By removing from the academic program students whom teachers could not easily teach, selection made it less necessary for schools and colleges to invent methods for dealing with nonstandard kinds of talent. Meritocratic, single-rank-order selection is only a shade less conservative than the aristocratic selection it replaced, since to a significant degree it also perpetuates advantage of birth.

We urge the social planner to be concerned not with running a fair competition but with running a talent-development operation that will bring everyone somewhere near *his or her* highest level of contribution (with due regard to distributional requirements of the society). The complex technical society needs a high percentage of persons in advanced occupations to maintain physical well-being and promote cultural development. It can use trained persons in large numbers, and it has almost no way to use untrained manpower. Any untrained segment is a source of social chaos and demoralization.

The traditional approach of schools has been to select by attainment. Whoever has a good school record to date is favored in the next stage, being admitted to whatever next program gives higher status and perhaps teaches more. Even at school entrance, vocabulary and work habits learned in the home give the pupil a chance to progress rapidly in basic skills. Early bloomers are favored. Those who do not fit the school as it is are shunted to a lower status at each choice point.

Rank-ordering on verbal, academic tests loses a vast number of talented persons who are in their own way much more excellent (along the lines of dexterity, or leadership, or musical insight, say) than those in the top academic quarter. Suppose that a society were determined to capitalize on the persons who are in the top quarter in any aptitude. Then selecting on just one aptitude would make use of 25 per cent of the population; selecting on two would use 44 per cent; and selecting persons who fall in the top quarter on any one of three aptitudes would classify 58 per cent as talented. (This figure assumes that the aptitudes are uncorrelated; it drops off when allowance is made for the intercorrelation of abilities. But it goes up as more aptitudes are considered.) There are great resources to be tapped if a society can open opportunities to persons who are excellent on dimensions of aptitude other than the traditional verbal-scholastic one.

If multivariate selection were to recognize the many specialized talents, however, it would simply flood advanced schools with prospective failures, so long as the educational methods are still tailored to persons high in verbal-academic accomplishments. Something similar can be said regarding training for skilled jobs, where the training is often verbally loaded even when the job is not. Talent that does not survive the training is lost. Identification of talent in the abstract is *not* the basic problem of aptitude testing; the basic problem is to identify those with readiness to take advantage of a particular niche in the social structure where their particular talent will be utilized or developed.

Aptitude measures and educational methods should form a mutually supporting system. Educational programs need to be designed for the student who does not fit the conventional instruction, and classification procedures need to be designed to choose the right participants for each such program. The old mandate was, "The institution is given; try to pick persons who fit it." The needed mandate is, "Try to design enough treatments so that everyone will be able to succeed in one of them, and route the person into a treatment he fits." That is an entirely different sort of "equality of opportunity."

The competitive, laissez-faire, quasibiological social theory of the first Darwinist movement was succeeded, in the Social Darwinism of Lester Frank Ward (1883) and his followers, by a program of environmental improvement through applied social science. Corwin (in Persons, 1950, pp. 190-191) describes the contrast in views:

    . . . [W]e are confronted with two interpretations of evolution for social application: The Spencerian, laissez faire interpretation and the reformist interpretation. Which one was best warranted by the Darwinian doctrine of biological evolution? Inasmuch as Darwin centers his attention upon the struggle for existence among *creatures* and treats the environment in which this struggle takes place either as relatively inert or as changing in response to factors beyond human control, the answer must undoubtedly be in favor of the Spencerian interpretation. . . .
    . . . Darwin saw all creatures engaged in a struggle for existence, which only those individuals which were best adapted to a particular environment survived to establish new species. From these general premises the laissez faire conclusion of "everyone for himself and the devil take the hindmost" was perfectly logical if not inevitable. . . .
    The transmutation of Darwinism into a gospel of social reform [by Ward in particular] *required a complete reversal of the formula of adaptation of creature to environment.* . . . The formula had to be read backward – instead of the creature being adapted to the *environment, the environment had to be adapted to the creature.*

The new social science was to help design a new social order, just as natural science had created an efficient industrial order. Reforms were pressed on many fronts, and from many different perspectives. Socialists and Progressives alike argued for active governmental programs to offset the advantages that accrued to wealth and centralized economic power. For Ward, the key to social reform was education for all; this is best seen in his *Applied Sociology* (1906), where chapter after chapter relates achievement to "opportunity," and the table of contents abstracts the sections in such uncompromising pronouncements as these:

All environments favorable in proportion as they are educational.
Possibility of creating men of genius at will demonstrated.
Equalizatio.: of intelligence the means to all other equalizations.

With the rise of pragmatism and the admiration of business efficiency, the Progressives pressed for similar efficiency in social institutions. Frederick Taylor and the other efficiency experts preached that there was one best way to do every job in industry, and had industrial structures redesigned on the basis of empirical evidence. The spirit appeared in the experimentalism of the Progressive social reformers, and in education it led to a fixation on efficiency in school management and instruction (Callahan, 1964). The "scientific movement in education" sought to resolve such general issues as the age at which the child should begin school, the best method of teaching reading, and the comparative benefits conferred by alternative curricula. The intent to design the best possible educational environment for children-in-general was but one manifestation of the intent to fit the society to the creature *Homo.* Whereas the first wave of Darwinists thought heredities could be placed in a single order of merit, the Progressive reformers thought of environments as capable of being ordered from good to bad.

The idea that environments and heredities can be rank-ordered still confuses thought. Thus, when an Heredity x Environment interaction is invoked, e.g., to explain differences and similarities in twins, the layman usually thinks of a ranking of heredities and a ranking of environments, whose merits combine multiplicatively as well as additively. Interaction is thus interpreted as merely the mutually reinforcing effect of two pushes in the "good" direction. This view is more wrong than right. Genetics has established a multivariate conception of environments and of heredities and recognizes that the ecology that benefits one genotype blocks the development of another. A similar complexity is required in thinking about social environments.

The interactionist formulation abandons the traditional questions of instructional theory and educational research, such as "What is *the best way* to teach reading?" That tradition—which assumes that environments can be ranked—asks that we engineer and standardize an efficient teaching practice, best for everyone. Interactions lead us instead to diversify treatments. Interestingly, this was the proposal of Ward himself (1906, p. 277): "The only thing that can be done is to equalize opportunities, so as not only to enable the really exceptional man to demonstrate the fact, but to make the open avenues so numerous and so easy to travel that he will be sure to find the one to which he is best adapted by nature." Ward wished not only to see multiple kinds of vocational training, but also multiple secondary curricula for teaching the same general truths to students having different "mental aptitudes" (1883, pp. 621-624). Ward was clearly ahead of his time. In his generation, the chief struggle was to open American education to children from all classes, and the refined interactionist view was only tacked onto the end of his larger argument.

In this century, educators often have adapted and diversified their treatments. An example is the change in American colleges, particularly the less elite ones, as college attendance spread across the population. Colleges have become less standardized, and now cater to a variety of styles and talents. Even so, the matching of students to colleges is almost entirely thoughtless and disorderly. There is little reason to assume, for example, that the person who scores highest on the College Boards should go to the most selective college. His personal style may be such that he will reach a higher peak of fulfillment or social contribution if he goes to, say, a small experimental school that is not especially selective.

Attempts to develop compensatory education can be described in similar terms. There is little payoff from a "Headstart" program designed to attune children to the same old one-track competition, one that seeks to put them on an equal footing only at the moment the starter shouts "Go!" in the first grade. Compensatory preschool programs have some short-term effects, but before long their graduates are falling behind the pack. An education that is merely remedial, in the narrow "training" sense, is insufficient; we have to design a true education that employs unique means wherever the child's distinctive development makes traditional methods ineffective for him.

The meritocratic selector and the experimental reformer alike missed the point of Darwin's theory. The theory did not posit that *generally* superior creatures evolve. Darwin's scientific writings were invariably concerned with fitness to survive in a *particular* ecology. To foster development of a wide variety of persons, then, one must offer a wide variety of environments. A social reform that would standardize the environment (whether to fit the average person, or the present elite, or the present proletariat) is inevitably procrustean, conservative, and self-limiting.

The argument that persons can develop in many ways is not to be confused with blurry values that assume every achievement to be worth as much as every other. In actuality, two kinds of social planning will blend in various proportions: (1) Distinct but honored roles are defined, for which different persons are enabled to prepare themselves. (2) Common objectives are identified, to be obtained in the greatest degree possible by all persons, by whatever method is necessary. Skill in musical performance is likely to be an objective of the first sort; skill in reading, of the second.

To date, differential measurement has served only the first type of social planning, capitalizing on the thought that different people can learn different things or can learn the same things faster. The orientation of this book is to the second type of social planning. It is assumed that information about the learner should help us to adapt instruction to him—to provide an environment in which *he* can thrive. Adaptation to the individual has been a slogan widely held among educators. But such adaptation has never been systematic because no one has known the principles that govern the matching of learner and instructional environment.

The plan of this book

The chapters which follow address themselves to two questions:

What person variables interact with what treatment variables?
What methods of investigation should be pursued in order to add to knowledge of this kind?

The fact that we pose the second question implies that psychologists are not yet in a position to give an adequate answer to the first question. The book has a heavy methodological burden. It would be wrong to offer a conventional review in which the conclusions drawn by the various original investigators are merely compiled. Often we have found an author's conclusions implausible, either because of inadequate analysis or because alternative interpretations of the data were over-looked.

We are candid in our evaluations of the work we review. We hold no scorn for the investigators we criticize and trust that our disagreements give no offense. We have modified our own methodological views substantially over the years. Many a practice or hypothesis we now find fault with we would have considered reasonable at the time the original study was done. This book cannot but mourn the waste of resources habitual in educational research, but we are conscious of our own sins and at various points in the book criticize some of our own previous work.

Chapter 2 offers guidance in matters of research strategy and design of studies. Chapter 3 covers significance testing, and Chapter 4 takes up various advanced topics in data analysis. These chapters are a mixture of discourse at two levels. For the reader with relatively little technical training and interest, they show how the commonplace research procedures must be modified and extended to give sound results in ATI studies. For the advanced reader, they draw attention to little-used techniques and to some techniques still in the process of development. While a full pedagogical effort is employed to make a few key ideas clear, the reader will need to bring to these chapters an understanding of analysis of variance, multiple-regression analysis, multivariate analysis, and true-score theory if he is to grasp everything in them. The reader whose interests are primarily substantive need not absorb every point, but he can and must understand the point of view of these chapters. We rely on them heavily when we move on to review past research.

Chapter 5 reviews the concept of "ability to learn" as it has developed in the psychological literature. This concept has always been on the periphery of research on learning, both human and animal, yet it has received little attention from experimenters. Likewise, it has always been on the periphery of intelligence testing, yet only a few research workers have tried to establish direct connections between tested intelligence and learning. It is inconsistent with an interest in interactions to suppose that there is a single, global "learning ability." What skills and habits make a person a superior learner no doubt depends on the task, the method of instruction, the conditions of practice, and the criterion against which learning is judged. We found it necessary, as a preliminary to work on interactions, to review the literature on learning rates, especially since some writers argue that mental-test scores never forecast success in learning. If that challenge were to be sustained—it is not!—the negative evidence would bear on ATI research. Studies of individual differences in learning reviewed in Chapter 5 point toward limitations of the studies of interaction that are summarized later.

Chapter 6 reflects on the strategy of ATI research in the light of the literature on aptitudes. For example, we have had to consider the implications of Guilford's array of 120 or more separately defined aptitudes. If his view of the structure of ability were to prevail, it would confront the investigator of ATI with a superhuman task of data collection, since any treatment contrast might interact with any of the aptitudes. The chapter attempts to lay a theoretical groundwork by discussing ways in which measured aptitudes might assist a person in responding to instruction, and so enter into an interaction. Some methods of analyzing tasks and of constructing hypotheses about ATI are suggested.

To categorize substantive findings on Aptitude x Treatment interactions presents an insuperable problem. Dozens of abilities and dozens of personality traits are used as aptitude variables (along with sex, age, and social class). Treatments are likewise heterogeneous, and there is no conventional basis for classifying them. A tabulation of the ATI work would have to be a grid of at least two dimensions, with a cell for each kind of AT combination, but a book has to be linear (in McLuhan's sense). Our final scheme is rather arbitrary and is influenced by the volume of research on various topics rather than by any judgment regarding importance. We settled on a plan of clustering that at best puts a study alongside others that raise somewhat similar questions. The studies discussed at greatest length are those that illuminate a procedural issue or offer rich substantive suggestions for future inquiries.

Chapters 7 to 11 examine the studies on interactions of measured ability with instructional variations. The whole of Chapter 7 is given to research on programmed instruction, not because the interactions found are outstandingly important, but because a remarkable volume of studies of interaction appeared during the flurry of interest in programmed instruction in the early 1960's. Chapter 8 deals with research on instruction in reading and with meaningfulness of instruction. These are placed together because meaning is a treatment variable in reading research and because the work on meaningfulness has also concentrated on primary-grade children. Chapter 9 continues the "meaning" theme, considering alternatives to verbal text and the popular but overly simple hypothesis that learning from pictures, symbols, or words calls upon spatial, symbolic, or verbal abilities, respectively. Chapter 10 is devoted to curricular research, including work on teaching via discovery. Chapter 11 collects small-scale experiments on intellectual processes under artificial, laboratory-like instruction. The research examines skills in observation, induction, and reasoning, along with specific instructional devices designed to influence information processing. Cognitive styles are also considered.

Chapters 12 and 13 concentrate on personality. Chapter 12 also takes up special methodological problems in personality research, developing further some themes from Chapters 2 to 4. It then reviews studies on anxiety and related variables. The two chief topics of Chapter 13 are the climate of the classroom or institution, and what we call "constructive motivation."

Finally, Chapter 14 offers our best synoptic answer to the question, "Do ATI exist?" and identifies variables most likely to interact. It reviews our methodological suggestions for future research. And it reflects on how school procedures may ultimately take advantage of knowledge about Aptitude x Treatment interactions.

Chapter 2 | Methods for research on interaction

An educator interested in a certain set of outcomes usually must compare alternative ways to attain them. His question is: *In what manner do the characteristics of learners affect the probable success of each one, in each program that might be considered?* Or, considering a particular learner: *To what degree will each program produce the desired changes in him?*

For readers new to research on interaction, this chapter and the next spell out the basic logic and applicable statistical methods. Chapter 4 examines sophisticated methods for squeezing meaning out of data. Some of these methods have only recently come into use in behavioral science and a few are introduced here for the first time.

Our scrutiny of research methods is a bit obsessive. We have been so thoroughly frustrated by the deficiencies of design, analysis, and reporting of past studies that we place the utmost stress on sound research techniques. Studies of interaction entail large contributions of subject time and extended effort on the part of the investigator. Far too many studies have ended in confusion or have reported conclusions—positive or negative—that the data did not warrant. Hence we shall sermonize about proper method with all the fervor we can command. But we are not without some sense of reality. While we shall suggest ways to avoid all manner of pitfalls, it is inconceivable that an investigator could follow all these recommendations at once. Indeed, some are inherently contradictory—notably, our interest in wide-ranging exploration of multiple variables, alongside our desire to reach solid, reproducible conclusions. Designing an experiment is inevitably an exercise in compromise; one must cut and trim within limited resources. We offer the investigator a repertoire of techniques. Which of them he will fit into any one study is for his art to determine.

Our review leaves us unhappy with practices in instructional research today. Studies are often conducted quickly, without pilot work, with a treatment so brief as to be unrelated to genuine instruction. Not often is there replication or follow-up to consolidate the sound findings or to expose fortuitous relations for what they are. More money was available for educational research during the last decade than ever before. Yet the truly substantial studies are as likely to come from the Depression years (for example, see pp. 245ff.) as from the 1960's. Fruitfulness has been sacrificed to statistical formalism. Thus a modern investigator often reduces his report to just the F ratios and p values that bear on his preconceived questions—indeed, sometimes to just those that reach significance. Such reports give none of the descriptive statistics that would inform the reader who is considering a somewhat different question or who wishes to apply a different model to the data. One cannot blame individual investigators, referees, or editors for the exaggerated emphasis on testing of *a priori* hypotheses; everyone is a captive of the *Zeitgeist*. But perhaps criticisms such as ours will help to reinstate a sturdier, earthier style in educational investigation.

To date, nearly all writing on interactions has assumed a very simple method of research: an aptitude is measured; persons are assigned at random to one of two treatments; an outcome is measured; and the interaction is tested for significance. This design, though of basic importance, is inadequate for many studies. Since characteristics of learners and of treatments are plural, it may be wise to measure more than one aptitude or to compare more than two treatments. Outcomes are also plural, since an instructional activity affects many aspects of the person. The aptitude-treatment combination that serves best to produce one outcome may have small effect on another outcome (or even a detrimental effect). To simplify this chapter, we deal primarily with studies limited to one aptitude, two treatments, and one criterion; but we shall repeatedly step back to take in a broader perspective.

The foregoing paragraph, and nearly all of what is to follow until we reach Chapter 13, envisions that ATI will be studied by controlled experimentation. A major role is also to be played by naturalistic studies and we have no intention to belittle them in devoting so much space to experiments. Chapter 13 will offer evidence that one kind of student does well under a teacher or in an institution where another kind does badly, not because of inferiority of the latter group but because of a mismatch. Naturalistic studies can consider more treatment variables than controlled studies can, and they can often provide richer observations. Much of what is said about planning formal experiments, the hazards resulting from nonrandom assignment of cases, etc., pertains to naturalistic studies as well.

A word of warning: In most of Chapters 2–4 we speak as if treatments were applied to independent individuals. This is a great oversimplification. Educational research is ordinarily conducted in classes, and the students in a class are influenced by each other and by the teacher. When we attempt to take class effects into account, at the end of Chapter 4, the complexities become serious. It appears that some of the most important questions cannot be resolved by the usual significance-seeking, statistics-bound strategy. Progress in the study of ATI will have to depend on insight which will come as much from naturalistic observation as from rigorous analysis of data. The methodological arguments into which we now launch leave many qualifications and elaborations to be worked out in the future.

The basic concept of interaction

Traditional correlational and experimental approaches

The usual concern in applied research on tests has been predictive validity. The investigator pursuing predictive studies has typically been interested in improving

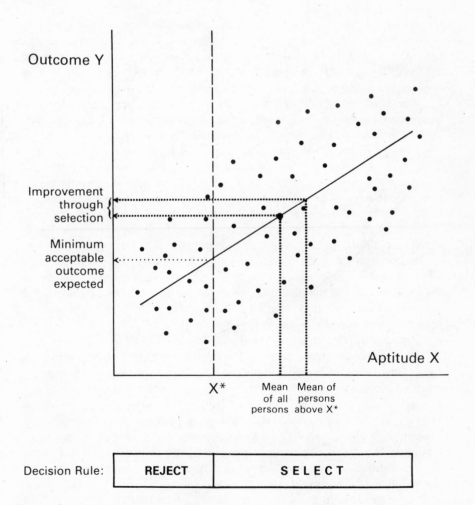

Figure 2.1.
The scheme for examining predictive validity.

net outcome—in instruction or industrial production—by selecting individuals likely to work effectively. He carries out a correlational study whose data can be depicted graphically as in Figure 2.1. The aptitude score and the criterion score for one individual together determine one point in the bivariate distribution. A trend line is drawn or a regression equation calculated to represent the relation of outcome to aptitude. We shall refer to these relations as "AT regressions." This distinguishes them from, for example, the relation of one aptitude to another aptitude, or the relation of a true score to an observed score.

In Figure 2.1, the AT regression has a positive slope; persons with higher aptitude tend to do better in the treatment under study. If this is a study of a college aptitude test in relation to grades in a certain college, the result implies that if the college hereafter admits only persons who reach the aptitude score X^*, cutting out all those to the left of X^*, the average outcome will be higher than it is when persons from the whole range are admitted. If the college were to make the cut at a point to the right of X^*, the average outcome would be still higher. The tendency is to seek predictor tests onto which the regression slope is steep, so that their use in selection can be expected to raise the average outcome.

When a test having validity for prediction is given to a new applicant, the AT regression equation can be used to calculate what outcome is expected for him. Where the decision is not constrained by a fixed number of vacancies to be filled, the standard practice is to admit those applicants for whom the expected outcome exceeds some minimum acceptable level. The minimum acceptable expected outcome implies the cutting score to be set. The regression equation indicates the aptitude score of persons whose expected outcome just reaches the allowable level. A cutting score of 500 on the College Boards, for example, might be used by a college admitting students if, in earlier years, freshmen who scored below this level did not typically achieve an average grade of at least "C".

The correlational study ignores the contrasting instructional environments that different students experience (or could experience). Whatever intervened between the aptitude test and the final measure of achievement is taken as a single undifferentiated treatment. In correlational analysis, the nature of the treatment is accepted without thought, as an institutional "given."

Experimental research *is* concerned with differences among treatments, but not with differences among persons. The experimenter attempts to remove effects of individual differences in aptitude from his comparison of treatment means. To minimize aptitude effects, he may distribute Ss over treatments at random or in matched pairs, or he may damp out the effects by means of analysis of covariance. Through successive comparisons of treatment means for experimental groups, the applied psychologist expects to determine the optimal treatment, the one best to apply to everyone. Thus, he might try to determine the best method of teaching college chemistry or the best sequence of curriculum content in elementary mathematics.

How the experimenter thinks is represented schematically in Figure 2.2. His emphasis is on the outcome means under the two treatments. He does not report AT regressions and seems ordinarily to assume that outcome relates to aptitude similarly in each treatment (as the dotted lines in Figure 2.2 indicate). If the investigator reports only that the mean outcome is higher in Treatment A than in Treatment B, the report suggests that Treatment A is better for everyone. In effect, a conclusion is generalized over all aptitude levels in the sample.

Nonparallel regressions as evidence of interaction

Figure 2.3 displays another pattern of results consistent with the same average superiority of Treatment A. The AT regression for Treatment B is steeper than

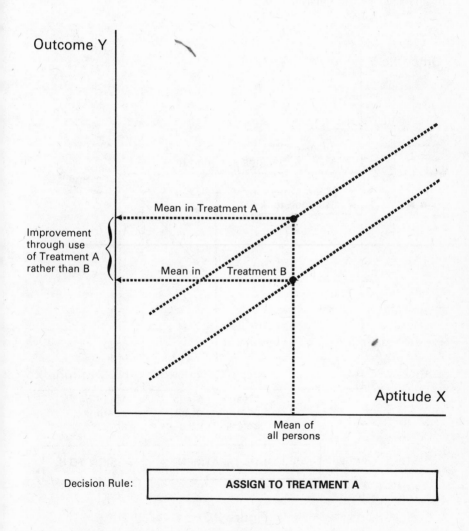

Figure 2.2.
The scheme for comparing treatment means.

that for A. Individuals with high aptitude generally do better if assigned to Treatment B. Treatment A tends to be superior for persons below X^* (the "crossover point" where the two lines intersect). Despite the difference at the mean, Treatment A is not superior in general.

Investigators should attend to differences in mean outcome and also to differences in relations of aptitudes to outcomes. The interaction study combines the correlational and experimental modes of inquiry and goes beyond them. Where policy makers have a commitment to universal education and a set of common educational goals, a principal aim of research on instruction becomes one of finding interactions and capitalizing on them.

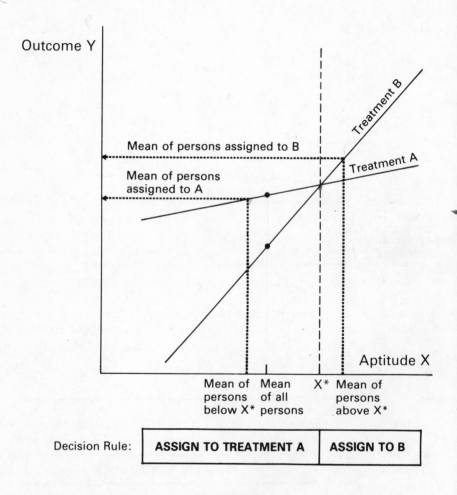

Figure 2.3.
The scheme for examining aptitude-treatment interaction.

Choosing instructional methods on the basis of interactions has the effect of reducing the correlation between initial status and outcome. In the end, it reduces the correlation of a child's status with that of his parents. A selective policy (Figure 2.1) tends to make outcomes strongly correlated with initial status. Selecting for extra education the persons with the highest initial status tends to widen the gap in outcome between those at the high and low ends of the scale. The treat-all-alike policy implicit in Figure 2.2 does nothing to modify the dependence of outcome on initial status, but it does not intensify it as the selective policy does. The placement policy (Figure 2.3) makes the outcome difference between those with high initial status, who are assigned to B, and those of low initial status, who are assigned to A, considerably less than it is under the other two policies. Capitalizing on interactions thus actively fosters social mobility. On the other hand, the model of placement decisions with sharp cutoff rules is only a model; it fixes ideas, but we as yet have no interactions that can be exploited in this way.

The interaction seen in Figure 2.3 is "disordinal": the expected outcomes have the order $A < B$ at one end of the X range and $B < A$ at the other end. In an "ordinal" interaction one line remains above the other (but is not parallel to it). We shall discuss the implications of ordinality later (p. 31).

Where there is an interaction, the aptitude measure has differential predictive validity. If we could put each person through both treatments and so directly obtain values of Y_{pA} and Y_{pB}, the correlation of X with $Y_{pA} - Y_{pB}$ would not be zero.

Although it is the regression slopes that define an interaction, attention ought also to be given to the standard error of estimate within each treatment. A difference in the two standard errors may be of psychological or practical interest, whether or not interaction is present. Interaction studies have generally failed to report these standard errors, though they can sometimes be inferred from published standard deviations and correlations. The conventional statistical methods for testing an interaction use a pooled error term; moreover, they ordinarily assume that the within-treatment residual variances are equal. Important as this point may be, we have not tried to trace methods of considering the difference through our methodological chapters, and have only rarely brought a comparison of such differences into the summary of a specific study.

The risk of oversimplification

A basic argument of this book is that considering regression slopes alongside the means probes deeper, and so avoids the experimenter's facile generalization in the form A-better-than-B. But is not a report regarding a single aptitude also a facile generalization? Might not consideration of a second aptitude variable or a second treatment variable disclose a still more complex truth? (Cronbach, 1975). The statement that persons high on Aptitude X_1 do better under Treatment A than under B is itself a statement about a difference in means; perhaps the size of that difference is conditioned by the level of Aptitude X_2. This warning

against simplified analysis can readily be extended: one can warn against confining attention to linear regressions, against assuming that relations are uniform
among subjects classfied by sex and educational background, and against assuming that what holds for the overall outcome measure will be true of the more
specific outcomes into which it could be divided.

The advisability of microanalysis. Just as we recommend going beyond the
comparison of means to look at the possibility of interaction, we recommend
that the investigator do what he can to examine the consistency of an interaction
over various segments of his data. He may, for example, break down his sample
to see if more or less the same interaction is found among the men and among
the women. If his aptitude measure has somewhat heterogeneous subtests, he
would do well to analyze them separately as well as together; his confidence in
his conclusion is enhanced if the relations for the several subtests are similar.
Likewise, he may check the conclusion by analyzing separate aspects of posttest
performance. But fine-grain analyses with smaller samples or less accurate measuring instruments inevitably generate inconsistent findings. These inconsistencies
may be due to unimportant variations or to higher-order interactions. They can
rarely be proven significant, and yet the ideas they suggest are not to be dismissed out of hand.

The intent to extrapolate. Throughout this monograph a concern with "external validity" will recur (Campbell & Stanley, 1963; Bracht & Glass, 1968;
Snow, 1974). One never wishes to confine interpretation to the kind of persons
who were given a certain treatment and measured on a certain test. The investigator is examining a broader hypothesis, generalizing not to what the population
would do in these identical circumstances but to what is expected in "similar"
conditions. Thus, the laboratory experimenter intends to generalize over pieces
of apparatus constructed to the same specifications, and perhaps over (say) all
tachistoscopes. He has little difficulty in this because such equipment is calibrat-
ed to reduce variability. Even when applicants for a program are chosen by a selection rule that was developed empirically in that setting the previous year, the
tester is generalizing to a somewhat different population. Generalization to other
institutions, to slightly different programs, or to a different kind of person goes
beyond the conclusion established by the data.

Extrapolation and broad interpretation are guided by theoretical understanding, based on intelligent consideration of findings from the whole corpus of research. No one study takes on great importance in the long-extended development of theory. The single study is open to a wide range of alternative interpretations, and varied predictions can be made about what will happen when conditions change. The investigator need not apologize that his one study is open to
diverse interpretations. Every study is. What is important is that he persist in his
research, assembling such a body of information that in due time he accumulates
substantial understanding.

When we point to counterinterpretations of a study that its design cannot
rule out, the obvious recommendation is to replicate the study, with modifications likely to resolve the original uncertainty. But no one strategy can be ad-

vocated. At times an investigator will be wise to repeat a study with little or no change in plan. At other times he will be wise to repeat the study after making one or two substantial changes of the variables or the population. There are also times when his second study should attack the same phenomenon from an entirely different direction. A stereotyped program repeating a single research formula will not be very illuminating. A hop-skip-jump activity in which each study moves to a new set of variables is equally counterproductive—as the literature on ATI to date makes evident.

Limitations of the trait model. An aptitude is thought of as present in greater or less degree, i.e., as a quantitative trait. The trait model is, like any other model, a simplification designed to permit analysis and prediction. It may be the only sensible model for the experimenter, at the present stage of our knowledge about interactions. But its simplifications leave certain aspects of the person out of consideration and thus create blind spots. The investigator who is aware of these simplifications can employ the model with relatively little risk, since he can step outside the model from time to time to consider his phenomenon more realistically.

One limitation of the model is that it is implicitly static. The investigator of ATI thinks of collecting data by means of a pretest, making a decision about the treatment to which the person will be assigned, and then holding him in that treatment until it is completed. This is entirely consistent with traditional experimentation, in which a treatment remains fixed throughout the term of the experiment.

Sometimes the treatment "works back" upon the aptitude, so that after a time the person's aptitude has changed. If so, it might then be advisable to modify his treatment. How important this is depends on the character of the aptitude. Variation in technique over a year's schooling probably will not have much effect on general mental ability. Where the aptitude test is closely related in content to the later instruction, the person's score (and his ranking) may change considerably. This is most obvious in the experiment of Sullivan, Okada, and Niedermeyer on reading instruction (pp. 162, 243), where a measure of ability to read unfamiliar words was used both as "aptitude" measure and as outcome measure. The efforts of Spielberger and others (p. 413) to study effects of "state" anxiety represent a valuable addition to studies of traits.

A second difficulty is that just a few dimensions are allowed for summing up a person. A test score is a fairly gross summary of a number of qualitatively distinct characteristics. Even in progressing through what appears to be tightly ordered instructional content, as in going from addition to multiplication, the person is acquiring several processes that he can add to his skill in different orders. (E.g., he can memorize multiplication combinations before or after he learns to "carry" in addition.) To say where the person stands on a scale of ability in arithmetic is at best a rough count of accomplishments, not a measurement of the strength of a growing property.

Writers such as Gagné (1970) who map out the components of arithmetic skill see the skills as forming a complexly branched and interlaced hierarchy, not a simple ladder. They recommend an educational strategy based on micromeasurement which identifies the particular skill or idea that a pupil lacks—among the many skills at his level in the hierarchy—so that his teacher can train him on precisely what he requires. This approach assumes the existence of ATI (Glaser, 1972). It conceives of aptitude not as a position on a quantifiable scale, but as a repertoire of specific responses to narrow classes of situations. It calls for taking inventory more than for measuring. And it prescribes a treatment, not in terms of a semester-long course taught in a vaguely defined style, but in terms of a next brief lesson chosen from a large collection of options. Students are sorted on characteristics such as "ability to arrange a set of addends such as 15, 105, 3.6, and 20 in a column with all 'units' aligned." Where a student lacks this ability, the treatment required is to explain this alignment task and give a few sessions of drill.

The inventory can be regarded as an elaboration of the trait model, since each element in the checklist of abilities is mastered to a greater or lesser degree and so is logically a narrow trait. But it is obviously impossible to experiment with all the dimensions and all the variant treatment patterns, to verify that the expected interactions occur. At most, one can apply a micromeasurement strategy over a period of weeks or months, and compare the end result with that from some less complexly branched strategy (cf. R.C. Atkinson, 1972). One can evaluate the strategy as a whole by a conventionally designed study, but evaluation of its myriad components cannot be complete and rigorous.

Relations of aptitude "dimensions" suggest broad policy recommendations rather than specific prescriptions for instructional acts. If a score interacts with a style of instruction, the school can adopt the policy of treating a student in a certain manner. E.g., a notation can be made that this student should be frequently evaluated by the instructor. The policy does not specify just what the instructor should do or when, but it suggests a style that is likely to improve the student's learning. Global though they are, such generalizations add to our understanding of the instructional process, and the policy may improve the school's success with the student.

The detailed assessment that identifies just what tasks the student can and cannot perform has a quite different function. It tells exactly what content to present at a given moment, but it says nothing about the persistent styles of student and teacher and gives no guidance to policy. The description of students in terms of specific "entering behaviors" and the description in terms of traits capture quite different aspects of readiness for instruction. They are supplementary, not competitors one of which must ultimately prove to be "right."

Interactions as functional relations

Before we embark on a technical discussion of research procedures, it will be well to comment on some unsatisfactory procedures that appear frequently in the literature.

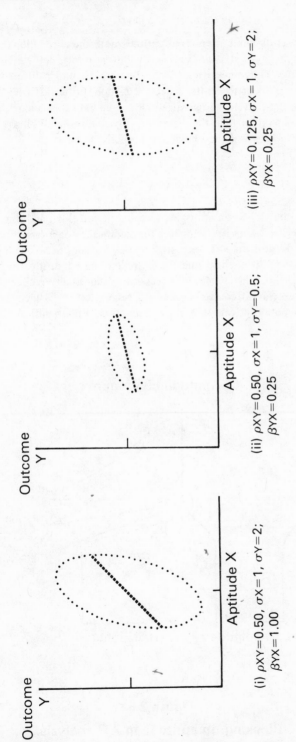

Figure 2.4.
Regression slope, correlation, and standard deviation of outcome: three combinations.

Common faults in analysis

Some studies report outcome means and aptitude-outcome correlations within treatments and do not report standard deviations. But an interaction can appear in a difference in s.d.'s. Outcomes often have different s.d.'s under different treatments; if so, regression slopes will differ when correlations do not. (Cf. Panels (i) and (ii) in Figure 2.4.) Even the investigator who reports s.d.'s is likely to discuss the correlations rather than the regression slopes; fortunately, his reader can calculate slopes to interpret the interaction properly, since

$$b_{YX} = r_{XY} \frac{s_Y}{s_X}.$$

It is common to "block" Ss on aptitude, grouping persons high and low in ability. This permits 2 x 2 anova as a test for the significance of interaction. As Figure 2.5 suggests, Treatments x Levels blocking distinguishes between some individuals whose aptitude differs little and treats as alike some individuals who differ greatly. Taking these differences into account would usually reduce the error term. Hence, a test on the difference between regression slopes will identify as significant some interaction effects that blocked anova calls nonsignificant. When

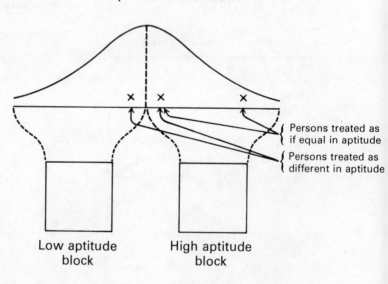

Aptitude continuum

Persons treated as if equal in aptitude

Persons treated as different in aptitude

Low aptitude block

High aptitude block

Figure 2.5.
Blocking on aptitude in ATI analysis.

the blocks are taken from the extremes of the distribution (e.g., high and low fifths), differences within each category are comparatively small; then the 2 x 2 analysis can be powerful. (See p. 60ff.)

We particularly discourage three-level blocking, i.e., forming high-, medium-, and low-aptitude groups prior to 2 x 3 anova. This loses power not only by disregarding within-block differences but also by disregarding the ordering of the three levels.*

Occasionally an investigator tests nothing but the main effect, even though he is in a position to examine interactions. This is likely to occur when he collects aptitude data only to describe his sample or to make sure that treatment groups are comparable. Even an investigator not interested in ATI ought to check for their presence, to determine whether his main effect can be generalized over the aptitude range.

Univariate regression equations

It is useful to express an observed aptitude-outcome relation as a linear regression equation:

$$(2.1) \quad \hat{Y}_{pt} = \overline{Y}_t + b_{Y_tX}(X_p - \overline{X}_t)$$

X_p is an aptitude measure for person p, and Y_{pt} is the outcome he reaches under Treatment T (with $\hat{Y}_{pt}$ denoting the estimated outcome). X_t and Y_t are the means for the sample assigned to Treatment T. A least-squares solution fitting the equation to points $[X_p, Y_{pt}]$ determines the slope.

Sample means within treatments differ. Comparison of equations across treatments becomes easier if one substitutes the grand means $\overline{\overline{X}}$ and $\overline{\overline{Y}}$ [which equals $\overline{Y}_t - b_{Y_tX}(\overline{X}_t - \overline{\overline{X}})$]. Where this notation is used, it will be convenient to think of two treatments and equal sample sizes, though this is not strictly necessary. Eq. (2.1) can be restated thus:

$$(2.2) \quad \hat{Y}_{pt} = \overline{\overline{Y}} + b_{Y_tX}(X_p - \overline{\overline{X}}).$$

We shall use the symbol β instead of b when discussing the population value of the unstandardized regression weight; b is the sample value. In an equation employing β, $\overline{\overline{X}}$ and $\overline{\overline{Y}}$ refer to population means.

Alternative scales for regression weights. The "beta weight" is the weight that applies to scores standardized on the basis of the sample s.d. In an ATI study, this would be a within-treatment slope. (We shall not use the symbol β for this.)

Psychologists have been inclined to report beta weights rather than raw-score weights, because raw scores, which depend on operational rules, vary arbitrarily

---

*While three-level blocking can help identify curvilinear relationships, curvilinearity can be more firmly identified by fitting quadratic or higher-order regression functions.

from one measure to another. Sociologists and economists have been inclined to report unstandardized weights because many of their variables (income, education) have "real" metrics. In all educational and psychological work, standardization can be detrimental. In a comparison from one kind of subject to another, or from a select population to the full population, standardized weights ordinarily fluctuate when the underlying relation is invariant. (See Wiley in Goldberger & Duncan, 1973, p. 71; see also p. 30 f. below.) Unstandardized weights are the correct choice in ATI research for a further reason: outcome measures standardized within treatments are not comparable over treatments. As we said earlier, s.d.'s must be taken into account in considering ATI.

The fact remains, however, that it is difficult to interpret unstandardized equations when the metric is arbitrary. To judge the importance of an effect, the outcome measure has to be related to some utility scale. But conversion to a utility scale is impossible in a general review of the literature; hence, we shall often invoke the standard deviation as a yardstick against which to evaluate effects. Thus, we shall argue that in many educational settings an improvement as large as 0.4 s.d. of the outcome measure is practically worthwhile.

To facilitate interpretation, we often rescale regression equations in this book. The rescaling is a kind of standardization based on the pooled within-groups mean square. Since we use the same multiplier in rescaling data for both groups, this in no way alters the relative magnitude of the regression slopes. It does not overlook differences in the standard deviations for the two groups, as conventionally standardized regression weights and correlation coefficients do. The reason for rescaling is that the reader then does not need to hold in mind information about the raw-score scales for various instruments.

Forms for expressing ATI. An interaction effect is a set of relations such that the $\beta_{Y_t X}$ in the various treatments differ. When an interaction is being examined, one would like an estimate of $\overline{\overline{Y}}$ and β for each treatment.

A numerical example is scarcely needed for equation (2.2), but providing one here will introduce a format. Suppose arbitrarily that, in the sample, X takes on the values 11 to 14. Suppose that the mean of Y among persons with a given X is as follows in the population:

	X	11	12	13	14
Mean Y	X in treatment A	40	44	48	52
Mean Y	X in treatment B	43	44	45	46

Now $\beta_{Y_A X}$ is 4 (i.e., there is a four-unit change in Y with each unit change in X), and $\beta_{Y_B X}$ is 1. If the X distribution is symmetric, the mean is at 12.5 and the regression equations are

$$\hat{Y}_{pA} = 46 + 4 \,(X_p - 12.5) = 4X_p - 4$$

$$\hat{Y}_{pB} = X_p + 32$$

Taking differences between outcomes, we have

X	11	12	13	14
Mean advantage of Treatment A	-3	0	3	6

There is a disordinal interaction, the crossover point coming at 12.

The separate equations can be embraced in a single expression by introducing a dummy variable T_p to identify the treatment to which person p is assigned. The dummy-variable technique is quite useful in some advanced computational procedures. To introduce it here we write X_1 even though no X_2 is in view at present. Where there are just two treatments, the value $T = +1$ is assigned to one treatment and the value $T = -1$ to the other. In the subsequent examples, Treatment A is coded +1. The person is characterized by a pair of numbers. E.g.: $[X_{1p} = 15, T_p = +1]$ indicates that p has a score of 15 on the aptitude X_1 and has been assigned to Treatment A. The outcome measure Y_{pt} is estimated by a function of the two "variables."

Disregarding the subscript p, the equation has the form

$$(2.3) \qquad \hat{Y}_t = \beta_0 + \beta_{0t}\,(T) + \beta_1\,(X_1 - \overline{\overline{X}}_1) + \beta_{1t}\,(X_1 - \overline{\overline{X}}_1)\,(T).$$

This is a generalized regression equation. β_0 is the general mean. The term β_{0t} represents the treatment main effect $\overline{\overline{Y}}_A - \overline{\overline{Y}}_B$; in the population this difference equals $\beta_{0t}\,(+1) - \beta_{0t}\,(-1)$ or $2\beta_{0t}$. The term $\beta_1(X_1 - \overline{\overline{X}}_1)$ describes the Y-on-X_1 regression slope derived from all cases considered together, without regard to treatment. This is what analysis of variance would report as an aptitude main effect, since it describes changes in Y as a function of X_1. The final term of the equation refers to the Aptitude x Treatment interaction. Suppose that persons who score high on X_1 do well in the first treatment $(T = +1)$, and less well in the second. Then Y tends to be high when the product $(X_1 - \overline{\overline{X}}_1)\,(T)$ is positive and low when the product is negative. This means that $\beta_{1t} > 0$. The multiplier β_{1t} reports the increment in the slope of the AT regression that arises from taking into account the treatment to which the person is assigned. The difference between the within-treatment slopes equals $2\beta_{1t}$; this is one measure of the strength of the interaction. An ordinary procedure for regression analysis with $T, X_1 - \overline{\overline{X}}_1$, and their product as three predictors estimates the four regression coefficients from sample data. (It is possible also to evaluate the weights using X_1 in place of $[X_1 - \overline{\overline{X}}_1]$. Deviation scores are preferable, to avoid problems arising from correlation among predictors.)

We may expand our first numerical example (p. 28) to illustrate these ideas. If the number of cases per cell is uniform, the Y means are 46 and 44.5 for Treatments A and B, respectively. To get β_1, we note the "column" means of 41.5, 44, 46.5, 49; the slope is 2.5. The terms in the regression equation are given at the left, and then applied to each X in turn:

	X	11	12	13	14
β_0		45.25	45.25	45.25	45.25
$\beta_{0A} = \beta_{0t}$ (+1) = 0.75		.75	.75	.75	.75
$\beta_1 (X_1 - \overline{\overline{X}}_1) = 2.5 (X_1 - 12.5)$		–3.75	–1.25	1.25	3.75
$\beta_{1A} (X_1 - \overline{\overline{X}}_1)(+1)$		–2.25	–0.75	.75	2.25
$\hat{Y}_A$		40.00	44.00	48.00	52.00

The reader can work out the table of values for B; we start him on the way by giving the values for the column under 11: 45.25, – 0.75, –3.75, +2.25, 43.00.

If we regroup terms in (2.3) we return to the population version of (2.2):

$$\hat{Y}_t = [\beta_0 + \beta_{0t}] + [\beta_1 + \beta_{1t}(T)](X_1 - \overline{\overline{X}}_1) = \overline{\overline{Y}}_t + \beta_{Y_t X_1} (X_1 - \overline{\overline{X}}_1).$$

Note, then, that $\beta_{\hat{Y}_A \hat{X}_1}$ is a combination of β_1 and β_{1A}.

Extrapolation to new populations. The conclusion from an experiment is more than a summary of findings about the population sampled. One may hope to find the same relation in populations other than the original one. For this reason it is unwise to report exclusively in terms of High and Low groups defined relative to the sample median. The description cannot be regarded as generalizable. It is much better to employ a reference scale that is independent of the sample, as in the statement:

Expected achievement = 13 + 6 (Mental Age in years).

This is an absolute statement.

The importance of a reproducible reference scale in stating a generalization can be made clearer with an example. A study has been carried out at one age or in one grade; the investigator urges that the study be repeated with Ss at other levels of maturity to confirm his conclusion. Suppose he found among fourth-graders that those with MA's above the median profited more from a "discovery" method of teaching while those below the median profited more from a "didactic" method. At the median (MA 10), the two methods were equally effective. The design can indeed by applied to younger and older children—but what finding would confirm the original one? In a *third* grade where the median MA is 9, would the investigator expect the MA-9 child to perform equally well regardless of method, as the median fourth-grader did? Or should the child do better under didactic instruction, as did the MA-9 subjects in Grade 4? Once this issue is posed, we see that the two regression functions of outcome on MA itself—without regard to the sample median—are the results to be confirmed. To state the original generalization in terms of the class median was misleading. To be sure, it may turn out that the regressions on MA differ from grade to grade in such a way that the child above the class median profits from teaching by discovery whereas the child below the median does better with didactic teaching. Then the result appears to be social-psychological, depending on the group as well as the individual. One conceivable explanation would be that the *relatively* able child takes a leading part in the discovery activity of the class and so profits more from it. If, on the other hand, the regression functions for Grade 3 as well as those for Grade 4 cross at about MA 10, the generalization in terms of the median is invalid. This finding would imply that *individual* mental development determines which method is advantageous. The absolute regression functions will hold up under replication if individual ability is the critical matter, whereas the crossover point of the two regressions—expressed on the MA scale—will be different in each group if relative ability is critical. Both kinds of effects could occur simultaneously, of course. (See p. 101 ff.)

Nonlinear relations. Floor and ceiling effects inevitably place limits on the validity of a linear hypothesis. Data from the extremes of a scale often depart from a trend found in the middle range. Nor need causal relations be linear. Where anxiety is a pretest variable, for example, generating mild stress may be advantageous for persons with intermediate scores and disadvantageous at the two extremes.

One can inform himself about nonlinearity by inspecting scatterplots. We advise the investigator to inspect his data for likely nonlinearities and to mention impressive ones to his reader, with the caution appropriate to any *post hoc* conclusion.

Much more will be said about curvilinearity in Chapter 12.

Ordinality of interactions. It is common to distinguish "ordinal" from "disordinal" interactions. Disordinal lines cross within the aptitude range of the sample (as in Figure 2.3). If one regression line remains above the other, the interaction is ordinal (see left panel of Figure 2.6).

At one time, writers stressed the value of disordinal interactions and tended to dismiss ordinal interactions. The ordinal interaction was regarded as a mere artifact of the choice of measuring scale for the dependent variable.

As Cronbach and Gleser (1957) originally traced the logic of classification decisions, assignment of persons to treatments was to be determined entirely by the crossover point of the AT regressions. Persons to the right of the crossover point were to be sent to one treatment and persons to the left were assigned to the other. An ordinal interaction (no crossing) would imply the same treat-

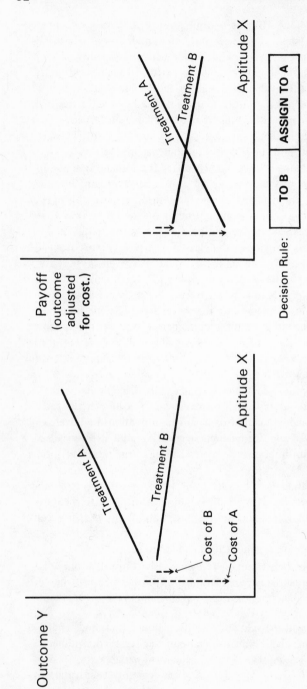

Figure 2.6.

Change of ordinality when cost is considered. The panel at left shows the AT regressions with outcome expressed on some utility scale, and also shows a value for the per-person cost of treatment. At right, the regressions have been moved downward, reducing the stated outcome by the pertinent cost figure.

ment for all persons. This argument about a decision rule needs to be modified; the cost of the treatment is to be charged against the benefit from the person's accomplishment. If the treatment that yields the greater outcome is much costlier than the other, the ordinal interaction effect on outcome becomes a disordinal effect on payoff (Figure 2.6, Panel ii). The more costly method should be applied only to those who will find it so advantageous that its extra cost is repaid in benefits. Even if the cost-corrected interaction is ordinal, differential assignment will be required when facilities for giving one treatment are limited. The scarce treatment will be given to those persons most likely to profit from it, i.e., persons from the end of the range where the payoff differential is greatest.

Apart from this conceivable application to placement, ordinal interactions should be taken more seriously than previous writings have suggested. In discussing personnel classification, Cronbach and Gleser assumed a fixed population, but a practicing psychologist may extrapolate to groups lower or higher in aptitude than the persons observed. The ordinal interaction in Figure 2.6 suggests— but does not prove—that the regression lines do cross, somewhere to the left of the range of the sample.

Nonparallel regressions can be brought into parallelism by some monotone transformation of the outcome scale. If the intervals of the scale for the dependent variable are truly arbitrary, theory is simplified by suppressing effects that arise from the scale itself. The ordinal effect should not be dismissed, however, if the scales have a real-world meaning. The science of genetics makes good use of ordinal interactions, such as that between the temperature during incubation and the number of eye facets developed in fruit flies of different strains.

The scale for reporting an instructional outcome is never truly arbitrary. The decision maker cannot decide whether a certain treatment is worth applying unless he can judge the cost and the benefit relative to each other; for a rational decision, outcomes have to be expressed on a payoff scale. One transformation of the outcome variable is "right" for expressing the values of decision maker Jones (or of the community or institution he speaks for). Hence all other transformations are wrong. It is most unlikely that the one transformation that makes the regression lines parallel is the scaling that coincides with Jones' utilities.

Correcting for error of measurement. Unreliability of aptitude measures needs to be taken into account. Theoretical interpretation is concerned with relations between true scores. Even an investigator seeking a practical decision rule needs to consider the effect of unreliability, since he can change the length of his tests in the future.

When two treatment groups are sampled from the same population, the point at which AT regressions cross will shift as the reliability of the aptitude measure is changed. This must be recognized if one is to think straight. Suppose that in a large sample the mean difference between outcomes in the two treatments is c and that the regression slope corresponding to the greater mean is $\Delta\beta$ units greater than the other slope. Then the point at which the regression lines cross will be $c/\Delta\beta$ units below $\overline{\overline{X}}$. Using (2.5) below, and writing ρ for the reliability, we find that the true-score regressions cross at $c\rho/\Delta\beta$. This shift can alter the ordinality of the regression, since the score $X_\infty = c\rho/\Delta\beta$ is closer to the mean of X_∞ (in units of σ_{X_∞}) than the score $X = c/\Delta\beta$ is to the mean of X (in units of σ_X). The same principle holds for regressions onto an observed score X_k formed by combining k parallel forms of X. Other things being equal, a more reliable predictor warrants assigning more persons to the treatment with the lower mean outcome.

Unreliability of the *outcome* measure does not bias the interpretation of ATI. The regression of Y_∞ onto X has the same equation as the regression of Y on X. An unreliable outcome measure, however, can make it harder to show statistical significance.

Ideally, every ATI study would examine the regression of outcome onto the true aptitude score, X_∞. The score $X_{\infty p}$ would be obtained if (hypothetically) we averaged an indefinitely large number of observed scores from person p on equivalent forms of the test. This AT regression will have a different slope than the observed-score regression, and under some circumstances the apparent interaction may be radically altered. Important as this matter is, it has been ignored in ATI research to date; and from past studies, we will be able to report only observed-score regressions (see also p. 48 ff.).

Equation (2.2) has the following true-score form:

$$(2.4) \qquad \hat{Y}_{\infty pt} = \overline{\overline{Y}}_t + \beta_{Y_t X_\infty} (X_{\infty p} - \overline{\overline{X}})$$

The means in (2.4) are the same as in (2.2), because we assume equivalent forms of the X measure.

$$(2.5) \qquad \beta_{Y_t X_\infty} = \beta_{Y_t X} / \rho_{XX'}$$

In a study with a single sample, (2.4) would be evaluated by substituting the sample means for X and Y and the sample coefficients b_{YX}, and $r_{XX'}$. In an ATI experiment, there are at least two samples. If there was random assignment the pooled samples provide the best estimate of the population mean and the reliability coefficient. (If the reliability has been calculated on a separate sample, one should bring forward the estimated error variance and calculate the reliability from the observed-score variance in the pooled treatment samples. One substitutes in (2.4) the means from the pooled samples, the value of $r_{XX'}$, and the b_{YX} for each treatment in turn. If the samples were not formed by random assignment, a different logic applies (see p. 49).)

Estimating the regression onto true score is a correction for attenuation. Correction for attenuation has a somewhat bad name because too low an estimate of $\rho_{XX'}$ can carry the estimate of $\rho_{X_\infty Y_\infty}$ above 1.00. An underestimate will also exaggerate the Y-on-X_∞ slope. But this only argues for estimating $\rho_{XX'}$ well.

To calculate AT regressions of Y on X_∞ will require reasonable estimates of the reliability of aptitude measures for the sample in the ATI study. The estimate should take into account the multiple sources of error of measurement (see Cronbach *et al.*, 1972, esp. pp. 90–92, 287–292, 325–328).

The correction increases the absolute magnitude of the regression coefficient. In a true experiment with strictly equivalent groups, the ratio of the AT regression slopes for two treatments (onto the same aptitude measure) will not be altered when true scores replace observed scores. When there is no observed-score interaction the regression lines will be parallel for true scores also. An observed-score interaction implies an interaction of true score.

Although the observed AT regression tells somewhat the same story as the regression onto true scores, the investigator would do well to interpret his results—at least impressionistically—in terms of true scores. Rather unreliable aptitude measures are commonly used in ATI studies, for the sake of increasing the number of variables on which data are collected. Moreover, the reliabilities of the aptitude measures may differ considerably. This means that a difference in regression slopes—even one that might seem to be of little practical importance—will appear more important after the correction is made. Unreliability may have especially powerful effects in the multivariate study (see below). Note also that when treatment groups differ in their X ranges the reliability differs with the group. Then, a finding of no ATI with raw scores implies ATI with true scores.

Multivariate regression

We usually speak of a single dependent variable Y. Where investigators have collected data on two or more outcomes, they have almost invariably treated them in turn. A multivariate consideration of outcomes could be profitable, but formal analysis of a vector of outcomes in an ATI study (e.g., a canonical analysis) would be hard to interpret. We do advise inspecting the within-treatment correlations of dependent variables, since it is possible that two treatments will generate different $\rho_{Y_1 Y_2}$. Such differences in outcome correlations were reported by N. Frederiksen, O. Jensen, and A. Beaton (1972), for example. Thus, in organizations where subadministrators were given freedom, the more thoughtful workers were more likely to communicate with peers ($r = 0.36$); where subordinates were closely supervised, the correlation between thoughtfulness and communication dropped to zero.

We recommend that plural *aptitude* variables be treated simultaneously. One may use multiple regression or may form a single composite, or may form several near-orthogonal composites. To open the discussion, we consider relationships in the population, and assume that only two aptitudes are measured.

Population equations in two variables. Adding a second aptitude calls for extending equations (2.1) to (2.3) in an obvious manner. If we employ the form of (2.2), we have

$$(2.6) \quad \hat{Y}_{pt} = \overline{\overline{Y}}_t + \beta_{Y_t X_1} (X_{1p} - \overline{\overline{X}}_1) + \beta_{Y_t X_2} (X_{2p} - \overline{\overline{X}}_2)$$

Note that the $\beta_{Y_t X_1}$ of this equation differs from the $\beta_{Y_t X_1}$ of (2.2) when X_1 and X_2 are correlated. An interaction is indicated if $\beta_{Y_A X_1}$ differs from $\beta_{Y_B X_1}$, or $\beta_{Y_A X_2}$ differs from $\beta_{Y_B X_2}$, or both—provided that the aptitudes are uncorrelated. If they are correlated, the two differences may offset each other. The weighted composite of X_1 and X_2 that best predicted the difference in outcomes under two treatments—i.e., that interacted most strongly in the sample—is given by $(\beta_{Y_A X_1} - \beta_{Y_B X_1}) X_1 + (\beta_{Y_A X_2} - \beta_{Y_B X_2}) X_2$. The weights which maximize the correlation of $\hat{Y}_{pt}$ with Y_{pt} are determined by the multiple-regression procedure. It is possible for the bivariate interaction to be statistically significant when neither univariate interaction is.

Equation (2.6) defines a regression plane for each treatment. The interaction is disordinal if the two planes cross within the joint distribution of the sample. It is possible for the planar regression to be disordinal when each univariate regression is ordinal, but not vice versa.

An attempt is often made to judge from the regression weights which variables are relevant to a prediction or interaction and which are irrelevant. Even if the population regression equation were known, the weights have to be interpreted with care. If X_1 and X_2 are correlated, various weighted combinations of them will correlate almost as strongly with outcome as did the weighting that maximized the multiple correlation. Only confidence-limit techniques (p. 86) allow one to define the range of X_1, X_2 combinations that may account for the interaction in the population.

The effects of error of measurement are more important in multiple-regression equations than in simple ones. Equation (2.6)—if known—is an appropriate basis for predicting success if the procedures for measuring of X_1 and X_2 are fixed. But if either or both measures will be made more accurate (or less accurate) when data for decision making are collected, the relative weights may be radically altered. The person making a theoretical interpretation should always be thinking of true scores. Where X_1 is the chief contributor in the raw-score equation, X_{2_∞} may be the chief contributor in the true-score equation. Sometimes, indeed, the sign of a regression weight is reversed by the correction.

Correction cannot be made by a simple extension of (2.5) to more variables. Instead, it is necessary to form the variance-covariance matrix for true scores, and to calculate the multivariate true-score regression equation from that. The covariance of true score with another variable equals the covariance of observed score with that variable, under certain assumptions. Under the same assumptions, $\sigma^2_{X_\infty} = \rho_{XX'} \sigma^2_X$. Methods of this kind have only recently been clarified

theoretically, and examples pertinent to ATI research do not exist. The few multivariate analyses reported in our substantive chapters are limited to observed scores. The methodological discussions on which future work will be based can be found in Tucker, 1971; Lord, 1974; Cronbach *et al.*, 1972, esp. Chap. 10; and Wiley, in Goldberger and Duncan, 1973, pp. 71ff.

In interpreting multiple-regression equations from the ATI standpoint, one should often think in terms of composite variables rather than of the original variables. Suppose, for example, that we have two predictors, Verbal and Nonverbal scores, and that both of these are perfectly reliable. Then the regression weights are perhaps as follows:

	Verbal	Nonverbal	Sum	Difference
Treatment A	1.3	0.8	2.1	0.5
Treatment B	0.8	0.5	1.3	0.3
Difference	0.5	0.3	0.8	0.2

Evidently, both Verbal and Nonverbal scores generate interactions, but the latter effect is smaller. The regression weight for the unweighted sum of the two scores is 1.3 + 0.8 or 2.1 in A, and 1.3 in B, implying an interaction effect of 0.8 in raw-score terms. And, on the other hand, the Verbal-Nonverbal difference has within-treatment weights of 0.5 and 0.3, a net effect of 0.2. It follows that the ability common to the Verbal and Nonverbal scores is the primary source of interaction. The effect for the Verbal-Nonverbal difference is modest; it would, however, appear larger in standard-score terms, since the s.d. of the difference is smaller than that for the sum.

Once a second aptitude variable enters the picture, second-order interactions are a possibility. In past research we find some indications that person characteristics do enter into higher-order interactions, although these effects have rarely been investigated and are difficult to establish without a large sample. To allow for a second-order interaction one adds a term

$$\beta_{Y_t X_1 X_2} (X_{1p} - \bar{\bar{X}}_1) (X_{2p} - \bar{\bar{X}}_2)$$

to equation (2.6). A difference between such regression weights for the two treatments implies that X_1 and X_2 *jointly* contribute to the interaction. With a greater number of aptitudes, one can represent triples, etc. But without better theory there is not much chance that third-order and higher interactions will be pinned down as significant.

Sampling errors with multiple aptitudes. Although this chapter is concerned with descriptive statistics rather than significance testing, it is vital to discuss here the effects of sampling errors in multivariate data.

Far too often, ATI studies have used samples of 20–60 cases per treatment; we shall discuss the sample-size requirements in detail below. Here, we may cite the instructive experience of Peters (1968). He randomly assigned 131 Ss among four experimental conditions. He was interested in two aptitudes, LCT and AS, in an experiment concerned with training in number conservation (see p. 375). He calculated the usual regressions of the posttest onto the aptitudes. Peters also had pretested on number conservation and he calculated AT regressions of the pretest onto the aptitudes. (Few investigators make this interesting check.) Peters found notable differences in the regressions at pretest, despite the random composition of the groups. (For a similar finding in an even larger study, see p. 246). The equation predicting the conservation pretest in one treatment was 0.8 LCT – 0.26 AS + constant, and in another was 0.01 LCT + 0.83 AS + constant. These differences were large and would have been considered important, if they were regressions of an outcome variable. Peters solved his problem as well as possible by entering the pretest as a third aptitude in his analysis of the posttest. We would of course recommend a larger sample, but it would have been possible for Peters to avoid much of the difficulty if he had defined subgroups homogeneous on both LCT and AS, and then randomly assigned to treatments *within* these subgroups. To use the pretest as a further stratifying variable would be still better.

When the population equation for the interaction is 0.5 Verbal + 0.3 Nonverbal, as in the example on p. 37, the regression equation accounting for interaction in a sample of 100 cases could turn out to be 0.4 Verbal + 0.5 Nonverbal, or 0.7 Verbal + 0.0 Nonverbal. There is no way to determine the population regression equation from sample data; even after making proper significance tests, one can only be confident that the sample equation probably defines *one* of the composites that will predict in the population. Confidence-band techniques can indicate how widely the possible weights range. A study of sample-size requirements by Gross (1973) concerned itself with the regression slope the sample regression equation would yield in the population, rather than with the weights themselves. His most striking conclusion was that the sample size required to achieve a given level of prediction in a crossvalidation sample increases in almost exact proportion to the number of predictor variables. This adds precision to an old principle: when more predictors are considered, the weights assigned to particular predictors become less and less stable. Sampling errors become particularly serious when there is a high degree of "collinearity," i.e., when one predictor can be estimated accurately from one or more of the others. For a recent statement on the problem, and references, see Linn and Werts (1973).

Two procedures are available for obtaining regression weights that are relatively likely to predict well in a crossvalidation sample, i.e., which better approximate population regression weights. One is the "free" stepwise procedure, which adds variables into the composite one at a time in order of their incremental predictive value, stopping when inclusion of the next variable would add little to the prediction. Various statistical criteria are used to guard against assigning weights that arise out of sampling error. This method in its usual form is not suitable for ATI research. (But see p. 71.)

The alternative procedure is a reduced-rank analysis. A limited number of composites of the original variables are formed by factor analysis or by clustering on the basis of judgment. Since only a few weights are fitted to the data, chance has less effect and the multiple correlation is likely to hold up under crossvalidation. Yet, since every original variable has a chance to enter the composites, all the variables may appear in the final equation. With 20 predictors, one could fit as many as 20 weights in a conventional within-treatment prediction equation. The reduced rank procedure, in contrast, might employ only six composites, and find that only four of those took on significant weight in either equation. By fitting four weights within each treatment, one nonetheless has brought most of the 20 variables into the prediction. The equation so formed may yield a higher or lower crossvalidation R than the equation obtained by weighting the predictors separately.

There is a disadvantage: reducing rank discards factors that appear in only one or two aptitudes, but that may nonetheless be valid predictors (Burket, 1964). The person contemplating any radical reduction of rank in his analysis should consult Browne (1970). Attention may also be drawn to Horst's (1974) comment on some new and powerful methods of crossvalidation for use with reduced-rank analysis.

Instead of forming composites on the basis of statistical analysis, one may of course establish them on the basis of some substantive theory. Thus, starting with a battery containing several conventional scholastic-aptitude measures and several of the Torrance tasks purporting to assess divergent productive abilities, one might form a simple total score to represent "general ability" (loosely but operationally defined), form a "convergent-vs.-divergent" score by subtracting the total Torrance score from the total of conventional tests (after weighting the two to make the variances nearly equal), and form a "verbal-vs.-figural" score based on the difference between two groups of subtests.

Table 2.1 Superficially different regression equations in two samples

Standardized regression equations derived from 16 predictors, in independent samples of about 100 cases	Multiple correlations in	
	Original sample	Crossvalidation sample
Sample A: 0.40 CMU + 0.23 MMT + 0.23 DMC	0.485	0.432
Sample B: 0.40 CMU + 0.37 MMT + 0.27 DST + 0.30 CMT + 0.22 EST + 0.17 NMT	0.667	0.420

After Hoepfner, Guilford, and Bradley, 1970

Whatever the procedure, it is essential that the regression equation for each treatment be calculated on the same set of variables. When a free-stepwise procedure is used, even though one starts every analysis with the same variable set, chance fluctuations in correlations will cause different variables to be dropped from the set in each sample. This is to be seen in Table 2.1. Hoepfner *et al.* calculated regression equations on two halves of a 200-case sample, after subjecting both halves to the same treatment. The predictor set consisted of 16 factor scores derived from a larger set of Guilford's tests. The analysis combined reduced-rank and stepwise methods. Even though the data sets differed only by chance, the variables retained in the stepwise equations differed from sample to sample. If the two sets of data had come from different treatments, the differences between the equations would have implied an interaction. In fact, however, equations made up with different weights or even with different variables may predict equally well within a treatment, in the next, independent sample. Thus, in Table 2.1, the B equation functioned in the A sample nearly as well as the A equation itself. The two R's were 0.420 and 0.485, respectively.

A side comment is to be made about the analysis. Hoepfner *et al.* reported standardized regression coefficients ("beta weights") and evidently used those weights in crossvalidation. This is technically incorrect (see p. 30). Standard deviations of predictors and criteria fluctuate from one sample to another, and consequently the standard score of +1 on CMU (say) corresponds to a different "raw" CMU score in each sample. Unstandardized weights have to be applied, in order to make the same prediction for persons in the two samples who have identical test performances.

In an ATI study, all variables in the regression equation for one treatment should appear in the equation for the second treatment, even if some weights are not significant. The reduced-rank procedure or the generalized regression analysis for ATI leads one naturally to apply the same predictors in all treatments.

The utility of placement decisions

From a scientific or explanatory view, small differences and small correlations often deserve attention. When a relation is to be the basis for an operating decision, on the other hand, one must ask whether it is strong enough to carry an appreciable practical benefit.

The model, as set forth by Cronbach and Gleser (1965), is abstract. Costs and benefits have to be expressed on a single scale of utility units, taking into account costs of testing, costs of the treatments, and the extra costs entailed by the placement procedure itself. Likewise, a single-valued assessment of the total benefit resulting from the immediate and future outcomes of the treatments is required. After these evaluations have been made, the net utility of any proposed decision rule can in principle be calculated. As we said earlier, the placement model is only a model, until dependable ATI are found.

To arrive at a general appreciation of the benefits from a certain kind of decision, one has to define hypothetical cases in terms of numerical parameters that are more or less characteristic of real cases. We shall set up a hypothetical place-ment problem with somewhat simplified assumptions, considering results in the population. We adopt the mathematical rationale of Cronbach and Gleser (pp. 307ff.). Consider two treatments, A and B, and an aptitude X. Express outcome U and cost of testing C in utility units. Assume that the X, U distribution is bi-variate normal. The within-treatment regression lines have slopes β_A and β_B and cross at $X = X^*$. By way of simplifying: we consider only population statistics; we set $\sigma(X) = 1$; we set the zero point on the U scale to the mean outcome in Treatment B; we write U_0 for the population mean in Treatment A, and assume that $U_0 > 0$. We write ξ for the ordinate of the normal distribution at X^* and ϕ for the area above X^*.

Suppose that $\beta_A > \beta_B$, which implies $X^* < 0$. Then the question before us is: What is the benefit when the group is divided, those above X^* being assigned to A and the remainder to B? For persons above X^*, the mean value of X is ξ/ϕ and the mean outcome is

$$(2.7) \quad \bar{U}_A = U_0 + \beta_A \, \xi / \phi$$

For the B group we have

$$(2.8) \quad \bar{U}_B = -\beta_B \, \xi / (1 - \phi)$$

Taking cost into account, we would have the following expression for the total utility when N students receive these treatments under the above placement rule.

$$(2.9) \quad \bar{U} = N\phi \bar{U}_A + N(1 - \phi)\bar{U}_B - NC$$
$$= N\phi U_0 + N(\beta_A - \beta_B)\,\xi - NC$$

We shall neglect C in what follows.

To learn more, we need to consider ΔU, the gain from making the placement into groups. Gain over what? Cronbach and Gleser—for reasons inherent in the structure of their book—compared $\bar{U}$ to the "*a priori* utility" attained when $N\phi$ random persons are assigned to A and $N(1 - \phi)$ to B. Here, however, it appears sensible to compare $\bar{U}$ to U_0, the outcome when everyone is assigned to Treat-ment A. Then, prorating over all persons,

$$(2.10) \quad \Delta U \text{ per person} = (\beta_A - \beta_B)\,\xi$$

The benefit, then, depends on the strength of the interaction and on the distance of X^* from the mean (since ξ has its maximum at the mean). But, since the $N\phi$ persons assigned to A would receive Treatment A if there were no differential placement, it seems equally appropriate to prorate the gain over the $N(1 - \phi)$ persons whose treatment changes:

$$(2.11) \quad \Delta U \text{ per person in B} = (\beta_A - \beta_B)\,\xi / (1 - \phi)$$

The gain has the trends shown in Figure 2.7. The per-person benefit is greatest in the "atypical" group when the crossover point is at the extreme left of the X distribution. Thus, a differential assignment that affects only a few persons may convey a sizable benefit to them. Essentially the same kinds of results would appear if we assumed $\beta_B > \beta_A$.

Hypothetical utility units become meaningful units only in discussion of a particular concrete case. But we can learn a good deal by proceeding on the assumption that one unit of utility equals the within-treatment s.d. of outcome. Here let us assume also that the outcome s.d. within treatments is the same, which means that we can speak of correlations rather than slopes. Now we learn from the figure that if the AT correlation is 1.00 in A and .00 in B (hence $\Delta \beta = 1$), and if $X^* = 0$, there is a gain of 0.8 units for persons in the B group, on the average. This seems to be appreciable. But of course AT correlations are far below 1.00. An institution might realistically hope to find one treatment where $\rho = 0.40$ and an alternative in which $\rho = 0.00$. That being the case, if $X^* = 0$, the utility-per-student-reassigned is about 0.3 s.d. (It is not impossible to obtain a larger $\Delta \beta$, especially when the slope of the regression is positive in one treatment and negative in another, as may occur with a bipolar personality variable.)

The utility for the students whose treatment is altered to capitalize on an interaction amounts to something like a rise from C to C+ in this example; that may be discouraging at first glance. But that benefit is averaged over all persons in Group B. We could not have expected to produce an appreciable improvement in outcome for persons near the cutting score. Their near-zero benefit holds down the overall average. The benefit to the student increases with his distance outward from the cutting score. Assuming correlations of 0.40 and 0.00, a person for whom $X = -2$ s.d. has a large probability of failing under Treatment A and (unless the crossover point is far to the left) a comfortably low probability of failing under Treatment B. *It is the expected benefit to the extreme cases that justifies the practice of placement.*

Design of ATI studies

Duration of treatment

From a formal point of view, an ATI experiment can be of any duration. In some experiments the entire treatment lasted only a few minutes. At the other extreme studies have sought to evaluate the impact of a college on its students, the treatment consisting of the entire four-year experience. Most of the ATI studies we have reviewed have been much too brief.

ATI research oriented toward the improvement of education should employ treatments of considerable duration. When testing hypotheses derived from theory within the experimental psychology of learning, one should often compare short,

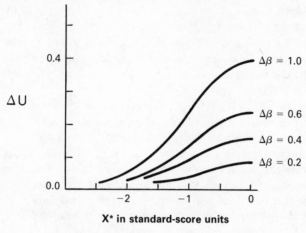

(i) Total benefit prorated over all men

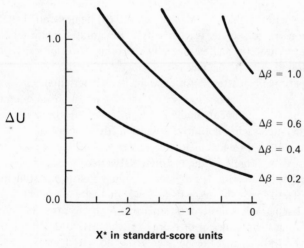

(ii) Benefit prorated over men assigned
to Treatment B

Figure 2.7.
Benefit from placement at different cutting scores.

sharply defined treatments. Even artificial experiments, however, must reckon with the troublesome fact that results from Ss exposed to a treatment for the first time are likely to differ from results obtained with experienced Ss.

Learning to learn is a well-established phenomenon in the laboratory (see Chapter 5); and the student in the classroom also learns to make use of an instructional procedure. Consequently, a kind of teaching that the person at first finds hard to handle can be considerably more effective later. In experimental comparisons, main effects among novices may differ from effects among those with experience (see p. 248). It follows that when a group is taught by a certain technique, some persons will proceed effectively and others will be inefficient. Whatever pretest variable reflects the relevant past experience will correlate with outcome. A contrast between a procedure with which everyone has had experience, and a treatment that is novel to some Ss, may lead to a finding of Aptitude x Treatment interaction. This is not of much interest if the interaction appears only during the first month of instruction. For example, Salomon *et al.* (1972) found that the attention given by lower-class children to *Sesame Street* (in Israel) increased considerably over a four-month period. On the contrary, the attentiveness of more mature children (older, middle-class) did not increase and may even have dropped off. Under such circumstances, an ATI found during the early application of an instructional treatment may actually be reversed in later months.

Many studies of teacher style or classroom climate have collected data by asking the teacher to adopt some style for just a few instructional sessions. Such comparisons are seriously limited. Mann *et al.* (1970) demonstrated that a class adapts over a long period to the teacher's style, the group climate shifting as anxieties abate or intensify and as mutually satisfying or reciprocally threatening strategies are found. The timing and pattern of the adaptation differ according to the students' personality patterns. An experiment that terminates before the climate has stabilized will necessarily leave the investigator with false impressions.

Just how long an experiment should last will depend on the investigator's resources, his intent to reach a definitive conlusion, the amount of effort required to install and maintain a treatment, the complexity of the response to be taught, and other factors. With most of the instructional variables examined in ATI research, a period of habituation is probably necessary before the student is working with full effectiveness; this leads us to think that an experiment lasting any less than ten class periods will be uninformative. A strong case can be made for experiments lasting for a semester or more. Yet there is no doubt a point of diminishing returns beyond which the AT regressions do not change.

Should an experimental design allow learning time to vary? Learning research can be designed either by carrying each subject "to criterion," allowing the instructional time to vary, or by holding the time constant and hence allowing attainment to vary over Ss. The former plan has been commonly used in laboratory research, even though interpretation of findings about, for example, differences in retention can become equivocal (see p. 113ff). Instructional research relied almost wholly on designs with time held constant, until programmed instruction became an object of research.

A fixed program is completed by students at different rates, and hence it seems appropriate to let time vary. But in fact one can reach an unequivocal conclusion about the main effect only when Treatment A produces better post-test scores than Treatment B *and* the average time of Ss in Group A is at least as short as the average time in Group B. If times and scores point in opposite directions, interpretation is impossible. Interpretation of individual differences and hence of ATI is even more puzzling.

Similar issues arise in the "mastery" strategy by which S is recycled through the original lessons or remedial activities until he reaches a satisfactory posttest score. Terminal attainment of different Ss is not uniform, even when they obtain the same score on the immediate posttest. Accomplishment assessed by transfer tests, retention tests, and tests of S's intellectual processes would surely show variations. The experimental design that allows time to vary, then, does not have the compensating advantage of "holding constant the amount learned."

We believe that investigators of ATI, and perhaps all investigators of educational learning, should try to hold instructional time constant in their designs. How much a student learns, over a year of instruction or over a fixed number of hours of work, meaningfully indicates the effectiveness of a treatment. This comparison bears directly on the problem the school faces of using each year of the student's school life effectively. Even where programmed instruction or a mastery strategy is used, it is fair to ask how much a person learns during a fixed time span, since in school the student goes on to other instruction once he has finished the first series of lessons. Not to appraise the surplus learning of those who finish early is to ignore a large part of their accomplishment. Or, conversely, it is to ignore the fact that those who spend extra time in recycling through lessons in one subject must be short-changed on other instruction. Costs as well as benefits ought to go into the overall appraisal.

It is sometimes hard to hold time constant. To study alternative modes of programmed instruction, for example, the investigator would need to prepare not only a first unit in each mode, which every S can complete within the time allocated for the experiment, but also follow-up units that would realistically represent how each technique would be extended if adopted in school practice. This is not an unreasonable demand. The basic issue in such a study is which mode to use as a regular policy throughout a course, not which mode to use for one isolated snatch of instruction. (In industrial training, our recommendation may be less reasonable. Whereas the school expects to keep the student through the year, industry might put the trainee on the job as soon as he achieves a criterion level on a worksample of task performance.)

Sample size

Persons validating selection tests or carrying out factor analyses are aware that sampling errors of correlations are large. They therefore take samples of 100 cases or more for each correlation, wherever this is practicable. Experimental psychologists are accustomed to deal with samples of 20 cases or fewer per treatment. In a two-treatment study, the risk of falsely accepting the hypothesis of no-mean-difference is then rather large unless the actual mean difference is great, but the experimenter manipulates effects and controls sources of error, and he intends to make effects great enough relative to error that a small experiment will detect them.

An ATI study is an experiment, and most investigators have followed experimental tradition, employing 40 or fewer *S*s per treatment. *This is radically wrong.* The ATI study must be much larger than a study where main effects or single correlations are at issue. The ATI effect is a difference in regression slopes. The sampling error of a difference in correlations is 1.4 times the sampling error of each correlation, and differences in slope are similarly hard to pin down. Even conventional experiments in education have typically been lacking in power, according to a survey by Brewer (1972; see also comments by J. Cohen, 1973; Dayton, Schafer, & Rogers, 1973; and Meyer, 1974). Consequently, published studies have often given little information, or misinformation. This problem is extraordinarily serious in the ATI literature.

Any rule of thumb regarding sample size must rest on assumptions and value judgments, and hence is to a degree arbitrary. We shall argue that an ATI study with *S*s assigned at random to one of two treatments ought to employ something like *100 Ss per treatment.* This recommendation must seem extravagant in the light of past practices. It casts doubt on virtually all past reports that accepted a null hypothesis regarding ATI. Their sample sizes made Type-II errors highly probable. That is to say, the hypothesis of no interaction has often been accepted when an important interaction was present.

One reason for insisting on power in ATI studies is that a psychologically and practically informative study of educational treatments must be of considerable duration, and the treatments often are costly to set up (considering preparation of instructional materials, etc.). Small experiments have an obvious place in the psychology laboratory where the experiment is usually suggested by a theoretical conception, and the conception is unlikely to be abandoned if a small experiment fails of significance. The usual response after disappointment is to modify procedures so as to strengthen the expected effect, and then to run a fresh experiment. The experiment that failed will probably not be published and so does not inhibit the field. In ATI research, however, negative results are likely to be sent to a journal for publication, if only because the investigator has invested much time and effort and wants credit for the work. We would be less concerned about power in an inexpensive experiment, likely to be repeated.

Our rule of thumb can be weakened when especially powerful experimental designs are used. An extreme-groups design using fewer than 100 cases per treatment can have satisfactory power (see p. 60 ff.). Stratification or matching of cases before random assignment to treatments can increase the power of the experiment. Sometimes a similar advantage can be gained by statistically controlling a variable that does not interact but that does predict outcomes; this control reduces the error term. A factorial design also can capitalize on a limited number of degrees of freedom. Thus in a 2 x 2 design with 50 cases in each of four treatments, one has 100 cases for testing the ATI of each "main" treatment factor; the study is almost equally powerful for detecting ATI at the cell level.

Before he collects data, an investigator ought to estimate the power of his design for testing effects of the magnitude that interest him. And every published report that "accepts" a null hypothesis ought to indicate how large an effect the experiment was powerful enough to detect.

Multistage experiments

We noted earlier that aptitude may change during the treatment period. This possibility can be taken into account by multiple-stage experimentation. The single-stage study assigns persons at random to Treatment A or Treatment B, applies the chosen treatment for i periods of instruction, measures outcome, and examines the AT regression. This could be replaced by a more complicated design:

1. Administer aptitude test.
2. Assign persons randomly to A or B and carry out treatment for $i/2$ periods.
3. Administer a further aptitude test (which may or may not be like the initial test, and which may be operationally like the outcome measure).
4. Reassign half the subjects initially in A, continuing half in A and reassigning the others to B; likewise for the initial B group. This assignment might be done in a random fashion, a stratified-random fashion, or a manner dicted by theory. (Theory might argue against shifting anyone from B to A, for instance.)
5. Carry out the treatments for $i/2$ further periods, and measure outcomes.

Many recent experiments have allowed working time to vary. In programmed instruction, for example, one may prescribe the same program to all Ss, but they will complete the program at different rates. (This does not mean a uniform standard of initial learning, however.) In so-called mastery-learning procedures in the classroom, it is recommended that students proceed through units "at their own rate," moving on to new assignments when they demonstrate adequate proficiency on each subsection of the course. More experiments on instruction are likely to adopt this scheme. We shall discuss some proposals of this type in Chapter 5. Here, it seems worthwhile to point out that designs that allow working time to vary are, in effect, multistage experiments.

Take a fairly simple example. A unit on magnetism is taught by programmed instruction. Students work through the material at their own rates, take a mastery test, and, if they fall short of the standard, work through the program again. No one is required to study the unit a third time. Some students finish the work in four class periods, some in eight. On Day 10 a final test is given, to judge the effectiveness of the teaching. It may include application tasks, and so go beyond the mastery tests. For the first three or four days all students are "in the same treatment." After that, they branch. On Day 5 some are still in the initial, first-encounter treatment. Some have taken the test, have failed, and are in a review treatment. Some have passed the test and are out of the "treatment" entirely. Hence by Day 5 the experimental group is divided between three treatments.

Quasiexperiments

In artificial experiments the investigator is usually able to assign subjects randomly, perhaps within aptitude levels. In educational experiments, randomization is rare, and sometimes it is out of the question.

Cronbach and Gleser, discussing the validation of tests for placement, spoke of dividing the validation sample at random between (say) sections covering a course at two rates of speed. But the school treads on ethically shaky ground if it permits an experimenter to assign students at random, so that half of the dull are taught at a fast pace and half of the bright are condemned to slow-section boredom. Still, tests for placement ought to be validated. What to do?

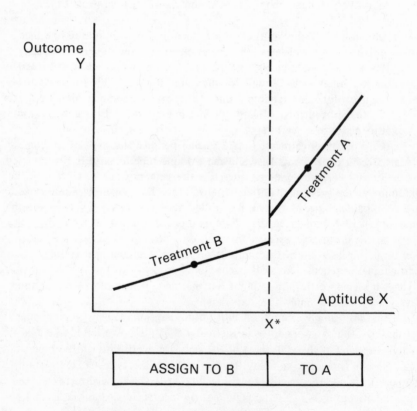

Figure 2.8.
Regression discontinuity in a quasiexperiment.

It is defensible to identify a score level (say, $X = X^*$) at which the treatments are thought to be equally suitable, and assign all persons above X^* to Treatment A, and all below X^* to B. Then the experimenter can examine the outcomes to judge whether the within-group AT regressions appear to be segments of a single linear trend. If the slopes appear to differ (as in Figure 2.8), extrapolation implies that the regressions cross. This "regression discontinuity" argument is an adaptation of the rationale put forward by D.T. Campbell and his collaborators (Thistlethwaite & Campbell, 1960; Campbell & Stanley, 1963; and Campbell, 1969). They take the discontinuity at X^* as evidence for a main effect.

In ATI research, one can consider the slopes of the two segments of the regression. This provides a somewhat dubious basis for claiming the presence of interaction, since a single curvilinear regression might account for what appears to be a difference in slopes between the two parts of the regression. On the other hand, this design does have one peculiar advantage over quasiexperiments where the assignment of cases is haphazard. With explicit selection on X (or explicit selection probabilistically related to X), the relation between the two regression slopes remains the same when a correction for error of measurement is made.

Equation (2.4) for estimating true-score regressions is based on the assumption that persons within a treatment group are representative of a population. The two sets of cases in a quasiexperiment are certainly not representative of the same population. If we treat the populations receiving the two treatments as distinct (because they are defined by unknown selection rules or by self-selection), we can estimate the true-score regression within each population. In general, we cannot expect the reliability of X to be the same in both populations, since with nonrandom assignment there is likely to be a different value of $\sigma^2(X)$ in each group. Thus, if regressions onto observed scores are parallel in a nonrandom experiment, the chances are that they are not parallel when disattenuated. It is the disattenuated regressions that are of fundamental interest.

Data from nonrandom experiments ought to be disattenuated before a conclusion is drawn about the presence of ATI. Suppose—to take a striking example —the two regression lines coincide, but the sample means on X differ. Then the disattenuated regression lines will not coincide, and whether they are parallel will depend on whether the two reliability coefficients are equal. For the current thinking on disattenuation, particularly with multiple predictors, see Cronbach *et al.*, 1976.

Many studies can be made only by comparing groups that have been formed in unknown or uncontrolled ways. The interpretation must then carry explicit warnings about the confounding of person characteristics with treatments and about the possible effects of unreliability.

Sometimes one can offer *a priori* reasons, plus distributional data, to persuade readers that assignment policies and other past events make the treatment groups representative of the same population even though the assignment was not fully controlled. Then there is warrant for reaching a general conclusion about, for example, the placement rules to be used in the future. One example is the use of operational data on successive college classes which, entering in different years, have received different treatments. Such comparisons often have to be made in evaluating a newly installed curriculum. Unless dramatic changes in population makeup are known to have been created by changed admission policy or the like, it is reasonable enough to think of such groups as if they were random samples from the same population. Comparison of mean outcomes and of AT regressions is then warranted, though it is not without hazard.

Chapter 3 | Testing hypotheses about interactions

This chapter describes and criticizes the established methods for testing the statistical significance of interactions. Less common, more elaborate analysis is reserved for Chapter 4, which expands upon various themes introduced here.

We shall recommend (p. 86) that ATI research use confidence limits instead of testing the null hypothesis as such. That shift seems likely to produce sounder interpretations. But since significance tests have been universal in past research they must be understood by anyone relying on the existing literature. For some purposes, moreover, F ratios will continue to be used even if confidence limits or Bayesian inference become the prevailing fashion.

We preface our description of significance tests with some discussion of the "philosophy" of significance testing. Though what we have to say has been said before in other contexts, a recapitulation is important here because students of interaction have too much emphasized the failure of interactions to reach conventional levels of significance.

Rigor vitae

The typical writer for psychological and educational journals seems to believe that significance tests sort relations into two classes: shadow and substance. A relation that "is significant" enters the enduring substance of the field. When $p \leqslant .05$, one has a real effect to explain. But when $p > .05$—to take the usual mystic number—the relation observed is a shadow, a chance perturbation. This treacherous dichotomy has two even less sensible variants. Some people seem to conclude that the nonsignificance of a relation itself provides a solid substantive finding, a demonstration that the null hypothesis is true. And others fudge the logic of the probability cutoff by once in a while taking as a substantive conclusion a relation for which p is .07 or .10 or even .20—rather in the spirit of Rip van Winkle's "I won't count this one." A person who thinks in this way is also likely to think that a relation for which $p < .001$ is known to be stronger in the population than a relation for which $p < .05$.

A p value reached by classical methods is not a summary of the data. Nor does the p attached to a result tell how strong or dependable the particular result is. Suppose that a journal carries 50 conclusions, for every one of which $p < .05$. Suppose that each study is now to be replicated on a further sample from its original population. The reader has no way to guess whether to expect 3, or 22, or 49 confirmations (p again $< .05$) of the original results. Writers and readers are all too likely to read .05 as $p (H | E)$, "the probability that the Hypothesis is true, given the Evidence." As textbooks on statistics reiterate almost in vain, p is $p (E | H)$, the probability that this Evidence would arise if the [null] Hypothesis is true. Only Bayesian statistics yield statements about $p (H | E)$.

All the findings of statistical studies are shadows on the wall of the cave. Some are likely to recur, but we do not know which ones. Significance testing is an act of discipline in social science. The scholarly community cannot attend to every relation or difference observed; in developing a body of knowledge it is necessary to restrict attention to some fraction of the propositions suggested by the shadows. Propositions are screened in an attempt to sift out a set of shadows of which a large proportion are likely to recur. One can make it a rule to attend only to results that have actually recurred in a second sample. One can give preference to statements that cohere when considered together as a theory. Insofar as these aids to selection are insufficient, social scientists have sorted shadows by attending chiefly to those for which $p < .05$.

Putting asterisks on a subset of the relations tested marks a class of relations which, taken as a class, yield more recurrences than a class selected by a more liberal standard would. It is fair enough to invite our friends to attend to these, to ponder their meanings, and to carry out confirmatory research. Without this kind of filtering, we would overwhelm each other by calling for attention to all the relations observed.

What we have said so far is pretty much the conservative, conventional wisdom. Another conservative remark is to be made, one which applies with especial force to research with multiple variables and multiple hypotheses. It is not uncommon for an ATI study to collect a large number of aptitude measures—some of them subtest scores—and to relate them to one or more outcome measures. Any relations for which a proper significance test reports $p < .05$ do indeed qualify for the pile of findings more likely to be reproduced. And yet, if an investigator has tested 100 pairs of regressions for significant difference in slope, he will almost certainly obtain a handful (five, or three, or eight) that meet the statistical requirement. If he has only a few "significant" findings, he ought to regard them as no more than a random five-per-cent sample from his proliferated hypotheses.

Look at it this way: He puts forth 100 hypotheses—in effect, 100 bets that he can identify variable combinations for which the null hypothesis will be disproved. He chooses to play on a wheel for which the house percentage—the α risk—is five per cent. When six rather than five of his bets pay off, he has no right to consider himself a born winner, or those six particular bets as acts of superior judgment. On his next plunge he may well lose to the house. The figure six out of 100 is a probability. Call it an estimate of $p\,(*\,|\,H_J)$—the probability that the conventional rules will reward with an asterisk the Hypotheses Investigator J states. Unless that probability is well above .05, J is not the bettor others are wise to lay their chips beside. Judging from the observed probability of .06, an asterisk in J's reports does not have the same meaning as an asterisk in the reports of Investigator K, for whom $p\,(*\,|\,H_K)$ is .30. If K can keep up such a record, he is obviously working on the basis of some sound understanding of the phenomenon he is dealing with. (The count must be based on all the hypotheses he tests seriously, not just the ones he publishes on! Note also that this argument is not complete, since nothing was said about independence of hypotheses.)

The investigator can properly use significance tests to discipline himself and to help readers focus their attention. He should not regard the table of F ratios or p values as a report of his observations. In our opinion, every report on an ATI study should carry basic descriptive statistics within each treatment. The needed statistics are the mean and s.d. of each aptitude and each outcome, plus the regression slope or correlation for each aptitude-outcome pair. This report can reasonably be simplified when a component analysis or the like has reduced the complexity of the data.

Interactions that do not reach significance should be described along with those that do, especially in analyses with low power. *Consistent* nonsignificant results are at least as valuable to a science as are incoherent significant results. Moreover, the implications of a nonsignificant result, for an hypothesis on which a significant result was previously reported, depend on the magnitude and direction of the relation in this second sample.

Discipline can be attained by forms of statistical inference other than tests of the null hypothesis. The confidence interval is a now-classical technique that enriches the descriptive interpretation and tells more about effects to be expected in the population (or in a replication) than the significance test does. We believe that associating confidence limits with regression lines (pp. 86ff.) provides a more satisfactory form of statistical rigor in ATI studies than conventional hypothesis testing. But in this chapter much must be said about conventional analyses.

How to think about exploratory studies

Abstract rules cannot advise investigators what hypotheses to put forward. Yet something can be said to help the investigator exploring ATI who has many relationships to test. Let us return to the two-aptitude problem of p. 37. Investigator J hypothesizes that Treatments A/B interact with IQ, and he has a hunch that Verbal/Performance IQs interact differently.* The conventional analysis is to

---

*Throughout this book we will use the slash (/) to imply a contrast: "A versus B," "Verbal as distinguished from Performance IQ."

run separate significance tests with V and with P. This is both inefficient and potentially confusing. For suppose that the interaction appears for each score, but only the Verbal interaction reaches significance. J has no justification for concluding that P fails to interact. He does not even have evidence that, in the population, V interacts more strongly than P.

Either of two procedures would reduce confusion. One is to rephrase the hypotheses. J had strong reason to think that IQ would interact; let him check the significance of the interaction of treatment with a Verbal-*plus*-Performance score. Since he then ought to be willing to bet on rejection of the null hypothesis, this analysis should count in his reckoning of p $(*|H_J)$. Second, J is curious about the possibly dissimilar relations for V and P. So let him form a Verbal-minus-Performance score and determine the nature and significance of its interaction. On this subordinate and exploratory hypothesis, no wager of reputation is warranted. Seen in this light, even a "significant" V–P interaction is not worth much thought until replicated.

An alternative procedure is a bit more subtle. Let J test the interaction of V+P as before. Then let him carry out a multiple-regression analysis, forming whatever weighted combination of V and P interacts most strongly with outcome. He can test whether weighting significantly reduces the residual outcome variance, i.e., whether the weighted combination predicts significantly better than the unweighted one. If so, J has some warrant for speculating about the meaning of the comparative weights of V and P.

We do not discourage hypotheses about complex aptitude combinations or specialized abilities. But the analysis ought to show clearly whether a differentiated hypothesis is actually better than alternatives.

When an investigator has measured aptitudes that intercorrelate, he should probably check out first the simple hypothesis that the sum of the aptitudes (or their first factor) interacts. Then, if he wishes, he may test whether the aptitudes enter differently into interactions. His complex psychological hypothesis amounts statistically to a forecast that the second, third, or later factors in the set of aptitudes will interact. If he tests the interactions for the several aptitude measures separately, he cannot say whether the variation *among* those several observed relations is likely to be replicable.

Similarly, conclusions implying higher-order interactions require direct testing. We have in mind particularly the study where the investigator, analyzing data separately for boys and girls, finds ATI significant for one sex and not the other. The disparity is not impressive until the investigator establishes confidence limits on the Sex x Aptitude x Treatment interaction itself. We shall discuss this matter more pointedly in Chapter 12.

Though we have no faith in significant relations seined out of a teeming swamp of *a priori* speculations, we encourage an exploratory attitude in the ATI investigator.

We shall later mention studies—some of them conducted by one of us or by an associate—that push the exploratory game to extremes. In the Carry study (p. 283) for example, "something interesting turned up" when he treated each item in his posttest as a separate independent variable (but the result did not reappear in a crossvalidation). When a Hidden Figures test was broken into two parts by Koran (p. 276), the first part interacted with treatment and the second did not. (There has been no crossvalidation of this.) Until replicated, unanticipated results of this kind are not "scientific findings." But it is just such first appearances of the unexpected that move scientific understanding ahead. The problem is to find a reporting style that gives due weight to obervations and does not trim the image of reality to conform to the published pattern of asterisks.

Given the complexity of the argument just developed, it seems well to quote another writer's expression of the same point of view (Cohen, 1968, p. 442).

> This, ultimately, is the reason that it is desirable in research that is to lead to *conclusions* to state hypotheses which are relatively few in number. This formulation is not intended to indict exploratory studies, which may be invaluable, but by definition, such studies do not result in conclusions, but in hypotheses, which then need to be tested (or . . . cross-validated). . . .
>
> A reasonable strategy depends upon organizing a hierarchy of sets of independent variables, ordered, by sets, according to a priori judgments. Set A represents the independent variables which the investigator most expects to be relevant to Y (perhaps all or some of the main effects and/or linear aspects of continuous variables). These may be thought of as the hypotheses of the research, and the fewer the better. Set B consists of next order possibilities (perhaps lower order interactions and/or some quadratic aspects). These are variables which are to be viewed less as hypotheses and more as exploratory issues. If there is a Set C (perhaps some higher order interactions . . .), it should be thought of as unqualifiedly exploratory.
>
> . . . The "perhaps" in the parenthetical phrases in this paragraph are included because it is not a mechanical ordering that is intended. In any given research, a central issue may be carried by an interaction or polynomial aspect while some main effect may be quite secondary. In most research, however, it is the simplest aspects of factors which are most likely to occupy the focus of the investigator's attention. . . .

Risks of false negative results

Chapter 2 (p. 45 ff.) offered a rule of thumb regarding size of sample. It is appropriate now to examine the arguments leading to that recommendation.

Just what sample size to recommend requires judgments on two points: what size of ATI effect an investigator intends to be fairly sure of detecting as significant; and what power level shall be chosen to represent "fairly sure."

Sample size for regression analysis. We would like to specify a certain difference in regression slopes that the investigator should be able to detect. But regression slopes have to be expressed in units, hence some form of standardization is required in a general discussion. Let us assume that $\sigma_X = 1$ in both treatments. We label A that treatment in which the regression slope is steeper, and scale Y so that the slope in Treatment A is positive and $\sigma_{Y(A)} = 1$. This standardization is not restrictive. (Writing ρ_A for $\rho_{XY(A)}$, etc., $\beta_A = \rho_A \geqslant \beta_B$.) Then, in principle, $\beta_B = \sigma_{Y(B)}\rho_B$ can differ from β_A either because $\sigma_{Y(B)} \neq 1$ or because $\rho_B \neq \rho_A$, or because in combination they produce a difference.

Within this framework we suggest that the investigator will wish to reject the null hypothesis if $\beta_A - \beta_B \geqslant 0.40$. Such a difference in slope seems likely to be theoretically important. In a particular practical context, costs and utilities could warrant specifying a greater or smaller effect size as important to detect. One might also make a "one-tailed" specification to place the burden of proof on an innovative or costly treatment. We believe, however, that a difference in slope of 0.40 will usually be of practical importance.

To reach a comparatively general statement, we shall assume in much of this discussion that the investigator wishes to detect a specified difference in correlations rather than in slopes. Ignoring possible variation in σ_Y probably does not greatly alter conclusions about sample size. *We shall assume an intent to detect an ATI represented by a difference between z-transformed correlation coefficients of 0.424*-a difference as large as that between ρ's of 0.00 and 0.40, or between ρ's of 0.40 and 0.69. We restrict the present argument to studies employing a single aptitude measure and a single outcome measure. More complex cases will be treated in Chapter 4.

We would like to set power at 0.90 (risk of Type-II error $\beta = 0.10$), when the two-tailed α risk is set at 0.05. With this power, an effect of the specified magnitude is likely to be reported as significant in nine studies out of ten. If the investigator replicates each study, he can expect that in eight studies out of ten this same effect will appear as significant. But we are mindful of Cohen's warning that power becomes costly (1969, pp. 53-54; notation altered):

> [F]or most behavioral science research (although admitting of many exceptions), power values as large as .90-.99 would demand sample sizes so large as to exceed an investigator's resources. Even when, with much effort or at much cost these large N's can be attained, they are probably inefficient, given the nature of statistical inference and the sociology of science.
>
> Why not seek . . . β risks close to zero? Why not use the simple principle, "the smaller the Type II error, the better"? . . . . [I]f β is made very small . . ., other things being equal, required sample sizes become very large. The behavioral scientist must set desired power values as well as desired α significance criteria on the basis of the consideration of the seriousness of the consequences of the two kinds of errors and the cost of obtaining data . . . .
>
> . . . [M]ore often than not, the behavioral scientist will decide that Type I errors . . . are more serious . . . than Type II errors . . . . The notion that failure to find is less serious than finding something that is not there accords with the conventional scientific view.

Moreover, the person who collects massive evidence locks his resources into the study of one hypothesis, whereas the person who revises his views as soon as he can analyze the first batches of data moves on more quickly to a better experiment, and so gets more for the same effort. But his decisions cannot rest simply on a premature, low-power significance test.

Table 3.1. Power of experiments of various sizes to detect a moderately strong ATI by regression analysis

Number of cases per treatment	Total	Two-tailed α risk			
		.20	.10	.05	.01
140	280	0.99	0.97	0.94	0.82
120	240	0.97	0.95	0.90	0.75
100	200	0.93	0.90	0.84	0.64
80	160	0.90	0.84	0.75	0.52
60	120	0.83	0.73	0.62	0.38
40	80	0.71	0.57	0.45	0.23
20	40	0.48	0.35	0.23	0.09

There are two treatments, and the z transformed within-treatment AT correlations have z values that differ by 0.424. Each entry above can be read as $1 - \beta$. Values are obtained by interpolation in Cohen's tables (1969, pp. 117–124). The values apply strictly to a test on differences in correlations, rather than to a difference in regression slopes.

Table 3.1 gives a basis for judging the benefits to be gained by increasing sample size when the alternative to the null hypothesis is $\Delta z = 0.424$. We shall discuss only the $\alpha = .05$ column. A sample of 40 cases (20 per treatment) will reject the null hypothesis only one time out of four, even though the variables actually enter into a rather strong ATI. An experiment of this size has a high probability of being misleading, of discouraging a line of investigation that rests on a valid hunch. Matters are a little better with sample size 80–120; half the time one is warned off a good line of investigation. By the time N reaches 160, the odds are 3-to-1 that a good hunch will be encouraged by the results of any one experiment. With a replicated experiment of this size, the probability is still only 0.56 (=0.75^2) that a z-difference of 0.424 will be detected as significant in both runs.

Investigators will differ in readiness to take risks. But we cannot recommend that an experimenter take seriously the failure of an appreciable observed ATI to reach significance unless N-per-treatment reaches the neighborhood of 100; even that leaves a substantial risk of overlooking a worthwhile interaction that is present in the population. It will be noted that the β risk drops by one-third as N per treatment goes from 100 to 120 or from 120 to 140. Hence, it may be quite worthwhile to collect a sample larger than the 100 cases our rule-of-thumb asks for. Large samples are somewhat less crucial when confidence intervals are reported, since they leave any "nonsignificant" relation in full view, and make it painfully evident when an experiment had too little power to give a clear answer.

The argument of this section again assumes that the ATI effects under examination are individual rather than group effects, and that individuals are sampled independently rather than by classes. When we examine the consequences of relaxing this assumption (p. 99 ff.), it will be apparent that even samples of 100 Ss per treatment leave the results of ATI experiments equivocal.

As we review the literature we shall apply the thinking of this section to decide which negative results to take seriously. This judgment will take into account the design, the sample size, and the statistical analysis. A study of low power may still be useful if it gives a positive indication of an effect, but absence of interaction in a small study will not be taken as impressive negative evidence. If several low-power studies report nonsignificant results of the same character, this is positive evidence *for* an effect. If low-power studies report strong effects in conflicting directions, they lend weight to the null hypothesis as against any single alternative. But they also suggest the possibility of higher-order interactions.

We act asymmetrically in casting suspicion on reports of nonsignificance while taking reports of significance from small studies more or less at face value. But the logic of significance tests does take sample size into account in guarding against false reports of the presence of effects. There is no reason to be more suspicious of a significant p in a small study than in a large one.

Significance is not to be accepted uncritically. The chief concerns are these: selective reporting of only those effects that appear to be statistically significant and suppression of studies with no significant result; testing of multitudinous hypothesis in some studies; calculating in terms of the number of individuals when the actual sampling or treatment unit was the class.

All of these practices require one to discount the isolated "significant" result that is not bolstered by replication or by a strong deduction from established theory. In some studies where we are particularly suspicious of inflation of probability levels we shall speak of an effect as "nominally significant," to imply a warning.

The reader will find that on occasion we dismiss a statistically significant effect as unlikely to be replicated in further research. We sometimes do this even though we can point to no specific flaw in the data collection or statistical analysis. The justification would have to be along Bayesian lines. Implicitly, when taking up a research report, any experienced reader sets some "prior probabilities" as to what outcomes would be consistent with his past experience, the relevant published research, and the current theories. Certain findings he would find credible; findings outside that range would be hard for him to believe. For example, when we encountered a report on the learning of boys/girls, given few/many examples of a concept, we expected that the treatment that worked better for one sex would also be superior for the other. That is, we placed a high prior probability on the hypothesis that the Sex x Treatment interaction is negligible. Though the investigator reported a significant interaction ($p < .05$), we dismissed it. Our judgment was influenced by the fact that the investigator had not anticipated the finding with a theoretical rationale. We shall likewise question many unexpected findings of V-shaped and Λ-shaped regressions.

Sample size in analysis of variance. Measuring an aptitude, dropping cases from the middle of the distribution, and randomly dividing cases in each of the tails to form treatment groups produces a comparatively powerful design. Interaction is usually tested by two-way anova. To evaluate the needed sample size, we follow a suggestion of Elashoff that applies directly only to the two-treatment study.

Again, X is fixed. It is scaled to have $\sigma = 1$ before mid-range cases are discarded. Bivariate normality of the within-treatment distribution before deletion of cases is assumed, and the difference to be detected in within-treatment slopes is set at $\Delta\beta$. We also assume that σ_Y has the same value for Treatment A as for Treatment B. The restrictions probably give results reasonably consistent with those we could obtain from a less restricted model. The assumptions, however, have the effect of underestimating the required sample size.

Let ϕ be the fraction of the population (i.e., of the intact distribution) assigned to either tail. Assume $N_A = N_B = N$, with $\frac{1}{2}N$ in each cell of the 2 × 2 design. N, then, stands for N-per-treatment. Let m be the mean value of X in the upper extreme group, in both treatments, and $-m$ the mean in the lower group. The value of m will be determined by dividing ϕ into the ordinate of the normal distribution at the cutting point. Let σ^2_{Xg} be the variance of X within each of the four extreme groups, and σ^2_{Yg} the corresponding variance of Y. Values of these can be obtained with the aid of the tables of N. Johnson and Kotz (1970). Then one can calculate the following index:

$$(3.1) \qquad d = 2m\,(\Delta\beta)\,(\phi/2)^{\frac{1}{2}}\,\sigma_{Yg}^{-1}$$

Entering Cohen's table for power of the two-tailed t-test, one determines the power corresponding to a specified α, N, and d; or, one enters the sample-size table and determines N. (A d' can be calculated if Dixon-Massey tables are to be used.) The use of the table for t or F is not entirely appropriate because the error variance consists of two components (regression and residual) rather than a single random error. Hence the results obtained should be regarded as a lower bound to the desired N.

An approximation can be developed by replacing $\Delta\beta$ with the product $\sigma_Y\,(\rho_A - \rho_B)$, and then assuming that $\rho_A = -\rho_B = \rho$. Then

$$(3.2) \qquad d = \frac{2m\,(2\rho)\,\sigma_Y\,(\phi/2)^{\frac{1}{2}}}{\sigma_{Yg}} = \frac{2mp\sqrt{2\phi}}{\sqrt{1 - \rho^2 + \rho^2\sigma^2_{Xg}}}$$

This centering of ρ on zero will rarely modify the result radically. Either ρ or $\Delta\beta$ may be specified as an effect size, but one cannot be derived from the other without also specifying σ_Y.

Table 3.2 indicates the sample size required to detect a significant ATI when, in the intact populations, the AT correlations are 0.00 and 0.40, or –0.20 and +0.20, etc. The column headed (50) is a base for comparison, derived as above,

(p. 57). (The two descriptions of the ATI effect are entirely comparable unless the larger of the two within-treatment correlations exceeds about 0.70.) The column headed 50 gives the sample size required when analysis of variance is applied after blocking cases at the median.

Comparison of the numbers in the (50) and 50 columns documents our earlier warning (p. 26) that the median split wantonly discards power.

Table 3.2. Sample size required to detect a moderately strong ATI by extreme-groups anova

Power	Percentage of cases entering upper or lower extreme group					
	(50)	50	33	25	20	10
0.80	90	151	81	59	49	31
0.90	121	202	108	79	65	41

The sample size is the required number of cases per treatment, both tails combined, in the first column, and a lower bound in the other columns.

It is assumed that in the population the correlations differ by 0.40, and that the β risk is .10. The analysis for ATI is anova with two-tailed α = .05, save in the column headed (50), which estimates the sample size required in a test of homogeneity of regressions using all cases.

A design treating upper and lower thirds of the population, or upper and lower quarters, is appreciably more powerful than a study with the same N distributed over the full aptitude range. Whatever the power desired, extreme-groups anova with cuts at the quartile points requires about 2/3 the number of cases that the regression analysis on a representative sample does. With more extreme selection of cases, the efficiency of the design is even greater. Unfortunately, the extreme-groups design is less practicable and less effectual when two or more aptitudes are under consideration. And it cannot disclose curvilinearity of regressions.

When samples extend over the full aptitude range, blocking of aptitude is an inefficient method of analysis. Table 3.2 demonstrates the loss of power in two-level blocking at the median. It appears worthwhile to give an indication also of the cost of three-level blocking.

Assume that blocking allocates Ss to three equal groups, with cuts at the 33d and 67th percentiles. Following Cohen (1969, pp. 363ff.), again assuming $\Delta \rho$ of 0.40 and α = .05, we have these required sample sizes per treatment: for power 0.80, $N \doteq 150$; for power 0.90, $N \doteq 198$. The test with three-level blocking has about the same power as a test made with two-level blocking of the same cases at the median. Treating the same number of cases from the extreme thirds would be more efficient. Indeed, in a full-range sample the analyst would increase his ability to detect a difference in slopes of linear regressions if he simply ignored scores of the middle group. When anova is to be used, the experimenter carries the middle third of his Ss through the treatment at some cost, yet gains no information about the linear regression. If he does carry all the cases, regression analysis is much more powerful than blocked anova.

These specific comparisons would not apply to other ways of dividing the group or to other effect sizes, but the general conclusion is clear: Investigators who have employed blocked anova have unnecessarily reduced the likelihood of rejecting the null hypothesis where it is false. Chapter 4 (p. 78) will offer a technique that can retrieve from a published table of mean squares much of the information lost by blocking.

Analysis of variance

The most rudimentary statistical test for the presence of ATI takes one of two forms: an analysis of variance with aptitude blocked and entered as a factor or a test on the hypothesis of uniform AT regression slopes.

The natural analysis for an extreme-groups design is Treatments x Levels anova. With High and Low aptitude groups and two treatments, the commonplace statistical procedure will produce mean squares for Treatments, Levels, Treatments x Levels, and Residual (Ss within cells). The F ratio for Treatments x Levels evaluates the significance of ATI. The procedure is readily extended to designs with multiple treatments. The test is generally applied soundly in the literature, but too often reports have given only the table of mean squares and F values, without cell means and s.d.'s or comparable descriptive information.

A common practice is to assign persons from the entire aptitude distribution to treatments, blocking them prior to assignment or for analysis only. As we said above, we do not recommend blocked anova except in the *extreme*-groups design.

A special fault of three-level blocking is that it often gives mystifying descriptive results. In a study by Fredrick and others (p. 265), outcome means (error scores) were 100 for Lows, 113 for Middles, and 61 for Highs. In a second treatment, the respective means were 95, 75, and 67. This is a contrast between a V-shaped and a Λ-shaped pattern of means. The linear regression slopes may not truly have differed and we cannot be sure that the curvilinearity implied by the three means is to be taken seriously. Choosing different cutting scores sometimes radically alters such a pattern, when N is modest. The possible nonlinearity of regression in the Fredrick results would be clearer if, instead of charting the means by blocks, the investigators had generated a moving average by plotting means for overlapping groups. Thus, starting with 150 cases within a treatment, one might aggregate the cases who hold ranks 1–20, 11–30, 21–40, etc., on the predictor, and calculate the X and Y means for each set. Plotting these means against each other would describe the curvilinearity in the sample while eliminating the presumably adventitious discontinuity reported above.

Testing parallelism of regressions

The regression test is familiar to most investigators as a standard preliminary to analysis of covariance. Investigators often are pained by significant heterogeneity of regression slopes because it casts doubt on the suitability of ordinary ancova for testing the main effect. But heterogeneity is the signal that an ATI is present, and the interaction should be interpreted.

Figures 3.1–3.3 have been constructed to aid in understanding the regression test. Figure 3.1 shows bivariate score distributions for the Ss of Groups A and B. Lines (1) and (2) are within-group regression lines (cf. Eq. 2.1). Deviation scores

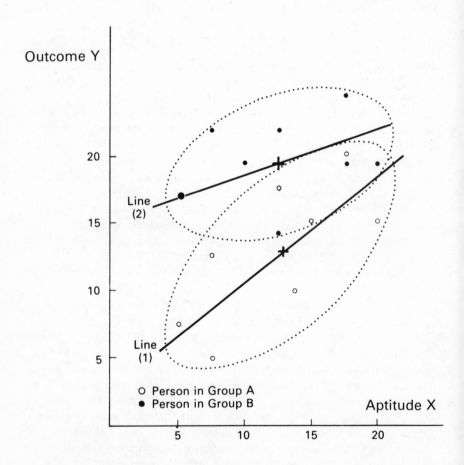

Figure 3.1.

Distributions of two treatment groups, with within-group regression lines.

$X - \bar{X}_A$ and $Y - \bar{Y}_A$ are calculated for each S in Group A; similarly in B. Distributions of these for the two groups are shown in Figure 3.2. The regression line (0) is then fitted to this pooled within-groups distribution; its slope may be designated b_{wg}. In Figure 3.3 regression lines (01) and (02), having the same slope as (0), are passed through the group means; these lines represent the null hypothesis. This allows the calculation of two kinds of deviation for each S; the deviation from the AT regression (1) and the deviation from line (01) in Group A.

In Figure 3.3, a dotted vertical line is inserted to represent the difference between the two estimates for one illustrative individual in Group A. For any person p in Group A there could be such a line of length

$$\hat{Y}_{p\,(01)} - \hat{Y}_{pA}, \text{ where}$$

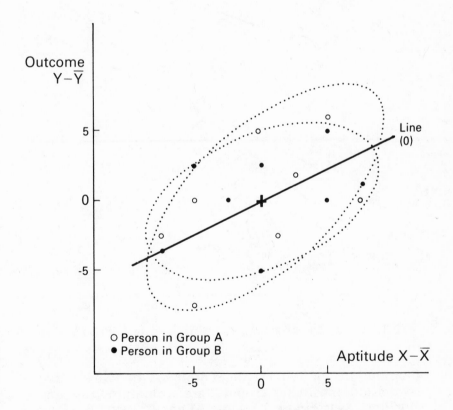

Figure 3.2.
Distributions of deviation scores pooled.

(3.3) $\hat{Y}_{p\,(01)} = \bar{Y}_A + b_{wg}\,(X_p - \bar{X}_A)$ = estimate from line (01)
using pooled within-groups
slopes

(3.4) $\hat{Y}_{pA} = \bar{Y}_A + b_{Y_A X}\,(X_p - \bar{X}_A)$ = estimate from line (1)
using within-groups slope
(special case of eq. (2.1))

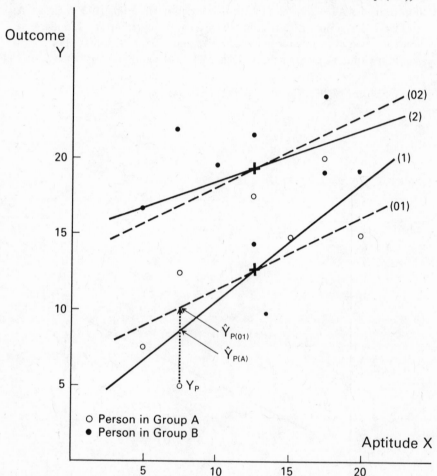

Figure 3.3.
Distributions for two treatment groups, with two kinds of
regression lines. Lines 1 and 2 are within-group regression lines as in Figure 3.1. Lines 01 and 02 have the slope
of the pooled within-groups regression as in Figure 3.2.

One squares this difference and sums over all persons in Group A. Adding in a similar set of values from Group B gives the sum of squared differences between the two estimates. Dividing by the number of groups minus one—here this value is 1—produces the corresponding mean square deviation. The dashed vertical line in Figure 3.3 represents the deviation of one individual's score from his own group's regression line. This has the form $Y_p - \hat{Y}_{pA}$, where Y_p is the actual criterion score for a person in Group A, and $\hat{Y}_{pA}$ is defined by (3.4). The sum of squares of these differences is divided by the number of degrees of freedom (the total number of cases minus twice the number of groups). This produces the mean square deviation within groups, the residual mean square.

Then the ratio

$$F = \frac{\text{MS} (\hat{Y}_{pT} - \hat{Y}_{p(OT)})}{\text{MS deviation about own-group regression}}$$

is calculated. The tabled F distribution is used to learn whether the obtained F ratio would be likely to arise under the null hypothesis. A significant F allows us to deny that the slopes of the regression lines for the two treatments are the same in the population; i.e., to deny that the difference in the slopes of lines (1) and (2) arises from sampling error. The test assumes that under the null hypothesis the joint outcome-aptitude distribution is normal and that values of X are fixed, rather than random. Further description of the process for testing homogeneity of regression may be found in many statistics textbooks (see, e.g., Walker & Lev, 1953; Winer, 1971).

Generalized regression analysis

We turn now to a form of regression analysis that embraces the procedures so far presented and opens up wider possibilities peculiarly suited to ATI studies. Generalized regression analysis is unfamiliar to most research workers in education and psychology, though some have used the variant put forward by Bottenberg and Ward (1963). The technique, prominent in mathematical statistics, dates back to the 1930's. Our readers are likely to find the following sources useful: Li (1964), Cohen (1968), Bashaw & Findley (1968), Walberg (1971), Dixon (1973, pp. 653–664).

In this chapter, we shall deal only with the case of two treatments, one outcome, and one aptitude. Elaborations are taken up later (p. 69). We start by repeating equation (2.3) of p. 29.

$$(2.3) \qquad \hat{Y}_t = \beta_0 + \beta_{0t}(T) + \beta_1(X_1 - \bar{\bar{X}}_1) + \beta_{1t}(X_1 - \bar{\bar{X}}_1)(T)$$

In the usual application of this form of the equation, with $N_A = N_B$, β_0 will equal $\bar{\bar{Y}}$. $\bar{Y}_t = \beta_0 + \beta_{0t}$ for Treatment A (if A is assigned the code +1 for T), and $\bar{Y}_t = \beta_0 - \beta_{0t}$ for B.

The equation states a general hypothesis. By specifying some β's to be zero, one can frame more limited hypotheses for test. One can then test contrasts between hypotheses, with appreciable economies in computing. Consider the most reasonable modifications:

If β_{1t} is set at zero,

$$(3.5) \qquad \hat{Y}_t = \beta_0 + \beta_{0t}\, (T) + \beta_1\, (X_1 - \bar{\bar{X}}_1)$$

If β_{1t} and β_{0t} are zero,

$$(3.6) \qquad \hat{Y}_t = \beta_0 \qquad\qquad + \beta_1\, (X_1 - \bar{\bar{X}}_1)$$

If β_1 and β_{1t} are zero,

$$(3.7) \qquad \hat{Y}_t = \beta_0 + \beta_{0t}\, (T)$$

One further equation is needed:

$$(3.8) \qquad \hat{Y}_t = \beta_0$$

Equation (3.7) expresses the hypothesis that Y is accounted for by a treatment main effect. β_{0t} equals the difference in population means $\bar{Y}_A - \bar{Y}$ or $\frac{1}{2}\,(\bar{Y}_A - \bar{Y}_B)$.

Equation (3.6) is a regression equation for pooled treatment groups. In the two-treatment case (3.6) expresses the hypothesis that, without regard to treatment, outcome is related to X_1.

In (3.5), the hypothesis takes both the aptitude and treatment effects into account. Equations (3.5) and (3.6) together allow a test of the main effect that is equivalent to an analysis of covariance, provided that assignment to groups was a random process with the X distributions fixed.

The hypothesis is typically encoded by writing 0 for variables irrelevant to the hypothesis and 1 for those that are relevant. We have these codes for the equations above:

	β_0	β_{0t}	β_1	β_{1t}
(2.3)	1	1	1	1
(3.5)	1	1	1	0
(3.6)	1	0	1	0
(3.7)	1	1	0	0
(3.8)	1	0	0	0

In this context, equation (2.3) is called the full model. Equation (3.8) expresses the hypothesis that treatment and aptitude effects are absent.

Each hypothesis is fitted to the data for both treatments pooled. The regression analysis for any hypothesis yields estimates of the β's for those variables coded as 1, a "sum of squares for regression"—i.e., SS $\hat{Y}$, the information predicted—and a residual sum of squares. Each SS has its proper d.f. which leads to the mean square (MS).

The simplest possible test is on the hypothesis $\beta_0 = 0$. Using (3.8) one divides

MS Regression by an MS Residual to get an F ratio. This tests whether $\bar{\bar{Y}}$ departs significantly from zero.

Equations (3.7) and (3.8) together allow a test on the hypothesis $\beta_{0t} = 0$.

Since SS $\hat{Y}$ from (3.7) embraces two "predictors" and SS $\hat{Y}$ from (3.8) considers only β_0, subtracting gives a sum of squares arising from the T effect. As there is 1 d.f. for this effect, this SS equals the MS for treatments. Dividing by an MSRes gives the F ratio for the treatment main effect. The difference between the SS $\hat{Y}$ of (3.6) and (3.8) leads to MS(X). The ratio of this to an MSRes is an F ratio testing the predictive power of X_1.

The strategy is to contrast one equation with another, asking whether adding a predictor to the equation raises the multiple correlation significantly. The test for ATI is of this kind. Equation (3.5) takes X_1 and T into account. Equation (2.3) adds an interaction term. The increase in SSRegr is achieved at the price of 1 d.f.

$$(3.9) \qquad F = \frac{\Delta \text{ SSRegr} / \text{d.f. for change}}{\text{MSRes}}$$

In all of these F ratios the denominator is usually based on the full model the investigator has set down. Above, (2.3) states the full model. One takes as the error term whatever Y variance is left after removing *all* the effects the investigator thought that it might be worthwhile to control when he planned the study.

Contrasts need not be restricted to equations that differ by only a single term. Sometimes it makes sense to consider several added effects at once. E.g., one might contrast a four-predictor equation with a two-predictor equation. Then it is necessary to use 2 d.f. for change.

The procedures of this section may be used with three or more treatments, with appropriate extension of the coding. The 2 x 2 factorial design will be treated below.

One can apply generalized regression procedures to extreme-group designs or to median splits. To represent high-low blocking on aptitude X, X can be encoded as +1/-1. The result is the same as that from 2 x 2 anova if cell sizes are equal.

Interpretation of findings is much clearer when one has a true orthogonal experiment in which Ss are assigned at random, the same number to each treatment. Results from designs where Ss are matched or stratified before assignment are also easily interpreted, although the analysis is more complicated. When treatment groups differ in aptitude or are unequal in size, serious difficulties of interpretation arise.

The procedure described above employs "step-up" F-tests, checking on the increase in R^2 as a variable is added to the equation, and the significance of the increase. A "step-down" procedure is also legitimate; from the full model one subtracts any variable and evaluates the decrease in R^2 and the F ratio for the change. The two procedures agree when the variables are orthogonal, but the step-down procedure can easily be misinterpreted when predictors are correlated.

A numerical example. We illustrate the generalized procedure with hypothetical numerical results. Suppose that $\overline{\overline{X}} = 3.0$ and that (3.5) is fitted, with these results:

$$b_0 = 7.10 \qquad\qquad b_{0t} = 1.32 \qquad\qquad b_1 = 0.60$$

Since $T = +1$ for Treatment A,

$$\hat{Y}_A = 7.10 + 1.32(1) + 0.60\,(X_1 - 3.0)$$

$$= 7.10 + 1.32 - 1.80 + 0.60X_1$$

$$= 6.62 + 0.60X_1$$

Entering -1 in the second term gives

$$\hat{Y}_B = 3.98 + 0.60X_1$$

These are parallel within-treatment regression lines, consistent with the hypothesis of no interaction.

If equation (2.3) is fitted, the terms given above will not change, but in addition we obtain b_{1t}. Suppose that this is 0.51. Then

$$\hat{Y}_A = 6.62 + 0.60X_1 + 0.51\,(X_1 - 3.0)$$

$$= 5.09 + 1.11X_1$$

$$\hat{Y}_B = 5.51 + 0.09X_1$$

These two equations describe the Aptitude x Treatment interaction. It is advantageous to put the equations in deviation-score form. In the raw-score equations above, it appears at first glance that $\hat{Y}_A$ tends to be smaller than $\hat{Y}_B$, since the intercepts at $X_1 = 0$ are 5.09 and 5.51, respectively. But in the deviation-score form the constant terms become 8.42 for A and 5.78 for B, bringing clearly into view the fact that, at the mean, A is the better treatment.

Chapter 4 | Statistical analysis: Advanced topics

This chapter assembles notes on statistical themes, most of which were introduced in Chapter 3. The chapter is disjointed, as it deals with topics at various points on the frontier of ATI analysis. While all the topics might be placed in the context of the overarching system with which we shall end the chapter, that would impose an overwhelming burden on comprehension at this time. Some of the points to be mentioned are parenthetical and speculative. Others we expect to be of major importance to the research of the next few years. We therefore hope that even the reader of modest statistical pretensions will scan the chapter.

Generalized regression analysis: Complex cases

In Chapter 2 (p. 29), we introduced the general regression equation in which a dummy variable T and its products give the analyses needed in an ATI study. We now take up more complex cases. The reader should connect this directly with pp. 65 ff.

Nonlinear regressions

The regression of outcome on aptitude can be curvilinear. Curvilinearity can be built into a model by adding further terms. Arches, half-arches, inverted arches, etc., can be described by adding quadratic terms to (3.5) and (2.3) to create these contrasting models:

	β_0	β_{0t}	β_1	β_{1t}	β_Q	β_{Qt}
(4.1)	1	1	1	1	1	1
(4.2)	1	1	1	1	1	0
(4.3)	1	1	1	0	1	0
(2.3)	1	1	1	1	0	0
(3.5)	1	1	1	0	0	0
(3.6)	1	0	1	0	0	0
(3.7)	1	1	0	0	0	0
(3.8)	1	0	0	0	0	0

The subscript Q identifies a quadratic term. The equation (4.1) contains $\beta_Q (X_1 - \overline{\overline{X}}_1)^2$ and $\beta_{Qt} (X_1 - \overline{\overline{X}}_1)^2 (T)$. A nonzero value of β_{1t} or β_{Qt} indicates an interaction.

Equation (4.3) is a quadratic function describing a pair of parabolas, that for $T = 1$ being displaced above that for $T = -1$ when β_{0t} is positive. Contrasting (4.3) with (3.5) tests whether curvilinearity is present in the population. If there is indeed curvilinearity, the contrast (4.2)/(4.3) is a more powerful test of linear ATI than the contrast (2.3)/(3.5).

The reader will have noted that deviation scores were used in the quadratic terms. It is possible to write terms in T, X_1, $X_1 \times T$, X_1^2, and $X_1 \times T$; indeed, most descriptions of generalized regression analysis use raw-score forms. We recommend routine use of deviation scores, which circumvents difficulties that arise when one predictor has a strong relation to some linear composite of other predictors. Starting with raw scores, the computer program may attempt to invert a correlation matrix some of whose roots nearly vanish. In such an operation, rounding errors may have large cumulative effects; this trouble is avoided by deviation scores. For example, X and X^2 are likely to correlate strongly if $\overline{\overline{X}}$ is large; but $(X - \overline{\overline{X}})$ and $(X - \overline{\overline{X}})^2$ are linearly independent. Deviations from $\overline{\overline{X}}$ and not $\overline{X}_t$ have to be used.

Linear regression with two treatments and two aptitudes

When a second aptitude is taken into account, the usual full model for an ATI study and the contrasting equation take this form:

	β_0	β_{0t}	β_1	β_2	β_{1t}	β_{2t}
(4.4)	1	1	1	1	1	1
(4.5)	1	1	1	1	0	0

The contrast with 2 d.f. for change is a test on ATI for both variables simultaneously. Equation (4.5) fits regression planes to each treatment, assuming a common slope, whereas (4.4) allows the slopes to vary. The contrast tests whether this variation is significant.

The model may be extended similarly to any number of aptitudes. One may enter terms stepwise, a procedure that is especially helpful when the number of predictors is large. It may be wiser, however, to use composite variables in place of the original scores. (Cf. p. 39.) In the two-variable case, one might write I for $X_1 + X_2$ and II for $X_1 - X_2$, and fit weights b_0, b_{0t}, b_I, etc. In this plan, one might well state the hypothesis:

	β_0	β_{0t}	β_I	β_{II}	β_{It}
(4.6)	1	1	1	1	1

The contrast (4.6)/(4.5) tests whether I interacts. To test whether II contributes further to the interaction one can contrast (4.6) with an equation having a β_{IIt} term [equivalent to (4.4)].

It is possible to add higher-order terms such as $\beta_{12t} (X_1 - \overline{\overline{X}}_1) (X_2 - \overline{\overline{X}}_2) (T)$.

An attractive feature of generalized regression analysis is that it enables one to ask directly which variable or which composite interacts most strongly with a set of treatments. This opens up the possibility of a free-stepwise ATI analysis in an exploratory study. Conventional stepwise analysis allows whatever variables to enter the equation that contribute most to the within-treatment multiple correlation, but those need not be the variables that interact most strongly.

Consider for example a study with five variables, two treatments, and a large N. The investigator decides not to form aptitude composites. He may set up a generalized hypothesis with β_{0t} and terms β_X, β_{Xt} for each variable. Then he can form the equation with β_{0t} and all the β_X; these have nothing to do with the interaction. At this point he shifts to the free-stepwise mode of regression calculation and allows variables to enter one at a time, according to the additional contribution made by their $\beta_{Xt} (X - \overline{\overline{X}}) (T)$ terms. No further interactions are fitted when one of these interaction effects proves to be negligible.

Interaction in a 2 x 2 factorial experiment

The flexibility of the general analysis in ATI work is to be seen in a study by Markle (1970; see our p. 281). Four treatments were derived from a 2 x 2 classification of conditions: verbal exposition with verbal exercises, pictorial exposition with verbal exercises, verbal-verbal, and pictorial-verbal. We assign the label

U to exposition; the alternatives are assigned codes $U = 1$ (verbal exposition) and $U = -1$ (pictorial exposition). The other classifying variable, kind of exercise, is labeled V. Then we might have the code $U = 1$, $V = 1$ for the verbal-verbal treatment, $U = -1$, $V = 1$ for the pictorial-verbal treatment, etc.

The full model needed to consider linear regressions and interactions of one aptitude is

$$(4.7) \qquad \hat{Y}_t = \beta_0 + \beta_{0U}(U_t) + \beta_{0V}(V_t) + \beta_{0UV}(U_t V_t)$$

$$+ [\beta_1 + \beta_{1U}(U_t) + \beta_{1V}(V_t) + \beta_{1UV}(U_t V_t)] \, (X_1 - \overline{\overline{X}}_1)$$

We may set up a few of the alternative hypotheses in coded form.

	β_0	β_{0U}	β_{0V}	β_{0UV}	β_1	β_{1U}	β_{1V}	β_{1UV}
(4.8)	1	1	1	1	1	1	1	1
(4.9)	1	1	1	1	1	1	1	0
(4.10)	1	1	1	1	1	1	0	0
(4.11)	1	1	1	1	0	0	0	0
(4.12)	1	0	1	0	0	0	0	0
(4.13)	1	1	0	0	0	0	0	0
(4.14)	1	1	0	0	1	1	0	0

Equation (4.14) is just like (2.3). It describes the hypothesis that X_1 interacts with treatment variable U. Equation (4.13) is comparable to (3.7), testing the treatment main-effect U. In (4.11), the fourth term allows for an Exposition x Exercise interaction (not an ATI).

Equation (4.9) has interaction terms for both main variables. Finally, (4.8) [coded version of (4.7)] brings in the hypothesis that the combination of exposition and exercises interacts with X_1 in a way not described by the separate interactions for U and V. The contrast

(4.8)	1	1	1	1	1	1	1	1
(4.15)	1	1	1	1	1			

provides an "overall" F test for ATI. If this is not significant, the separate interactions are not. If it is significant, the contrast (4.8)/(4.9) tests the significance of β_{1UV}, and the contrast (4/10)/(4.15) tests β_{1U}; this test is more powerful than the contrast (2.3)/(3.5) unless V effects are small. The reader can trace out other significance tests.

The coefficients from (4.11)—the model equivalent to two-way anova—were as follows in the Markle data:

$$b_0 = 14.67 \qquad b_{0U} = 2.15 \qquad b_{0V} = -0.32 \qquad b_{0UV} = 0.17$$

Then, for the verbal-verbal treatment ($U = 1$, $V = 1$),

$$\hat{Y}_{11} = 14.67 + 2.15(+1) - 0.32(+1) + 0.17 \, (+1)$$

$$= 16.67$$

The reader can verify that for the pictorial-verbal treatment the mean is 12.03, etc. The coefficients for terms in X are combined similarly, when these have been fitted.

Gain scores as the dependent variable

Gain scores—i.e., changes of level between two points in time—are often used to analyze learning data. Their use is particularly common in studies of school learning, where data are collected only before and after instruction. Although the simple difference between pretest and posttest seems to measure learning rate, such scores are likely to produce misleading results. One has to assume that test scores form a meaningful interval scale. This common assumption is rarely troublesome in ordinary measurement. But in dealing with gains the assumption of equal intervals is critical and it almost never can be defended. Also, the gain score is likely to be highly unreliable, since it combines the errors of two fallible measures. Errors introduce systematic biases; for example, the person who happens to be unlucky in his guesses on the pretest will for that reason show what seems to be an especially fine improvement.

Lord (1956, 1958, 1963), McNemar (1958), and Cronbach and Furby (1970) have suggested how true gain can be estimated so as to overcome many kinds of bias, though no estimate of a gain score can overcome the problem of scale intervals. Cronbach and Furby, however, after considering how to improve estimates, argued that estimates of change scores should rarely or never be employed. For describing and testing treatment effects they advocated use of the observed posttest score, or some composite of posttest scores, as the dependent variable.

Regarding interactions, Cronbach and Furby advised examining the within-treatment regression of posttest on pretest, or the multiple regression onto the pretest and other aptitude measures. They suggested determining regressions onto true scores (see p. 33 above) and pointed out that the regression onto true scores can be calculated directly from a variance-covariance matrix without estimating true scores for individuals. These remarks still appear to be sound, but we have turned up some new relationships. These relationships help us to interpret studies already in the literature where gain scores or residual gains have been analyzed.

We shall set up a simplified case by assuming that a very large group of Ss is divided at random between Treatments A and B. Both the pretest X_1 and another aptitude X_2 have mean 0 and s.d. 1. This standardization simplifies equations with no loss of generality. Y is measured on the same scale as X_1, but its means and s.d.'s are not constrained. We define β_{1A}, β_{2A}, etc. as within-treatment regression coefficients for the predictors taken singly, and define corresponding correlations ρ_{1A}, etc. We define β_1 as the pooled within-treatments regression coefficient relating Y to the pretest X_1 and write $\overline{\overline{Y}}$ for the mean of $\overline{Y}_A$ and $\overline{Y}_B$. We write ρ_{12} for the covariance of X_1 and X_2, since their s.d.'s are set at one.

Analyses of the same data with three different indices of the outcome are to be compared:

a.   Analysis of Y, the unadjusted outcome.
b.   Analysis of Y_{adj}, the outcome adjusted by β_1 as in ancova. Y_{adj}, is often referred to as "residual gain."
c.   Analysis of G, the gain, equal to $Y - X_1$.

The residual gain in Treatment A is

$$(4.16) \qquad Y_{adjA} = Y_A - (\overline{\overline{Y}} + \beta_1 X_1)$$

There is an analogous equation with B substituted for A.

Under our assumptions, the AT regression coefficient for X_2 is given by the covariance of X_2 with the outcome measure. For the three cases we have these coefficients in Treatment A:

a. β_{2A}
b. $\beta_{2A} - \beta_1 \rho_{12}$
c. $\beta_{2A} - \rho_{12}$

The difference between this slope and the corresponding slope for Group B is the same in all three analyses. The same conclusion is reached with X_1 as the aptitude whose AT regressions are examined, and also with an analysis that considers X_1 and X_2 together in the adjusting equation. The statement holds in quasiexperiments where the groups are not equated on X_1, and it also applies to the regressions onto true scores. The three raw-score regression equaitons all pass through the group mean; hence, the crossover point of the regressions will come at the same point on the X_2 scale no matter which form of the dependent variable is used.

This is important to our intended review of ATI studies because it means that previous workers who have taken gain or adjusted outcome as a dependent variable *have* reported accurate information about the difference in slopes. The same difference would have been reported if unadjusted outcome had been the dependent variable.

We must next examine the error about the AT regression under each mode of analysis. Since the effect size is the same for all procedures, the significance test for presence of ATI is least powerful for whatever procedure generates the largest error mean square. We refer to the error in the three cases as e_a, e_b, and e_c.

We need to derive the variance of errors only in Group A, since the equation for B will be the same except in notation. All variances and covariances should have a subscript A, but we omit it for ease of reading.

     a. We take $\sigma^2(e_a)$ as a baseline.

(4.17) $$e_a = Y - \hat{Y}|X_2 \qquad \text{(read } \hat{Y} \text{ as "} Y \text{ estimated from } X_2 \text{")}$$

(4.18) $$\sigma^2(e_a) = \sigma^2(Y{\cdot}X_2)\ [= \sigma^2(Y)(1 - \rho^2_{2A})]$$

     b. We next take up raw gain.

(4.19) $$e_c = G - \hat{G}|X_2$$

(4.20) $$= Y - X_1 - \hat{Y}|X_2 + \hat{X}_1|X_2$$

(4.21) $$\hat{X}_1|X_2 = \rho_{12}X_2$$

(4.22) $$e_c = e_a - (X_1 - \rho_{12}X_2)$$

(4.23) $$\sigma^2(e_c) = \sigma^2(e_a) + \sigma^2(X_1) + \rho^2_{12}\sigma^2(X_2)$$

$$- 2\rho_{12}\sigma(X_1, X_2) - 2\sigma(Y{\cdot}X_2, X_1{\cdot}X_2)$$

     Noting that $\sigma(X_1) = \sigma(X_2) = 1$, hence $\sigma(X_1, X_2) = \rho_{12}$,

(4.24) $$\sigma^2(e_c) = \sigma^2(e_a) + 1 - \rho^2_{12} - 2\sigma(Y{\cdot}X_2, X_1{\cdot}X_2)$$

(4.25) $$\sigma^2(e_c) - \sigma^2(e_a) = 1 - \rho^2_{12} - 2\sigma(Y{\cdot}X_2, X_1{\cdot}X_2)$$

(4.26) $$= 1 - \rho^2_{12} - 2\sigma_Y(\rho_{1A} - \rho_{2A}\rho_{12})$$

One cannot say, in general, whether the error mean square from use of gain scores will be larger or smaller than the error from use of Y itself. For example, if $\rho_{12} = 0$, the sign of the difference (4.26) depends on the size of σ_Y. With some parameters, analysis of raw gains is more powerful, as a means of testing interactions for significance, than analysis of Y directly (!)

  b. For adjusted outcome, assuming the population value β_1 known,

$$(4.27) \qquad\qquad e_b = Y_{adj} - \hat{Y}_{adj}|X_2$$

$$(4.28) \qquad\qquad Y_{adj} = Y - (\overline{Y} + \beta_1 X_1)$$

$$(4.29) \qquad\qquad \hat{Y}_{adj}|X_2 = \hat{Y}|X_2 - \overline{Y} - \beta_1 \hat{X}_1|X_2$$

$$(4.30) \qquad\qquad\qquad = \hat{Y}|X_2 - \overline{Y} - \beta_1 \rho_{12} X_2$$

$$(4.31) \qquad\qquad e_b = e_a - \beta_1 (X_1 - \rho_{12} X_2)$$

$$(4.32) \qquad \sigma^2(e_b) - \sigma^2(e_a) = \beta_1^2 (1 - \rho^2_{12}) - 2\beta_1 \sigma_Y (\rho_{1A} - \rho_{2A}\rho_{12})$$

Whether analysis of Y_{adj} gives greater or less power than analysis of Y or $Y - X_1$ depends on the several parameters. One cannot begin to say, then, which form of dependent variable will generally give the least error variance and hence the greater power.

As we leave this section, mention may be made of a dependent variable used in the first wave of research on programmed instruction: gain expressed as percentage of possible gain. Use of this measure is surely inadvisable. It compounds the problems of gain scores in various ways. For example, it magnifies the already large error of measurement among those Ss with high initial scores.

Improving the interpretation of anova

Estimating components of variance

  While some persons regard the F ratio as the main fruit of the analysis of variance, another line of interpretation opens up if one estimates "components of variance." The rationale and procedures are discussed thoroughly in such sources as Winer (1971) and we need give only a brief account.

  The person's score is seen as a sum of a number of components. The Treatment effect $\mu_A - \mu$ is the difference between the mean of Treatment A in the population and the general mean; it is equal to β_{0t} of generalized regression analysis. If sex is a factor in the experiment, there is an effect for males of magnitude $\mu_M - \mu$, and an equal and opposite effect for females. One may similarly have an effect $\mu_H - \mu$ for persons high on an aptitude that has been blocked into two levels, and an equal and opposite effect for Lows. Then there are various interaction effects; for males in Treatment A the effect is $\mu_{AM} - \mu_M - \mu_A + \mu$. Finally, there is a residual, the deviation of the individual's score from the population mean for the cell to which he belongs. One can estimate the variances of the components, e.g., a variance for the Treatment effects $\mu_T - \mu$, a variance for the Sex x T interactions, etc.

While it is customary for an investigator to judge the magnitude of a Treatment effect by inspecting the means, the square root of the variance component for Treatments gives a better indication, since it has been adjusted for sampling errors. Interpretation of variance components has considerable potential value when interactions are of interest, particularly those of higher order. The component of variance (or its square root) enables one to judge at a glance whether the interaction effect is large or small relative to the influence of other factors in the design and relative to the residual variance.

The equations for estimating variance components differ, according to whether the levels of the various factors in the experimental design are regarded as fixed or as random samples from some universe of levels. In virtually all ATI experiments it appears that the fixed model is appropriate; only persons (or classes) within cells are random. (An exception would be a study that considers teachers as randomly selected "treatment" levels.) The equations take into account the factor mean square and the number of levels of other factors. Thus, if we have three treatments and wish to estimate the variance component for Sex in a Sex x Treatment design, the equation is

$$MS_{Sex} = MS_{Res} + 3n\hat{\sigma}_{Sex}$$

Here σ^2_{Sex} is the variance of $\mu_{Sex} - \mu$, and n is the number of cases per cell of the design. The reader should see Winer for the entire system of equations. (At

---

Table 4.1. Analysis of variance components under a fixed model

Effect	Output from anova				Estimation equations		Estimated component of variance	Square root
	SS	d.f	MS	F				
Treatment	800	2	400	4.0	$(MS_T - MS_{Res})$	$\div (2)(50)$	3	1.73
Sex	400	1	400	4.0	$(MS_S - MS_{Res})$	$\div (3)(50)$	2	1.41
SxT	400	2	200	2.0	$(MS_{SxT} - MS_{Res}) \div 50$[a]		2	1.41
Residual	29400	294	100		MS_{Res}		100	10.0
	31000							

[a] Assumed number of persons per cell

times, for an effect whose F ratio is less than 1, the equations produce a negative variance estimate. This may be converted to zero.)

To illustrate the estimation of components, we start with a hypothetical 3 x 2 anova, which gives the output at the left in Table 4.1. According to the F ratios, Sex and Treatment effects are significant. The interaction is not significant, yet the estimated variance component proves to be as large as that for Sex. Moreover, both these effects are of the same order of magnitude as the Treatment effect (see the square-root column); hence, if one of the three is practically important, the others are also important. While the effects account for only a small proportion of the total variance, there may nonetheless be a practical advantage in raising the mean by choosing the better treatment, or selecting on the basis of sex, or assigning to treatment on the basis of sex. Once again, we have seen descriptive statistics (here, estimates of components) contradicting an impression given by inferential statistics.

Adjustment for two-level blocking

When a continuous Aptitude X is blocked into two levels, one can estimate a variance component due to X and its interactions just as was done for Sex above. No information is lost when Sex is treated in two levels, but information is discarded by blocking a continuous variable. Its variance components and the associated F's are systematically underestimated, compared to the results that would be obtained from regression analysis.

In order to correct these underestimates, we assume that the joint distribution of outcome and X is bivariate normal for Ss who are similar with respect to the other factors in the design (e.g., Treatment, Sex). Also, we have to assume that the *sample* distribution of X is the same in all these groups. Here we develop a correction for blocking at the overall median. A similar correction could be developed for any other division point and for an extreme-groups analysis. With further assumptions the methods could be extended to blocking on more than one aptitude. These corrections are to be employed when one must make sense of published results from blocked anova. Regression analysis of the original data is always to be preferred.

The basic argument is this: In the population the between-blocks variance of X is a known proportion of the X variance. With a median split, this proportion is $(0.798)^2$ or 0.637; and the within-blocks variance is the remainder, 0.363 of the total variance. Anova in effect determines how much of the variance in Y is predicted when each person is assigned the Y value that corresponds to the mean Y in his X block. If there is linear regression in the population, this variance is 0.637 times the variance of Y that could be predicted from the continuous X. That is, the potential contribution of X as a predictor is underestimated. If we represent that potential contribution by $\text{Var}'(Y_X)$, the estimate of the component of variance obtained from blocked anova applied to the population will (on average) be 0.637 Est. $\hat{\text{Var}}'(Y_X)$. The correction is to multiply the estimated value by 1.57. (This same multiplier is used in changing a point-biserial correlation to a biserial correlation.) Since with two-level blocking an interaction effect is a linear regression effect describing a difference in outcomes (between treatments or sexes, etc.) as a function of aptitude, the same proportionate reduction of components for interactions of X occurs, and a similar multiplication is needed.

Consider the simplest possible example: one treatment, Aptitude X blocked. This generates only two mean squares, for regression and residual. MS_X is the mean square for regression obtained directly from anova and MS'_X is the adjusted value; primes will also denote other adjustments. Note that there are mean squares, variances, etc., of the outcome measure, not of X itself.

(4.33) $\text{Est. Var}(Y_X) = (MS_X - MS_{Res}) \div 2n$

(4.34) $\text{Est. Var}'(Y_X) = 1.57\ \text{Est. Var}(Y_X)$

(4.35) $MS'_X = 2n\ \text{Est. Var}'(Y_X) + MS_{Res}$

(4.36) $SS'_X = MS'_X \times \text{d.f.}_X = MS'_X\ ;\ SS_{Tot} - SS'_X = SS'_{Res}$

(4.37) $MS'_{Res} = SS'_{Res}/\text{d.f.}_{Res}$

In principle, the above analysis should be iterated, as MS_{Res} had to be used in (4.35). One could apply (4.33) to MS'_X and MS'_{Res} to get a $\text{Var}''(Y_X)$ obtaining MS''_{Res}, etc. This sequence could be repeated. But the value of $\text{Var}'(Y_X)$ will be close to the final value from iteration. One can divide each mean square (original or adjusted) by MS'_{Res} to get a corrected "F ratio." Neither the original F values nor ours truly have an F distribution, however; hence, statistical inference is approximate at best.

Table 4.2   Components of variance, mean squares, and F ratios adjusted for two-level blocking

| Original results | | | | | Revised | Estimated component | Estimated |
Effect	σ^2	F	MS' (MS)	SS' (SS)	F	of variance	Square root
Treatment	3	4.0	(400)	(800)	4.0	3.01	1.73
X	2	4.0	571	571	5.8	3.15	1.77
X x T	2	2.0	257	514	2.6	3.16	1.78
Residual	100		99	29115		99.0	9.95

The general procedure, for designs with one aptitude blocked at the median, is as follows:

1. Estimate components of variance for effects involving X.
2. Multiply those by 1.57.
3. Work backward to get the corresponding SS'.
4. Add the SS' and the original SS for all other effects save the residual. Substract this subtotal from the original SS Total to get SS'_{Res}.
5. Calculate MS'_{Res}. Iterate if desired, omitting Step 2.
   Calculate new pseudo-F ratios for all effects.

This is illustrated in Table 4.2, using the numerical values from Table 4.1 but letting X replace Sex. The adjustment from Step 2 gives the entries 3.14 for components, along with 100.00 and 3.00. Step 3 gives the MS' of 571 and 257, from which the corresponding SS' follow. Subtracting 1885 from 31000 gives MS'_{Res} of 29115. $(257 - 99) \div 50 = 3.16$. And so on.

These corrections raised the F ratios for the terms involving X, but in this instance did not alter the judgments regarding significance. Whereas originally it appeared that the treatment effect was larger than the Aptitude and $X \times T$ effects, these effects are slightly larger than the treatment effect, after adjustment.

For a further example, with a more complex design, see p. 314.

More on power in significance tests

We have pointed out that an investigation with a small sample is likely to accept the null hypothesis as tenable even though a powerful effect is present. In Chapter 2 (p. 46), we introduced a rule of thumb for ATI research where the null hypothesis is to be tested: the sample size ought to reach 100 cases per treatment unless extreme groups are used. (This rule can be softened if a factorial design is imposed on the treatments. Suppose there are two treatment variables, A/B and a/b. Fifty cases, in each of the four cells of the design, would provide 100 cases for testing the interaction of the A/B contrast with aptitude, and for testing the interaction of the a/b contrast. The sample size would be insufficient, however, for a reasonably powerful test of the second-order interaction, of aptitude with Aa/Ab/Ba/Bb.) We now go more deeply into the rationale of power analysis, to provide background for the technically minded.

Comparison of required sample sizes: main effects, simple interactions, higher-order interactions

Our recommendation of large samples may have suggested that interactions are peculiarly hard to detect. This impression is reinforced by statements in Cohen's book on statistical power (1969). In many of his examples the power for tests of interactions was less than the power for testing main effects on the same sample, and the power for testing higher-order interactions was extremely low (his pp. 367ff.). Cohen said:

Although generally overlooked by behavioral scientists, the power of tests of interactions in a factorial design is distinctly lower than that of the main effects for constant . . . [effect size and α risk]. The reason for this lies in the fact that the n which governs the power of an $R \times C$ interaction test is the *cell n*, while the n for testing a main effect is a multiple of the cell n which depends on the number of levels of the other main effect(s). . . . Further, this relative weakness of interaction tests progresses sharply with higher orders.

This statement is misleading in its generality. Cohen's power was low because his examples were experiments with three or more levels of the treatments.

When one sticks to two levels per factor (for both aptitudes and treatments), power does not drop appreciably. Consider, for example, a $2 \times 2 \times 2$ design, with aptitude(s) blocked at the median; correction for blocking will not be made. Let us ask what sample size is required to detect, with power $1 - \beta = 0.80$, effects of the following magnitude:

main effect: cell means $+0.4\sigma$, -0.4σ;

first-order interaction: $\mu_{ij} - \mu_i - \mu_j + \mu = \pm 0.4\sigma$

second-order interaction: $\mu_{ijk} - \mu_i - \mu_j - \mu_k + \mu_{ij} + \mu_{ik} + \mu_{jk} - \mu$

$$= \pm 0.4\sigma$$

For comparability we define σ in all these cases as the population variance within the eight cells of the design. The respective effect sizes for entering Cohen's table are 0.4, $0.4\sqrt{2}$, and 0.4(2). Now, interpolating in Cohen's table for the F test with $\alpha = 0.5$ and 1 d.f. for the numerator (his p. 304-305), we read the required cell n's to be 25, 13.6, and 7.2, respectively. Multiplying by the number of cells (i.e., the number of means contrasted), we get the required sample sizes: 50, 54.4, and 57.6. While these values seem to increase, the increase comes from errors of interpolation. It can be shown (Rosedith Sitgreaves, personal communication) that the required sample size in all 2^k designs is exactly the same, for fixed α and β risks and fixed strength of effect. There is no "relative weakness of interaction tests" and weakness does *not* "progress sharply with higher orders."

Perhaps this will seem intuitively more reasonable if we refer to the generalized regression model with two treatments. In that analysis one tests, in turn, the significance of a string of β's representing the main effect of treatment, the main effect of each aptitude, the first-order interactions, and so on. Now if the residual MS and d.f. from the full model define the error term of each F test, the power for detecting a β of a certain size is the same no matter whether it is for a main effect or an nth-order interaction.

The weaknesses to which Cohen referred do appear in designs with three or more levels per factor. Any 2^k design assigns just 1 d.f. to an interaction of any order. In 3^k designs, the number of d.f. for interaction increases rapidly—4, 8, 16, ... This makes for greater variance of sample interaction effects when the null hypothesis is true, and hence requires larger samples to achieve a specified power. In a fully crossed design of size $n_r \times n_c \times n_f$, the number of cases required to test the highest-order interaction is a function of $(n_c - 1)(n_r - 1)(n_f - 1)$. The sample size for one of the first-order interactions is a function of $(n_c - 1)(n_r - 1)$.

Before moving ahead, let us pinpoint why our recommended sample size of 100 cases per treatment is so much larger than has been customary in experimental research. We reached our recommendation on the assumption that an aptitude will often predict an outcome (within treatments) with $\rho = 0.40$, and that this level of prediction is practically useful. One would be much interested in finding that a treatment where $\rho = 0.40$ could be contrasted with another where ρ is zero. The interaction (after adjustment for the main effect) is represented by a ρ of ± 0.20 or the corresponding β or, with a median split on aptitude, by a cell mean of ± 0.16. In a 2^k orthogonal design the cell mean for all interactions is at this same 0.16 level. This is simply a much smaller effect, harder to detect than a ρ of 0.40 or a block mean of ± 0.32. Thus, we need 100 cases per treatment, whereas the test on main effects needs 70. A smaller sample size tends to dismiss a main effect of ± 0.32. That may be reasonable in experimental psychology where σ is small, thanks to precise control of conditions and perhaps of much subject variation. It will rarely be reasonable to run an educational experiment that is likely to dismiss a net difference of 0.64σ as insignificant; so large an effect is almost always practically important.

Differentiating among outcomes

When two or more outcomes have been measured, most investigators treat them separately (i.e., successively) as dependent variables. When a significant interaction is found for one outcome and not for another, the investigator is tempted to give this disparity a psychological interpretation. Whether one interaction is stronger than the other is a meaningful question only if Y and Y' are scaled in a comparable manner. This seems to require a judgment in terms of utilities.

An evaluation is needed of the hypothesis that the rescaled interaction effects do not differ: H_0 is

$$(\beta_{Y_A X} - \beta_{Y_B X}) - (\beta_{Y'_A X} - \beta_{Y'_B X}) = 0$$

This can be converted to a significance test on the effect of interaction on the difference in rescaled outcomes. The null hypothesis becomes

$$\beta_{(Y - Y')_A X} - \beta_{(Y - Y')_B X} = 0.$$

That is, one can find out whether the difference between outcomes is affected by ATI.

In order to gain some impression of the power of ATI studies for detecting such differences, we shall consider a special case. Assume that $\sigma_Y = \sigma_{Y'} = 1$ within each treatment and that $\sigma_X = 1$. Assume also, for simplicity, that $\rho_{XY_A} = -\rho_{XY_B}$ and $\rho_{XY'_A} = -\rho_{XY'_B}$. We shall set ρ_{XY_A} at 0.197, rounded to 0.20. The corresponding Δz is 0.400 rather than the 0.424 used earlier, an unimportant difference. We assume that $\rho_{XY'_A} = \rho_{XY'_B}$ and denote it by ρ_{12}. Its magnitude determines what $\rho_{XY'_A}$ must be if the difference in interaction effects is to be detected as significant. Even with our assumptions, there are four variables in this system: $\rho_{12}, \rho_{XY'_A}, \rho_{Y_A Y'_A}$, and $\rho_{Y_B Y'_B}$ These constrain each other; fixing the last three implies a maximum and a minimum ρ_{12}.

Under our assumptions,

$$(4.38) \qquad \rho_{X(Y-Y')_A} = \frac{\rho_{XY_A} - \rho_{XY'_A}}{\sqrt{2}\ \sqrt{1 - \rho_{12}}} = \frac{0.20 - \rho_{XY'_A}}{\sqrt{2}\ \sqrt{1 - \rho_{12}}} = \rho_{X(Y-Y')_B}$$

Assume that the sample is just large enough--about 100 cases per treatment--to detect the interaction effect on Y (where $\Delta \rho = 0.40$) with power 0.80. Now $\rho_{X(Y-Y')_A}$ must be at least 0.20 in absolute value, to be detected as significant with power 0.80. Substituting 0.20 and simplifying, we have

$$(4.39) \qquad \rho_{Y'_A X} = 0.20 \pm 0.28 \sqrt{1 - \rho_{12}}.$$

To represent the case where the interaction effect on Y is not significant, we consider the negative value only. For any value of ρ_{12}, then, this equation indicates the maximum value of $\rho_{Y'_A X}$ that will allow the difference to be detected in interaction effects with the specified power. The following values show the trend:

ρ_{12}	= -0.50	0.00	0.50	0.75	1.00
$\rho_{Y'_A X}$	= -0.14	-0.08	0.00	0.06	0.20

Thus, unless $\rho_{12} > 0.50$, the experiment is not powerful enough to detect a difference in the interactions when the correlations ρ_{XY_A} and $\rho_{XY'_A}$ have the same sign. The higher the correlation ρ_{12}, the easier it is to establish the significance of a difference between interaction effects of a given size. Further detail on these trends will be given in the next section.

This result appears paradoxical at first. It is well known that as ρ_{12} increases the difference score becomes less reliable and has a smaller variance. Consequently, its relationships should be harder, not easier, to detect. The conflict is resolved when we distinguish between the likelihood that a certain relationship exists in the population and the likelihood that we will detect it if it exists. The fact that the variance of the difference becomes smaller with increasing ρ_{12} is what makes a mean difference of a given size easier to detect (size being expressed in the common metric of the rescaled Y and Y', and not restandardized on the basis of $\sigma_{(Y-Y')}$). As a difference between correlated variables is comparatively unreliable, a relatively small proportion of its variance is predictable. Consequently, X is not likely to have a practically important relationship with the difference in the population. Our power index states the probability of rejecting the null hypothesis about an interaction under the condition that the interaction effect in the population does reach a specified magnitude. This conditional probability could be multiplied by a Bayesian conjecture as to the probability that, over a population of experiments and with the given ρ_{12}, interactions of the specified magnitude will occur. The product—i.e., the probability that interactions *will* be detected—will decline as ρ_{12} increases, with any plausible conjecture.

Differentiating among predictors

A similar problem arises with two or more *predictors*. The X_1 interaction may be significant, and the X_2 interaction not significant. Do the two predictors really behave differently? This calls for a test of the significance of the interaction of $X_1 - X_2$ (or of their standard-score difference) with treatment. Perhaps instead the interactions for both variables are similar but short of significance. This raises the question, Does the sum of the two variables interact significantly? While we discuss the questions here in terms of significance testing, we shall see below that confidence-limit calculations are more informative.

An equation similar to (4.22) may be written for the correlation of $z_{X_1} - z_{X_2}$ with Y. We shall assume that $\rho_{X_1 Y_A} = -\rho_{X_1 Y_B}$ and we set this value at 0.197; this is the smallest interaction effect that can be detected with power 0.80 and α .05 when N per treatment is 100. Then Panel (ii) of Figure 4.1 shows the relations between N, $\rho_{X_1 X_2}$ (coded as ρ_{12}), and $\rho_{X_2 Y_A} = -\rho_{X_2 Y_B}$ (coded as θ). When $N = 100$, any combination of ρ and θ appearing below the line labeled $N = 100$ will, in 80 experiments out of 100, generate a significant difference between the interactions for the two variables (under the conditions specified). This result is the same as that for a difference between two outcomes, and the figure can be reinterpreted to apply to that problem. The figure indicates also the power of larger and smaller experiments. It is to be remembered that some values of ρ_{12} to the right of the figure are impossible, the constraints being most severe when the other correlations in the system are large.

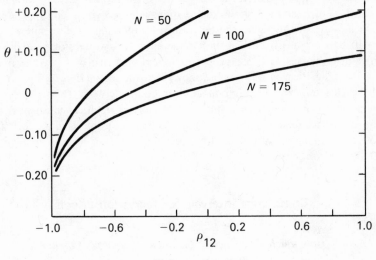

(i) Sum of variables

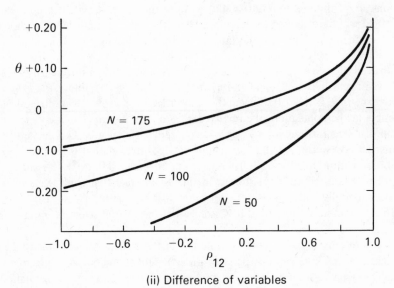

(ii) Difference of variables

Figure 4.1.

Sample size (per treatment) required to detect interaction with power 0.80, α 0.05, when a sum or difference of aptitudes is the predictor.

$$\rho_{12} = \rho\, x_1 x_2;\ \text{assume } \rho\, x_1 y_A = -\rho\, x_1 y_B = 0.197;$$
$$\rho\, x_2 y_A = -\rho\, x_2 y_B = \theta$$

The same kind of equation can be developed for the sum of two variables, and Panel (i) of Figure 4.1 shows the relations among N, ρ_{12}, and θ. The important message of this figure can be grasped by focusing on the point where $\rho_{12} = 0.18$ and $\theta = 0.16$. (Then the interaction of X_2 would not generally be significant in samples of 100 cases per treatment, and that of X_1 would only barely reach significance.) The figure shows that the interaction of $X_1 + X_2$ would reach significance with a sample of approximately 75. That is to say, when correlated predictors yield interactions short of significance, there is a good chance that the interaction for their sum will be significant. This supports the use of reduced-rank analysis or multiple-regression analysis instead of treating aptitudes *seriatim*.

Confidence intervals for regression effects

How much difference does choice of treatment make?

We have urged greater attention to the description of effects and less to decisions about the null hypothesis. But without the dikes of statistical inference the field will be swamped by fortuitous findings. One does not have to choose *between* the descriptive and the inferential; by establishing a confidence interval on each effect he can have both.

Instead of reporting that two means were 8.0 and 10.0, a difference of +2.0 not significant by t test, one can report that the confidence interval for the mean difference is –3.0 to +7.0. Since either a positive or negative mean difference is possible in the population, the observed +2.0 does not carry much conviction. If, instead, the interval is –0.02 to +4.02, a zero difference is acknowledged as a statistical possibility, yet the strong hint of a positive relation is kept in view. Similarly with a "significant" difference: the intervals +0.02 to +3.98 and +1.98 to +2.02 tell different stories. In view of the fact that confidence intervals are logically and numerically consistent with the traditional statistical tests, yet provide more information, it is strange that behavioral scientists rarely report them.

We note only in passing the possible use of Bayesian statistics, which take into account information acquired prior to the experiment and so set a different—usually narrower—limit on the presumed range of the effect in the population. Such methods are currently being applied in educational prediction and in principle can be applied to regressions in ATI studies. But that development is too far beyond present practice, and in too much dispute, for formal consideration here. (Note added in proof. A paper by Novick and others (1972) lays out procedures for adjusting regressions in a Bayesian manner. The paper arrives at a posterior distribution for the treatment effect, not for the slope itself.)

Many texts in statistics discuss the confidence interval for a simple regression equation (e.g., Dixon & Massey, 1969, pp. 197ff.). The rationale is a simple extension of that which yields a confidence interval for a mean. Instead of setting limits on the population mean μ_Y, one sets limits on $\mu_Y| X$. The interval is relatively broad when $| X - \bar{X} |$ is large. Over the whole X range the confidence limits sweep out a region bounded by an hyperbola (see Figure 4.2). The two lines that envelop the hyperbola are the steepest and shallowest (or steepest negative) regressions consistent with the sample data. The method extends to multiple regressions and to extreme-group designs.

One might apply this technique to the regression within each treatment in turn. A more direct statement about the limits of the interaction effect is obtained by setting confidence limits on $(\mu_{Y(A)} - \mu_{Y(B)})| X$. These are the population differences corresponding to the differences in outcome that describe the sample interaction. The technical formulation of the problem is given by Potthoff (1964); he requires the assumption, rather inappropriate to ATI work, that the σ^2 is uniform over the treatments.* We shall give one computing formula below. Wunderlich and Borich (1973) extend the technique to quadratic regressions.

Confidence limits with one predictor: a hypothetical example. We carry forward the hypothetical values from p. 28 to give a first illustration. Suppose that the variances, the sample size, and the chosen confidence level lead to these confidence limits:

$\underline{X}$	11	12	13	14
Estimated $(\bar{Y}_{(A)} - Y_{(B)})| X$	-3	0	3	6
Upper confidence limit	-1.2	1.1	4.1	7.8
Lower confidence limit	-4.8	-1.1	1.9	4.2

As Figure 4.2, Panel (i) shows, the region is narrowest at $\bar{X}$ (=12.5). In the sample, Treatment A was better than B on the average when $X > 12$. In the population, A is better than B when $X > 12.3$. The advantage lies with B when $X < 11.5$. Between 11.5 and 12.3 we are uncertain; on the average over all persons at this level, the advantage may lie either with A or B.

The region bounded by 11.5 and 12.3 is a "region of significance." The Johnson-Neyman technique for establishing such regions** has been discussed frequently in connection with ATI and has been applied in a few studies. The confidence intervals and the significance region are calculated from the same formula. The confidence limits, plotted as a function of X, carry information in addition to the significance region, and we therefore favor calculating them.

---

*We believe that a much weaker assumption can be employed, but have not located technical studies of the problem. A further unresolved question is whether these methods apply as they stand to ATI studies where assignment was nonrandom.

** This technique also assumes equal Y variances. We have not examined the effect of violations of the assumption, which are to be expected when ATI are present.

One can read off the maximum and minimum interaction effects. The table above suggests that the slope difference may be as large as

4.2 (= [7.8 −(−4.8)] ÷ [14 −11])and as small as 1.8 [=[4.2 − (−1.2)] ÷ 3).

This is not precisely accurate; the true limits, the asymptotes of the hyperbola, are shown by the dotted lines in the figure. Ordinarily they are calculated from the equation for the hyperbola. These limits give a sense, which no other technique offers, of the possible strength and possible weakness of the interaction in the population.

The results in this example are not fully understood until one brings to bear some sense of the utility of differences of 3 points or so in Y means, and also considers the range of X in the population. If the range of X is from 11 to 14 — cf. (a) in the figure—then the region of significance includes many persons. But if the range of X is from 12.2 to 12.8, no persons are found in the region where B is significantly better than A. (The preceding statements can easily be amended to recognize small fractions in the tails of the population.)

Aitkin (1972) has recently put forward an alternative to the Johnson-Neyman technique, based on an adaptation of work by Gafarian. Whereas the Johnson-Neyman method considers the range of the aptitude variable to extend indefinitely in either direction, the Aitken technique fixes a finite range symmetric about the mean. This allows for a smaller region of nonsignificance in some bodies of data, but makes for a larger one in others. The method presumably has a counterpart technique for arriving at confidence limits.

Confidence intervals provide information on the ordinality/disordinality of the interaction in the population. Figure 4.2 displays possible configurations that can arise with the same interaction effect in the sample (broken line). In Panel (i), assume that the sample range is (a). Then both the sample interaction and the population interaction are disordinal. With range (b) the sample interaction is ordinal and the population interaction may be. But the population mean difference can be negative at 12, and if so the true interaction is disordinal. The minimum degree of disordinality in the population can be described by noting what proportion of the sample falls in the region of indifference and in each tail of the region of significance.

The sample interaction (slope of broken line) is the same in all three panels. Wider separation of the upper and lower curves comes with larger s_Y or smaller sample or a higher confidence level. In the second hypothetical result, plotted in Panel (ii), there is no region of significance, perhaps because the sample is small. The F test for interaction would not reject the null hypothesis, as the population slope might be positive, zero, or perhaps slightly negative.

In Panel (iii) the lower branch of the hyperbola cuts the X-axis at two places and the upper branch never cuts it. The regression slope could be positive or negative in the population, hence the interaction is not significant. A is better than B when X lies between 12.4 and 14.1, but the issue is in doubt outside that region of significance. Here the region of uncertainty has two tails. It is particularly to be noted that this analysis allows a strong generalization when the range is narrow. When the range is (b), A is better than B for virtually all persons. When the range is (a), there is again a main effect, but not necessarily throughout the entire range. Thus, the interaction analysis adds information about the main effect even though the presence of interaction is questionable (cf. Ferster, 1971).

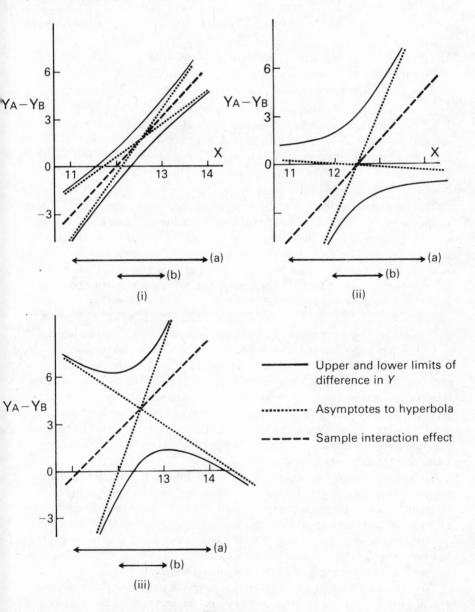

Figure 4.2.
Confidence intervals for interaction effects.

Extension to two predictors. We give the equation for only one of several variants of the technique, simplifying Potthoff's formula (his 3.1). For *one* predictor and two treatment groups of size N_A and N_B, one forms the following quantity:

$$(4.41)\,\delta^2 = 2F_{2,\,\text{d.f.}}\left(\frac{1}{N_A} + \frac{1}{N_B} + \frac{(X - \bar{X}_{(A)})^2}{(N_A - 1)}\cdot\frac{1}{s^2_{X(A)}} + \frac{(X - \bar{X}_{(B)})^2}{N_B - 1}\cdot\frac{1}{s^2_{X(B)}} \right)s$$

The *F ratio* corresponds to an α risk equal to 1 minus the intended confidence level, and d.f. is the number of degrees of freedom for SS_{Res} (here, equal to $N_A + N_B - 4$). The sample residual mean square, s^2_e, is the mean square of the deviations from the regression lines, pooled over treatments. The value of $\hat{Y}_A - \hat{Y}_B = \Delta\hat{Y}$ is obtained by subtracting one within-treatment regression equation from the other. This function of X describes the interaction. $\Delta\hat{Y} \pm \delta$, likewise a function of X, is the equation of the hyperbola that describes the confidence limits. When there are r predictors, the coefficient within the brackets is replaced by $(r + 1)F_{r + 1,\,\text{d.f.}}$.

This calculation is stated in terms of a "simultaneous" confidence limit. To set a "successive" confidence limit one uses a smaller value of F (see Potthoff). The asymptotes deriving from the F defined above will fan further away from the sample regression line than those describing the successive limits, making the region of uncertainty wider. The successive limit was embodied in the traditional Johnson-Neyman calculations, but we accept Potthoff's argument (his pp. 243–244) that the simultaneous limit is better suited to ATI research. The existing computer programs for the Johnson-Neyman method (e.g., Borich, 1971; Borich & Wunderlich, 1973) can readily be modified to generate simultaneous limits.

Confidence techniques are, in a sense, conservative. When the confidence level (=1 - α) is set at .90 and N per treatment is below 100, the region of uncertainty is likely to extend over the entire X continuum. The use of confidence intervals is precisely the way to bring this uncertainty into the open. One may prefer, however, to accept a less conservative level of confidence. A 70-per-cent confidence level (α = .30) may be suitable, in Potthoff's view. It will be recalled that when test scores are converted to confidence intervals for use in guidance, a 68-per-cent confidence level is commonly set.

The confidence intervals apply to data from a true experiment, with random assignment to treatments. In a quasiexperiment, the treatment groups were differentiated on unknown bases (including self-selection). Then one can infer from each sample to its own population, but population and the treatment are confounded (cf. p. 48). Hence it appears illogical to test the interaction as if one had two samples from the same population. One can, however, establish the confidence limits for the regression in each group separately.

Confidence limits with two predictors: a numerical example. These methods extend to two or more predictors. With two predictors the confidence intervals outline an hyperboloid of two sheets, one above and one below the sample regression plane. The region of significance, instead of consisting of one or two line segments, will be a space defined within an ellipse or hyperbola. The envelope of the hyperboloid is an elliptical cone.

To show concretely the direction in which data processing should evolve, we work through an example from an old study by Austin Bond (1940). Bond used statistical methods closer to our suggested ideal than most recent studies have. Our descriptive report of the study (p. 304 ff.) illustrates how Bond applied the Johnson-Neyman technique; here we shall form a confidence interval. We shall relate a posttest called Evaluation of Authorities (EA) to the EA pretest (X_1) and a scholastic aptitude test (X_2). We label the experimental and control treatments A and B, respectively.

The data needed for the calculations were given by Bond (his p. 56) in the form of within-treatment means, s.d.'s and r's. The regression equations within-treatment suggested that the scholastic aptitude test was more relevant to the experimental treatment and the pretest more relevant to the control treatment. Bond gave the following raw-score equation relating D ($= EA_A - EA_B$) to the predictors:

(4.42) $D = 0.0589\ X_2 - 0.1747\ X_1 + 2.7392$

That is, persons high in scholastic aptitude and low on the pretest profited most from the experimental treatment. This plane is plotted in Figure 4.3. The interaction was disordinal, in the sample at least. (Such a relation of outcome to an achievement pretest and a general-ability measure appears with some frequency in the ATI research we shall review.)

To set up intervals for the interaction effect we need a standard error. The current method of computing this is to set s_e^2 equal to MS_{Res} from a generalized regression analysis; the Bond report permits a within-treatments residual to be calculated from s_{EA}^2 and the multiple correlation. Second, we need to fix a confidence level. We chose 0.90 for a successive interval, which corresponds closely to 0.55 for a simultaneous interval in this case. Any other confidence level would lead to an hyperboloid of much the same shape. If a higher level is chosen, the surface will pull further from the D plane and will have less curvature. The simultaneous intervals corresponding to confidence 0.70 would be about one-sixth wider than those pictured.

Instead of applying the Potthoff equation, we parallel Bond's calculations; the result will be the same. In his Johnson-Neyman calculation Bond formed a quadratic. Our expression differs slightly from Bond's, presumably because of differences in rounding.

(4.43) $2.2323\ X_1^2 + 0.2666\ X_2^2 - 0.4369\ X_1X_2 - 104.6694X_1$

$- 29.5731\ X_2 + 2960.3805 = \delta^2\ (d.f.)/t$

The number of degrees of freedom is 105 and $t = 1.66$. Substitution into (4.42) and (4.43) of values suitably spaced along the X_1 and X_2 ranges provides values of D, $D + \delta$, and $D - \delta$. The results are plotted in Figure 4.3.

The region blocked out in the X_1, X_2 space of the figure covers most of the range in the Bond sample. The cross-marks locate the mean. At the mean, and over most of the range, Treatment A produced better results, in the sample. The

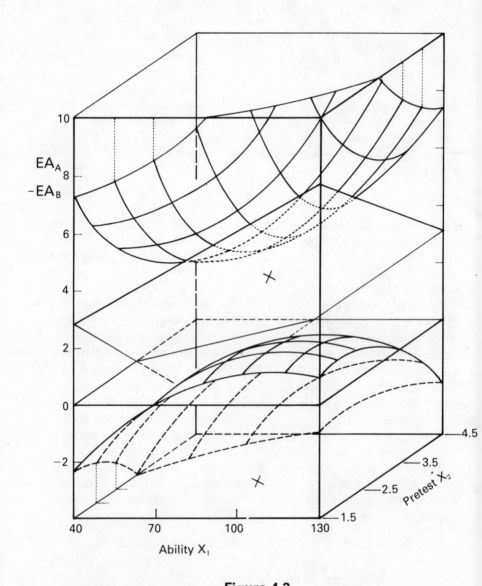

Figure 4.3.

Surfaces defining limits of the interaction effect on Evaluation of Authorities.

lower shell of the hyperboloid cuts through the $D = 0$ plane to define an elliptical region of significance, about one-fourth of which lies within the figure. A is presumably the better treatment for persons whose X_1 and X_2 locate them inside the ellipse. There is uncertainty outside the region. For persons at 15, 40, for example (front left), the population mean difference may be +7 or -2 or anything between. The within-treatment s.d. of the EA score is about 8 points; hence this uncertainty is a substantial one. The regression plane in the population might be horizontal; hence Bond's study, with 111 cases for this dependent variable, was not able to provide conclusive evidence that interaction is present in the population.

Reasons for rejecting an alternative test of ordinality

Examining whether the region of significance has two tails within the range is the only "test of ordinality" we can recommend. But another test has been put forward.

Bracht and Glass (1968, p. 446) proposed that any significant interaction be interpreted as ordinal unless the relation satisfies a severe test for disordinality. They called for a t test (or the like) on differences between treatment-group means among Ss in the left tail of the distribution, and for another test on Ss in the right tail. If and only if there is a significant difference in one tail and a significant difference of opposite sign in the other tail, the observed-score regression would be considered disordinal.

We do not consider this criterion appropriate. Bracht and Glass originally called the test "imperfect" and we understand from personal communication that they are now prepared to discard it. The proposal followed from their view that it is parsimonious to call an interaction ordinal until disordinality is proved beyond dispute. Bracht and Glass thus assigned ordinality a preferred position in scientific strategy, akin to that given the null hypothesis. But ordinal interaction is not a more parsimonious hypothesis than disordinal interaction. Once a significance test has established the presence of interaction, one has agreement that the regression function (2.3) for these treatments includes a nonzero β_{1t}. That term is required to describe either an ordinal interaction or a disordinal interaction, and one is not fitting additional parameters when he entertains the idea of disordinality.

Bracht and Glass required that two independent t tests display significance. If t is required to reach 1.96, when the null hypothesis is true the first test will be "significant" with $p < .05$. And the second test will reach significance in the opposite direction with $p < .025$. The Bracht-Glass paper, then, proposed to accept the hypothesis of disordinal interaction only with α risk .00125—the joint probability of these two occurrences. This implies that when the null hypothesis is valid they would report an ordinal interaction with risk .00475. Hence their test is strongly biased against a report of disordinality.

Confidence limits are a more powerful test of ordinality than the Bracht-Glass two-stage test, so long as the assumptions are satisfied.

Structural regression

Psychologists and educational research workers have generally classed variables as independent/dependent, and have chosen statistical procedures consistent with that scheme. In interaction research the independent variables are subdivided into those measurable prior to the experiment ("aptitudes," or "entering behavior") and those manipulated ("treatments").

Sociologists and economists are accustomed to thinking of chains of events: initial states, later causative variables, intermediate variables that reflect both kinds of influence, and terminal states. It is possible to tease apart these relations by means of path analysis, structural equations, and related techniques. Such methods are becoming increasingly significant in educational research, and they may be peculiarly valuable in studies of learning and ATI. We cannot deal thoroughly with the techniques and their limitations; the reader is referred to Goldberger and Duncan, 1973, and the annual editions of *Sociological Methodology* (Borgatta & Bohrnstedt, 1970; Costner, 1973).

A learning experiment often employs two or three "dependent" variables that are ordered in time—e.g., time required to reach criterion during the treatment, immediate posttest performance, and delayed posttest performance. The first is sometimes unmistakably a measure of learning rate, but in self-paced work it may have other interpretations. The usual analysis takes up the dependent variables one at a time, and tests treatment differences for significance.

A structural analysis presupposes directional relationships such as Figure 4.4 displays. The arrows represent effects, and a coefficient is associated with each effect. Here we write a, b, c, etc., instead of using the β notation. The zero value at the left implies that Treatment is independent of Aptitude. The effects U_1, U_2, U_3 refer to unexplained variance. Thus the c and U_2 effects, combined, are hypothesized to account for all variance in Y_2.

This hypothesized structure attends to the presumed causal direction of effects: Y_2 depends on Y_1, and not on Y_3. Completion rate is seen as an intermediate variable. The structure assumes that some effects are negligible. For example, the diagram shows no arrow connecting Treatment to Y_2. It thus states that any influence of Treatment on Y_2 is wholly reflected in (mediated by) Y_1.

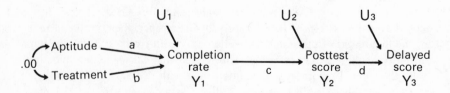

Figure 4.4.
Possible structural model in a learning experiment.

This working hypothesis may be contrary to fact. For example, two treatments might require about the same time-to-complete for persons of a certain aptitude level and yet produce quite different posttest scores. Figure 4.5 shows a structure with more parameters to fit (less restrictive). This structure could reduce to the first one, if the data show $e, f, \ldots$ to be negligible.

The structure in Figure 4.4 can be expressed in terms of these equations:

$$Y_3 = d(Y_2) + q_3 U_3, \text{ hence } \hat{Y}_3 = d(Y_2)$$

(4.44) $\hat{Y}_2 = c(Y_1)$

$$\hat{Y}_1 = a \text{ (Aptitude)} + b \text{ (Treatment)}$$

The "path coefficients" a to d can be evaluated by regression analysis. The more complicated structure in Figure 4.5 leads to

(4.45) $Y_3 = d(Y_2) + f(\text{Treatment} \cdot Y_2) + h(\text{Aptitude} \cdot Y_2) + q_3 U_3$

and other more elaborate equations. The dot implies that Y_2 is partialed out. Thus, f evaluates the direct, unmediated effect of treatment on delayed performance. If f is not zero, Treatment partly accounts for differences on the delayed test among persons who scored the same on the immediate posttest.

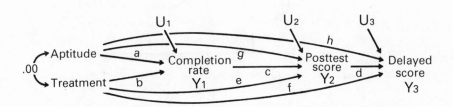

Figure 4.5.
More complex structural model.

We expect effects of Aptitude and of Treatment on outcome and want to entertain the possibility that the product Aptitude x Treatment has *additional* power to predict effects. The easiest way to represent ATI in the path diagram is to introduce a partial variate $AT \cdot A,T$. This device, however, leads to some problems of interpretation which Darlington and Rom (1972) have discussed. A more direct approach is to carry out the structural-regression analysis *within* each treatment postulating the same structure in all treatments.

Application of structural analysis to learning data

In Chapter 2, we recommended holding training time constant for all Ss rather than attempting to bring learners to a common criterion. In many studies, however, both time and amount learned are allowed to vary. If that is the case, it is necessary to consider time and level scores simultaneously rather than separately. Just how this is to be done remains obscure, but we have some hope that structural regression can be useful.

Structural regression has an importance for studies of retention and transfer quite independent of its use in ATI studies. In the typical study of forgetting, for example, each group of Ss is exposed to its own treatment. The Y_1 and Y_2 of the models above represent two aspects of "original learning," and the investigator seeking to explain the forgetting process ought to be primarily interested in the effect of the treatment on Y_3, the delayed test, after differences in Y_1 and Y_2 are controlled. If he tries to bring these under *experimental* control, he faces a dilemma. He can fix the number of trials, so that Y_1 is the same for everyone, but then Y_2 will vary as a function of treatment. (Y_2 may be total errors during learning, or score on the last trial, or score on an immediate post-test.) If he controls Y_2 by continuing training until S reaches some predetermined level of performance, he makes Y_1 a function of the treatment. This difficulty is discussed by Underwood (1964) and Keppel (1965), among others. For studies of short-term memory* they advocate controlling Y_2. This leaves Y_1 uncontrolled both experimentally and statistically.

It should be advantageous to examine the regression surface relating the delayed test to Y_1 and Y_2 (and to aptitudes). We suggest that in most studies of educational learning the experimenter should control the number of trials Y_1, perhaps setting different limits for different samples, rather than allow Y_1 to vary according to each S's learning. But the plan has to depend on the investigator's theoretical concerns and the character of the instruction.

We illustrate structural analysis with data from an experiment by Gagné and Gropper that we shall discuss more adequately in Chapter 9. For present purposes, the reader needs only a few facts about the design. In the first phase, Ss worked through an instructional program on certain background topics. This provided a time score ("Pre-Rate") and an achievement score ("Pre-Ach"). This preliminary phase was the same for all Ss. Ss then worked through a series of verbal lessons under one of three conditions: Visual supplement, Verbal supplement, no supplement. The rate of completion ("Rate") and a posttest ("Achievement") were taken as dependent variables. The test was repeated a month later ("Retention").

Rate can affect Achievement, the preliminary measures can forecast performance in the experimental material, and Achievement can forecast Retention. All regression coefficients called for by this structure are represented by arrows in Figure 4.6. To obtain a preliminary overall picture, we calculated these coefficients for all Ss pooled, using within-treatment deviation scores. Relatively important influences are identified with solid lines in the figure. The coefficients

---

*Underwood has dealt with the method of anticipation in verbal learning, and has "projected" a score to replace the number of correct responses on the last trial. In his specific research, delayed performance is not related to Y_1, when this projected score is held constant.

given are *unstandardized;* to aid in interpretation, the standard deviation of each
variable is shown in parentheses beneath the variable means. Interpretation is not
simple, both because this kind of reasoning is unfamiliar and because small
samples cause fluctuations.

Rate of work was forecast to some degree by Pre-Rate, which may reflect
either a consistent tempo or a consistent tendency to find both sets of lessons
easy or hard. The U variables are residuals–variance not accounted for by whatever variables come earlier in the system. These have been scaled with an arbitrary s.d. of 1.0. This small s.d. inevitably makes these weights disproportionate-
ly large compared to weights for variables with larger s.d.'s. Even allowing for
this, it appears that Rate was not so much influenced by Pre-Rate and Pre-Ach
as by unmeasured influences and chance. Likewise, Pre-Ach was little affected
by variations in Pre-Rate.

Achievement is affected by whatever enters into Pre-Ach and Pre-Rate, that
is, by abilities and prior knowledge. The negative weight for Rate (–0.27) is of

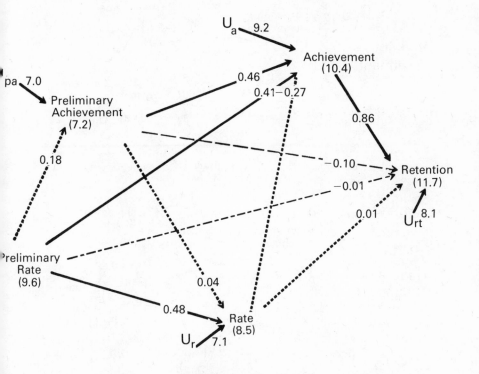

Figure 4.6.
Unstandardized path coefficients for all treatments
pooled. Numbers in parentheses are standard deviations.
S.d. for residual variables U is arbitrarily set at 1.0. Data
from Gagné and Gropper.

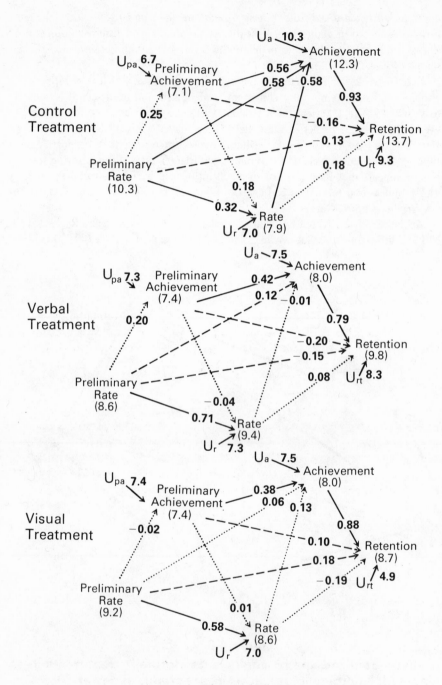

Figure 4.7.
Path coefficients for three treatments.

interest. The interpretation must take into account that any regression coefficient predicting Achievement is attached to a partial variate; the negative weight refers to Rate with Pre-Ach and Pre-Rate held constant. Among persons who came to the instruction with similar competence, and similar tempo as measured by Pre-Rate, those who worked through the main program faster achieve somewhat less. This makes sense.

Retention depended to a striking degree on initial achievement, but residual causes (including unpredictable vagaries of memory) also accounted for much variance. The tiny coefficient for Rate implies that the student who worked through the program rapidly was not thereby handicapped in his permanent learning, relative to others with the same Achievement.

Figure 4.7 presents similar diagrams for the treatment groups separately. The coefficient relating Pre-Rate to Pre-Ach varied from –0.02 to 0.25, most likely as a result of sampling fluctuations. This makes us cautious in interpreting variations among the coefficients later in the sequence. In fact, none of the differences between comparable coefficients turned out to be significant. Even so, some attention to the differences will increase our understanding of path analysis.

With regard to Retention, the striking difference is the smaller coefficient of U_{rt} in the Visual treatment; for unknown reasons, posttest scores were rather well accounted for by prior data in this group. With regard to Achievement, the notable difference is again in the residual; performance of Controls was highly variable and comparatively unpredictable. Note also that Pre-Rate was more relevant for Controls than others. Rate was more related to Pre-Rate among treated Ss than among Controls. The findings will be considerably augmented when aptitude measures are added to these pictures (p. 266).

This exercise probably is more confusing than clarifying to the reader who encounters path coefficients for the first time. Many of the clearest findings—the small values and very large values—would have been seen directly in the correlation matrix. Path analysis, however, can bring out facts not at all evident when outcomes are handled as separate dependent variables. Here, for example, the negative coefficient linking Rate to Achievement could not have been observed without path analysis, since the correlation itself was positive (but near zero).

A radical reappraisal of the ATI model

It oversimplifies to assume, as we have to this point, that individuals are independent units sampled from the population and treated independently.

It is widely recognized that cluster sampling biases the usual significance tests. When four classes are selected from a population of classes, the a risk calculated on the number of individuals is understated. Strictly speaking, one ought to carry out the calculation with the class as the unit of sampling. Thus one could test the hypothesis that the outcome mean is zero by comparing the mean of the four class means to the s.d. of those means.

While this argument about statistical inference from group data has been presented frequently, practically nothing has been written about the implications of grouping for hypotheses about learning. In instructional research, social effects are not unlikely. Even in programmed instruction, some students finish faster than others, and this is evident to their classmates. Such dramatization of differences may tend to demoralize the slow learner, in a way that would not happen if he were working by himself.

Regressions and interactions divide—at least in principle—into group and individual components that have distinct substantive meanings. Recognition of these distinctions forces a radical change in thinking about ATI.

Components of outcome in a classroom study with one treatment

For the moment we limit attention to one Treatment A, and simplify by assuming classes uniform in size. On the pretest X, each Class C has its own fixed mean X_c in this model.

Person P's score X_{pc} can be restated in terms of the class mean X_c and the population mean $\overline{\overline{X}}$:

$$(4.46) \qquad X_{pc} = \overline{\overline{X}} + (X_c - \overline{\overline{X}}) + (X_{pc} - X_c)$$

Now, to simplify notation and to indicate that our concept is *multivariate*, we write X_1 for $X_c - \overline{\overline{X}}$ and X_2 for $X_{pc} - X_c$. X_1 and X_2 may have different causal effects. $\overline{Y}$ is the expected outcome in Treatment A when $X = \overline{\overline{X}}$; it equals the mean of class means Y_c over the population of classes and also the mean of the individual scores Y_{pc}.

We may also divide the outcome score:

$$(4.47) \qquad Y_{pc} = \underset{\mathbf{1}}{\overline{\overline{Y}}} + (Y_c - \overline{\overline{Y}}) + (Y_{pc} - Y_c)$$

Since the class mean Y_c is predicted by X_c,

$$(4.48) \qquad Y_c - \overline{\overline{Y}} = \underset{\mathbf{2}}{\beta_1 X_1} + \underset{\mathbf{3}}{(Y_c - \overline{\overline{Y}} - \beta_1 X_1)}$$

Term 2 describes the between-groups regression—the tendency, perhaps, of abler classes to learn more. Term 3 is a residual, possibly useful in singling out exceptional classes for intensive study.

Decomposition at the individual level gives

$$(4.49) \qquad Y_{pc} - Y_c = \underset{\mathbf{4}}{\beta_2 X_2} + (Y_{pc} - Y_c - \beta_2 X_2)$$

Term 4 describes the pooled within-groups regression (an alternative to it would be the weighted average of the β_{2c}, the separate within-class regression coefficients.) We can carry the decomposition down to

$$(4.50) \qquad Y_{pc} - Y_c = \beta_2 X_2 + (\beta_{2c} - \beta_2)X_2 + (Y_{pc} - Y_c - \beta_{2c}X_2)$$

$$\qquad\qquad\qquad\quad \mathbf{4} \qquad\qquad \mathbf{5} \qquad\qquad\qquad \mathbf{6}$$

The regression equation within Class C can be written[*]:

$$(4.51) \qquad \hat{Y}_{pc} = \overline{\overline{Y}} + \beta_1 X_1 + \beta_2 X_2 + (\beta_{2c} - \beta_2)X_2$$

$$\qquad\qquad\qquad \mathbf{1} \qquad \mathbf{2} \qquad \mathbf{4} \qquad \mathbf{5}$$

Terms **3** and **6** together constitute the error of estimate. As a descriptive report on Class C, it is not adequate to give a regression equation in the form $a + bX$, (plus X_c, r_{XY}, and a standard error of estimate). When data on additional classes are available, one can and should report estimates of **3**, β_1, β_2, β_{2c}, and the within-class variance of **6**. One can also report the amount of Y variance accounted for by each of the components.

For purposes of statistical inference, one needs an unusual model. The model can specify that individuals are sampled from a population. Then they are assembled into classes by some mechanism which gives each class its own distribution of X. The mechanism may reflect some explicit policy of grouping students or may result from self-selection, neighborhood, etc. No student falls into more than one class. This forms a population of classes. Classes are then sampled (without replacement). An alternative model is simply to treat persons within classes as fixed, leaving classes random.

For establishing confidence intervals or testing the significance of effect **2** , classes are to be considered the unit of sampling. It appears most reasonable to evaluate **4** with reference to the variance of the β_{2c} over classes. Statistical inference with this two-stage model presents some unusual issues, and the appropriate procedures remain to be worked out.

The within-treatment regression equation applying to the population of classes is

$$(4.52) \qquad \hat{Y}_p = \overline{\overline{Y}} + \beta_1 X_1 + \beta_2 X_2$$

If one were to process the data by the conventional equation (2.3), ignoring the distinction between β_1 and β_2, the obtained regression coefficient would, in a very large sample, approach $\rho\beta_1 + (1 - \rho)\beta_2$, where ρ is the intraclass correlation of X. The more widely the class means vary, relative to the total X distribution, the greater is ρ .

This model has substantive consequences. It allows for Aptitude x Class interactions within a treatment. That is, some classes may have steep regression slopes and some may have shallow ones, because of the teachers' contrasting policies

---

[*]The model can be made more complex. It would be reasonable to consider a term in X_1 x X_2 or to divide β_{2c} into a part predictable from X_1 and a residual.

or because of subtler dynamics. A few studies in later chapters support this conjecture. Second, the model distinguishes two AT regression slopes, β_1 and β_2. It is possible to have β_1 large and β_2 small, for example, if able classes cover more ground and so learn more, while differences within the class are ironed out by remedial tactics. The reverse—β_1 small and β_2 large—could happen, for example, when the number of days the group spends on a topic is allowed to vary and the teacher leaves the topic as soon as the group has, on the average, reached satisfactory proficiency. This would hold down β_1 but would allow individual differences within the class.

Interactions at the class and individual levels

With two or more treatments, one must assume that after classes are sampled they are assigned to treatments. If the assignment mechanism is not random, the confounding of class characteristics with treatments complicates interpretation. Unequal numbers of classes per treatment also may cause trouble. We extend (4.51) into a more general model with the aid of a dummy variable.

$$(4.53) \qquad \hat{Y}_{pt} = \beta_0 + \beta_{0t}T + \beta_1 X_1 + \beta_{1t}X_1 T + \beta_2 X_2 + \beta_{2t}X_2 T + (\beta_{2ct} - \beta_{2t})X_2 T$$

The ATI is divided into a between-classes and a within-classes-pooled component. (Note that the within-treatment β_1 used earlier equals the $\beta_1 + \beta_{1t}T$ of this general notation and the former β_2 now becomes $\beta_2 + \beta_{2ct}T$.) In principle, one could identify a further interaction component specific to Class C. As it is almost never practicable to expose a class to more than one treatment, this last elaboration is not very profitable. With one treatment per class, β_{2ct} and β_{2c} are indistinguishable. There is no way to separate β_{2ct} into the Class x Aptitude interaction and the Class x Treatment x Aptitude interaction.

A reasonable procedure is stepwise prediction of Y_{ct} from X_1 and T, which gives equal weight to each class. One would fit b_0, b_{0t}, b_1, and b_{1t}, in turn. The second phase of the analysis predicts $Y_{pc} - Y_c$ from X_2 and T. One would fit b_2, b_{2t}, and b_{2ct} in turn. An alternative computational procedure gives equal weight to individuals.

Discussion

Ambiguity of traditional reports of ATI. Once we conceive of two distinct interactions, it becomes apparent that previous ATI studies have not asked as penetrating a question as they should. Except for a few studies of teacher effects, the investigator of ATI has reported a single composite ATI, calculated either between classes or on classes pooled.

The between-classes analysis ignores within-class effects. The pooled analysis leaves effects mingled. It is possible for β_{1t} and β_{2t} to be opposite in sign, and in that case the pooled-classes analysis will suggest less interaction than is present.

When β_{1t} and β_{2t} are unequal—regardless of sign—their comparative influence in the composite interaction depends on the intraclass correlation of X. When classes vary considerably in X (ρ large), the combined effect depends increasingly on β_{1t}. (Note the implication for experimental design: one cannot learn about effects of type β_{1t} if the several classes are formed with uniform X_1.) Unless classes have been formed by deliberate homogeneous grouping, ρ is likely to be in the neighborhood of 0.30, we find.

In the study with just one class per treatment, the reported aptitude effect arises wholly from X_2. Regression effects of X_1 are entangled within the reported Treatment effect. Hence, an ATI from such a study is always to be interpreted as a β_{2t} effect.

At times in the past an investigator has chosen to analyze "at the class level" an ATI study having several classes nested within treatments. That is, he has taken Y_c as the dependent variable, X_1 as the predictor, and the number of classes as the number of observations. This approach has enabled him to estimate the $\bar{\bar{Y}}_t$, the β_{1t}, and their difference (interaction). He has had nothing to say about β_{2t}.

Limitations placed upon statistical inference. The recognition of effects at the class level creates serious difficulties for statistical inference. The number of classes in the study determines the precision with which the important effects are evaluated. Analysis at the individual level is not a legitimate basis for statistical inference, as it greatly understates the α risk.

In testing a Treatment main-effect, it costs little to take the class as unit of analysis, so long as there are, say, five or more classes per treatment. While the number of degrees of freedom is small, the variance of class means—which generates the error term—is also small. The F ratio for the main effect is likely to be about as large as it would be if individuals were taken as the unit of analysis.

With regard to the Aptitude effect β_1, the significance test with the class as unit of analysis is likely to lack power. With the usual design, a sample of about 100 *classes* would be required to detect a $\rho_{X_1 Y_c}$ of 0.20 as significant ($\alpha = .05$, beta risk = .33). A similar statement is to be made about the interaction effect β_{1t}. Consequently, failure of a between-classes ATI to reach statistical significance is meaningless.

In inference from classes pooled, the number of degrees of freedom is derived from the number of persons. This appears to be unjustified when the effect tested is a mixture of group and individual effects. It is legitimate only if one is prepared to assert that the experience Person P has in Class C does not differ from the experience he would have had if he had fallen into Class C'. That is, one must assume absence of teacher effects, rivalry effects, contagion effects, and chance effects that operate systematically on members of a class. (Another option might be to change the model, regarding classes as fixed. That seems not to be sound in ATI research, and it is of questionable relevance in an evaluation study.) It seems obvious that the rule of thumb for sample size offered earlier—100 cases per treatment—is much too conservative, unless one is prepared to deny *a priori* the existence of group effects.

This thinking makes it even more evident that research on ATI cannot place the usual emphasis on the significance of results. Confidence limits preserve the investigator and his readers from premature closure. But closure in the end will have to come more from the theoretical coherence of results than from the statistics alone. The costs of experimentation, and the need to generalize, make it impossible to rely on the conventional statistics-based strategy.

One further limitation must be recognized. The experimental classes were formed according to some policy or practice, and the findings apply only to classes formed in that same manner. Thus, the fact that certain classes have higher X_1 than others may, in the settings where the experiment was carried out, result from the tendency of abler students to sign up with teachers who have the reputation of being demanding. This confounding of teacher characteristics with X_1 is one of the experimental conditions. In another school, class sections in English may differ in X_1 because the ablest students enroll in physics at 10 A.M. and so are not free to take English. Then the effect attributed to X_1 may derive from science interests instead. To consider a third possibility, a school may scrupulously equalize the ability level of sections of its English classes. This would be an ideal setting for an experiment to determine the β_{2t} for some treatment pair, even if it would not shed light on the β_{1t}. But note that β_{2t} then describes the aptitude-outcome relation within a wide-range class. There is no warrant for assuming that similar social-psychological effects will exist if next year's students are grouped by ability, narrowing the range of X_2.

Where a formal placement rule is proposed for use, validation will evidently have to be done by forming classes according to the rule and examining the regression discontinuities (p. 49). Generalization from one set of classes to classes assembled in other ways is not to be trusted. This point has been made independently by Porter and Chibucos (1974).

Limitations implied for the "placement" concept. Such psychologists as Woodworth, Hull and Lewin long ago advised stating psychological laws in terms of both the individual and the situation. For most research workers of the past decade (and for a few pioneer workers of thirty years ago who adopted the then-new Johnson-Neyman technique), this concern has become identified with the comparison of within-treatment regression slopes. This way of thinking about the problem fitted the argument of Cronbach and Gleser (1957; Cronbach, 1957) that most tests are used for "placement" decisions, and that such tests can be validated only by establishing differences in regression slopes. The representation in Figure 2.3, on which nearly every development in Chapters 2–4 save this last section was based, derives directly from Cronbach and Gleser. After establishing a disordinal ATI for aptitude X, one might assign individuals to treatments by establishing an appropriate cutting score X*. But this regards individuals as independent and ignores the β_{1t}, β_{2t} distinction.

Once we distinguish β_{1t} from β_{2t}, we see that the X* placement rule is legitimate only as an interpretation of β_{1t}. The crossing of the between-class regressions tells us how we might assign *classes* to treatments. The rule applies rigorously only to new classes formed by the same mechanism as those in the experimental sample. A rule for placing *individuals* will assemble classes in a new manner. The old study tells nothing about ATI of the new classes.

A pooled-classes analysis can be given no practical interpretation. Consider the simplest case: two treatments, with many classes. Each class extends over the whole range, so that ρ is close to zero. Then the interaction slope for cases pooled will be approximately the same as β_{2t}. Suppose the regression lines cross at X = 0, Y = 0. When we form new classes by cutting the next year's students at X* = 0, the intraclass ρ rises to about 0.64. We can assign classes made up of high-X students to whatever treatment had the steeper regression slope. Will this pay off? We might speculate that β_{2t} has the same value in these new, more homogeneous classes as before. But it is β_{1t} that does most to determine the effect of placement, and any statement about β_{1t} for the homogeneous classes has to be entirely a leap in the dark. Only an assumption that effects are entirely individual, and hence not related to the range of X in the class, warrants the X* assignment rule.

How circumstances of grouping can alter regression slopes is illustrated by the history of "payment by results," in the British schools of a century ago (B. Simon, 1970). The system previously in use had seen schoolmasters lavishing their attention on their ablest pupils, the ones most likely to continue in school. The rear ranks were nearly ignored. The within-class slope of accomplishment and of remaining in school onto aptitude was steep, judging from the contemporary complaints. The between-class slope no doubt was positive but less steep. To promote more equal treatment, Parliament began to make its grants in support of the schools contingent on results. E.g., for every pupil who met the official standard on an end-of-year reading test, the school received 1s.6d. In a proprietary school, this was money in the teacher's pocket. As a result, the teacher was soon spending all his time on the laggards, bringing them to the point of payoff while the able scholars were cut adrift. This generated a rather flat AT regression slope within the class. ATI created by administrative manipulation! (The between-classes slope may have changed very little.)

To think about classifying pupils in the light of such an ATI leads into a paradox. The abler students had an advantage over others without payment for results; the less able students did their best with payment. Suppose that the placement rule is now to pay off on results of class members with poor initial scores and not to pay on results of Highs. One would—on psychological grounds—expect about the same regression slope among Lows as when there was payment at all levels. Putting the Highs in the "no payment" treatment *within* a class, while Lows are in the "payment" condition, would not put Highs in the social situation that originally generated excellent results for them. The benefits of the ATI might be salvaged by putting the Highs in a no-payment class by themselves.

But we reach this judgment through a psychological argument, not by looking at regressions.

An additional consideration reduces the usefulness of the attempt to establish generalizations in a form that justifies a placement rule. As we proceed through the literature, it will be increasingly apparent that dozens of person and treatment variables may enter into interactions. While some benefit can be obtained by classifying persons on a single variable and assigning each to one kind of treatment, classes supposedly conducted in the same style will almost certainly vary in many significant ways, and hence benefits from placement will be far from predictable.

We conclude that formal models of placement are primarily important as heuristics which place the informal practices of the schools in a new light. It is just such an heuristic function that other parts of the Cronbach-Gleser decision theory have performed. ATI findings likewise are most important for the light they shed on instructional processes. Both the grand effects β_{1t} and β_{2t} and the irregularities expressed in the β_{2ct} call for explanation, and so advance instructional psychology.

This section sets out a view that came into focus late in our work. It opens a new phase of ATI exploration. The literature we review in later chapters, and the methods presented prior to p. 100, were almost invariably based on the tacit assumption that all ATI effects occur independently in different individuals. This probably is true for instruction administered to students singly, but one cannot be sure that it is true when students work side by side, even with programmed materials.

Some data from past studies can in time be reanalyzed on the basis of a model that separates group and individual effects (e.g., p. 245). Our remarks have sketched the possible character of such analysis, but experience will modify these ideas. As it becomes clearer which sources of variance are comparatively large, this will suggest new ideas for efficient experimental design in ATI studies. Sooner or later the conceptual and statistical separation of the several kinds of ATI will give more valuable results.

Note added in proof: A much more extensive study of the separation of between-group from within-group effects was carried out by Cronbach in 1975. A draft of a monograph is to be available in the ERIC system by late 1976. The separation is required in any statistical study of data collected in classrooms, according to these later developments. It is found that confusion on this subject has been rampant in evaluation of compensatory education.

Chapter 5 | Learning rates as a reflection of aptitude

Individuals differ in the facility with which they learn, and the study of these differences is at the heart of research on ATI. Psychologically, aptitude is whatever makes a person ready to learn rapidly in a particular situation (or, more generally, to make effective use of a particular environment). To speak more formally: Working on any particular body of instructional material and with any instructional procedure, students are presumed to differ in expected rate of learning. The term "expected" is used in the sense that if the learner were hypothetically to experience that instruction many times independently, his time-to-criterion would vary; its average value we could call his expected rate of learning under these conditions. The premise of ATI research is not that some persons are invariably fast learners and some slow, but that the instructional conditions determine what kind of person will learn most rapidly. The relatively fast learner in one condition can be a laggard in another condition.

Reasons for interest in learning rate

Ability to learn remained for a long time in the background of psychology and educational psychology. During the 1960's, however, several independent lines of work drew attention to rate-of-progress as a variable to be considered alongside the level of achievement after instruction.

In this chapter, we explore at length the notion of learning rate or learning abilities. As will shortly be seen, problems of great current interest to educators and psychologists are stated in terms of such a notion. While the intuitive con-

cepts of learning ability or abilities and learning rate(s) will continue to be useful, the attempt to give theoretical meaning to them or to reduce them to operational terms is blocked by a number of difficulties.

Our thinking has gone through an almost complete turnabout. We—along with
many other writers of the 1960's—were once convinced that direct measurement
of learning rate (as distinct from measurement of posttraining performance on
previously learned tasks) would be the appropriate way to attack many critical
problems of research and evaluation. This kind of measure had been unduly neglected, we thought. We shall review some of these hopeful arguments, but we
shall recommend against rate measures in the end. It is not that the questions
encountered in this first section must remain unanswerable, but that apparently
they can be framed in terms of learning rates only under quite specialized circumstances.

Arguments about curriculum

Rate of learning is surely altered by experience. This has been taken for grant-
ed throughout the history of research on learning; thus, transfer of training has
been defined, since Ebbinghaus, in terms of "savings" in time required to learn,
i.e., of increase in learning rate. Many of the basic issues in curriculum theory
really have to do with alternative methods of improving aptitude. This broadens
our interest considerably; the statement refers to aptitude as an outcome of instruction rather than as solely a predictor.

Obvious as that may seem, it played little part in discussions of curriculum
until developers of the new science and mathematics curricula, in the years around
1960, said that one of their objectives was to improve ability to learn in those
fields. Knowledge, they said, is developing rapidly and therefore the school has
to create an ability to comprehend findings and concepts as they emerge, rather
than transmit an established body of knowledge for lifelong use. This thought
was Deweyan, but Progressive curriculum theory never carried it as far as it was
carried in 1960. In writings of the post-Sputnik reformers, the empirical claim
was made that each new curriculum developed aptitude for learning (of science,
or mathematics, or foreign language, etc.). It was hoped that study of a certain
curriculum would shorten the time a person would later require to master a new
scientific topic, or an additional language, or whatever.

If aptitude is an ability to learn, and a curriculum is intended to develop such
an aptitude, the obvious way to test its success is to assess how easily its graduates master subsequent lessons covering fresh content from this subject area. The
transfer measure usual in educational experiments is not a learning measure; the
common procedure is to present a novel problem and observe how well the
graduate reasons through to a solution, aided neither by instruction nor opportunity for overt trial-and-error. Such a one-trial insight or application task does
not show ability to learn. To inquire about a person's learning rate, one would
observe his progress during extended study or practice on a new unit of material,
with or without "instruction."

The enthusiasts for programmed instruction did not write of learning rate as an outcome, but they emphasized it as the chief or even the only kind of individual difference the school need adapt to. Inspired by Skinner's 1954 paper, they took the arch-environmentalist stance that with proper linear programming of lessons every person could master anything. It hasn't worked out quite that way, but the influence of the movement on educational thinking has been enormous. Stimulated in part by his experience with programmed instruction, but also by his career-long study of instruction in foreign language at all ages, Carroll (1963a, in Krumboltz, 1965; also in Block, 1971) put forth a "model of school learning" in which learning rate was the chief source of individual differences in educability. This was used by Bloom (Bloom, Hastings, & Madaus, 1971; Block, 1971) as underpinning for revival of a suggestion, dating back to Locke, that students should be kept at work on a unit until they reach "mastery." These arguments are carried too far, we believe, when it is suggested that individual differences in achievement can be eliminated (p. 498).

Carroll emphasizes the importance to the educator of differences in the time required to learn, once lessons are pitched at a level low enough that the person's general ability enables him to understand them. As a first step in adaptation, Carroll has proposed to take general ability into account in setting a ceiling on the complexity of the instructional materials assigned to a person. Time-to-learn is expected to depend on specialized abilities. In the case that most concerns Carroll, these are the phonetic and auditory abilities that contribute to foreign-language skills. While Carroll seems to speak of a generalized ability to learn, he expects different abilities to apply to different lessons. Moreover, personal communication makes it clear that he expects to find ATI: learning will proceed at different rates with different instructional tactics, and the tactic best for one student need not be best for another. Carroll tends to favor an eclectic combination of instructional procedures in the classroom (as in intensive foreign-language courses). He expects an eclectic procedure to serve almost as well as methods differentiated to fit the individual. For this reason Carroll gives little attention to choice among instructional styles.

Carroll proposes an alternative to the century-old Galtonian tradition in which ability defined the level a person could attain in any educational or occupational line. The traditional policy for taking ability into account was to assign the student to a curriculum where he would not be set goals "beyond his reach." Here again, Carroll's interest in foreign language may be reflected in his ideas. Until very recently, enrollment in foreign language was restricted to the intellectual elite, in most Western school systems. Carroll takes the position, for the sake of argument, that any nondefective child can be brought to any level of accomplishment in any subject, given enough time. He is well aware that a lifetime may not be long enough to carry some students to competence in, say, theoretical physics—but the hyperbole has a proper rhetorical function. His position is implicitly an attack on use of tests solely to predict success. An argument similar to Carroll's was made in the Cronbach-Gleser decision theory.

Challenges to mental testers

There has always been a loose identification of the concept of intelligence or aptitude with learning rate. In distinguishing one's general mental ability from the proficiency created by one's education to date—even though the two are strongly correlated in a group who have had equivalent education—the testers of 1900–1940 were thinking about an ability-to-learn. Achievers presumably had employed this ability more fully than others with the same IQ. Binet aimed to separate those able to profit from school instruction from those who require special education. This implies that contrasting predictions can be made about students who, though similar in school achievement to date, reach different levels on his test. Moreover, it implies that the two kinds of student should be treated differently, and so assumes an Intelligence x Treatment interaction!

Testers came to think of the IQ as constant, to see ability to learn as a fixed quantity, and to assume that if students were exposed to much the same treatment over many years their paths would inevitably diverge. This was taken as support for educational tracking, starting at an early age. As longitudinal studies came to fruition, their findings challenged the constancy position. Many young people rose or fell in IQ during the school years, and one explanation was that the changes in ranking reflected greater or less learning than the norm. The learning was of skills in problem solving and of conceptual tools, rather than of school lessons in the narrow sense. Did this imply differences in ability to learn, independent of IQ?

Americans focused on the long-term stability of mental-test standings to a far greater degree than Binet did, and at least prior to 1945 they commonly interpreted the IQ as a measure of "ability to learn." While it is obvious that greater mastery of vocabulary or arithmetic will aid in subsequent school learning to which these are relevant, it is not so obvious that mental-test scores indicate anything about efficiency of learning *per se*. This comment fits with Carroll's formulation that general ability may limit what one can comprehend, but it is not "ability to learn."

A 1939 paper by John Anderson is particularly interesting in historical perspective, since an idea surfaced briefly there that is only now revived. Anderson thought that a test of childhood IQ, to be sound, should forecast adult intellectual performance. Binet had employed a wide range of tasks all of which required efficient mental functioning at the time of testing. Anderson proposed to reject a task proposed for (say) Age 4 if it proved not to correlate strongly with performance at Age 18. Accepting Galton's "capacity" notion, Anderson thought the mental test should predict who will reach the highest terminal performance when maturation and schooling have done their work. Since Anderson was inclined to emphasize the hereditary aspects of intellectual development, it is probable that he saw changes from early intellectual accomplishment to adult accomplishment as more maturational than environmental in origin.

Anderson noted that correlations of mental tests close together in time are higher than those of widely spaced tests. By a Monte Carlo procedure he showed that such a pattern of correlations would be generated if gain in IQ from one year to the next is uncorrelated with IQ on the first testing. The implication seemed to be that the person's mental growth to date tells nothing about any continuing property that will affect his later development. Anderson put forth a strong "Overlap Hypothesis" to the effect that the correlation between IQs at Times t_1 and t_2, squared, equals the percentage of the person's experience to t_2 that had been laid down by the earlier t_1. I.e., the IQ is a credit for past general learning. This hypothesis was not solidly supported by Anderson's data, and it languished until revived by Bloom (1964) to support his strongly environmentalist convictions. Before turning to Bloom, however, we need to take up some intervening ideas.

Woodrow (1938a, 1938b, 1940, 1946) launched a blunt attack on psychologists who had equated tested intelligence with ability to learn. He measured learning rate on tasks from the psychological laboratory (e.g., mazes, paired associates), and concluded that the learning scores were not very consistent and not correlated with mental tests. Woodrow's challenge was simply ignored by testers and theorists, no doubt for a mixture of good reasons and bad.

By this time psychologists were ready to deny that mental tests can directly measure some inborn quality, and they were receptive to such suggestions as Hebb's distinction between Intelligence A and Intelligence B (potential and attained status, one might say). This emerging view was captured in two provocative papers by Ferguson (1954, 1956). He discussed functional aptitude as an end-product or by-product of learning.

Aptitude is attained over some period of time, Ferguson said, and is consolidated through regular use. This does not deny a genetic substrate, but it emphasizes the indirect development that occurs from the ubiquitous exercise of steadily improving attentional and analytic skills. Ferguson expected aptitudes to influence learning by a transfer mechanism. The nineteenth-century notion of transferable powers or faculties had long been in disrepute, and most writers had come to expect transfer only for specific knowledge and skills. Ferguson was reinstating the concept of ability as transferable; but, as the transferable acquisition, he emphasized what would today be called information-processing skills and habits. While he expected abilities to reach a plateau in the normal course of development, he did not suggest that development has to stop at any age.

Research in experimental and developmental psychology

Empirical research on the learning-ability relationship was revived in the course of attempts to explain learning. Hull and other theorists, developing formal principles to explain the course of learning in prototype laboratory situations, had brought in a parameter to represent the learning rate of the organism (see esp. Hull, 1945). The chief investigations of person parameters were undertaken by Gulliksen and his students. We shall treat many of these papers in detail.

In the 1950's developmental psychologists also turned to the study of children's learning in the laboratory (Stevenson, 1971). Their tradition, unlike that of experimenters, made it natural to relate outcomes to mental tests. It was from research on performance in grossly similar laboratory tasks that Jensen (1969, 1973) came to distinguish two kinds of ability to learn: Level I ("associative") and Level II ("conceptual"). The latter is represented in reasoning tests and achievement tests, whereas the former has to be assessed directly from efficiency in rote learning. The distinction is rather speculative, and open to both theoretical and empirical challenge (Rohwer, 1971).

The final work to mention in this historical overview is Bloom's *Stability and change* (1964). Reviewing longitudinal studies of ability, Bloom calculated correlations of IQ or achievement at Time t_1 with gain to Time t_2, and found these to be zero or negative (see p. 143). He therefore accepted Anderson's Overlap Hypothesis and reached a conclusion that became famous: "General intelligence appears to develop as much from conception to age 4 as it does during the 14 years from age 4 to age 18." To modify the course of intellectual development one has to take action during the early years of life, said Bloom. If modifying the environment has little power to affect intelligence or ability to learn after Age 6, then after that age the school has to take the learning ability already present and adapt instruction to it.

We find, then, a strange convergence. Bloom, one of the most environmentalist of current writers, joins Jensen, one of the most hereditarian, in seeing the person's learning rate as largely fixed at school ages. Bloom rejects the idea of "capacity," yet joins Anderson who saw capacity as the central issue. IQ constancy is a significant assumption for Bloom's advocacy of "mastery" in education. Bloom's policy turns its back on the curricular optimism of the 1960's which set out to augment intellectual, analytic skills. It is at least as pessimistic about transfer as was the curricular stance E.L. Thorndike adopted following the early Thorndike-Woodrow experiments.

Critical remarks. We find many of the arguments cited unconvincing. In defending the idea that ability to learn is independent of tested ability, Woodrow and Bloom employed gain scores, and conclusions based on such scores are misleading. Moreover, the very formulation appears to be illogical. It is suggested that a person compiles experience in proportion to elapsed time. Hence, 75 per cent of the 12-year-old's experience and 75 per cent of his mental bonds (or the like) were laid down at Age 9. Hence, the squared correlation of Age-9 score with Age-12 score will be 0.75. But this implies that all individual differences in the intellectual inventory at Age 9 also appear as differences in the Age-12 inventory. That is not the case. Nine-year-olds differ in mastery of the lessons for that age; for example, some of them are capable of reproducing the essentials of a one-paragraph anecdote they are told, and some are not. But by Age 12 this ability will have been developed by almost everyone. Not being a source of individual differences, it does not contribute to "overlap."

The Overlap Hypothesis was not well-supported by either the Anderson or the Bloom data; many other hypotheses—including the hypothesis that present IQ predicts gain in IQ—can account for the correlations. At the end of this chapter we shall reach a conclusion quite different from Bloom's. The Overlap Hypothesis is sure to fit the trend of the correlations under some one transformation of the measurement scale. Bloom achieved his fit, and his estimate of amount gained to Age 4, only by an arbitrary *post hoc* choice of scale. The reader may also wish to examine Jensen's reevaluation of the issue (1973, Chap. 3).

For all our discontent with writings on rate of learning, the various arguments have unquestionably placed clarification of the concept of learning rate(s) high on the educational psychologist's agenda.

The person's "learning rate" may be no more than a summary statement about the intellectual distance he has travelled during the past year. If so, it is a non-explanatory, purely operational statement about a fact in his personal history. It says as much about his circumstances during that time as about his own qualities. Such crude operationalism is not palatable to psychologists, who are inclined to regard learning rate as an attribute of the individual, something within his skin. How fast he will learn his next lessons depends on what he brings to them. His rate may differ with the character of the instruction, but few writers have yet attempted to specify how a change in instruction can alter individual learning rates.

Whether there exists just one ability to learn (one "rate" for learning practically anything) or a great many has been the subject of research by measurement specialists (reviewed by Gulliksen, 1968) and by child psychologists (e.g., Stevenson *et al.*, 1968). Improvement in some tasks proves to be independent of mental-test score and of social or ethnic background, but in many other tasks improvement *is* correlated with conventional mental tests or with demographic characteristics. The concept of "learning rate" will evidently have to be subdivided. Beyond doubt, learning of particular content is facilitated when the person has command of the particular concepts and discriminative abilities called for by that content. Less is known regarding the learning styles that might affect response to different kinds of instruction on similar content.

Learning curves and learning rates

Rate measures compared with level measures

Although ATI research has concentrated on the level of accomplishment persons reach after treatment, much of the learning in the laboratory is usually assessed by the amount of time S requires to reach criterion. As we have seen, learning rate is also stressed in the Carroll and Bloom discussions. Both aspects of learning can be described by a learning curve, but in most research a single score is taken as a summary. This reports either what level of performance S reached after a fixed amount of practice or how long he required to advance from one level to a next predetermined level. The two kinds of score do not carry the same information.

The "level" describes degree of mastery or proficiency after some specified amount of training. Thus, a learning experiment may provide for a certain number of trials; a score such as number of errors or time on target is recorded on the final trial or block of trials.

To assess "rate," one must set two performance levels—a low and a high

standard—and determine how much practice time S needs to work his way from
the first level of performance to the second. This has been called the "common
points" measure of learning. In a pursuit-rotor experiment, for example, one
might take 40 per cent time-on-target as the low standard, and 90 per cent as the
high standard. S will start with a performance somewhere below 40 per cent on
the initial trial, cross the first standard at Time t_1 and reach the high standard at
Time t_2. Then $t_2 - t_1$ represents his rate of progress. The first standard must be

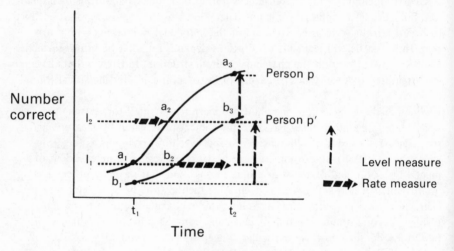

Figure 5.1.

Rate and level measures for persons p and p′

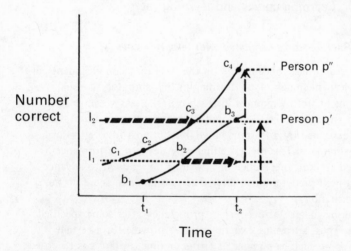

Figure 5.2.

Rate and level measures for persons p′ and p″.

set somewhere above the score of the poorest performer on the first trial. The high standard must be low enough to be reached by every S during the course of the experiment.

Rate and level scores are not interchangeable. Figure 5.1 gives an example. It displays learning curves for Persons p and p'. Levels ℓ_1 and ℓ_2 and Times t_1 and t_2 have been selected for the purposes of our argument. Six data points—$a_1, \ldots$ b_3—are labelled. a_1 and b_1 are the levels of proficiency at Time t_1, and a_3 and b_3 are the levels at Time t_2. a_1 and b_2 correspond to ℓ_1, a_2 and b_3 to ℓ_2. The broad arrows represent rate measures and the narrow arrows represent level scores. The rate measures are derived from points a_1 and a_2, and b_2 and b_3; the level measures are derived from a_3 and b_3. Here the order of the two persons is the same on the two measures, as a short horizontal arrow and a *long* vertical arrow both report good performance. The two systems of analysis, however, select different parts of the data for attention.

While in Figure 5.1 the two kinds of measure agree in describing p as superior, this is not inevitable. Figure 5.2 has the same curve for p' as appeared in Figure 5.1. Person p'' has the same score as p but was superior to p at t_1 and progressed less rapidly just after t_1. As a consequence, his rate measure (c_1 to c_3) shows him inferior to p and p'.

The rate measure has some advantages. It is not affected by transformations in the scoring scale. Any monotone transformation of the scale on which level is recorded will generate the same rate measure, since the latter is stated in terms of practice periods, or in terms of units of time. The rate measure is less subject to floor and ceiling effects than the level measure.

The most obvious disadvantage of the rate measure is that it requires several successive observations of performance with equivalent instruments. Rate cannot be assessed if data are collected only before and after treatment. There are practical difficulties in using equivalent measures at successive times in the ordinary classroom, since lessons progress to new content. Data for assessing rate do become routinely available in some of the newer instructional procedures, notably in computer-assisted instruction.

The reliability of learning measures is suspect. Error is thought of as the departure of Ss performance on any one series of trials from the performance that would represent his true ability. Departure from the true learning rate is inevitable not so much because of errors of measurement as because of uncontrolled processes in the learning itself—fluctuations of attention, confusion, and "chance" selection among competing responses. Such errors were demonstrated by R. Bush and Lovejoy (1965), who set up an all-or-none learning model and generated hypothetical scores for individuals stochastically. The individual was assigned a value of the learning-rate parameter. Successive learning curves generated from the same value of the parameter differed considerably. The average of those curves could be taken as S's "true" learning curve. The trials-to-criterion score proved to be extremely sensitive to chance; from one run of the model to another, the score fluctuated over a range of many trials. Bogartz (1965) reached a similar conclusion and used it as a basis for criticizing transfer and retention studies where an attempt is made to bring all Ss "to criterion" on original learning prior to running the transfer condition. Another significant difficulty is that the "common points" conception seems not to fit multivariate learning (see below).

All this leads us to conclude that rate measures or common-points methods are not satisfactory. Outcomes in learning research, especially educational research, then, ought to be expressed in terms of level scores collected at some terminal point (and perhaps at intermediate points also). In evaluating those results, one will have to take the varying initial status of learners into account, usually by making it a covariate. The reliability of these measures will, of course, be limited by the chance character of many events during learning.

Change in performance seen as multivariate

Many writers seem to view learning ability as a unitary construct. Even the person who expects each kind of instruction to require a different learning ability is likely to speak of a subtype of ability as unitary; Jensen's references to Level I are an example. All that we have said about ATI to this point (save for our passing mention of path analysis) has also referred to a single outcome in any instructional study, and all the statistical methods offered in the last two chapters dealt with single dependent variables. Learning is multivariate, however. Within any one task a person's performance at a point in time can be represented by a set of scores describing aspects of the performance. Hence, typical discussions of "learning rate" simplify drastically. They lead the investigator to collect a single score at each point, and so limit him to asking simple questions. Here we can do no more than mention the larger questions. Multivariate studies of the course of learning being almost nonexistent, no review of findings can be undertaken.

Trials-to-criterion or any other rate measure is defined in terms of a single measure of performance. But even in laboratory research on rote learning, performance can be assessed by multiple indices: errors, latencies, and resistance to extinction, for example. These are only moderately correlated and do not necessarily develop at the same rate. In the paired-associates task, subskills have to be acquired: discriminating among and becoming familiar with the stimulus terms, being able to produce the response terms, and tying response to stimulus. If these attainments were separately measured, each would generate a learning curve, and there is no reason to think that the curves would echo each other. The multivariate nature of educational learning should be obvious. To follow Carroll in using foreign-language learning as an example: vocabulary, conjugations, auditory comprehension, and pronunciation are separately observable attainments.

Learning curves for aspects of performance have different shapes. This is seen, for example, in Lindahl's data for workers being trained on a disk-cutting machine. Lindahl measured the worker's speed, smoothness, and (avoidance of) overthrow. In Figure 5.3, it is seen that these develop differently. The chart

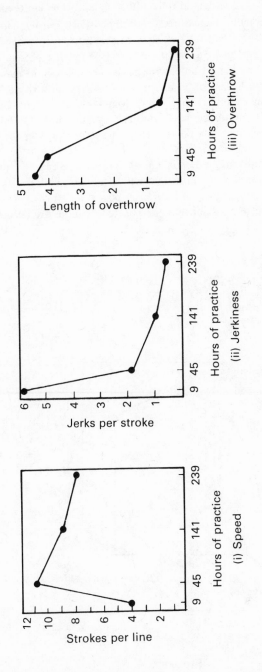

Figure 5.3.

Learning curves for three outcomes. Data from Lindahl, 1945. After Cronbach, 1963, p. 298.

describes only one person, and data at only four points in time are reported.

If two or three outcomes are measured, multidimensional learning curves can be plotted. We have put the data for Lindahl's worker into three dimensions in Figure 5.4 (interpolating to make a smooth curve). One might represent several curves by wires twisting within a frame, with beads on each wire to mark the time scale. Since individuals can form quite different tracks through the space, two multivariate learning curves are unlikely to coincide at any point. One learner will advance rapidly in pronunciation. Another may outstrip him in mastery of grammar while still pronouncing poorly. They are never truly "in the same stage" of learning.

In some studies, a multivariate description of performance can be reduced to a few dimensions, or even to one dimension, with little loss. Within a group all exposed to the same treatment, one has for each person an array of scores at each of several points in time. Relatively complicated methods are needed to

	S	J	O
9	4	5.9	4.4
45	11	1.9	4.1
141	9	1.0	0.6
239	8	.8	0.1

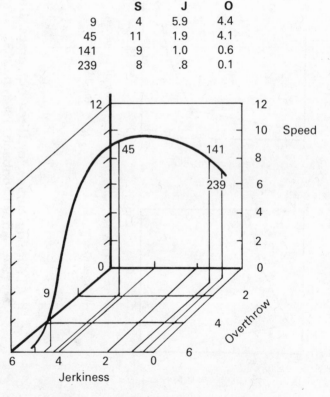

Figure 5.4.

Three-dimensional curves Points at 9, 45, 141, and 239 hours of practice from data reported in Figure 5.3.

reduce a matrix of size n x v x t, that is to say, a matrix of scores of n persons on v variables, each measurement repeated at several times t. Modern scaling methods (Shepard, Romney & Nerlove, 1972) seem likely to be applicable. They may capture most of the information in a two- or three-dimensional plot.

One study that moves toward multidimensional learning curves is that of Love and Tucker (1970). S's task was serial learning of 20 low-meaning CVC trigrams. While one can think of this as a unified task of mastering a list, and score the performance in terms of trials-to-criterion (or total errors), Love and Tucker recorded scores on the ten successive pairs of trigrams. (Partial credit was allowed when, for example, S recalled the correct consonants but the wrong vowel.) The matrix of scores for Persons x Pairs x Trials was subjected to three-mode factor analysis. There were the familiar findings that some persons do better overall and that some who rank relatively low on early trials rank higher later (or vice versa). A further "person" factor was found. Persons at the "bad" extreme on this variable had greater difficulty in mastering the syllables in the middle of the list than in mastering first and last syllables. Persons at the "good" extreme on this factor made more or less uniform progress across the whole set of syllables. One suspects that these two kinds of Ss were encoding and rehearsing differently.

Love and Tucker did not present individual learning curves that would trace the ten-pair vector of performance scores through time. They did plot group data for each type of S, using the position of the syllables in the list as the abscissa. They give one curve for each point in time, for each kind of S. The several curves for successive times, if arranged behind each other, would form a three-dimensional chart. Each front-to-back slice of the chart represents a learning curve on one "outcome" measure, for persons with similar factor scores. One could reduce the number of slices by grouping adjacent pairs of syllables. Two or three factors would adequately summarize the ten outcome dimensions and allow plotting of a multidimensional curve for each S or each kind of S.

Final outcomes that are highly correlated need not have been reached by one-dimensional learning tracks. Conventional factor analysis works from the correlation matrix connecting scores at one point in time. Even when this matrix has a single factor, the course of learning might not be describable by a composite index of outcome.

To clarify this, Figures 5.5 and 5.6 present hypothetical data for three persons on a task measured by scores Y and Y'. First, we see the plot of scores for three persons at Times t_1 and t_2; a single dimension describes individual differences at either point in time. In Figure 5.6, identifications are assigned to the points. In Panel (i) the order of the persons has been kept the same; arranging persons on a single dimension would adequately describe these differences. But in Panel (ii), with another labeling, the order changes between t_1 and t_2; person p'' reached very nearly his ceiling on Y by t_1. Panel (ii) is an extreme tortoise-and-hare case; there is a correlation of -1.00 between scores at t_1 and t_2. The reader can prepare diagrams representing zero correlations or modest positive correlations; in these also, bivariate learning curves cross. Apparently, the entire matrix of intercorrelations for the several scores, within *and between* trials, must be close to unidimensional before one parameter per person can adequately describe individual differences in learning.

It seems difficult to justify the concept of rate of learning (or of "savings transfer"), once learning is recognized to be multivariate. A learner "reaches criterion" on different variables at different times. One wonders, then, about the appropriateness of Carroll's model of school learning (p. 109 above), identifying aptitude with the "time a student needs to learn a given task." Carroll says (personal communication) that he thinks of applying his model to foreign-language learning only because experience suggests that the several outcomes do proceed in step with each other when excellent, mixed teaching methods are used. Such methods stress the various aspects of performance equally and require the student to use them simultaneously in communication. Perhaps the instruction would create data such as Figure 5.7 displays, where the multivariate learning curves follow in the same track rather than separate tracks. If the point marked by an arrow is taken as criterion, the students reach it in order: p'', then p, then p'.

Learning-rate concepts are of restricted value if they apply only under such a special condition. Carroll is willing to reinterpret his model to recognize multidimensional learning curves, he says—but then the concept of time-to-criterion or time-to-mastery is inadequate. So far we have talked about correlations among persons all exposed to the same treatment. Carroll envisions that for some methods of instruction in foreign language the outcomes will not develop in tandem. This would be the case, presumably, where drills on grammar are largely inde-

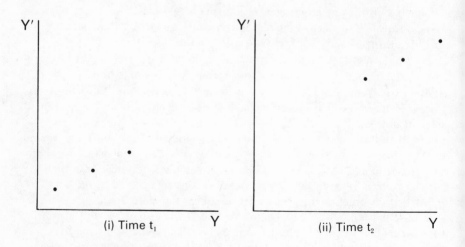

Figure 5.5.

Scores of three persons on two outcomes

pendent of conversational activities designed to promote fluency and comprehension. Even if there were unidimensionality *within* each of the alternative
treatments, the between-treatments correlations need not be unifactorial. Modern
thought on evaluation, in fact, presumes that this will be the case, when it is

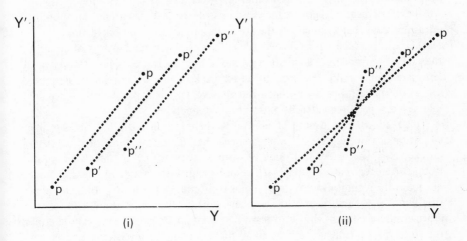

Figure 5.6.

Two sets of bivariate learning curves consistent with Figure 5.5.

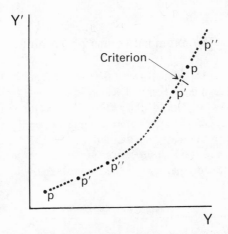

Figure 5.7.

Bivariate learning curves in which persons reach the same criterion at different times.

argued that the profile displaying mean attainment of two or more outcomes is likely to differ in shape from one instructional plan to another; e.g., one method will best promote fluency, another will best promote correct conjugation of verbs.

If one thinks of educational growth as the piecemeal acquisition of unitary skills and associations, the lessons during a week can be pointed directly toward whichever elementary performances are least developed. Then one can speak of a learning rate that summarizes the student's progress on the broad front the teacher is concerned with. This is rather like describing the progress of an army; the rate of movement is a function of the rates for advance units, infantry, artillery, and supply train. It is meaningful to speak of rate of movement, as some armies do move faster than others. But the events that make the difference are microevents, each regulated by rates of specific actions.

This reconciliation cannot be used, if we believe that many outcomes in liberal education are side-effects or epiphenomena that cannot be established by head-on exercises. The reader will think of many outcomes that are largely or wholly in this "transfer" category: e.g., self-respect, ability to foresee ecological consequences of a technical innovation, moral convictions, ability to formulate scientific hypotheses, ability to criticize a new work of literature or art, and—of especial interest to us—ability to learn new content in a field. One can determine the stage the student has reached in all these concurrent intellectual and personal developments. But the growth rates for various outcomes need to be understood separately. There is evidence, for example, that methods excellently able to produce content mastery may be inferior for producing some broader outcomes. There is no overall criterion—even in a single field—toward which instruction can press.

The extended course of learning

The typical learning experiment treats the data as representing a single process, but learning is a succession of events. Even within a single continuous series of practice trials on the same task, distinct "stages" of accomplishment can often be identified. The person becomes a more competent learner as his experience extends. He attends to the material differently, encodes it differently, and perhaps modifies his storage and retrieval processes. An analysis of learning ability, then, ought to make a place for changes in what the learner does.

Stages of learning

A changing relationship between aptitude and learning, as the learning extends in time, has possible implications for ATI work and for educational practice. The well-known research of Fleishman (1966) on motor skills established that under certain circumstances the abilities that account for individual differences during early practice trials have little to do with final standings. In that research, the "early stages" were the first portion of a two-hour practice period. Cognitive tests did predict motor performance during early trials, but it was motor speed and coordination that predicted performance at the "late stage." One might argue that something different was being learned during the early stage and the late stage, or that the acts of the learner or the character of the learning process changed.

We once thought, wrongly, that Fleishman's finding might appear in educational treatments extending over long periods. The findings now in hand support the opposite conclusion, but there has been far less study of the question than its social importance deserves. If a fast start implies talent, then teachers and aptitude tests ought to place much weight on early data. If the tortoise often overtakes the hare, it is bad policy to make early decisions.

Some writers have hinted that aptitude tests are of only short-term relevance. Thus, Humphreys (1968) correlated aptitude tests given to freshmen with their grades in later years, and found that correlations with junior and senior grade-averages were appreciably less than those with freshman grades. This, however, is open to any number of explanations, as the early and late data were not comparable. Advanced courses are diverse, and grading practices vary from course to course. Ferris (1962) reported that, in certain innovative high-school courses in physics and chemistry, correlations of unit-by-unit tests with aptitude tests declined as the year progressed. This was true also when the aptitude tests were given at the end of the year. But Ferris's report was not convincing, as he did not formally summarize his evidence. Ferris's hypothesis was that the new curricula, being tightly integrated and intellectually cumulative, generated divergent paths of individual success. The student who grasped the main threads of the argument—who might or might not have scored well on aptitude tests—was in a position to profit continually from this advantage. Gagné has elaborated the view that, in sequential or hierarchical learning, tested aptitudes are important to individual differences chiefly during early phases of instruction. In traditional courses made up of more disjointed units, each unit might be said to represent a fresh start. Where that is the case, late as well as early success could depend on general abilities, according to Gagné and Ferris, whereas this would not happen in a course with cumulative content.

We are now inclined to dismiss these notions, though there is little evidence on the correlation of aptitudes with success at various points in an educational sequence. This chapter will show that, in short-term learning of a nonmotor sort, aptitudes correlate with performance at early and late stages. In other chapters, it will be seen that aptitude measures do correlate with educational learning that extends in time, even when—in programmed instruction, for example—the content is sequentially organized. In many of the recent science curricula, there is now evidence that the ability-outcome correlation holds up in later units (see p. 310, 311). Thus, it now appears that aptitude tests at the outset of a course do indeed predict late-stage performance. The hare maintains his advantage over the tortoise.

A further analytic question can profitably be asked about the Fleishman studies. Fleishman and his various coworkers correlated the score on each trial (e.g., number of correct responses) with aptitude tests. The aptitudes that predicted such a score differed from one block of trials to another. Persons high on cognitive tests generally did well on the early blocks. This is sensible; understanding directions and the patterns of the task is a cognitive activity, and those who are good at it should start fast.

For the Complex Coordination Test (Fleishman & Hempel, 1954), the percentage of score variance predicted from cognitive tests at different points in practice is approximately as follows:

Elapsed practice time (min.)	10	30	50	70	90
Percentage of variance predicted in test on latest segment	35	20	10	7	5

The fact that the "influence" of cognitive abilities dropped off with the passage of time has been misinterpreted as showing that cognition is largely irrelevant on later trials. According to the data above, cognitive abilities correlate *negatively* with the improvement in score between (e.g.) 10 and 50 minutes. This seems paradoxical, but there is a perfectly clear psychological explanation (which rests on some of Fleishman's own thinking). A certain amount of cognitive work is to be done in a task like this. When S has analyzed the task and has grasped the basic patterns, he can perform more efficiently. Hence, whenever he masters the cognitive part of the task, his score should rise. Ss high on cognitive tests evidently grasp the intellectual aspects of Complex Coordination early in practice and so earn high early scores. Presumably, Ss low on cognitive tests gain the same understanding, but more slowly. On some of the later trials (say, around the 20th minute) they are achieving what High Cognitives achieved early. As the gains accruing from this cognitive achievement are now being made by the Low Cognitives, the gains on these trials correlate negatively with the aptitude measures. Instead, then, of accepting the common interpretation that cognitive ability is important in early learning and not later, we conclude that cognitive learning is taking place early for some persons and later for others. The same argument would apply to any study of correlations for successive trials or period, where the task remains the same on every trial and continues to be judged by the same criteria. That condition rarely describes a sequence of school lessons.

Learning to learn

Any study of aptitude-outcome relations ought to take "learning-to-learn" (LTL) into account. A learner does considerably better after he has had experience with many tasks of the same kind. The learning ability he displayed on the first few tasks of that series may not be the most significant indication of his ability to perform in an instructional situation or in any long-continued learning. Very little of the research on aptitudes has taken LTL into account (and vice versa), even though recognition of LTL traces back as far as Webb's study in 1917, and LTL was given substantial attention by McGeogh and Irion (1952).

Permanence of gains. Notable among these early studies is a little-known report by Husband (1947). His college students learned one maze, and several months later learned a second maze. A contrast group relearned the original maze. The savings on the transfer maze were compared with the savings in relearning. There were several paired groups, each pair with a different delay interval. While the transfer (new maze) groups were slower to learn the second maze than the relearning groups, transfer groups did show improvement over their own first performance. The comparative advantage the relearners gained from previous acquaintance with a particular maze vanished as the elapsed time approached six months. The "forgetting curve" for relearning groups had the usual form of dropoff over time. The trend for transfer groups, however, was essentially flat; i.e., savings in learning time were the same no matter what the interval between tasks. Thus, whatever improved ability to learn a maze may consist of, it evidently is retained to a remarkable degree. Essentially the same finding appears in studies by Bunch (1936, on Peterson's rational maze) and Bunch and McCraven (1938, on paired associates). In none of these studies, however, was the learning period very long; the single initial experience must have served chiefly to acquaint S with this kind of task.

Discrimination learning set. LTL was brought into prominence by Harlow's well-known experiments (1949). His monkeys worked day by day on a long series of discrimination-learning problems. They eventually could perform with great efficiency, attaining the correct solution on the first or second trial. Harlow's research left an unfortunate conceptual heritage, since two fundamentally different types of experiments were commingled. One is represented by the famous oddity problem, where the correct answer is determined not by the choice of one stimulus as correct but by the application of a concept. In a group of three stimulus objects, two of which are alike, choice of the odd object is rewarded. An S who discovers that this rule is operating is able to solve a new problem (i.e., a new set of objects of which one is odd) on the *first* trial. In the other type of problem, one of two objects is *arbitrarily* chosen as correct. S cannot choose correctly on the first trial save by chance, but he can achieve perfect success on the *second* trial. Some writers now call the second type of improvement "discrimination learning set." The second type of study gives evidence of LTL. In the oddity problem, however, S is acquiring a set to favor one response category over another. That set is useful only because S is playing a game with an experimenter who agrees not to change the rule. To be sure, if S is acquiring a generally applicable concept that is new to him (such as "dissimilar"), there is some transferable residue of the experience. But once the concept is in his repertoire his reliance on it is a trivial phenomenon of "learning to read the experimenter's mind." Our primary interest is in discrimination learning set.

There has been considerable work on such sets in children, much of which is reviewed by Reese (1964). In the laboratory, Ss clearly do learn to discriminate more quickly after they have considerable experience in learning which alternative brings reward.

The complex information processing required in advanced learning also shows LTL. Freibergs and Tulving (1961) had college students perform concept-attainment tasks of the sort where a concept is defined in terms of selected attributes of patterns (e.g., red circles present). On each trial, S sees one pattern and is to say whether it is an instance of the concept. Ss solve the problem much more readily when the successive instances are exemplars of the concept (positive instances) than when they encounter a series of non-exemplars of the concept (negative instances). This is the case even though, for the patterns used, the two kinds of instances give equal amounts of information and, hence (logically), allow equally early solutions. In the Freibergs-Tulving experiment many successive problems were given; each S received only positive instances, or only negative instances, on all problems. The superior performance of positive-instance Ss on early problems did not continue; their advantage nearly vanished by the twelfth problem. Though given no instructions, Ss in the negative-instance group had learned to process such information.

Individual differences. Regrettably, studies on LTL have rarely reported on individual differences. It would be important to know whether persons who do relatively well on early tasks maintain their advantage. If not, whether mental tests correlated with success in an isolated learning task is irrelevant to questions about predictive power in the educational situation where a person accumulates experience with similar tasks. It would be valuable also to know how the person who forms learning sets rapidly differs from the person slow in this respect.

We have already argued for ATI studies of considerable duration (p. 42); let us tie this to the issue of learning-set formation. An ATI finding that could be a basis for policy would presumably take some such form as this: "Learners with the following pattern of characteristics benefit more from instruction of the following type." But this generalization is practically significant only if individual differences in learning are fairly consistent throughout an extended instructional program where new lessons are presented each day. If individual differences prove to be stable and predictable, one can capitalize on findings from the experiment in which learning is observed only for a short time, perhaps on just one task or topic. If individual differences are radically altered during learning-set formation, the short-term experiments on ATI will not give practically useful conclusions. Under this hypothesis, persons who learn most efficiently, among a group all of whom have become thoroughly familiar with a problem, would not generally be the ones who learned most efficiently at the outset; hence, they would not have been among the most successful learners in a short experiment. The educator ought to ask who is going to learn well after he is some weeks into the course, when his approach to lessons of a given type has been stabilized. There is not much point in identifying the student who will be off to a running start, if he is likely to fade back into the pack.

Rate of LTL—at least in brief learning sequences—is strongly related to mental age. After reviewing findings of Harter and Katz, who have related discrimination learning-set to MA, we shall go on to the more complex inquiries of Alvord and Bunderson, who related LTL in concept attainment to multiple aptitudes.

Harter used the standard Wisconsin task in which one object of a pair is arbitrarily chosen as correct. The child understands that a marble is hidden under one object; whether he selects the right or the wrong object on the first trial, he can always succeed on the second trial, once he grasps the principle. Four trials were allowed on each pair of objects. Children of high, average, and low IQ, ranging from CA 3½ to 13, were used in Harter's 1965 study. The number of problems required to reach consistent good performance (i.e., to master the task of making a good inference from the first trial) was strongly related to MA with a constant age group. With MA constant, the bright children (younger) surpassed average children, but there was no great difference between average and dull (older) Ss. Fewer Ability x Age cells were used in Harter's 1967 study, and less complete conclusions can be drawn. The relation of LTL to CA-with-MA-constant appeared to be weaker in this study. Studies such as Harter's do not give information on individual differences following LTL. The series of discrimination-learning tasks is essentially a single problem into which the child achieves insight. Once he has the insight, any remaining individual differences are due to lapses of self-discipline.

Katz (1967) used a task similar to Harter's. Nursery-school children obtained marbles for guessing which of two geometric figures was correct. There were four groups, each of which received difficult problems on Day 3; on these problems, the right and wrong figures differed in few respects. Group A had received gradually more difficult discrimination problems on Days 1 and 2, leading up to the Day-3 level. Group B had received easy problems on Days 1 and 2. Group C received difficult problems on all days. Control Ss were given no problems on Days 1 and 2. Trials-to-criterion on Day 3, served as the dependent variable. With Ss divided at the median on IQ, it was shown that *Highs improved gradually over the three days under all experimental conditions, while Lows showed consistent improvement only when difficult problems were given* on all three days (Group C). This is an ATI finding.

Six months later a random half of the Ss, representing all experimental groups pooled, were matched with a new control sample and given three additional difficult problems. There were no differences between experienced and inexperienced Ss on the first problem, indicating no simple transfer from the earlier experience. On gain from the first to the third problem, however, Ss with earlier experience improved much more than control Ss. *High-IQ Ss displayed more improvement than Lows, in the experimental group.* (In the new control group, Highs improved less than Lows.) Katz demonstrated, then, that both learning-set formation and transfer were greater for Highs than for Lows. One regrets that Katz could not compare his experimental groups in the delayed learning task. The value of measuring transfer with several successive new problems rather than with just one is to be noted.

Alvord (1969) asked fifth-grade children to work on seven consecutive concept-attainment problems, five on one day and two on the next. The design was carefully counterbalanced so that peculiarities of displays and solution rules would not affect the results. Alvord had to use quite simple problems in which the concept was defined by one attribute (e.g., red). His naive Ss, working without memory support, were unable to cope with complex concepts.

Alvord was interested in the possibility of distinguishing "learning ability" from "ability to transfer." Transfer of two kinds was examined. Within a family of concepts all pertinent to the same set of stimuli, each solution rule is a subset of the same fixed set of attributes. In such a family, LTL is demonstrated if S is faster at identifying the pertinent attribute on a late problem than he was on early problems. When a problem outside the family presents stimuli with other attributes, somewhat more complex transfer is perhaps required to set up an information-processing strategy.

Alvord's Ss learned to learn. The number of trials to solution dropped from a median of 12 on the first problem to a median of 5 on the fifth problem. Introducing stimuli with new attributes as the sixth problem did not impair scores; evidently Alvord had not complicated matters sufficiently to require a higher order of transfer at this point. (The most surprising finding about the central tendency was that control Ss nearly equalled the experimental Ss on the last learning task. These Ss had been given only one problem on the first day, identical to the first task of the experimental Ss. On the second day, the two groups received the same two tasks. Two problems separated by a 24-hour interval improved learning ability as much as a series of six problems, five on the first day and one on the second. This extrapolates into a powerful argument for spaced practice in learning to learn.)

In the experimental group, intercorrelations of learning scores on Problems 2–7 were high. Except for Problem 1, each problem correlated about 0.60 with its neighbors, and correlated about 0.50 with tasks three or four places removed from it in the series. This implies that individual differences are rather stable even when LTL is taking place. Unusual attenuating factors held down correlations between problems in this study. Because of the counterbalanced design, the nth problem was different for different children, some receiving a relatively easy problem and some a relatively hard one. Furthermore, even on an easy concept-attainment problem, confusion can arise unpredictably. One lapse in memory may confuse S and make him slow to attain the concept. Likewise, it is possible for him to form a "lucky" hypothesis; when it is confirmed, his information processing is much simplified. And, on the other hand, confusion on one problem can inhibit performance on the next, and so raise the correlations.

Bunderson's study (1967) has many points of similarity with Alvord's. With Princeton undergraduates as Ss, Bunderson could use relatively complex solution rules. He presented 26 problems (but only eight trials for each one). S was allowed to record information as he obtained it, whereas Alvord's S had to rely on memory. Performance across the problem series was expected to involve three LTL processes: problem-analysis (to identify what information was needed to solve the problem); search (to find operations for reducing the amount of information needed); and organization (to integrate the operations into a program for problem-solving).

Bunderson recorded, at each of several stages of practice, scores for positive process (positive instances marked correctly), negative process (negative instances marked correctly), and solution process (number of correct final solutions). All three scores gave evidence of LTL, though Ss were far from perfect on the last block of problems. Variances were substantial and much the same at all points in the series of problems. Bunderson did not report problem-to-problem correlations. He did relate learning scores to pretested abilities, and the correlations differed somewhat with stage of practice. A review of these relations appears below (p. 135). The results suggest that different abilities were used in processing positive and negative instances, and ability to solve these problems developed by stages (as hypothesized). The study offers a useful model for future work on processes in LTL.

LTL has ordinarily been regarded as incremental. It is thought that S gradually learns to direct his attention so that he processes information efficiently. But the gains of the individual S may be all-or-none in character, in the sense that he acquires a particular insight or technique and then holds onto it firmly. Such jumps are masked in group data. More attention will need to be paid to the course of LTL in the individual in order to determine whether it is gradual, as the group curves suggest, or sharply discontinuous. Concept attainment may not be the best experimental vehicle for studies of this kind, because the performance curve of an individual is typically irregular, thanks to transient confusion and local insights.

Tuning

A number of studies have demonstrated the possibility of "tuning" the learner. The LTL study invariably leaves the learner to his own devices, and under those circumstances efficiency is likely to grow slowly. In the studies below, there was some minimal training to clarify the nature of the task and perhaps to suggest a strategy for coping with it.

Jensen and Rohwer (1965) asked children of various ages to learn syllable pairs. Older Ss were able to do considerably better than younger ones and there was a marked social-class difference. There was, however, no class difference in serial rote learning. It was hypothesized that middle-class children excel on paired associates because they habitually use mediation, that is, connect a pair of syllables through some meaningful association. Doing this transforms the task from rote learning to meaningful learning, and so makes it much easier. This device will not serve in serial learning, as it is too difficult to make up a meaningful linkage for a long series of unrelated words. Jensen and Rohwer next suggested to lower-class Ss that *they* attempt to form meaningful connections. This bit of advice immediately improved their performance, and the social-class effect disappeared. A difference in "learning ability" was erased simply by instructing children to use an ability they possessed but had not considered relevant.

Tuning was similarly effective for Eimas (1966). He asked children to respond in a four-choice situation, not telling them that two of the four choices had arbitrarily been selected as correct. *S* thus received a reward for either of two responses; this made the task very difficult for younger *S*s. When Eimas did no more than explain that *two* of the choices had been baited with candy, young children learned effectively. Age-related aptitudes were no longer relevant.

An extended discussion of this kind of tuning is to be found in papers by Flavell and his associates (for example, Moely *et al.*, 1969). Their research tends to show that at certain stages of development the child simply does not use skills that he possesses; this has been called a "production deficiency." Rather simple instruction can remove the deficiency and so improve learning.

This is evidence that tuning the learner alters his task and greatly alters his performance. We know of no attempt to tune *S*s for efficient concept attainment, although both Alvord and Bunderson used a warmup procedure to make sure that the basic rules were clear.

These comments echo the complaint that David Hawkins (in Shulman & Keislar, 1966) made in a too-little-noticed criticism of research on learning. The following extracts (pp. 4-6) indicate the tenor of his argument.

> . . . most experimental work in the psychology of learning and teaching has not been very relevant to learning or teaching. A teacher friend of mine put it thus: "Most psychologists," she said, "have never really *looked* at children." . . .

> To interpret: Let me say something first about the concept of *preparation,* as when one talks about preparing an experiment. I do not mean the preparation which consists in getting oneself ready, but the preparation of the subject of the experiment, a light-beam, or a colony of paramoecia, or a child, or classroom of children. . . .

> There are many psychological experiments I know, which require comparatively simple preparation. . . . [T]he preparation involved in pedagogical investigation goes up very sharply with the significance of their results and . . . an experiment which takes a half-hour or a day or a week to prepare is, in general, not worth doing. . . .

> To call something an independent variable is not to use a name but to claim an achievement. . . . In biology another dimension looms as crucial, that is preparation time. To put a complex system in a prepared state takes time. The good biological experiments have such a long preparation time that husbandry becomes the dominant characteristic of the lab or station; in the short run, at least, its resident prepared species determine its experiments. . . .

> Situations of optimum learning require a great deal of preparation. If we do experiments in learning with only superficial preparation—instructions, "training", etc., of short duration—then the rare things get swamped by statistical noise.

Just as the animal psychologist familiarizes his *S* with the laboratory, the existence of food boxes, and other things the animal needs to know to be a good experimental S, so the educational psychologist ought to be tuning his S to give an optimum performance. Otherwise, the learning data arise out of whatever tendencies, a residue of his uncontrolled past experiences, are now haphardly activated. The school situation to which we wish to generalize is one in which S is indeed tuned. The teacher presumably does show the pupil how to work effectively, and will not present tasks where the principal difficulty is to figure out what rules the teacher is following. (Perhaps this is not the case in every classroom, but educational psychology should be more interested in advising the competent teacher than in generalizing about ill-managed classrooms.) Superficial individual differences that result from inadequate understanding of the task or from failure to hit upon an effective strategy should be systematically eliminated by helping the S to achieve his best style of work within the prescribed instructional technique—before the experiment proper starts.

What has just been said about learning experiments applies with equal force to those miniature experiments called mental tests. Once it was thought that placing S in a novel situation and observing how rapidly he adapts was the obvious way to measure his intellectual powers. Now it is recognized that his choice of an effective or ineffective strategy may be fortuitous, or conditioned by his past experience with intellectual tasks. Particularly as a result of their experience in developing countries, the more self-critical testers now seem agreed in recommending some form of coaching or intensive familiarization before testing proper begins (Cronbach & Drenth, 1972). But there have been few investigations of the effect of tuning on validity, and the findings are inconsistent (Dague, in Cronbach & Drenth, 1972, pp. 63-74).

The fact that familiarization is likely to alter scores has sharp implications for the topic of our next section, the correlation of learning scores with other measures. The data that we shall be able to summarize come almost exclusively from naive Ss who first encounter a kind of task on the series of performance trials from which their learning score is taken. Note Alvord's experience. His concept-attainment problems correlated highly with each other and correlated with external measures. But this was not so true for scores on his first problem. Despite elaborate warmup and introductory procedures, superiority or inferiority on the initial problem seemed to be a transient phenomenon. With some materials several problems would no doubt be required, before familiarization is complete enough for everyone's strategy to have stabilized. The fact that Alvord's problem-to-problem correlations rose notably when Ss became familiar with his task causes us to doubt the usefulness of studies of individual differences in learning where S has little opportunity to learn to learn. While many studies of naive Ss show little relation among learning tasks, we should not be much interested in scores made by "untuned" Ss on their first attempts at some kind of learning.

The need is for studies of learning ability as measured after LTL has been largely completed. By then the nature of the problem is thoroughly familiar, though the solution rule or the associations for the new task are not. One would have to investigate this with progressively more difficult tasks "of the same kind." On Alvord's tasks the solution is logically determinable, hence S could achieve the correct answer on the second or third trial when he became fully efficient. If later tasks remain as simple as the early tasks, individual differences in learning may vanish. Learners who have attained this outstanding efficiency in extracting concepts from displays that vary in only two attributes, however, can be expected to differ when they attempt tasks with three or four attributes.

Learning abilities: Their number and aptitude correlates

Our concern in this section is with correlations among measures of learning ability. One question is the analogue of the much pursued question regarding the structure of mental abilities. To what extent can success in various learning tasks be accounted for by a single "general" learning ability? To what extent must comparatively specialized learning abilities be called upon to account for different kinds of performance? Another question has to do with the relation of learning abilities to aptitude factors.

We are handicapped by the character of the data available. The data almost always come from naive Ss rather than from Ss who have stabilized a strategy, and they come from learning through practice rather than through instruction. Correlations are often calculated from gain scores, and hence are virtually uninterpretable. And the learning scores in many studies seem likely to be so unreliable as to guarantee low correlations with other measures. (This is particularly to be suspected in any task where insight or a lucky guess can speed up a person's attainment of the criterion. Even where the data do give a pattern of correlations, it is difficult to reach persuasive interpretations.

We quote the long-standing conclusions of Herbert Woodrow before turning to more recent research. From his own evidence and that of others, Woodrow (see esp. 1946, pp. 148-149) reached the following generalizations:

1.   The ability to learn cannot be identified with the ability known as intelligence.
2.   Individuals possess no such thing as a unitary general learning ability.
3.   Improvement with practice correlates importantly with group factors, that is, relatively narrow abilities, and also with specific factors.
4.   Even the group factors involved in learning are not unique to learning, but consist of abilities which can be measured by tests given but once.

Woodrow's conclusions were a deliberate challenge to the many testing psychologists who had, over the years, identified the IQ as a measure of "ability to learn." None of them rose to the defense of the interpretation. Instead, they simply ignored Woodrow's papers. During the 1960's, there were occasional references to the Woodrow work, usually in defense of the view that learning rate depends on instruction and not on ability. This was the thrust of Stolurow's (1966, p. 138) citation of Woodrow while advocating programmed instruction. It was Stolurow's view that PI depends on an "ability to learn" but not on scholastic aptitude as usually measured.

The 1960's saw a good deal of research on individual differences in learning. The evidence now in hand undermines Woodrow's first and second conclusions; this chapter and Chapters 7-11 will show that learning tasks often correlate with each other and with tested abilities. But the results have been mixed rather than obviously coherent. With regard to Woodrow's third and fourth conclusions, the evidence defies summary. Some "relatively narrow learning abilities" clearly exist; but there is insufficient evidence that specialized aptitudes of the Thurstone or Guilford sort are implicated. Only rote memory seems to appear as a factor both in aptitude batteries and in analyses of learning data.

Ability correlates at various stages of learning

Alvord had tests from the French and Guilford sets, plus scores from the Lorge-Thorndike Intelligence Test and the Stanford Achievement Test, as predictors. The best single predictor of attainment of a concept was success in attaining the immediately preceding concept. Combining several preceding tasks gave a still better prediction. The squared multiple correlations when scores on Problems 3 to 7 were predicted from scores on preceding problems fell in the range 0.40 to 0.48. (Hence the correlations were in the range 0.65 to 0.70.)

Tests, considered by themselves, predicted concept attainment. Scores on Problem 1 were more difficult to predict than scores on later problems. Across Problems 2 to 7, any test had nearly uniform correlations. Lorge-Thorndike, Stanford, and Hidden Patterns scores correlated with learning; $r = 0.20$ to 0.30. The zero-order correlations for Lorge-Thorndike Total IQ ($N = 147$) are representative:

Problem	1	2	3	4	5	6	7
r	0.29	0.35	0.32	0.31	0.40	0.29	0.29

The abilities that accounted for performance did not differ early and late in practice, nor did transfer relate to different abilities than initial learning. The pattern of correlations was quite unlike that of the Fleishman studies.

Combining aptitude tests with scores on prior concepts did not predict attainment of a concept appreciably better than did the prior scores taken alone. It is not that the abilities the tests measure are irrelevant on later trials. Rather, the information on such individual differences is carried in the learning scores themselves, so that the test has no added predictive information to report. Superior tested ability translates into a modest advantage in solving the first and second problems, and this in turn leaves a residue of skills and insights that help on the third problem, and so on. Late in practice the effects of ability are mediated through the specific skills acquired early. Among those who perform equally well on the fourth or fifth problem, tested abilities do not indicate who will do best on Problem 6. Conversely, the student who gets off to a good start on the first few problems is likely to maintain his standing even if his ability tests gave a poor prognosis. Though his initial success may have been the result of happy accident, once he learns the trick of such problems successive experiences are likely to maintain this skill.

After removal of the variance predicted from aptitudes, the residual matrix of interproblem correlations had a superdiagonal form, the correlations diminishing for problems spaced further apart. Such data suggest that some individuals were making gains in analytic skill, on any given trial, that helped their work consistently thereafter. So far as we can judge, these gains were fortuitous and unpredictable, in the way that flashes of insight are.

Alvord's correlations for ability of fifth-graders are not in agreement with the conclusions reported for high-school students by Dunham, Guilford, and Hoepfner (1966), but we find consistency when we reinterpret the latter data. The concept-attainment task of Dunham *et al.* was unlike Alvord's and the design provided little opportunity for learning to learn. Three problems were presented, one on each day, scores being collected at various points in S's work on each problem. Dunham analyzed scores on stages within a problem, whereas Alvord's scores came from successive independent problems.

To illustrate the Dunham procedure, consider the figural task given on the second day. S guessed which of four classes each successive figure belonged to; one class, for example, consisted of figures with two intersecting lines. Given feedback after each trial, S could eventually infer the defining rules for the classes. There was also a symbolic task (first day) and a semantic task (third day). A large number of Guilford tests, selected primarily to emphasize the "class" type of "product," were administered. The usual Guilfordian factor analysis was carried out. The investigators retained 16 pincipal axes (some of them accounting for little variance) and rotated them. As nearly as can be judged from the report without laborious calculation, the first of the unrotated principal-axis factors correlated with the concept-learning scores—and nothing else did. The investigators' rotation simply clouded interpretation by fragmenting this broad factor.

To reach a summary impression, we returned to the correlations, confining attention to the five tests having the highest loadings on the first unrotated factor. These tests (Figure Class Inclusion, Letter Grouping, Verbal Classification, etc.) clearly involve reasoning and are rather like conventional mental-test tasks. A straight vocabulary test ranked only slightly behind these tests in first-factor loading. We then determined the median of the five correlations of these tests with each successive concept-formation score. The correlations rose as Ss gained experience (Figure 5.8). The correlations are somewhat lower than Alvord's, probably because the short tests in the Dunham study were unreliable. We see no convincing evidence that the three kinds of problems related to different abilities, nor that scores on the third problem had a pattern of correlations dif-

ferent from those on the first. The data firmly support the idea that general
ability does correlate with concept learning and hence they confirm the Alvord
result except in details.

In the Bunderson study (p. 128) the correlations seemed to be much like
those we extract from the Dunham data. Multiple correlations for predicting
Bunderson's most basic measures of learning rose steadily, from 0.45 on the first

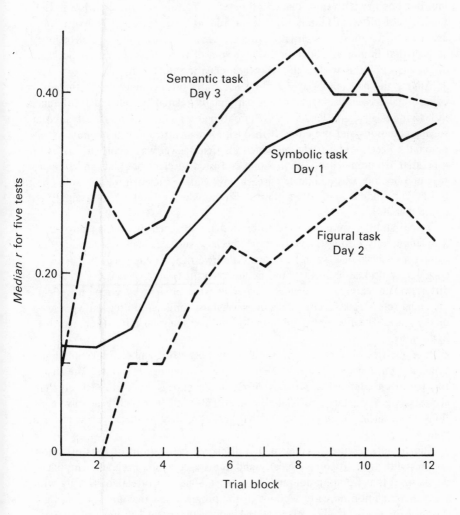

Figure 5.8.

Correlation of "general" ability measure with concept-attainment scores on successive blocks of trials. Data from Dunham et *al.*

block of problems to 0.60 on the last two blocks. These correlations, however, are inflated by capitalization on chance.

Among Bunderson's reasoning tests, two factors correlated highest with Blocks 2 and 3, and two others peaked during Blocks 3 to 5. Three memory factors peaked on Blocks 2 or 3, and one gave a flat function over Blocks 3 to 6. Two miscellaneous factors showed declining patterns. At face value, this argues that different kinds of ability were important at different stages of learning. But one needs to note that the Bunderson factors are intercorrelated. The tendency of different factors to be influential at different stages is a weak one, and two of the most influential factors are aspects of reasoning. We strongly suspect that in a crossvalidation a simple sum of these tests would predict learning at each point as well as the regression equation did.

Among the papers of Gagné and his associates on hierarchical structures of educational accomplishments, one is particularly related to individual differences in learning. Gagné and Paradise (1961) outlined a hierarchy of subskills used in solving equations and presented it through a linear instructional program. S was required to review any frame on which his first answer was incorrect. Errors thus generated a time penalty. The program consisted of eight booklets and it appears that one booklet was administered each day, with sufficient time for everyone to finish. The student marked his place in the booklet at 3-minute intervals, to give a rate measure.

Tested abilities were expected to be relevant to speed in working through the program chiefly during the early stages, because such tests epitomize what the learner already knows when he enters. The investigators expected that in later stages conventional abilities would be less relevant to rate of mastery. Individual differences in learning of advanced materials were thought by Gagné to reflect "learning sets"—task-specific skills or bad habits—built up during earlier stages of the work. The Fleishman findings no doubt influenced him in reaching this hypothesis.

Five abilities were measured: Vocabulary, Speed of Symbol Discrimination, Computation Speed, Associative Memory, and Following Directions. The first two had been intended to serve as "irrelevant" controls, but it turned out that all tests save Vocabulary correlated around 0.50 with final ability to solve equations. Once again the implication is that general ability predicts success in learning.

The authors' Figure 3a (their p. 12) displayed correlations of tests of various abilities with time to complete early and late stages of the program. The figure emphasized that Computation and Associative Memory correlated strongly with time-to-completion on early sections of the program and that the correlations dropped off gradually. For Associative Memory the gradual dropoff of r's was a plausible effect. The early, elementary rules and equivalences could be acquired largely by memorization, whereas later stages required increasing amounts of analysis and foresight. The downward trend for Computation requires reevaluation. The successive median r's were 0.83, 0.69, 0.60, 0.53, 0.51. (The figure showed values of 0.83, 0.69, 0.42, 0.36, and 0.25, which do not agree with the tabled values on their p. 22.) The very high correlation of 0.83 reflects only that in units where the tasks were computational the students high on Computation worked rapidly and accurately. The correlation says nothing about rate of *learning.*

The correlations of Following Directions with completion rates did seem to support the stage hypothesis. Median correlations in successive phases of the program were as follows: 0.54, 0.47, 0.37, 0.28, 0.30, and 0.20. Since Following Directions can be regarded as a measure of *g,* this alone would have supported the view that general ability has greater influence on speed of progress during early stages of complex learning. Posttest data, however, alter the picture. One posttest had included items specific to the subgoals of each section of the program. The median correlations of Following Directions with the subtests matching successive phases were 0.17, 0.30, 0.42, 0.39, and 0.41. Thus there was no decline in the relevance of general ability to *success* in learning. And the memory test, the computation test, and even the supposedly irrelevant test on speed of symbol discrimination showed markedly greater correlations with final knowledge of the late subprocesses than of the early subprocesses.

This study controlled neither level of mastery nor time allowed for study; consequently, the student was free to reflect on trouble spots or to move ahead after superficial review, so striking his own balance between time invested and amount learned. Time and attainment as *separate* dependent variables could not adequately reflect success in learning. Probably the best recourse in this kind of study is to examine the regression of each section of the posttest on completion rate for the corresponding section of the program, so as to learn something about the exchange rate between speed and mastery. The design offers possibilities of path analysis, though far more cases probably would be required to obtain stable path coefficients. It might be possible in this kind of study to control level of attainment by giving a posttest at the end of each subsection of the program, and requiring those who fail to drop back. This would make completion rate a meaningful indicator of learning, but it would be cumbersome. The alternative of setting a uniform time limit would resolve no ambiguities. If all students did work carefully, one could take the posttest as an indicator of what was learned, but would have to give an arbitrary weight to the later sections of the content that some did not reach. If some students worked carefully and others chose to complete the program even if this meant minimal reflection, the scores would be as hard to appraise as are those of the original study.

Before leaving the Gagné-Paradise study, we should note one finding that tended strongly to confirm Gagné's mode of analysis. The authors had introduced Following Directions as a measure of "integration," and their analysis of content had led them to predict that integration would be required in two particular sub-sections, one early and one late. The correlations of Following Directions with both the rate and level scores for those particular subsections were distinctly higher than the correlations for subsections adjacent in time. Hence, whether or not integration is distinct from g, the armchair analysis of content succeeded in identifying instructional material to which the ability was peculiarly relevant.

All the foregoing studies taken together lead us to think that general mental ability does predict success in learning even after Ss are well into a cumulative learning task.

Particularly impressive evidence of pervasiveness of general ability in diverse learning tasks is found in the work of Taylor and Fox (1967). They used six realistic tasks, devised to represent complexities ranging from stimulus-response association to learning of principles. All tasks resembled military-training activities. For five tasks, posttests correlated substantially with the Armed Forces Qualification Test. (The sixth, a monitoring task, required alertness but can scarcely be said to involve learning.) As the report contrasted extreme groups—with a middle group sometimes added—it is difficult to estimate the size of the correlations. The Highs performed better than the Lows throughout the practice or training trials, but ceiling effects made it possible for the dull to come closer to the bright in the end. The report states that those who did poorly on one kind of learning did poorly on all, but no numerical results on this were given. (See also p. 182.)

While we have concluded that general ability is related to ability to learn or learning rate, a body of recent work from an important laboratory argues just the opposite, seeming to echo Woodrow. The Individually Prescribed Instruction methods pioneered by Robert Glaser and his group employ a kind of "contract" plan in which the teacher determines just what work the student is to do on the basis of pretest information, monitors his performance, and moves him on to a new unit when he reaches mastery. J.L. Yeager and Kissel (1969) cited several studies within that program that purportedly found no relation of tested general ability to rate of learning under IPI. They went on to offer evidence of their own to support the same conclusion. For purposes of understanding this conflict in views, it will suffice to summarize the Yeager-Kissel study.

Eight units on computation skills in arithmetic were taught. For each S the file included the score on a pretest for each unit, given at the time the student reached that unit, and the "number of skills," within a list of microobjectives, that the student lacked when the unit began.

The number of days of work—from the start of the unit to the point where the student was declared to have reached mastery—was correlated with the two pretest measures, with age, and with IQ. The IQ range was somewhat limited (s.d. about ten) and the CA range was wide (s.d. about one year). This no doubt reflected the classification policy of the school in some manner. Now the pretest correlated highly (median r beyond -0.60) with time-to-completion, and so did skills-absent-at-pretest (median r beyond $+0.60$). But IQ did not correlate, only one r being outside the range -0.17 to $+0.17$. This puzzled us, and so did the fact that IQ failed to correlate with the pretest. Then we realized that we were reading about an extraordinarily large age range. Looking further, we saw that age correlated with time-to-completion (median r beyond -0.40). It appears likely that the students of lower IQ were also the older ones in this sample of children, who were taking the same lessons.

Of course, no one should expect IQ as such to correlate with learning, in school or out. It is mental age that reflects level of present ability, and only in an exotically selected sample will IQ rather than MA be the more relevant variable. If CA correlates with time to completion, as Yeager and Kissel found, MA does also. There is no way to judge from their report whether the regression of learning rate on MA was steep or not. And one should look at the regression rather than the correlation because of the peculiar distribution of CA and MA in the sample.

One other matter that beclouds the IPI studies is that teachers used pretest information as a basis for scheduling the child's work. Hence, there was a direct causal link, rather than a merely predictive link, of pretest and skills-to-be-mastered with time-to-completion. In fact, one suspects that if chance values were assigned to students at the time of pretest and made known to the teachers, such arbitrary "predictors" would correlate with time-to-completion. On the other hand, we doubt that the teacher's schedule of work would be much modified by giving him a vague impression of each child's age and mental ability. All in all, then, we find this line of research irrelevant to the psychological questions this section has dealt with.

Similar issues arise with regard to "mastery" procedures. In Block's dissertation (1970), lessons in matrix algebra were taught under a mastery regimen. A certain percentage score on an immediate posttest was required before the student could go on to the next lesson. The percentages were set at 65, 75, 85, and 95 per cent for different Ss. According to Block, "Despite the individual differences in the entry resources (pretest and previous achievement measures) of students in the 85 and 95 per-cent groups, these differences were *not* reflected in final achievement. Most students in each group learned to approximately the same high level." Block claimed that, with the higher standards, mean scores were higher. On a close reading of the dissertation, we find that some students in each group had been discarded. A student in the 65-per-cent group (for example) was discarded by Block if his score was above 70 per cent or below 60. A student in the 95-per-cent group was discarded if he did not reach 90 per cent during the experiment. This obviously reduced the range of attainment, in a biased manner. We have no way to judge how much closer the 65- and 75-per-cent groups would have come to the 85- and 95-per-cent groups if the samples had not been trimmed.

Correlations among distinct tasks, and related aptitudes

The literature on individual differences in learning has emphasized correlations among learning rates on distinct tasks. Glaser (in Gagné, 1967) reviewed many of the older studies. Most of this research allowed for neither tuning nor thorough familiarization, and provided contradictory results. Hence, we shall do no more than cite a few representative studies. As we review these, we include whatever evidence the authors reported on correlations of learning rate with tested ability.

Allison (1960) had 315 Naval recruits work on 13 learning tasks, including verbal, symbolic, and spatial code-association learning, verbal and spatial concept formation, mechanical assembly, polar-coordinate grid plotting, maze learning, and rotary pursuit. For each task, he reduced scores to three parameters by a curve-fitting technique; these parameters reflected learning rate (related to both total errors and level attained), curvature (degree of negative acceleration), and goodness of fit (trial-to-trial regularity). He employed 39 reference variables representing abilities and personal characteristics. He factor-analyzed the learning and ability data separately, and then related the two sets of factors by means of Tucker's (1958) interbattery analysis. This is one of many studies where an ambitious factor analysis seems to have clouded essentially simple results. In studies with numerous variables, tests are usually short and correlations are small. Factor patterns then are likely to rest on small amounts of variance. We shall look at the correlations and ignore the factor analyses.

Most of Allison's correlations among learning-task parameters were quite low. Of 378 intercorrelations among learning parameters, only 28 exceeded 0.30. The four correlations that exceeded 0.40 were spurious, arising from variables that were not experimentally independent. There were 481 correlations of learning-rate measures with reference measures. Only 62 of these reached 0.30; 55 of the 62 were attributable to just three of the 13 learning tasks, and just four tasks accounted for 60 of the 62. For the three most predictable learning tasks (CIC Plotting, Verbal Concept Formation II, and Spatial Concept Formation II), the appreciable correlations spread over almost all the tests in the reference group. The best predictors included Number Series, Letter Sets, Vocabulary, and General Classification, all of which reflect v:ed or g. Learning-rate parameters for the three predictable learning tasks intercorrelated 0.32, on the average. Thus, we account for virtually all the sizable correlations if we simply say that these three learning tasks are interrelated and somewhat dependent on general ability. Counting correlations as low as 0.20 also, two or three more learning-rate measures could be predicted, almost always by the tests most like conventional mental tests. Similar results obtained for the curvature parameter. Of 481 possible learning-ability correlations 54 correlations reached 0.30 and 42 of these were attributable to three learning tasks (CIC Plotting, Verbal Concept Formation I and II). Again a core of general ability accounted for most of the correlations.

It does not appear, however, that mental tests are very good predictors of the learning tasks. Take as an example the concept-attainment tasks, as predictable as any of Allison's measures. When we regard the four measures in this category as samples from a domain of such tasks, we can estimate the correlation of the universe score on omnibus mental-ability tests with the universe score on concept attainment. This correlation was only about 0.50 even though "corrected for attenuation." So ability to attain concepts includes a large component not assessable from g, v:ed, or Allison's special abilities.

On the whole, then, Allison's most important finding appears to be that general ability was related to learning in conceptual tasks. This finding has reappeared repeatedly. It is important also to note that correlations of ability tests with success in some kind of learning tended to be larger than correlations between two measures of learning.

Stake (1961) factor-analyzed learning parameters and ability tests given to 240 seventh-graders. There were 12 learning tasks, designed to represent contrasts between relational and rote learning, verbal and nonverbal materials, game-like and scholastic tasks, and individual and group administration. The reference battery included 37 measures representing nine ability factors, general ability, and school grades. Stake extracted several ability and achievement factors along with four learning factors. We shall again concentrate on the observed correlations rather than the factor loadings.

Of the 66 task-to-task correlations for learning scores, 16 exceeded 0.30. Of those, three exceeded 0.40. There were 432 correlations between such learning scores and mental tests; 250 reached 0.30, and many reached 0.40 or 0.50. As in Allison's study, the correlations were distributed across most of the reference tests. Just two learning tasks failed to related appreciably to the tests. One was a difficult classification task, the other a rote-memory task.

Stake found strong evidence of a consistent relation between conceptual learning and diverse mental tests. As in Allison's study, relations of ability tests to learning scores were stronger than relations from one learning task to another. Among the tests relating most consistently to learning were subtests of the Stanford Achievement Test, school grades, the Otis intelligence test, and subtests of PMA that measure reasoning.

Manley (1965) had 119 ninth-graders work on three types of concept-attainment tasks: a nonverbal series derived from Goldstein, a card-sort series derived from the Wisconsin and Kendler techniques, and a verbal series derived from Allison. The correlations among tasks within any category were substantial; for the Allison tasks the correlations were around 0.70. The correlations from one category of task to another were generally very small. Among 32 correlations of Allison tasks with other concept-attainment tasks, the highest was only 0.20 and few exceeded 0.10. The scores could be predicted to some extent by measures of reasoning or fluid ability, the best single predictor being Logical Reasoning. In this study, however, card-sort concept-attainment tasks and another kind of nonverbal concept attainment were not predictable.

Duncanson (1964) employed card-sort tasks of the Wisconsin type with 135 sixth-graders. The tasks correlated with each other, as in the Manley study, but they had very little in common with paired-associates learning and rote memory.

Some other studies have added bits of evidence. Stevenson and Odom (1965) found discrimination and concept-attainment tasks correlated ($r = 0.40$ or more), but unrelated to PA learning and anagram problem-solving which did relate to one another. However, a later study by Stevenson et al. (1968) did find correlation between discrimination and PA learning. Olson et al. (1968) studied several similar types of laboratory learning and found that these correlated about 0.50 with verbal IQ.

Considering all studies together, it appears that learning rates on closely similar tasks do correlate, whereas correlations among moderately different tasks are usually rather low. Presumably "narrow" factors influence performance on specific types of task. Task-specific factors limit the extent to which aptitudes can predict learning. But aptitude measures do correlate with learning to a greater extent than two independent learning scores correlate with each other. The unreliability of learning measures puts a ceiling on all such correlations. A concept of general mental ability is adequate to account for nearly all the correlations observed, except where a separate rote-memory factor is pertinent. Allison and Stake both found rote-memory tests related to rote learning, and forming factors rather distinct from conceptual tests and tasks.

The Overlap Hypothesis revisited

Early in this chapter we referred to the Anderson Overlap Hypothesis and its revival by Bloom, who defended the hypothesis on the basis of an analysis of the Bayley longitudinal study of mental tests. Here we shall reanalyze those data, partly because of their substantive interest and partly for the sake of illustrating some techniques. First, we shall examine correlates of gain in ability and then we shall apply path analysis to the data.

Bayley tested 40-odd children from very early ages until, ultimately, the middle 30's. Bloom relied on her 1949 report, which stopped at Age 17; we also shall use these data and ignore tests other than the Stanford-Binet.

J.E. Anderson (1939) entertained the idea that the mental test summarizes intellectual growth to date, but that a high score does not forecast that subsequent mental *growth* will be superior. As he saw it, mental development may accrue through increments in accomplishment that are randomly distributed, without relation to the child's status at the start of the period. To simulate such progress he generated a series of scores on successive trials for hypothetical persons by accumulating randomly chosen numbers. These artificial scores had a matrix of intertrial correlations that resembled in its superdiagonal form the year-to-year matrix of correlations for actual tests. Since the artificial data were generated by assuming a zero correlation of score at Stage t with the increment from Stage t to Stage $t+1$, the similar pattern of the actual correlations led Anderson tentatively to accept the notion that mental growth also has zero correlation with initial status. Bloom reexamined this question with a more satisfactory series of correlations (from Bayley, 1949) than Anderson had.

Change analysis

Bloom (1964) applied the conventional psychometric algorithm for calculating a correlation of $y - x$ with x, from the correlations and standard deviations of x and y. Figure 5.9 is his figure, with his title. We quote the part of his interpretation that bears on Ages 6 and above (his p. 63):

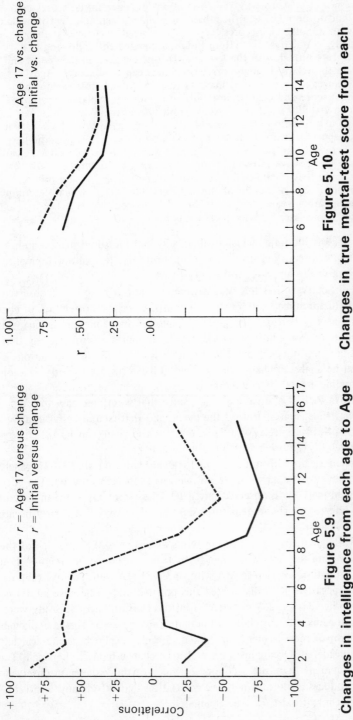

Figure 5.9.

Changes in intelligence from each age to Age 17 correlated with intelligence at Age 17 and with intelligence at the beginning of the change period. After Bloom, 1964, p. 62. Data from Bayley, 1949.

Figure 5.10.

Changes in true mental-test score from each age to Age 17, correlated with true score at Age 17 and with true score at the beginning of the change period. Derived from Bayley data, 1949.

> We are not clear as to why the correlations between initial scores and
> changes tend to be negative other than for a general ceiling effect in which
> persons with initially high scores tend to make smaller changes than persons
> with initially low scores. . . . [Here Bloom appended the following in a
> footnote.] In contrast with the low correlations between initial scores and
> changes are the relatively high correlations between final scores (Age 17)
> and the changes. These serve to make clear that the low correlations be-
> tween initial score and changes are not to be entirely explained in terms
> of the low reliability of change scores. [End footnote.] Much the same
> patterns of low or zero correlations between initial position and changes in
> I.Q. were reported by Roff (1941, p. 385) who states . . . [that] the cor-
> relations between test scores at one age and gain in scores at a later age are
> as likely to be negative as positive, and fluctuate around zero. . . . These
> results indicate that the so-called "constancy of the I.Q." is due primarily
> to the retention by each child of the skills and knowledge which determined
> his scores in earlier years, and is not due at all to correlation between
> earlier scores and later gains or increments.

The Anderson-Roff-Bloom conclusion, then, was that measured mental ability
has a negligible or even a negative relation to future intellectual development.
This mystifying result turns out to be an artifact.

The first difficulty is that the studies were carried out in terms of observed
IQs or MAs. This produced spurious correlations. A positive correlation of change
with final status is to be expected simply because errors of measuring final status
add to (or subtract from) both variables. Hence, Bloom was wrong to say that
unreliable data could not have produced sizable correlations. A more serious difficulty is that he analyzed change *in IQ*. The IQ has a fixed standard deviation
(save for sampling errors). It is impossible for persons at the high end of the
scale to improve their IQs, on the average, since that would increase the standard
deviation. They must regress toward the mean, and that guarantees a negative
correlation. A positive correlation of initial status and change in IQ is a *mathematical* impossibility (ignoring sampling fluctuations).

Roff correlated gain with initial status for data from four studies. The analysis
most like Bloom's used data from Hirsch, who had reported only IQ. The correlations of gain in IQ with observed initial IQ were essentially zero. In view of
the artifacts referred to above, it is surprising that they were not clearly negative,
as in Bloom's analysis.

Two of Roff's analyses were made in terms of observed MA, and one of these
was for Bayley data for Ages 6 through 9, from one of her earlier reports. Four
out of five correlations of gain in MA with observed MA were positive (about
0.40) and one negative. Roff discounted this positive finding because he did not
find it in his other data sets. When MAs from the Harvard Growth Study were
correlated with gains, the correlations fluctuated around zero. This is explainable
in terms of error of measurement. In these data, only gains over a one-year interval were considered. Over a brief interval, true change tends to be small. The
error of measurement therefore accounts for much of the variance in observed
change and produces a spurious negative correlation that offsets any positive
correlation that might exist for true change.

Roff's fourth analysis, of raw scores collected by Freeman and Flory, yielded negative correlations. Again, the fact that he examined change over only a one-year interval means that some or all of the negative correlation is a spurious effect arising from error. But it is also to be noted that the raw-score s.d.'s were much the same from year to year, and this would have the same effect that the standardization of IQ data did, in forcing a negative correlation. The stable s.d. arose because Freeman and Flory, to avoid a ceiling effect, had allowed item difficulty to increase steeply at the upper end of their scale.

Our reanalysis started with the data Bloom used, but we did not look at change in IQ, which is artifactual. Nor did we consider change in MA, which is perturbed by error. Instead, we asked how change in true mental age correlated with initial mental age, which is the question most pertinent to the Anderson hypothesis. We estimated covariances and correlations for true scores from an extension of the observed-score covariance matrix. Bayley's correlations were somewhat irregular because the sample was small, so we smoothed the correlation matrix. The smoothed data enable us better to estimate trends in the population; we believe that no bias is introduced. Our first step in smoothing was graphical. We took into account that correlations over a short interval should be larger than those over a longer interval that includes the short one and that, in general, correlations over a given elapsed time should be larger for older children. (But, consistent with the Bayley data—where there may be a ceiling effect on the Binet—a small drop in correlations for Age 17 was allowed.) After a first smoothing, the data were fitted analytically with a quadratic surface, to express r_{tt} as a function of $X_t, X_{t'}, X_t^2, X_{t'}^2$, and $X_t X_{t'}$. New correlations were calculated from that function. Our modification of the data was not drastic; here, for example are the original Bayley correlations for Age-8 MA with MA at other ages, and our adjusted values:

Age	6	7	9	10	11	12	14	17
Bayley r	.85	.88	.91	.89	.89	.91	.91	.84
Our final r	.848	.875	.894	.884	.874	.860	.842	.824

(While our correlations for Age 8 happen to be consistently smaller than Bayley's, our r's were higher at some other ages; there was no general bias.)

Since the continuous surface enabled us to estimate a correlation between independent tests separated by any time interval, we could let $t = t'$ and so estimate the following reliabilities (different forms, different days close together):

Age	6	7	8	9	10	11	12	14	17
r_{tt}	.855	.879	.898	.915	.924	.929	.927	.921	.913

This procedure is justified if we assume that the Bayley tests were experimentally independent, with no proactive effects. The reliabilities are smaller than those reported for the Stanford-Binet by Terman and Merrill, but Bayley's sample had a somewhat restricted range.

Our final step in this analysis was to calculate covariances of true gain (i.e., change between two accurately measured MAs) with true score at the beginning of the interval and true score at Age 17. These covariances led to the correlations charted in Figure 5.10. To simplify, final calculations were made only for alternate years. We find that true mental age does predict gain in subsequent years; all initial-vs.-change correlations are positive. True MA at Age 6 (or true IQ) predicts change in true MA between 6 and 17 with an r close to 0.60.

Path analysis

Path analysis (i.e., structural regression analysis) is another way of examining data collected at successive points in time. In applying path analysis to the Bayley data we added information on parental education (from Bayley, 1954). "Midparent Education" is the average of father's and mother's years of education. We smoothed Bayley's correlations of this with MA.

To give a clearer impression of the application of path analysis, we present a full set of true-score statistics for a brief age span. The reason for using true scores where possible is that a path diagram for observed scores is inevitably more complicated than that for true scores. The complications are a consequence

Table 5.1. Correlations and regression slopes relating true mental age to earlier variables

Variable	s.d. (months)	Correlation with true MA at			Standardized regression weights for predictors		
		Age 10	Age 12	Age 14	Age 10	Age 12	Midparent Education
Midparent Ed.	2.9	.610	.623	.638			
True MA, Age 10	27.7		.975	.960			.610
True MA, Age 12	30.5			.987	.948		.045
True MA, Age 14	30.5				-0.049	1.011	.038

Data from Bayley, 1954

of the errors of measurement, and hence of no scientific interest. For true MA, Table 5.1 gives the estimated standard deviations expressed in months and the intercorrelations for Ages 10, 12, and 14. Then, for each true MA in turn, the regression weights are given that forecast it from the variables that are temporarily antecedent and therefore could be causal.

These weights are organized into Figure 5.11 by the conventions of path analysis. The several U's represent unidentified causes (including such scattered events as serious illness, emotional disturbance, or unusually effective educational experience). Each U is a variable with s.d. one, having zero correlation with variables coming earlier in time. Mathematically, the several U's might represent "random increments," but from a psychological viewpoint they are influences not accounted for by other terms of the linear model. The variance unexplained at Age 10 includes many influences that could have been identified in the child's earlier record; but the only predictor available in Table 5.1 was Midparent Education.

Age-14 MA is forecast by an equation that gives heavy weight to Age-12 MA, recognizes some influence of Midparent Education, and includes a negative weight for Age-10 MA. This negative loading—the "direct influence" of Age-10 MA on Age-14 MA—requires some explanation. It is not a "cause" as such. Rather, it is to be thought of as a partial variate. Of two children with the same Age-12 MA and the same Midparent Education, which one can reasonably be expected to do better at 14—the one who ranked higher at 10, or the one who ranked lower? The one who ranked lower, according to the negative weight. And this makes sense. The child was moving from second place at Age 10 to a tie at Age 12 and was evidently in some sort of intellectual growth spurt; his curve of progress is comparatively steep, and hence he moves out front by Age 14. This is interesting but of no practical significance; including Age-10 MA as a third predictor adds only 0.0001 to R^2. The increment due to inclusion of Midparent Education is also nonsignificant.

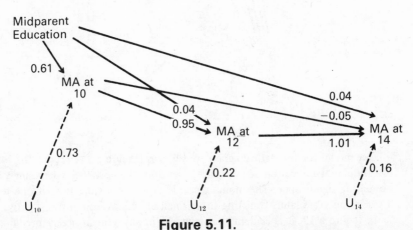

Figure 5.11.
Path diagram for true mental age at Age 14 (standardized coefficients).

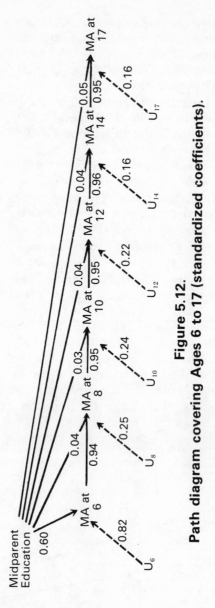

Figure 5.12.

Path diagram covering Ages 6 to 17 (standardized coefficients).

Our model for the path diagram for all ages (Figure 5.12) retains the loadings for Midparent Education at every age, even though the values taken singly are of borderline significance. The model discards the direct connection of one test with a test some years later. Omitting these small effects oversimplifies slightly.

In Figure 5.12, it is evident that true MA in any year is largely predictable from true MA two years or so earlier. A small part of the increment at each point can be predicted from Midparent Education. Although numerically small, this effect is important, as it denies the hypothesis that parental influence acts like a single-stage rocket booster which would send the child into an intellectual orbit where he continues on his own power. From this set of results, it appears that the parental contribution makes a steady, small input. There is no evidence that over this age range the effect of the home becomes gradually less important. One must be hesitant, however, to interpret the effect as an environmental one; it is equally consistent with the data to envision "timed-release" hereditary influences that express themselves in differential biological maturation.

One has the option of reporting standardized path coefficients, essentially beta weights, as in Figure 5.12, or of reporting regression weights in terms of the units of measurement. For Midparent Education the unit is years of schooling and for the tests it is months of mental age. The unstandardized weights for predicting true MA are as follows:

Age predicted	6	8	10	12	14	17
Midparent Education	2.1	0.2	0.3	0.4	0.3	0.7
Preceding true MA		1.57	1.58	1.37	1.15	1.18

The largest value of 1.58 tells us that if a child has a true MA 6 months above average at Age 8, our best prediction from that fact alone is that he will be about 9½ months above average at Age 10. Insofar as we accept the mental-age unit as a basis for discussion, then, he increases his lead. Such increases are comparatively modest beyond Age 10. If the values dropped to 1.00 for any period, one would conclude that gains in true MA during the period are not related to true MA at the start. For Midparent Education a coefficient of 0.5 would imply that each extra year of education for both parents gives the child 0.5 months of advantage in mental growth during the period.

Given all the data, then, we reject the Anderson-Roff-Bloom conclusion that increments in mental development are a random process. The semi-constancy of ranks in ability is rooted in part in the fact that, under ordinary conditions of development, the child who starts the period with an intellectual advantage is likely to improve his ability to answer test questions more rapidly than his age-mates. Such increments in performance are certainly not random.

On the other hand, the question of the correlations of gains with initial status is to some extent a false one. Whether the correlation of true gain with true initial status is positive, negative, or zero depends upon the metric chosen and upon the construction of the instrument used.

Consider an example. Persons start the year with vocabulary of size X and, to make a simple assumption, each of them adds 500 words before the next measurement. Then the correlation of gain with initial status is indeterminate (and the regression slope is zero). If instead of using X as the score we use $log\ X$, it turns out that gain determined on this scale has a strong negative correlation with initial score. If we use e^X as the score, there is a strong positive relation of gain to initial status. Testers rarely make this kind of conversion, but their practices in item selection have similar consequences. One might build up a vocabulary test by sampling (say) one word from the easiest 100, one from the next easiest, and so on. This test would give a raw score more or less proportional to vocabulary size, i.e., like X. Or one might sample one word from the first 100, one from the next 200, one from the next 300, etc. This would have somewhat the same effect on scores as would conversion of vocabulary size to $log\ X$; it would produce a negative correlation of gain with initial status. The test-construction plan of Freeman and Flory produced just this effect. It is obvious that we could design another vocabulary test where a positive correlation between true score (in raw score units) and subsequent true gain would be anticipated.

The relationship of gain to initial ability is specific to the scale used to measure ability. While it is valuable to be able to deny that gains in mental ability are random increments, it is only by an arbitrary definition of scale units that we can speak of a generally positive relation of initial ability to gain. Our argument may appropriately end with the statement with which R.L. Thorndike concluded his analysis of the matter (1966, p. 127):

> . . . [U]nless and until scales are developed that are truly homogeneous in the functions that they tap at all levels and are truly expressed in equal units, we will have to forego serious attempts to give a quantitative answer to the simple but tantalizing question: To what extent will the children who have grown rapidly in intellect up to the present moment continue to grow rapidly in the future?

Chapter 6 | Conceptualizing aptitudes and treatments

ATI research seeks to establish generalizations relating treatment variables to measurable characteristics of the individual. Treatment variables and aptitudes are numerous, hence the combinations to be tested are virtually inexhaustible. The task becomes hopelessly extended if one confronts two unorganized lists, each with hundreds of variables considered equally worthy of attention.

Throughout the modern history of differential psychology there has been a tension between those who wish to concentrate on a few key dimensions of aptitude and those who emphasize how very many dimensions are required to characterize an individual fully. It seems best to focus on a short list of especially significant traits for scientific purposes and also in any rule for assigning students to instructional groups. Guilford's classification of abilities gives us particular concern, since if 120 or more rubrics must be used to describe mental abilities properly, a programmatic search for ATI will be endless. We therefore make a particular effort to appraise Guilford's structure.

Personality factors proliferate even more than abilities. The problem is compounded because personality measurement suffers severe handicaps in methodology and so far has not based theory on those few methodological foundations that are available to it. Personality scales that measure the same trait are interpreted differently, scales that measure different traits are labeled similarly, and the vast list of traits now in hand is little organized. Yet variation of personality and style is extremely important, since some of the most interesting ATI findings to date rest on such variables. In turn, ATI research can help bring order to the personality domain. Sound theory can be built on demonstrations that personality-learning relationships can be manipulated by treatment variations.

Treatments also vary in numerous ways. The contrived tasks of laboratory experimentation can be categorized well enough. Distinctions suggested by the laboratory will describe some aspects of educational treatments, but such a taxonomy does little to organize the infinitely variable treatments that occur in education. Instructional media and methods, organization of groups, social climates, and teacher characteristics and practices have to be considered. No investigator has yet been able to see the range of treatment variations as a system.

This chapter reviews structures that have been suggested for the ability domain and deals with issues of generality, stability, and modifiability of aptitudes. While much of this applies to personality variables as well as to abilities, discussion of personality will be postponed to Chapters 12 and 13. No taxonomy of treatments can be offered, but some heuristic concepts are given for distinguishing treatments with respect to their aptitude requirements. Since progress in taxonomy for all these domains has to come from better task analysis, we describe some methods of analyzing tasks. At most, this chapter indicates directions in which parsimonious description of aptitudes and treatments may lie.

Intellectual abilities and their organization

The evolution of factor-analyzed abilities

Arguments about the complexity of the ability domain never end. Models range from modest elaborations of the Spearman structure, dominated by a general factor, to the Guilford model, which enthrones a multitude of abilities in Baritarian equality.

Spearman hypothesized a general factor of intelligence g, pervading all mental tests to some degree, and a host of specific factors, one in each test. His data on English and Scottish school children offered crude support for the claim. He was inclined to interpret g as an inherited, unitary intellectual power. But his contemporaries disagreed. Thomson regarded factors as categories reflecting similarities of test content (i.e., of stimuli) rather than as directly reflecting anything about the organization of psychological processes (responses). E.L. Thorndike held a similar view, suggesting that mental tests served only to weigh up one's repertoire of independent associations, embodying no more order or unity than a pile of leaves. A bit later, Thurstone and others challenged the Spearman monocracy of intellect by describing seven or more "primary" mental powers. Adopting the Thurstone procedures of factor analysis, Guilford undertook to catalog abilities (see Guilford, 1967; Guilford & Hoepfner, 1971). During World War II, his Air Force research team studying classification tests had extracted dozens of distinct factors—some intellectual, some psychomotor. After the war, Guilford began to postulate many further abilities and to invent tests for many of them. In time he organized his search by means of an egg-crate model he called "the structure of intellect." Guilford's present hypothesis embraces 120 or more abilities, nearly 100 of which purportedly have been identified with distinct test operations.

The British school—Spearman, his American colleague Holzinger, Burt,

Vernon, R. B. Cattell, and others—also moved beyond the original scheme. Their later models retain a general factor atop a hierarchical system. They place at the second level verbal-educational ($v:ed$) and spatial-mechanical abilities, two major group factors which tie together subordinate group factors roughly analogous to Thurstone's primaries. At the base they locate test-specific abilities. In principle, various intermediate levels can be added.

What accounts for the conflict among proposals about the number and interrelation of abilities? Choice of factor-analytic procedure has been one source of contention; to some extent, changing the procedure does change the results. When the omnibus, heterogeneous tests of the 1920's were later replaced with many narrow tests, each having items that are minor variations on a single task, test variety increased. This salted the data with numerous "small" factors. Conceivably, some of the conflicts also arose from the use of different subject pools.

Differences among theories no doubt have been exaggerated by investigators' predilections. The early British position has been criticized as a rationalization of Victorian England's single-rank-order view of human merit, and Guilford's many-celled structure has been called "scatterbrained." But the alternative structures are not inherently at odds. One can describe any system in terms of minute particles or in terms of large unities; each scheme brings a different set of relations into view.

The hierarchical model. Hierarchical arrangement of abilities has been endorsed by many theorists, and a widely shared view is now coming into focus (Vernon, 1969, p. 22; Cattell, 1971). At the apex of a hierarchy is something called g or fluid ability or analytic ability. Fluid ability—Cattell's term—is distinguished from "crystallized" ability and achievement that depend directly on training. Guttman (1965) arrived at a similar distinction between tests measuring "analytic ability" and those measuring "achievement." Guttman categorized even some of Thurstone's "primary" factors as achievements, and this is now supported by the results of Claeys (in Cronbach & Drenth, 1972, pp. 381-390).

Fluid ability is probably best seen as a complex assemblage of intellectual skills and strategies whose makeup differs a bit from person to person, rather than as a unified process or a biological parameter. Complex tasks (Matrices, Block Design, Dominoes) that require deployment of strategies in combination seem to provide the best measures. Observation of performance under varying conditions could tease out many component mental processes, and perhaps these could be separately appraised, but a "whole" ability is more than a sum of subordinate acts. The adaptive process that schedules, monitors, and reschedules the separate acts of attention and transformation of information is the *sine qua non* of excellent performance.

Some arrangements recognize more than one peak. Cattell has suggested that a second "fluid" ability has to do with ideational fluency. Both he and Eysenck consider mental speed to be a separate domain. Furthermore, rote memory appears to be distinct, and it is possible that a hierarchy for that domain can be elaborated.

No level of the ability hierarchy merits the entire attention of the psychologist. Sometimes g or another broad composite serves a particular purpose; sometimes one wants to use a profile at the level, say, of verbal, spatial, and numerical abilities; and sometimes one wants to move down to narrowly specific abilities. Those concerned with programmed instruction are forced to move down to minute abilities—e.g., "possesses the concept of numbers as an ordered series," or even, "counts '... 9 - 10 - 11' with a latency between numerals of no more than 750 milliseconds." Microanalysis is neither more nor less correct than gross analysis; the size of the bundle into which abilities are tied should be adjusted to the theoretical or practical context. At times, elaboration is needed to communicate an elaborate thought. At other times, it confuses.

The facet model. The chief modern competitor to the hierarchical notion is the facet model (Guttman, 1966). Tasks can be described in terms of two, three, or more rubrics or "facets." Within each rubric are several "levels" (not necessarily ordered). The array of task categories is given by the Cartesian product of the levels. Facets A (a_1, a_2, a_3) and B (b_1, b_2, b_3, b_4) imply twelve cells—$a_1 b_1$, $a_2 b_1$, ... $a_3 b_4$. Within each category it may be possible to define many tasks. The facet model is best known in the specialized version christened the "multitrait-multimethod" design by Campbell and Fiske (1959). The two-facet structure used in these studies, however, does not fully exploit Guttman's idea. (In passing, let us distinguish the ideas mentioned here from the multifacet generalizability theory of Cronbach *et al.*, 1972. In generalizability theory the "levels" of a facet are considered to represent a universe and to be in a sense interchangeable. The Guttman "levels" and the Campbell-Fiske "traits" are fixed, and each enters a theoretical statement in its own right. Whether the Campbell-Fiske "methods" are random or fixed varies from one application to another.)

It may not be necessary to choose between facet and hierarchical models. If one facet is "content," then it clearly is possible to develop one or more hierarchies within the content area. A hierarchy within such a process area as memory is also easily imagined. A process and a content hierarchy could cross to form a structure combining the hierarchical model with the facet model.

Guilford sets forth a facet structure, with content, operation, and product as the facets. It is easy to form the impression from Guilford's writings that he sees his cell factors as independent, and does not expect coherence among factors that share, for example, the same content. In personal communication, however, Guilford makes it clear that this stance is one of suspended judgment more than one of conviction. Since oblique factor structures cannot be established in an objective manner at present, he prefers not to argue about patterning within his cube. He foresees that, in time, evidence will support a systematic grouping of cell factors, more or less corresponding to "slabs" cut from the cube.

We quote from a letter dated Sept. 13, 1972:

> Although the fact that I have always rotated axes orthogonally is probably largely responsible for the impression that I believe the SI abilities to be mutually independent, I really do not believe this, nor have I, as far as I can recall, ever said so. I have not made oblique rotations because I do

not trust them to give dependable information regarding correlations among first-order factors. True, they give better simple structure, as Thurstone defined that concept, but my many years of experience in factor analysis have led me to reject simple structure as a dependable criterion for the location of axes. A simple-structure solution is too much dependent upon what test variables happen to be analyzed together. This route is not the way to invariance, one of the demands of science.

There are indications in our results, and Merrifield's special analyses bear this out, that when higher order factors are properly located, they will be along the lines of the categories of the SI model.

A partial assessment of the Guilford system. Reviews of ATI studies employing Guilford factors will appear later, especially in Chapters 9 and 11. We shall argue that the differentiated Guilford factors usually do not explain results as well as does an interpretation at the level of g or $v{:}ed$. We shall be equally skeptical of most reports of ATI findings where the interpreter has stressed Thurstone or French-kit group factors. But in the present chapter we report only our attempts to judge how coherent the Guilford factors are.

Guilford has constructed tests to reflect particular cells of his cube. In the typical study he administers dozens of such tests and reports the intercorrelations. He factors the battery and rotates the factors by a technique designed to bring the results into harmony with the originally postulated factors. While this approach is not open to criticism as a strategy for exploring his system and trying out new test ideas, it is not satisfactory for workers standing "outside" the system. The fit of the data to the hypotheses is not well tested by such a method, because the fit is allowed to capitalize on small differences among correlations in the particular sample. Horn and Knapp (1973; see also Guilford, 1974) demonstrated this by showing that Guilford data can be rotated to fit randomly generated hypotheses about as well as they fit Guilford's hypotheses.

Decisions about the Guilford system are important for the future course of work on ATI. We need to know whether much would be sacrificed by adopting some simpler system; even if all of Guilford's postulated factors do exist in some sense, they may not be worth much attention if they serve only as "trace elements." If as many abilities as Guilford recognizes *must* be recognized, hypotheses about ATI will have to be finely differentiated and very large samples will be needed to establish weightings for separate abilities. The prospects for successful ATI research would be much enhanced if it were decided that a system simpler than Guilford's accounts for the ability differences of long-run practical importance.

Aggregating tests that have high intercorrelations allows one to make some check upon postulated structures (though factor analysts rightly contend that this need not disclose the most useful dimensional structure). Ordinarily, among tests of similar reliability, one expects a higher correlation between tests loaded on the same factor than between tests loaded on different factors. If this fails to occur for a particular test, there may be an explanation consistent with the original hypothesis; but if such attempts at verification fail repeatedly, the postulated structure is untenable.

Correlations between pairs of tests assigned to Guilford cells having three facets in common (e.g., same content, same operation, same product) may be compared with correlations for pairs drawn from cells having just one facet in common, or two, or none. For example, CSI (cognition of symbolic implications) might or might not be more closely related to CMI (cognition of semantic implications) than to DMU (divergent production of semantic units), even though CSI has two facets identical to CMI and no facets identical to DMU. Guilford does expect higher correlations of tests that share all three facets than of tests that share one, two, or none. Tests sharing one or two facets are not necessarily expected to correlate to a greater degree than tests taken from cells that share no facet.

Hoepfner and Guilford (1965) administered 57 tests to ninth-graders, most of the tests being measures of divergent thinking. They judged the validity of the theoretical structure by tallying how often a test was strongly loaded on the supposedly relevant factors. Thus a test hypothesized to represent the DFC cell ought to have its highest loading in the DFC factor. Hoepfner and Guilford looked not only at cells. They also tallied facets separately and so seem to have taken factors at the facet level as working hypotheses, reasoning much as we have done. They asked, for example, how often tests coded as DFC, DMU, etc., were indeed assigned to D factors *of any sort* in the factor analysis. The system was confirmed, they said, with the following degrees of success:

"Operation" classification	74 times out of 81	
"Content" classification	71	81
"Product" classification	52	81

This result, like other reports from the Guilford laboratory, seems to argue for the validity of the system. Though the "hit" rate for product assignments was comparatively low, there are six kinds of products, hence the rate of 64 per cent is well above chance.

We carried out a limited tabulation of the Hoepfner-Guilford correlations, examining only the correlations of the divergent tests with each other. We sorted these into pairs of four kinds: CP, where both tests supposedly reflect the same content and product; Cx, where both tests involve the same content but different products; xP, same product but different content; and xx, products and content dissimilar. We then asked, for any one category of test (DMC, for example), what fraction of the correlations of each kind exceeded 0.40. (The results to be reported here were confirmed using other cutoff levels.)

For DMC, 33 per cent of the CP correlations (i.e., correlations of one DMC test with another) exceeded 0.40. Corresponding values were 40 per cent for Cx correlations, 7 per cent for xP correlations, and 7 per cent for xx correlations. Tests with similar *content* indeed tend to correlate. According to this analysis, however, tests calling for the same kind of *product* are not functionally similar. The figures for DMC are typical of our results for all cells from Guilford's "divergent" domain on which the study gave data. CP and Cx correlations tended to be equally large, and both exceeded xx correlations by a considerable margin. While the xP category fell between CP and xx (all data considered), the effect was weak; the order xx > xP was not uncommon. This result implies that the product classification accounted for little or no variance in this domain. Other findings, however, give some support to the use of the product rubrics.

Table 6.1	Structure of findings in two analyses by Merrifield	
Theoretical relationship within test pair	*DEGREE OF CORRELATION WITHIN PAIR*	
	Study I	*Study II*
Three facets shared	Highest correlations	Highest correlations
Two facets shared	No data	No data
One facet shared: Operations	No special coherence	Cognition tests showed some coherence
One facet shared: Content	Considerable coherence within semantic or symbolic test-pairs	Semantic tests cohered; figural did not
One facet shared: Product	No special coherence	No special coherence

Merrifield (in Dockrell, 1970) chose the same study for reanalysis by another technique. He selected two sets of eight tests, each set fitting an ingenious factorial design. The first set consisted of two tests from each of these cells: CSR, CMI, DSI, DMR. The second set had two tests each of types CFC, CMU, DFU, DMC. When the first matrix was factored, it was found that most of the common variance was accounted for by the content distinction, semantic/symbolic (−M−/−S−). In the second matrix, most of the common variance had to do with the convergent/divergent distinction (N−−/D−−). The content distinction in that set, semantic/figural, was detectable but weak. Looking at the correlations within blocks of the two matrices, we arrive at the summary in Table 6.1. The coherence of test-pairs sharing no facet was used as a baseline against which to identify "special coherence" for purposes of this summary. The Merrifield analysis implied that the product classification considered in isolation accounts for little variance, but that the concept "product within an Operation x Content category" may have some power. That is, tests referring to a given product, such as "transformations," are not likely to be especially correlated unless the Content and Operation classes for the tests are also the same.

We applied Kruskal's (1964) program for nonmetric scaling to two correlation

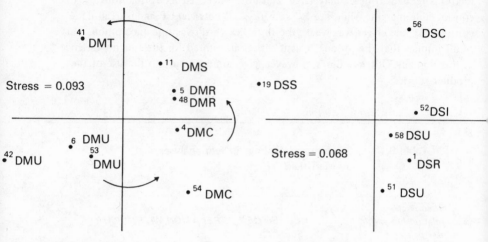

(i) Nine tests of the divergent-semantic (DM_) type

(ii) Six tests of the divergent-symbolic (DS_) type

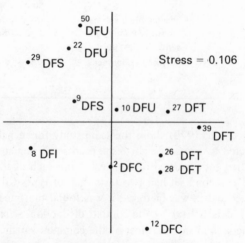

(iii) Twelve tests of the divergent-figural (DF_) type

Figure 6.1.
Three results from application of nonmetric scaling to tests
differing only with respect to their "product" classification.
Stress values (Kruskal's goodness-of-fit measure) below 0.10
represent fair to good fit using two dimensions. Numerals
identify variables as numbered by Hoepfner and Guilford,
1965.

matrices from Guilford's laboratory (Hoepfner & Guilford, 1965; Hoepfner, Guilford, & Merrifield, 1964). Clusters seemed to have more to do with content than with products considered in isolation. Figure 6.1 shows two-dimensional plots obtained by applying the Kruskal program to divergent-production tests grouped in three content categories. In the DM_ and DF_ charts, tests involving the same product do appear as a cluster. The DS_ data included too few tests to give useful evidence on this question. The finding supports the concept of cell factors for products within an Operation x Content rubric. This agrees with Merrifield's finding.

We also asked whether product factors are ordered. It might be supposed *a priori* that units (U), classes (C), relations (R), systems (S), transformations (T), and implications (I) constitute a set ordered from simple to complex. This idea was supported only in the DM_ chart (Panel i of the figure), where the series may be traced from U to C, then through R and S to T. (The apparent turning back of T toward U may result only from the compression of the data into two dimensions.)

A number of other small analyses lead us to think that the Guilford structure is unprofitably elaborate. Even a reproducible difference between two classes of tests may have no practical consequence. A calculation from one set of Guilford data indicates that four hours of testing (!) would be required to estimate with reliability 0.70 the difference score for NSC minus DSC factors (convergent/divergent symbolic-classification tasks). If these data are representative, even the famous convergent/divergent distinction accounts for remarkably little of the patterning of abilities.

We anticipate that ATI, when found, will be explainable in terms of abilities broader than that of the typical Guilford cell. We are inclined to think that those who start from the Guilford model should work with scores for Operation x Content rubrics (pooling various products), and obtain AT regressions by reduced-rank multiple-correlation methods. Crossvalidation will be a necessity, especially if the components of Guilford scores seem to interact differently. If the basic analysis succeeds in locating ATI for differentiated abilities, a final exploration of products within those Operation x Content cells that give interesting results might be warranted. To keep products separate in the main analysis is likely to produce more confusion than information.

Versions of our doubts about the power of Guilford's system have appeared in other places, and Guilford (1972) has explained why he considers our criticisms not to be well founded. But when all the work now available is put together with Guilford's recent communications, the criticism reduces to questions of utility. How much variance is accounted for by a relatively simple system of (say) content factors? How much by moving to the Operation x Content level? And how much by the further step down to the cell level? If Guilford accepts this hierarchical mode of thought, the next step is to work out these percentages of variance for sets of tests. The variances need to be estimated in a sample other than the one used to establish test classifications or factor-estimation equations.

We follow C. W. Harris (1967) and Carroll (1972) in recommending a vigorous program of reanalysis of the Guilford data according to schemes other than the hypothesis-determined simple structure he has employed. Two reports have moved in this direction: M. L. Harris and C. W. Harris (1970), Haynes (1970). Haynes actually succeeded in deriving a hierarchical structure within a set of tests of "cognition."

The issue of generality

Any conclusion regarding a specific ability is open to bothersome alternative interpretations, unless its generality is tested. Suppose, for example, that the Cubes test is found, in several experiments, to interact with a certain treatment variable. Is one to attribute the effect uniquely to this form of the Cubes task? or to the Cubes task, regardless of form? or to Spatial Visualization? or to Spatial Ability (undifferentiated)? or to Fluid Ability? Since these broader constructs do account to some extent for the Cubes score, the meaning of the empirical result is obscure until a multitrait-multimethod design is brought to bear.

To confirm that the result is explained by "spatial visualization" (i.e., the ability to visualize the rotation of objects in three-dimensional space), the investigator must employ at least two distinct tests of that construct, perhaps DAT Spatial Relations along with Cubes. That meets the multimethod requirement. If the several tests representing the construct show the same interaction, the conceptualization is supported. Broader interpretations have also to be ruled out, however. The hypothesis implies, among other things, that unless spatial tests require three-dimensional visualization they do *not* enter into this kind of interaction. To confirm this too, the study ought to include as a minimum a test such as Spatial Orientation or Minnesota Paper Form Board (rotation in a plane) and a test of fluid ability (Figure Series or Embedded Figures, perhaps). Obviously, when more tests represent the hypothesis and each counterhypothesis, the conclusion is sounder; but there are practical limits. The multitrait-multimethod desideratum has not yet been taken seriously in ATI research.

The issue of stability

Factor analysis has inquired into the relations among tests given at a single point in time. While one can be interested in momentary states, any theory of aptitude surely should be based on an organization of more lasting traits.

Stability of differences between aptitudes (i.e., of profiles) and the stability of aptitude organization have received little attention. Suppose that a hierarchical structure appears in a certain domain, in data collected simultaneously. A stability study could tell us whether the finer differentiations in the profile have long-term meaning. At the second level of the hierarchy, differences between factor-scores U and V at one testing might predict similar differences six months later. But third-level information perhaps has negligible stability; within factor U, for example, score differences found among subfactors $U1$, $U2$, and $U3$ on the first testing might not predict profile shape at the later date. $U1$ of the first testing might correlate no higher with $U1$ of the second testing than with $U2$ and $U3$ of the second testing. If such is the case, the third-level distinction is useless for any decision reaching as much as six months into the future. This is not to say that fine distinctions or short-term descriptions of aptitude have no use; these can serve theoretical purposes and can be useful in response-sensitive adaptations of instruction. But any long-term recommendations as to a strategy for teaching a student would need to be based on aptitudes that are likely to remain stable for months, if not years.

Interbattery factor analysis, developed by Ledyard Tucker (1958), is useful for studies of stability. Nanda (see Cronbach et al., 1972, p. 324) illustrated the potential of this approach, comparing two forms of the Differential Aptitude Test administered in a longitudinal framework. Of the eight factors available from each form, four proved stable enough to be worth reporting separately. Two other factors had inadequate but not negligible stability, and two were totally incongruent over the time period studied.

While the method adopted by Nanda is serviceable, there are alternative ways to formulate the stability problem mathematically, and alternative computational procedures. Several investigators have applied canonical correlation to the problem (Harnqvist, n.d.; Conger & Lipshitz, 1973). Whatever the method, the general point remains: Aptitude distinctions that guide educational decisions must be based on clear evidence that such distinctions are stable over the period governed by the decision.

The issue of modifiability

The language used in discussing aptitudes usually does imply that aptitudes are fixed. We speak of some persons as "having" high aptitude—high g or high spatial ability, or high CFU, or whatever—and others as low. Yet all cognitive psychology and all developmental psychology argue that aptitudes grow out of learning and experience, and that they are continually changing. Even if *ranks* in aptitude were to remain essentially stable during the school years, that would not justify the use of a concept of fixed aptitude in discussing ATI. For, as we argued earlier (p. 30), aptitude-outcome relations are to be described on an absolute scale rather than in terms of ranks or comparative standings. A particular treatment produces a good outcome for the person whose spatial skills have reached a certain level; *that* is the form a scientific finding and a causal explanation can reasonably expect to take.

The conventional design measures aptitude prior to instruction and carries out instruction for some period of time. The studies most relevant to education will use treatments of appreciable duration. When the posttest score, which reflects the whole training, is compared with the initial score, the implication is that the initial level of aptitude was operating throughout the training as a continuing causal factor. Whether this is plausible or not depends on the duration of the training, and on the intimacy of the relations between the processes tapped by the aptitude measure and the processes used in learning and in the criterion measure.

The issue was brought sharply into focus by the ATI study of Sullivan, Okada, and Niedermeyer (1971). An elegant two-treatment design obtained striking results with a remarkably small sample. On its face, the finding provides about as clear a prescription for instruction as any ATI study yet conducted. The study dealt with first-graders already well into reading instruction. For about a month, the experimenters trained the students to associate certain sounds with certain letters or letter combinations, to break up a word into those units and sound out the units, and then to reassemble the sounds into a pronounceable word. One treatment (SL) taught this through the use of single letters—*s* to be translated into an "sss" sound, *i* into an "ih" sound, etc. Another treatment (LC) presented the same letters and also introduced, within the same total training time, letter combinations (*it, nd, end*).

The children were given a pretest and paired on the basis of that score. One member of each pair was assigned to each treatment; 24 pairs finished the experiment. A strong interaction was evident in the following mean scores (from parallel forms of the pronunciation test) for three levels of pretest performance:

	Low	Medium	High
Percentage correct on pretest	0 - 14	15 - 39	40 - 97
Number of pairs of subjects	8	8	8
Mean percentage correct on posttest			
SL training	46	72	86
LC training	27	77	99

The interaction is significant and would perhaps have been even more striking save for the ceiling effect in the LC treatment.

The implication appears to be that the LC treatment is to be preferred for all pupils who score above 20 (or thereabout) on the pretest and the SL treatment for those who start with very little ability in word analysis. If only children who score above about 20 on the pretest are ready to profit from LC training, assignment of those below this point to SL training is justified as a *temporary* expedient. It would be wise to monitor each child in the SL group, and introduce him to letter combinations as soon as he has built up basic analytic skills.

The static ATI experiment, where two sharply distinct treatments are maintained throughout the period of data collection, only hints at the proper transition rule. A sequential experiment comparing various rules for making the SL-to-LC transition would provide a better guide to practice than the one-stage experiment (see also p. 2.14). The argument may generalize to all ATI findings:

Aptitude develops as training proceeds, and any assignment to treatment has to be reconsidered when the aptitude has increased significantly.

This dynamic conception of assignments is quite different from the one usually discussed in personnel classification. The two are not inherently in conflict, however, so long as research conducted within the static framework is given sophisticated interpretation. Above, we were able to draw a dynamic conclusion, though not a precise sequential-assignment rule, from a one-stage study. Sequential experiments are considerably harder to conduct than static experiments, because the number of alternative hypotheses is great.

The Sullivan experiment required a dynamic interpretation because the pretest measure of "aptitude" was just like the posttest. The aptitude score had to change if the training worked. A similar circular relation is encountered whenever the "aptitude" measure taps elements of the criterion task, and the treatment repairs deficiencies in those elements. In remediation one must monitor progress and alter the treatment once the deficiency has been overcome.

Some "aptitudes" are formed through years of cumulative experience. Deficiencies in such skills or habits may be difficult to overcome. Then the static model is appropriate. Any statement that a deficiency is difficult to overcome is subject to challenge. However long the fruitless efforts to remedy a certain deficiency may have extended, we can never say that all hopes are false. Tomorrow may bring the educational invention that succeeds. Nonetheless, the finding that an ability resists training has to be taken seriously. There is, for example, much reason to think that the young adolescent attains formal operational thought in his own good time, and that training pointed toward that end rarely produces more than a hollow simulacrum of such thought. If we are powerless to remedy logical deficiencies in short order, and if we wish to teach science, then for logic-deficient students we shall design science instruction that makes minimal demands on formal logic. The more rigorous approach would be reserved for students who have acquired formal operational thought.

So it is whenever we think of designing contrasting instructional approaches —concrete/abstract, complex verbal presentation/simple verbal presentation, modelling/self-discovery, etc. The person who sets up an experimental comparison of two treatments assumes that, in the learners under study, aptitude is in pretty much a steady state. In traditional experimentation, aptitudes are measured only at the start of the study, if at all. This implies a steady-state assumption, for if relevant aptitudes were likely to change in the course of the experiment, a conclusion about method main-effects would apply only to naive entering Ss. In a follow-up experiment in which the same two methods were used to teach some further content to the same Ss, the treatment difference found in the first experiment might be reversed.

On the whole, it appears that the aptitudes one can regard as stable and employ as a basis for static assignment are those generalized aptitudes that can be seen as transfer phenomena (Ferguson, 1954; 1956). In reading, for example, the vicious circle of incomprehension, dislike for reading, faint-hearted practice, and further incomprehension leaves some students weak in reading comprehension, and this deficiency crops up whenever they are given relatively difficult material to read. Entries at the upper levels in hierarchical models of ability seem to have this generalized character, pertaining to many different tasks, measurable by many different tests, and pervading response to instruction. At the lowest levels of the hierarchy, abilities are too specific to be thought of as constructs. They are narrow, directly teachable skills: knowledge of a particular letter sound, or of the meaning of a particular word, for example. Describing the person's microabilities may profitably point to content for remedial lessons. Appraising his global, transferable abilities may help select a style of instruction.

Insofar as an instructor is commissioned to teach the student science in an allotted number of months, the question becomes one of selecting a teaching method in the light of the hard-to-change aptitudes. Any easy-to-change "aptitudes," such as inability to read a scale accurately in the laboratory, can be diagnosed and remedied along the way. Beyond this, the instructor will want an instructional strategy for students who are limited in their use of formal logic, or in spatial ability, or in reading comprehension. For him to attempt to remedy these would be to digress from his primary assignment. The counter-argument takes the form: "Which is more important to develop: the student's science? or his logic (spatial ability, reading)?" The tradeoffs between near and distant payoffs cannot be entirely reduced to issues that experiments settle. Stealing time from science instruction to improve reading is clearly warranted, if gains in reading will be so rapid that the student can then make up the lost ground in science. On the other hand, to give such high priority to the Three R's, or the Seven Primary Abilities, or other supposedly basic elements may be to impoverish the student in the end. Between taking the course of least resistance and the course of most resistance, the choice is not to be resolved by maxims or by season-to-taste recipes. There is a time for each kind of effort. Once it is agreed that at least sometimes the educator will choose to adapt his methods to the student's deeply rooted weaknesses, the importance of ATI research is undeniable.

Analysis of instructional treatments

We have seen that aptitudes, at least in the cognitive sphere, can be organized into a reasonably coherent taxonomy. Despite its limitations, this organization at least can serve as a guide toward parsimonious interpretation of ATI research. We need a comparable organization of instructional treatment variables. While some progress has been made in categorizing tasks from the laboratory (see, e.g., Melton, 1964), taxonomies of instructional treatments or other natural situations are almost totally lacking. Sells (1963) has long advocated the development of such taxonomies. He made a start toward classifying a wide range of environmental variables. Moos and his coworkers (see Insel & Moos, 1974) have been defining general dimensions of social ecologies, including school classrooms as one kind of setting. But these variables have little direct relation to instruction.

The potential value of a taxonomy of instructional situations is suggested by the work of Fleishman (1972, 1974) and his associates. Fleishman, concerned with psychomotor and vigilance tasks, has collected most of his data under conditions of practice, with no instruction. Independent of the data, such task characteristics as demand for verbal comprehension, demand for perceptual closure, and demand for fine muscular adjustment are rated. In some experiments, parameters of the task (e.g., the orientation of the display vis-a-vis the control levers S manipulates) were varied from one group of Ss to another. It turns out that what aptitudes correlate with rapid learning depends upon such parameters, varying in a reasonable manner. Moreover, changes in the parameters interact with such treatment variables as massed/distributed practice and knowledge of results. A taxonomic analysis of instructional situations that considers the stimulus properties of the task, the stimulus properties of the instructor and the instructional displays, and the conditions of practice and reinforcement would be of substantial help in collating and understanding interactions.

The compilation of ATI studies to be reviewed in this book might be expected to suggest categories of treatments that produce similar effects. But many strong studies will need to be in hand before categories with theoretical import emerge. Sorting through such studies, the theorist might adopt a style much like that of the biologist classifying specimens by their apparent features. This may be the only feasible approach to taxonomy in instruction for some time to come. Ultimately, though, we would hope to identify the significant underlying dimensions along which complex treatments vary. There appear to be two principal approaches to use. One of these derives from the experimental, laboratory spirit of task analysis. The other takes a naturalistic, correlational view.

Dimensional analysis

The multivariate methods can in principle be used to analyze situations, just as they have been used to analyze aptitudes. One can imagine five, ten, or even a hundred alternative treatments: e.g., various text or film renderings of a body of material, or alternative teacher presentations. Characteristics of the stimuli could be quantified and the interrelations of these variables across the "sample" of texts, films, or teachers, could be calculated, just as tests are intercorrelated in a sample of students. Dimensions of such a matrix can be obtained. N. Frederiksen (1972) discussed some of these possibilities, citing research on college environments as a prime example (see our p. 486). There have also been some attempts to obtain dimensions of classroom climates (our p. 298), and of the climates of Upward Bound projects (our p. 376). Magnusson (1969) worked out a way to use similarity judgments from students for such purposes. Decades of research on teacher effectiveness has aimed at identifying dimensions of teaching style. But this work has rarely been concerned with ATI (see e.g., Rosenshine, 1971; Dunkin & Biddle, 1974; our p. 320), nor has it generated taxonomies of instructional treatments.

Beswick and Tallmadge (1971) sought to specify dimensions in the instructional features of one-day Navy training courses. Earlier results had suggested that these ten courses differed in eight respects related to arousal of curiosity: information presented, structure, role of examples, role of response production and practice, reliance on unusual stimuli, etc. Treatments were ranked on these characteristics, the rankings were intercorrelated, and the correlations were factored. Two orthogonal factors were identified as ideation/substance and implicit/explicit task structure. Examining aptitude data from previous studies, Beswick and Tallmadge concluded (for example) that "Set toward education" correlated with outcome more strongly when the structure was explicit. But this result is an inference from only one significant correlation. A conclusion of similar form regarding measures of learner curiosity is also questionable. The patterns may have emerged by chance. The study's value lies in its suggestive technique of rating and factoring treatment dimensions.

Some other pilot studies have investigated dimensions of instruction by motion picture. O'Connor (1950) ranked 27 commercial films according to achievement effects on elementary school children and also according to experts' ratings of the effectiveness of the films. He then quantified 21 characteristics of each film and showed that 10 of these correlated above 0.35 with one criterion or the other. Variables like "number of nouns with a concrete referent," "dramatic rating," "ratio of words to scenes," and "words with a personal referent" gave correlations (over films) of 0.59, 0.49, −0.47, and 0.45, respectively, with achievement. Snow (1963) measured these and other auditory and visual aspects of a series of films on college physics. He identified such factors as audio-visual stimulus complexity, temporality, video and audio iconicity, and artificiality. Artificiality perhaps entered into an ATI. The factor had to do with the number of "contrived" visual experiences in each film: slow-motion, zooms, and other effects that cannot exist in nature. Experienced film learners seemed to profit more than others from the more artificial films. This implies that aptitude for film learning, developed through prior experience in learning from film, is particularly important for films that rely on special devices. O'Connor and Snow used only small samples of films, with varying content. Their reasoning relating student outcomes to film characteristics is at best indirect.

M. E. Smith and Seibert (1966) made a somewhat similar analysis of frame sequences in the Holland-Skinner program *Analysis of behavior.* They isolated such factors as quantity of instruction, sentence complexity, and concrete/abstract. Heckman (1967) then used these treatment factors in combination with aptitude factors to predict criterion scores in a Person x Frame matrix for the Holland-Skinner program. (This is an unusual method of exploring ATI in correlational data, developed by Seibert and Snow, 1965, and otherwise untried. In Heckman's study, aptitude dimensions accounted for a good deal of the variance on the criterion test; treatment dimensions accounted for relatively little. AT combinations had negligible predictive power.

Stimulus dimensions of potential use for instructional research have come from some isolated analyses of prose samples (*e.g.,* Carroll, 1960; Funkhouser & Maccoby, 1970). Studies of the objective features of text as they influence readability provide further examples. Carroll (1971) reviewed this voluminous literature, including both correlational and experimental analyses, so we need not reiterate. Carroll also noted comparable studies dealing with auditory presentation and some experiments on the characteristics of pictorial communications. We know of one correlational study of illustrations: Twedt's (1952) analysis of characteristics of magazine advertisements as they relate to readership indices.

Such work has produced a long list of potential treatment dimensions that differ in generality, just as ability factors do. But no one has yet sought to organize these into some hierarchical or other taxonomic structure. Most dimensions are either too specific (*e.g.,* number of affixes per 100 words, or size of illustration) or too general (*e.g.,* difficulty or complexity of presentation) to provide convenient descriptions of treatments for educational research. An intermediate range of dimensions is probably needed to characterize variations in instructional method.

Even with an improved sense of dimensionality, it will be impossible in educational research to explore systematically all the parameters of the stimuli. Very likely a useful tactic is to shift to a "matrix-sampling" design (Shoemaker, 1973; Clark, 1973). Every subject need not study the same passage. It would be possible in an experiment on, for example, learning from text, to have twenty or more passages, sampled so as to represent the range of assignments actually made in typical courses. These could be distributed at random over the Ss in each treatment group, so that every group is reading the same mix of selections. Then the experiment would be analyzed just as before, the only difference being that the error term would be greater. If that sampling can actually be made representative with respect to dimensions of typical course assignments, then these dimensions can be used in the analysis and the error term reduced proportionately. Additional interactions can be explored. The error term will always be larger than in the single-passage experiment. But this higher price purchases a more secure generalization. In the single-passage case one is entitled strictly to conclude only that an effect is present in the population when that fixed passage is used. If the experiment with many passages produces a positive result, one gains confidence that the significant effect will hold up over the range of assignments studied, even if it does not hold for every separate assignment.

Matrix sampling is easier to apply in a short, highly controlled experiment than in a large study. But one wants an educational experiment to be carried out in many classrooms if that is practicable, so that he can more safely generalize over classrooms, teachers, etc. An investigator going to this effort can apply different lessons in different classrooms. For example, if an experiment on algebra is to be conducted, it may be practicable to apply each treatment to several topics within algebra, no classroom working on more than one of the topics. One would also want to represent classroom or teacher dimensions in such a design. The information obtained should be more valuable than data from the same number of student-hours where the same content was taught in every class.

Process analysis

Increasing effort is being devoted to the analysis of particular instructional tasks in information-processing terms. Improved task analysis is a vital need in instructional psychology generally, as Glaser and Resnick (1972) have emphasized. Their review, and that by Carroll (1971) already noted, appear to be the best summaries of the present state of knowledge. But neither of these is primarily concerned with ATI; most studies still ignore individual differences.

At present, methods for task analysis are not well developed. The analyst must rely largely on intuitions and on scattered bits of theory. Beyond traditional experimental methods, and the correlational approaches suggested in previous pages, there are some techniques for disclosing processes. Two that may be adaptable to ATI research involve the specification of behavioral hierarchies and the use of computer simulation.

Behavioral hierarchies. Behavioral analyses of tasks were introduced to specify job and training requirements in the military and in industry (R. B. Miller, 1962). Gagné (1970; 1974) has carried on the educational applications of this approach, identifying various classes of learning outcomes. Regarding a given instructional outcome, Gagné would contrast final performance with the performance that is one step short of the complete, successful act. He would ask: What must the learner know or be able to do before he is ready to take this final step? Having specified what attainment(s) come just before the final attainment, Gagné then asks the same question about the next preceding step. Continuing in this way, Gagné constructs a converging hierarchy of steps, with each step defined in terms of observable behavior. A hierarchical network of steps is laid out, from the rudimentary base to the complex final objective. The hierarchy suggests where positive transfer occurs during acquisition, and guides the sequencing of instruction. Gagné gives many examples.

The approach allows for individual differences in prior knowledge and skill by permitting learners to enter the hierarchy at different levels. Some subskills, particularly those at the base of the hierarchy, turn out to resemble ability constructs. (See, for example, the hierarchy for number series, Gagné, 1970, p. 234). Extra time on the early steps of the hierarchy is allowed the learner weak in such abilities.

Unfortunately, the analysis of treatments in these terms has been restricted to the learning outcomes and to the intermediate skills and processes demanded by the content of the lessons. Analyses have not been made of the demands imposed by the methods and media used to convey the content; yet these may be where interactions originate.

Computer simulation. A second approach to task analysis derives from computer simulations of cognitive processes, and from the current psychology of information processing. The goal is to set up a flowchart or other account of the sequence of decisions and operations used in performing a task. The investigator asks questions like these: What alternative decision, storage, etc., sequences are possible? How do effective and ineffective learners differ in their choice of alternatives? The simulator frequently enlists the cooperation of a learner, asking him to "talk his way through" as he works. Introspections from several learners serve as prime data for identifying steps and strategies. The components hypothesized can be checked in small experiments. The approach is at least as specific as that of Gagné. Further, one can presumably characterize learning tasks and aptitude tests in common terms by this means. Simon and Kotovsky (1963; Kotovsky & Simon, 1973), for example have simulated performance on the Thurstone Letter Series test, a measure of inductive reasoning ability. From introspective protocols and error records, these authors were able to build rules by which a computer could generate responses to each test item, making errors similar to those of human Ss. Such simulation forces task description to a level of detail rarely obtained by other means. And, since descriptions of tasks and tests are stated in a common language, their coordination may suggest ATI hypotheses.

Although this form of theorizing has gained increasing acceptance in experimental psychology, it has as yet seen little application to ATI research. A first step was taken by Carroll (1976), who developed a coding system based on a cognitive process model and applied it in task analyses of 24 ability tests. We expect information-processing ideas to be uniquely useful in gaining an improved understanding of instructional treatments. And increased efforts in this direction can provide a new kind of theory of aptitude. Beyond these, however, we need ideas about aptitude-treatment matching.

Matching aptitudes and treatments

Forms of matching

Although previous ATI research has not shown the cumulative use of any kind of strategy and so gives no base of experience, a perspective on possible strategies is needed. We suggest that aptitudes and treatments can be matched in at least three ways: "capitalization of strengths," "compensation," and "remediation." (All of these tactics assume that ATI effects operate on the individual, ignoring social-psychological factors operating at the group level.)

Building upon the learner's assets—it will be convenient to call this a "capitalization" strategy—tailors instruction to capabilities of the learner. Thus, some writers have suspected that learners high in spatial ability will do better when more diagrams are used in teaching. Likewise, a student high in verbal ability might be expected to respond best to a more verbal treatment. (This is a handy

example, but in fact spatial/verbal aptitude has not interacted in this way. See
pp. 266 ff.) Other capitalization hypotheses will be seen later in this book.
Some rest on personality variables rather than abilities as aptitudes. Thus, Domino (p. 442) showed that students characterized as "achieving via conformity"
do best when courses require conformity, while "independent achievers" do best
in courses arranged to encourage independence.

One variant of the strategy is to capitalize on student preferences. Conceivably, a mode of instruction a learner is more comfortable with is one to which
he can and will respond well. Hence one might expect self-selection among materials, work schedule, etc., to be beneficial. Catering to preferences assumes that
the learner has distinct preferences, that the learner really does know what treatments serve his purposes, and that the learner's goals are fully compatible with
those of the instructor. In the few studies testing this strategy, the results indicate that basing instructional adaptations on student preferences does not improve learning and may be detrimental (see p. 478).

But a capitalization strategy need not rest on Ss's stated preferences. Results
like Domino's could arise from differences in the learning strategies that each
kind of S typically adopts, consciously or not. These may or may not be con-
sonant with what S says he prefers. More detailed diagnoses of these typical
strategies or styles is needed.

A second form of aptitude-treatment matching may be referred to as compensation. A treatment can be made to do for the learner what he cannot do
for himself. If the usual treatment requires the learner to use some skill or mental process that is not inherent also in the criterion performance, it may be possible to add to the treatment a prosthetic substitute for the learner to use just
as an artificial limb is provided for the amputee. If the learner is weak in organizing, it will help to organize the instructional material for him. The poor reader
can listen to the material if it is put on tape. Those whose minds tend to wander can be given a text studded with questions to prompt attention. (For examples of these possibilities, see Ch. 11.)

To pursue the simplest example used earlier, perhaps the learner with low
verbal ability is poor at formulating in words what he observes. It would then
be reasonable for the treatment to provide verbal statements for him. If he has
high spatial ability he perhaps needs few diagrams, since he can visualize their
extensions and transformations. The high-verbal learner who is weak in visualization might be supplied with extensive diagrams and left to generate his own
verbal representation. Each treatment can be preprocessed by the needed "aptitude," to compensate for a particular weakness. Cost, time, and the risk of
boredom weigh against predigesting or elaborating the material in all possible
respects, hence one ought not to do for the learner what he can do for himself.
Compensation that helps Lows can produce a negative relation between aptitude
and outcome, if unneeded elaboration damages motivation or produces interference among Highs.

A third form of aptitude-treatment matching is remediation. In its simplest
variation, a remedial loop merely fills specific holes in the student's initial knowl-

edge. But one can think of more general remediation of inaptitude. Where a general skill in learning is weak, it usually ought to be remedied rather than bypassed through a compensatory treatment. Thus one would help the poor reader to learn by training his reading. To teach him science by a prosthetic treatment that eliminates the need for reading is only a stopgap.

The tactic of supplying bits of information to the learner is of no psychological interest, and training in such skills as reading needs no discussion. But research is needed on the possibility that intervention can promote ability to learn.

The three forms of matching can be combined. One can think of capitalization and compensation as complementary. Treatments might be designed to favor Highs on one aptitude who are Lows on another by coordinating several capitalization and compensation devices. CAI programs might be designed to provide remedial and compensatory subroutines within several streams planned on different capitalization strategies. (For further discussion of the three forms, with examples, see Stolurow, 1965; Snow, 1970; Salomon, 1972.)

Finding ATI when treatment alternatives are fixed

Often the educator has to choose between competing methods of instruction, each of which has its advocates and its research support. Often, educational research has failed to identify one of the alternatives as best. For example, a review of experiments on teacher-centered (authoritarian)/learner-centered (democratic) classrooms showed eight studies favoring the first mode, 11 studies favoring the second, and 13 studies showing no difference (R. C. Anderson, 1959). Among comparisons of televised/live classroom teaching, 83 studies favored television, 55 favored conventional teaching, and 255 found no significant difference (Schramm, 1962). In a comparison of lecture/discussion in college, the tally was 45 studies on one side, 43 on the other (Dubin & Taveggia, 1968). Some reversals of significant main effects from one study to another very likely result because studies used dissimilar Ss. Subject differences should produce reversals if the treatment variable enters into disordinal within-group ATI. A review of past studies may suggest what aptitudes distinguish the Ss in studies yielding contradictory main effects.

Instead of launching a trial-and-error search for aptitudes that relate to a contrast between two treatments, the investigator should try to specify the learner skills or styles important in each treatment, the processes each treatment calls for, and the prerequisite information each calls upon. The various forms of task analysis and of thinking about aptitude-treatment matching should prove helpful in identifying likely aptitude variables. In choosing abilities, attention will need to be paid to competing hypotheses suggested from a hierarchical view of ability organization. Once some aptitude choices are made, the best approach will probably be to investigate ATI through a series of iterative experiments. We stress iterative research here because it is only through successive approximation that new kinds of aptitude or treatment dimensions are likely to be defined. If a first attempt shows some interaction, successive studies would add, subtract, or otherwise modify aspects of the aptitude or the treatment conceptions in line with the interpretation of results. To strengthen the interaction, one might modify a treatment by elaborating an explanation, adding or dropping cues to direct attention, changing the pace, etc. Alternatively, multitrait-multimethod analyses, item analyses, and the like could clarify just what the interacting aptitude is and improve its measurement.

Finding ATI when aptitude. is fixed

An investigator may be primarily interested in a particular aptitude. Starting there, he will choose experimental contrasts that seem likely to relate to the construct of interest. Experiments that successfully manipulate a construct's relation to other variables provide a key demonstration that the psychological nature of the trait is becoming understood. Thus, ATI research can play a fundamental role in construct validation. A good example of this process in action is seen in the work on achievement motivation. (See J. Atkinson & Feather, 1966.)

Just as with treatment variables, task analyses of aptitudes are essential. One example comes from P. Jacobs and Vandeventer (1971, 1972) who sought to develop programmed instruction for improving scores on figural reasoning tasks like those in Raven's Matrices. The analysis provides a fairly detailed account of learners' activities in solving matrices.

Given an aptitude variable and some analysis of the processes it reflects, one than asks: What instructional techniques would make this competence especially relevant to learning? What would a treatment have to provide to make learning easy for the low-aptitude S? What training would improve the aptitude itself? In constructing likely treatment variables, the implications of the aptitude construct and of previous validity studies on it need to be considered. If it has been observed that related instruments predict performance strongly under some conditions but weakly under others, these contrasting conditions should be examined for treatment elements worth incorporating into an ATI experiment. Once treatment elements are identified, a factorial design in which all these elements can be varied independently is an option.* An alternative is to design only two treatments, each of which combines several treatment elements whose contrasts are hypothesized to produce interaction. Here, one sacrifices tests of specific contrasts in order to obtain enough Ss in each treatment for a powerful statistical test of the overall contrast. As argued earlier, an experiment with sufficient sample size and covering a sufficient segment of school experience is necessary to test ATI ideas. Costs of experimenting will, we think, preclude elaborate Fisherian designs for testing ATI. The strategy of pinning down interactions of a few well-controlled, isolated variables and building toward complex treatments is un-

---

*The most elaborate example we have found of such a design is a study by Allen, Filep, and Cooney (see p. 211). The analysis of the data, however, was unfruitful.

likely to pay off in this realm. Once an interaction has been substantiated using a more global contrast, there will be time for experimental elaborations from the initial pair of treatments to arrive at a superior combination of treatment elements.

Microadaptation of instruction

The ATI approach envisions modifying instruction by periodic decisions that assign the person to one or another style of instruction for at least a few months. More nearly continuous alteration of instruction obviously is possible if one employs data collected at the end of every week or every day. At the extreme, adaptation of instruction can be as detailed as computer-aided instruction (CAI), where a single response determines what task or explanation the student confronts on his terminal at the next moment.

These response-sensitive training procedures—to adopt a term from R. C. Atkinson (1972)—assume the existence of interaction. They, however, match instruction to a highly specific appraisal of faults seen at a given moment, not to a broad and stable aptitude. Research on response-sensitive instruction may be simpler in some ways than research on ATI. The generalization established by such research is a rule for selecting the next unit of instruction. The designer of the system can try a limited number of strategies, and find out which works best. With microadaptation, the "best treatment" may not differ substantially from one learner to another. That is to say, there may be a uniform strategy, even though the sequence of frames displayed changes according to the person's errors. ATI data may be used for revision of the program, as in Bunderson's work (1969), even where there is no intent to classify learners into alternative tracks.

We suspect that a single treatment plan, even with microadaptation, will never be fully efficient. There probably are broad classes of learners for whom different streams of instruction are appropriate. One can imagine CAI programs in two or three distinct syles; microadaptation of instruction can take place within these. It is also possible that for some learners the expensive CAI style is unnecessary or even dysfunctional. The economics of education demand concern for ATI. But whether economies are actually obtainable through allocation on the basis of aptitude remains an open question.

Perspective

We have reviewed the present state of thinking about the organization of aptitude, some means of reaching an organization of treatments, and ideas about matching the two. Through this and previous chapters the reader should have become aware that ATI research is fraught with conceptual and methodological difficulties. Traditional research approaches are inadequate to deal with ATI. And the ATI issue calls many accepted "truths" into question. While progress has been made in sharpening an attack on these problems, this very process creates uncertainties about previous ATI studies.

The next seven chapters bring together evidence on the presence or absence of ATI. The survey is broad but not exhaustive. There is no efficient way to search the literature thoroughly, and no established categories into which to sort it. We have no illusions that our sorting and reinterpretations of past research gives even a taxonomy on which theory can be built. The immediate aim is more modest: To identify ATI hypotheses worth more exacting, more powerful study.

Chapter 7 | Interaction of abilities with variations in instructional programming

The largest body of research on ATI has to do with programmed instruction (PI). This technique leads the learner through instructional content step-by-step, obtains an overt response which is corrected if necessary, and informs him when he is correct and ready to move on to another bit of content. In the early 1960's, enthusiasts for this emerging technique believed that it would have special value for students of low ability—an ATI hypothesis. The hypothesis was elaborated into predictions about how alternative methods of programming would interact with aptitudes. Hence, it became almost commonplace to administer at least one aptitude measure and to search for interactions, providing us with a large body of research.

All these studies consider some form of general or verbal-educational ability. An achievement test, covering a broad content area such as mathematics or the specific content of the program, is sometimes used as a pretest. And (rarely) a comparatively specialized ability test such as Hidden Figures is used. Virtually all the tests, however, appear likely to correlate substantially with an overall IQ and with Verbal IQ. The collection of results, taken as a whole, is evidence on whether general ability interacts with the treatment variables.

It could be important educationally to learn that fluid ability and crystallized ability (or any other such pair) do not interact with treatments in the same way. But few studies contrast two well-measured aptitudes. Hence, we will not be able to establish separate conclusions about subdivisions within the domain of general abilities.

175

Table 7.1   Comparisons of PI and conventional instruction.

I. Studies with less steep slope under PI

Investigator(s) and content	Duration of treatment	Did aptitude predict PI success?	Was there ATI?	Treatment giving best outcome with		Remarks
				Low ability	High ability	
Bhushan (biology)	4 weeks	Yes	Yes a,b,c	PI	No difference	Results for two posttests added. Aptitude was SES with ability partialled out.
Cowan (physics)	A few weeks	Yes	Yes a,b	PI	Conventional	Result for science pretest not like that for IQ.
Goldberg et al. (statistics)	18 hours	Yes	Yes a,b	PI	Conventional	Interaction for transfer test only.
Knight (trigonometry)	6 hours	Yes	Yes a,b	PI	Conventional	Interaction, if any, for delayed posttest only.
Little (educational psychology)	Full course		Yes	Pressey feedback	No difference	Not a PI study. No significant test on ATI.
Meddis-Bowditch (statistics)	5 lessons		Yes a,b,c	Machine	No difference	Ordinal interaction.
Owen et al. (electrocardiogram)	14 hours	Irregular	Yes a,b,c	PI	Conventional	
Porter (spelling)	Several weeks	Not reported	Possibly b,c	PI	Little difference	
Roebuck (physics)	2 weeks	Yes	Yes a,b	PI	Conventional	
Schurdak (programming)	4 hours	Not for CAI Yes for PI	Yes a,b	CAI	Little difference	Smaller difference when PI/conventional compared.

Table 7.1

| Investigator(s) and content | Duration of treatment | Did aptitude predict PI success? | Was there ATI? | Treatment giving best outcome with | | Remarks |
				Low ability	High ability	
Stukat (grammar)	Full course	Yes	Yes	PI	Little difference	Interaction in Grades 5 and 6 but not 4.
Taylor Fox (plotting)	Single sitting	Yes	Yes	Small-step TV	Little difference	Ordinal. Not a PI study.
Taylor Fox (map symbols)	Single sitting	Yes	Yes	Self-regulated	Self-regulated	Much greater difference for Highs. Not a PI study. Structured treatment unsuccessful.

aWeakly significant or not significant.
bSample size inadequate for powerful test.
cProcedure inadequate for powerful test.

Comparisons of programmed and conventional instruction

We start with studies comparing programmed, computer-aided, or other highly structured methods with more conventional classroom procedures. Some of these studies also compare alternative techniques of PI. What we label "conventional" instruction is not the same from study to study, nor is it controlled enough to be a reproducible "method."

Tables 7.1–7.3 list the studies of the PI/conventional contrast. Though our primary concern is with interactions, we have also noted whether aptitudes correlate with success in PI. When PI was first introduced, dull students were expected to do nearly as well in it as bright students. Instead, as the tables show, pretests and aptitude measures correlated with outcome from PI or CAI in nearly every study. (Many other studies reported similar correlations, but did not deal with ATI.)

In few studies of PI was the time devoted to instruction and study controlled. If S completes the program in less time than is allowed for the conventional instruction, PI saves time he could use to learn more. But the experimental comparison ignores that bonus. If the abler students finish sooner, the correlations and regression slopes for PI are underestimated, compared to what they would be with time held constant. This failure of experimental design (compounded by the failure to record time differences and adjust for them) is sufficient to account for the mixed results in the literature.

Interactions where PI had the lesser slope

Many investigators believed that programming would compensate for the limitations of dull learners. They expected a shallow AT regression in PI, in contrast to the steep regression likely in conventional instruction. In a fair number of studies (see Table 7.1), the regression slope for the more programmed instruction was indeed smaller. We take up first the studies with the longest series of lessons.

Stukat (1965) pitted conventional classroom instruction in grammar against PI as the main instructional vehicle for an entire course. There was no interaction in Grade 4 with IQ, and in Grades 5 or 6 there was none with a grammar pretest. An interaction with IQ appeared in Grades 5 and 6. Stukat gave detailed data for 345 Ss in Grade 6. *Children of low ability learned significantly more from the program than from conventional instruction.* For Highs, conventional instruction was at least as good as PI. Analysis at the class level was needed. One might have expected the program to serve better in Grade 4 than conventional instruction, since the fourth graders are "Lows," compared to the Grade-6 mean. But the mean difference in Grade 4 favored the conventional treatment.

Programmed materials were developed to teach PSSC physics in rural high schools having no physics teacher (Cowan, 1967). In nine scattered schools, 22 Ss worked through two units of the course, seeing all the films and following the usual laboratory guide along with the programmed text. A control group of 48 Ss was formed from teacher-taught classes in three other schools. The experimental group seemed to have a slight advantage. In the sample, there appeared to be *some disordinal interaction.* Persons low in reading and IQ were helped by PI, but those low on STEP Science did a bit worse in PI.

Interpretation of electrocardiograms was taught to advanced medical students by 14 hours of lectures and assessed by a three-hour examination (Owen *et al.*, 1965). The 41 Ss in this group were compared with 36 who covered the same material by means of PI on which they spent from 7 to 33 hours. Examination scores did not relate to time spent. Ability was judged from grades in two previous medical courses. The mean posttest scores were as follows:

Baseline	Poor	Fair	Good	Superior
Lecture group	62	79	86	118
PI group	86	77	82	107

At the extremes, the means are based on four to seven Ss. Even though slicing the ability range into four parts lowered the power of the analysis, the *ATI was nearly significant* ($.10 < p < .05$). The lesser regression slope was found with PI.

Instruction in descriptive statistics was given to 47 clerical workers by programmed text/programmed machine/classroom lecture and discussion, with 18 hours of work for each group (M. Goldberg, Dawson, & Barrett, 1964). Achievement was strongly related to a pretest on mathematics in all groups. *No ATI* was evident on an achievement test based directly on program frames. There was a *weak ATI,* according to an understanding-and-application criterion. Classroom instruction was slightly better for Highs than machine or programmed text, but slightly worse for Lows.

Teaching machines were compared with conventional instruction in spelling during several weeks of the school year by Porter (1961). Individual differences were examined only for sixth-graders. There were only 37 Ss, for both treatments together. The data (his page 86) show that Highs made about the same progress under both kinds of instruction, while *Lows did much better with PI.* Either IQ or the spelling pretest may have accounted for the ATI.

A most dramatic *disordinal interaction* was reported in Roebuck's (1970) Nigerian study. The slope of the posttest-on-pretest regression in one treatment was eight times that in the other! A pretest was given to each of two classes in secondary-school physics. The class Ns were 30 and 23, so that none of the statistical results is dependable. The pretest means were 7.0 and 8.5 (out of 12 possible). During the two-week treatment, the first group worked on PI supplemented by experiments; the second group had the same experiments, plus conventional instruction on the same topics. The posttest means were 19.3 and 16.2 (out of 23), suggesting an advantage for the program. The regression information is startling:

	Slope	MS deviations
With PI	0.37	3.7
With conventional instruction	2.99	13.8

Adults were taught trigonometry in groups or on machines ($N = 59$; Knight, 1969). The treatments yielded equal results on the posttests, but instructional time for the classroom treatment was twice that for the machine. There is a *hint of disordinal interaction:* mental ability correlated 0.81 with the delayed posttest in the live-instruction group, 0.40 in the machine group.

Schurdak (1967) evaluated a short CAI course in FORTRAN programming, comparing CAI/programmed text/conventional text. Forty-eight college students spent about four hours in the experiment. The Henmon-Nelson test was the aptitude measure. CAI was clearly the best treatment on the average, with programmed text next, and conventional text last. The respective AT correlations were 0.17, 0.42, and 0.52 . Scatterplots in the report indicate that *the corresponding regression slopes were about 0.1, 0.4, and 0.8.* The slope differences were not statistically significant, the sample being tiny. For students with Henmon-Nelson raw scores above about 80, either sort of text appeared to give results nearly as good as CAI did. But perhaps a ceiling effect prevented differences from appearing among Highs. Among students below 80 (roughly half of Schurdak's sample), CAI was clearly superior; its cost may be offset by gains in outcome.

A statistics program for 12-year-olds was compared with results from live instruction by Meddis and Bowditch (1966), with 48 Ss overall, in a 2 x 2 design. While the *ATI for mental ability was not statistically significant,* Highs outperformed Lows to a greater degree with the live teacher, and the sample was small.

SES rather than ability was the subject of a study of biology instruction for 9-year-olds by Bhushan (1971). There was a *zero or negative slope of outcome on SES* when PI was used, and a small positive slope in teacher-text instruction. The interaction was nearly significant ($N = 105$) but hard to interpret; ability had been covaried out rather than treated as a source of possible interaction, and two outcome measures gave differing results. If we add the two posttests, we find PI advantageous for low SES students.

Little (1934) studied Pressey's early devices for teaching by testing. His 420 Ss, students in educational psychology, all received conventional instruction, including 12 quizzes spaced through the course. Some class sections used Pressey's test-scoring device during the quizzes, obtaining immediate knowledge of results. In some other sections, students drilled on a revolving drum that provided the correct answer following each student response. The student worked through each quiz until he had answered all items correctly. Still other sections received knowledge of results a day later, after the instructor had scored the quizzes. Ss were matched on pretest and IQ. Little reported that the drill condition was best, that immediate knowledge of results was better than the conventional delayed scoring, and that *the new methods seemed to benefit most the students in the lower half of the ability range.* The implied ATI was not reported in numerical terms, nor was it tested statistically.

Two studies by Taylor and Fox (1967) can be placed in this category though PI was not used. One study used a television presentation with pictorial examples. New ideas were introduced in small steps during ten trials in a single sitting. Practice with knowledge of results was provided for 76 Ss. The topic of instruction

Table 7.2   Comparisons of PI and conventional instruction.
II. Studies with steeper slope under PI

Investigator(s) and content	Duration of treatment	Did aptitude predict PI success?	Was there ATI?	Treatment giving best outcome with Low ability	High ability	Remarks
Berliner-Melanson (Morse code)	13 weeks	Yes, but weak	Yes[a,b,c]	Conventional CAI		One out of 11 ATI tested reached significance, but effect for general ability is suspected.
Cavanagh (applied math)	1 hour	Yes	Yes	Lecture	PI	No interaction with a pretest. ATI found with a mental test.
Gropper-Lumsdaine (physics)	Single lesson	Yes	Yes	No difference	PI	ATI found for only one of two units of instruction.
Maier-Jacobs (Spanish)	One year	Yes	Yes[a]	Conventional PI plus innovative teacher		Attitude outcomes also showed ATI. Analysis of between-groups data unusual.
Wallis-Wicks (trigonometry)	9 hours	Yes	Yes[a,b,c,]	Conventional Autotutor		Interacting aptitude was a pretest on the topics taught.

[a]Weakly significant or not significant.
[b]Sample size inadequate for powerful test.
[c]Procedure inadequate for powerful test.

was complex plotting of military data. Another 20 Ss had a conventional lecture and practiced without knowledge of results. The TV method, which simplified the learner's task, was superior—strikingly so for the dull learner. The *interaction was ordinal* (though not tested statistically), implying that TV was helpful for all men. But the conventional method appeared to be efficient for abler men, and TV is costly. A strong ceiling effect limited the possible differences among able men. Without a ceiling, the interaction might vanish.

Taylor and Fox (1967) also taught military map symbols to 109 enlisted men. In one method, the trainee was allowed to study symbol meanings from cards, by procedures of his own choice. In a second method, practice was controlled; the stimulus was presented, S responded, and the correct response was presented for confirmation or correction. The order and timing of stimuli were controlled. Free pacing worked better for all men, but was particularly superior for abler men. *The more structured method had the lesser slope.*

Interactions where PI had the steeper slope

We now turn to the studies (Table 7.2) where the more structured treatment had a steeper slope and therefore had a relative advantage for students of high aptitude. The studies are so diverse that there is no satisfactory way to group them; we have again put first the studies of greater duration.

Maier and P. Jacobs (1964; or see Jacobs, Maier, & Stolurow, 1966, p. 60ff.) contrasted pure-PI/a-combination-of-programmed-and-live-instruction/live-instruction-only. A year-long televised series of PI lessons in Spanish was given to fifth- and sixth-graders. PI only was used in 48 classes; 15 had PI plus lessons from a teacher; and 14 had live lessons with no PI. There were three aptitude variables: Kuhlmann-Anderson IQ, Spanish pretest, and pretest on attitude toward Spanish. Significant main effects appeared for ability and for treatment, with pure PI yielding relatively poor results. The AT correlations for class-mean achievement against class-mean IQ were consistently high; there does not appear to have been a between-classes interaction effect, but we lack information about s.d.'s. An analysis at the individual level (classes pooled) again suggested *absence of ATI effects on achievement.*

An interaction was found when attitude toward using Spanish was examined as an outcome. The correlations of IQ with final attitude were as follows:

	Pure PI	PI-plus-Live	Live only
Class as unit of analysis	− 0.20	− 0.35	0.57
Individual as unit of analysis	0.10	− 0.06	0.23

The individual analysis mingles between-groups and within-groups effects. Intuitively reasoning along the lines of p. 99 ff., it appears that the within-group correlations were moderate in the two PI treatments and quite low in the live treatment. But it is impossible to draw firm conclusions without information about s.d.'s. It does appear that the class of high average ability responded (relatively) favorably to live teaching and that attitude was unrelated to IQ. Such a class responded more adversely to instruction that included PI. Within a PI class, abler students perhaps were more favorable.

The between-class correlations of the Spanish pretest with final attitude were as follows: 0.07, 0.48, 0.71. This is only partially consistent with the data for IQ. Analysis at the individual or within-class level was not reported.

Some teachers got better results than others, which produced *higher-order interactions.* Maier and Jacobs recommended that *High-IQ students should have teacher-instruction-plus-PI from a teacher who favors innovative methods, and low IQ students should be taught by a live conventional teacher,* without PI.

The many excellent features of this study should be noted: reproducible treatments (at least insofar as the PI component was concerned); use of two treatment dimensions (extent and character of live teaching); use of more than one aptitude variable and more than one outcome variable; instruction extending over a realistically long time with real course content; and a large sample (77 classes with some 900 students). Maier and Jacobs carried out a mixture of analyses: between classes, within single classes, and for individuals pooled. They did their best to make sense of the complexly patterned results, wisely not stressing significance tests. Today one could propose refinements: reporting of regression slopes in place of correlations; calculation by multivariate methods instead of treating aptitudes separately; fuller reporting of within-class regressions; separate interpretation of within-class and between-class regressions. Maier and Jacobs came close to these refinements when the technique of ATI research was in its infancy. (See also their second study, p. 197.)

Berliner and Melanson (1971) compared CAI and conventional instruction in Morse code. Ss were 83 enlistees, randomly assigned to one of two treatment conditions for a 13-week course. The conventional treatment used large classes, group pacing, teacher scoring of exercises, and delayed feedback, with little attention to the individual. In the CAI group, there was individual pacing, immediate feedback, and considerable attention to individuals. The criterion score was derived from tests of decoding during the sixth week of training. Aptitude information came from the Army Classification Battery administered at induction. The intercorrelations of the aptitude measures were fairly high in this study and their interactions with treatments were much the same. An interpretation in terms of general ability would be parsimonious, but we have not been able to calculate the regression slopes for a pooled ability measure.

Correlations of aptitude with outcome were low, the highest being 0.26. Ten of eleven *aptitude tests were negatively related to performance in conventional instruction;* and nine of eleven were *positively related to performance in CAI.* Only one of these eleven ATI contrasts was significant at the .05 level, so the trend was quite weak. The negative AT slopes in conventional instruction might be explained by the boredom of Highs held back to the pace of their less able peers. In this study, CAI appears to have accentuated ability differences among learners;

this is contrary to the usual premise and to the Schurdak result (p. 180).

A study for the British Navy (Wallis & Wicks, 1964) was intended chiefly to compare a live teacher/a "scrambled book" form of PI/a teaching machine. The course covered basic trigonometry in nine hours. Ss were 67 teenage recruits. A pretest on mathematics had been given to restrict the sample. For obscure reasons, this pretest was carried forward as a covariate, whereas scores on mental ability and reading were used only to show that the treatment groups were similar. On a delayed posttest the machine group did best, with the teacher-taught group second. Despite the restriction of range, there was a striking relation of posttest to pretest in the machine group ($r = 0.69$), some relation in the text group ($r = 0.48$), and none in the teacher-taught group ($r = 0.14$). The data strongly suggest a *disordinal interaction*. The programmed materials depended more on initial knowledge than did live teaching.

Cavanagh, Thornton, and R.G.T. Morgan (1965) taught airline employees to carry out calculations regarding the loading of airplanes. Instruction by lecture was compared with brief machine instruction. Aptitude measures were a pretest and a general mental test. Of chief interest to us is a strong correlation (ca. 0.60) of outcome with general ability in the machine group vs. one of about 0.30 in the lecture group. (S.d.'s did not differ enough to affect the comparison.) The *interaction appears to be significant and disordinal* (overall $N = 158$). The pretest did not interact.

Though the study of Moore (1964) showed no interesting relation of the posttest score to treatment or to ability, Moore manipulated instructional time in a way that produced a hint of an interaction. The study makes evident the need for better control of the time factor. Moore translated an instructional unit on voting into programmed material that could be completed in about six class periods. The control classes studied the same material from a brochure and recited on it. There were 300 Ss, with one control and one experimental class in each school. A reading test was taken as an aptitude measure; Ss were blocked on this variable. If only the posttest had been available for consideration, one would conclude that there was no treatment effect and no ATI. But Moore had made a record of the instructional time. Control classes in four schools were taught for 270 minutes; in the same schools the PI groups finished their work much more quickly. Pooling schools, we have the following contrasts between controls and experimentals:

		Controls	Experimentals
Good readers	time	270 min., score 38	188 min., 37
Intermediate readers	time	270 min., score 34	194 min., 32
Poor readers	time	270 min., score 26	204 min., 26

Since the differences between treatments in posttest score were negligible, one has to see this as an *ordinal interaction;* PI saved time, and saved somewhat more time for good readers. (A fifth school is left out of our account because the teacher

Table 7.3   Comparisons of PI and conventional instruction.
III.   Studies finding no interaction

Investigator(s) and content	Treatment	Did aptitude predict PI success?	Remarks
Burnkrant-Lambert (writing)	PI/conventional	Yes	Threat improved performance of Lows.
Carroll-Leonard (Arabic writing)	PI/conventional	Yes	b
Davis et al. (mathematics)	PI/conventional	Usually, but low	See p. 194.
Deep (arithmetic)	Individually prescribed/conventional	Yes	Power of experiment hard to evaluate.
Duncan (trigonometry)	Machine/PI/conventional	Mixed	Insufficient information reported.[b]
Jacobs et al. (Bill of Rights)	PI/text/conventional	Yes	Transfer test showed interaction steeper slope in PI; possibly a floor effect.[b]
Karraker (educational psychology)	Test with/without feedback	Does not apply [b]	
Miller (multiplication)	Mixed devices/conventional	Yes [b]	
Reed-Hayman (grammar)	PI/conventional	Yes	Large study, well-controlled except with regard to time. One interaction significant, according to authors.
Ripple et al. (vocabulary)	PI/conventional	Yes	
Smith (statistics)	PI/conventional	Yes	b
Schurdak (programming)	Scrambled book/conventional	Yes	Very weak slope difference. [b]
Tagatz (handwriting)	PI/conventional/diagnostic	Yes	b
Unwin (algebra)	PI/conventional	Yes	[b]Maybe ATI on retention. [b]

[b]Sample size inadequate for powerful test.

used 370 minutes for control instruction, and the data were peculiarly irregular.)

One cannot be sure that Moore's data are generalizable. To understand the phenomenon, one needs to know how scores in each kind of instruction increase as the available time increases. Furthermore, one needs to examine working times of individuals, not to use a group mean as Moore's report forces us to do. Even so, the moral is clear: No conclusion about the interactions of aptitude can be drawn on the basis of posttest results if working time is not equated operationally or statistically.

Gropper and Lumsdaine (1961) used PI and conventional presentations via closed-circuit television in physics. For a lesson on heat, Ss were 140 high-school students, and 158 for a lesson on nuclear reactions. On the first topic but not on the second, high-IQ Ss did better with PI; there was no difference for Lows. This, then, is a *poorly established ordinal interaction*.

Studies with no interaction

In a third set of studies, PI/conventional instruction did not interact with ability

A mammoth study by Ripple, Millman, and Glock (1969) had 22 matched pairs of eighth-grade classes and 1040 Ss. It compared 10 hours of PI, designed to increase reading vocabulary, with conventional English teaching. Sex, mental age, and several personality variables were the aptitudes. The conventional treatment appeared to be slightly more effective; apparently more instructional time was allowed for it.

The analysis took a strange form. For each class, scores were reduced to 16 cell means, each based on a few students. Thus, there would be, in each class, one mean for able, anxious males. This analysis lost power, as the authors acknowledged. No separation of between-class and within-class regressions was attempted. However that may be, the data given in the ERIC report on the study do indicate that *interaction was absent or weak*. If anything, the slope onto IQ was greater in PI. (See also p. 426.)

A small study compared teaching of the Arabic writing system by programmed drills with teaching by a live teacher (Carroll & Leonard, 1963). The results clearly favored the experimental method. There was a strong correlation of achievement with the Modern Language Aptitude Test (0.70 within treatments, pooled). But the regression *slopes were virtually identical* for the two treatments.

N. Smith (1962) compared a programmed text in statistics with conventional lecture instruction during 12 lessons of a college course. Achievement, and time needed to complete the work, served as dependent measures. Prior mathematics achievement predicted performance in both treatments ($N = 128$), but no main effects for treatment and *no ATI* were found nominally significant. Means were not given.

A great body of data was collected by J. Reed and Hayman (1962), who gave three months of PI in grammar to 10 classes, and conventional instruction to control classes from the same school and ability track. There were three grammar pretests, an IQ, and a grade average; IQ and GPA correlated very strongly with outcome in each treatment. Means are reported for the students in high, medium, and low tracks in the two treatment groups. For any aptitude and posttest, we can plot the track means and draw a conclusion about the AT regression slope for each treatment. *No interaction occurred;* the regression lines nearly coincided. The authors' ancova reported a significant Method x Level interaction for one posttest. We are unable to detect whether they made an error or whether a very large mass of data and a very powerful analysis enabled a microscopic effect to appear as significant. There would be a place, of course, for examining between-class and within-class effects separately.

J. Miller (1964) taught four sixth-grade classes (N = 114) to multiply fractions. The experimental treatment used a written lesson plan, flannel-board demonstrations, teacher discussion, and automated practice devices that provided immediate knowledge of results. The conventional treatment relied on a standard textbook and workbook. The teacher gave feedback on computations a day or two later. Each group received nine 45-minute lessons before a posttest on computation was administered. A computation pretest was positively related to performance in both treatments. *There was no ATI.*

In a study of handwriting, Tagatz *et al*. (1968) compared traditional group-instruction aided by a text/commercially available PI/an individualized diagnostic approach which emphasized self-evaluation plus practice on material S himself chose. Third- and fourth-graders (N = 163) were assigned to treatments after stratification on sex and ability. Instruction continued for nine weeks. Indices of speed and legibility were derived from pretest and posttest handwriting samples. Individualized approaches were superior to the traditional method for third-graders, but not for fourth-graders. A main effect of ability was also apparent. The authors noted one ATI as significant, but the discussion and reported data prevent us from verifying or understanding this finding. Apparently one erratic group caused the result. We conclude that *no interesting ATI occurred.*

A nine-hour instructional program on solving equations was developed for technical-school students by Unwin (1966) and compared with conventional instruction. There were only 45 Ss. Correlations of mathematics pretests with the posttests were greater under PI, but differences were not statistically significant. On the immediate posttest, a larger s.d. under conventional instruction indicates that interaction was absent. On retention, however, the regression difference might well have been significant in a larger sample; PI gave a steeper slope.

Burnkrant and Lambert (1965) studied high-school students' improvement in writing skills ($N > 500$) under PI/conventional conditions. Every posttest score was expressed as a residual gain over the pretest. Half the Ss learning in each way were told that their grades would be influenced by this unit of work and its post-test. Incentive and general mental ability interacted significantly. The Lows did better when told that their work would affect their marks. But it appears that *PI/conventional treatment did not interact with ability;* Highs had better adjusted scores than Lows in both treatments.

Mention may be made of Duncan's several comparisons of machine teaching with conventional or scrambled-book instruction (1966). In each, he tested for significant differences in slopes of AT regressions onto an aptitude composite; he found no significant ATI. Since his samples never exceeded 23 *S*s per treatment, and since he gave no descriptive information on aptitude-outcome relations, *we cannot confidently accept this as evidence against ATI.*

J. N. Jacobs, H. Yeager, and Tilford (1966) assigned 60 eleventh-grade classes to learn "The Bill of Rights" by PI or text, either at home or in school. A conventional classroom condition was also used. Instruction spread over three days. No aptitude measure was included, but class makeup ("academic," "general," "basic") supposedly reflected levels of ability. PI was best, whether worked through at home or school. Students from the highest track outperformed those from the lowest track under all conditions. An information posttest showed *no ATI.* A borderline-significant interaction effect on a posttest of application of civil-rights concepts reflects the fact that Lows did equally badly under all methods, whereas classes at other levels showed treatment differences. *This could well be an artifact,* from a floor effect on the test.

Two final studies are somewhat outside the PI territory. Deep (1966) investigated "individually prescribed instruction" (see p. 5.) Comparing this to conventional instruction in arithmetic, Deep found *no ATI.* He had 66 experimental and 399 control *S*s. Karraker (1967) evaluated feedback on a single multiple-choice test in educational psychology ($N = 72$). The experimental group took the test and was given a report the next day. One control group took the test and got no feedback. A second control group did not take the test. Performance on a later constructed-response test over the same material showed that *treatment did not interact* with IQ.

A study of performance contracting

Perhaps the largest study of PI ever undertaken arose out of the interest of the Office of Economic Opportunity in educational "performance contracting." We have not entered it in any table.

The study included some 25,000 *S*s in Grades 1, 2, 3, 7, 8, and 9 from 18 geographically scattered school districts. In each district, a private company specializing in educational technology contracted to provide remedial-reading and mathematics instruction to the lowest achievers. Each company was free to use instructional arrangements and materials of its own design. All used PI, adding incentives for achievement. An independent research agency evaluated the program. Their final report (H. Ray, 1972) is the basis for our summary.

In each district, the school showing the largest deficiency in reading and mathematics was designated as "experimental"; the next most deficient was called "control." In each school, attention was given to the 100 *S*s in each grade whose initial achievement was lowest. Occasionally, to obtain the number of *S*s needed in a district, more than one school was used as experimental or control. Assignment to treatment was not random; racial, socioeconomic, and pretest differences between experimental and control groups appeared at many sites. Instruction continued for one school year. For first-graders, the Stanford Early Achievement

Test was used as pretest and the California Achievement Test as posttest. For all other grades, forms of the Metropolitan Achievement Test were used as pretests and posttests.

At almost every site, children of superior aptitude achieved most; pretest-posttest correlations were usually above 0.50. The scattered main effects for treatment that appeared within sites sometimes favored the experimental classes and sometimes the controls. The analysis of interest to us calculated the AT regression of each posttest on the corresponding pretest, within each grade within each site. Some 232 tests of heterogeneity of slope for paired schools were made. Of these, 40 were nominally significant (p $<$ .05), where only about 12 would be expected by chance. And many contrasts had fewer than 100 Ss per treatment. Of the 40, nine were ordinal. There were 17 disordinal ATI showing the experimental treatment being superior for Lows and inferior for Highs, and 14 disordinal interactions showing the experimental treatment superior for Highs and inferior for Lows.

We do not trust these findings; at the present writing, we have not been able to ascertain which, if any, of these ATI represent meaningful results. Perusal of the reported analyses suggests the presence of severe scaling problems. Routine assumptions underlying the statistical tests may be untenable at many sites. The variations from site to site clearly are substantial, which reinforces our recommendation that in all such large studies attempts be made to trace why interactions take different forms in different classes.

Summary

There is overwhelming evidence that tested abilities relate to success under PI. Despite a few teasing exceptions, the evidence adds further weight to our rejection (p.132 ff.) of the Woodrow hypothesis and its close relatives.

As for ATI, we have found a number of studies to support each of three conclusions: no interaction, steeper slope for PI, or less steep slope for PI. On the whole, the "no interaction" findings are unimpressive; only the studies of Reed-Hayman (grammar) and Ripple (vocabulary) are substantial negative evidence. In the OEO study alone, there appear to be a number of significant interactions running in each direction. Rather than accept the null hypothesis or relapse into sheer confusion, we would argue that one cannot generalize about PI as a variable. The specifics of content, duration of instruction and its variation within and between treatments, teacher enthusiasm, outcome measured, and unidentified local factors produce ATI. PI often generates a lower AT regression slope—but the opposite finding occurs often enough to discourage generalization.

Where PI is used to present drills, or content with little internal organization, interactions in each direction are about equally frequent. ATI often are absent; nearly all the studies that accept the null hypothesis (Table 7.3) used drill-like instruction. We are unable to see any principle that distinguishes the studies of Table 7.1 from those of Table 7.2.

On the whole, the evidence encourages further search for ATI where PI/conventional is the treatment contrast. It is essential to bring working time under experimental or statistical control. The aim in further research should not be to test a general ATI hypothesis. The aim should be to pin down the variations within PI treatments that generate steeper or shallower slopes (within and between classes). This moves toward a theoretical account of the role aptitude plays in response to instruction.

Most of our readers can now jump to page 213. The bulk of what follows documents the failure of one extensive line of research: the attempt to relate abilities to such variations within PI as branching, use of small steps, requiring *S* to construct his own response, etc. It is important to document this failure, because all these various ATI hypotheses were widely held a decade ago and research on these treatments continues to appear. As some positive results have been reported, the existence of such ATI perhaps still commands belief among those who develop PI.

For the reader not concerned with hypotheses about PI as such, there are still some things to be learned from the section. A few studies display novelties of method or give us a chance to demonstrate a useful analysis, and a few contain the germs of theoretical ideas with wider applicability. The reader may find it most profitable to scan the reports on the following studies (listed in order of appearance): Burton-Goldbeck, Carroll-Spearritt, Maier-Jacobs, Leone Smith, Vincent Campbell, Kress-Gropper, Kropp *et al.*, Allen-Filep-Cooney.

Overtness of response as a treatment variable

The basic form of PI presents a frame asking a question or making an incomplete statement. The learner writes an answer and then is shown the correct answer; he may or may not be required to cycle through the program until he can complete all frames without error. As a contrasting treatment another learner may be presented the identical material with all blanks filled in, but with the key response underlined. This is much like study from any text. As he reads through these statements he is said to be in a "covert response" mode, on the presumption that he is thinking about question and response. Instead of presenting the content in programmed form, the "covert response" treatment may simply use conventional connected text to present whatever content the program develops frame-by-frame.

In most investigations of the overt/covert contrast, the working hypothesis was that the AT regression slope would be relatively flat, or even negative, for the overt treatment. In actual data, however, correlations of aptitude with outcome are positive enough to contradict the expectation and to confirm that general ability correlates with learning rate on new material. We shall not recapitulate the data on this point in detail, since the preceding section has amply documented the relation of general abilities to performance in PI. Our final conclusion in the section will reject the working hypothesis. The studies do not cohere around any alternative interaction hypothesis.

Interactions where overt response produced the lesser slope

Lambert, D. Miller, and Wiley (1962) compared overt written and covert response modes in mathematics (sets, relations, and functions) on 534 ninth-graders. There was no main effect for treatment. There was a weak ATI for Henmon-Nelson IQ. The *covert mode was slightly better for Highs,* whereas writing out the response produced a slight advantage for Lows.

Wittrock (1963) tried a short program on science in first and second grades, contrasting overt and covert response. Comparing *S*s of high and low MA, he found the *Lows helped by overt oral responding* and the Highs slightly handicapped by it. The regression of outcome on MA was essentially flat in the overt mode and fairly steep in the covert mode; the interaction was significant ($N = 80$). The interaction did not appear on a retest one year later.

In a study by McNeil (1962), 188 kindergartners were taught word recognition by PI. Children received 15 minutes of PI daily over three weeks under one of two conditions. In one group, Ss were instructed to look at each stimulus word and to select the corresponding pictures from a display. In the second group, naming of each stimulus word was required in addition. There was also an uninstructed control group. On a written posttest, *oral response was particularly effective for those low in IQ,* though it benefitted all *S*s.

Another study of word recognition at the primary level was that of McNeil & Keislar (1963). Thirteen children observed each frame while listening to the sound track; a matched group made oral response. The mean scores were as follows:

	Low IQ	Medium IQ	High IQ
Overt oral response	25	32	34
No overt response	17	24	30

Overt response was best at all levels. *The weak ordinal interaction* was not significant in this small sample.

Interactions where overt response produced the steeper slope

In two studies, overt response was advantageous for Highs. A three-hour linear program teaching about operator graphs was applied to engineering students by Entwisle, Huggins, and Phelps (1968). Some *S*s had to construct responses to the difficult problems before checking answers. Others were directed to read without trying to solve the problems for themselves. Previous achievement was treated as an aptitude. A second study with the same design used another program of the same general sort. In the two studies ($N = 44$ and 48), the achievement posttest means were as follows:

Previous achievement	First study		Second study	
	Low	High	Low	High
Reading	15.2	16.1	8.5	9.7
Constructed Response	12.0	18.7	6.3	10.5

Although not every contrast was significant, the two studies confirm a *disordinal interaction, with the covert mode having the near-flat slope.* It was suggested that the covert-response condition directed the attention of Lows to the pertinent stimuli, while Highs benefited from constructing responses. The investigators *failed to find ATI on a delayed posttest* in the first study. There was no delayed test in the second study.

Just 47 boys were allocated among three versions of a short program on number bases (Buckland, 1967). An immediate test was given, with a transfer test a month later. The ability measure was a mathematics examination. There were three treatments: Covert 1. Reading the program with blanks filled in; Covert 2. Thinking what went into the blank before examining the answer given; Overt. Writing an answer before examining that given by the author.

Covert 2 was best for Lows, but the poorest of the three treatments for Highs. Overt was worst for Lows, best for Highs; perhaps Lows who write wrong answers create interference for themselves. Covert 1 results about matched results for Overt, among Lows. Among Highs, the immediate test result on Covert 1 was good but scores were poor a month later.

If the Buckland and Entwisle results were found on substantial bodies of instructional material and substantial samples, we would conclude that *Highs should write their responses and Lows should only "think them".* But other studies in the preceding section, and the Lambert study above, suggest the opposite.

Studies with no interaction

The studies above, which give positive results, are probably to be dismissed. Most of them employed small samples and brief treatments. The overwhelming majority of studies of the overt/covert contrast found no interaction, and, as many of these studies had good-sized samples, we conclude that this contrast is not a treatment variable deserving of further research. It is necessary to document by summarizing the studies that found no interaction. We place first studies that have interest apart from their negative results.

The most thought-provoking is the study of Burton and Goldbeck (1962). A short program (35 frames) taught isolated facts; three versions were developed. Each frame was a sentence with a key word missing. Treatment DA (multiple-choice) gave the correct answer along with highly confusable alternative responses. Treatment EA gave the correct answer along with highly discriminable alternatives. Treatment NA—most overt—used the constructed-response technique. The correct answer was supplied on the feedback frame. Verbal reasoning was the aptitude measured. By happenstance there were sizable differences among treatment groups on the pretest. For all groups together, $N = 108$. *Aptitude did not interact with method in its effect on the total score on the posttests.*

A complex breakdown (planned in advance) led to a *strange but highly significant interaction.* Items on the test were classified according to whether the response was a high-frequency word, readily available in S's response repertoire when he thinks of a category such as "animal," or was rare, low in the repertoire. Table 7.4 gives the results: each number is the proportion of correct answers (over all items and Ss). The Highs had no advantage when the item was difficult (DA) and the response a common one. The Highs also had little advantage when the response alternatives were easily discriminated (EA) and the correct response was a rare one. The Highs had a considerable advantage in three of the other cells. This interaction is essentially ordinal, if we disregard the small reversal in the cell at the upper left.

Table 7.4   Proportion correct on posttest items requiring common and rare words as responses

Aptitude	Response availability	Treatment		
		DA	NA	EA
High	Common	0.70	0.80	0.84
Low	Common	0.74	0.58	0.68
High	Rare	0.57	0.54	0.63
Low	Rare	0.29	0.42	0.56

After Burton and Goldbeck, 1962.

The following extracts from the discussion, although not completely clear out of context, are illuminating:

> We have hypothesized that the learning method for group EA with easy alternatives emphasized response training, while the learning method for group DA with difficult alternatives emphasized discrimination training. The test data indicated . . . that [rare] responses not strong enough to be elicited easily . . . benefit more from response training as provided in group EA. The advantage of group EA for these responses was substantially greater for Low verbal aptitude subjects. Apparently the response training provided in group EA was most appropriate for low aptitude students learning responses that were not well established in their response repertory.

> We might expect the discrimination training provided in group DA would be relatively more effective for responses that are well established in the response set. The data lend some support to this expectation in the case of low aptitude students. . . . for high aptitude subjects the reverse was true.

> It is worth noting that without analysis of subject and response characteristics, the "findings" for this study would have been simply that no differences occurred among the three methods of learning.

It is not inconsistent with our summary on p. 189 to learn here that effects reverse themselves when the difficulty of the content to be learned is changed. In this study, it was possible to use the theoretical distinction between association learning and discrimination learning to generate an hypothesis to guide the analysis.

Two other studies suggested that personality or attitude may be relevant to the choice between overt and covert modes. Della-Piana (1961) developed four versions of a program for college students:

A. Constructed written response. Correct answer printed on next page.

B. Constructed response, with the initial letter of the response given as a hint. Correct answer printed on next page.

C. Correct answer already filled in. S required to copy it.

D. Constructed response to be given orally. Proctor approves or requires S to try again if he responded incorrectly.

The American Council Psychological Examination-Verbal was the aptitude measure. Grade averages were also available. As the standard deviations of outcome variables were reasonably similar from treatment to treatment, we can interpret correlations directly. Within-treatment correlations of outcome with verbal aptitude differed little, the higher values occurring in Treatments A and D. The correlation of grade-point average with outcome was again high in D but quite low in A. (With 50 cases or fewer per cell, these differences could be fortuitous). We conclude that there was *no ATI*, nor any main effect.

A further analysis employed a Semantic-Differential measure of attitude toward PI. This had modest positive correlations with outcome under the constructed-response Treatments A and D and no relation in Treatments B and C. Persons who began with a favorable attitude tended to learn better from the constructed-response treatment. *The interaction effect is too small to arouse much interest.*

Another college-level study (Lublin, 1965) employed the Holland-Skinner programmed text for college psychology ($N = 219$). All the frames were left to be filled in, or 50 per cent of them (alternate items), or 50 per cent selected at random, or none. Success correlated 0.46 with a scholastic aptitude score (all cases pooled). There was *no significant interaction* between amount of responding required and ability, but N per group was too small for a powerful test.

The remaining studies are ordered alphabetically. Ashbaugh (1964) compared overt/covert responding to short programs on molecules-atoms (120 Ss) and sets-relations-functions (238 Ss). Mental ability was highly related to performance in both treatments; *ATI were absent.*

R. C. Anderson, Kulhavy, and Andre (1971) found that verbal ability interacted with error rate in various kinds of CAI on electrocardiogram interpretation, but the result did not appear in a second sample. ($N = 168$ and 188 educational-psychology students.) Some conditions allowed peeking before responding; some gave feedback only after correct response, etc. *The interaction found in the first sample seems not to be important.*

R. H. Davis, Marzocco, and Denny (1967) conducted two experiments in a semester-long remedial mathematics program. One compared overt/covert, multiple-choice/constructed-response, and choice-of-treatment conditions/no choice. 189 Ss (college freshmen) received PI. Another 180 received conventional text and lectures. But N within treatments dropped to 50 or less in many comparisons, and different rates of dropout confounded the interpretation. Aptitude variables included attitude toward math, several college-qualification tests, and special-ability tests. Criteria were midterm and final departmental examinations. The analysis examined 100 pairs of correlations, obtaining only one significant contrast. Descriptive data were reported only on three relatively large contrasts. The soundest conclusion appears to be that *ATIs were absent*. The second experiment compared feedback/no-feedback conditions in two programmed units from introductory psychology. 246 Ss gave at least partial data. Analysis was based on pretest-posttest gains, which did not correlate with any aptitude measure. Insofar as we can judge, *ATI were absent*.

A further section of the paper by Entwisle *et al.* (see p. 191) compared constructed-response/reading-only versions of brief instruction in FORTRAN arithmetic. Ss were 100 engineering undergraduates stratified on ability in mathematics. Main effects and *ATI were absent*. The overall correlation of aptitude and posttest was 0.87.

In a study by M. Feldman (1965), programs in college psychology were written at three levels of readability. The pretests and posttests given the three treatment groups differed (N = 144). Furthermore, ceiling effects were likely. A transfer test, uniform for all Ss, apparently gave a fair basis for comparison, but persons with low ability were dropped from the analysis and we are given no information as to their distribution over treatments. Reducing readability seemed to impede Lows but not Highs. *We could call this an ordinal interaction, but we do not trust the analysis.*

A 2 x 2 x 2 design was used by Leith and Eastment (1970) to investigate the answer-given (prompting)/answer-not-given; overt-response/covert-response; and programmed-text/machine procedures. The content was on probability, the work required about four hours, and the Ss were 130 adolescent boys. The only significant interaction with a verbal reasoning score was for a nine-week-delayed posttest. This result hinges entirely on the fact that Lows did as well as Highs in the two machine-with-answer-given cells. Each mean came from eight Ss. The fact that time-on-program varied radically from treatment to treatment, plus the irregularity of the trends observed leads us to conclude that *no conclusion about ATI is warranted.*

Seidel and Rotberg (1966) put 60 high-school Ss through an eight-hour course on computer programming. A "rules" group wrote out the rules used for programming; a "naming" group wrote out the names of rules but not the rules, and a control group wrote programs directly. Half of the Ss in each group wrote their answers after being prompted with the information needed for response, and half wrote their answers before receiving information. Aptitude was significantly related to posttests in all conditions. *No ATI* with the Army Classification Test were observed.

Constructed response was contrasted with reading of a program on medical content for undergraduates (Tobias, 1969). There were apparently *no ATI* with verbal aptitudes.

Todd and Kessler (1971) compared the effects of overt/covert responding at three levels of difficulty, where the content to be learned was a story. There were main effects for sex and reading ability, but *no ATI*; a main effect for response mode appeared only for one dependent variable out of four. (*N* = 180 college students overall.)

Two studies by Williams investigated the multiple-choice/constructed response contrast. The better of the studies (1963) employed four kinds of response (completion/multiple-choice/reading with key response words underlined/straight reading). The latter two covert modes were definitely inferior for the Holland-Skinner material used. The two forms of active response gave these results:

	Mean	s.d.	r
Completion	23.5	2.1	0.57
Multiple-choice	23.0	3.3	0.23

(The correlations in the covert treatments were around 0.35.) The slopes of regression on aptitude standard score were 0.76 for choice and 1.20 for completion. *The interaction was ordinal*, which would seem to argue for requiring completion response of all students. But since completion takes longer, this may not be the best decision.

It is uncertain what conclusion should be drawn from Williams' 1965 study on sixth-graders, with content from zoology. Comparing completion items with multiple-choice items, she found a supposedly significant interaction. But this was calculated from raw gain scores divided by working time. This surely is *meaningless*, judging from the means given for the test scores.

Another study not involving choice response was also *equivocal*. Williams and Levy (1964) contrasted constructed-response training/straight reading of filled-in text, again on the material from zoology. The correlations of verbal ability with posttest were very strong. The groups being small, the variation among the correlations has to be regarded as nonsignificant. The pretest should have been used along with the aptitude scores to give meaningful information on the authors' correlational questions.

Redundancy and regularity as programming variables

Various studies have investigated treatment variations that make it easier or harder for the learner to respond correctly. One set of studies contrasted orderly linear programs with the same frames exposed in scrambled order. We shall use the generic terms "smooth" and "rough" to encompass the variants of this technique. Another set of studies dealt with "size of step", i.e., pitted a program that covered a body of content in rather few frames against a longer program that elaborated each point carefully. A few miscellaneous studies dealt with other ways of manipulating the probability of anticipating answers. There are some difficulties in classifying instructional materials as more and less smooth. Briggs (1967) has pointed out that the concept of sequencing in instruction is ambiguous; any generalization couched in these terms can be no more than a first approximation.

"Smooth" vs. "rough" programs

All but a few of the studies of program sequence are rather unsatisfactory. Instruction was brief, sample size small, and the analysis unacceptable. In some studies, the less orderly program was beneficial to Highs, and the regression slope was often steeper than that of the smooth program. But this effect was not always present and the reverse was the case in some samples. In most of the studies in this section, general abilities correlated with success in PI. We shall not detail that aspect of the results.

We earlier summarized the Maier-Jacobs comparison of PI with teacher-led instruction in elementary Spanish. Another study of theirs (1966) had a similar style: a year-long series of brief lessons, with two pretest measures (IQ and attitude to Spanish) and three posttests (achievement, attitude to Spanish, and attitude to PI). Seventeen classes worked on a small-step, orderly program; 22 classes, on a scrambled program with no regular progression of frames.

The means for the two versions were similar (Section I of Table 7.5). The s.d.'s for the achievement posttest varied somewhat more from class to class following the scrambled treatment.

With achievement as outcome, there was a *modest difference in the between-groups slopes* (Section III) onto IQ. Abler classes did better on the scrambled version, less-able classes better on the orderly version. The effect arose from the large between-classes s.d. of achievement under the scrambled program. This could be a morale effect, some classes being stimulated by the scrambled version and and others frustrated.

Abler classes had a more positive attitude toward PI than duller classes, when exposed to the orderly version; there was a small effect in the opposite direction for the scrambled version. The slopes (Section III) are small because the s.d. of attitudes was very small. Finally, we note that classes favorable to the idea of studying Spanish tended to do better with the scrambled program.

Jacobs calculated for us the statistics on individuals (classes pooled) that appear in Section II of the table. From this we calculated a pooled-within-classes slope for the regression of outcome on IQ in each treatment. These values—0.55/0.52— imply that there was no consistent trend in the within-class slope as a function of treatment. Nor did the pooled-within-class s.d.'s for outcome differ. The most intriguing result is the contrast between 0.77 (between-classes slope) and 0.52 (within) for the scrambled version. This may not be replicable, but one can believe that an able class would, as a group, use a scrambled text more effectively than would a dull group.

Table 7.5   Results of an experiment on orderly/scrambled PI in Spanish

	Orderly version		Scrambled version	
I. Means and standard deviations of class means				
	Mean	s.d.	Mean	s.d.
Pretest variable				
Kuhlmann-Anderson IQ	106.5	6.6	103.5	8.3
Spanish attitude	4.5	0.5	4.7	0.7
Posttest variable				
Achievement	20.5	4.7	20.2	7.8
Spanish attitude	10.5	1.1	10.3	1.6
Attitude to PI	0.5	0.2	0.5	0.3

II. Statistics calculated for individuals (classes pooled)				
	Mean	s.d.	Mean	s.d.
IQ	107.1	12.1	104.3	13.3
Achievement	20.8	11.0	20.9	12.9
Correlation	0.59		0.64	
Slope, achievement on IQ	0.53		0.62	

III.   Correlations and regression slopes calculated between classes*

	Correlations for			Univariate regression slope for predicting outcome from	
	IQ	Sp attitude (pre)	PI attitude (post)	IQ	Sp attitude (pre)
IQ		- 0.01	0.75		
		- 0.02	- 0.32		
Spanish attitude (pre)	- 0.01		- 0.08		
	- 0.02		- 0.03		
Achievement	0.70	0.07	0.74	0.50	0.7
	0.82	0.21	- 0.27	0.77	2.3
Spanish attitude (post)	0.04	0.50	- 0.11	0.01	1.1
	- 0.19	0.71	- 0.01	- 0.04	1.6
PI attitude (post)	0.75	- 0.08		0.02	- 0.03
	- 0.32	- 0.03		- 0.12	- 0.01

*Orderly above in each pair; scrambled below.

Data from Maier and Jacobs, 1966.

J. L. Brown (1970) compared logically-ordered/scrambled versions of a program on number series. Tenth- and eleventh-graders worked about 100 minutes on the programs in class. Although the 2 x 2 analysis of variance using IQ as aptitude did not show a significant interaction ($N = 37$), the power of the significance test was slight. The descriptive data indicate an *ordinal interaction* with the smooth treatment better. As with Buckland, the scrambled treatment was very bad for Lows.

In a small study by Buckland (1968), a 50-frame conventional program on number bases was "block-scrambled" by reordering logically distinct sections; in the alternative treatment, items were scrambled ($N = 78$). General ability had been measured previously. The program in conventional "smooth" order showed virtually no difference between Lows and Highs. The block-scrambled program was at least as good as the smooth program for Highs, and very bad for Lows. The item-scrambled program produced bad results for everyone. This was an *ordinal interaction favoring the smooth program.*

An instructional program on solving equations was carefully sequenced in accord with a Gagné hierarchy (Spencer & Briggs, 1972). This was then given in regular/scrambled order ($N = 175$). The scrambled sequence produced poorer results on an immediate test. The Ability x Treatment Interaction reached significance for an attitude measure. Unlike what Maier and Jacobs found, Lows rather disliked the scrambled program. They also did very badly on it, and a statistical analysis not involving three-level blocking would surely have shown *significant ATI for the immediate posttest.*

Regular/scrambled PI were contrasted in a 17-day series of lessons on geometry for second grade (G. Levin & Baker, 1963). There were only 18 cases per group; the report was incomplete (e.g., no s.d.'s reported), and the study had little power. *The scrambled program may have been best for those with high IQ.*

Suggestive results appeared in Olivier's (1971) study of alternative sequences in Xenograde science, but the complexities of design and analysis prevent us from drawing a conclusion. At the heart of the study was an index (HSCI) describing how closely a sequence of frames corresponded to an "ideal" sequence that covered subordinate ideas before moving to ideas higher in the hierarchy. Fifty-two Ss were allowed to call up sections of the material in the order they preferred. The HSCI for these sequences ranged from 1.00 (ideal) to .00 (a reverse hierarchy, in which S worked down the hierarchy from the terminal concept to the elementary ones). Intermediate values indicated various degrees of non-conformity to hierarchical order. Each of these stimulus-choosing S's was yoked to an S who was required to work with the program the first one had chosen. Finally, another 52 Ss had to work on predetermined programs. In the analysis, these last two groups were pooled, but as they were divided unevenly over five levels of HSCI there were as few as 13 Ss per treatment. It may be that self-selection of program was disadvantageous. The self-sequencing group was not considered in the ATI analysis. Memory predicted outcome among the controlled-sequence Ss, but did not interact with HSCI. Induction seems to have interacted;

in the strongly ordered sequence (whether in forward or reverse order), Highs did only slightly better than Lows, but *irregular sequences produced very bad results for Lows.* This relation is plausible.

A significant interaction in the opposite direction was reported by Pyatte (1969). He taught eleven concepts having to do with measurement in science. One program arranged the material in an intellectually consecutive order. The "rough" version put sections in the order 1, 4, 3, 2 so that the base for sections 3 and 4 was not systematically developed. Subjects were 156 fourth-, fifth-, and sixth-graders. Scores on the Iowa Test of Basic Skills in Arithmetic, and grade level, allowed a 2 x 3 x 3 analysis of variance of immediate achievement and another of transfer. For achievement, a significant ATI was obtained: *Lows did better in the rough treatment* whereas Highs did better in the smooth treatment. Ability was positively correlated with achievement in all groups, more highly in the structured groups. *No ATI were found for the transfer test.*

Payne, Krathwohl, and Gordon (1967) taught statistical concepts to 238 college students by eight variant programs of 164 frames each. There was no main effect. Correlations of outcome with an arithmetic pretest varied erratically. Regression slopes indicated ATI. *A completely scrambled version had a slope about one-seventh of that associated with the least scrambled.* The correlations among scores on part-tests were higher for material taught by smooth programs than for "rough" presentations. Smooth programs, therefore, produced more variability of outcomes.

Wodtke *et al.* (1967), like Maier and Jacobs, found about twice as large an s.d. of outcome from a *rough* program as from a smooth one. A 74-frame program on number bases other than 10, requiring about 2 hours, was administered to 80 college students in either a linear or scrambled form. Aptitude information was available only for 43 Ss. The correlation of SAT Total with a posttest was 0.80 with the rough program, 0.57 with the smooth program. These together with the s.d.'s imply a disordinal interaction, *Highs doing better on the scrambled program* than on the ordered one. Unfortunately, the pilot work had given just the opposite result. It used another version of the program, with remedial loops. With 48 Ss, the pilot-study interaction was near to significance. The scrambled-program regression slope was slightly negative, while the orderly-program slope was positive and steep. *Highs did much better on the ordered program.* Time spent on the program varied with both the treatment and S's aptitude; without a sound control on that, the experiment suffers.

Sixth-graders (208 in all) were taught an artificial language by Carroll and Spearritt (1967). A "rough" program gave the rules in a haphazard sequence, several rules being studied at the same time; moreover, the learner's errors were identified to him as errors without explanation. A "smooth" program developed one rule at a time, explained errors, and made sure that each rule was learned before the student took up a new one. Several dependent variables were examined. A short test was given after page 60 of the booklet. Students of high IQ did better on the smooth program and others did better on the rough program. The authors took time-to-reach-page-60 as the main variable. Those who did badly on the test at this point were ignored in the analysis of working times. Among those who earned adequate test scores, cases were discarded at random within cells, for the sake of balancing the design. This reduced N to 96. Though no significant interaction effect on working time appeared, there was an irregular trend (see below). As the last step in data collection a difficult task was offered, on which students were allowed to work as long as they wished. The work period was generally under five minutes. The relation of persistence to ability was again irregular. The differences in the time measures were as follows (mean, in minutes, for the "rough" group, less the mean for the "smooth" group):

	Low ability	Inter-mediate ability	High ability
Time spent on program ("learning rate")	5	1	4
Time spent on extra problem ("perseverance")	- 1	1	- 1

This minor study, requiring only a single class period, was intended as a first attempt to use the Carroll "model of school learning" (p. 109). Analysis proved to be awkward, since eliminating Ss who failed to reach criterion created biased, noncomparable samples from the several Ability x Treatment cells. Such difficulties would be aggravated in an experiment of longer duration. *It does not appear that any conclusions can be drawn.* We would try to examine the regression of test score on working time and aptitude jointly, or to use path analysis, but the Carroll model makes time the dependent variable and test score an *a posteriori* control variable. The importance of this study is that it demonstrates some of the difficulties in research on "mastery learning."

Tobias (1973) found no interaction of ability with rough/smooth sequence, but ability did combine with anxiety to produce interactions under some circumstances. (See pp. 401 ff.)

Three orders of presenting a program in ninth-grade mathematics were compared by Niedermeyer, J. Brown, and Sulzen (1969). There were only 64 Ss in four groups, but the regression lines were close to parallel.

The possibility that homogeneity/heterogeneity of practice material would differentially influence student learning was entertained by Traub (1964). Three days of instruction were given regarding graphical addition, on the number line, of positive and negative integers. The first two days of instruction were common to all groups. On the third day the problem sets were heterogeneous for one group, and homogeneous for the second. The control group had a time-filling activity. There were approximately 100 sixth-graders in each group. Traub collected 36 aptitude measures from tests or school records. A main effect favored the group that worked on heterogeneous problems. Traub concluded that there was *no significant interaction.* The 36 aptitude variables were reduced to 12 by factor analysis, so as to sacrifice fewer degrees of freedom. Traub then compared regression slopes onto each of the twelve variables. A full multivariate test would have been more powerful.

A "by-passing" technique was studied by V. Campbell and Briggs (1962). In this, as in the British "skip-branching," the student is moved rapidly through or past material on which he passes pretest questions. The early studies, often informal, found bypassing advantageous for able students in some grades and disadvantageous in others. A large study in several grades then was carried out (N = 780). This produced convincing evidence that there was *no interaction in any grade* (V. Campbell, 1964).

We shall discuss at length the equivocality of results in two dissertations by Cartwright and Smith, where positive results were originally reported.

Cartwright (1962) taught fractions to small samples of mentally retarded adolescents by means of two programs. One was arranged to show the successive fractions in a systematic, natural manner (e.g., 1/2 and 1/3, 1/3 and 1/4, 1/4 and 1/5, etc.). The other presented the sequence in an irregular order. Groups differed in retention and transfer, not in immediate learning. The smooth treatment produced superior retention; the scrambled treatment produced superior transfer. This result is not unbelievable, since the intellectual activity required to organize scrambled material might well produce greater comprehension.

Cartwright (1962) reported correlated criteria with several pretest variables including general ability, language, prior knowledge of arithmetic fundamentals, and simple mathematical reasoning. He himself did not look for interactions. Stolurow's secondary account (1964, p. 352) emphasized that general ability correlated strongly (0.61) with performance on the rough program and negligibly with performance on the more regular one.

We reanalyzed to obtain better evidence on interaction. The results are presented in Table 7.6. F tests on pairs of slopes yielded only one effect approaching nominal significance (p < .10): the scrambled program produced a stronger relation between Full Scale IQ and the immediate posttest. The number of cases is small, hence statistical significance is not to be expected, but the *inconsistency of the various slope differences argues against taking them seriously.* One cannot build a case on this one significant relationship, when the retention and transfer tests failed to confirm it.

L. Smith (1962) placed 133 fifth-graders (four classes) into various groups and gave three kinds of PI, with more/less fine steps and more/less strong prompts. Four other classes received regular classroom instruction. Seven concepts about fractions were taught. The aptitude measures included PMA tests and Guilford divergent-thinking tests. A "criterion" test was given as a pretest and twice later; residual-gain scores were the outcome measures. Correlations were calculated between the residuals and the aptitude tests. The pretest should, we think, have been entered into a multiple-regression analysis instead of residualizing. Smith interpreted correlations rather than regression slopes. Rather large differences in s.d.'s within groups occurred in both pretests and posttests, and examination of slopes is called for. The information on correlations is of little use, since Smith

Table 7.6   Correlations and regression slopes relating outcomes to
aptitudes in orderly/scrambled instructional programs
for a retarded group

Aptitude measure	Criterion measure					
	Immediate posttest		Retention test		Transfer test	
	r	slope	r	slope	r	slope
Pretest	0.72	0.58	0.66	0.42	0.55	0.34
	0.49	0.50	0.57	0.53	0.56	0.30
Arithmetic Reasoning	0.68	5.12	0.48	2.86	0.51	2.89
	0.64	4.88	0.60	4.17	0.48	1.94
Arithmetic Fundamentals	0.74	7.14	0.67	5.12	0.54	3.99
	0.41	3.23	0.44	3.16	0.23	0.98
Total Arithmetic	0.73	6.52	0.59	4.16	0.55	3.71
	0.55	4.38	0.54	3.92	0.37	1.58
Total Reading	0.47	3.47	0.62	3.62	0.63	3.54
	0.57	5.40	0.64	5.63	0.43	2.21
Total Language	0.40	2.58	0.51	2.58	0.52	2.53
	0.63	6.67	0.40	3.90	0.24	1.37
Total Achievement	0.56	4.30	0.60	3.67	0.60	3.47
	0.62	6.25	0.57	5.30	0.38	2.03
Full Scale IQ	0.19	0.28	0.33	0.39	0.38	0.43
	0.61	1.57	0.16	0.38	0.27	0.37

Data from Cartwright, 1962. For each set, figures for the orderly program appear above, for the scrambled program below. N = 20 and 16 for orderly and scrambled programs, respectively.

reported only "significant" correlations. She correlated 15 ability scores with several outcome measures, in eight groups; and any single group had 20 or fewer cases. This means that the scattered "significant" correlations very likely reached that level by chance, whereas consistent but nonsignificant correlations were suppressed. Smith's view was that programmed and conventional instruction produced different aptitude-outcome correlations. *We are unable to accept or deny this ATI.* A laborious experiment was rendered worthless by faulty analysis.

Step size and pacing

Many PI studies have examined effects of step size, usually defined by probability of correct response on the average frame or by the amount of material to be read between responses. Step size may alter difficulty of comprehension, probability of positive reinforcement, pacing, etc. Some studies have examined pacing directly, without manipulating step size. We list the two kinds of studies together. But this makes the studies in this section heterogeneous. (In this body of literature, general ability again correlated with outcome under PI.)

Most studies placed in this classification showed only faint hints of ATI or none at all. Since the studies had small samples, the issue is not closed. Work in this area may connect with laboratory studies of the sort reported by Katz (our p. 127). There, however, Lows improved only when given a series of difficult problems. This is the opposite of the usual PI hypothesis.

The Kress-Gropper (1966) study of televised instruction asked complex questions about pacing, with a reasonably large sample. Audio-visual programs on elasticity and on direct and inverse relationships were prepared. Three levels of prompting were crossed with four presentation rates ("tempos"). 168 eighth-graders were matched on IQ and on estimates of the pace they characteristically set for themselves. An ATI was observed but not tested for significance.

> Subjects who were characteristically fast under self-paced conditions out-performed the characteristically slow Ss only when both worked under *fast*, fixed-tempo conditions. The superiority of the fast workers was evident in all six [criterion] measures. Surprisingly, however, in five of six measures, the opposite effect was observed under *slow*, fixed-tempo conditions. Here, the fast workers committed more errors and achieved lower scores than did the slow workers. Thus, though fast workers were matched with slow workers for IQ, under the *slow* fixed-tempo, where impairment would not be expected to be great for either group, fast workers did more poorly.
>
> The general pattern, then, . . . revealed that mean performance was highest when characteristically fast students worked under a fast fixed-tempo, and when characteristically slow students worked under a slow fixed-tempo. *Lowest means resulted when characteristic work rates and externally controlled tempos were not matched.*
>
> (From p. 277 of source; italics added.)

Regression analyses using IQ and characteristic work-rate together to predict criterion performance could have shown more clearly the nature of a pacing interaction, and would have reduced the uncertainty that arose from imperfect matching.

In teaching of the passive voice in Spanish to 110 high-school students (Gallegos, 1968), fast/slow pacing was regulated by tape recorder. A third alternative allowed S to move at his own pace. With a translation test as criterion, a *nonsignificant ATI* was noted: Highs on IQ seemed to do better with self-pacing, while Lows did better with slow, externally-regulated pacing. This does not concur with our finding from the Woodruff data (see p. 205).

Several investigations comparing linear PI with methods allowing more student self-direction have been summarized by V. Campbell (1964). Self-direction meant that Ss were provided with outlines, short test sections, supplementary examples, explanations, and self-testing questions with feedback. Each organized his own study procedure and paced himself. In a small sample of ninth-graders, mathematical ability correlated 0.75 and 0.49 with learning of two topics in mathematics by self-direction, but only 0.41 and 0.26 when learning was by PI. In the absence of a main effect, this is weak evidence that *self-direction may be better for high-ability Ss*, with standardized PI better for Lows. No direct test of the ATI was made. In one experiment, self-direction proved superior to other methods on the average after *S*s were coached in self-direction. Even after coaching, some *S*s read the materials straight through instead of trying to organize and evaluate for themselves.

Judd, Bunderson, and Bessent (1970) taught remedial college mathematics by computer in four modes which allowed students varying degrees of control over what they would study at any point. The plans varied from a skip-branching procedure that allowed no learner control to one leaving many decisions to the learner. On three units of work, *N* varied from 32 to 76. Posttest-on-pretest regressions differed, but there was no consistent patterning from unit to unit. The authors accepted the null hypothesis, but the number of cases per treatment (as low as 6) *scarcely warrants any conclusion.*

With regard to step size, *no ATI* were found by Rogers and Quartermain (1964), Furukawa (1970), Lewis and Gregson (1965), or Showel (1968). Only errors-on-program interacted for Shay (1961).

Woodruff, Shimabukuro, and Frey (1965) had 74 eighth-graders take a complete programmed course on general science (TMI-Grolier). The *S*s were randomly divided between teacher-regulated/self-regulated pacing conditions and again between in-class/out-of-class conditions of use. At the end of the first and second semesters, the number of frames correctly completed and a posttest score were recorded. The 40 scores originally analyzed include 21 scores from Torrance tests of divergent thinking, two grade averages, three reading scores, two Lorge-Thorndike IQs, a pretest on science, the two measures of performance on the program, two posttests, and various redundant composites.

With only 20 *S*s per treatment, the absence of significant main effects means little. Only scattered correlations of the Torrance measures with achievement were found. Previous grades, IQ, and reading ability correlated with most measures of achievement. The relation of mental ability to achievement was much higher in the first semester than in the second, perhaps because of a decline in rate of progress among Highs. The authors seemingly had intended to study ATI, but the report did not directly examine them.

With the help of E.I. Sawin, we computed the complete intercorrelation matrix within each treatment group. Of 256 pairs (32 aptitude variables, 8 criteria), 103 correlated significantly in at least one of the four groups. Regression comparisons were obtained across four treatments wherever at least one correlation was significant. Twenty of these F tests of slope heterogeneity reached $p < .05$—approximately 8 per cent of the original 256 pairs. Chance clearly played a large part in this study.

Most of the nominally significant ATIs arose with number-of-correct-frames as a criterion. *Several Torrance scores correlated substantially with outcome in the self-paced, out-of-class condition* (but *N* was only 16). In other treatments, these slopes were negligible. Highs completed more of the program correctly working out-of-class; Lows completed more when self-paced, in class. Those lowest on flexibility did better when teacher-paced, working out-of-class. *If the sample findings were based on more cases, it would appear that for these programs, students with average or low IQs should be assigned to self-paced, in-class conditions,* whereas abler students should work out-of-class, pacing themselves. Those with low grade averages did best with self-pacing, in class. Those with high grade averages did best on the program itself in the teacher-regulated, out-of-class condition. On the posttest, however, the teacher-regulated, in-class condition served students with good grade records best. A similar finding was obtained using reading speed as the aptitude dimension.

Time compression of speech could increase pace and perhaps put more information into a given instructional time. Sticht (1971) examined this variable with Army trainees (N = 150) classified as high or low extremes on the Armed Forces Qualification Test. Several versions of an audiotape presentation, differing in speech rate and amount of additional information included, were used. Lows benefited somewhat from additional information. *Differences were not statistically significant.*

Valverde and R. L. Morgan (1970) collected evidence on interaction of IQ with redundancy of instructional material. Airmen (88 per group) were taught medical terminology by five procedures, ranging from a pack of summary cards, one card for each term, up to three hours of small-step PI. The Otis means of the groups differed slightly, but we may ignore that to give the following results:

	Small-step PI	PI	PI	Terse text	Card
Posttest mean	67.5	67.9	71.9	71.7	70.4
Slope of regression on Otis IQ	0.37	0.44	0.25	0.17	0.35

The more redundant treatments are in the leftmost columns. The report allows no firm conclusion. It seems *possible that there were ATI.* Except for the card presentation, the trend in slopes was regular: terse instruction was less related to ability than redundant instruction. This is the opposite of the usual working hypothesis.

Hershberger (1964) stripped material from a redundant program to create a terse version. Each version was presented with/without quiz questions. The questions improved results. A California Reading Test score was the aptitude measure. Performance was strongly related to aptitude in two treatment cells, moderately in the other two, giving *some indication of interaction.* With the redundant text, added questions were far more helpful to Highs. Without quiz questions, the terse text was better for Highs than the redundant text. Results were not well reported, and the author's statements are not wholly consistent with the published figure.

One study dealt with redundancy of reading material rather than of PI (Kropp, Nelson, & King, 1967, pp. 27ff.). Over 200 sixth-graders with generally low IQs and presumably low socioeconomic status were the *S*s. Half of them read a textbook statement about a scientific topic; the others read an especially prepared "redundant" version, nearly 20 per cent shorter (!) than the original. A multiple-choice posttest on the content common to both versions was given. As aptitude measures *S*s had taken three Primary Mental Abilities (PMA) tests and a syllogistic test from the California Test of Mental Maturity (CTMM). The data showed a *clear disordinal ATI.* Highs did better, particularly on the simplified version. Although the brief passage was redundant (by the cloze test), this redundancy was achieved by removing detail and simplifying, not by paraphrasing and expanding on the content.

Various aspects of the analysis may be questioned. The dependent variable was the pupil's achievement divided by his study time; the arbitrary combining rule could have distorted results. Second, interaction was tested by comparing regression slopes for each aptitude variable in turn. A reduced-rank analysis would have been more satisfactory. With aptitudes treated singly, only the PMA Reasoning test showed a significant interaction, but the trends for all four aptitudes were similar. It seems best to account for the results in terms of a general factor.

Leith (see p. 424) found a steep slope of posttest onto IQ in straightforward PI with either large steps (general principles only) or small steps (details following every principle). When the large-step program followed the small-step program as review, the overall average was not improved (!) but the regression slope became zero. A branching treatment produced the same result. *The interaction could be important,* though it did not reach significance.

Nothing about ATI can be learned from the report of Hassinger (1965), but the study perhaps helps us to understand how the legend that mental ability has nothing to do with success in programmed instruction took root. Hassinger gave more/less redundant variants of a program in statistics to 132 *S*s, calculated gain scores, and correlated gains with IQ; $r = -0.02$. If IQ were uncorrelated with true gain, it would have a negative correlation with observed gain in raw score. Hassinger's zero correlation probably results from a counterbalance between a real positive relation and a spurious negative relation. Many other early studies of PI stressed gain scores or even more treacherous indices such as gain-divided-by-possible-gain.

Quasi-independent study

A few studies compare regular classroom instruction with instruction that allows the student to draw on a library of programmed lessons, audiotapes, or the like, so as to proceed through the work in his own way. In addition to the two studies to be described here, the studies of Oosthoek and Ackers and of Szabo and Asher described later (pp. 452 ff.) indicate an interaction with ability. Here we shall see steeper regression slopes in the conventional treatment, and that is also the Szabo-Asher finding. In the Oosthoek study, however, the interaction was more complex, being moderated by anxiety. In all the studies, the variation in working time between the two treatments complicates the interpretation.

B. W. Tuckman and Orefice (1973) contrasted four methods of teaching accounting, with only 120 Ss. There was a conventional lecture-discussion-textbook treatment/a combination of lecture with programmed text in the classroom/PI only, in the classroom/and independent study with taped lectures and PI. Instruction extended over eight class meetings. Students kept a record of time spent, including classtime. As a measure of the abstract/concrete variable (somewhat like the CL variable of David Hunt, see p. 376 ff.), Tuckman used a questionnaire of his own devising. We are inclined to think that variables of this character strongly overlap with intellectual ability. On the posttest the results were poor for all students in the two-classroom PI treatments. *In the conventional treatment and the independent treatment, the abstract students (high CL) did well.* The steep slope in these treatments did not depart significantly from the flat slopes in the PI treatments. A borderline significant interaction of the time measure seems to suggest that abstract students did less work than others in the independent condition and more than others in the conventional condition. The abstract students liked PI-without-lecture fairly well; concrete Ss did not. The abstract Ss given PI-plus-lecture disliked the treatment, whereas concrete Ss responded favorably. The slopes differed significantly, but the result is too mysterious to be trusted with these small samples. We are not told whether liking had any relation to achievement.

Conventional and audio-tutorial (a–t) procedures in college physics were contrasted by Ott and Macklin (1974). A student group of superior ability (N about 300) was divided between the two plans. Some were assigned at random and some were given the treatment of their choice. Working time was not closely controlled; indeed, there is reason to think that some preferred the a–t plan because it gave them more free time to use on things other than physics. No adjustment was made for differences in working time.

Two mathematics aptitude tests had similar regressions, but the investigators analyzed them separately. Course grade served as the criterion. Ott and Macklin have provided us with regressions separating the preference and random subgroups. The chief ATI finding appears to be *a steeper regression slope onto mathematical aptitude in the conventional treatment,* contrasted with a modest slope in the a–t groups. Within the a–t treatment, the slope was steeper among the assigned (random) Ss. This is consistent with the view that able students who chose the a–t method did not work as hard as those assigned to it. A replication is in progress.

Another study comparing conventional/a–t conditions was reported by Stuck and Manatt (1970). 219 college Ss were divided for about seven hours of instruction in school law. Splitting groups on prior achievement gave main effects favoring high prior achievement and a–t, but *no interaction.* The statistical test was weak and cell means were not reported.

Variations of technique in PI

This final section deals with miscellaneous variations of technique in PI.

Few studies of branching considered aptitude. D. Beane (1965) divided high-school students ($N = 48$) into four treatment groups to receive two weeks of PI in plane geometry. One group received linear PI exclusively, one group received branching PI exclusively, and two groups were shifted, half-way through the unit, from one technique to the other. Achievement, time, and attitude measures were collected. For analysis, Ss were divided at the median IQ. There were no main effects of treatment on achievement or attitude, and *no ATI*. It was noted that high-IQ Ss tended to favor the linear program to a greater extent than did Lows.

J. Hartley (1965) compared linear PI on logarithms with a skip-branching program in which Ss who answered correctly could move ahead quickly. The branching program included remedial loops for each incorrect response. Ss were 68 British high-school girls from two ability tracks. IQ and mathematics scores were available. IQ was strongly related to outcome (particularly to retention) in the branching group, but not in the linear group. Improved analysis *might have shown a weak ATI.*

Senter *et al.* (1964) reported *no interaction* between college grade average to date and alternative programs in computer arithmetic. There were about 20 Ss per treatment group and the program required about 6 hours of work. One program was linear and comparatively brief; the other two versions were branched. High-GPA students did much better than others on the posttest, but they had also done better on a pretest. An attempt to investigate the relation of the programs to numerical ability led to a confused report, because only gain scores were analyzed.

A conventional linear program on the topic of electricity, with a branched program, was contrasted by Larkin and Leith (1964). Work extended over three class periods ($N = 48$ 10-year-olds). *The linear program was conspicuously better for Lows,* whereas the two programs gave essentially equal results for Highs. A retest after 12 weeks showed a similar pattern.

The four studies, taken together, do not support a generalization. Generalization could come only from instruction over a considerable period, with respectable samples, that considers amount of content learned within a fixed instructional time and observes attitude and transfer outcomes. Even so, results may differ with the content and with specifics of the programming technique.

Eigen (1962) compared teaching machine/horizontal programmed text (frames on separate pages)/vertical programmed text (frames in columns down the page). The program consisted of 65 frames on mathematics. Ss were 77 eighth-graders. No main effects for mode of presentation were found. From correlations of Pintner IQs and s.d.'s we computed the regression slopes. Machine gave the steepest, and vertical text the shallowest, slopes. According to the author's anova the machine/vertical-text comparison had a barely significant disordinal interaction. Apparently, Ss with IQ below about 118 did better with vertical text, while *Highs were better off with machines.*

Nagel (1968) prepared two versions of PI on celestial navigation, one formal and impersonal, the other "conversational," with personal asides, humor, and cartoons. Among 80 Navy reservists, *Ss without previous experience in PI or in the subject matter learned more from the conversational style.* The two styles were about equally effective when *S* had experience.

Nuthall (1968) taught two sociological concepts to 432 high-school students. Four alternative teaching strategies were used in PI booklets requiring 30 minutes of work. In one treatment, all frames described concepts; another added comparisons with other concepts; another added instances and examples; and the fourth was composed only of comparison and example frames. The analysis took into account whether or not *S* had previously studied a related topic and his knowledge at pretest. Learning was assessed by an essay and a delayed multiple-choice test. *It appears that a program including instances and examples was better* than descriptive or comparative *programs for Ss with moderate and high levels of prior knowledge.* Treatment means did not differ among *S*s low on prior knowledge.

Scharf (1961) provided varying amounts of feedback in programs on logic. *S* was required to write his answer to each question. In the middle sections of the program, one group was given a correct answer on every item. The other groups had feedback on every second item, feedback on half of the items in mixed order, or feedback on a quarter of the items in mixed order. There was a strong main effect for IQ, but *no interaction* of treatment with IQ ($N = 69$, giving an extremely weak test of ATI). Skimpy reinforcement increased the number of errors Lows made in working through the program; but this did not handicap them particularly on the posttest. At both IQ levels, 100 per cent reinforcement produced the best scores. Thus, ability failed to interact with feedback and reinforcement conditions.

A German study on spelling drills (Klauer, 1969) did find some hint of interactio with the same variable as Scharf's. The study was repeated, making the total *N* about 170. *S*s were classified on a "pretest" as High or Low. It is uncertain whether the pretest on the 30 words of the experimental lesson or the cumulative record from prior lessons was used. Both should have entered into the analysis. Each day (two days in one run, four days in the other) the words were dictated. In one group, *S* had a chance to check his spelling of every word against a master list on the blackboard; other *S*s saw the correct spelling for only a random half of the words. There was a weak, nonsignificant interaction; *complete feedback was advantageous for Lows.*

Federico (1971) gave four classes of military trainees ($N = 112$) seven hours of PI on medical fundamentals, then divided them between audio-visual PI/printed PI and pretest/no pretest conditions. Instruction was brief, lasting 20 minutes in the audio-visual condition and 80 to 120 minutes in the printed condition. Ancova showed no significant main effects or interaction.

The investigator had six or more aptitude measures, but made only a weak attempt to search for ATI. He split at the median on the Armed Forces Qualification Test and discarded cases to square off a Treatments x Levels design. The interaction reached only the .10 level of significance. The unadjusted means (20 cases each) showed a disordinal interaction, as follows:

	Low AFQT	High AFQT
Audiovisual	18.0	20.9
Written	18.8	19.7

It is likely that a test on regression slopes would show a significant interaction.

A second "aptitude" was a test that had been given on content presented during the first seven hours of PI. With this predictor there was *no interaction.*

A multifacet study. The most complexly designed of all ATI studies admits of only a negative conclusion. A comprehensive sample of 1400 students from Los Angeles eighth-grade classes was tested on a dozen aptitudes, then divided at random among 54 (!) systematic variations in programming. Ss were trained on teaching machines and tested individually. Complete data were available for 1232 Ss. The original report (Allen, Filep, & Cooney, 1967) dealt with effects other than ATI by means of analysis of variance and covariance. All statistics relevant to ATI appeared in that report, however. A supplementary report by Filep (1967) carried out a correlational analysis and drew conclusions about ATI, but these seem to be entirely unconnected with the statistics he reported. We have attempted to derive information about possible interactions from the tables of the first report; our reading of the data has little in common with Filep's conclusions.

Elements of crystallography were to be taught by PI, each program requiring 40 minutes of working time, more or less. Three "syllabi" were taught, to develop three distinct kinds of performance. What the authors call "nonconcrete" we shall refer to as "verbal-abstract"; S learned to spell and interpret words such as *crystal-lography.* The authors' "concrete" content required verbal responses to figural presentations, for example, the naming of crystal shapes. Thirdly, there was "action-process" content, having to do with processes such as crystal growth. The content and tests being different, the authors considered these variations as three distinct experiments to be analyzed separately, by parallel techniques. We would not criticize this, but we shall aggregate some results across experiments; this can be done since the three tests had the same score range and much the same s.d. within treatments.

As aptitude the authors used the Lorge-Thorndike Total IQ. They also administered a set of Guilford's tests of convergent and divergent thinking and pooled to form one score, which we may label G. IQ and G were substantially correlated.

Their technology could display visual and auditory stimuli automatically. The visual displays took three forms: "Text," in which all messages were conveyed in words on the screen; "Figural," in which words on the screen were accompanied by still pictures or diagrams, and "Motion," which added motion photographs and animated drawings. These variations were crossed with three auditory modes: "Silent;" "Redundant," in which the words appearing in the visual display were read aloud; and "Directive," in which comments were made about what the student should notice on the screen. Each of the nine programs on each of the three syllabi was modified to provide branching loops for half of its Ss. Tables reported the posttest means and s.d.'s for Ss with IQ above/below 100. We shall take the difference Δ between any such pair of means as an indication of the regression slopes. We do not know the means of the 108 subject groups on IQ itself; with about 11 Ss per cell, the High-Low difference in IQ varied from cell to cell and this is needed to get the proper slopes. We averaged within-treatment means over comparable treatments without weighting them to take into account the varying N (from loss of cases).

The overall mean outcome was approximately 29 for Highs and 20 for Lows; the within-cell s.d. (within IQ block) ranged from 3 to 12, but was usually around 7. We considered s.d.'s in deciding which differences in Δ to treat as potentially important. The overall Δ was 9 -. (We use this crude form of presentation to avoid any implication of precision.)

There was little difference in Δ between linear/branching treatments, nor among silent/redundant/directive audio treatments. There was a smaller Δ for motion than for the other visual treatments, but this appears to be a second-order effect (see below). Comparing experiments, outcome means were highest for verbal-abstract, lowest for action-process. Δ was 11 for the former, 7 for the latter, with concrete intermediate. That is to say, Highs ran farthest ahead of Lows on the material that was easiest to learn.

Within experiments, linear/branching did not interact, and differences in audio treatment probably did not. One within-experiment difference for visual treatments was sizable. With concrete material, the figural treatment showed the greatest Δ, 10+, compared to 8+ for text and 6+ for motion. This interaction must be nominally significant, with 18 cells in the analysis. Four of the six figural cells were among the five with largest Δ's, and four of the motion cells were among the five with smallest Δ's. But the comparison is one of dozens. Third-order and fourth-order combinations did not show any contrast large enough to take seriously.

The same analysis can be made from tables on the G score. This score was not so strongly related to outcome, the overall Δ being 7 -. There was no first-order interaction of audio variations or of linear/branching. For the text/figural/motion comparison, the Δ's were 6, 9 -, and 6 -. This agrees with the result for IQ. Each of these means is based on about 400 Ss. In all three experiments, the figural treatment showed greater relation to G than other treatments did.

The experiment-to-experiment comparison was not at all like that for IQ: for verbal-abstract, $\Delta = 6$ -, for concrete, 7 -; for action-process, 8. Those High on G ran farthest ahead of Lows on the material *hardest* to learn.

Within experiments, there was no interaction for linear/branching. As for audio comparisons: with verbal-abstract content, directive produced the smallest Δ (4, vs. 6 - overall); with concrete content, silent produced the smallest Δ (16 -, vs. 7 -). For process content, Δ for redundant was low (7 -) and that for directive high (9+). The visual within-experiment comparisons suggest interactions; those will be detailed below.

At the third level, there were two possible effects in the concrete experiment. Within the visual motion treatment, Δ for linear was 4 - and for branched was 7. Within the redundant audio treatment, the respective values were 5+ and 10. There is one fourth-order effect to mention for the concrete experiment: the text treatment with no sound gave a steep slope ($\Delta = 13$) for the linear version and a shallow slope ($\Delta = 4$) for the branched version.

The inconsistencies between the two aptitude measures are mystifying, since there is no psychological reason to expect them. A proper regression analysis that identified which component(s) in the Guilford battery interacted differently from IQ would have been helpful. While the authors actually employed a general-linear-hypothesis computer program in their work, they did not use it in such a way as to disclose or test interactions. In fact, when they carried out an analysis of co-variance, they ignored interactions that Filep believed to be present.

The important conclusions are that programmed instruction by no means over-came the effect of aptitude on learning and that fairly substantial *contrasts in programming technique did not often generate interactions, within a one-hour training session*. The suggestion that the visual modes entered into an interaction is too inconsistent to be trusted, as is seen by comparing across rows in Table 7.7. If one were to have made a guess *a priori*, it would surely have been that interpreting concrete (figural) ideas to the learner through figural displays would make learning easier for Lows and reduce Δ. Such effects as appear here are in the opposite direction.

Table 7.7   Differences between means (Δ) of high and low aptitude groups in nine PI treatments

	Δ for IQ			Δ for G		
	Figural	*Text*	*Motion*	*Figural*	*Text*	*Motion*
Abstract	10+	12-	11	6	4	5+
Concrete	10+	8+	6+	8-	4-	5+
Process	7-	7+	7+	10+	7+	7-
Pooled	9	9+	8+	9-	6	6-

Based on study by Allen, Filep, and Cooney (1967).

Conclusion

The studies reviewed in this chapter range from nearly trivial studies involving fewer than 20 subject-hours per treatment to year-long studies in a sizable number of classes. Taken together, they represent the most extensive body of cumulative knowledge that exists regarding any one kind of ATI. Even if programmed instruction has now been stowed in that closet where educators keep yesterday's panacea, the findings should help us think about other kinds of instruction and about strategy for ATI research.

The initial claim that PI enables Lows to learn as much as Highs was thoroughly disproved. Outcomes from PI were correlated with initial test scores (whether on general abilities or on the content to be taught) in the overwhelming majority of studies. The current propaganda for "mastery learning" appears to make almost precisely the claim that this review has overturned. One simply cannot eliminate individual differences in learning. To be sure, one can confine attention to a finite body of content and extend practice to the point where a ceiling effect removes individual differences. Indeed, in a fair number of the studies reviewed here, work on the program was extended to the point where all persons had "mastered" the responses to the program frames. But on tests that rephrased the content, or required application, or examined retention over a few weeks, individual differences reappeared.

We were prepared to entertain the hypothesis, arising from Gagné's work, that carefully sequenced instruction can carry the person past the handicaps with which he enters, give him the intellectual keys to the new content, and so make his progress in subsequent lessons dependent on specifics rather than general aptitudes. In the studies of long-extended instruction reviewed in this chapter, that simply did not happen. General aptitudes predicted outcomes.

The hypothesis that PI would produce a smaller AT regression slope than conventional instruction is weakly supported, provided that we can rationalize away the many studies where no ATI appeared and some in which the direction of interaction was reversed. The difficulty, of course, is that neither "PI" nor "conventional instruction" defines a treatment condition; within each of those classes there is an infinite variety of treatments. Outcomes from PI may be strongly correlated with aptitude or very little correlated.

From a strategic point of view, the most important message from this compilation of research is that any attempt to generalize about a class of educational treatments is suspect. In reaching an operational decision in a particular institution about the teaching of a particular course, an experimenter can reasonably assign groups of students to alternative packages of instructional material. Determining which one is most efficient, or which kind of student each package serves best, enables one to adopt the more promising instructional procedure for that specific setting in subsequent years. There is hazard in applying that knowledge in other institutions that teach the same course; but one can monitor results in the new setting without a full experiment.

What one cannot do is generalize about instructional techniques in the abstract. Strong generalizations cannot be established about treatments characterized only as (e.g.) "linear programmed instruction with overt response." Findings may depend on whether the response is oral or written, whether the content is logically continuous and integrated or episodic, whether it includes concrete instances, whether the instruction is tedious for abler students, how the teacher feels about programmed instruction, etc. No experiment can manipulate all the pertinent variables, but the experimenter can at least eschew simple generalizations.

Any one classroom study is a case study of instruction in a certain body of material, by a teacher who sets a certain tone and emphasizes certain objectives, in a group that establishes a certain kind of morale. Each class is a single case. The more completely the investigator observes and informs himself about the social psychology of his group and its intellectual progress as the instruction proceeds, the more likely he is to know why he attained the results he did. The apparent positive findings for more connected content do imply that if psychological research is pursued in an analytic fashion we may be able to discover modes of programmed or computer-based instruction that, extended over a semester or more, will nullify many of the predictions of failure that would have been valid for conventional treatments.

It was once supposed that Lows would be aided by the requirement of active response and that small steps or smoothly ordered programs would aid Lows. Most often, no interaction has appeared in such studies; the interactions that did appear were not consistent.

Chapter 8 | Interactions in reading and arithmetic instruction

Chapter 7 showed that general abilities (whether fluid or crystallized) frequently predict learning in the classroom, presumably because they aid the learner in processing the lessons. But the widely held expectation that PI would produce flat AT regression slopes proved to be unsound and overly simple. We turn now to two other issues of long-standing interest: Can we improve upon basal, whole-word reading instruction? Does meaningful instruction, particularly in arithmetic, serve better than drill? A few studies with older Ss and with content other than reading and arithmetic set the stage for Chapter 9, on alternatives to verbal instruction. We locate research on reading beside that on meaning, since much discussion of reading methods revolves around the question of meaningfulness.

ATI hypotheses have been implicit in much of the work, and, in contrast to work on PI, the data do suggest some consistencies worth following up.

The teaching of reading

Reading is the main task of school beginners. Children arrive at school without systematic preparation, differing widely in their relevant prior experiences and, consequently, in skills. From available instructional treatments, the teacher must shape a program that fits each child's assortment of characteristics, to develop not only reading skills but also aptitude for further learning. Success or failure will influence the child's response to almost all later instruction. Findings of ATI in reading are thus of great moment.

The voluminous literature on reading is filled with thorny issues. The experiments

217

on instructional method reviewed by Chall (1967) generally were cast in "horse-race" terms, seeking to show that one method or another produced a higher mean outcome. Yet the concept of readiness has always been prominent in reading re-search, and there is much reason to expect that the readiness required by one method of instruction differs in character and in level from the readiness required by another. Some methods presumably demand greater overall mental develop-ment, some place greater demands on visual perception, and some may be sensitive to anxiety or dependency.

As long ago as 1935 Guy Bond suggested that memory span contributes to reading under "whole–word" teaching methods, but interferes with learning via phonics. Likewise, Dolch and Bloomster (1937) argued from limited data that phonic methods can be used effectively only with pupils of MA 7 or over, whereas pupils below this level can learn to read from whole-word methods. And Chall (1967, p. 138) considered ATI when she hypothesized that Lows need an emphasis on decoding (as in phonics), whereas Highs can respond to either a code emphasis or a meaning emphasis.

These ATI hypotheses span 30 years, and they conflict. While much of the intervening (and subsequent) research on reading instruction might have shed light on such interactions, little of it has been thoroughly analyzed or reported. We shall first discuss one program of experiments we consider exemplary in scope, planning, and execution. Then we shall review other informative studies. But this section cannot cover all the reading research that is potentially related to the study of individual differences in learning to read.

Comparisons of whole-word instruction with other methods

The primary question through decades of reading research has been whether the conventional whole-word, or basal reader, methods can be improved upon. The most extensive study of this question has been the Cooperative Reading Program.

Plan of the Cooperative Reading Program. In the middle 1960's, a program of 27 coordinated studies of beginning reading was sponsored by the U. S. Office of Education. Each investigator was asked to include elements of a standard design no matter what unique question he was pursuing (G. L. Bond & Dykstra, 1967). Specified aptitudes were to be measured, classes were to be assigned at random to one of the treatments (though assignment of pupils to classes was not random), and one treatment ("basal reader") was to be used along with contrasting treat-ments chosen for the particular subproject. The period of instruction between pretests and posttests was fixed at 140 days in every project. Posttests were also given at the end of Grade 2 in some projects.

The investigators made their own analyses and reports, and not all those analyses were powerful. Most of the studies were reported in some detail through the ERIC system, and popularized accounts appeared in *The Reading Teacher.* The data from all the studies were supplied to the program directors, who analyzed them as a whole, paying particular attention to main effects for methods and to interactions (Bond & Dykstra, 1967; Dykstra, 1968). Because samples were large, it was possible to analyze both between and within projects. Lo (1973) later reanalyzed the data. Lo's aim was more to demonstrate sophisticated procedures for reducing ATI data than to extract substantive conclusions. His report has potential methodological interest for our readers, though it is of little help in interpretation. The entire programmatic effort, then, collected extensive aptitude data and analyzed them in alternative ways with great sophistication. There was explicit interest in identifying ATI. We know of no comparable effort in other curriculum areas.

Six kinds of treatment entered into comparisons within projects. First, every investigator agreed to collect data from "basal reader" instruction, to provide a common benchmark. This was a whole-word method (WWM), ordinarily following the Scott-Foresman series or other books in the Dick-and-Jane pattern. Some investigators compared this with a "linguistics" approach (LM), a "phonics" approach (PM), or a combination of linguistics and phonics (PLM). Such teaching systematically develops skill in decoding graphemes and recognizing phonemes, and teaches the child to dissect words and recombine elements. Some investigators tried a WWM, PM combination. In some projects, one of the treatments used materials printed in the Initial Teaching Alphabet (i.t.a.); though i.t.a. was designed to facilitate phonic analysis, it can be used in a story-reading, whole-word curriculum. The sixth category of treatment was "language experience" (LE). In LE classes, students and teachers conversed and told stories to build a vocabulary they then employed in homemade stories. Learning to read was thus made an integral part of meaningful work. Among the 27 projects, 17 provided data on WWM (4266 Ss, 187 classes). For i.t.a., there were five projects, 1055 Ss, 48 classes; for WWM-plus-PM, four projects, 1104 Ss, 46 classes; for LE, four projects, 1431 Ss, 60 classes; for LM, three projects, 760 Ss, 31 classes; and for PLM, three projects, 488 Ss, 23 classes.

The aptitude scores common to all projects were Pintner-Cunningham Intelligence; Murphy-Durrell Phonemes, Letter Names, and Learning Rate; Thurstone Pattern Copying and Identical Forms; and Metropolitan Word Meaning and Listening. The principal outcome measures were subtests of the Stanford Achievement Test (Word Reading, Paragraph Meaning, Vocabulary, Spelling, and Word Study Skills). Many of the projects measured additional outcomes.

The Bond-Dykstra analysis. Bond and Dykstra (1967) studied each pair of treatment contrasts in a Sex x Treatment x Project design. The analysis was carried out on the means for boys and girls in each class; hence, the half-class was treated as a sampling unit. Treatment x Project interactions were frequently significant; i.e., the "same" treatments did not operate in the same way in different projects. This could have arisen from nonrandom assignment of students and teachers to treatments within projects, from the fact that the projects served different populations, or from uncontrolled variations in method of teaching. The prevalence of such findings persuaded Bond and Dykstra to examine the data project-by-project. We are strongly in accord with this shift in strategy. With regard to main effects, their final judgment was that programs other than WWM tended to produce superior recognition of words—but the most striking finding was the class-to-class variability within treatments, even within the same project.

The within-project analyses for interactions blocked on three variables—Pintner-

Cunningham, Phonemes, and Letter Names—each in a separate set of analyses. There were four, three, and four levels, respectively, of these variables. The number of significant interactions was at the chance level consistently—save in one project, Stauffer's, where Lows did better in WWM, while Highs did better in LE. This conclusion was dismissed when Bond and Dykstra found that Stauffer's treatment groups differed at pretest, in a direction matching the outcome difference. Other nominally significant interactions were not examined further or interpreted. The overall conclusion, then, was *no ATI.*

But blocking on aptitude led to extraordinarily weak statistical tests. Furthermore, applying uniform cutting scores across all projects created markedly uneven cell sizes within projects, undermining the anova. For example, Stauffer's low, middle, and high blocks on Phonemes contained 292, 70, and 95 Ss. In the Kendrick project, these respective blocks contained 292, 340, and 657 Ss. Cell sizes also varied between treatments within projects. Regression methods would have minimized these difficulties, and would have made it possible to compare relations across projects. We note that several nominally significant interactions, discarded by Bond and Dykstra as attributable to chance, involved the same outcome variable (vocabulary) and similar treatment comparisons (WWM/LM and WWM/PM). Such consistency in patterns adds weight to the evidence that the F test as such cannot recognize.

Regression analysis can be applied even now. The Bond-Dykstra report of Grade 1 data and the Dykstra followup data gave r's and s.d.'s for each treatment with all cases pooled. For present purposes, we chose to compute AT regression slopes for a combined outcome measure with the pooled Grade-1 data, as background for examining Lo's more extensive reanalysis. Some differences in slopes were apparent. Those of WWM-plus-PM and of LM seemed steeper than those of other treatments, for example. Particular readiness tests yielded slopes in i.t.a. or in WWM that were different, in a plausible direction, from those in other treatments.

However, inconsistencies between our findings and those of individual project reports led us to abandon this effort, and we shall not report our computations here. Exploration of this sort in large data pools can be of value, but it is evidently hazardous in this case. Moreover, an analysis carried out while this book was in press shows that unstable between-class interactions had a large influence in the previous analyses. See note, p. 106.

The Lo reanalysis.   The Lo dissertation (1973) is more methodological than substantive; indeed, the relations he found significant were described only briefly, if at all. Lo's methodological arguments are consistent with our Chapters 2 to 4 in most respects. He gave theoretical elaborations and detailed examples that our reader may wish to examine and pursued some techniques of analysis that we do not emphasize. Some of the techniques he applied (e.g., blocked anova), we recommend against.

Lo chose to pool the data over those projects where the same treatment was ostensibly represented, though he acknowledged that Ss were not independently sampled. His Chapter 4 used data for only 215 Ss chosen from one project that compared WWM/LE. He reduced the aptitude data to two dimensions: a first principal component reflecting a general ability (G) and a perceptual-speed factor (PS).The latter is in essence the Identical Forms test with G partialed out. Lo formed a composite Grade-1 criterion, and also a Grade-2 composite. The dissertation demonstrated the application of anova (3x3 blocking on aptitude factors), a test of homogeneity of regression, generalized regression analysis, and the Johnson-Neyman technique. Then the Grade-1 and Grade-2 composites were treated simultaneously in the multivariate extension of each of the first three methods. (The pertinent computer programs appear in Lo's appendix.)

There was significant ATI, persons above average on perceptual speed doing better in LE and persons very low on perceptual speed doing better in WWM. This result is not consistent with the slopes we computed from the pooled data nor with the report of Bond and Dykstra (esp. their p. 110). We attribute the discrepancy to the different sets of cases entering these analyses.

Lo's Chapter 5 selected 3963 Ss from the ten projects that had conducted follow-up evaluations in Grade 2. Five factors were extracted from the eight pretests: G, PS, narrowly defined factors for space and short-term memory, and a mysterious bipolar factor that Lo called "listening." The criteria were reduced to a single composite in each grade, since the Stanford subtests were accounted for by one factor. *Nearly all contrasts of WWM with other treatments showed significant ATI* (p often $<$ .001). Lo was wrong to attribute this significance merely to the "enormous number of degrees of freedom" for the F tests (his p. 127). The logic of statistical inference applies to large studies as well as to small ones. To be sure, when N is very large, the assumptions underlying the test become more critical. Here the number of degrees of freedom was exaggerated by the decision to treat persons as the unit of sampling. To put it differently, when Lo allowed the assumption of independent sampling to be violated, he probably reduced the estimate of error variance drastically and so exaggerated the significance levels.

Lo found interactions of all five aptitude dimensions with the WWM/LE contrast. (These results included the Stauffer data whose ATI Bond and Dykstra had dismissed as reflecting nonequivalence of treatment groups at pretest.) Other interactions, particularly those for the space factor (which were consistent in both grades), may also be meaningful. Lo's within-project analyses also located several significant ATI, but apparently these were not consistent. In fact, if one looks only at the asterisks in Lo's tables, no Aptitude x Treatment pairing gave consistently significant results across projects. Lo did not attempt to describe the ATI findings in the overall analysis or to interpret the inconsistencies among projects.

Inconsistency across studies can have many causes, the first of which is uncontrolled variance. A replication is rarely able to duplicate fully the original conditions. Treatments are multivariate in nature—to characterize a treatment as "phonic" is to leave a great deal unspecified. Even in following detailed specifications for a treatment one mixes the ingredients variously in the classroom and inevitably adds unplanned variations. Chall and S. Feldman (1966) observed that teachers who described themselves as using PM (or WWM) varied considerably in their actual classroom procedures. This may explain contradictions between studies that ostensibly investigated the same treatment. In the Bond-Dykstra and Lo reports, contrast labels gloss over potentially important variations within and between treatments, making treatments appear to be the same though they are not. Some of Lo's labels seem false to the projects whose descriptions are given by Bond and Dykstra. But Bond and Dykstra also confused matters occasionally— for example, when they lumped radically different i.t.a. treatments in the same table. One cannot rely on labels; interpretation must be based on the more detailed (though still limited) treatment descriptions in individual reports. We infer from Lo's analyses that an aptitude measure often had similar effects in specific instances of "different" treatments, and dissimilar effects in specific instances of "the same" treatment. If one were to group instances that show similar AT slopes for a certain aptitude, regardless of the treatment ostensibly illustrated, he might find a basis for generalization. At least, once clusters of treatments identified in this way are located, one can look at the multiple aspects of the classroom methods rather than stop with a label.

Another source of inconsistency is statistical. In some projects, there were only about 120 d.f. for the error term (roughly 60 cases per treatment). Even a powerful method of processing the data from a small project would probably not have rejected the null hypothesis. Other projects had more than 200 cases per treatment. When analyses differ in power, significance tests may show inconsistency from study to study even though the relationships themselves are consistent.

Given the striking class-to-class inconsistency, seeking generalizations like "Basic WWM is good for students high on SR" is premature, if not fundamentally inappropriate. It is easy to believe that means and AT slopes vary from community to community and from school to school, as well as from teacher to teacher. Even with the same teacher and the "same method," classes develop their own dynamics; each may generate a different pattern of outcomes and regression slopes. It follows that a statistical sifting of ATI must be amplified by clinical, anthropological, idiographic study. For survey purposes it is necessary to organize results grossly around treatment categories, as Bond-Dykstra and Lo did and as we do in this book. But this can provide only a superficial summary.

A project-by-project reading of the results. Because the overall analyses described treatments only superficially and let significance tests dominate the interpretation, we turned to the individual project reports. We hoped to augment the Bond-Dykstra and Lo results with more detailed descriptions of treatments and with judgments about consistencies in ATI patterns. Table 8.1 summarizes our findings along with those of Bond-Dykstra and Lo. We have labeled treatment contrasts on the basis of our own reading; these labels differ somewhat from those used in the overall analyses. It should be clear that treatments are spread along a spectrum and do not fall into a few distinct categories. Our judgments about ATI patterns are impressionistic at some points, because many original reports were incomplete. Collating all the readings of the data, we reach several ATI hypotheses, stated in the rightmost column. We cannot conclude that these hypotheses have

Table 8.1 A summary of project-by-project results in the Cooperative Reading Program

Project (by principal author)	Treatment contrast (label as inferred from original report)	Interactions called significant				Interactions of G inferred from original project report	Character of ATI hypotheses worth further test
		Lo analysis		Bond-Dykstra analysis			
		Aptitudes[a] Gr. 1	Gr. 2	Aptitude(s)	Outcome(s)		
Stauffer	WWM/LE	G	G LA	G PD LN	All All All	G and special abilities show many ATI, all slopes steeper with LE.	1
Cleland	WWM/LE	STM	STM	G	Vocabulary	Ordinal ATI in Grade 1; LE best for Lows on Vocabulary; in Grades 2 & 3, ATI disordinal; three slopes steeper with LE for boys.	1
Kendrick	WWM/LE	----	----	G PD — LN	Vocabulary Word Reading Vocabulary Word-Study Skills All	Report inadequate.	1
Manning	WWM+PM/ WWM+PM+LE	----	----	----	----	Several ATI for boys, few for girls; all slopes shallower with LE.	1
Ruddell	WWM/LM+LE	LA	LA	----	----	Several ATI patterns, all slopes steeper with LE.	1
Ruddell	LM/LM+LE	----		----	----		1
Sheldon	WWM/LM+LE	SR	none	----	----	First-year report inadequate. Second-year report shows two ATI for girls, slopes steeper with LE.	1
Hahn	WWM/LE	PS	none	LN	Paragraph Meaning	Most slopes steeper with LE, steepest with LE+i.t.a.	1
Hahn	WWM/LE+i.t.a.	LA	G LA	none			1,2
Mazurkiewicz	WWM+LE/ WWM+LE+i.t.a.	PS LA	none	LN	Spelling	i.t.a. slope shallower for Paragraph Meaning only.	2

Table 8.1   A summary of project-by-project results in the Cooperative Reading Program

Project (by principal author)	Treatment contrast (label as inferred from original report)	Interactions called significant Lo analysis — Aptitudes[a] Gr. 1	Gr. 2	Bond-Dykstra analysis Aptitude(s)	Outcome(s)	Interactions of G inferred from original project report	Character of ATI hypotheses worth further test
Fry	WWM/WWM+DMS	PS?	PS?	—	—	PM+i.t.a. slopes steeper on para mean. Low boys best	2
Fry	WWM+DMS/ PM+i.t.a.	—	—	—	—	with WWM, low girls best	2, 3
Fry	WWM/PM+i.t.a.	none	none	PD LN	Paragraph Meaning Vocabulary	with DMS added.	2, 3
Tanyzer	WWM/PLM+i.t.a.	STM	none	PD	Paragraph Meaning	All WWM slopes shallower, all i.t.a. slopes shallower	2, 3
Tanyzer	PLM/PLM+i.t.a.	—	—	—	—	for girls. Special ability may interact.	2, 3
Hayes	WWM/PLM+i.t.a.	none	none	G	Paragraph Meaning	Several WWM slopes shallower.	2, 3
Hayes	PLM/PLM+i.t.a.	—	—	—	—	No interaction; sex not studied.	2, 3
Tanyzer	WWM/PLM	none?	none?	G PD	Paragraph Meaning Paragraph Meaning Word Reading Word Study Skills	All WWM slopes shallower.	3
Hayes	WWM/PLM	none	none	G	Vocabulary	Several WWM slopes shallower.	3
Wyatt	WWM/PLM	—	—	none		Ordinal on two outcomes for boys; PLM steeper.	3
Ruddell	WWM/LM	none	none	PD LN	Spelling Word Reading Word Study Skills	Probably no ATI.	4
Sheldon	WWM/LM	none?	none?	none		Slight or no ATI.	4

Table 8.1   A summary of project-by-project results in the Cooperative Reading Program

Project (by principal author)	Treatment contrast (label as inferred from original report)	Interactions called significant				Interactions of G inferred from original project report	Character of ATI hypotheses worth further test
		Lo analysis		Bond-Dykstra analysis			
		Aptitudes[a] Gr. 1	Gr. 2	Aptitude(s)	Outcome(s)		
Hayes	WWM/WWM+PLM	none?	none?	none	Spelling	Probably no ATI.	4
Bordeaux	WWM/WWM+PM	---	---	LN	Paragraph Meaning	Report inadequate.	4
Bordeaux	WWM/ WWM+PM+AV	---	---	---			4
Manning	WWM/WWM+PM	---	---	LN	Vocabulary	Probably no ATI	4
Murphy	WWM/WWM+PM	---	---	LN	Word Reading Paragraph Meaning	Report inadequate	4

[a] All relations took the first principal component as outcome.

WWM	= Whole-Word Method	G	= General Ability
LE	= Language Experience	PS	= Perceptual Speed
i.t.a.	= Initial Teaching Alphabet	LA	= Listening ability
PM	= Phonic Method	SR	= Space Relations
LM	= Linguistic Method	STM	= Short-Term Memory
PLM	= Combination of PM and LM	PD	= Phoneme Discrimination
AV	= Audio Visual	LN	= Letter Naming
DMS	= Diacritical Marking System		

? = labeling of treatment contrasts in Lo report makes assignment of this result uncertain

Code for hypotheses:

1. G slope is steeper in LE and shallower in WWM, primarily with Vocabulary and Paragraph Meaning as outcomes. LM, PM, Sex, and SES may moderate this interaction.

2. G slope is steeper in i.t.a. and shallower in WWM, primarily with Paragraph Meaning as outcome. PLM and sex may moderate this interaction. Special abilities may also interact.

3. G Slope is steeper in PLM and shallower in WWM, primarily with Vocabulary and Paragraph Meaning as outcomes. ATI is probably ordinal, with PLM giving higher average outcome. i.t.a. may moderate this interaction. Special abilities may also interact.

4. Conflicting evidence on G. Interaction (if any) is complex, involving special abilities.

been adequately tested, only that they are plausible and generally consistent with the Cooperative data. On these grounds they deserve further test.

The table begins with studies that contrasted WWM with LE; some of the latter added i.t.a. to an LE treatment. These studies shade into contrasts of WWM/PM or WWM/PLM, sometimes with i.t.a. added. Finally, there are contrasts of WWM/ LM and of WWM/WWM-plus-PM. We have indicated wherever possible what series of materials was used for each treatment (except for LE, which is a diffuse treatment with no particular series of readers regularly used). Below we treat each project in turn, the review more or less following the sequence of the table.

The WWM/LE contrast. Data from the Stauffer-Hammond (1965), Vilscek-Cleland (1964, 1968), and Hahn (1965) projects showed ATI, according to Lo, who considered them to be studies of different treatment contrasts. We, however, perceive much the same contrast in all three projects. Lo reported similar ATI in the Ruddell (1965) and Sheldon (1966, 1967) projects. Bond and Dykstra found ATI in two of these projects (Stauffer, Cleland) and in another not studied by Lo (Kendrick, 1966). A study by Manning (1966), where we found ATI, was not included by either Bond-Dykstra or Lo.

Hahn (1965) tried three methods in 36 classrooms ($N = 900$) roughly matched on SES and general ability. Two methods stressed LE with discussion and writing, one treatment being based on i.t.a. and one on traditional orthography. The third, more direct method was WWM, with books from Scott-Foresman, Ginn, American Book, and Houghton Mifflin. No one method was consistently superior. All correlations between initial IQ and later achievement were positive and higher in LE than in WWM. IQ gave much the same ATI pattern in Grades 2 ($N = 210$) and 3 ($N = 166$). Paragraph Meaning gave the largest spread in correlations: $r = 0.62$ for LE, 0.52 for LE-plus-i.t.a., and 0.47 for WWM. Tables of means within aptitude blocks, however, suggested that *slopes were steepest for LE-plus-i.t.a.* Highs did best and Lows worst in this treatment. Paragraph Meaning also gave a markedly disordinal interaction in both later grades. This interaction did not appear with the initial readiness tests.

Stauffer and Hammond (1965; $N = 433$) compared WWM (books from American and Ginn) and LE. Here, as in Hahn's study, LE included much discussion and writing. The ten LE classrooms included two from a black school and some from a partially integrated school, while the ten WWM classes were white. Pretest differences favored LE on Phoneme Discrimination and Alphabet Knowledge, but WWM on Identical Forms. Other pretest differences were not negligible (e.g., one-month differences in CA and MA, indicating that the LE group was younger and brighter). On posttests, several main effects favored LE. All pretests correlated higher with outcomes in LE than in WWM, and many interactions were disordinal. Since the regression slopes of three readiness tests onto MA differed from treatment to treatment at pretest, the univariate regressions are virtually impossible to interpret. Even so, the Hahn and Stauffer results agree in suggesting ATI: *shallower slopes on G in WWM, steeper slopes in LE.*

Imperfect support for this hypothesis came from the Cleland project (See Vilscek & Cleland, 1964, 1968.) WWM was not the standard Scott-Foresman treatment here, since multi-ethnic materials were included. Also, all students had IQs above 110; this suggests that "Low" groups here were more like the middle groups in some other projects. There were 649 children in 24 classes divided between WWM/LE. Grade 1 showed little in the way of ATI patterns consistent with the Hahn or Stauffer results. In fact, on Vocabulary LE was better than WWM for Lows! This ordinal ATI was statistically significant in the Bond-Dykstra analysis. However, in Cleland's follow-up studies for Grades 2 and 3, distinct ATI did appear that were consistent with Hahn's and Stauffer's results. *LE gave steeper slopes and WWM shallower, but only for boys.* Word Study Skills, Spelling, and Paragraph Meaning showed markedly disordinal ATI among boys in both later grades. Among girls the pattern was again ordinal, as in Grade 1: LE superior, and especially for Lows. The ATI were not significant in Grade 2, with $N = 396$, but they were significant in Grade 3 with $N = 251$.

Ruddell (1965) found some indication of a similar ATI. He studied 24 classrooms (533 urban middle-class and low-income children). He had a basic WWM treatment using McGraw-Hill books. To form two additional treatments, each of these was augmented with LE activities. MA was blocked in thirds. On the average, LM gave best results. There appear to have been *interaction effects on four of five Stanford scores.* In each case, LM-plus-LE appeared best for Highs. WWM produced higher Paragraph Meaning scores for Lows. On other outcomes LM succeeded best for Lows.

Sheldon (Sheldon & Lashinger, 1966; Sheldon, Nichols, & Lashinger, 1967) studied 467 low-to-middle-income children, urban and suburban. Treatments were WWM (Ginn), LM (Bloomfield-Barnhart books, with no illustrations), and a modified LM that included LE activities (Stern structural reading series). Seven classrooms were assigned to each. There were no treatment main-effects. Data for the first year of the study were not adequately reported, but we could examine the follow-up report for ATI ($N = 346$). Here we observed two ATI patterns among girls, none among boys. *The slopes of Word Meaning and Paragraph Meaning on girls' IQ were steepest with modified LM-plus-LE, slightly shallower with LM, and shallower still with WWM.* This is consistent with the Ruddell results. Two other outcomes showed no ATI among girls.

Manning's (1966) data, however, contradicted the hypothesis suggested by the other studies. He used the Ginn series for WWM. For another treatment, ability grouping and individualized training in PM skills was added to WWM. To all this, Manning added LE writing materials to form a third treatment. His 959 children came from a rural low-income population. Data were divided into four IQ blocks for analysis. WWM was inferior on the average. Manning reported no significant ATI on Stanford outcomes, but found four significant ATI on writing measures. In the tables of means, we perceived ATI on six of eleven outcomes among boys and on two of eleven among girls. All had the same trend: *steeper slope under WWM-plus-PM, shallower slope under WWM-plus-PM-plus-LE.*

The Kendrick (1966) results on the same hypothesis are equivocal because of weak analysis and sketchy reporting. Kendrick compared LE with WWM (Ginn and Sheldon Series; $N = 1302$). Pretest differences favored the LE group on G, while favoring **WWM** on readiness tests. Main effects were not consistent: **WWM** was superior on Stanford Paragraph Meaning and on speaking, and LE was superior on writing samples. Among 225 tests of ATI the number of significant findings did not exceed chance. The analysis was blocked anova, hence weak, and the data were not given in a form that allows us to probe further. Nor can we determine the nature of the ATI that Bond and Dykstra found significant in this study.

Considering all these analyses, their strengths and their weaknesses, we conclude that the data predominantly showed steep slopes in LE treatments and comparatively shallow slopes in **WWM** treatments. This effect was sometimes moderated by sex, at least when LE was combined with LM instruction. The effect was reversed in one study where LE was combined with PM in a low-income rural population. The outcomes most often affected were Vocabulary and Paragraph Meaning. The hypothesis is contrary to what our estimates of slopes from pooled data indicated. One difference is that this conclusion rests on studies that amalgamated LE with other treatments, as well as those using LE alone. In the pooled data, moreover, larger studies weighed more heavily; in our examination within projects, we took little account of sample size, since all studies were reasonably large. In view of the variations among individual projects, we regard the overall analyses (ours, as well as those of Lo and Bond-Dykstra) as uninformative.

Studies including i.t.a. Bond-Dykstra and Lo considered i.t.a. as a distinct treatment, to be contrasted with instruction using traditional orthography (TO). In practice, i.t.a. was included in several kinds of treatment: PM or PLM instruction in three projects, LE or **WWM**-plus-LE in others. This must be considered in interpreting results.

Hahn's study, mentioned above, combined i.t.a. with LE. Slopes onto G were steeper in these treatments than in **WWM**, as we said above. There were differences between LE-plus-i.t.a./LE-plus-TO. On three of five outcomes, the correlation of outcome with G was lower with i.t.a.; on one it was higher. These correlations may be misleading, however; inferring from the block means *the slopes in LE-plus-i.t.a. were as steep and occasionally steeper than those in LE.*

Combining treatments like LE and i.t.a. may intensify interaction, bringing both G and special abilities into play. Lo found that some special abilities interacted in studies of i.t.a.; hence, it is possible that G is relevant to learning in LE, with special skills operating also when i.t.a. is used. In the Mazurkiewicz (1965) data, for example, Lo found two special abilities, PS and LA, interacting in the first year (but not in the second). Mazurkiewicz had compared two **WWM**-plus-LE treatments, one using i.t.a. In the course of his work, he matched 163 pairs of Ss on IQ and sex. In the data on G and on outcomes for these pairs (his appendix), we observed an ATI pattern for one outcome only. *Adding i.t.a. to WWM-plus-LE seemed to reduce the positive slope of Paragraph Meaning onto G; the slope was steep with TO.* Beyond this, we are blocked. Mazurkiewicz did not report special ability scores for his cases, and Lo did not describe the interactions he found significant. Hence, we cannot contrast the effects of G and special abilities.

Fry, Tanyzer, and Hayes added i.t.a. to PM or PLM. Fry (1965) chose the Sheldon Readers (WWM) and for another treatment added a diacritical marking system (DMS) to these books. A third group received PM-plus-i.t.a. (This same treatment appeared in the Tanyzer and Hayes projects.) Seven classes were assigned to each method (N = 396). There was no main effect for treatment. The report provided only one table, on Paragraph Meaning, relevant to our purposes. While the ATI was not significant, the means for three IQ blocks showed a distinctly disordinal pattern, *the slope being steepest for PM-plus-i.t.a.* With the sample divided by sex, the steeper slope of PM-plus-i.t.a. appeared in both sexes; the shallowest slope was in WWM-plus-DMS among girls and in WWM among boys.

Tanyzer and Alpert (1965) divided 643 first-graders into three IQ levels to compare PLM (Lippincott series)/PLM-plus-i.t.a./WWM (Scott-Foresman readers). The composite Stanford score showed main effects for IQ in all three methods, and both PLM treatments gave better average results than WWM. ATI was not significant in the author's blocked anova of the composite or part-scores within sexes. But we perceive clear indications of ATI among girls. On each part-score, girls showed a distinctly steeper slope onto IQ in PLM than in PLM-plus-i.t.a. For each outcome the regressions crossed within the IQ range. The WWM condition, with a shallow slope, was significantly inferior to PLM at all IQ levels. Boys showed no such interactions; slopes for them were often less steep than those for girls. Thus, despite the Tanyzer-Alpert statistics, we judge that *G probably interacted with PLM-TO/PLM-i.t.a. for girls.*

Hayes and Nemeth (1965) studied the same PLM/PLM-i.t.a./WWM contrast as Tanyzer and Alpert, with the same kinds of materials. A fourth treatment added phonics workbooks to Scott-Foresman books. With 415 Ss, PLM and PLM-plus-i.t.a. were superior for high-IQ and middle-IQ Ss, and PLM-plus-i.t.a. was superior for low-IQ Ss. The results were similar in the Grade 2 follow-up. Slopes were about alike in PLM-TO and PLM-plus-i.t.a. treatments. In WWM, slopes tended to be shallow. Sometimes a WWM regression crossed that for PLM, the former being better for Ss of low IQ. This was the case with several measures of silent and oral reading. Thus, though the authors found ATI not significant (and did not analyze by sex), *the findings are much like those of the Tanyzer and the Fry projects.*

ATI do seem to appear with i.t.a./TO contrasts. The strongest hypothesis is that adding i.t.a. to PM, PLM, or LE increases the AT slope (Fry, Tanyzer, Hayes, Hahn). Adding i.t.a. makes for a greater departure from the shallow slope of WWM. Thus, Highs are helped by i.t.a. while Lows are hurt, at least on some outcome measures. But this picture is complicated by the Tanyzer and Mazurkiewicz findings. Tanyzer's girls showed a shallower slope in PLM-plus-i.t.a. than in PLM-plus-TO. And Mazurkiewicz found that adding i.t.a. to a combination of WWM and LE reduced the AT slope on the very outcome measure that gave other investigators some of their steepest slopes. There is the further possibility that i.t.a. and DMS bring special abilities into play.

The WWM/PLM contrast. It is impossible to disentangle i.t.a. effects from the basic WWM/PM or WWM/PLM comparison. We are inclined to think that ability relates strongly to performance in PM and PLM with any orthography; both

Tanyzer and Hayes found steeper slopes in PLM-TO as well as PLM-plus-i.t.a. One
other study adds further data. Wyatt (1965) studied 30 classes of urban and
suburban children (N = 633) divided among three treatments: WWM (using Scott-
Foresman plus other readers), PLM (Lippincott plus other linguistic readers), and
sex-grouping within WWM. Main effects favored PLM. While ATI were not significant, some ordinal ATI patterns appeared, particularly on two outcomes for
boys; *PLM gave steeper slopes.* Thus, the hypothesis of ATI with WWM/PM or
WWM/PLM appears tenable.

The WWM/LM contrast. The results on WWM/LM differ markedly from those
on WWM/PLM, where PLM is based on Lippincott books. The Ruddell and Sheldon
studies (above) do not indicate ATI with WWM/LM. Ruddell's data contained
some divergent regression patterns, but these seemed to be more a consequence
of mixing LE with LM than of LM alone.

The Bond-Dykstra tables indicated ATI of special abilities with WWM/LM, but
no report provides enough data to describe these. Sheldon did find heterogeneous
slopes on two of four outcomes among girls, but the largest difference in slope in
each case came from the WWM/LM-plus-LE contrast, with the LM slope intermediate. LM alone did not contrast strongly.

Moreover, the Schneyer project found ATI of a sort quite different from those
found in contrasts of WWM/PLM. Schneyer, Schultz, and Cowen (1966) compared Scott-Foresman WWM with an LM treatment based on the work of Fries.
There were 674 first-graders, divided for the analysis on IQ and sex. Apparently,
for several Stanford subtests, *the WWM slope was steeper,* WWM being significantly
superior to LM for Highs. At the end of Grade 2, a slightly steeper slope in WWM
again appeared. Among Lows, differences between methods were not significant.
For middle-IQ Ss, one of five part-scores showed significant differences favoring
WWM, and for Highs, all five part-scores showed such differences; one of these,
on Word-Study Skills, is of clear practical importance. Bond-Dykstra also found
ATI in this study, but on Vocabulary only. The fact that the WWM group started
out with higher average MA should be noted.

A study not in the Cooperative Program lends support to Schneyer's otherwise
isolated finding. Edward (1964) compared WWM/WWM-plus-LM for 810 parochial-
school fourth-graders. WWM-LM was generally the better treatment. The report
gave few details, but it suggested that the difference was smallest for those with
high nonverbal IQs. If so, *WWM produced the steeper regression slope.*

Thus, Schneyer's remarkable result, supported only by Edward, suggests that
LM works in a way opposite to that of PM and PLM, the other methods of its
genre. This we find rather implausible. Apart from this possibility the evidence
is that ATI do not occur with G as aptitude and WWM/LM as the treatment
contrast.

Mixtures of WWM and PM. Four projects added phonics to WWM, but the
reports of two of these (Murphy, 1965; Bordeaux & Shope, n.d.) were inadequate
for our purposes. Lo did not include these studies in his work, so we have only
the Bond-Dykstra conclusion of no ATI. Four of eleven ATI were significant in
the Manning study, all on outcome measures other than Stanford scores. But these
seem to result more from the addition of LE to WWM than from the addition of

PM. Bond and Dykstra reported ATI of Letter Naming in both the Murphy and Manning data, but we lack data to describe the interaction. Hayes included WWM-plus-PLM alongside the WWM/PLM contrast mentioned earlier. WM-PLM yielded slopes similar to WWM alone. A study outside the Cooperative Program (Sabaroff, 1963) tried similar mixtures of WWM and PM. The finding of no ATI cannot be taken seriously with only 54 Ss divided among three treatments. One would have to conclude on the basis of these studies that ATI of G with WWM/WWM-plus-PM are highly unlikely. However, a reanalysis of data from one Cooperative study not included above reopens the question.

The Reid project (H. C. Reid & Beltramo, 1965) had compared seven treatments: WWM (Ginn), PM (Houghton-Mifflin) two idiosyncratic methods, and three kinds of combined methods, one of which was essentially WWM-plus-PM. The study did not appear in the Bond-Dykstra or the Lo reanalyses. We ignored it, since the original report gave no data relevant to ATI. But Newman and Lohnes (1972); see also Cooley & Lohnes, 1976, p. 68) reanalyzed a portion of the original data, as part of a longer term follow-up study, with a remarkable result. Scores on 310 Ss, who represented the lowest third of the original sample on reading readiness, generated nine aptitude factors, of which the two largest were G and Alphabet (including Letter Naming). From the outcomes the investigators derived three orthogonal factors: General Intellectual Development, Vocabulary, and Paragraph Reading. This last step is an improvement over all previous analyses which used the Stanford subtests individually or in a single composite. With these clarified measures, regression analysis unearthed a striking ATI. In WWM, the standardized regression slope of Paragraph Reading on G was +0.55; in WWM-plus-PM it was -0.40. When the Alphabet factor (which is presumably alphabet knowledge with G partialed out) was added to the multiple, its weights were -0.05 and +0.30, respectively. The interpretation of this interaction would be that, among children showing low overall readiness, with Paragraph Reading as criterion, Ss high in G do best in WWM, while Ss low in G but high in Alphabet can profit from the addition of PM training to WWM.

This isolated finding does not negate the other studies cited above, particularly since it is based on only one-third of the data from one study. Rather, it suggests an improved model for reanalyzing studies of this and other contrasts. Multiple-regression methods, using orthogonal factors for outcome, provide a powerful analysis, as we have argued throughout this book. The Newman-Lohnes application is better tuned than were the earlier reanalyses, or our rereading of original reports, to the apparent character of the data. Vocabulary and Paragraph Meaning were the outcomes most frequently cited as entering ATI. The ATI hypotheses so far gleaned from the Cooperative data could be reexamined with this approach, on a project-by-project basis.

Subsidiary questions

Various projects in the Cooperative Program dealt with subsidiary questions that connect with other bodies of research. We shall treat only a selection of these questions.

Sex as a moderator. Investigators of reading often expect results to be mode-rated by sex. But Bond and Dykstra found no significant Sex x Treatment inter-action in the pooled data. Girls showed greater reading readiness at the start of Grade 1, and this seemed to account for subsequent sex differences in achieve-ment. No treatment had a particular within-sex effect. As noted above, a few studies did suggest that sex might moderate the relation of outcome to IQ, but only one project showed this clearly; there, ATI occurred for girls but not for boys (Tanyzer & Alpert, 1965). Wyatt's Cooperative study (1965) taught boys and girls separately, adapting WWM materials appropriately and comparing this with ungrouped WWM and PLM. This did bring boys to the achievement level of girls, whereas they were inferior to girls in other treatments. But for boys as well as girls, PLM with no grouping was better than WWM with grouping by sex. Sex seemed not to influence regressions onto pretests appreciably.

Sex may interact under specific conditions. McNeil (1964) studied programmed (machine) instruction in reading during kindergarten, followed by conventional teaching in Grade 1. Whereas boys and girls (N = 93) had been equal on a pretest, *the boys were superior after PI but inferior after four months in Grade 1.* Both differences were significant. The author speculated that PI reduced social distractions, helping boys. It appeared that the live teacher did not give boys as much opportunity to learn as girls.

A similar conclusion resulted from research on CAI in beginning reading (Fletcher & R. Atkinson, 1972). Forty-four like-sex pairs matched on a reading pretest were divided between CAI/conventional teaching. Ss in CAI spent about 10 minutes per day at the terminal from January to June. Other instruction was similar for the two groups. Posttests included the Stanford Achievement Test and the Cooperative Reading Test. *Boys seem to have been much better off with CAI than with conventional teaching;* CAI was beneficial to girls, but not so markedly.

Morgan and Light (1963) compared PM/WWM. One study (N = 40) covered a full school year; a spelling test and the Gates Basic Reading Test were the de-pendent variables. Another study (N = 100) extended for three years, using the California Achievement Test in reading as criterion. There were main effects favoring WWM and favoring girls. While sex did not interact significantly with method, N was very small. On just two of ten criterion measures girls seemed slightly better off with WWM, boys with PM. *If there was interaction it was quite weak.*

It is at least possible that the tighter control over instructional elements in PM, PI, and CAI helps boys. But that is not what the Tanyzer-Alpert results indicated, or the results from a small study by Hartley to be presented later (p. 242). A test of the hypothesis could be derived from a study like that of L. W. Johnson (1966). He compared two treatments during the first 100 days of Grade 1. One, PI, was largely self-paced; the second, phonetic demonstrations, was teacher-centered and teacher-paced. Six sections were composed of boys only; in six others, boys and girls were mingled (N = 147). There was no treatment effect on the Stanford Achievement Test in reading. *Low-IQ boys did far better in a mixed-sex group,* while Highs were slightly better off in an all-boy group.

This is partly consistent with Wyatt's result. But instructional treatment was ignored in Johnson's blocked anova, since some cells had only one observation. This difficulty could have been circumvented by regression analysis.

We are left with the impression that sex is not the all-important moderator in reading that some have assumed it to be.

Individualization and ability grouping. Some studies have looked at the effects of dealing with students individually instead of, or in addition to, teaching in groups. One of the Cooperative Projects (MacDonald, T. Harris, & Rarick, 1966) combined WWM and PM in Grade 1. Of 20 classes ($N = 540$), they assigned 10 to a condition in which all formal instruction was individual. Teachers and pupils met for 20-minute conferences about twice a week. Each teacher individualized in his own manner. All used some group sessions for oral reading. The second condition (group instruction) allowed for some subgrouping of pupils, but the teachers followed conventional procedures during 20-minute reading periods, twice a day.

There was a very weak, nonsignificant ATI of IQ. The slope was slightly steeper under the individual condition. Highs achieved slightly more with individualization than with group work; the opposite was true for Lows. The group method produced higher achievement at all levels on the Metropolitan Readiness Score (significantly so among Highs). The data taken as a whole imply that the group method was a trifle better and that *ATI were negligible.* Nothing is known about within-teacher slopes, which might have differed in a meaningful way.

D. Spencer and Moquin (1965; 1966) tried a similar comparison of individualized, primarily PM, teaching and conventional WWM (Scott-Foresman). With 347 children children in Grade 1, some main effects favored individualization. No trace of ATI appeared. In a Grade 2 follow-up, a few slight ATI patterns appeared, with shallower slopes for WWM; these must be regarded as negligible.

Marita's Cooperative study (1965) gave different results. Here, whole-class LE was compared with two kinds of ability-grouping, one of which included individualized work and teacher conferences. The small groups were composed of three to five children, working with WWM (Ginn) materials. There were 810 children distributed across 32 classes. Ability grouping produced higher reading outcome on the average. On three Stanford subtests (including arithmetic) slopes were steeper with the whole-class organization. Lows (MA $<$ 77) did much better with either form of ability grouping than with whole-class LE, with no difference among methods for Highs. Other outcomes yielded no ATI pattern. (One apparent exception is obviously a typographical error.)

Ungraded programs presumably allow greater individualization and these have been compared with conventional graded and/or ability grouped programs. In one such study, Hopkins, Oldridge, and Williamson (1965) set out to compare graded/nongraded primary programs, using posttests on reading vocabulary and comprehension. There were 20 nongraded and 25 graded classrooms (from four schools). Only children who had spent their previous school careers in the same (graded) program were included in the analysis. The California Test of Mental Maturity and California Reading Test were administered at the start of Grade 3, and the reading test was readministered at the end of Grade 3. At pretest there was an average difference, on both reading vocabulary and comprehension, favoring the group who remained in the graded program. Ancova showed no effect of non-graded organization. The regression of posttest on aptitude did not differ between graded and nongraded classes, indicating *no ATI*. Scores collected at the start of Grade 4 yielded similar results.

Brody (1970) contrasted performance of 268 first- and second-graders in a graded school and in two ungraded schools on Stanford tests in reading and arithmetic. With a median split on IQ, there were ordinal interactions for reading, not for arithmetic. In Grade 1, Lows scored highest in ungraded schools, often doing as well as their abler schoolmates; among Highs the condition means were near equal. In Grade 2, the condition means did not differ among Lows, but Highs did better with nongrading. It may be that nongrading is particularly helpful to Lows at the start of school and to Highs during the second school year; but the data are far from conclusive.

One other study lends support to this hypothesis, but two others do not. Green and Riley (1963) evaluated nongraded reading instruction. *S*s from several grades were mixed during the reading period, groups being somewhat homogeneous in reading level. Four schools participated, providing 38 classes ranging from Grade 3 to 7. Fourth-graders provided most of the data. Stanford Achievement Tests at the beginning and end of the year provided a gain score. Data for a control group were obtained from the records of similar students during the previous year. This group was matched to experimentals on several background variables. The non-graded plan proved superior to grouping by grade. Among fourth-graders *IQ correlated 0.39 with gain in the experimental group and 0.24 in the control group.* This difference could be of some importance, especially considering the large *N;* but the report is insufficient for ATI analysis.

Kierstead (1963) compared a nongraded plan with ability grouping within Grades 3 to 8. (*N* = 258). Iowa Tests of Basic Skills (Reading Comprehension and Vocabulary scores) served as pretests and posttests. He found graded ability grouping *somewhat superior for students high on IQ and pretest,* with no difference between conditions for Lows. Slope differences were nonsignificant, but the analysis lacked power. And Skapski (1961) compared ungraded reading instruction in one school with ability grouping in two other schools for third-graders (*N* = 110). With Paragraph Meaning as outcome, ungraded *S*s did best; there was *no ATI*.

Another study pitted graded ability grouping against conventional grading. Berkun, Swanson, and Sawyer (1966) reorganized 18 of 46 classes in Grades 3, 4, and 5 into homogeneous ability groups within grades (*N* approximated 1100). The California Reading Test was administered at the beginning and end of the year. For analysis, *S*s were classed as above and below the school mean on the pretest. Main effects favored ability grouping in Grades 3 and 5; there were *no ATI*.

Treatments characterized as nongraded or ability-grouped or individualized may be similar or quite different. One cannot tell from most reports just what form individualization takes in such conditions. The studies reviewed here hardly justify a strong conclusion. If there is an advantage for abler students in individual work or in homogeneous ability groups, the effect is slight. And the Marita and Brody data suggest that individualization can be effective for Lows.

Readiness training. Training for reading readiness is one of the commonest examples of differentiating instruction to fit individuals. Schools divide primary children on the basis of test performance, sending the advanced group into reading instruction and giving the others a "readiness training" that is essentially remedial. This policy deserves to be tested thoroughly by an ATI design, but we find only three substantial studies, two of them from the Cooperative program. The fact that their findings are utterly contradictory only points up the need for solid research.

The two Cooperative projects are those of Spache *et al.* (1966) and Horn (1966). Spache *et al.* studied 816 first-graders, black and white. Experimental *S*s received intensive reading-readiness instruction. At two month intervals, readiness tests were administered. Pupils who reached the 75th percentile on two of three reading-readiness skills moved into regular reading instruction at that point. The others received further readiness training until the next test date. In March, regular reading instruction began for those whose readiness scores were still below criterion. Control *S*s in other school districts received only regular reading instruction from the start. The Stanford Achievement Test in reading served as the year-end criterion.

Control whites achieved better than the whites with differentiated treatment. Perhaps the adaptive program cut too far into the time for formal reading instruction; a test given a year later might tell a different story. Among blacks, the readiness training produced better results than unadapted reading instruction. *This significant Race x Treatment interaction was ordinal. Sex, age, reading readiness, and IQ did not interact* with treatment, within races.

Horn dealt with Spanish-speaking first-graders, plus a limited number of English monolinguals. He divided 28 classes (*N* = 584) among three treatments: intensive language instruction in oral-aural English, using "culture fair" science materials as the vehicle/similar instruction in oral-aural Spanish/control instruction in science without special language work, but with work to develop reading readiness. The across-classes regression of posttest (Metropolitan Reading Readiness) on ability (in Spanish) was evaluated. (For an across-classroom effect, even this large sample of children lacks power.) There was little or no main effect; an ATI was significant. While all three regression slopes were positive, that among classes receiving only readiness instruction (third treatment) was much shallower. The regressions crossed near the average of the ability distribution. *Low-ability classes apparently could make better use of readiness instruction than language instruction.* The reverse was true among *high-ability classes; oral-aural instruction was best* for them, particularly if given in English. The printed posttest on perceptual aspects of reading probably gave an inadequate evaluation of oral-aural instruction, however.

Kelley and Chen (1967) gave readiness instruction to some kindergartners while an equivalent group began reading instruction (*N* = 197). End-of-year posttests measured reading skills, reading habits, and attitude to school. Direct reading instruction gave better results. Both a general mental test and a readiness test correlated positively with all outcomes save self-reported attitude. There was *no significant ATI,* but achievement-on-aptitude slopes were somewhat steeper in the formal-reading group. This weakly supports Horn's result.

All in all, the data suggest that weaker students can use readiness training, but the effects are neither consistent nor particularly impressive. How can it be that a widely adopted and seemingly sensible grouping practice should be so little supported by tangible evidence?

A study of teacher training. One Cooperative study fits nowhere else in this review, yet deserves mention for its implications. Heilman (1965) provided in-service training for 15 randomly chosen teachers. The training sessions included discussion of research findings on teaching methods and much sharing of ideas and experiences among participants. It is reported that these teachers tried a variety of new classroom approaches during the year. They sought increased individualization and enrichment of learning activities, introduced mixtures of LE, i.t.a., and PI materials, and visited one another's classrooms. The basic teaching method (and also of 15 control teachers) was WWM. Data for 603 students showed significant main effects favoring teachers in the training program on four of five Stanford outcomes, but the mean differences were only one to three raw-score points.

We determined regression slopes from r's given by Heilman. (See Table 8.2.) There were clear interactions, some of which were disordinal. With more than 100 Ss per slope, this finding is worth pursuing. For boys, slopes were consistently steeper when teachers were not in the training program; slope differences were greatest with G as aptitude. Girls followed the same pattern, except that on two outcome measures steeper slopes appeared with trained teachers. It is not clear that weight should be attached to the sex difference, especially since there was inconsistency of slope within girls on one outcome. An important addition to this analysis would have been to study within-class slopes and to relate results to what each teacher actually did, whether specially trained or not. Teacher variation is important in its own right, and evidence on each teacher would allow us to connect these findings to previous work on particular teaching methods in the Cooperative program.

Studies of special skills

According to Lo, some special aptitudes entered into interactions. The Perceptual Speed, Space, and Listening factors, in particular, seemed to interact with the choice between WWM and PLM, PM, LM, or i.t.a. Bond and Dykstra looked at Phoneme Discrimination and Letter Naming in addition to IQ, and they also turned up a few ATI. There is in this a hint that auditory/visual distinctions may be important. Some further research has pursued this idea, as well as the analysis of other, fairly specific word skills. We review these efforts next.

Auditory/visual contrasts. Auditory and visual skills develop unevenly in children, a fact considered in diagnosing those who make slow progress in reading. It is natural to suggest that the instruction emphasize visual processing for some

Table 8.2   Correlations and regression slopes relating outcome to aptitude within classes of two kinds of teachers

Aptitude	Outcome	Sex	Ss with teachers in inservice training		Ss with teachers not in inservice training	
			r	b	r	b
Pintner-Cunningham	Word reading	M	0.41	0.34	0.55	0.42
		F	0.37	0.30	0.48	0.41
	Paragraph meaning	M	0.32	0.33	0.55	0.56
		F	0.32	0.37	0.47	0.53
	Vocabulary	M	0.51	0.37	0.62	0.52
		F	0.51	0.43	0.40	0.35
	Spelling	M	0.29	0.21	0.46	0.34
		F	0.22	0.18	0.47	0.36
	Word-Study Skills	M	0.44	0.56	0.40	0.63
		F	0.33	0.44	0.29	0.56
Metropolitan Reading Readiness	Word reading	M	0.56	0.26	0.67	0.27
		F	0.52	0.23	0.59	0.26
	Paragraph meaning	M	0.47	0.27	0.27	0.34
		F	0.53	0.33	0.61	0.35
	Vocabulary	M	0.59	0.24	0.60	0.27
		F	0.59	0.27	0.54	0.24
	Spelling	M	0.45	0.19	0.60	0.23
		F	0.47	0.21	0.63	0.25
	Word-Study Skills	M	0.55	0.40	0.50	0.42
		F	0.52	0.37	0.31	0.31

Data from Heilman, 1965.

children and auditory processing for others. The Robinson and Bateman studies below failed to find interactions for such treatments, and Stallings' suggestive results can be interpreted in terms of general abilities.

Bateman (1967) considered two scales of the Illinois Test of Psycholinguistic Abilities (ITPA). Ss higher in auditory memory than in visual memory she labeled "auditory." Those with the opposite pattern she called "visual." Ss were assigned to Lippincott (PLM)/Scott-Foresman (WWM), the treatments being expected to suit "auditory" and "visual" Ss, respectively. Groups were matched in IQ and sex. (N = 182.) At the end of Grade 1, reading and spelling were tested. PLM was consistently superior to WWM even for "visual" Ss. "Auditory" Ss achieved better than "visual" Ss regardless of method. There was no ATI.

From a pool of 448 first-grade Ss, Robinson (1972) chose 162 children who represented extreme groups on tests of auditory and/or visual perception. About half the Ss were in school systems using WWM (Scott-Foresman, Ginn) and half in schools using Lippincott PLM. Four districts, 11 schools, and 22 teachers participated. Forms of the Metropolitan Achievement Test in reading were given at the end of Grades 1 and 3. One other outcome measure was added at each grade. The sample reduced to 116 by Grade 3. There was no significant difference between methods on the Metropolitan, nor were there interactions for ability groups or sex. The low-visual, high-auditory group appeared to do better in PLM on both Grade-3 outcomes, but no ATI conclusion was justified.

In a similar vein, Stallings (1970) hypothesized that learning by PLM requires "sequencing" ability—the ability to construct and reconstruct strings of letters and sounds from short-term memory. She further distinguished auditory/visual sequencing. Children deficient in these skills would not learn well from PLM, she thought and might show anxious and avoidant reactions as well. Those with sufficient sequencing ability could be expected to do quite well in PLM. Stallings reasoned that WWM makes no demand on sequencing and would be preferable for children low in this ability. But the opposite hypothesis could be argued (and was argued by Snow when the study was planned). PLM might make sequencing proficient by providing training in it. Moreover, word recognition may require sequencing even if the learner is never shown how letter sequences are assembled. By this hypothesis Ss would do well in WWM only if already capable of sequencing. Hence, a positive relation of sequencing ability to outcome under WWM might be predicted. Lows might be expected to do well in PLM, perhaps even better than their more able peers who would be inhibited by extensive practice in PLM. Hence, a zero or negative relation might be expected here. Other sources provided anecdotal evidence that some subscales of ITPA relate negatively to reading achievement under PLM.

Three studies were conducted to examine these competing hypotheses (Stallings, 1970; Stallings & Snow, in preparation). Two experiments were pilot studies, each with only 20 Ss randomly divided between treatments. In the third, a large-scale study in the public schools, random assignment was not possible.

The pilot studies were conducted in successive years in a small private elementary school. Each year, the same procedure was followed. The aptitude measures were auditory and visual sequencing tests, both those from ITPA and newly constructed ones. After aptitude scores were collected, 20 first-graders were divided into comparable groups. During the first two months of school, one group received PLM (but based on the Fries materials called LM by Bond and Dykstra) while the other group was taught by Scott-Foresman WWM. Children moved into these two groups each day for reading instruction (at opposite ends of the large classroom), but worked as a united class during the rest of the school day. Two teachers (unaware of Ss' sequencing scores) alternated between the two groups daily, to balance teacher effects. The experiment was terminated after two months so that the instruction could be modified for children not showing progress. At this time the California Achievement Test in Reading (CAT) was administered; a total score and a Reading Comprehension criterion were obtained. The Murphy-Durrell Reading Readiness Analysis served as a supplementary pretest and posttest in the first study. In addition, observers checked Ss periodically for behavior suggestive of "learning avoidance." Indicators included excessive fidgeting, distracting neighbors, fighting, chair-rocking, etc. The frequency of avoidant acts during reading instruction was treated as an outcome, though it is perhaps more nearly an intermediate variable. This frequency correlated 0.82 with similar observations made in the children's other classes.

There were no main effects for treatment. Table 8.3 presents regression coefficients for the interactions of primary interest in each of the two pilot studies. The number of cases did not warrant multivariate analysis, nor can significance tests be taken seriously. Frequency of learning avoidance related to the ITPA score for Visual Sequencing, but differently in the two treatments. The similar result in the two pilot years is a clear replication. In PLM, students High in ITPA Visual Sequencing were attentive in their work; in WWM, they tended to be inattentive. Stallings' own test of visual sequencing did not give this result in the first pilot study, but the result did appear in the second. "Avoidance" was not significantly related to accomplishment, and the reading posttests showed no interaction. For the pretests of auditory sequencing, there were scattered, inconsistent interactions.

ble 8.3   **Regression slopes relating reading performance**
to sequencing abilities in two pilot studies

		Outcome measure					
*titude *asure	*Treat-ment*	*Frequency of learning avoidance after two months*		*CAT Reading Comprehension*		*CAT Total*	
		Study 1	*Study 2*	*Study 1*	*Study 2*	*Study 1*	*Study 2*
PA Visual	PLM	3.93*	3.90	-0.29	0.35	-1.49	2.00
quencing	WWM	-1.09	-5.20*	-0.38	0.66	-0.79	3.44
allings Visual	PLM	-1.50	1.99	0.08	0.80	1.00	3.32
quencing	WWM	-0.97	-5.32*	-0.01	0.86	-0.15	4.11
PA Auditory	PLM	2.02	0.53	0.01	0.43	-0.61	1.92
quencing	WWM	0.92	-0.74	0.53	0.15	1.17*	0.68
allings Auditory	PLM	-3.16	-0.38	-0.42	0.79	-1.04	3.07
quencing	WWM	-1.15	1.05	0.91*	0.41	1.48	-0.01

ta from Stallings, 1970. N = 20 in each study. Asterisks refer to statistical comparisons, of regression pes, the asterisk being placed alongside the steeper slope (positive or negative); $p < .05$

In the public-school study, N was 246. Six PLM classrooms followed a new curriculum developed by the school system. Seven other classrooms were assigned to WWM. Classroom visits confirmed that teachers adhered adequately to the treatment plan. Again, there were aptitude measures—the sequencing tests and the Macmillan Reading Readiness Test—at the start of the school year and observations of learning avoidance during later months. January posttesting employed the CAT, the sequencing tests (for a second time), and a reading test based on phonic-linguistic content (RTLA). There were 10 aptitude measures and 11 dependent measures, counting part and total scores. Stallings (1970) pooled classes and compared regressions between treatments. Of 110 statistical tests, 49 showed significant ATI. There were also main effects for sex, girls being superior to boys on some criteria. Table 8.4 gives the ATI findings of principal interest.

The tests of visual sequencing yielded significant ATI resembling that found in the pilot studies, with learning avoidance as dependent variable. Highs showed more learning avoidance under PLM, while Lows showed more avoidance under

Table 8.4   Regression slopes relating reading performance to sequencing abilities

Aptitude measure	Treatment	Frequency of learning avoidance after one month	after two months	CAT Reading Comprehension	CAT Total	R
ITPA Visual	PLM	−0.01	0.14*	0.29	1.27	
Sequencing	WWM	−0.28*	−0.12	0.12	0.49	
Stallings Visual	PLM	0.08	0.07	0.50*	2.17*	
Sequencing	WWM	−0.46*	−0.20*	0.16	0.57	
ITPA Auditory	PLM	0.07	0.02	0.26*	1.19*	
Sequencing	WWM	0.08	−0.05	0.03	0.27	
Stallings Auditory	PLM	0.11	−0.01	0.31*	1.15	
Sequencing	WWM	−0.03	−0.01	0.10	0.53	

Data from Stallings, 1970. $N = 246$. Asterisks refer to statistical comparisons of regression slopes, the asterisk being placed alongside the steeper slope (positive or negative) $p < .05$

WWM. Reading achievement gave a result unlike that in the pilot studies. Here, both tests of auditory sequencing and Stallings's own visual sequencing test had significant ATI effects on the CAT scores and on RTLA. All slopes were positive, with those for PLM steeper. Highs did better in PLM than in WWM and, despite the main effect favoring PLM, several regression lines crossed. In the pilot studies, the slope differences went in both directions. We consider the larger public-school study as deserving more weight.

In the public-school data there was another ATI pattern (not anticipated). Though weak, this effect is notable for its implications concerning development of aptitude. The four principal aptitude tests were given both before and after treatment. There was no important effect on means and variances, but the pretest-posttest relations seemed to show treatment effects. Correlations between visual pretests and auditory posttests, and between auditory pretests and visual post-tests, were distinctly higher in PLM than in WWM. Thus, the PLM treatment may have reduced some of the separation of visual and auditory abilities. There is reason to believe, however, that this result is due in part to differences between the treatment groups at the start of the study. A new experiment with random assignment would be needed to check this out.

Simple regression analyses cannot make parsimonious sense of complex data. In a reexamination, composite variables entered into a multiple-regression analysis (Stallings & Snow, in preparation). A composite aptitude, C, was defined as the sum of the four principal pretests, and a bipolar score, D, was defined as the sum of the visual pretests minus the sum of the auditory pretests. The composite presumably represents a general sequencing ability similar to rote serial learning. Learning avoidance, CAT, and RTLA served as criteria. Treatment (T) was coded as PLM = 1, WWM = -1. Predictor variables were entered in the following order: T, C, D, TC, TD, CD, TCD. Preliminary analyses had indicated that sexes could be pooled without loss of information. The computer program evaluated the further contributions of sex and the four specific aptitude scores to prediction, but they added little.

The results in Table 8.5 were interpreted with the aid of scatterplots. Within-

Table 8.5   Multiple-regression equations with composite sequencing scores C and D as predictors

Outcome measure	Predictor[a]	Regression coefficient[b]	Cumulative R^2
	constant	13.72	
	T	-10.97*	0.11*
	C	0.60*	0.30*
CAT	D	- 0.41	0.30
Total	TC	0.26*	0.33*
	TD	- 0.11	0.34
	CD	0.01	0.34
	TCD	0.00	0.34
	constant	- 4.03	
	T	-12.11*	0.08*
	C	0.43*	0.25*
RTLA	D	- 0.49	0.25
	TC	0.23*	0.29*
	TD	- 0.33	0.29
	CD	0.01*	0.31*
	TCD	0.00	0.31
	constant	9.49	
	T	- 0.94	0.00
Frequency of	C	- 0.01	0.00
learning	D	- 0.06	0.00
avoidance	TC	0.02	0.01
at two months	TD	0.18	0.03
	CD	0.00	0.03
	TCD	0.00	0.04

Data are the same as in Table 8.4.

[a] T = Treatment; C is an additive composite; D is a visual-minus-auditory difference.

[b] Asterisk indicates stepwise F-to-enter significant ($p < .05$).

class slopes of both CAT and RTLA on D proved to be heterogeneous in PLM classes, so teachers must have influenced these relationships substantially. All other within-treatment slopes (for both C and D) were homogeneous. Two inter-actions of general sequencing ability with treatment were significant. The D variable added little to the prediction or the interaction. The simple *ATI effects reported earlier are to be interpreted primarily as results of a general ability to store and recall,* not of skills specific to one sense modality.

Learning avoidance was not well predicted and interactions were not statistically significant. It appears that the ATI reported earlier arose more from D than from C. *Learners with visual skill superior to auditory showed more avoidance in PLM. The reverse was true for WWM.*

The implication of all this is that PLM makes the strong stronger and the weak weaker, relative to what they would have accomplished in WWM. PLM may also have consolidated auditory-visual skill, perhaps by promoting transfer. In the process, PLM produced a comparatively high frequency of learning avoidance in able learners, while WWM had this effect on the less able. But learning avoidance was uncorrelated with accomplishment. Perhaps the interpretation of this variable needs reconsideration, since some kinds of bodily activities may well accompany effective learning in some pupils. All these results deserve to be checked in formal experiments.

Specific analytic skills. Research on reading has been moving toward finer analyses of component skills and stimulus characteristics. Some of this work has examined ATI. We cite here a few investigations that bear on the PM/WWM or PLM/WWM contrast or on the distinctions between sense modalities.

We begin by recalling the study of Sullivan *et al.* (p. 162), in which first-graders were instructed for months by "single letter" (PM?)/"letter combination" (WWM?) methods. An alternate form of the posttest was taken as an aptitude measure. There was no treatment main effect, but the ATI was significant. *WWM was superior for Highs, but PM was far better for Lows than WWM.* The result held up on transfer tests with words not taught.

Such ATI did not appear in a brief study by Jeffrey and Samuels (1967). Sixty kindergarten *S*s were divided among letter-training/word-training/control groups. In the letter-training condition (PM?), *S*s learned single correspondences between non-English graphemes paired with English phonemes. In the word-training condition (WWM?), these correspondences were included in simple words. A transfer list of nonsense words made of the same graphemes served as the criterion task. Apparently *S*s trained by PM were superior on the transfer tasks to those trained by WWM. Response on the first transfer trial showed a significant ATI of treatment with IQ, due to a ceiling effect in the PM group. *No ATI oc-curred on trials-to-criterion or for total-correct-responses.*

As a miniature treatment, R. Hartley (1968) organized a master list of words into four-word, "minimum-contrast" lists where all phonemes but one remained constant (e.g., *hen, pen, men, ten*), and maximum-contrast lists (e.g., *men, swing, bow, cake*). The lists were presented under three cue conditions: with little meaningful context/with accompanying colored pictures/in meaningful sentences. The same 16 words were learned under each of the six conditions. *S*s were 127 beginning first-graders. The ability measure was Murphy-Durrell Reading Readiness. Each *S* received ten study- and ten test-trials on each of four word lists, one list per day. There were two delayed posttests and a transfer test, all calling for pronunciation of words.

There were complicated, significant three-way interactions, but these were not consistent from one dependent variable to another. High boys did best with maximum contrast and High girls did best with minimum contrast. For Lows, these effects were at times reversed (but all Lows did poorly). An Ability x List x Cue-condition interaction complicates the picture. Embellishments (sentence context) were useful to Highs but sometimes distracted Lows.

Hartley followed textbook anova routines. She used a median split and gave data only to describe the nominally significant differences, so we are unable to see the results as a whole. Interpretation is difficult because the study lacks power; one cannot be sure that in the population Hartley's effects would be as complex as they were in the sample.

Another miniature study lends some support to Hartley's findings that embellishments impede Lows. *S*s read a story with/without pictures (Samuels, 1967). *N* was only 26. Lows recognized significantly more posttest words when given no pictures, while the picture condition helped Highs. This is a *borderline disordinal interaction.*

Compton (1970) taught word recognition to 36 educationally handicapped second- and third-grade boys. Each *S* received 80 minutes of a visual treatment (focusing on word length, configuration, and picture cues), with a new list on each of four consecutive days; and also 80 minutes of a multisensory treatment (adding sound blending, tracing, and writing to the visual work), again with four lists of words. Aptitudes assessed were auditory-visual integration and tactile-visual integration, with two tests for each in a multimethod design. Compton based a V score on immediate and delayed performance on those particular words the pupil had learned in the visual treatment. There was an M score for the words taught by the multisensory method. Her hypothesis was that different aptitudes predicted learning of each type, but in fact V and M correlated 0.86, leaving little differential information. Her aptitude measures did predict V + M. The aptitude scores all had larger correlations with V than with M, but this small hint of *interaction is undependable.*

The best study in this group is that by Sullivan, Okada, and Niedermeyer. They dealt with a well-specified instructional task of sufficient duration, though their sample was too limited. Their finding that WWM was best for Highs may tie to Hartley's finding that maximum-contrast lists were best for High boys and with the results of Schneyer *et al.* and Wyatt reported earlier. The Jeffrey-Samuels study is not really inconsistent, since it related IQ to learning of a bit of nonsense material by kindergartners, whose performance might be comparable to those for low-ability first-graders. On the other hand, several major studies suggested that PLM either is best on the average or that it is best for Highs. (Tanyzer-Alpert and Hartley found this only for High girls.)

The data do not support an ATI hypothesis based on auditory/visual distinctions. The studies investigating this either found no ATI or obtained interactions which can be accounted for by a more general aptitude construct. The findings of Robinson and of Stallings are consistent with the hypothesis derived from the Cooperative program regarding WWM/PLM contrasts; steeper slopes were obtained for PLM.

Discussion

Reading is a complicated process, only now being subjected to truly penetrating analysis. Except for the Cooperative studies, research on reading has gone off in many directions and only the contrast between WWM and various mixtures of PM and LM has received sustained attention. As aptitude data have almost always been collected, the frequent failure to examine ATI is a missed opportunity. But enough data are now in hand to suggest that, while ATI may not be ubiquitous in reading instruction, they can be found when satisfactory samples are collected. (And if this is true in reading, is it not likely in most other instruction?)

On the other hand, the results do not add up to really convincing conclusions. Several studies support the contention that general ability interacts with WWM/PLM and WWM/LE, WWM yielding the shallower slope. But how such findings should be interpreted is unclear. PLM stresses word analysis and underplays meaning, whereas LE stresses meaning even more than does WWM. Possibly PLM and LE are good for different kinds of Highs, i.e., those with strength in fluid or crystallized ability, respectively. As for WWM/LM, isolated evidence suggests that general ability interacts with *steeper* slopes in WWM. Yet LM and PLM are kindred. We need further studies to pin down the variables that moderate such results. Method variations within these gross contrasts, including teacher behavior, deserve attention. Distinctions between PM, LM, and PLM need clarification, since it seems unlikely, at least in studies of long duration, that PM can be kept distinct from LM. Sex and special abilities will need to be considered on the learner side. Higher-order interactions have been given only passing attention.

In the next round of research on reading, we would recommend reduced-rank regression analyses with orthogonal dependent variables, such as Lo demonstrated. It is essential to think about the regression coefficients for the several aptitude factors, as Stallings and Snow did, not to stop with the F's that Lo concentrated upon. We would prefer to examine all the within-treatment regressions, rather than merely the significant interactions. But beyond that we would want to trace the components of regression through their several subdivisions: within treatment, between projects or localities within treatment, within projects, between teachers or classes within projects, and between classes and pupils within teachers. This will produce a maze of results, but if such regressions can be examined alongside reports of what each teacher was trying to do, what activities he emphasized, etc., we will learn about the interplay between aptitudes and instructional treatments.

Meaningfulness of instruction

Rote/meaningful presentations in arithmetic

In the 1930's, educators reacted against Thorndikean emphasis on drill and correspondingly welcomed ideas from Gestalt psychology. Many studies of this era sought to demonstrate the superiority of "meaningful" over "rote" instruction. Individual differences in response were neglected, however, and data on them appeared only in a few reports. The most noteworthy is that of G. L. Anderson (1941).

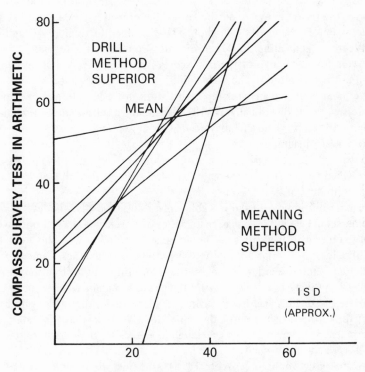

MINNEAPOLIS SCHOOL ABILITY TEST

Figure 8.1.
Lines where regression planes for less-able classes crossed in the Anderson study. Each line refers to a different outcome. (Data from G. L. Anderson, 1940. This figure reproduced by permission from Robert Gagné, (Ed.) *Learning and individual differences.* Merrill, 1967, p. 33.)

Fourth-grade classes were assigned to conventional arithmetic instruction emphasizing practice, or to instruction that made a deliberate attempt to develop meanings. Instruction continued for a year, in 18 classrooms, making this an exceptional study for those times or ours. Anderson discarded three ill-matched classes and split the remaining classes into able and less-able subgroups so that variances would be more homogeneous. The Johnson-Neyman analysis, within subgroups between treatments, pooled classes and counted individuals as the sampling unit. There were more cases in the low-ability classes (5 drill classes, 3 meaning classes; total $N = 234$), and these comparisons had a greater likelihood of showing significance. Eight outcomes were regressed onto the Compass Survey Test in Arithmetic and the general ability test. Among lower-ability classes, a region of significance was located in seven of the eight instances. The region in Figure 8.1 shows where the regression planes crossed. The drill method was superior in the region above or to the left of the crossover line; i.e., it was advantageous for "overachievers." In about half the plots, the region of significance was a hyperbola, indicating significant disordinal interactions. Regions of significance were found for two of the four scores Anderson regressed against the van Wagenen arithmetic pretest. The high-ability subset of classes had only 114 cases altogether, and only five analyses reported significant results. In just one analysis was there significant disordinal ATI. The high-ability results were somewhat inconsistent with each other, and they tended to show the drill method superior in the lower-*left* quadrants.

Anderson's design, analysis, and interpretation were of a quality rare even today. But when we reanalyze to separate between-class from within-class effects, the original finding of ATI becomes suspect.

The Anderson findings in the less-able classes suggested that the less-meaningful instruction should be given to classes made up of "overachievers" in arithmetic, whereas the meaningful instruction should be given to those who show good general ability along with poor arithmetic skills. Anderson's findings seemed to have a commonsense interpretation. In 1939, the prior arithmetic instruction of his pupils had very likely been relatively meaningless. A student who has achieved well to date presumably has study techniques or aptitudes that make him a good prospect for further instruction of the same kind. Where a student's standing in achievement is below what his general ability predicts, an alternative treatment sounds like a good investment.

In a reanalysis (Cronbach & Webb, 1975), a number of students having missing data were eliminated, regression estimates of missing scores were made for others, and one very small class was dropped that Anderson too had discarded. This left 434 cases. The reanalysis did not subdivide on the basis of ability. A composite dependent variable (Zach) was formed by combining the four subtests of the Compass posttest and the four subtests of the van Wagenen posttest. As aptitude variables, the Compass pretest (Precom) and a partial variate defined as Ability-minus-0.042-times-Precom were used. This latter variable, hereafter referred to as Abil, correlated zero with Precom over all cases pooled, but of course the correlation within a subgroup often departed from zero. All three variables were rescaled to mean zero and s.d. 100, over all cases pooled.

We confine attention here to descriptive statistics. Since the experiment attempts to generalize over classes, the number of degrees of freedom comes from nine drill classes and eight meaning classes. This number is so small that the confidence interval for any regression line is very wide. Considering students to be fixed-within-classes is a defensible model, and under this model there is no way to use the number of students as the basis for degrees of freedom. The Zach means in the two treatments differed very little; hence, we shall disregard the small constant terms in the regressions we report.

We report within-treatment multiple regressions of the class means, with the means weighted by the number of cases per class rather than weighted equally. (The unweighted calculation would lead us to the same conclusion.) The analysis was made stepwise, with Precom entered before Abil. The univariate regression for Abil was also calculated.

A dissimilarity in Anderson's treatment groups—which he evidently overlooked —greatly complicates interpretation and in the end undercuts the experiment. Precom and Ability were strongly correlated across drill classes, with the result that the partial variate Abil had only a small between-class-within-drill variance; i.e., a problem of collinearity arose, making the regression weight for Abil in drill classes virtually indeterminate.[1] (Collinearity was not a problem in the meaning classes.) In the face of this difficulty, we find it necessary to examine both the simple regressions and the multiple regressions (Table 8.6). Before moving to the interpretation, we note that something like a ceiling effect occurred, which accounts for low slopes in some able classes. The between-class regression was not made curvilinear by this ceiling, however.

The between-class multiple regressions (third line of table) indicate that class means depended to the same degree on Precom in both treatments, and that Abil contributed to the class mean in the Meaning treatment only. If we focus on the simple regressions, we again see a greater influence of Abil in the meaning condition. The dramatic negative slope in the drill condition cannot be taken seriously; it is a consequence of lack of variance in Abil. The difference in the simple regression slopes onto Precom is not artifactual, but it is probably due to the small number of classes. In the meaning condition, a small negative correlation between Precom and Abil means caused the multiple-regression equation (which applies weights to partial variates) to differ from the simple regression. The simple regressions give a clearer picture.

The within-class regressions of Zach onto Precom were the same in both treatments. Likewise, standing within the class depended on Abil to the same degree

---

[1]Anderson assigned treatments to the teachers according to their preference. Assignment of classes to teachers must have been haphazard. With hindsight, we can recommend forming pairs of classes with similar pretest means and assigning treatments within pairs. But that is not easy to arrange.

Table 8.6   **Between-class and within-class regressions**
              in drill and meaning treatments

| | | Coefficients predicting outcome in | | | | | |
| | | Drill treatment | | | Meaning treatment | | |
Analysis	Predictor	b	b	r or R	b	b	r or
Between	Precom	0.74		0.88	0.47		0.48
classes [a]	Abil		-0.47	-0.20		0.22	0.31
	Precom + Abil	0.75	0.06	0.88	0.70	0.42	0.73
Within	Precom	0.73		0.70	0.71		0.70
classes [b]	Abil		0.39	0.39		0.51	0.52
	Precom + Abil	0.75	0.41	0.81	0.65	0.42	0.82

Data from G. L. Anderson, 1941.

[a]Means weighted by class size.

[b]Calculated by pooling deviations from class means, over cases within treatments.

in both treatments. This makes it clear that *if Anderson actually had ATI for overall achievement, the effect occurred between classes.*

The between-class slopes seemed to differ dramatically between treatments, in a way consistent with Anderson's conclusion. The negative slopes onto Abil in the drill group, however, is clearly a chance result. When we plot the means, no difference between treatments appears save that the range of Abil is narrow. The difference in univariate slopes for Precom (0.74 vs. 0.47) suggests a more meaningful interaction, but the plots were again quite similar. *The Anderson study with only a few classes per treatment was entirely lacking in power to detect between-class ATI effects.*

Within a treatment, within-class slopes showed a good deal of variation. There were also large differences in R and MS_{Res}. The classes where R was lower were not the ones with especially large MS_{Res}. It is hard to know how seriously to take such effects, when class sizes ranged from 13 to 36. The effects are large enough to suggest comparing class slopes within treatments in future studies.

A few methodological points are worth emphasis. It is critically important in research on classroom instruction to state hypotheses and conclusions so as to distinguish between-class effects from effects at the individual level. Even if the number of classes is small, the analysis can examine the individual-level effects with class effects removed. Very large samples will be required to pin down class-level interactions. Our study of regressions within treatments gave a clearer picture of Anderson's data than he obtained by the Johnson-Neyman analysis. Finally, we remark on the clarity gained by converting the predictors to orthogonal variables, and the important role a plot of data points played in clarifying the descriptive statistics.

A few years after the Anderson study, Brownell and Moser (1949) reported a magnificent study of meaningful/mechanical instruction in subtraction. A brief account of the main themes of the study is given by Cronbach (1963, pp. 342-344). What concerns us here is a finding on individual differences. Dozens of schools participated. In half of them, a major effort was made to explain why certain steps were performed in (e.g.) borrowing. But third-graders in some of the schools seemed unable to profit from these explanations. The authors tell us that for students whose instruction had been by rote in the two preceding grades the whole concept of explanation in arithmetic was strange. They could not incorporate the meanings offered. *Some children, then, had actually developed an inaptitude for meaningful instruction, whereas other children had been led to the point where they could profit from explanation.* This is important, first, in undermining the concept that aptitude or readiness is simply a matter of intellectual maturity. Second, it challenges Jensen's suggestion that there is a native incapacity to profit from meaningful instruction. Third, it destroys any lingering hope of defining "one best way" of instruction. Fourth, it urges us in the direction of combining techniques when trying to help the student who does not make good use of meaningful instruction. The school has to advance his skills without relying on comprehension, but ought at the same time to advance his ability to comprehend. It would be wrong to write off these third-graders as doomed never to comprehend, but it will take more than simple tuning to enable them to absorb explanation.

Brownell and Moser offered only anecdotal evidence on this overwhelmingly important ATI. So far as we know there has been no follow-up on their research. Indeed, there has been a remarkable absence of research on what makes instruction meaningful, what prepares a student to profit from meaning, and how the student who is so prepared goes about learning. Experimental and developmental psychologists have worked on mediation, but their stimuli have been remote from educational materials and their short-term treatments unlike those in education. Here, then, is a major topic where ATI questions can profitably be combined with an attempt to understand basic processes of intellectual development and performance.

Thiele (1938) taught addition facts to second-graders by "generalization" (meaningful) or drill (rote) methods. The study covered 15 weeks of daily lessons and included more than 500 Ss in nine schools. *The meaningful treatment was much better for those of IQ 105 and above.* Differences below that level were in the same direction but small. Findings based on gain scores (his page 59) suggest that the generalization method had its greatest advantage for students low in arithmetic at pretest, but this is suspect because of a ceiling effect. Taken at face value, Thiele's findings are much like Anderson's.

Equivocal results on the same problem were reported by McConnell (1934). He found a modest advantage of instruction by discovery on transfer tests, offset by a modest advantage drill gave on direct tests of speed in computation. The study used 400 cases per treatment, and the instruction continued seven months. There was a puzzling but presumably random difference between groups prior to treatment. The group means and s.d.'s on IQ and the arithmetic pretest were similar, but the correlations differed by 0.13. Correlations of the posttests with IQ showed similar differences. The correlations are as shown in Table 8.7, where tests are ordered according to the critical ratio for the difference in group means.

The tests that involved greater transfer (and on which meaningful teaching gave better results) generally correlated more with IQ in the drill group than did the straight computation tests. After instruction by drill, children low in IQ found the transfer tests hard.

Table 8.7   Correlations relating outcomes to aptitude for drill and meaningful instruction in arithmetic

Outcome measure	Critical ratio	Treatment with higher mean	r (IQ x posttest)		
			Drill	Meaning	D.
2 Speed	4.2	Drill	0.25	0.10	0.
5 Detecting computational errors	2.6	Drill	0.26	0.20	0.
6 Learning a new skill	0.5	Meaning	0.26	0.21	0.
1 Accuracy	0.7	Meaning	0.33	0.21	0.
4 Verbal problems	0.8	Meaning	0.39	0.28	0.
3 Transfer	1.7	Meaning	0.39	0.26	0.
7 Maturity of process	3.1	Meaning	0.40	0.18	0.
(Arithmetic pretest)			0.34	0.21	0.

Data from McConnell, 1934.

The s.d.'s were so nearly comparable from group to group that the correlations may be used to judge the interaction. The two correlations are most nearly equal for Tests 4, 5, and 6, and least alike for 7. In view of the difference of 0.13 in r's at the time of the pretest, *one cannot conclude that ATI were present.* If the data show an ATI, the effect is the opposite of Thiele's, with drill serving the brighter students best. We have no information on the predictive power of the pretest.

Both Thiele and McConnell made deliberate efforts to keep facts unconnected in teaching the "drill" group, which seems unduly artificial. And Thiele criticized the "meaningful" procedure of the McConnell study as not truly meaningful. Hence, these studies may not fairly evaluate the two kinds of instruction. There are also some technical difficulties in McConnell's study. All in all, one cannot consider McConnell's failure to find clear ATI a contradiction of the other studies.

Orton, McKay and Rainey (1964) contrasted a systematic development of the topic of Roman numerals through rules-followed-by-examples/a straight drill-and-practice method with no general rules. *S*s (overall $N = 52$) were at three levels, from third-graders of IQ above 111 to a group of older mentally handicapped students. Instruction was confined to four sessions. There were seven outcome measures: immediate, delayed, and transfer. The ablest group had its best results on the rule-and-example method. The group of average ability nearly equalled the bright group on direct learning but not on transfer; for the average students, the differences between methods were inconsistent from one outcome to another. The dull group got consistently better results from drill, at least equalling the normal group. They learned somewhat less than other groups from rule-and-example training. The sample is small and the differences small, but the trend is for explanation or rules to help bright students and to handicap the dull.

Instruction in arithmetic by conventional/Cuisenaire methods was carried out in six Canadian schools (Lucow, 1964). The Cuisenaire student manipulates wooden rods of varying lengths to get a concrete sense of relationships. 254 third-graders were taught multiplication and division for six weeks. Treatment groups were not constituted randomly, and the Cuisenaire groups had had extra prior instruction. Lucow analyzed gain scores by ancova with the pretest as covariate, and took IQ into account by blocking into three levels. Insofar as we can judge from the report, the Cuisenaire materials worked best, and *the curriculum contrast probably did not yield ATI*. But IQ was strongly related to outcome in two groups: Cuisenaire method in rural schools and conventional method in urban schools. This relation was weak or absent in the other groups. The oddity of this result and the defects of the study keep us from taking it seriously.

The large-scale studies in this section cohere around a finding of positive evidence for ATI, though just what variables interact, and just where the interaction can be expected, must be left vague. The evidence is especially valuable because the studies were on genuine school lessons and of considerable duration. Some employed several dependent variables. Evidently, treatments that attempt to explain relationships within mathematical content, or to lead the student to organize the material intellectually, benefit the student with superior mental ability or the student who combines good mental ability with inferior achievement to date. This was the finding of Anderson, Thiele, and Orton. The Brownell study was consistent with this conclusion. We can to some extent discount the equivocal or contradictory findings of McConnell and of Lucow.

Instruction intended to be meaningful may or may not be meaningful. Supplying the meaning is unnecessary if the able student can supply the meaning for himself; where that is possible, the meaningful presentation benefits the Lows rather than the Highs. Meaningfulness inheres not in the lessons presented, but in the way the learner processes the lessons. Good mental ability does not guarantee that the student will have the skills and attitudes required to capture the meaning, even when he knows the facts upon which the explanation rests, the words employed, etc.

Some students are ready to use meaningful presentations, thanks to a combination of general ability and sound ways of approaching instructional material. Some others who score equally high on conventional tests are unprepared to profit from explanations. In the Orton study, providing explanations was harmful to Lows. No mental test assesses directly the ability to take in, comprehend, and use an explanation. While this ability (or habit of work) is probably correlated with both fluid and crystallized abilities, it seems to call for some special skill in coping with connected discourse. Perhaps it can be measured by learning samples.

We face once again the need to specify an ATI hypothesis by means of task analysis. Some meaningful presentations are demanding. The explanations given are only potentially meaningful, useful only to the person who brings considerable powers to them. With a demanding presentation we might expect a comparatively steep regression of outcome onto whatever aptitude test measures the powers needed to grasp the explanations. At the other extreme are simplified presentatons, redundant to the point where the ideas are almost inescapable. They should provide a prosthesis for the learner who lacks the insight and ability to organize for himself. With such explanations one expects the slope of regression on ability to be shallower than with conventional instruction.

Distinguishing rote from meaningful instruction is an outworn notion. Rote is rote, if the content cannot possibly be given meaning; but even paired-associate lists can be given meaning by the learner. An ideally coherent argument, on the other hand, is meaningful only for the learner who follows the argument. "Meaningful" refers not to a treatment variable but—by definition—to an interpretation that takes place in the learner.

Some support for the view that one man's meaning is another man's rote is found in Tanaka's (1968) study of classification skills among first-graders. In one treatment (called "manipulative"), children grouped objects on the basis of color, number, etc. The teacher led them through exercises on grouping by inclusion and exclusion. A second treatment (called "verbal") dealt with abstract shapes and terms referring to concepts. Again the teacher led Ss in practice. A control group received no training. A test on picture classification served as pretest and posttest. Although the AT slope was positive in the manipulative and control groups, that in the verbal group was markedly steeper. *The verbal treatment was superior for children with relatively high pretest scores,* while the manipulative condition was superior for Lows. As in the Sullivan study (p. 162 f.), one wonders how long the manipulative condition would continue to be superior if training were extended in time.

Some further remarks need to be made about the thinking of Arthur Jensen, as his distinction between Level I (rote learning) and Level II (fluid) abilities makes him an advocate of ATI research. It might be thought that Jensen advocates teaching by rote for children who are high on Level I abilities and low on Level II. But he states that no study has yet identified methods of instruction suitable for such children. Traditional school methods are ill-adapted to the High-I, Low-II child, but the substitute is not at hand.

At present we do not know how to teach to Level I ability. Although Level I is manifested in rote learning, it is not advocated that simple notions of rote learning be the model for instruction. Instructional techniques that can utilize the abilities that are manifested in rote learning are needed, but this does not necessarily imply that the instruction consist of rote learning *per se.* We also need to find out to what extent Level II abilities can be acquired or stimulated by appropriate instruction to children who possess good Level I ability but are relatively low on Level II. . . . (1973, p. 190).

This last sentence will surprise those who believe that Jensen thinks Level II deficits to be irremediable. The whole passage will surprise those who have thought that he intends to capitalize on Level-I ability by introducing rote teaching. But in evaluating the drill/meaningful interaction above we were by no means setting up a straw man. Proposals to teach via conditioning and drill abound, particularly in compensatory education.

A study of verbal elaboration in programmed instruction. A miscellaneous study by Silberman *et al.* (1962) undertook to develop programs in plane geometry that would appeal differentially to "overachieving" and "underachieving" students. They expected the underachievers to be challenged by an unconventional approach. A three-week study was carried out in three high schools, with 258 students selected according to whether their first-semester geometry achievement was at/above/below what would have been predicted from the California Test of Mental Maturity. Equal numbers of students of the three types were retained in the study. One instructional program developed each topic in a step-by-step, straightforward "rote" manner, with no surprises or challenges. A contrasting "conceptual" program worked back and forth from what was given to what was to be determined, directing attention to methods of attack and including more abstract discussion. A posttest measured both recall and application. The means for the three types of students were almost identical under the two treatments, and the authors reported that there was no interaction. A refined analysis within each school, for each type of item separately, did produce significant interactions the investigators found difficult to explain.

Training research

Two experiments modified job training to make it more meaningful. The ATI in these studies are unlike those typically found in mathematics; adding meaning helped men of low general ability.

DePauli and Parker (1969) compared a class of Navy sonar technicians given a special training device with two other classes given instruction with conventional equipment ($N = 59$). Training was part of a 14-week course. There was *a substantial interaction,* though not as strong as the investigators thought. Table 8.8 presents means and correlations that DePauli and Parker interpreted, plus regression slopes. The aptitude measure was a combination of the General Classification Test and Arithmetic Test (GCT/ARI). The school mark was based on the regular tests given in the course of training; the special "criterion test" was a reliable, difficult comprehensive examination. The groups had been equated on an aptitude test for technicians that was not entered in the analysis of results.

Failing to recognize the difference between groups in GCT/ARI, DePauli and Parker overlooked the superiority of the experimental treatment. They did note the dramatic differences in correlations. From the regressions it is evident that the trainer gave much better results for men below 124 on GCT/ARI. Among men above 130 the conventional course gave better results. Whereas the Navy had been ruling out of electronics training any man with GCT/ARI below 110,

Table 8.8   Effects of a training device for electronics maintenance

	Aptitude		School-mark criterion				Special criteri		
	Mean	s.d.	Mean	s.d.	r	b	Mean	s.d.	r
Conventional Class I	128	6.66	85.50	7.47	0.56	0.62	54.35	8.50	0.71
Conventional Class 2	124	5.89	83.20	5.25	0.56	0.49	54.93	10.14	0.71
Class using trainer	119	7.55	85.79	3.99	0.01	0.01	54.61	12.49	0.2

Data from DePauli and Parker, 1969.

it appears that the new trainer would allow men at this level to succeed. The trainer was a simplified set of circuits representing the main features of sonar sensors, designed to allow the student to make a ready match between the theor of electronics and the practical setting. This made the training less verbal in character and seems likely to have made the theory clearer to the student. (A side study showed that, on average, graduates of the experimental training were more adept at carrying out actual repairs. ATI were not examined in the side study.)

Happily, the trainer is much less expensive than the operational sonar equipment used in teaching the conventional course. The question remains open whetl the conventional course has advantages over the trainer for men of superior aptitude; when cost is considered, the disordinal interaction very likely becomes ordinal.

Interactions of multiple abilities were examined in a training course for aviatic mechanics ($N = 150$; Edgerton, 1958). The alternative treatments were largely verbal. One method of instruction was rote; trainees were to memorize what the were told and to reproduce it on examinations. In the other method, the instructor was directed to explain and to urge students to raise questions. Instructors, however, did not vary the classroom work as much as had been intended. (For another Edgerton study of training see p. 317 ff.) The group taugh meaningfully did best (posttest mean of 77.9, vs. 75.7 for the rote group).

The original report emphasized correlations within treatment groups and their significance. We calculated slopes for the final achievement composite against the ability tests, from the Tests of Primary Mental Abilities, and rescaled them to make the within-treatment s.d.'s close to 1. In each pair of lines in Table 8.9, the upper line refers to the rote treatment. This slope is higher than its companion.

It was not feasible for us to determine the significance of the differences in sl Taking differences in s.d.'s into account may have raised to significance some interactions that did not show up as significant in the correlations. It appears tha

Table 8.9   **Correlations and regression slopes relating outcome to aptitudes in technical training**

	Mean	s.d.		rescaled b
Number	54.8[a]	16.9	0.322	0.35
	56.8	18.6	0.205	0.19
Verbal	62.2	16.8	0.614*	0.50
	63.9	16.0	0.403	0.40
Space	56.3	20.1	0.444	0.48
	57.7	21.9	0.376	0.35
Fluency	53.9	15.4	0.409*	0.40
	51.9	14.1	0.184	0.19
Reasoning	28.3	8.7	0.609*	0.64
	29.0	8.9	0.387	0.37
Memory	8.3	3.9	0.260	0.29
	8.9	4.5	0.230	0.21
General Classification	53.3	6.6	0.747	0.74
Test	54.6	6.0	0.631	0.64
Outcome measure	75.7	9.7	—	—
	77.9	9.1	—	—

Data from Edgerton, 1958.

[a]Upper row gives value for less meaningful treatment.

*Difference in r's reported to be significant.

general, verbal ability was more highly correlated with success under the rote treatment than under the more meaningful treatment. The net effect, then, was for the explanations to overcome some of the learning difficulties of duller men. Reasonable enough, if the explanations were easy for a dull person to grasp, and easy for a bright one to invent for himself. (A further, more limited study gave essentially similar results.)

The author's multiple-regression analysis included twelve predictors (including parts of GCT). The multiple correlation for all predictors was 0.83 in the rote treatment and 0.70 in the meaningful treatment. We are suspicious of the weights reported for specific predictors, since when two tests are correlated both receive weights lower than their separate relevance would indicate. We therefore do not accept the author's conclusion that Fluency was relevant only in the rote treatment and that Memory interfered in the meaningful treatment (where it had a negative weight in the multiple-regression equation). Our conclusion is that $v{:}ed$ was a more powerful predictor than the more peripheral abilities. A better analysis for the purpose of studying differential abilities would be to partial out the first principal component of the aptitude tests and then determine if any of the residual aptitudes had predictive value.

A multiscore interest test had also been given. Correlations were rarely large, but there were some significant differences. The rote treatment seemed to get best results from men interested in the kind of content being taught, which is not surprising. Performance in the meaningful treatment showed no relation to interests; meaning overcame whatever handicap lack of interest entailed.

We come away from these studies with a revised view of "meaningful" instruction; meaningfulness can be defined only with reference to student ability. Adding explanation can make arithmetic meaningful for the child with sufficient ability to understand and to use the concepts given. Capitalizing on this ability may be particularly important for children who have not benefited from previous, unelaborated instruction. But in other cases (e.g., adult military trainees), explanation primarily helps those who lack the ability to make concepts meaningful themselves.

Chapter 9 | Interactive effects of making instruction less verbal

Education is necessarily verbal to a large degree, but making instruction exclusively verbal unduly burdens the student who is below average in vocabulary, or reading, or motivation for abstract learning. Work on concrete projects, presentation of lessons in some audiovisual form, and other devices are available to augment or replace verbal instruction. The DePauli-Parker study reviewed in the last chapter shows how a training device can serve this function. But most ATI research on this topic compared more and less verbal forms of communication. Many of the studies were motivated by the belief that specialized abilities in the Thurstone-Guilford tradition are likely to predict learning when a treatment is low in its verbal demands. The first section of this chapter takes up instruction by means of abstract symbols. We then move on to various forms of pictorial and diagrammatic communication.

Communication using symbols

Several ATI studies were inspired by Guilford's distinction between "semantic" and "symbolic" abilities. Though we shall conclude that this contrast is not an important source of interaction, the substitution of symbols does often alter the degree to which a treatment depends on general or verbal-educational abilities. The available studies have to do with mathematical and grammatical content.

Studies of mathematics

J. B. Davis, Jr. prepared instructional material on vector multiplication and on the taking of derivatives, in forms that might capitalize on semantic/symbolic

257

abilities. This work was included in the project report of Kropp *et al.* (1967, pp. 152–203). Figure 9.1 illustrates corresponding parts of frames in the two treatments. Following the lines displayed here, the rest of the frame was stated verbally in the first treatment, algebraically in the second. Both treatments were rather demanding.

Definition

The product of two vectors, when the two vectors are expressed as ordered pairs of real numbers, is defined by the following three steps:

. . . .

(a) Semantic treatment

Definition

The product of two vectors

$$\text{written } \begin{Vmatrix} x_1 \\ x_2 \end{Vmatrix} * \begin{Vmatrix} y_1 \\ y_2 \end{Vmatrix}$$

is defined by:

. . . .

$$\begin{Vmatrix} x_1 \\ x_2 \end{Vmatrix} \text{ and } \begin{Vmatrix} y_1 \\ y_2 \end{Vmatrix}$$

(b) Symbolic treatment

Figure 9.1.

Contrasting frames illustrating semantic and symbolic treatments.

Table 9.1   Tests that interacted with semantic/symbolic treatment in three studies by Kropp et al.

Tests for which slope was greater under the _semantic_ treatment

Study I	Study II	Study III	
CMC	CMC		
CMR	CMR	CMR	
NMR	NMR	NMR	Semantic
NMT	NMT		tests
	NMI	NMI	
NST	NST	NST	
NSI		NSI	
	CSR		Symbolic
	NSR	NSR	tests
		CSC	

Tests for which slope was greater under the _symbolic_ treatment

Study I	Study II	Study III	
NMI			Semantic test
	NSI		Symbolic test

If slopes are the same in sign, the greater one is at least 1.5 times the smaller for any test admitted to this table. If opposite in sign, the positive slope is greater in absolute value than the negative slope.

Ten semantic and symbolic tests from Guilford's system were the aptitude measures. Apparently, the dependent measure differed in form between the two treatments. A faceted test, like that constructed by Markle (see our p. 281), would have been preferable.

Three experiments were performed, illustrating the unusual readiness of Kropp and his group to do pilot work and to replicate their studies. Study I and Study II were essentially similar and employed similar Ss. College psychology students (about 70 in each study) worked through one or the other program during a three-hour period. The symbolic treatment seemed easier on the average, significantly so in Study II. The authors computed the regression slope for one aptitude at a time within each treatment. Some significance tests for differences in slope were calculated. Table 9.1 lists certain key differences which refer mostly to total achievement scores rather than to subcriteria. It will be recalled that, in Guilford's system, semantic tests are coded -M- (e.g., CMR) and symbolic tests -S- (e.g., CSR). The ATI findings in these two studies were strikingly similar, the more so when we realize that the aptitude tests were rather unreliable and the sample size modest. Differences in outcome depended on measured aptitudes to a much greater degree under the semantic treatment than under the symbolic treatment. Whenever a test appeared to relate more strongly to outcome from symbolic treatment, this finding failed to replicate.

As the S and M categories did not cluster appreciably, no strong generalization regarding these aptitude classes could be established. The tests had generally positive intercorrelations. It would have been wise to identify one or two main components and to calculate regression slopes on these comparatively reliable composites. There would have been a near-general factor embracing tests of *both* kinds. The reported data suggest that a general factor would have had a steeper slope in the semantic treatment. No factor extracted from the remainder of the test variance would have had a significant relation to outcome, we judge.

In Study III, the same instructional materials were used with 177 tenth-graders. This time the instruction extended over three days, one hour per day. The program was clearly too difficult for the Ss, at least under spaced conditions. Kropp *et al.* were inclined to view the Study III interactions (Table 9.1) as inconsistent with the other two studies, but this interpretation takes too seriously the fragmentation of the aptitude domain. The first principal component among the tests would almost certainly have displayed a significant interaction in this study also. The three tests that interacted in all three studies were verbal analogies (CMR), vocabulary completion (NMR), and camouflaged words (NST). We judge that a reduced-rank regression analysis would tell the same story in all three studies.

Here is fairly solid evidence that *the "symbolic" presentation served test-weak pupils better than a conventional, more difficult verbal treatment did.*

A dissertation by Yelvington (1968) followed in the Florida State program. He compared verbal/numerical booklets on the topic of correlation in statistics, using only 11 minutes of instruction ($N = 463$ college Ss). Aptitudes were vocabulary and arithmetic tests from the ETS kit. A test of achievement (immediate and after five weeks) had items of four types: verbal, numerical, hybrid, and spatial. The difficulty and value of the instruction, and liking of it, were also rated.

Outcome measures were regressed onto verbal and numerical ability separately in each treatment, but ATI was tested by an unusual ancova procedure, on a subsample representing extreme aptitude groups. Reporting was complicated and incomplete, but we can reach some general statements. Both verbal and numerical ability predicted total achievement and some subtests of achievement and retention. Ss in the numerical treatment showed higher achievement and retention on one subtest, but found the program less "entertaining" than did Ss in the verbal treatment. Some disordinal ATI were nominally significant; *high-verbal Ss said that the verbal treatment was less difficult and less valuable than the numerical treatment, but they performed better on numerical achievement items following verbal instruction. Low verbal Ss showed the opposite pattern.* With most other cognitive outcomes, however, steeper slopes onto both verbal and numerical ability in the numerical treatment appeared. The analysis did not take advantage of the sample size or the multivariate character of the data.

Petersen *et al.* (1963) carried out companion experiments in "general mathematics" and algebra. We discuss the results here even though the work was not explicitly designed to study the semantic/symbolic contrast. The study has many excellent features: extensive data, thoughtful analysis, and unusually complete reporting.

A certain school taught four courses to ninth-graders: Basic mathematics and and Non-college algebra, both of which emphasized numerical computation; and Regular and Accelerated algebra. We shall refer to these as Courses 1, 2, 3, and 4. The four groups had different ability levels, the mean MA's ranging from 12.8 to 15.7. We shall give most of our attention to Courses 1 and 2 (where N's for any one analysis were ca. 80 and 100, respectively). Course 2 included more formulas than Course 1; and the posttest for those courses covered the full range of objectives of the broader Course 2. Within each treatment the authors reported ten AT regressions for different subsets of the aptitude measures. They compared shrunken multiple R's and reported standardized regression weights. To examine ATI one has to compare unstandardized regression weights. The report allows us to do this only to a limited degree.

The abler group in Course 2 did better and had a lower criterion s.d. The simplest regression equations, combining two CTMM scores, lead us to a conclusion that the Peterson analysis overlooked. The rescaled regression equations for predicting the outcome were:

Course 1 $\hat{Y} = 0.40$ Language $+ 0.10$ Non-Language $+$ constant.

Course 2 $\hat{Y} = 0.38$ Language $+ 0.24$ Non-Language $+$ constant.

The respective shrunken R's were 0.34 and 0.40. The constants are such that one regression plane lay more than one s.d. above the other: there was an *advantage for the more comprehensive course over the entire range of both groups*, i.e., a main effect. If the regression was linear over the range, as assumed here, the school was seemingly wrong to assign the Lows to Course 1. Course 2 would teach even these weaker students more, by Petersen's criterion.[1] The greater weight for Non-Language ability in the more symbolic course was probably not significant.

Another pair of rescaled regression equations can be calculated for four DAT scores:

Course 1 $\hat{Y} = 0.12$ Verbal $+ 0.55$ Numerical $+ 0.11$ Abstract
                $+ 0.13$ Clerical $+$ constant.

Course 2 $\hat{Y} = 0.25$ Verbal $+ 0.36$ Numerical $+ 0.25$ Abstract
                $+ 0.37$ Clerical $+$ constant.

---

[1]The configuration of the data might have been different if regressions on estimated true scores were considered. To make proper corrections, it would be necessary to know whether the CTMM scores were themselves a basis for assignment to courses and, of course, to know the reliability of each score in each treatment group.

The R's were 0.57 and 0.53.

The authors calculated 13 factors scores representing cells in Guilford's system and entered them into a further set of equations; we neglect terms with very small weights.

Course 1 $\hat{Y}$ = 0.42 MSI + 0.18 NMS + 0.13 CSR + 0.15 DSR − 0.04 NSS
              + 0.04 EMR + constant.

Course 2 $\hat{Y}$ = 0.36 MSI + 0.01 NMS + 0.13 CSR − 0.03 DSR + 0.15 NSS
              + 0.19 EMR + constant.

R = 0.46 and 0.45, respectively. As the factor scores were correlated, there is *no way to judge whether the differences in weights imply appreciable interaction*, even in the sample. As a minimum, the Course 2 weights should be applied to the Course 1 data, and vice-versa. Unless each obtained unshrunken "cross" R is well below the shrunken R originally obtained for the equation fitted to the target group, there was no worthwhile interaction. We conclude that general ability— loosely defined—did not interact with this course contrast.

In the Regular/Accelerated comparison (Courses 3/4), with an algebra test as criterion, Course 4 had a higher average and a slightly higher s.d. We shall look at only the equations for four DAT variables, rescaled:

Course 3 $\hat{Y}$ = 0.12 Verbal + 0.22 Numerical + 0.09 Abstract
              + 0.27 Clerical + constant.

Course 4 $\hat{Y}$ = 0.47 Verbal + 0.50 Numerical + 0.15 Abstract
              + 0.46 Clerical + constant.

R's were 0.24 and 0.70; N's, 118 and 75. *Almost certainly a significant disordinal interaction* was present, though without knowledge of the within-group correlations we cannot reach a firm conclusion. Evidently, a general factor would account for the interaction, Highs doing better in the accelerated treatment.

Petersen *et al.* had been interested in contrasting Courses 3 and 4 with Courses 1 and 2, where the outcome measures were different. They drew some conclusions from the regressions of the standardized scores, neglecting the different character of the measures. This direct numerical comparison makes sense only if one aims to put the student in a class where he will *rank* well. What matters is whether a student learns more or learns material whose total value is greater in one course than the other; his rank may be lower in the class were he learns more. For a sound decision one would have to ask the school or the parents of the students to judge what raw score on the algebra final has the same worth in their eyes as a score of 20 (say) on the general math test. This may seem to be an impossible decision, but it has to be made before the school's assignments to courses can be defended empirically. No defense can be founded on statistics alone. (The reader may be interested in the latest interpretation of the study [Guilford & Hoepfner, 1971, pp. 291 ff.] which covers issues other than ATI.)

Another comparison of regressions in algebra/general math was made by Seder-berg (1966). He compared 222 ninth-graders in general mathematics/simplified introductory algebra/no math. Assignment to treatment was random, but as it happened the 70 students assigned to the control treatment were superior in aptitude and on pretests. The peculiar results suggest that the teaching was quite bad. Students of average and low mathematical-reasoning ability made little progress during the nine-month math course. There was an ordinal interaction in a direction that one would not have predicted. For Highs, the general mathematics course gave best results even on an algebra posttest. The algebra course gave considerably worse results (!).

Studies in grammar

King *et al.* (1969) investigated the semantic/symbolic contrast by comparing two linear programmed textbooks in high-school grammar. The texts dealt with the same grammatical concepts, one (traditional) presenting descriptions and explanations primarily in verbal form, while the other (transformational) presented symbols and tree diagrams. There were two studies; the smaller Study II served primarily to crossvalidate equations produced in Study I. Instruction covered five months and three months of the school year, for 174 and 115 tenth-graders, respectively.

In Study I, 174 tenth-graders were assigned randomly to treatments. The major criterion measures—a test requiring Ss to rewrite and improve a given passage (yielding several subscores) and a multiple-choice test of structural relationships—were administered as both pretests and posttests. Part 1 of STEP Writing and Part B of the Stanford Achievement Test (English and Spelling) were also used as posttests. Aptitude measures were nine Guilford tests, chosen to emphasize the semantic/symbolic distinction. Study II was similar; we shall not detail the changes in variables and design.

Preliminary analyses suggested to the authors that quadratic and cubic terms should enter the regression equations. Aptitude scores together with their quadratic, cubic, and interaction forms and with a dummy variable for treatment were entered into the general-regression model. No main effect was found in Study I, nor was there a significant interaction of any one aptitude test or the pretest with any one of the three posttests. When fourth-degree equations were formed that combined an aptitude and the pretest called Aluminum Rewrite, out of 27 combinations tested six interacted significantly. The authors rested their case not on these regression equations but on the crossvalidation in Study II.

Out of four aptitude tests that related to their complexity-of-writing criterion, the investigators carried only one into Study II. They justified this simplification on the ground that the equations relating each of the aptitudes to this outcome were similar in form. The regression equation to be validated had terms for treatment T, aptitude Z (Correlate Completion, a Guilford NSR test), and the pretest X. Beyond these terms it had X^2 and X^3 terms, and nine interaction terms (e.g., TX, TX^3, TZ^2, TZX^2, . . .).

An estimate was made of the criterion score each S would have if assigned to each treatment. On the basis of the difference between the two estimates S was placed in one of three categories: better suited to Treatment A, better suited to B, or uncertain. Then the persons who actually had taken Treatment A were identified, and the actual outcome means of those in each category were calculated, as reported in Table 9.2. Likewise for the B subjects. Among persons in Study I this tabulation did no more than assess the power of the classification system on the data from which it was derived. Study II gave independent evidence.

Table 9.2   Attempt to crossvalidate a classification scheme

Judgment about S derived from regression equations of Study I	Mean outcome score (and N) of persons actually receiving each treatment		
	Traditional treatment	Transforma-tional treatment	Mean difference
I (Original) — Should do better in traditional	11.23 (34)	10.21 (28)	1.0
Uncertain	10.15 (29)	9.31 (37	0.8
Should do better in transformational	7.28 (10)	10.62 (3)	- 3.3
II (Cross-validation) — Should do better in traditional	9.91 (29)	10.74 (31)	- 0.8
Uncertain	7.87 (8)	8.54 (18)	- 0.6
Should do better in transformational	8.71 (8)	7.31 (5)	1.4

Data from King *et al.*, 1969. Prediction was based on a pretest and the Correlate Completion test.

The favorable (but spurious) result in Study I was reversed in Study II. A tabulation of the same kind was made for Word Classification (a Guilford CMC test). There was no interaction in Study II. Further complex analyses give no satisfying evidence of interaction.

We regret to say that the authors were following a recommendation we had made for applying generalized regression analysis in ATI studies (a recommendation renewed in Chapters 3 and 4 above). They elaborated on this idea, and complicated matters too much. We shall comment on two aspects of their method. We find no indication that each of the nine interaction terms in the equation reproduced above added significantly to the multiple correlation in Study I. (The same is true of their other comparable equations.) Composites should have been used to reduce the number of variables, or the terms that added negligibly to prediction should have been discarded. In another analysis, the authors did factor the aptitudes and then formed a regression equation with cubic terms. They reported significant interactions. (The data for Study II did not permit an attempt at crossvalidation.) But to combine reduced rank with cubic terms is self-defeating. If Z^2 and Z^3 are worthy candidates for the variable system, they—or rather $(Z - \overline{\overline{Z}})^2$ and

$(Z - \overline{\overline{Z}})^3$ – should go into the factor analysis just as an additional test would. Components resulting from such a factoring would give more interpretable regression equations, more likely to crossvalidate.

It is fairly clear that Highs (on the ability running through many Guilford tests) had higher scores on both treatments. We conclude that *no interaction was established,* though the analysis may have obscured a weak relation of some kind.

There is one other study of symbolic instruction. Fredrick, Blount, and Johnson (1968; see also Fredrick, 1971) divided 72 eighth-graders among four experimental groups. One group received five PI lessons on structural grammar constructed without symbols or figures. A second group received a version of the program that used symbolic notation, and a third group received a "figural" version with the symbols organized in tree diagrams. Control lessons on poetry were given to the fourth group. Instruction lasted one week. A posttest (two days later) and a delayed posttest (two weeks later) were given.

The programs using symbols and/or diagrams were superior to purely verbal lessons. Significant ATI with Lorge-Thorndike IQ were obtained on both criteria. IQ was entered as a three-level factor in the analysis of variance, providing six Ss per cell; the cell means appear in Table 9.3. The figural treatment was best for Highs and very bad for Lows. No difference between symbolic and verbal treatments appeared among Lows. One suspects that the anomalous low score on the verbal treatment of the half-dozen Ss in the middle group contributed heavily to the significance of the interaction. Given the small sample and the weak analysis, *the ATI finding is best regarded as undependable.* Perhaps, however, the inability of the Lows to use the diagrams would stand up under crossvalidation.

Table 9.3   Mean errors in four treatments as a function of IQ

Treatment	Mean posttest error score within each IQ classification		
	Low	Medium	High
Figural	121	72	50
Symbolic	95	75	67
Verbal	100	113	61
Control	117	105	102

Values are read approximately from a figure
of Fredrick, Blount, and Johnson (1968).

In this section we have seen appreciable evidence that easier, more symbolic treatments can reduce the advantage of those high in general ability or *v:ed,* and therefore can be advantageous for Lows. This was crossvalidated by Davis and supported by the Fredrick study and the low R in regular algebra in the Petersen study. The failure of other studies to support the conclusion carries no weight, in view of their inadequacies of design and analysis. The evidence for interaction of *differential* abilities is not impressive.

Pictorial presentations

Drawings and photographs can fulfill various instructional functions. Some supplement the verbal text and make it easier to understand. Some provide images that the learner can remember in an iconic form or can encode for storage in his own words. Some may provide problematic material that has to be manipulated or transformed, as a way of coming to comprehend the subject matter. Various working hypotheses have been applied in studies of visual materials. Some investigators have thought that adding illustrations would reduce the correlation with general ability that is typical of verbal lessons, while others have hypothesized that "spatial" ability somehow affects learning from diagrams.

This section will take up treatments in which the illustrations are more or less iconic. We first examine the Gagné-Gropper study at length, as it permits us to demonstrate path analysis in an ATI study. We follow this with notes on related studies by Gropper. Another subsection contrasts film and television with more conventional instruction. Some minor studies of imagery are appended.

Iconic diagrams

Path analysis of the Gagné-Gropper results. Chapter 4 introduced some aspects of the study by Gagné and Gropper (1965) in which rate of learning, achievement, and retention were measured. Now we bring in aptitude data and examine ATI. With about 40 Ss per treatment, the suggestive, complex findings may not be replicable.

Eighth-graders took four tests: Otis (omnibus ability), DAT Verbal Reasoning, DAT Space Relations, and DAT Abstract Reasoning. The authors supposed that the treatments would interact with Verbal and Space only. Our reanalysis employs two composites: "Ability" is the sum of raw scores on all four tests, with Space weighted 0.5 to compensate for its larger s.d.; and "Ver/Sp" is a bipolar variable formed by doubling Verbal and subtracting Abstract and Space, the latter weighted 0.5. To keep Abstract and Space separate would confuse our report to no good purpose; their correlations with other variables were much the same.

The central instruction—the same for all Ss— consisted of seven self-spaced programmed lessons on mechanical advantage. The dependent variables were time to work through the lessons (Rate), score on an achievement test given after the lessons (Achievement or Ach), and score on the same test a month later (Retention or Ret). There were two preliminary programmed lessons on content basic to the main lessons. These lessons not only repaired some deficiencies but generated two further "aptitude" measures: Pre-Rate (time to work through these self-paced lessons) and Pre-Ach, a posttest score. The total set of nine lessons constituted the entire treatment for the Control group.

Two randomly selected experimental groups were given special introductions to each of the seven main lessons. The Visual group saw film demonstrations of concepts the lessons would develop. The verbal group saw no pictures; the same demonstrations were described in words.

The authors tested main effects by 3 x 2 x 2 anova after reducing the sample

Table 9.4 Correlations and univariate regression slopes relating delayed posttest to aptitude

	Mean of retention test	s.d.	Relation of Retention to								
			Otis	Verbal	Abstract	Space	Ability	Ver/Sp	Pre-Rate	Pre-Ach	
Verbal			0.22	0.48	0.22	0.09	0.30	0.28	0.02	0.09	Correlations
Visual			0.16	0.36	0.39	0.30	0.42	-0.12	0.19	0.36	
Control			0.33	0.47	0.29	0.35	0.48	0.07	0.27	0.23	
Verbal	33.5	9.8	0.30	0.63	0.27	0.05	0.11	0.17	0.02	0.12	Regression slopes
Visual	37.8	8.7	0.20	0.59	0.47	0.14	0.18	-0.07	0.18	0.43	
Control	32.2	13.7	0.66	0.85	0.47	0.24	0.26	0.04	0.36	0.45	

Data from Gagné and Gropper, 1965.

from 133 to 95, in order to equate groups on IQ and Pre-Rate. An obvious difference in Achievement favored the treated groups. (For all cases, the means were 39.0, 37.5, 33.9; s.e.m. = 1.2 to 1.9). On Retention, the authors reported no significant difference, but the Verbal group dropped in score and finished little better than the Controls (see Table 9.4). The Verbal/Visual difference may in fact be statistically significant, but the presence of interaction makes it pointless to discuss the main effect. The s.d. of Controls was notably larger than that of the treated groups on Ach and Ret.

From the correlations and blocked anova, Gagné and Gropper concluded that there was no interaction. Our reanalysis first examined the regression slopes for single variables. Table 9.4 deals only with Retention; there was no interaction effect on Rate or Ach. The impression given by the slopes is often different from that given by the correlations, because of the larger s.d. of Retention among Controls. This is to be seen, for example, in the Otis column, where the correlations are in the ratio 3:2:4 and the slopes in the ratio 3:2:7. Several slope differences hint at interaction.

We next undertook a sketchy path analysis. Experience with this kind of analysis is limited, and some of our procedural decisions are surely open to criticism.

1. From correlations and s.d.'s we calculated a variance-covariance matrix within each treatment. From these we calculated variances and covariances of Ability and Ver/Sp with other variables. Thereafter we disregarded the original aptitudes.

2. We formed a variance-covariance matrix for treated Ss by adding the matrices of the Verbal and Visual groups and dividing by two. We formed a further matrix for all Ss by adding the matrices for treated Ss and Controls and dividing by two. (This method added weight to the control cases.)

3. In each sample, we calculated raw-score regression weights. A predictor was included in an equation if it was truly antecedent and if there seemed to be a possible relationship within at least one treatment. The decision to include variables in the final equations was thus influenced by the data.

4. We tested each Verbal/Visual contrast for significance, by examining whether the mean square for regression calculated from the two within-treatment sums of squares taken together significantly exceeded that calculated from pooled-within-experimental-treatments covariances for the same variables. We also tested the contrast between Control and pooled-treatment data.

At the end, we had comparable path diagrams for the three treatment groups and the two combined groups. In order to help the reader think about the data, we offer a simplified summary in Figures 9.2-9.4.

Figure 9.2 pulls Rate out as a single dependent variable, since Rate had little influence on Ach and Retention (see p. 96). The Visual group was a bit slower than the other groups; significantly so, according to Gagné and Gropper. The single diagram in Figure 9.2 considers all Ss together.

Rate was predicted by Pre-Rate and, to a lesser degree, by Pre-Ach. Presumably, the style of work reflected in Pre-Rate carried over into Rate on the later lessons. The coefficient for the residual U_r seems overpowering, but that reflects its arbitrary small s.d. The standardized weights of Ability and Ver/Sp were of the same order of magnitude as the weights of Pre-Ach. The negative coefficient of Ability has to be read in context; Ability had a positive relation to Pre-Rate and Pre-Ach, and the negative sign refers to the contribution of Ability *with these two held constant.* Bright students who did relatively poorly on the preliminary program were relatively slow on the main lessons. Partial regression coefficients onto true scores would differ from the coefficients for observed scores given here.

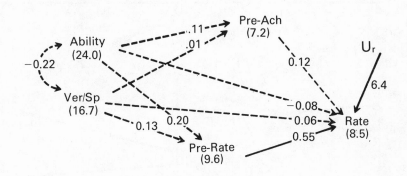

Figure 9.2.

Unstandardized path coefficients forecasting Rate (all treatments pooled). Numerals in parentheses are standard deviations.

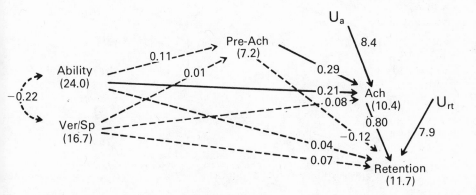

Figure 9.3.

Unstandardized path coefficients forecasting Achievement and Retention (all treatments pooled).

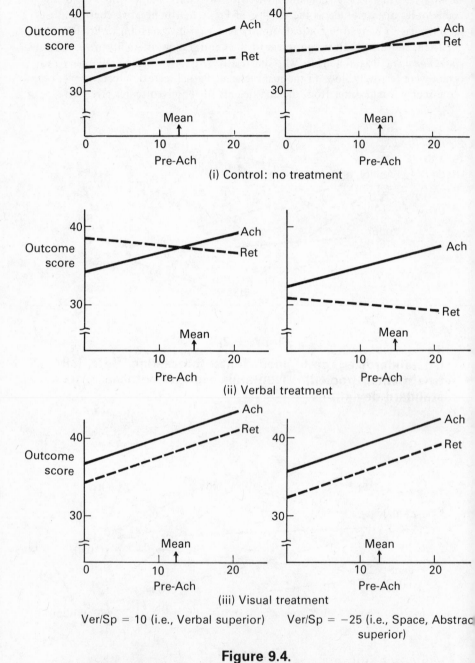

(i) Control: no treatment

(ii) Verbal treatment

(iii) Visual treatment

Ver/Sp = 10 (i.e., Verbal superior)   Ver/Sp = −25 (i.e., Space, Abstrac
superior)

Figure 9.4.

**Regression lines for Achievement and Retention in three
treatments (Ability fixed at 180).**

Lacking reliability coefficients, we were unable to take error of measurement into account. Here there is a special difficulty: errors on Pre-Ach and Pre-Rate may be correlated.

The Control-group coefficient relating Pre-Ach to Rate was 0.31; this r was close to zero in each experimental group. The contrast did not reach statistical significance.

Figure 9.3 presents another diagram for all Ss pooled, keeping Ach and Ret as outcomes. Pre-Rate, which had little independent relation to these outcomes, is disregarded. Ret depended heavily on Ach, as reported in Chapter 4. Aptitudes had positive relationship to the learning outcomes. The negative relation of Pre-Ach to Ret does not imply that those with good Pre-Ach retained relatively little. Rather, Ach tended to determine Ret, whether or not Ach was consistent with Pre-Ach. Ability influenced Ach, and those for whom verbal ability was high compared to spatial and abstract abilities tended to achieve more. Among those who achieved equally well, Ability and Ver/Sp superiority went with somewhat better Ret. With Ach as dependent variable we found *no ATI* (Fig. 9.4).

With regard to Ret, the only difference between Controls and pooled Experimental Ss was the larger residuals of Controls. *The predictors interacted with the Verbal/Visual contrast* (nominally significant). The path diagram of Figure 9.3 implies the following regression equation for predicting raw scores on Ret, treatments pooled:

Ret =   0.04 Ability + 0.07 Ver/Sp + 0.80 Ach - 0.12 Pre-Ach

We have ignored the constant; hence, have predicted the deviation from the group mean. The equation within the Control group ($R^2 = 0.58$) is much the same:

Ret =   0.06 Ability + 0.05 Ver/Sp + 0.81 Ach - 0.18 Pre-Ach.

The other slopes are described as follows:

Verbal group ($R^2 = 0.43$)

Ret =   0.06 Ability + 0.18 Ver/Sp + 0.68 Ach - 0.25 Pre-Ach

Visual group ($R^2 = 0.69$).

Ret =   0.00 Ability - 0.01 Ver/Sp + 0.87 Ach + 0.09 Pre-Ach

We have not tested the separate significance of the several contrasting weights. The contrasts imply that Ret from the Verbal treatment depended less on Ach than Ret from the Visual treatment, that Pre-Ach had a greater negative weight and Ver/Sp a greater positive weight.

With Ach omitted, the deviation score AT regressions were as follows:

Control group ($R^2 = 0.25$).

Ret =   0.27 Ability + 0.12 Ver/Sp + 0.07 Pre-Ach

Verbal group ($R^2 = 0.22$)

Ret =   0.15 Ability + 0.22 Ver/Sp - 0.07 Pre-Ach

Visual group ($R^2 = 0.27$).

Ret =   0.18 Ability + 0.07 Ver/Sp + 0.36 Pre-Ach

Removing Ach from the equation allowed Pre-Ach and Ability to take on weight. For Controls, the influence of Ability was partly a direct contribution, but mostly it was an effect mediated through Ach. Even though the weights for Ability were similar in the Verbal and Visual groups, a "direct" effect appeared only in the Verbal group. Holding Ach and other variables constant, test-bright Ss retained no more after Visual treatment than test-dull Ss. It is this kind of "causal" analysis to which path coefficients lend themselves.

Figure 9.4 lays out some of the relationships for inspection. Each panel shows the regressions for two outcome variables under one treatment. No one panel alone portrays an interaction. All regressions were calculated inserting the value of 180 (near the mean) for Ability. The left-hand column assumes Ver/Sp = + 10 (about 1 s.d. above the mean) and the right-hand column assumes Ver/Sp = – 25 (about 1 s.d. below the mean).

With some caution, in view of the sample size, we reach these conclusions:

1.   General ability forecast achievement and retention. Advance organizers somewhat reduced the importance of general ability. In fact, *able Ss were some-what better off under the Control treatment.*

2.   Differences in the treatment means are scarcely interpretable in view of the interactions.

3.   *Pre-Ach interacted.* The Verbal treatment was better for persons with low Pre-Ach and the Visual treatment better for those high on Pre-Ach.

4.   Other things being equal, *persons with Spatial and Abstract stronger than Verbal ability* (right-hand column of the figure) *profited more from the Visual treatment.* This is consistent with the basic Gagné hypothesis. For persons with comparatively strong Verbal ability, which treatment was advantageous depended on Pre-Ach .

The study tended to support the potential value of research on the Verbal/Visual contrast.

Under the Visual treatment, the relation of Ret to Ach was what one might expect: loss of a fraction of the initial achievement. The relation under Verbal and Control treatments was paradoxical; there were great losses for those who did well on Pre-Ach, and no loss at all—perhaps even a gain—for those poor on Pre-Ach. This sleeper effect could be important if confirmed in other samples. It constitutes a strong argument for using a delayed test in classroom ATI studies.

Gagné and Gropper concluded that they had found no interaction, and went on to say that the abilities most tests measure are too general. If ability to learn from visual materials depends upon specific abilities, these will be abilities directly related to the way information is to be processed in this task. Some such abilities are: ability to abstract a class concept from exemplars, ability to discriminate visual objects by multiple cues, ability to resist interference from reversal of cues, ability to code unfamiliar figures for retention, and ability to identify correct verbal statements of principles from visual exemplars. Such abilities, not measured by present tests, are measurable. Gagné and Gropper advocated analyzing the aptitudes required in the particular tasks to be used in instruction.

The Gropper studies. Work that Gropper (1965) had previously carried out differed from the study just discussed. The Visual/Verbal contrast was between two main bodies of instruction rather than between two preliminary ground-laying treatments.

An investigator is rewarded for reporting dramatic positive results, not for conflicting, ambiguous, or insignificant results. Gropper's work was selected by his organization, the American Institutes for Research, as one feature of their Annual Report for 1965. A multicolored chart displayed a negative relation of gain to ability, in the Visual treatment, the implication being that Lows should be taught visually. These dramatic results were highly selected. *Interactions appeared only sporadically in the data.*

Gropper had taught principles of physics by visual displays on closed-circuit television or by programmed verbal materials (also presented on a video screen). On a verbal posttest the respective means of outcome (not gain) for students with low and high IQs were 13.2 and 15.7 for the Visual presentation, implying a modest relation to ability; and 12.8 and 17.8 for the Verbal presentation, implying a strong relation. Interpretation is made bewildering by the fact that there were eight treatment groups, allowing such treatment combinations as repetition of lesson with active response, and shift from Verbal and Visual lesson with no active response. It is impossible to figure out which subgroups entered into the two "treatment means."

The second study was if anything more complicated in design, and the report even less clear. On the delayed achievement test only, in half the cases only, IQ was steeply related to performance in a treatment that called for verbal responses. IQ was little related to outcome when the student responded by marking pictures in his booklet.

There is a recurrent suggestion in the work of Gagné and Gropper that adding diagrams to text reduces the usual advantage of the student with high IQ or high verbal ability. The studies of Eastman and Behr (p. 285, 286) support this. The regression slopes usually do not differ greatly and are not consistent from one sample to another or from one item of knowledge to another. The later investigators have converged in criticizing simple hypotheses about pictorial-spatial correspondence. Hypotheses ought instead to characterize pictures in terms of the kind of processing (iconic storage, verbal translation, rotation, etc.) that is required to learn from them. While spatial aptitudes may be relevant to learning that requires mental rotation or other such transformation, they probably have nothing to do with other kinds of processing. It is not certain that any current aptitude test is relevant to iconic learning. It is especially important to check on the possibility that adding pictures is detrimental to the learning of some high-Verbal students. In future work with pictures, the instruction should be of considerably longer duration than in these studies.

Presentation by film and television

We have not examined all the reports that pit filmed or televised instruction against other presentations. Many of these studies have been gross comparisons, without well-defined experimental variables. (Some studies with well-defined variables fit into other parts of our discussion.)

A comparison that suggests ATI and also implies learning-to-learn-from-films was reported by Snow (1963). Measures of personality, attitude, and ability, and reports of prior experience, were collected on Ss observing filmed/live lecture-demonstrations in college physics. N = 437 freshman engineers. The alternative treatments constituted the major portion of a semester's work for one course. Immediate and delayed recall were assessed. Blocking procedures were used to form a series of three-way unweighted-means analyses, though regression methods would have been more powerful and more parsimonious. Results for personality and attitude variables will be discussed in Chapter 13. Here we concentrate on abilities.

Treatments did not differ on the average. The blocking procedure provided nine subgroups: High/medium/low aptitude, crossed with high/medium/low prior knowledge of physics. Some modest ATI were statistically significant using either verbal or numerical scores as aptitude. Numerical ability was related to performance in the live condition more than in other conditions, for all levels of prior knowledge. *Live demonstration was consistently superior to film for Ss high on numerical ability.* For low-numerical Ss having high prior knowledge of physics, film was superior to live demonstrations on both immediate and delayed criteria. For other subgroups, differences were negligible. Only one verbal effect reached significance: the live condition was superior to film for high-verbal, medium knowledge Ss. For other subgroups the methods did not differ. As no complex curvilinear relations had been predicted, we conclude that *verbal ability did not interact.*

Of potentially greater importance was an effect of prior experience in learning from films. S was asked to estimate the extent to which he had previously been taught by film. An affirmative report of *experience with instructional films was associated with better performance in the film condition.* This effect became more pronounced as the semester proceeded. Experience was not related to performance in the live condition.

Snow's finding about prior experience fits with earlier work on instructional film by Vandermeer (1950). A three-month general-science course was taught to ninth-graders by a series of 44 films (shown twice)/by films plus study guides/by conventional classroom methods; N = about 120. There was a small difference favoring the film groups on a three-month delayed posttest. On a subsequent series of geography and natural-history films, it was found that Ss who had had the extensive film-learning experience learned more from these later films. This advantage has been called "film literacy."

An ordinal interaction suggested the *advantage of film for persons of low aptitude* in a World War II Air Force study (Gibson, 1947, pp. 246ff.). The small scale of the study left the significance of the findings uncertain. One hour of training was given on a technique of aerial gunnery that depended on the gunner's insight into the relative motion of the attacking and defending planes. The instruction was by film/by illustrated manual/by illustrated lecture. Instead of looking at aptitude, the investigators compared the men high and low on the immediate posttest, contrasting the top and bottom 30 per cent within each treatment. This deceptively simple technique of dramatizing differences in within-treatment s.d.'s translates information about means and s.d.'s within treatments into an implied ATI. In the Air Force study the top performers in the film group were very little better than the leaders in the other groups. Among the Lows, the film group was considerably ahead on both immediate and delayed tests. There was, then, an ordinal interaction of an aptitude that was not identified.

Crowley and Rudy (1969) used DAT Verbal and Space tests to form High-High, High-Low, Low-High, and Low-Low samples. Random halves from each cell were taught by videotape/a printed transcript with illustrations ($N = 64$). The 14-minute lesson covered mitosis, reviewing material Ss had studied one year earlier in tenth-grade biology. A Semantic Differential assessed interest. Ss rated how well the presentation had covered a list of cues. And knowledge was tested. Multivariate analysis of covariance indicated that the printed transcript produced better knowledge. *No ATI were significant,* but the experiment and analysis were not powerful.

Older literature on the TV/live contrast has been discussed by Campeau (1967) and by Snow and Salomon (1968). Campeau (p. 105–106) summarized findings thus:

> Differences in effectiveness between instruction by TV and by conventional methods have sometimes been found to vary with ability level. High-ability students learned significantly more by TV than by conventional methods in psychology (Dreher and Beatty, 1958) and in science ([J. N.] Jacobs and Bollenbacher, 1959); . . . conventional methods of instruction were most effective for low-ability students in science (Curry, 1959, 1960; Jacobs and Bollenbacher, 1959). However, conventional instruction was significantly better than TV for high-ability learners in English composition (Buckler, 1958) and mathematics (Curry, 1959), while TV was significantly better than conventional instruction for low-ability learners in economics and psychology (Dreher and Beatty, 1958) and math problem solving (Jacobs, Bollenbacher, and Keiffer, 1961).

Whatever the final verdict on the adequacy of the original studies, the TV/conventional contrast is evidently not a variable about which one can safely generalize.

We warn against accepting any author's conclusion about ATI of film or TV without careful reconsideration of the statistical treatment. A case in point is the Jacobs-Bollenbacher finding. When the fine print of their report was examined, the alleged strong interaction proved to be spurious. The school system had labeled classes as having high/medium/low ability, and the authors related outcomes to these labels. But one of the "low" classes was a comparatively weak class in a superior school and clearly better on a pretest than the low class in the other treatment. *TV/non-TV did not interact* perceptibly with measured ability.

A microteaching study and its sequels

In microteaching, a teacher in training leads a few students through a ten-minute lesson. The session is videotaped and can be criticized when played back. The trainee replans his lesson and tries it again with other students. Koran (1969) sought to improve the teacher's ability to ask analytic questions. In a video-modeling treatment (VM), a videotape showed a teacher performing the required skill. The sound track from the tape was typed out and read by Ss in a text-modeling treatment (TM). Teacher interns ($N = 121$) were randomly assigned to treatments. Control Ss (C) had no model and no critique. The number and nature of analytic questions asked by S of his students in subsequent microteaching trials, and a printed test of his ability to identify analytic questions, served as criteria. Pretest aptitude measures were taken from the ETS Kit and from Seibert and Snow (1965). A strong main effect favored VM. All criterion measures entered into ATI.

Criterion measures were paired with aptitude measures for regression analysis. Some aptitude part-scores were entered separately. This practice is questionable, since more analyses implies more results significant by chance. Among Koran's 73 regression analyses, 13 yielded *nominally significant ATI* (compared with 4 expected by chance).

Two aptitude measures had especially strong interactions with the number of analytic questions actually asked after training, the most important criterion. The relation of criterion performance to Hidden Figures Part 1 (HF-1) showed ATI. The TM treatment worked best for those high on HF-1, while VM was best for Lows. Indeed, under VM, Lows outperformed Highs. Hidden Figures may be an index of general nonverbal ability, of Thurstone's flexibility of closure, or of Witkin's field independence. Strangely, an ATI appeared only for HF-1, and the pattern of regression slopes for HF-2 was nonsignificant in the reverse direction.

An interaction similar to the result for HF-1 was obtained for Part 2 of Maze Tracing Speed, a perceptual scanning test. (The intercorrelation of HF-1 and Maze Tracing Speed was only 0.28.) No ATI was obtained with verbal comprehension, auditory memory, expressional fluency, or other tests of perceptual speed.

An experimental test, Film Memory, had a positive regression slope in VM and a negative slope in TM. Memory for photographically displayed live action apparently helped in learning from videotape; but why was this ability a drawback in TM?

It may be that VM is best for trainees with relatively good Film Memory and poor HF-1. TM had no clear advantage for Ss with the opposite pattern. In practice, the less costly *TM treatment could be chosen for Ss with low Film Memory and high HF-1*, reserving VM for the type of learner most likely to profit from it.

The interacting measures were unconventional. Film Memory is one of a number of cine-psychometric devices developed to explore mental processes not accessible to printed tests (Seibert & Snow, 1965; Seibert, Reid, & Snow, 1967). The content portrays complex human behavior, largely nonverbal, that is hard to encode fully in symbolic or verbal terms. And, as noted before, HF-1 is just half of a test whose meaning is uncertain. Such measures may represent information-processing skills relevant to learning, which conventional tests do not reflect.

In three brief, small studies, Marantz and Dowaliby pursued Koran's hint that HF-1 warrants attention, working with classroom instruction rather than micro-teaching. In Study I (1973a), 65 college Ss viewed a 45-minute film/a 25-minute videotape lecture on obedience. The content was identical to that used by Jacobs and Bollenbacher (see our p. 275). Factual multiple-choice and fill-in sections of the posttest were analyzed separately.

HF-1, HF-2, and the Taylor Manifest Anxiety Scale served as aptitude measures. Only HF-1 related significantly to achievement, and results were reported only for this part score. With a median split on Anxiety and on HF-1 in a 2 x 2 x 2 anova, the multiple-choice posttest showed Treatment and Anxiety main effects (lecture < film; Low A < High A) but *no first-order ATI*. On fill-in items, there was a Hidden Figures main effect and no Treatment effect. HF-1 related strongly to fill-in performance in the lecture group but not the film group. *This ATI was similar to Koran's.* Among anxious Ss, the lecture/film slopes for HF-1 differed greatly; this suggests a second-order ATI. (Cf. Oosthoek, p. 452.)

Studies II and III were reported together (Marantz & Dowaliby, 1973b). In Study II, 224 college Ss were divided between movie/lecture, each shown by film/videotape. The movie, entitled *Conflict,* lasted 18 minutes. The lecture took 15 minutes. Here, only HF-1 was administered and only upper and lower quartiles were included in the analysis, reducing the sample to 112. A verbal-ability measure was said to yield no important results. The posttest on facts consisted of 17 fill-in items. Main effects were significant: movie > lecture; video > film. HF-1 interacted significantly and ordinally; the movie was superior to the lecture for Lows, whereas the treatments were equal among Highs.

Study III used 116 college Ss in four conditions: audiotaped lecture/audiotaped narration of the movie/typed transcript of the lecture/audiotaped lecture plus the lecture transcript. The movie, lecture, and immediate posttest were the same as in Study II, and again the data came from high and low quartiles on HF-1 (N = 64). Treatments means did not differ. The correlation of HF-1 with outcome was negative (!) in the audio-lecture-plus-transcript treatment, and positive in other conditions.

The authors then computed regression slopes for each treatment of Studies II and III. Figure 9.5 combines two of their figures. Johnson-Neyman analyses were made for eight pairs of slopes[1]. The upper bound of every region of non-significance was beyond the aptitude range. The HF-1 score defining the lower bound ranged from 3.8 to 7.1, with an average at 5.5. Using the code of Figure 9.5, the following contrasts generated at-least-nominally significant ATI:

---

[1] The Johnson-Neyman assumption of uniform outcome variances was probably violated, and we do not know the consequences of such violations for the reported regions of significance.

AL + TL/TL or FL or AL or VL or AM
FM/FL
VM/TL

This finding has considerable resemblance to Koran's.

The results for audio lecture-plus-transcript are puzzling. Why should two conditions which produced positive slopes when used separately have a negative slope when combined? The authors suggested that the movies, with parallel audio and video channels, and the added task of reading transcript along with an audio lecture, assures that the attention of Lows will be directed to critical details. This helps Lows who do not identify details on their own. Highs may do better when concentrating their analytic skill on a single channel.

The Marantz-Dowaliby data move us closer to a credible ATI hypothesis. But the studies taken together still do not suffice as replication or extension of Koran's result. Interpretation of HF-1 remains uncertain unless we know how HF-2 would function.

We append here another study with similar results, though the aptitude was verbal ability. Ketcham and Heath (1963) divided 154 college Ss between film with sound/sound only. Two groups received one presentation of the material, and two received three presentations. Another group was allowed three film showings plus notetaking. Still another received conventional classroom instruction. Treatment means showed film to be better than sound alone, and three showings to be better than one. When the posttest was regressed onto aptitude, slopes for the six groups did not differ significantly, but N was small and the contrast of principal interest is lost from view among six slopes.

The pairs of slopes showed ordinal ATI. *With one presentation, film gave a shallow slope, sound gave a steep one.* (These groups correspond to Treatments 1 and 7, respectively, of Marantz and Dowaliby.) Three presentations gave a similar but weaker pattern. Notetaking and conventional teaching also gave shallow slopes.

Auditory presentations. While studies of instructional media have at times considered an auditory (e.g., audiotape) presentation as an alternative to text (e.g., Marantz & Dowaliby, p. 277), only two minor studies concentrated on this contrast.

In a study of reading comprehension, Oakan, Wiener, and Cromer (1971) obtained a finding with clear ATI implications. We ignore other aspects of the work. Fifth-grade students ($N = 96$) were classified as good/poor readers. Brief stories were presented in audiotape/printed form with good/poor input characteristics. In "good input," S read the original printed stories, or listened to the taped reading of a skilled fifth-grader. "Poor input" was a tape of a poor fifth-grade reader, or a transcript of such a reading. Each S spent slightly less than an hour reading or listening to stories. An immediate posttest measured comprehension.

ATI was significant and disordinal. Good printed input was best for good readers. Good auditory input was best for poor readers. The regression slope for story comprehension onto reading level was strongly positive for good printed

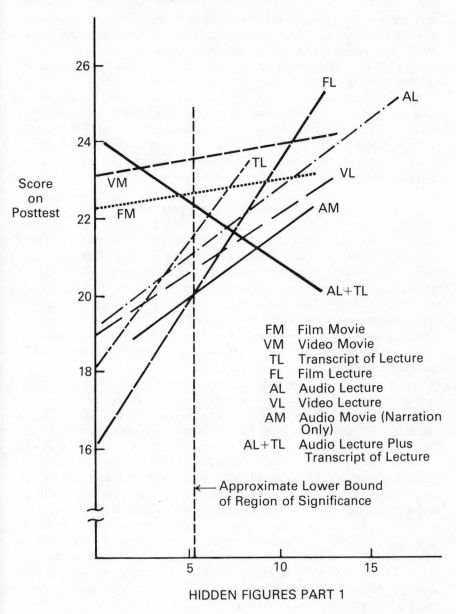

Figure 9.5.

Regression lines under audio, video, and text presentations. After Marantz and Dowaliby, 1973b.

input and zero for good auditory input. The implication of this miniature study is that *poor readers should receive information by ear:* "compensation by prosthesis." Weakness in reading ability could be circumvented in this way; instruction in other school areas could proceed by audio communication while the reading weakness is being remedied.

Budoff and Quinlan (1964) lend some support to this suggestion. Among seven- and eight-year-olds of average IQ, those reading below/at grade level were identified. Word pairs were presented by audiotape/by flash card. With trials-to-learn the paired associates as criterion, audio presentation was best for both groups but particularly good for the poor readers. Extrapolation suggests that excellent readers might learn better from the flash cards.

Spatial and figural supplements to text

The recurrence of spatial ability measures in the ATI studies of the preceding sections reflects the persistent view that special abilities in the Thurstone tradition ought to be useful in fitting instructional methods to the individual. The Thurstone approach has been significant in guidance. No one doubts, for example, that mathematical training is relevant to advanced work in engineering. The prospective engineering student is encouraged if he does well on mathematical tests and advised to consider other career goals if he does badly. This kind of guidance makes use of ATI of a sort. But our interest is in the possibility of achieving the *same* educational goal by alternative methods.

A common suggestion for matching method to aptitude has been to distinguish various modes of communication (e.g., verbal, symbolic, or figural) so that persons who do well on a test in one medium can be instructed via that medium. Gagné (1960, pp. 53, 112), for example, predicted that persons high in spatial ability "should acquire mediating spatial concepts more readily than they do symbolic or verbal ones." Moreover, "high verbal ability should facilitate the learning of verbal concepts; and high numerical ability should facilitate the learning of symbolic concepts." As we shall see, this kind of hypothesis has rarely held up under test, though some scattered findings could be worth pursuing.

In the typical experiment in this vein, *S* takes a test from the spatial-figural-visualization domain which requires him to recognize how some diagram will look when rotated, folded into a solid object, or otherwise transformed. He also takes a test of vocabulary, verbal analogies, or the like. Half the *S*s are asked to learn from a verbal presentation, while the other half are given diagrams or photographs, perhaps with verbal accompaniment.

Only rarely does a figural treatment truly call for spatial reasoning, where areas or volumes must be rotated, unfolded, or otherwise transformed. Graphs, pictures, and diagrammatic schemes may aid communication, especially for the verbally deficient student, but it is hard to see that they capitalize on any kind of spatial ability.

Allison's study (1960) is an example. He administered four concept-attainment tasks. In two tasks, the stimuli were words and the solution rules semantic, while in the other two the stimuli were shapes and the solution rules had to do with their classification. Among Allison's aptitude tests were three measures of vocabulary or verbal reasoning and three spatial tests. (We ignore Cubes, which had low correlations with all variables.) Ss were 315 Navy recruits.

Concept-attainment tasks call for discovery or inference, and are rather unlike typical instruction. Moreover, Allison's Ss had to classify figures rather than to visualize transformations. Even so, the hypothesis that verbal content should make the task easier for those high on verbal tests (and similarly for spatial) fits Gagné's line of reasoning. *Results for the verbal tasks (Table 9.5) supported the expectation.*

Table 9.5   Correlations of parameters of concept-attainment scores with two kinds of aptitude

Task	Parameter	Correlations of outcome with verbal tests	Correlations of outcome with spatial tests	Higher r's
V1	Rate	0.23, 0.28, 0.30	0.15, 0.17, 0.19	V
	Curvature	0.33, 0.34, 0.40	0.14, 0.18, 0.25	V
V2	Rate	0.42, 0.50, 0.51	0.15, 0.23, 0.23	V
	Curvature	0.42, 0.45, 0.45	0.09, 0.12, 0.23	V
S1	Rate	0.10, 0.14, 0.14	0.07, 0.08, 0.18	?
	Curvature	0.17, 0.22, 0.25	0.20, 0.20, 0.28	?
S2	Rate	0.33, 0.35, 0.38	0.24, 0.26, 0.30	V
	Curvature	0.05, 0.10, 0.15	0.05, 0.09, 0.20	?

Data from Allison, 1960. Correlations within a set are listed in order of magnitude and there is no row-to-row correspondence.

The analogous statement regarding spatial content was not supported. The two kinds of ability were equally relevant to spatial tasks.

After many such reports, we come to realize that a task is to be characterized not merely by its stimuli and the required responses, but also by the way a good performer processes the information. In classifying spatial material and generalizing a rule, verbal processes can be as important as spatial ones.

Our latter-day skepticism about the spatial/verbal hypothesis was strongly influenced by a dissertation carried out under our supervision, and we shall discuss it at some length before rounding up other studies. Approximately 200 junior-high-school Ss were given PI in crystallography (Markle, 1968). One program was entirely in words. The alternative presentation was largely diagrammatic; words were used in a limited way, for names of crystals and key terms. The aptitude measures were a Wide-Range Vocabulary Test, a test derived from Thurstone's Cubes, and the Punched Holes test.

These treatments and aptitudes have a notable resemblance to some of those in the study of Allen *et al.* (p. 211 ff.). Markle's criterion measure balanced various forms of representation: verbal items, spatial items, items with verbal stems and spatial alternatives, and items with spatial stems and verbal alternatives. A transfer test was also constructed.

Regression equations taking all predictor variables into account, fitted within each treatment, did not predict significantly better than a single regression equation for all cases pooled, adjusted for treatment means. Significance tests for more specific hypotheses, therefore, could not be justified, and *the null hypothesis regarding ATI was accepted.* The regressions within treatments were examined, of course, and there was only one hint of an effect that in a larger sample could prove significant (see below).

A new hypothesis is needed to replace the supposition that verbal ability implies ability to learn from verbal treatments, and spatial ability implies ability to learn from spatial treatments. What do we mean by "a spatial treatment"? Obviously, we mean a treatment that makes use of diagrams. But a spatial treatment may be designed so as to demand considerable spatial reasoning, or it may be so brilliantly executed that the program serves as a prosthesis for the student who has *poor* spatial ability. That is to say, the program can do the spatial reasoning for him.

While educators have insufficient experience with spatial instruction to say just how this is to be accomplished, we do have such experience with verbal instruction. Text material can be entirely explicit, with every idea developed slowly and reiterated until even the student with low verbal aptitude comprehends. Or, *per contra,* the argument can be elliptical, leaving the student with responsibility for tracing connections, summarizing, etc. It is not obvious that the more explicit treatment is better; it can be time-consuming and tedious for the able student. Moreover, the able student who organizes for himself will probably learn more than when he passively absorbs premasticated materials. Once this has been said, regarding verbal materials, it seems obvious that with regard to any other ability one can design materials either to capitalize on the ability (forcing the student to exercise it) or to avoid demands on it. This means that research on ATI ought not simply to contrast "verbal treatments," "spatial treatments," "numerical treatments," etc.

Markle found remarkably similar correlations in her two treatments. The Punched Hole test (which requires mental rotation of plane figures) correlated 0.46 with the principal outcome measure in one treatment and 0.50 in the other. The Cubes test was unrelated to either treatment; $r = 0.13, 0.15$. (This test had proved irrelevant for Allison also.) The correlations for Vocabulary were 0.51 for the figural treatment and 0.36 for the purely verbal treatment, almost the opposite of the original expectation. The figural instruction used few words—but it therefore offered little redundancy and so placed a burden on the less-verbal student. The verbal treatment was not so lucid as to remove all the difficulties of the less-verbal *S*, but the burden on him was evidently reduced. The substantial correlation of Punched Holes with outcome in a verbal treatment surprised us. But transforming words into images was probably needed to comprehend the statements about crystal forms.

None of the remaining studies was spatial in the usual sense. Bracht's miniature study (1969) compared figural/verbal PI on addition of signed numbers. The figural program emphasized directional arrows on a number line. It was intended to demand spatial reasoning and little verbal reasoning. The reasoning, however, had to do entirely with lines superimposed or laid end to end, whereas spatial tests invariably involve two or three dimensions. Ss were 159 sixth-graders. The average time spent in instruction was less than 15 minutes. The eight ability measures— numerical, verbal, and spatial—had much the same regression slopes, though in 12 out of 16 pairs (considering both an immediate and a delayed posttest) the slope in the verbal treatment was a bit larger. Bracht thought he detected a complex interaction with three-level blocking; among Ss low in spatial ability, those in the middle verbal group did best with the figural treatment, while Highs did best with the verbal treatment. But the relationship is based on some cells where $N=4$ and appears to be a chance result. We conclude that *interaction was negligible.*

Carry (1972) attempted to design alternative treatments, one of which would capitalize on Spatial visualization. The interaction he predicted did not appear in his study, but he pursued the idea by guiding Webb (1971) and Eastman (1972) in later studies of the same variables. The instructional material was revised, the posttests were extended, and new aptitude variables were introduced. At the end, Eastman could conclude that his data "support the original hypothesis of Carry . . . which both Carry and Webb failed to confirm." This work deserves a close look because, on the one hand, it demonstrates that persistent, self-critical, large-scale work is more profitable than hit-and-run hypothesis testing—and, on the other hand, it illustrates the difficulty of replicating and interpreting ATI.

The topic of instruction was quadratic inequalities. The following posttest item, used by Webb and Eastman, is illustrative.

The truth set for $(p^2 - 9) < 0$ is

1. $\{p \mid p < 9\}$
2. $\{p \mid -3 < p < 3\}$
3. $\{p \mid p < 3\}$
4. $\{p \mid p < -3\} \cup \{p \mid p < 3\}$
5. The empty (null) set

The analytic (A) treatment had much symbolic material similar to this item, along with verbal exposition. The "graphical" treatment (G) started much like that in the Bracht study, with the symbolic and verbal material interpreted by vectors on the number line. Later, linear graphs were used to divide a plane into regions, and then sketches of quadratic boundaries of the form $(x - 1)(x - 2) > 0$ were introduced. No "spatial" analysis or transformation of the figures was required, though the student did have to reason from symbol to chart. Table 9.6 summarizes some main aspects of the three experiments. In each of them, Ss were randomly assigned to treatment within classes.

Carry gave both a direct test of learning and a transfer test. Carry's direct test showed no hint of interaction. Webb carried a direct test through his pilot work, but did not use it in his main study. All three investigators emphasized a transfer test that required comparatively difficult applications of the technique.

Each study included the test Necessary Arithmetic Operations (NAO) as a measure of "general reasoning." This is a verbal test which requires no numerical work; S is given a word problem and reports that to solve it one must (for example) add, then divide. Carry's visualization tests were French's Paper Folding (PF) and Form Board tests; because of some faults in the data, Form Board results were ignored. Carry's direct posttest did not correlate with the aptitudes.

As there were only very small differences in means and s.d.'s in these studies, the report of correlations in Table 9.6 gives an adequate picture of the ATI. In Carry's data NAO considered by itself interacted. According to the multiple-regression analysis, the transfer test was predicted by NAO in Treatment G with no weight for Paper Folding and by PF alone in Treatment A. An unpublished reanalysis by Borich established a hyperbolic region of significance, with *the low NAO subject doing better in the analytic treatment* (unless he was also low on PF) and the high NAO, low PF subject better in the graphical treatment.

Table 9.6. Comparison of studies in the Carry series

| Investigator and subjects | Comments on instruction | Tests used | Correlation with transfer measure | | | |
| | | | Reasoning | | Visualization | |
			A	G	A	G
Carry (181 geometry students)	Two periods ample for completion and review	NAO; Paper Folding	0.05	0.44	0.24	0.14
Webb (249 students in second-year algebra)	Mean time to completion about 60 minutes	NAO, Mathematics R2; Paper Folding, Spatial Visualization II	0.18 0.31	0.29 0.33	0.09 0.13	0.22 0.11
Eastman (70 geometry students)	Allowed two class periods	NAO; Abstract Reasoning	0.69	0.18	0.45	0.37

NAO = Necessary Arithmetic Operation   A = Analytic treatment, G = Graphical treatment

This was the opposite of Carry's expectation. Noting that his transfer test lacked internal consistency and that just two of the eight items showed an interaction effect, Carry called for replication.

Webb made editorial improvements in the Carry programs and lengthened them somewhat. He adopted a multitrait-multimethod design for aptitude measurement (see table). He developed a 20-item transfer test whose reliability proved to be about 0.65. While he recorded time-to-completion as a second dependent variable, it had small correlations with other variables and can be ignored here. The transfer test showed *no interaction.* In the regression equations, the only hint of interaction is the slightly steeper slopes in Treatment G, onto PF and NAO. The result for NAO resembled Carry's, but that for PF did not. The two specific items that had shown an interaction in Carry's data showed no such effect in Webb's.

Eastman made an effort to sharpen the distinction between treatments and to obtain reliable transfer scores. For reasons that are not clear he abandoned the multimethod principle and discarded Paper Folding in favor of the DAT Abstract Reasoning test (AR). He regarded this as a measure of spatial visualization, but the test is usually regarded as measuring general reasoning with figural stimuli. Following up Webb's impression that Treatment A was comparatively deductive, Eastman deliberately made his A treatment as deductive as possible, while making the G treatment highly inductive. The modification of the A treatment was slight. At the outset Eastman added a page of abstract verbal axioms. In most of the text, the axioms added only a pedantic note. Thus, the development in time reaches the example $(x+2)(x-3) < 0$. Webb's A text had said, "We have seen that a product including an ——— number of negative factors is negative." Eastman repeated Webb's ten frames on this example verbatim except for changing this sentence to "We know from axiom A_3 that a product. . ." Webb's G text was augmented with a small amount of intuitive material.

Eastman's sample was uncomfortably small, and he complicated matters by splitting each treatment group into advance-organizer/no-organizer subtreatments. This variable had no apparent effect and the samples were recombined for analysis of the main hypothesis. The correlations were much higher than before, excepting NAO in Treatment G. The interaction was significant. It could be described entirely in terms of NAO, but the sample interaction is fitted a trifle better by the weighting 0.60 NAO - 0.22 AR. According to Borich's unpublished calculations the interaction was ordinal, with *Treatment A significantly superior for Ss above the NAO median.* The approach through figures helped the less able students but was somewhat disadvantageous to Highs. This resembles the hint given by a subset of the Bracht data. There is no reason to accept Eastman's interpretation of AR as a test of visualization and no reason to conclude that AR played a distinctive role in his results. The three studies together provide *only negative evidence on the possible relevance of visualization* to a presentation that uses graphs.

It is rare to find a shallower AT slope in an "inductive treatment" (see p. 311), but Eastman's Treatment G required very little inference by the student. We find it strange that the correlation of NAO with outcome should be so much higher for Eastman than for Webb or Carry. The small sample may be responsible. But it is not unlikely that the forbidding page of axioms discouraged Lows at the outset of Eastman's A instruction. This series of near-replications underscores the value of persistent effort, and yet it leaves us with no basis for a conclusion.

Borich's chart of Carry's data shows Treatment G significantly better with NAO 16 or better (over much of the PF range). His chart of Eastman's data shows G significantly *worse* with NAO 16 or better. Would a study pitting Carry's A text against Eastman's A text find an interaction?

Behr (1967) contrasted "figural symbolic"/"verbal symbolic" PI, supposing that figural tests would predict the former and semantic tests the latter. More than 200 teachers in training were asked to study numerical operations in modulus-seven arithmetic. Again, the figural-symbolic material was not "spatial." On post-tests there were no mean differences. The verbal treatment produced a higher s.d. on the delayed posttest than the figural treatment did.

Behr had crossed seven outcome measures with 14 tests from the Guilford system (producing a breeding ground for chance relationships). Emphasizing the principal dimension(s) in the outcome data would have been advisable. But Behr calculated regression slopes for one Guilford test and one outcome measure at a time. His interpretation emphasized those scattered tests for which regression slopes seemed to differ from treatment to treatment.

The slopes Behr calculated enable us to examine a simpler hypothesis. Do figural tests relate more strongly to the figural treatment and verbal tests more to the verbal treatment? Taking all figural tests (CFU, MFS, etc.), we summed the regression slopes for the main outcome (total score on learning test). We repeated this for each treatment, and for semantic tests also, with these resultant slopes, all in the raw-score metric:

	Figural tests	Semantic tests
Figural treatment	7.45	4.28
Semantic treatment	9.21	7.45

The numbers may not be compared from one column to the other, as predictor variances differed. Tests of *either* type predicted better in the semantic (verbal) treatment than in the figural treatment. It follows that a more or less *general factor had greater relevance to the verbal treatment than to the figural treatment.* At the level of single tests, Behr's most striking slope differences were for measures that Guilford codes as CFU, MFU, CMU, and MMR—a thoroughly mixed bag. And all of them gave higher slopes with the verbal treatment.

Kropp, Nelson, and King (within whose project Behr did his work) also carried out a study of the verbal/figural distinction in mathematics instruction, crossing it with an inductive/deductive contrast (Kropp *et al.*, 1967, pp. 69ff.). They found *no significant interaction of verbal/figural treatment with tests,* but they did find other interactions. The study is discussed in detail in our section on discovery learning, p. 370, Kropp *et al.* (1967, pp. 98–112) also made a study of concept attainment that resembled Allison's, stimuli being in figural/verbal form. A pilot study with 16 cases had suggested that Hidden Figures was associated with better figural performance and poorer verbal performance. There was *no hint of suc a relation* in the main study, however. The concept-attainment scores were unreliable and N was only 51.

A disappointing study by Hancock (1972) contrasted short verbal/figural programs for teaching mathematical topics. The figural program made only minimal use of geometric schema, however; it surely is better described as verbal-plus-symbolic. Six Guilford aptitude tests were used. Hancock tested for interactions in a strange way. He first checked the AT regression slope within each treatment for significance; if and only if both slopes were significant, he examined whether the regression lines crossed within the sample range; if so, he then tested for homogeneity of slope. As it happened, none of his 144 ATI comparisons generated an ATI that this routine classed as significant and disordinal. But Hancock's procedure was bizarrely inappropriate, even if one wishes to locate disordinal relations only, since it knocked out of consideration the relations where one regression was steep and the other flat. Since Hancock gave no descriptive statistics we *can only discard the study.*

A later study (Peterson & Hancock, 1974) compared verbal, symbolic, and figural materials on the mathematics of network tracing. Instruction lasted only 35 minutes. (N = 170 college Ss.) Aptitudes were nine Guilford tests. Three composite scores were also formed, to represent the three kinds of content. Posttests were given immediately, then one week later and five weeks later. Treatment main effects, though not tested, appear to have been inconsequential. Nonsignificant AT regression slopes were not discarded, but Hancock's criterion of disordinality was again applied. Homogeneity was thus tested for 67 of the 108 possible pairs of slopes (treatment groups being taken two by two). Of these, 14 were judged nominally significant, using α = .10. This is hardly above chance expectancy. If we ignore the many individual significance tests and look only at the three composite aptitude scores, a simpler though weak pattern emerges. The outcome-on-verbal-ability slope was shallower in verbal instruction than in figural or symbolic instruction. This was true of all three outcomes. (At five-week delay, these contrasts were statistically significant.) With the immediate posttest, figural and symbolic ability gave similar patterns, i.e., shallower slopes when test content matched instructional content, steeper slopes with mismatched content. On the two retention measures, however, figural and symbolic ability showed steepest slopes when matched with like instructional content. These patterns are reminiscent of our discussion of capitalization and compensation in ATI (p. 169 ff). But differences here are slight and the analysis is insufficient. *No conclusion is warranted.*

This brings us to the end of the review of instruction by means of figures. There was no evidence that spatial abilities interacted in this mass of work. It was found, with some frequency, that general ability had a weaker relation to outcome in partly figural instruction than in straight verbal instruction. We shall now summarize two lines of scattered work, each of which has some relevance to the topics of this section. The studies are usually small and isolated, so that they can lead to no conclusions.

Contrasts between mathematics courses. Petersen *et al.* (p. 261) showed an appreciable interaction of aptitudes with demands of alternative ninth-grade mathematics courses. A few other studies have similarly contrasted alternative courses. Two of them contrast "old math"/"new math" in the ninth grade. Osburn and Melton (1963) took PMA and DAT variables as predictors (N = 155). The correlations originally reported were puzzling. Later analysis of the raw data (see Cronbach & Gleser, 1965, p. 176) gave information on regression slopes. The experimental (modern) treatment produced a significantly higher s.d. of outcomes. There seemed to be interactions, the regression slope onto spatial and abstract tests being greater in the experimental treatment. Thus, *the new-math approach somehow did capitalize on spatial ability,* at least in the sample; we do not know enough about the instructional method to understand the result.

In Sabers' (1967) study of the same contrast, the interaction was weak. Over 1000 algebra students in many high schools were scored on the Iowa Test of Basic Skills and on a new version of the Iowa Algebra Aptitude Test. Schools were classed as offering "traditional" or "modern" math. The outcome measures were teacher marks and two achievement tests, one traditional and one modern. Since each group took only one achievement test, no comparison of r's or regression slopes gives directly meaningful evidence for or against ATI. Teachers' marks are an equally uncertain criterion for an ATI study.

The ITBS composite score had about the same predictive value in both courses and results from the arithmetic section of ITBS were equivocal. We read Sabers' data as indicating that all subtests of Algebra Aptitude (reasoning and learning samples) *related to outcomes in the modern course a bit more strongly than in the traditional course.* This steeper slope is consistent with the Osburn-Melton finding, but the interaction was not strong enough to be practically important.

A mystifying finding on spatial ability merits passing mention. Hills (1957; N = 148) contrasted spatial measures with visualization measures, namely the clock-rotation test of Guilford and Zimmerman vs. the boat-prow pictures from the same battery. *The spatial test was strongly related to success in mathematics for engineers* but not in sections taught for physics majors. *The visualization test, however, correlated better in the physics sections.* Regression functions in the two kinds of classes were not given; we cannot judge how much range was restricted; and we know nothing about the way the courses were conducted. There has been no replication.

Imagery as an explanatory variable. We have stressed the importance of identifying the processes involved in ATI. One old connection between aptitude and process variables is the concept of mental imagery, suggesting that some Ss use "mental pictures" to hold ideas in mind during learning, and to associate and elaborate them. Experimental psychologists have lately returned to the study of imagery, though most of the work with laboratory tasks has little relevance to instruction. Investigators such as Levin (1972) have argued that the concept may be particularly helpful in work on ATI. A few studies have tested this.

Two dissertations, by Kuhlman (1960) and Stewart (1965), predate the current interest. Both identified children as High or Low on imagery using spatial tests (e.g., DAT Space Relations, Thurstone Flags).

Kuhlman found *Highs faster than Lows in learning nonsense names for objects shown in random order, but slower in seeing these object names as instances of a concept.* There were two studies, one with extreme groups drawn from Grades 1 and 2 ($N = 20$), the other with 49 pairs from the extremes of a Grade K-4 pool. In the latter, Grade x Imagery interactions appeared, with the effect largest in Grade 1. In the total sample ($N = 490$), correlations of imagery with visual memory, drawing ability, and susceptibility to distortion in Carmichael's classic convergence task were significant but modest. Even larger were correlations of imagery with reading comprehension ($r = 0.35$) and an arithmetic test ($r = 0.34$).

We have not seen Stewart's study, but DiVesta and his colleagues tried a replication and summarized the Stewart work at length in their report (DiVesta *et al.,* 1971, p. 7-8). Apparently, Stewart's data supported Kuhlman's results. In recognition learning, pictures were superior to words for Highs but inferior to words for Lows. Highs perhaps tended to code words as pictures in learning, while Lows tried to code pictures as words.

DiVesta *et al.* (1971, p. 7ff.) used extreme groups of 50 college *S*s. The tests used by Kuhlman and Stewart, plus Embedded Figures, defined Highs and Lows. A list of 50 words and 50 pictures of common objects, derived from Stewart, was presented in random order. Then, a recognition trial presented half of the words and pictures seen earlier, mixed with words and pictures not seen earlier, plus some words seen earlier as pictures and vice versa. After this, the original list was presented for a second time and tested by free recall. Pictures shown originally as pictures were most often recognized and recalled, with words shown originally as pictures a close second. *There was no ATI.* A slight, nominally significant ATI appeared when Highs recalled pictures better than words. DiVesta judged that this result might be due to general ability and not imagery, concluding that Stewart's ATI was not replicated. Note, however, the disparity in age of *S*s in the two studies; imagery in children may be qualitatively different from that in adults.

A second study (their p. 37ff.) showed concrete nouns as words/geometric shapes, each paired with a random numeral. Aptitudes were imagery tests as before, plus the Stroop Color-Word Test and a test of speed in naming pictured objects. $N = 198$ college *S*s. Along with the score on PA learning was a transfer task presenting words and shapes related to the original stimuli. Again, the main effect favored pictorial stimuli. *The only ATI appears unimportant;* speed-of-naming and sex entered into a four-way interaction effect on transfer.

In Study III (their p. 57ff.), interaction appeared in recall of lists of words ($N = 219$). Concrete words were recalled best on the average. The effect was disordinal but not large. *Highs did better than Lows on concrete words while Lows did better than Highs on abstract words.*

In Study IV (their p. 115ff.), a new sample of Highs and Lows ($N = 130$, extreme groups) were given noun-adjective pairs to learn in two study-recall trials. Each word appeared as either stimulus or response, and each was rated high or low on concreteness. ATI appeared only in a four-way interaction; *Highs did better than Lows when stimulus terms were low in concreteness. All Ss did well on concrete words.* The modest effect conflicts with the previous finding.

Study V (their p. 135ff.) compared *S*s learning word lists by using the words in pictures/sentences, with the help of mnemonics in jingle form. The jingles were composed of concrete/abstract words. Extreme groups ($N = 160$) on spatial tests were defined. The jingle with concrete words led to fewer errors in recall. *Several interactions of little consequence were obtained.* Ignoring differences among word lists, one would conclude that all Ss should draw pictures using jingles with concrete words for best results. Ignoring mnemonics as well, we find Lows better off writing sentences.

We see no way to go from this work on variations in imagery of college students in the laboratory to implications about instruction. The Kuhlman and Stewart results with school children might be followed up by larger experiments with children. But cautious interpretation is in order. Kuhlman found imagery related to other ability and achievement measures. A factor analysis of college data by DiVesta *et al.* (their p. 89f.) did not separate imagery from general ability or SAT-Mathematics. The tests used to identify "imagery" are usually called tests of "spatial ability." Future work will need to prove that image generation, and not a broader construct, accounts for results.

The one apparently consistent finding across these studies is that pictures are better learned than words. Pictures, and the imagery they prompt, very likely provide a kind of elaboration useful in learning. This is the implication of many of Rohwer's experiments. We include one of his studies here, because it also suggests an ATI worthy of note. Rohwer and Matz (n.d.) presented three prose passages aurally to 128 middle-SES white and low-SES black fourth-graders. Half of the sample also saw the printed text on slides, whereas half saw pictures illustrating the information given on the audiotape. Another treatment variable compared Ss given memory support (reference copies of text or pictures) with Ss who had to rely on memory. On the posttest S had to state whether each of a list of assertions (presented both aurally and in print) was faithful to the original passages. Pictures were significantly better than print, markedly so for the low-SES black Ss. *The cell means showed a clear ordinal ATI,* which can be attributed to general-ability differences between the two samples. Further analysis suggested that pictures helped middle-SES Ss particularly in verifying true assertions, but helped low-SES Ss more on false assertions.

A generalization that pictures are better than words would be premature, however. Three miniature studies can be appended here to indicate various qualifications We noted (p. 243 ff.) a study by Samuels suggesting that adding pictures to text can distract Low-IQ children. Kulm *et al.* (1974) support this. They divided ninth-graders ($N = 116$) into three IQ blocks, then assigned them to work on algebra word problems in one of five conditions: text/pictures/text plus pictures/text generated by other students, with/without pictures. Of five performance scores, two showed ATI. The presence of pictures caused Lows to use incorrect methods on some problems; text was better for them. The conditions did not differ for more able Ss. The picture condition also elicited more sketching during solution among able Ss, but not among Lows.

A laboratory experiment by Anderson and Kulhavy (1972; $N = 62$) presented text with/without instructions to S to form images during learning. Finding no treatment effect on a posttest, the authors then classified Ss according to whether they reported having used imagery with none/half/all of the text booklet. Reported imagery was positively related to the posttest and an ordinal interaction was nominally significant. Ss *not* using imagery when asked to do so learned less than other non-imagers; the two conditions did not differ among Ss using imagery. The implication seems to be that instructions to use images are harmful to Ss who are not inclined to use them naturally.

Finally, we note a dissertation by Coffing (1971). His finding deserves to be checked in further work on pictures. After taking six tests of verbal, spatial, perceptual-speed, and reasoning abilities, 38 high-school Ss saw slides showing paired associates. The stimulus pairs were such that either or both members of a pair could be represented by a picture of an object/a printed name. A recorded voice named each pair as it appeared on the screen. In a pretest series, each slide presented a pair, showing both the pictures and the names. By recording eye fixations Coffing could infer which form of representation S preferred to attend to. Subsequently, S encountered 12 slides that paired pictures *and* 12 that paired words, all with taped voice accompaniment.

The pictorial treatment was superior. Among a dozen scores on paper-and-pencil tests of ability, it is possible that a maze test interacted but not significantly. Among 17 indices of pretest attention patterns, two did yield significant ATI. The verbal treatment was very poor for Ss who fixated predominantly on the pictorial *stimuli* (not the response terms, not the words) at pretest. Given the tiny sample and the shotgun nature of the analysis, no confidence can be put in this result as it stands.

Summary

Most of the research of this chapter searched for interactions of specialized abilities. Rarely were the original hypotheses confirmed in even one study. The bulk of the evidence again indicates interactions of a vaguely defined general ability, and absence of expected effects of more specialized abilities.

Treatments designed to capitalize on spatial ability presented information diagrammatically or required reasoning about diagrams. In these treatments, the regression of outcome onto spatial ability was not often steeper than the regression onto verbal ability.

This negative result was found in the following studies: Allison, Hamilton, Bracht, Carry, Behr, Kropp *et al.* mathematics, Kropp *et al.* concept attainment, and Crowley-Rudy. Studies by DiVesta on imagery gave no additional leads. The positive findings were as follows. In the Gagné-Gropper study, persons standing higher on spatial than on verbal aptitude profited from the figural treatment. (But interactions of general ability and of prior knowledge were more impressive.) Koran's Hidden Figures part-score related positively to an iconic (not figural) presentation and negatively to a verbal one. Marantz and Dowaliby produced similar interactions with a film/lecture contrast. There were inexplicable miscellaneous findings (e.g., Hills, Osburn-Melton).

Symbolic presentations were contrasted with semantic ones that made more use of words. These did not interact with the corresponding distinction among Guilford tests (Davis, King grammar).

There is a bit of evidence that measures of specialized kinds of learning ability interact. A test of ability to learn from film interacted with pictorial/verbal presentation (Koran). This is consistent with the findings of Snow and Vandermeer that persons with more experience in learning from film profit more from instruction via film. One can make a parallel argument about the Brownell-Moser finding (p. 248) that some children know how to take in a meaningful explanation and some do not. The apparent interaction of a radio-code test (Berliner-Melanson, p. 183) should also be recalled.

Taking Chapters 8 and 9 together reinforces the view that general ability enters into interactions. The data do not indicate whether the effect is more attributable to fluid ability, or general verbal development and reading ability, or relevant knowledge, or memory, etc. One might generalize that "meaningful" treatments relate to the general-ability complex to a greater degree than "less meaningful" treatments. We have concluded that this is a poor way to state the issue. "Meaningful" is a response-defined construct. Meaning is not directly provided to the learner; it is constructed by him as he processes the material. Generalizations ought to be stated in terms of directly manipulable characteristics of the treatments. Materials that use more words or that conceptualize more abstractly give steeper AT slopes onto general abilities than do less-verbal materials. (The only study that clearly points in the opposite direction is that of Edgerton, where a treatment not intended to make meanings readily apparent was beneficial to Highs.) The Fredrick study reminds us that the learner must extract meaning from diagrammatic as well as verbal presentations; hence, diagrams too may place a burden on Lows.

Students who have been doing well in the kind of instruction they have been receiving, as shown by their achievement to date or by measures of their ability to learn from kind of instruction, probably should continue to receive instruction of that kind. But students who do well on general mental tests, and less well on measures of past instruction, presumably have talents that have not been used, and one can hope that some other instructional approach will enhance their learning. This is of course the usual assumption behind remedial instruction. It presupposes an interaction of what has often been called "underachievement"— the difference between fluid and crystallized abilities—with conventional/alternative instruction. Evidence of this kind is to be found in the Anderson, Thiele, Petersen-Guilford, and Gagné-Gropper studies. The studies of specialized learning ability also support this notion.

We need more sophisticated hypotheses, based on a careful analysis of the information processing required in the course of learning, and a corresponding analysis of tests to identify the processes that account for high scores. To label a treatment as "spatial" merely because it uses diagrams is simple-minded. To label a treatment as "meaningful" is equally to overlook the significant questions about who is able to extract the meaning and how. To date, no major study has framed hypotheses in terms of the acts the learner must perform. We have seen some small studies—and shall meet a few more—where striking shifts in aptitude-outcome correlations were achieved by altering treatments according to detailed conceptions of the act of learning or retrieval.

Even though this chapter forces us to reject the conclusion that spatial treatments demand spatial ability, and the notion that the differentiated Guilford abilities will interact with "treatments of the same name," the door is not closed to positive findings in the future. Analysis of a certain set of lessons might suggest that certain specific internal manipulations are needed to encode and transform what is given. It should then be possible to select or invent at least one directly relevant test which will identify the superior learner. The test might be even more specific than the constructs of Guilford. This is not a simple kind of theorizing; even when the effort to work analytically fails, it will enhance our ability to theorize about aptitudes.

Chapter 10 | Interactions of abilities with variations in curriculum and instruction

Chapter 10 looks at further experiments on classroom instruction, most of them extending over some weeks. Studies closer to the laboratory in spirit are reserved for Chapter 11.

Research on innovative curricula

Curricular research is rather unlike the experimental research that compares alternative teaching techniques for conveying the same facts or developing the same skill. Curricula differ in content. Two geometry curricula will employ different kinds of problems, different theorems, and perhaps different degrees of emphasis on formal proof. Alternative chemistry courses will differ in choice of units, choice of theoretical terms, and sequence of topics. Each curriculum in literature will have its own list of authors to be read. Which, among the competing curricula, yields best results is only in part an empirical question, since educators place different values on the specific content of each set of lessons. The issue of effectiveness can be joined at the transfer level, if the competing courses have the same broad aim. The lessons in chemistry are a vehicle through which the course is to develop ability to comprehend scientific arguments, including those the course did not touch upon. Likewise, each literature course is to alter the student's reaction to whatever literature he will read after the course ends. Such transfer outcomes are of primary importance in curriculum studies.

Instruction in mathematics

Data on interactions were collected in the National Longitudinal Study of Mathematical Abilities (see *NLSMA Reports,* esp. No. 26, 1972), but the interactions were not brought to the surface. This enterprise compiled data over at least three years on "over 112,000 students from 1,500 schools in 40 States". Various abilities and many separate outcomes of mathematics instruction were measured. Data were analyzed separately for students who followed the "new mathematics" curriculum of the School Mathematics Study Group, for students who followed any of several conventional texts, and, in some reports, for smaller groups of students who followed particular other texts. Analyses of individual differences were left wholly without interpretation. Thousands of pages of statistical results relate performance in mathematics to the other individual variables, teacher variables, and curriculum differences—all as a do-it yourself kit from which the reader is to construct hypotheses.

The statistical analyses underlying the tables were intricate, and one would have to study the whole five-foot shelf of reports with care to reach substantive conclusions. NLSMA was not directly concerned with ATI, and regression equations were not reported. Treatment effects were tested by ancova, the covariates being Lorge-Thorndike scores and some basic mathematical abilities. A first step in each of these analyses was to test homogeneity of regressions. Significant heterogeneity of slopes of one or another dependent variable was usually (!) reported; but as a large number of significance tests were made, it is *hard to judge whether to take these interactions seriously.* The within-treatment regressions were not described in the reports; hence, we know nothing about the character of these ATI.

Numerous tables reported how diverse cognitive and affective measures related to performance in mathematics. Tables on relations of cognitive variables to dependent variables in various groups spread over 1200 pages of reproduced computer printouts. Regarding Hidden Figures alone, nearly 100 pages were published. Plunging in at random, *one easily finds what might be significant interactions,* but a full review of the data would be a project in itself.

The data can be illustrated with the first test to appear in Report No. 22: Pick Two Pictures (PTP). This, one of Kagan's measures of "analytic style" or impulsiveness (see p. 382), had been given in the Fall of Grade 4. Fourteen achievement tests had been given in the Spring of Grades 4, 5, and 6. (We ignore tests in the Fall of Grade 7, for simplicity.) The statistical significance of the relation of PTP to each achievement test in turn was tested separately within each Treatment x Sex combination. We consider boys first.

No descriptive summary was given of any relation that fell short of significance; as there were more than 500 cases per sample, nonsignificance implies nearly no relation. Examining the tables, we discovered that computation posttests had a pattern of regressions different from that typical of tests of comprehension or analysis. (Here, "analysis" is used in the sense of the *Taxonomy of Educational Objectives,* not in Kagan's sense.)

Among the six computation tests, we found

1 test significantly related to PTP in both treatments; slope steeper for SMSG.
3 tests significantly related to PTP in SMSG only; slope steeper for SMSG.
1 test significantly related to PTP in Conventional only; slope steeper for
  Conventional.
1 test significantly related to PTP in neither treatment.

Among the six comprehension tests we found

3 tests significantly related to PTP in Conventional only; slope steeper for
  Conventional.
3 tests significantly related to PTP in neither treatment.

Of two tests classed as measures of analysis, one was more related to PTP in the conventional treatment. A test classed as application had the same positive slope in both treatments.

The PTP test, then, appears to have had a *complex interaction pattern.* SMSG did somewhat better in teaching boys high on PTP to compute, but had no advantage for Lows. On the other hand, SMSG was superior in improving comprehension of Lows and less beneficial for Highs. The data on girls support a different conclusion. Neither comprehension tests nor any other outcome had a steeper regression onto PTP in the conventional treatment. I.e., there was an interaction effect on most outcomes, probably ordinal, with SMSG tending to generate the greater slope.

No weight is to be put on these conclusions. But if such patterns appear for the first aptitude examined out of several dozen, a thorough interpretation of the tables should be made. A truly adequate analysis would return to the original data tapes and determine confidence limits for the within-treatment regressions. It might be possible to separate within-school and between-school components of regression.

Two other studies in mathematics hint at interactions, but the reporting or analysis was seriously inadequate. In all, 126 pairs of ninth-grade classes entered a series of comparisons of three modern curricula (SMSG, UICSM, and Ball State) with conventional curricula (J. Ryan, 1968). Attitude and interest were emphasized as outcomes, not competence. The research consisted of many small substudies: e.g., nine classes taught SMSG math were contrasted with nine taught conventional math by the same teachers. The regressions of end-of-year attitude on start-of-year attitude were examined. *Some indication of interactions* appeared at a few points. Thus, girls in UICSM classes showed a comparatively flat posttest-on-pretest regression on the Dutton Mathematics Attitude Scale. There was also a tendency for girls to respond more favorably in UICSM than they did in other treatments. On the whole, the data suggest that UICSM "shook up" preexisting attitudes more than did other curricula. Another analysis considered initial ability and sex as moderator variables. Ryan's anova generated F ratios for Teacher, Teacher x Treatment (modern/conventional), Teacher x Pretest, and Teacher x Pretest x Treatment effects. The F ratios rather often reached significance, but Ryan offered no descriptive information on the effects.

An experimental curriculum emphasizing discovery methods (Madison project) was compared with conventional instruction in Grades 4 to 6, with 200–300 students in each grade. W. F. Brown (1963) divided at random 26 teachers from a larger group of volunteers. Special training was given to the teachers assigned to the experimental method. The analysis was deficient and the tables in the report incomplete and largely incomprehensible.

An appendix reported means for so-called "high," "middle," and "low" IQ blocks and for the total group, on four posttests within each grade, within treatments. But the mean for the whole group should be an average of the block means weighted by their N's, and when we attempted to estimate N's on that premise we found a negative N for Lows in Grade 5. Hence the Grade-5 data are worthless. Whether we can trust the data for Grades 4 and 6 is uncertain. We calculate that in Grade 4, 66 per cent of Ss fell in the high group (!)—with 22 per cent middle and 12 per cent low. The means indicate a disordinal interaction in Grade 4 with Lows better in the experimental treatment and Highs better in the control treatment. The percentages in Grade 6 we calculate to be 51, 27, and 22. The Lows again did less well in the experimental group, but the regressions coincided for middle and high groups. The Grade-5 means give still another picture, but these we must dismiss. Insofar as we can judge, the innovative curriculum helped Lows. Later we shall find, however, that the weight of evidence is for a steeper slope with discovery methods—just the opposite of what seemed to be the case here.

The research of Harvard Project Physics

A major curriculum project of the 1960's was Harvard Project Physics. The HPP staff included a research-and-evaluation team who carried out an exceptional program of studies.

Most important for our purposes is their nationwide experiment in which teachers who said they would be willing to teach the new course were divided strictly at random (Welch & Walberg, 1972; Welch, Walberg, & Watson, in preparation*). Experimental teachers taught the HPP course. Controls were asked to teach whatever they had been teaching previously. This was the experimental PSSC course for some teachers, and for others a conventional course using an established textbook. Because the project leaders wanted to avoid invidious comparisons, the reports did not subdivide the control group.

Among the pretests, the analysis paid greatest attention to start-of-year IQ. There were end-of-year measures of scientific knowledge, comprehension, and attitudes. A particularly interesting instrument—applied in midyear—is the Learning Environment Inventory (LEI). The LEI is a set of statements describing the class-

---

*Criticism of this manuscript may not apply to what is ultimately published. We thank the authors for allowing us to use this draft material. We believe that they now share many of the methodological views we have developed since the HPP data were processed.

room climate and the teacher's style. LEI scores thus describe a complex of intermediate variables caused by student and teacher characteristics. The class atmosphere reflects the success of instruction and the resulting morale, and also has its
own causal effect on the final outcomes.

Cognitive outcomes. The investigators decided that the HPP/other contrast
should be examined with classes as the sampling unit and that the many dependent
variables should be assembled into sets prior to multivariate anova.

In order to take ability into account, as a covariate and as a source of ATI,
classes were blocked on the basis of their mean IQs. Cuts were made at IQ 112.1
and 119.3, to locate classes in three blocks; these fractions represented thirds of
a larger distribution of classes. The 34 HPP teachers divided into 9 High (class
mean IQ above 119.3), 12 Middle, and 13 Low. The 19 "other" teachers divided
5, 8, and 6. These could have been further divided: 1, 4, 1 in PSCC physics, and
4, 4, 5 in classes following one or another conventional text (Welch, personal
communication).

The study lacked power to reject the null hypothesis for large ATI effects with
the class as the sampling unit* and it is no surprise to find that F ratios for ATI
of cognitive outcomes were small. Three-level blocking made matters worse. Though
it would have been pointless to separate the 19 "other" teachers into tiny PSSC
and conventional subgroups for the purpose of significance testing, it was equally
pointless to treat them together as from a single population. In a Brunswikian
sense the "other" treatment had ecological validity as a sample of what was going
on in the country in one particular year, but that seems to be a poor baseline in
an expensive study intended to guide future policy.

Before the HPP staff decided to use class means as the unit of analysis, analyses
had been made of the scores of individuals, pooling classes. These may be instructive
even though persons were not sampled independently, and though the pooled
regression mixes between- and within-class effects. The only such report comparing
courses is embedded in a methodological paper by Walberg (1970). Data were from
a sample who took the same achievement test as pretest and posttest ($N = 250$
boys for HPP, 127 boys for "other"). The achievement measure was converted
to a residual-gain score, i.e., to the deviation from the posttest-on-pretest regression
for all Ss pooled (both sexes, both treatments). Individual IQ was blocked into
three levels.

Treatment interacted with IQ, a physics pretest, and a pretest on the Test on
Understanding Science (TOUS) to influence final achievement. Scattered relations
of personal data probably can be ignored. Judging from Walberg's charts, there
was no difference in achievement between HPP and "other" treatments for able
students, but there was a *marked difference for Lows, who did better in HPP.*
This makes sense, as HPP was intended to be a less technical course.

Effects on attitude. Student opinion about the courses was more favorable

---

*The study was large enough to assess main effects reasonably well. These were said to be
the chief concern—though it is hard to know what a main effect implies if ATI are present.

to HPP. The multivariate interaction F of IQ was not significant, with class as unit of analysis.

For a posttest on attitudes about science, *what at first appears to be a flood of significant ATI were reported.* The HPP developers had particularly wished to generate a positive feeling about science in a population of students to whom conventional physics does not appeal. There was no significant main effect when end-of-course attitude was assessed by a Semantic Differential. There was a significant F for multivariate interaction (p < .01 despite the low power of the analysis). Tests were run on 14 separate attitude variables; plots of the block means for the nine that reached significance were displayed.

A typical pattern is the rating of the stimulus word *Physics* on Interesting/Uninteresting, a cluster score derived from the Semantic Differential. A high score represented a favorable attitude. The cell means were as follows (number of classes in parentheses):

	Low IQ	Middle IQ	High IQ
HPP	4.7 (13)	5.3 (12)	5.0 (9)
Other	5.7 (6)	4.7 (8)	5.2 (5)

The V-shaped regression for the "other" classes was found in nearly every plot, and that for HPP usually was a shallow $\wedge$, as here.

This strange pattern probably means little. Considering the small cell numbers, the dramatic drop of the middle group could be an accidental result—one that could be wiped out by a small change in the cutting scores. Matters are confounded by the fact that the PSSC classes fell in the middle group. Also, classes with deviant means may well have been smaller.

There is a counterargument to be made in the authors' defense. Their null hypothesis was pitted against the hypotheses of linear interaction and nonlinear interaction by their experimental design. The significance test was unbiased. While the positive result may have been the one-in-a-hundred chance represented in the α risk, only twelve multivariate F tests were made; hence, the authors cannot be accused of guaranteeing some "significant" results just by shotgun testing of hypotheses.

A slightly different instrument also generated significant F ratios for interaction. This instrument asked for straightforward ratings of physics. The data for Interesting were almost identical to those from the Semantic Differential, and the same comments apply. Several other scales, however, showed a more regular trend. For example, for ratings of physics on the adjective Technical (where a low rating is desired), these means appeared:

	Low	Middle	High
HPP	5.8	5.5	5.4
Other	5.4	5.9	6.3

On the whole, the data indicate that HPP was more successful at producing the desired attitude in High-IQ classes than in Low groups.

Classroom climate as an "effect". The Learning Environment Inventory (LEI) combines into scales the responses to items such as "Members of the class don't care what the class does." Fourteen scores are formed by averaging the responses of the class members over a subset of items. The item just quoted is scored in the Apathy cluster.

Welch *et al.* treated LEI as a dependent variable. The multivariate F for HPP/ other (main effect) reached significance. While the multivariate F for interaction was small, the lack of power leaves us unable to decide for the null hypothesis.

HPP classes were seen as more diverse than "others" in activities, as less difficult, and as less plagued by teacher favoritism toward star students. The very low F for IQ x Course interaction implies (insofar as we can rely on an analysis of low power) that the difference in LEI ratings of HPP/other was about the same whether the raters were in High-IQ or Low-IQ classes.

In the paper of Walberg and in the work of Anderson and Bar-Yam (see below), some analyses treated LEI as a predictor. Walberg found, for example, that HPP had an advantage over "other" courses in more formal classrooms, whereas there was no important difference in less formal classrooms. This bears on ATI research only in showing that it is well to recognize nuances of the treatment as actually delivered to the student.

Interactions of ability and climate. None of the analyses asked how ability and LEI *and* HPP/other interacted to produce outcomes. Dissertations by G. J. Anderson (1968) and Miriam Bar-Yam (1969) did relate outcomes to ability and LEI *within* HPP. These studies were completed during the earlier period, when individuals were taken as the unit of analysis by this team of investigators. (Bar-Yam included personality variables as aptitudes; on this, see p. 463.)

Some of these analyses may be seen as studies of Aptitude x Treatment interaction *within* HPP. Certain LEI scales (e.g., Goal-Direction) seem to describe treatment characteristics that are under the control of the teacher. Other scales (e.g., Apathy) are resultants of teacher, course, student characteristics, and uncontrolled events. A class mean on one of these other scales is more an index of an intermediate outcome than of a manipulable treatment.

Anderson and Bar-Yam used the same data pool: a national sample of 113 classrooms taught by 56 teachers, all using HPP. Most analyses were restricted to subsamples. Anderson treated boys and girls separately, about 200 boys and 70 girls providing each score. Bar-Yam pooled the sexes and had over 500 cases for each analysis.

One of Anderson's dependent variables was an achievement test, residualized by partialing out a pretest of the same kind. For each of the 14 LEI scales, Anderson carried out a stepwise regression analysis, entering scores on these variables in turn: IQ, LEI, IQ x LEI, IQ^2, LEI^2. The quadratic term for LEI seems not to have had effects beyond the chance level, and the scattered weights for IQ^2 have nothing to do with interactions. Among boys there were no significant interactions. Among girls, there was a strong effect of Difficulty, seen in this equation for standard scores:

Est. of residual achievement $= 0.51z_{IQ} + 0.28z_{Diff} - 0.25z_{IQ} \times Diff.$

The successive R's were 0.51, 0.60, and 0.63. Girls learned more in classes that perceived the work to be difficult than in "easy" classes; this was especially true of girls with average and low IQs.

Also, brighter girls tended to achieve more in classes where there was more Friction and in classes with more Goal Direction by the teacher.

TOUS (residualized) as a dependent variable also showed no interactions among boys. Among girls there were four strong ATIs. Brighter girls did better in classes characterized by low Friction, low Apathy, low Cliqueness, and more Intimacy. A third cognitive outcome was measured with a Science Process Inventory. On this the boys showed a weak interaction for Cliqueness. Among girls there was no ATI.

Anderson's data for boys were consistent: no interactions of LEI scales with IQ (save for one that may be due to chance). There were several strong and significant interactions for girls. Anderson ran more than 100 significance tests for interactions and it seems *best to dismiss the six "significant" results as chance effects.* This spares us the necessity of explaining how Friction can have positive, negative, and negligible ATI with three cognitive outcomes. The contrast of the results in the two sexes means little, since the criteria were residualized by means of within-sex regression weights, making them noncomparable across sexes.

Although Anderson had found only scattered evidence that Goal Direction, Formality, and Organization had any relation to outcomes, Bar-Yam made these the focus of her study of a set of data that overlapped Anderson's. Her anova blocked LEI in two levels and IQ in three levels, with the student as unit. Bar-Yam did not residualize the achievement score, nor did she take the pretest into account in any other way. The p values for interaction of IQ with the three LEI scales were greater than .05. Bar-Yam also ran a t-test at one point and reported that High-IQ Ss did better in less-firmly-directed classes. The effect was modest and *perhaps should be dismissed,* since no such result appeared in Anderson's analysis. There was no difference for Lows.

Bar-Yam found one believable interaction for IQ x LEI when the students' rating of the course was taken as criterion. Students were better satisfied when the class was perceived as Organized. Pooling the more Organized classes, the AT regression slope was positive.

In more disorganized classes it was negative. I.e., *organization made a difference for Highs,* not for Lows. An attempt to use a biographical inventory of science activities as an aptitude turned up nothing of interest.

Methodological notes. We are critical of the statistical procedures used by HPP, but we note that the staff used first-rate statistical consultants. This apparent divergence of views may reflect only the passage of time. Certainly, the criticisms we make now would not have occurred to us in the mid-60's, when the study of HPP was in full swing. On the other hand, it may be that the statistical experts who worked on the study would not be impressed by our criticisms even today.

To begin, let us ignore LEI and ask about interactions of IQ with course. Instead of debating whether to take the course or the student as unit for analysis, we would favor describing effects at several levels (cf. p. 99). Instead of using global F tests to make sure that the null hypothesis is taken as the conclusion wherever possible, we would describe all the discernible effects in these expensive data. The effects (main and ATI) can be described in this manner:

student within *sex* within *class* within *teacher* within *course*

Noting that there were comparatively few girls (two per class or fewer) and that girls are expected to react differently to physics, we would be inclined to do a thorough analysis for boys only. Once this set of findings is digested, the limited data for girls could be processed intelligently.

We would propose to fit a linear equation relating each outcome to IQ within each class. One could then compare plots of those equations so as to judge whether consistency appeared between classes within teachers (in adjusted mean and/or in slope) and whether teachers differed appreciably within course classifications. This would allow separate examination of the several "other" courses. It would allow examination of within-class regressions within treatments, separate from between-class regressions. Once the description of all effects is fully in mind, confidence intervals can evaluate the dependability of the finding and so encourage caution in the use of the information. plots of variables could be inspected for curvilinearity but we would not build curvilinearity into the central hypothesis.

Another general remark: We would much prefer to enter the pretests alongside IQ in the regression analysis. The HPP investigators residualized the outcome, tacitly assuming that the pretests did not interact.

LEI is an intermediate variable. Hence in principle a structural regression analysis would be illuminating. More simply, one could summarize the within-class regressions of groups of classes having contrasting LEI scores. Given a composite display of regression lines for outcome against IQ for all the HPP classes, for example, one could simply trace over the lines for high-Formality classes with a red pencil. Any effect not disclosed by this is probably of little value.

Walberg (1970) has discussed the application of generalized regression analysis to such data. This can be a superior way to lay out prominent effects, but when calculated for persons pooled the regression function is a puzzling mixture of within- and between-class effects. And a between-class generalized regression loses much information. As a minimum, then, it appears that a generalized analysis for IQ along with any LEI scale must include terms for $\overline{IQ}$ and LEI (the class means),

$(\overline{IQ} - \overline{\overline{IQ}}) \times LEI$, $IQ - \overline{IQ}$ (within class), and $(IQ - \overline{IQ}) \times LEI$, with the individual outcome as the dependent variable.* This assumes that teacher is fully confounded with class and that all classes take the same course. There are some treacherous

---

*An alternative suggested by Bock (personal communication to Walberg) starts by calculating means within the class for high-IQ and low-IQ subgroups. Then the sum and difference of this pair of means provide, respectively, a level and slope index that together describe the within-class regression. One may examine these simultaneously or separately. An analysis of this character for a sex interaction was used in a study of mathematics (NLSMA, 1969, Report 10, Chap. 1), to which Bock was a consultant.

problems of statistical inference, since both students and classes can be regarded as units of sampling.

A socially-slanted course in genetics:
A Johnson-Neyman demonstration

A one-quarter college course on genetics with an emphasis on the social implications of the facts and theories was evaluated in a classic study by A. D. Bond (1940). For the control group, the course was almost entirely on technical aspects of genetics. About 200 Ss participated. Bond, working under the guidance of Helen M. Walker, analyzed results entirely by the Johnson-Neyman technique and

Table 10.1.   Outcomes from two methods of teaching genetics

Test and sample[a]		Posttest (Y) M	s	ACE[b] (X_1) M	s	r_{X_1Y}	b	Pretest (X_2) M	s	r_{X_2Y}	
Knowledge											
Selection of Facts I (FS)	E	35.3	9.34	83.3	24.0	0.340	0.132	25.4[f]	9.53[f]	0.387	0.3
	C	38.0	9.94	83.6	23.8	0.335	0.139	27.3[f]	9.89[f]	0.452	0.4
Selection of Facts II (FS)	E	37.7	8.76	83.3	24.0	0.606	0.221	25.4[f]	9.53[f]	0.481	0.4
	C	36.5	8.76	83.6	23.8	0.396	0.146	27.3[f]	9.89[f]	0.397	0.38
Selection of Facts I or II (FS)	E	35.8[f]	9.18[f]	83.3	24.0	0.327[f]	0.125[f]	25.4[f]	9.53[f]	0.268[f]	0.2
	C	36.3[f]	8.57[f]	83.6	23.8	0.249[f]	0.089[f]	27.3[f]	9.89[f]	0.476[f]	0.4
True-False Test (facts) (Sp)	E	38.4	9.70	82.7	22.3	0.507	0.220	20.5	8.75	0.768	0.8
	C	30.6	10.50	79.8	21.5	0.301	0.147	17.6	8.42	0.544	0.6
Superstitions[9] (Sp)	E	-16.7	13.70	82.7	22.3	0.252	0.155	22.0	17.90	0.562	0.4
	C	-30.9	22.20	79.8	21.5	0.300	0.310	30.4	23.20	0.744	0.7
Reasoning											
Application of Principles I (FS)	E	21.6	6.49	83.3	24.0	0.302	0.082	13.7[f]	6.15[f]	0.076	0.0
	C	22.2	7.80	83.6	23.8	0.202	0.066	14.6[f]	5.62[f]	0.118	0.16
Application of Principles II (FS)	E	18.9	6.37	83.3	24.0	0.231	0.061	13.7[f]	6.15[f]	0.283	0.2
	C	17.5	6.78	83.6	23.8	0.327	0.093	14.6[f]	5.62[f]	0.292	0.3
Interpretation of Data (FS)	E	8.9	3.64	83.3	24.0	0.472	0.072	6.5	3.18	0.148	0.1
	C	7.7	3.25	83.6	23.8	0.475	0.065	6.1	3.42	0.182	0.1
Evaluation of Authorities (Sp)	E	36.1	5.75	82.7	22.3	0.268	0.069	31.4	7.09	0.282	0.22
	C	33.9	6.27	79.8	21.5	0.153	0.045	31.4	8.11	0.467	0.36
Attitude											
Opinions on Intern'l Questions (FS)	E	106.6	21.60	83.3	24.0	0.407	0.366	101.4	20.00	0.862	0.93
	C	103.8	18.60	83.6	23.8	0.275	0.215	101.5	19.30	0.843	0.75
Opinions on Imperialism[h] (FS)	E	23.7	5.92	83.3	24.0	0.400	0.099	22.6	6.22	0.651	0.62
	C	22.7	5.87	83.6	23.8	0.433	0.107	22.8	4.83	0.782	0.95
Attitudes toward Ethnic Groups (Sp)	E	71.0	29.50	82.7	22.3	0.488	0.646	59.9	28.18	0.653	0.68
	C	59.1	29.40	79.8	21.5	0.098	0.134	50.0	24.99	0.787	0.92

Based on data from Bond, 1940.

[a]FS identifies data that combine the Spring and Fall replications, Sp identifies a test given to the Spring sample only.

[b]American Council on Education Psychological Examination.

[c]X_1 is scaled to give a mean of zero and an approximate s.d. of 1 within each treatment group. Likewise for X_2 and Y.

[d]The sum of absolute differences for the two pairs of regression weights. This is roughly proportional to the interaction effect for both predictors combined.

his report displays the technique to good advantage. Tests of knowledge, reasoning, and attitude were given both before and after instruction. The results of Fall and Spring classes were combined, except for a few tests given only to the Spring sample. Considering each posttest in turn, Bond used the corresponding pretest and the ACE scholastic aptitude test as predictors. We would suggest some changes in the analysis—in particular, we would favor taking all pretests into account simultaneously, presumably by forming composites. But Bond was ahead not only of his time but of the usual current practices.

In Table 10.1 we reproduce many of the statistical results, adding regression slopes we have calculated. The main results are indicated in the rightmost columns.

x st — 2	Rescaled[c] multiple-regression equation ignoring constant	Strength of interaction[d]	Direction,[e] from center of region, where $E > C$ / Region of significance / Interaction if any in sample
f f	$0.25X_1 + 0.31X_2$ $0.27X_1 + 0.41X_2$	0.12	WSW / None / Negligible
f f	$0.51X_1 + 0.35X_2$ $0.34X_1 + 0.33X_2$	0.19	ENE including center / Ellipse toward ENE / Weak, disordinal
f f	$0.28X_1 + 0.20X_2$ $0.16X_1 + 0.42X_2$	0.34	ESE including center / None / Disordinal
	$0.26X_1 + 0.64X_2$ $0.11X_1 + 0.53X_2$	0.26	NE, but includes entire range / Ellipse, center and NE / Weak, ordinal
	$0.02X_1 + 0.47X_2$ $0.27X_1 + 0.77X_2$	0.45	SE, but includes most of range[g] / Hyperbola, including center and SW quadrant in one branch / Strong, near to ordinal
f f	$0.27X_1 + 0.05X_2$ $0.22X_1 + 0.08X_2$	0.08	ESE / None / Negligible
f f	$0.21X_1 + 0.25X_2$ $0.34X_1 + 0.32X_2$	0.20	SW, but includes most of range / Ellipse around center in NE/SW direction / Weak, near to ordinal
	$0.49X_1 + 0.06X_2$ $0.44X_1 + 0.07X_2$	0.07	E, including entire range / Ellipse around center in E/W direction / Negligible
	$0.20X_1 + 0.24X_2$ $-0.01X_1 + 0.46X_2$	0.43	SE, including center / Ellipse, center and SE / Strong, near to ordinal
	$-0.03X_1 + 0.92X_2$ $0.05X_1 + 0.78X_2$	0.22	NNE, including center / Ellipse, center to N / Weak, disordinal
	$0.29X_1 + 0.53X_2$ $0.36X_1 + 0.85X_2$	0.39	WSW, including center / Hyperbola spanning S third / Strong, disordinal
	$0.25X_1 + 0.52X_2$ $-0.01X_1 + 0.84X_2$	0.58	SE, including center / Hyperbola spanning SE quadrant / Very strong, disordinal

[e] Directions are described relative to a standard-score compass rose, with good ACE scores at East and good pretest scores at North, centered at the location of the means on X_1 and X_2.

[f] These means and s.d.'s mix pretest data for both forms, each of which was given to half the Ss at pretest. The two forms were closely matched. The posttest is whichever form S did not take at pretest.

[g] A subset of the items of the True-False test. See also Figure 10.1. We have revised Bond's scoring of Superstitions so that a larger negative score indicates acceptance of more superstitious statements. Moreover, we have multiplied each score by 10, so as to keep 3 significant digits in the table.

[h] A subset of the items of Opinions on International Questions.

The strongest interactions were with these outcomes: a test of superstitions (in which a score near zero is desirable), a test of ability to evaluate the adequacy of support for various contentions, and a measure of opinions about ethnic groups. Figure 10.1 gives information on two of these. In examining these figures, the reader should think of outcome as a third dimension perpendicular to the page. Then he can visualize two regression planes hinged at the 0——0 line. On one side of the hinge members of the E group tended to earn better scores, while the C's did better on the other side. The hyperbola in Panel (i) locates the points where the data indicate with high probability that in the population the E mean exceeds the C mean. In general, the E treatment was more effective than the control in eliminating superstitions of students at and below the mean on ACE. It is understandable that no difference should emerge for students (top of chart) who had no superstitions at the start. About half the cases lie outside the region of significance and in theory the 0——0 line could move to any position outside the hyperbola. The second branch of the hyperbola is far to the northeast, outside the figure; hence, the population 0——0 line could fall far outside the distribution. The interaction, then, may be ordinal or disordinal in the population. We do not entirely trust the result on Superstitions, as pretest and posttest scores had skewed distributions and the regression surfaces must have been curved rather than planar as the Johnson-Neyman technique assumes. Skewness seems not to be a problem with Bond's other scores.

On ethnic attitudes, the experimental method had its great advantage with the students who initially had superior ability and undesirable attitudes. In Panel (ii), the region is an ellipse. For nearly half the distribution, the C outcome was better; but the 0——0 line in the population could move far off to the top or left, or it could swing to a vertical or horizontal position. If Bond had plotted the .05 rather than the .01 region, the ellipse would be much fatter and would come closer to the 0——0 line.

The next largest interaction, on Evaluation of Authorities, was nearly ordinal, the experimental treatment again producing better results for most Ss. The patterning is rather like that in Panel (ii) of Figure 10.1, save that the 0——0 line moved toward the upper left and the hyperbola narrowed to an ellipse encompassing the center. Able persons who could not evaluate authority for statements about genetics at the outset of the course benefited greatly from the experimental instruction. Dull students who already were competent at this task performed equally well in both treatments. (See also Fig. 4.3, p. 92.)

We can consider now the whole set of outcomes, making use of the rightmost column of Table 10.1. The three analyses on Selection of Facts give conflicting pictures. For every other test, $E > C$ over more than half of the bivariate distribution and usually over nearly all of it. For the attitude tests and for one analysis of Application of Principles, the 0——0 line splits the group near the middle. Only when the region of significance is an hyperbola is disordinality in the population established, and then only if both branches cut through the distribution. This never occurred in Bond's data. Hence, the basic picture is one *favoring the E treatment on all outcomes*, with the possibility that the C treatment

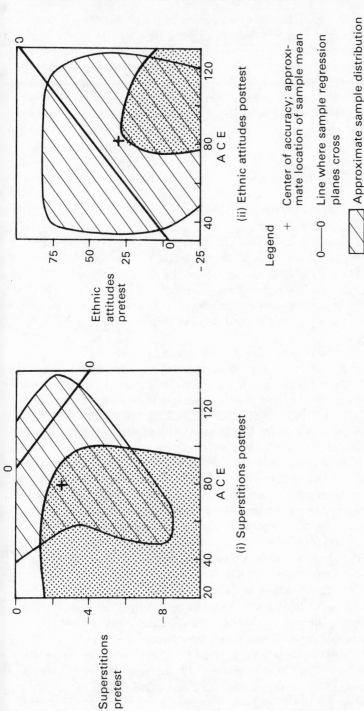

Figure 10.1.
Results of Johnson-Neyman analysis for two posttests that in-teracted with pretest and A C E. After Bond, 1940.

achieved some outcomes better for some minority of the population. There is considerable agreement among the findings for cognitive tests. The line of greatest E-C difference in slope fell in a sector from approximately East (Selection of Facts II) to SSE (Selection of Facts I) for six analyses; the outliers are Application of Principles II (SW) and True-False (NE). It appears then, that *the control treatment tended to be as good as or better than the experimental treatment for students low in scholastic aptitude who were superior on initial achievement and attitude.* The three attitude measures gave radically inconsistent (though significant) results.

It should be clear by now that Johnson-Neyman results are thought-provoking. Similar descriptions would emerge if confidence limits for interaction effects were established in the Potthoff manner.

Other studies in science

Instruction in chemistry. An innovative chemistry course was evaluated by J. S. Anderson and by Herron. Each of them collected pretest and posttest data in high schools where chemistry was being offered by the conventional or the CHEM-Study curriculum. The posttests were intended to fit both courses. If an item intended to test reasoning required certain factual knowledge, it was accompanied by a reading passage sufficient to make these facts available to the student.

J. S. Anderson (1964) allowed five months between pretests and posttests. A total score on the School and College Ability Test (SCAT) was available as an aptitude measure. Anderson chose to block on this. While her 638 Ss provided reasonable samples in the High and Middle ranges, the numbers in her Low block (lowest third of the national norm distribution) were too small to warrant consideration. The differences between CHEM and traditional groups were large at pretest, the traditional groups being superior even within ability blocks. Anderson's statistical analyses were crude; she interpreted gain scores, and made inadequate use of the available covariates. Since the two curriculum groups represented different populations, even an analysis of covariance would not have been without bias. The most satisfactory report would have taken the form of multiple regressions relating outcome to pretests and SCAT within each treatment— preferably, to true scores on those variables. Insofar as we can judge, the CHEM Study group gained about ¼ s.d. more on knowledge than the other group; there was no interaction. There was no effect on Comprehension, if we ignore the handful of Lows. On Application and Analysis it appears to us that students high on SCAT gained more from CHEM study. Anderson drew entirely different conclusions, accepting the null hypothesis on all these points; *we are not sure that a proper analysis would have shown a significant interaction.*

A quite similar study by Herron (1966) changed the procedure in several ways: the Iowa Test of Educational Development was the aptitude measure; synthesis and evaluation were added to the outcomes measured; nine months of instruction was assessed; the sample was divided into thirds, not cut at tertile points of the national norms. This means that Herron's "Low" group ranged as high as the

80th percentile on the national norms for ITED, but it was of good size. In all, Herron had 479 Ss. Of the six outcome measures, *only the "analysis" subtest showed an interaction.* Highs did better in this after CHEM Study, while the so-called Lows did better after the conventional course. The absence of interaction for the many other categories of achievement makes the effect seem peculiarly specific. Perhaps it was unwise for Herron to rely so heavily on the *Taxonomy.* It would have been instructive to examine ATI for each posttest item, and then to characterize the items that did show interaction effects.

Some rubric that cuts across *Taxonomy* categories might have accounted better than "analysis" for the interaction. (For another piece of research on CHEM Study see p. 332.)

A study by Lucow (1954) compared text-centered/laboratory-centered courses over a year of high school chemistry ($N = 60$). Although aptitude was not measured, about half the Ss were classed as college preparatory and half not, so the groups presumably differed in general ability. The final examination showed ATI. *Highs did well in either treatment; Lows did more poorly in general, but lab was better than text for them.* Lucow's analysis focused on pre-post differences in variance rather than means because, in 1954, he valued instruction that *increased* individual differences in achievement. (Note the contrast with today's mastery emphasis.) Only Lows in the text group (the treatment with the lowest mean) failed to show marked increase in variance over the year.

Instruction in physics. Records of students who had taken a certain College Board physics test were drawn from Board files and classified into PSSC students, non-PSSC students, and an unclassified group which was discarded (Wasik, 1971). Items in the achievement test were classified according to the *Taxonomy.* For 370 students with each kind of history, SAT-V and -M scores were obtained from the file. These tests were presumably concurrent with the physics test and followed the course (or were taken late in the instructional year). Wasik demonstrated significant main effects favoring the PSSC group on all four categories of achievement. There were significant ATI effects on Comprehension and Application, the effect being traceable to SAT-M rather than SAT-V. *Highs on SAT-M did somewhat better on Comprehension and Application and extreme Lows did worse, when taught the PSSC course.* An interaction of similar magnitude and character for Knowledge did not reach Wasik's standard of significance. There was no interaction effect on analysis items. Caution is required here. The aptitude measure followed the physics course. Moreover, the two groups of Ss may have differed in many respects.

One curriculum study that failed to test ATI deserves mention for its evidence on change in aptitude. Brakken (1965) asked whether the PSSC curriculum differed from a conventional program in its effects on intellectual abilities. The Holzinger-Crowder Unifactor tests and the Watson-Glaser Critical Thinking Appraisal were given to 533 suburban high-school students at the start of the year and in alternate form near the end of the year. The PSSC curriculum was taken by 309 students and the conventional curriculum by 224 students. The groups were comparable on general scholastic ability, though the conventional group started higher on numerical ability and on the Watson-Glaser test. Relations of PSSC unit-tests with abilities were the same on the late units as on early units (contrary to Ferris' report, p. 123 above).

Factor analyses were made, separately on data from each group at each testing. Similar verbal, spatial, numerical, and critical-thinking factors were identified in the Fall data for the two groups. The within-group factors appeared to be less similar after instruction. In the conventionally treated group, the verbal and critical-thinking factors merged into a single factor, while a pure-reasoning factor separated out. Brakken inferred that the conventional course was more dependent on verbal ability. Fall-to-Spring changes suggested that PSSC students gained significantly more in critical thinking and numerical ability (on which they had been low in the Fall), while conventional students gained significantly more in "pure reasoning." There was little change in verbal and spatial scores in either group.

Comparing factor patterns is treacherous, especially when simple correlation matrices are not made available for examination. Chance shifts in correlations from matrix to matrix alter rotated factor solutions substantially (Horn & Knapp, 1973). Comparing simple gains computed from different starting points is also questionable, so *the stated conclusions are dubious,* in our view. We would prefer to regress various end-of-year measures (or composites of them) onto composites of pretests, the composites being the same in all groups.

Instruction in biology. A strong indication of interaction appeared in one piece of work within the Biological Sciences Curriculum Study (Cain, 1964). As part of the national evaluation, experimental classes and control classes had been set up. Cain used only those experimentals (*N* over 500) who were studying the BSCS "yellow version," a text emphasizing genetics and development. The 500+ controls were in traditional biology classes; for some reason their aptitude was better than that of the experimentals. As a posttest, Cain used a final examination for the BSCS course which was patently "unfair" to the controls. Be that as it may, the experimentals did better than the controls on the posttest and *the ATI regression was very much steeper among experimentals,* with either DAT Verbal Reasoning or Numerical Ability or previous grade in algebra as the predictor. Using teacher's mark in biology as criterion, the same slope difference appeared with Numerical Reasoning; the slope differences with the other predictors was slight. Finding ATI of Numerical Reasoning makes sense, since BSCS-Yellow places unusual emphasis on mathematical content. But an interaction of verbal ability is harder to explain. Incidentally, Cain found that correlations of unit tests with aptitude did not decline over the course of the year, which appears to drive the final nail into the coffin of the Ferris observation.

Discussion

The wave of curriculum research of the past decade missed an opportunity. Data were collected on many very large samples, but ATI were examined in only a few, and then incompletely. Curriculum contrasts evidently do interact with ability.

But the work tends to show how complicated the relationships are, not to establish a general conclusion.

A curriculum is a treatment, but to say this is to generalize at a high level. Classes receiving the "same" treatment are taught in different ways and develop different climates. Consequently, it is desirable to analyze for class or teacher effects. It also appears that interactions need not generalize over outcomes. In studies in mathematics, genetics, chemistry, and physics, ATI were found for one outcome and a contradictory ATI or no ATI for another. This is not to be dismissed as an artifact; certain of the curricula aimed to develop reasoning skills where the contrasting curriculum did not, so that patterned outcomes are to be expected. More powerful analyses are needed, however, to verify that the patterning is not a chance effect.

Sometimes the conventional curriculum gave better results and sometimes the novel curriculum. Most of the results suggest that ability is relevant to the choice of curriculum. Interactions were not the same from study to study, but slopes were more often steep in the experimental treatment than in the control treatment. The only apparent reversal of this effect was in HPP (and in the suspect evidence on the Madison project). Since HPP is less technical than the courses it was compared with, whereas BSCS, PSSC, and CHEM are more technical, this need not be regarded as a contradiction. The Bond study considered simultaneously the interactions of general ability and past subject-matter achievement, and found the innovation beneficial to all *S*s save those with a High-Low pattern. This more subtle hypothesis could and should have been tested in other bodies of data.

Inductive teaching

Much instructional theory and research is concerned with learning "by discovery," or with guided discovery that leads the learner from specific examples or experiences to general principles. These inductive methods contrast with the didactic-expository technique in which the teacher states the principle and then gives examples or exercises to consolidate the learner's understanding of it. Other contrasts, such as self-reliance/teacher-dominance, and insight/association, are implicit in this debate. Despite the popularity of the theme, there has been little substantial research on it under genuine pedagogical conditions and confirmed conclusions even about main effects are lacking (Shulman & Keislar, 1966). The studies of ATI are even fewer, and many of them are of little value. A limited number of studies have compared two styles of "live" teaching, and these we place here alongside the curricular studies. This seems fitting, since many of the curricular innovations in mathematics and science adopted deductive tactics. In Chapter 11, we will consider other inductive/deductive studies where instruction was brief and comparatively artificial. While those findings supplement the ones examined here, they are of more value to the theorist than to the educator.

Instruction in mathematics

Mathematical subject-matter has been used in the majority of the longer studies, partly because innovators in mathematics teaching favor the inductive approach and partly because mathematics lends itself to this kind of experiment. Representativ of the better studies is that of Sobel (1956), who had teachers guide students in discovering how to apply concepts of ninth-grade algebra. The control teachers taught in a conventional deductive manner. Teachers and their 14 classes were assigned to treatments nonrandomly for the four-week period of instruction. *The inductive treatment appeared to be superior among classes with a high mean IQ.* There was no treatment difference in classes of lower ability. These findings held for both immediate and three-month delayed posttests. No within-class analysis was reported.

Much the same ordinal interaction was found by Maynard and Strickland (1969) when they compared discovery/guided-discovery/teacher-presentation-and-application during three units of eighth- and ninth-grade mathematics. $N = 400$. Scores on immediate and delayed posttests for each unit were related to Otis mental-ability scores. *Three weak ATIs* were obtained. Among Highs, discovery was slightly advantageous in two units and guided discovery somewhat advantageous in the third. Among Lows, the deductive method was as good as the inductive method. (The same curriculum was the subject of a very large study by Berger and Horowitz [1967], which is useless for our purposes. Ability levels were defined differently in different classes. No data were reported and we are unwilling to interpret the original inappropriate analysis.)

No interaction appeared in a study by Barrish (1970), in which general ability and measures of divergent thinking were the aptitude variables. With a total of only 96 fifth- and sixth-graders, the experiment lacked power. There was *no hint of a consistent trend* over the two grade groups and the two dependent variables, save for an ability main effect. The novel, elegant design merits some further description. Four teachers were selected. These teachers worked in an "open plan" arrangement with various subgroupings of the total group. *S*s were stratified on both IQ and divergent thinking, and then randomly assigned (within strata) to groups to be taught mathematical topics by discovery/didactic methods. Midway in the four-week period teachers were interchanged, so that at some point each teacher applied each method to one group of students.

We judge that interactions were absent in a year-long study in fourth-grade mathematics with 374 students and 13 teachers (Olander & Robertson, 1973). Both treatment groups used the same textbook, but the teachers were asked to use contrasting discovery/expository styles. Pretests (three subscores of the Stanford Achievement Test plus a homemade test over the content of the instruction) were treated separately as aptitude measures in interaction analyses. The same tests served as posttests. The authors made no significance tests for interaction, but they plotted regression lines and discussed the differences in slopes. The original regression slopes were incorrectly calculated, one of the authors informs us. We base our interpretation on the revised calculation (which will become the basis for a published erratum). The slopes seem not to have differed greatly between treatments and were inconsistent from one measure to another. *We doubt that any interaction in the population is indicated by these data.* We would have preferred to see a reduced-rank analysis of this study, since the tests were probably strongly correlated.

Some readers may be interested in a report on 41 black kindergartners who studied a three-week workbook unit on mathematics (Anastasiow *et al.*, 1970). The conditions compared were discovery/guided-discovery/didactic. The authors analyzed at great length data collected during the instructional period and reported interaction effects on them. ATI were also investigated by correlating the post-tests with picture-vocabulary and geometry pretests. There were large but not significant differences in the correlations. Their irregular pattern and the small N lead us to regard the study as *inconclusive*.

Other courses

We find single studies in subjects other than mathematics. Interactions appeared in every subject, but the effects were not simple or consistent.

Thomas and Snider (1969) gave six weeks of instruction to eighth-graders, in guided-discovery/didactic form. The course concerned early man in America. In the discovery treatment, the teacher guided discussion to preclude learning of unsound responses, but retained a basically inductive approach. In the didactic treatment, the teacher presented generalizations and illustrations according to a detailed outline. Originally there were two teachers, each of whom employed both methods with different Ss; after finding a large teacher effect, the investigators unwisely confined the analysis to one teacher and 85 students. Data included the Henmon-Nelson measure of IQ and three outcome measures: an achievement posttest, the Watson-Glaser test of Critical Thinking, and a test on solving science problems (a measure of remote transfer). At all IQ levels more content was learned from didactic teaching. Critical thinking and problem solving, however, showed disordinal ATI effects. *Guided discovery was advantageous for students with high IQ,* whereas below IQ 120 direct exposition gave better results on all outcomes.

Rizzuto (1970) looked for interactions arising in one month of inductive/ deductive instruction in English. Verbal ability (SCAT) and sex were taken as aptitudes in six eighth-grade classes ($N = 165$). Three teachers gave instruction in a formal, precise manner (deductive) while three other teachers (inductive) were instructed to act as catalysts for discussion, asking open-ended questions and directing students' attention. Instruction extended over 20 45-minute class periods. Recognition and transfer posttests were administered immediately after the instruction and again after a two-week delay. Rizzuto did not report the crucial descriptive statistics. According to his anova, the Sex x Treatment interaction was significant on the delayed posttest; girls did much better in the inductive treatment while boys found it only moderately advantageous. The interaction for ability on the immediate test fell short of significance; but three-level blocking diluted the analysis and we are unwilling to accept the null hypothesis. The study is *inconclusive*.

The two approaches to laboratory instruction in freshman chemistry that Hittle (1969) contrasted were both somewhat inductive. Ss in both treatments carried out the same experiments. In Treatment 1, they discussed the experiment with the instructor both before and after making their observations, so as to advance their understanding of the procedure and the results. Treatment 2 used the same experiments, but directions were supplied in writing and the student was left largely on his own. The most relevant outcome measure was an examination closely matched to the laboratory work; it tested recall, interpretation of data, and understanding of the laboratory rationale. There were 146 Ss blocked 2 x 2 on SAT-V and SAT-M. Hittle's weak analysis found no significant interaction. In his charts, we find a puzzling effect. In three of four cells, the outcome was good in Treatment 2; only the Low-Lows did badly. In three of four cells, the outcome was poor in Treatment 1; only the High-Highs did well. In each case, the outlier was at least ½ s.d. from the other groups. How could it be that extra discussion and explanation (didactic?) handicapped all but the best students and was of no help to the best ones? *This second-order interaction should be regarded with suspicion,* since it rests on a blocked analysis.

We shall go into greater detail regarding two other studies.

Teaching Archimedes' principle: Demonstration of variance components

A particularly well-planned study by Babikian (1971) contrasted methods of teaching Archimedes' principle. We shall use it to demonstrate the adjustment technique for blocked anova introduced in Chapter 4. About 250 eighth-graders were taught for three weeks by one of three methods:

A. Expository. Teacher explanation, largely verbal. Worksheets for practice and review. No laboratory.
B. Laboratory. All ideas developed by means of laboratory worksheets. Students tested each principle for themselves. Exercises and review.
C. Discovery. Students worked in the laboratory and observed much the same events as the second group, but were never given the statement of the principle.

All groups worked on the same concepts and used the same exercises and review questions. Babikian analyzed part scores of the posttest as well as the total. This proved to be illuminating, since the pattern of results was only partly consistent from outcome to outcome. Before detailing these results we shall use the overall result for our methodological demonstration.

Results on overall achievement. Babikian made a 2 x 2 x 3 analysis of variance with Sex and IQ as factors; he had 18 cases per cell after squaring off his design. He reported means and variances within cells. Table 10.2 is the output of his anova, augmented as explained below. The IQ main effect was the expected one, Highs superior. Boys surpassed girls in each IQ x Sex comparison within treatment, generating a Sex main effect; but the effect was close to zero in some cells and as large as 1.5 s.d. at the other extreme, suggesting an interaction. The significant Treatment effect arose from the very poor performance in Treatment C of

Table 10.2 Estimates of variance components and adjusted F ratios to describe interactions in a study of physics

Effect	SS	d.f.	MS	F	m^a	σ^2	Revised σ^2	Revised MS	Revised F
Treatment	829	2	414.5	15.94*	72	5.40	5.40	(414.5)	16.92*
IQ	439	1	439	16.88*	108	3.82	6.00	674	27.51*
Sex	228	1	228	8.77*	108	1.87	1.87	(228)	9.31*
IQ x T	19	2	9.5	0.37	36	b	0	26	1.06
Sex x T	151	2	75.5	2.90	36	1.37	1.37	(75.5)	3.08`
Sex x IQ	21	1	21	0.81	54	b	0	26	1.06
Sex x IQ x T	100	2	50	1.92	18	1.33	2.09	63.6	2.60
Residual	5305	204	26.0			26.0	24.50	24.5^c	
Total	7092								

Original anova from Babikian, 1971.

[a]Multiplier recognizing number of levels of other factors, and cell size.

[b]Calculation gives a negative value, implying that the component is small.

[c]Revised SS_{Res} = 7092 - 2087 = 5005.

*$p < .01$ `$p < .05$ after adjustment

every group except boys of high IQ. Results in Treatments A and B differed very little, but A was better for Lows on most subtests.

No interactions were significant, yet rather large differences in slope were evident from the reported means. Boys did much better than girls under Treatment C (mean difference 2.3 points) and only a little better than girls (<1 point difference) in A and B. The slopes of the regression onto IQ were flat for A boys and C girls. To get a clearer picture of Babikian's effects we estimated variance components and adjusted them to restore the information lost by blocking on aptitude (Table 10.2). The components showed very strong IQ and Treatment main effects. The Sex x Treatment interaction became significant after adjust-

Table 10.3   Adjusted estimates of variance components on tests of diverse outcomes

Effect	Variance components relative to residual				
	Total test	Subtest			
		Verbal recall	Recognition	Numerical	Transfer
T	0.22**	0.23**	0.11**	0.26**	0.04*
IQ	0.24**	0.13**	0.13**	0.13**	0.05*
Sex	0.08**	0.00^a	0.05**	0.03*	0.09**
IQ x T	0.00^a	0.10*	0.05	0.00^a	0.11* ··
Sex x T	0.06˙	0.10*	0.03	0.05˙	0.00^a
Sex x IQ	0.00	0.00^a	0.00^a	0.03	0.00^a
Sex x IQ x T	0.09	0.21* ··	0.00	0.00	0.22* ··
Residual	1.00	1.00	1.00	1.00	1.00
Treatment(s) with highest mean(s)	A,B	A	A,B	A	B,C
Group doing better than others in each treatment:					
A. Expository	Highs	b	b	Highs	Boys, High girls
B. Laboratory	Highs	Highs	Highs, esp. boys	Highs	Boys, esp. Lows
C. Discovery	High boys	High boys	Boys, esp. Highs	High boys	Highs, esp. boys

Data from Babikian, 1971.

*,**$p < .05, .01$ in original analysis

· ,·· $p < .05, .01$ after adjustment, if different from original

^{a}Calculation gives a negative value.

^{b}Differences small; regression on IQ and Sex rather flat.

ment. The Sex x IQ x T effect was actually a bit stronger than the Sex and Sex x Treatment effects, but it fell short of significance even after adjustment. The three-way interaction arose from the fact that High girls in the sample did no better than Low girls in Treatment C, whereas High boys did well, For boys, then, we have in the sample the same result that appeared in the Sobel, Maynard, and Thomas studies: *a comparatively steep regression on IQ with discovery learning.* But even for High boys Babikian's *discovery method was somewhat disadvantageous.* For girls, *the discovery method gave disastrously poor results* and nothing like a steep regression on IQ was found.

Results for subtests. Four subtests were scored by Babikian.

V. Verbal statement of principles (6 items).
R. Recognition of principles (10 items).
Tr. Transfer to new situations (10 items).
N. Numerical applications (10 items).

Instead of interpreting from Babikian's calculations, we made the full adjustment of variance components. We rescaled components to make the residual 1.00 in each case, to simplify comparison across columns. The components for total score are similarly rescaled in Table 10.3.

The treatment effect was fairly large on V and N items and favorable to the expository Treatment A. Discovery (C) was at least the equal of the other treatments in promoting transfer, however. Sex effects were especially large on transfer items. The IQ effects on V, N, and R subtests were similar. There were IQ x Treatment effects on V and Tr items. Persons low in IQ had superior recall after expository instruction. The interaction on the transfer test reflected the very steep slope of its regression on IQ after discovery training. Large Sex x IQ x Treatment effects, different in character, appeared on the V and Tr subtests. All in all, the estimates of variance components, along with the adjustment for blocking, has given a more sensible summary of data than the conventional anova.

While the overall finding strongly supported the use of didactic treatments (A or B) under Babikian's conditions, the analysis by subtests raised a serious issue. On the transfer test discovery had a clear advantage for Highs. This means that the overall effect could be reversed if transfer were given greater weight in the outcome measure. Such a patterning of results is not hard to believe and may be of great educational importance.

Interactions of primary abilities in a training program

Treatment, thoroughness of measurement, and sample size set an old inquiry by Edgerton (1956) apart from more artificial studies of the deductive/inductive contrast. The investigators posed a question regarding vocational training: Should theory or technique come first? This is not the traditional question about "discovery," of course; in some ways it echoes the earlier Edgerton question (p. 253) about meaning in training.

The *S*s were enlisted men in a 14-week program to train weather observers. For purposes of the experiment the curriculum was arranged to present explanations

Table 10.4   Regression slopes relating outcomes to primary mental abilities in how-why/why-how instruction

Item classification[a]	Basis for subject classification	How-Why treatment			Why-How treatment			Mean difference[b]	Slope difference
		Mean for Lows	Mean for Highs	Slope	Mean for Lows	Mean for Highs	Slope		
How–RN	R	72.7	77.5	4.8	76.1	79.6	3.5		-1.3
	N	72.5	77.5	5.0	78.1	78.6	0.5		-4.5*
	Others	73.9	77.7	3.8	77.5	80.2	2.7	3	-1.1
How–M	M	73.6	75.4	1.8	73.1	72.0	-1.1		-2.9
	Others	73.3	76.2	2.9	72.5	74.1	1.6	1	-1.3
Why–R	R	72.6	75.2	2.6	69.1	77.5	8.4		+5.8*
	Others	72.2	75.1	2.9	73.5	75.8	2.3	1	-0.6
X–VM	V	79.5	82.4	2.9	83.6	86.6	3.0		+0.1
	M	77.2	83.6	6.4	85.7	86.6	0.9		-5.5*
	Others	79.8	82.5	2.7	83.8	86.6	2.8	4	+0.1
X–M	M	78.1	80.3	2.2	78.9	80.9	2.0		-0.2
	Others	78.1	80.0	1.9	79.0	80.9	1.9	1	0.0

Data from Edgerton, 1956.

[a] See text for code.

[b] Highs and Lows weighted equally. Positive difference favors Why-How. All means and slopes are expressed on a percentage scale.

* Interaction indicated.

first in the sequence of units and also first within units, for half the Ss (Why-How condition). The other Ss (How-Why condition) received practical instruction first, insofar as possible. Six scores on the Chicago Test of Primary Abilities were obtained for the 251 Ss. Achievement tests at various points in the course contributed to the outcome data. The ATI analysis blocked Ss at the median on each PMA score in turn, and compared Highs and Lows within treatments. There was no ATI attributable to a general or composite ability. A number of modest interactions of specific abilities appeared, but Edgerton made no direct test of their significance. The regression slopes of total achievement onto Space (S), Word Fluency (W), and Reasoning (R) were steeper in the Why-How condition, while the slopes onto Verbal (V), Number (N), and Memory (M) were steeper with the How-Why order. There is no obvious explanation of this split between the tests.

The report broke down results by type of item. For categories containing at least 20 items, considering all examinations together, category means were reported for Highs and Lows on each PMA score, within each treatment. The effects were small, but there is suggestive patterning. As listed in Table 10.4, *Why* items asked for explanation or recall or use of theory; *How* items called for use of a procedure (usually in a computation); *X* items were not classifiable as *Why/How*. Each item was also coded by identifying which ability—R, N, or M—it made demands on.

The first three lines of the table refer to *How* questions that demanded reasoning and memory. There was a rather steep regression of performance onto R in each treatment, with little or no interaction. But with N there was a steep slope in How-Why and none in Why-How; the slope difference in the last column indicates that there was a modest interaction of treatment with N. To consider the alternative hypothesis that a general ability interacted, we formed the first entry in the third row of the table by averaging the mean on *How-RN* items of the persons within the How-Why treatment who were low on M, V, S, and W; and so on. The slope difference was small enough to imply an absence of interactions for the ability composite. In each section of the table, the aptitudes not given a line of their own are included in the "Others" composite. There was evidently little or *no interaction of treatment with overall ability,* but there were *interactions with specific abilities at three points* (starred). These interactions may or may not have been significant. On *How-RN* items, for example, Why-How teaching improved performance, being especially beneficial for Low-N's. This makes sense, as Low-N's might well have found the instruction in computing routines troublesome when it came first. So long as such findings are regarded as tentative, much is to be gained in ATI studies by similar subdivisions of criterion scores.

To summarize: The comparisons of inductive/deductive treatments turn up interactions with considerable frequency, while main effects are rarely large. Three studies (Sobel, Maynard, Thomas) found that inductive teaching benefits Highs and is equal to or worse than the deductive approach for Lows. This tends to be consistent with the trend in curricular comparisons. Of the studies that found no interaction, only one (Olander) was of good size.

The two most interesting studies generated extremely complex conclusions. Babikian confirmed the trend in other studies toward a steeper regression slope on general ability in the inductive treatment, but that treatment produced inferior results on most outcomes. The inductive method showed to some advantage on the especially important transfer test, and there was a strong interaction. The importance of subdividing outcomes is seen again in the Edgerton study. Main effects were fairly strong on two categories of items. Interactions with general ability were lacking, but mysteriously patterned interactions of specific abilities, treatment, and item type appeared. It is evident that the response of students to inductive/deductive instruction is worth studying, but that we should abandon the search for a simple generalization about the main effect or the first-order interaction.

Types of classroom interaction

The classic Boy's Club experiment of Kurt Lewin and his collaborators had a great impact on the thinking of educators, especially after it was elaborated by the group dynamics movement and the experimental social psychologists into a theory of role relationships. Much of the research on democratic, dominative, and other leadership patterns in the classroom assessed main effects, neglecting variation among students. The studies that did check for ATI usually assumed that personality differences would account for reactions to classroom practices or considered personality and ability jointly. We shall review here the handful of studies that investigated the ATI of abilities with the permissiveness of the teacher and similar variables. Studies of personality data will follow in Chapter 13.

The two earliest reports in this vein were studies at Michigan that broke the ground for the extensive investigations of McKeachie and his colleagues. For his doctoral dissertation, Wispé (1951) asked eight instructors of sections of a college social-relations course to play a directive/permissive role for a semester. Directive teachers were formal and subject-matter-oriented, while permissive teachers were informal and student-oriented. The four sections of each type were matched in several respects. N was approximately 200. Section meetings were observed in order to document the teaching styles. Attitudes were assessed along with achievement at the end of the course. Most students preferred directive instruction for its clear definitions of tasks and the direct preparation it gave for examinations, but they found permissive instruction more enjoyable. Directive instruction produced somewhat higher achievement for persons low on SAT and the pretest than permissive instruction did. There was no method difference for Highs. The interaction was ordinal, with *a steeper positive slope in the permissive treatment.*

Guetzkow, Kelly, and McKeachie (1954) compared three methods of conducting psychology classes: recitation, discussion, and tutorial. They reported *no interaction* of final examination scores with ability or student preference for method. The study lasted for a semester, with 805 students. Eight teaching assistants were assigned three sections each, with each of the three series of section meetings to be handled in a different manner. There were, however, common lectures, a common text, and common assignments, which limited the possible effect of treatment variations.

One other McKeachie study analyzed results by ability level in classes where the investigator allowed more/less opportunity for students to speak up with comments and questions. The sample was that of McKeachie's Study I; for details, see p. 444. The *able students did much better when allowed more freedom* to assert themselves. The Lows did their best when instructors did the talking.

Flanders (1965) compared directive/permissive teachers in Grade 8. The posttests were adjusted for differences at pretest and then compared with IQ. Two tables in the report gave means in geometry and social studies for three IQ blocks within two categories of teachers. In both courses, the permissive teachers got better results. There was *little or no interaction*, though the advantage of permissive teaching was a trifle greater for Highs. The studies used 16 and 15 teachers, respectively, and over 300 students each.

J. N. Ward (1956) compared the lecture-demonstration method with a more interactive procedure in college physics for teachers ($N = 119$). With instructor-chosen objectives, and required readings, the lecture was teacher-dominated if not authoritarian. In the more "democratic" group method, readings were suggested, but the group decided on the topics and materials to be dealt with in class. Physics tests were given at the beginning, middle, and end of the semester-long course. ACE Quantitative scores were used as an aptitude measure. No clear description of the ATI can be gleaned from Ward's report. It appears that *lecturing was superior to the group method for Lows* and that the methods were about equal at other levels.

In Grade 5, *little or no interaction* was found by Herman *et al.* (1969). Eighteen classes were blocked on the class mean ability score, so that the interaction investigated was (as in HPP) that of group ability, and not of individual ability. Sex was a variable within the class. The teacher's personal style was brought under statistical control by pairing teachers on the basis of prior observation. During the experiment half the teachers were to teach a unit on explorers in a teacher-centered manner and then to teach a unit on colonization in the student-centered manner. The order of instructional procedures but not of the topics was reversed for the other teachers. The anova was exceptionally low in power. (It took no advantage of the initial pairing of teachers or the repeated measures design, blocked class ability on three levels, and treated cell-within-class as the unit of sampling). There was a report of significant Ability x Treatment interaction when interest was taken as dependent variable, in the second unit only. Given the lack of consistency between units and the strange V shape of one of the regressions, this seems likely not to be a real finding. The achievement posttest gave no hint of interaction.

G. Brown (1958) treated "overachievement" rather than ability as an interacting variable, in a study of classroom climates where classroom means were the chief concern. He gave the Stanford Achievement Test in January and in June, and divided his 300-odd elementary-grade Ss into thirds on the basis of their January reading scores, relative to the reading score predicted from their individual MA's. He then correlated the pupil's score on a June achievement subtest with a measure of his teacher's style, pooling classes. Brown partialed the January score on the same subtest out of the correlation. This is a strangely complicated way to describe the dependence of the June subtest on four predictors: MA, January reading, January achievement subtest, and teacher style. It is vulnerable to artifacts. Moreover, pooling of cases confounded within-class and between-class regressions. It would be highly desirable to evaluate correlations and/or slopes of regression of the posttest on true scores for prior achievement and aptitude, to check on hypotheses such as Brown's. The techniques suggested by Cronbach and Furby (1970) need to be extended to separate between- and within-class relationships.

Brown's index of teacher style was obtained by observing teachers with the aid of Withall's system for categorizing teacher remarks. The Brown results are adequately summarized by the data for a composite score (Withall's scores 1 + 2 - 6 - 7), which describes the teacher's tendency to give encouragement and support rather than to reprove or make teacher-defensive statements. Table 10.5 presents the relevant partial correlations. The more supporting teacher tended to elicit better results from both overachievers and underachievers, whereas teacher differences did not affect the normal achievers. All the patterning seen in Table 10.5 can be explained as an artifact of restricted range, since the middle group must have been less variable, in reading and probably in other scores also. *One would need data on more teachers, more adequately analyzed, before concluding that a curvilinear ATI was present.*

A short experimental procedure with permissive/authoritarian climates was carried out three times by Calvin, Hoffman, and Harden (1957). In each replication, groups of six to eight undergraduates were formed; members of each group came from the upper or lower extreme in general ability. Problems of the "Twenty Questions" type were presented by a permissive experimenter (informal, round-table, "Bethel") or an authoritarian experimenter (formal, concise, businesslike). Groups were compared on the number of questions they had to ask to solve a problem and on the percentage of problems solved. This is not a learning outcome, of course. While only one difference was significant by itself, the three sets of results agreed, pointing to a distinct disordinal interaction. Pooling three sets

Table 10.5   Partial correlations, calculated by pooling students over classes, relating an achievement posttest to teacher supportiveness

Achievement subtest	Correlation of teacher supportiveness with achievement posttest, holding pretest constant		
	Underachievers	Normal achievers	Overachievers
Paragraph Meaning	0.09	- 0.02	0.13
Word Meaning	0.14	0.04	0.15
Arithmetic Reasoning	0.33	0.14	0.28
Arithmetic Computation	0.22	0.00	0.07

After G. Brown, 1958.

of data gave us Table 10.6. *Abler Ss did their best under permissive treatment, while Lows did their best under the authoritarian treatment.* According to comments made by *Ss* after the session, Highs appeared to enjoy the experiment and so did Lows in the authoritarian condition. Lows in the permissive condition were restless, uncertain, and disorganized.

In the work reviewed above, no interaction appeared in the weak fifth-grade study of Herman and in the highly constrained experiment of Guetzkow; and the Brown results must be regarded with suspicion. Four other investigations— Wispé, McKeachie, Ward, Calvin—showed essentially consistent evidence of interaction. The weak Flanders interaction was in the same direction. In each study, the more permissive or more conversational method had a fairly steep positive slope, Highs gaining more from it than Lows. When the teacher was dominant, the difference between Lows and Highs was much smaller and sometimes favored Lows. The McKeachie and Calvin interactions were disordinal, while those of Wispé, Flanders, and Ward were ordinal. This warrants somewhat greater confidence in Bar-Yam's ordinal interaction (p. 302) of IQ with teacher-direction (measured by the LEI); her Highs did their best in more permissive classes. (G.J. Anderson's companion analysis in the same data pool, however, found the opposite effect in a small sample of girls and no effect in a large group of boys.) We can draw a parallel between the directive or lecture instruction of this section and the didactic teaching of the preceding section. The preponderant finding in that section was of a shallower slope for deductive teaching and a steeper slope for inductive teaching. Both inductive teaching and permissive teaching presumably put more responsibility on the student than do directive, didactic methods.

One might seek to explain interactions as a consequence of classroom dynamics rather than of individual reactions. For example, the Highs within a heterogeneous class may participate in the discussion to the exclusion of their duller classmates. This could generate the steep slope in the permissive treatment. Comparing a class of Highs with a class of Lows we would find no such slope, if the effect is wholly one of within-class dynamics. (This may explain the absence of interaction in Herman's between-groups analysis.) There is need for research where homogeneous/

Table 10.6   Effectiveness of groups in solving problems as a function of ability and group climate

Style of leader	Number of questions needed		Percentage of problems solved	
	Low ability	High ability	Low ability	High ability
Permissive	71.0	47.5	56.3	91.7
Authoritarian	61.0	54.5	77.1	87.5

Data from Calvin, Hoffman, and Harden, 1957. Results of three experiments have been averaged.

heterogeneous grouping is crossed with permissive/directive instruction and where both within-class and between-class regressions are examined. It would be advisable to collect intermediate data on participation and on perceived climate.

One study conflicts with the generalization suggested above. In it, Lows profited from a more interactive teaching style. This innovative treatment, however, was unique and the sample small. In a class of students preparing to teach elementary science, basic scientific ideas were taught by a conventional lecture-discussion procedure (Harvey, 1970). A comparable class studied the same materials but used its class time in what Harvey called "gaming." The activity consisted of playing the role of a teacher answering a student question about a key concept from the text, or the like. There were 76 Ss, and the instruction extended over eight weeks. The gaming procedure generated higher scores on a posttest of knowledge and on attitude measures. *The regression slope for posttest knowledge onto pretest knowledge was nearly flat in the gaming group* but steep in the group receiving conventional instruction.

We have chosen not to review the scattered studies on learning and problem-solving in small groups. They are diverse, artificial, and inadequate in sample size. The findings do suggest that when small groups work on intellectual tasks there may be complicated interactions of the ability level(s) within groups with other conditions. The study of Lott and Lott (1969) is probably the best known of these studies; we also include a study by Amaria, Biran, and Leith (1969) in our bibliography.

Style in compensatory education. The practical importance of increasing the effectiveness of compensatory education has led to mammoth studies contrasting alternative "models," and—within the limits of a quasiexperimental design—one could hope to obtain useful information about ATI from such studies. We have seen only one substantial effort at ATI analysis in such programs, and we have such serious questions about the analysis that we are unwilling to accept the author's conclusions that strong ATI were present. The conclusions would be highly important if true, and other readers may see the methodological issues differently than we do.

In the Head Start Planned Variation study, comparable data were collected in various preschool sites. The educational operation in each site followed one of eight "models." Featherstone (1973) classified as "more directive" the Engelmann-Bereiter and Bushell models; the "less-directive" models were Far West, Tucson, and EDC. The remaining models entered into analyses that we shall pass over. Data were available for over 600 cases in some analyses. When the IQ was used as a covariate or outcome or interacting variable, N dropped below 200.

The outcome measures were the Caldwell Preschool Inventory (PSI, consisting of simple questions assessing intellectual development) and the Stanford-Binet. The 1969-1970 data were processed in an exploratory fashion. Even though Featherstone tried to take the inevitable bias in gain scores into account, the statistics she reported on them cannot be interpreted with any confidence. The 1970-71 data were used to test various prespecified hypotheses about the interactions of directiveness. For continuous predictors, generalized regression analysis of posttests (not gains) was used.

When the aptitude under consideration was a continuous variable (not a categorical one), Featherstone proceeded as follows to establish ATI. Some forty predictors (characteristics of the child and of the program, their products, and some higher-order terms) were considered as possible covariates; the ones that made a significant contribution in a stepwise multiple regression were combined and used to adjust the posttest. Then—if we understand the report—the Aptitude x Treatment product was introduced as the last predictor. This might be, for example, PSI x Directiveness-of-program.

As we read the paper, faults in the analysis may distort the interpretation. The most serious is that the author did not orthogonalize the predictor set and reduce rank. Several product terms (e.g., Directiveness x Sex, Directiveness x IQ) were removed from the dependent variable before Directiveness x IQ was entered in the regression. This in effect determined the regression of one partial variate on another: the PSI posttest, minus the part predictable from all variables save PSI, was regressed onto Directiveness x (PSI pretest minus the predictable part). Now when this interaction was large—and it was—we have no reason to doubt that interaction occurred in the sample. But IQ and PSI overlap, and to study IQ · PSI or PSI · IQ as a predictor is to leave out most of the central ability factor that would be represented by a weighted sum of IQ and PSI.

Nor is it correct to speak of the interaction of PSI ·(IQ, Sex, Age, . . .) as the interaction effect of PSI. The author was surprised to find significant interactions "of PSI" and "of IQ" that were opposite in sign(!). She thought that this might be due to the use of the IQ in place of a raw score or MA, since the latter properly assesses *level* of ability. We agree that MA is preferable as a variable in a young group that varies in age. Partialing out age effects ought to have taken care of that difficulty, however. The real problem is that the two predictors are radically different. Who knows the psychological meaning of PSI with IQ and age (and other things) removed? Whereas zero-order PSI correlated positively with age, the zero-order IQ correlated negatively with age (especially at posttest). Who knows how to interpret the residualized IQ, as either predictor or outcome? Quite possibly, interaction effects important in magnitude were present in the Head Start data. But their interpretation is obscured to the point of disaster.

This study cries out for between-site analysis (within treatment). If the interaction effects in Featherstone's sample were between-site rather than within-site effects, then they are likely to be accidental. The number of degrees of freedom was not always powerful even for the analysis with individuals-as-units that Featherstone did, especially when the partialing soaked up dozens of d.f. But the d.f. for a between-classes effect (main or interaction) was of the order of magnitude of the number of d.f. used for regression. It is even possible that the latter number of d.f. was larger. *If so, and if the between-site effects in the sample accounted for much of the variance, the reported ATI are wholly spurious.* (The Office of Education [in a 1974 "request for proposals"] has directed that, in the next stage of Follow Through analysis, within-site and between-site effects— including ATI—be carefully separated. This will only generate further misleading results, in a study costing dozens of millions, unless the technical quality of the analysis rises far beyond all precedents.)

The power of analyses with 183 d.f. at the individual level is entirely too small to permit a powerful test for ATI, even of the original predictors. Power is reduced toward the vanishing point when aptitudes are stripped down to their unique components by the partialing technique. This means that effects of the first principal component of the aptitude space (which can reasonably be interpreted as intellectual readiness at pretest) was largely discarded! Given the quasi-collinearity of a set of 40 or more predictors, all the meaningful variance must have been stripped out of some predictors. Hence, Featherstone's negative conclusions about some variables cannot be trusted.

When the aptitude was categorical, Featherstone used analysis of covariance. That is, scores were adjusted by partialing out some number of predictors, and the adjusted scores were entered in an analysis of variance.

One such variable is presence absence of prior preschool experience.

In just one program (Tucson, intermediate in directiveness) were adjusted PSI posttest scores of experienced children higher than those of inexperienced children. This interaction actually had been predicted from the 1969-1970 results, but other predictions of the same kind were not borne out. Whereas directiveness did not interact with experience to affect PSI, the interaction did affect adjusted IQ at posttest significantly; by that index, the experienced child was much better off in a less-directive program. This contradiction may arise from a methodological complication that we have not tracked down.

Response styles observed during the Stanford-Binet pretest were also used as aptitude variables. In the 1970-71 data, programs differed greatly in their effects on children who made "competence" responses (i.e., who spoke of their own inadequacies while taking the Binet). Children of this kind were at a disadvantage in the directive programs, as predicted. The technical information given regarding the adjustment is not clear enough for us to judge the trustworthiness or the magnitude of the effect.

Featherstone concluded that generalizable effects of sex, age, and black/white were not found. As for SES, prior studies had led to the expectation that low-SES children would respond better to more-structured programs, but the 1969-1970 data did not seem to show this. The 1970-1971 report says that the SES x Directiveness interaction was insignificant. Again, the use of numerous predictors in the adjustment leaves the result in doubt. Featherstone referred to a Harvard doctoral dissertation by J. S. Bissell (1970) which did show "enrichment" programs (e.g., Montessori) having outcomes positively related to SES, whereas the relation was weak or negative in highly structured programs.

Interactions of teacher characteristics with student ability

Various studies of instructional style have taken classroom variables as they come, asking whether some teachers are particularly effective with able students and some with less able students. The research question may be formulated in any of several ways.

(a)   For a specific teacher, what is the regression of outcome on one or more aptitudes? If regression slopes vary from teacher to teacher, can this be explained on the basis of observation?

(b)   Classifying teachers with respect to style of instruction or general procedure, do regressions for students taught in one style differ from those for other groups?

(c)   When students are assigned to teachers on the basis of some principle (e.g., abler students with abler teachers), are the results better than when the assignment is random? Better than assignment on some other principle?

It is evident that (c) is a gamble on a strong hypothesis and that (a) goes to the opposite extreme of open-eyed exploration. We know of only a very few studies of each type in the ability domain. We will encounter far more studies of teacher style in Chapter 13; the studies of personality and belief that we encounter there are mostly of type (b).

Regressions for individual teachers

We strongly favor examining the regression slope for outcome on aptitude within the class(es) of each teacher, even in those studies where several teachers are supposedly using the same method or style. We expect final attainment to correlate strongly with pretest score under some teachers, weakly under others. Such contrasting teachers perform different social functions. The first kind conserves and enhances already apparent talents, while the second kind of teacher overcomes deficiencies. An important followup question is, What do these types of teacher do differently in day-by-day activities? Although pertinent data must have been collected hundreds of times, we find no study that deals directly with this possibility. Rosenshine (1971) reviewed some 70 studies attempting to relate teacher variables to student achievement. In most of these, however, the class was the unit of analysis. The between-class correlation of average achievement with teacher behavior, sometimes with class-average ability partialed out, was examined. Even in those rare instances where homogeneity of within-class AT regressions has been tested, a report accepting the null hypothesis tells nothing about ATI, especially as classes are too small to allow important differences in slope to emerge as statistically significant.

That different instructors should produce different AT regression slopes seems to be an obvious hypothesis, but we rarely find published data on it. Marr *et al.* (1960) set out to compare instruction in psychology with/without regular class-meetings for lectures. An instructor taught an experimental and a control section, and within each class just 18 *S*s, stratified on prior GPA, were used as the sample. When data for the four instructors were analyzed together there was a strong treatment effect, a strong effect for ability, and an appreciable effect for instructors. Miniscule though the sample was, the weak 4 x 3 x 2 blocked anova showed a *significant Ability x Instructor interaction.* The authors thought that the interaction might have been due to irregularities of examination scheduling rather than to lasting characteristics. (The Ability x Treatment interaction and the three-way interaction had negligible estimated components of variance, which makes it probable that these effects were negligible in the population.)

One of the writers has examined microteaching data on 31 teachers-in-training (Baker & Snow, 1972). Each trainee prepared a 40-minute lesson and then taught approximately 20 secondary-school students at the start of his summer training in June. In August he taught another group. Each group of students was tested on the content taught and on verbal and reasoning aptitudes. A positive AT slope was found in nearly every class, with the majority tending to be less steep in August. Some variation in slope between teachers was observed. Teachers whose slopes decreased from June to August seemed to be those who in August were more inclined to reinforce and to probe. *These data do not justify a conclusion,* but they suggest the value of more extensive investigations. One further study in this vein, by Cleare, is discussed under another heading (p. 332).

Divergent thinking as a teacher characteristic

The Michigan studies reviewed earlier (p. 320) were of type (b); two more (b) studies happen to have been concerned with divergent thinking. The investigators supposed that this characteristic, assessed by tests of fluency of ideas, is distinct from more conventional fluid and crystallized abilities (but see our p. 159). Teachers high in divergent thinking might teach differently and might have a beneficial effect on certain students. The well-known Heil study (p. 459) can be interpreted in this vein, since his "spontaneous" teachers had characteristics often attributed to divergent thinkers.

Yamamoto (1963) adopted very nearly a conventional ATI formulation; students were classed with respect to divergent thinking and exposed to a high-divergent/low-divergent teacher. These alternative "treatments" were defined by splitting a group of 19 fifth-grade teachers at the median on two of Torrance's tests. In October and again in March, the reading and arithmetic subtests of the Iowa Test of Basic Skills and the California Test of Personality were administered to the children. Lorge-Thorndike IQs were obtained in October. Standardized, scorable observations were made on each teacher at times during the intervening five months. Teachers also filled out a personality inventory.

Yamamoto's analysis was unnecessarily complex; the general linear hypothesis taking simultaneously into account reading and arithmetic pretests, IQ, and creativity would have served this study well. This choice of analyses would have alleviated problems of unequal cell size, would have checked whether there is any merit in distinguishing "intelligence" from "creativity," and would have avoided fallacies inherent in Yamamoto's analysis. Yamamoto tested homogeneity of regressions within treatment groups; those of arithmetic and personal adjustment onto their respective pretests were significantly heterogeneous. Even though he had rejected the homogeneity assumption, Yamamoto proceeded with ancova on each outcome. (The power of Yamamoto's test of homogeneity of regression was reduced by blocking; there might have been heterogeneous regressions onto IQ and the reading pretest.)

The rejection of the homogeneity assumption implied interaction effects of the arithmetic pretest with at least one of the blocking variables: teacher characteristics student sex, or student ability. But Yamamoto gave no descriptive information about this pattern. His illegitimate analysis of covariance within the blocked design indicated that teacher creativity interacted significantly with student creativity. Insofar as we can trust the cell means from the blocked data, which confound between-class and within-class effects and treat the "creativity" pretest in isolation, we learn that students who scored low on Torrance tests learned much more arithmetic when placed with a teacher who scored low on Torrance tests. Differences for middle and low students were negligible.

Reading achievement seemingly did not show an interactive effect of the teacher's creativity.

Emotional adjustment at posttest (self-reported) depended in part on some interactive effect of IQ and/or adjustment at pretest. No descriptive information on this effect was given. Ignoring the interaction and comparing posttest scores "adjusted" for both these pretests, Yamamoto found an indication of significant interaction effect of Teacher Torrance scores x Student Torrance scores x Sex— on the "personal adjustment" but not the "social adjustment" posttest. Insofar as we can trust the cell means, High-Torrance girls became much better adjusted when placed with Low-Torrance teachers. Boys tended to have better final adjustment when placed with teachers whose Torrance scores matched their own.

Teacher self-reports and classroom observations did not shed much light on the interactions. Low-Torrance teachers tended to score much lower on "complexity" and "theoretical orientation." Perhaps this style reduced the stress on Low-Torrance pupils. But the analysis of the Yamamoto data so obscures the effects that *the study warrants no conclusions.* In Chapter 13, we shall encounter evidence that conforming Ss respond to teachers differently than independent students. It would not be surprising to learn that students who are lower on divergent thinking than on measures of crystallized ability tend to be conforming or even compulsive, and that they are most comfortable in classrooms where the instruction is structured and predictable.

An experiment by Hutchinson (1963) had the same design as Marr's: four instructors, each teaching an experimental and a control class. In the experimental classes, teachers tried to elicit independent thinking of all types. In the control classes, teachers gave information and elicited recall. This in some ways resembled the inductive/deductive contrast of studies reported earlier. Pretest and posttest data were collected on a unit about transportation and communication. There was a small mean difference between treatments.

Hutchinson was concerned with interaction because he regarded the conventional school as suited to the "high IQ" student. He hoped to encourage a kind of teaching that a different type of able student would profit from. Groups were initially matched on mental age. It is the interactions of treatment with MA that can be examined; Hutchinson gave seven pretests on divergent thinking, but did not report these data in usable form.

Hutchinson analyzed correlations of gain scores. It will reinforce our methodological message to compare the author's report with our own conclusions from a different analysis. Hutchinson's correlations between mental age and gain are to be seen in Table 10.7. He read these as indicating a significant interaction in Classrooms A, B, and C. Even the simple replacement of gain with the posttest

Table 10.7   Correlations and regression slopes relating outcomes to aptitudes within teacher and instructional method

	r, MA x Gain		r, MA x Posttest		b, Posttest on MA	
	Control	Experimental	Control	Experimental	Control	Experimental
Teacher A	0.51	- 0.02	0.64	0.56	0.24	0.16
Teacher B	0.41	0.19	0.54	0.63	0.22	0.20
Teacher C	0.44	- 0.16	0.72	0.20	0.17	0.04
Teacher D	- 0.50	- 0.17	0.39	0.47	0.09	0.12

Data from Hutchinson, 1963.

itself (middle columns) radically alters the impressions regarding Teachers A and B. We would prefer to form a regression equation in three pretest variables: MA, total score on divergent-thinking tests, and score on the content pretest. We could not do this from the data reported, but we could calculate posttest-on-MA regression slopes for raw scores (rightmost columns of Table 10.7). According to the regression slopes, some *interaction occurred for Teachers A and C;* their experimental teaching did have a shallower AT slope. Contrary to Hutchinson's report, there was no interaction for B.

Table 10.8 gives more detail regarding the data for Teacher A. We observe the fortuitous difference in the correlations of pretest with MA. That difference could have been avoided if Ss had been stratified on MA and pretest jointly, before assignment to groups. The disparity at pretest explains much of the large difference in correlations and slopes for the gain score. The univariate regressions have been rescaled to make it easier to compare the two predictors. The posttest had a much steeper regression on MA in the experimental group than in the control group. The posttest-on-pretest slopes did not differ much.

As a more powerful way of getting at the principal results we calculated correlations and regression slopes for two composites: 4 Pretest + MA and 4

Table 10.8   Correlations and regression slopes relating a gain score and a posttest to other variables

Score	Control group				Experimental group			
	s.d.	Correlation with			s.d.	Correlation with		
		Pretest	Posttest	Gain		Pretest	Posttest	Gai
MA	18.3	0.35	0.64	0.51	18.3	0.67	0.56	-0.(
Pretest	4.7		0.61	- 0.08	4.3		0.67	-0.
Posttest	7.0			0.74	5.2			0.(
Gain	5.5				4.0			

		Rescaled slope of univariate regression of				Rescaled slope of univariate regression of	
		Posttest	Gain			Posttest	Gai
MA	18.3	0.73	0.58	18.3		0.47	-0.
Pretest	4.7	0.66	- 0.09	4.3		0.59	-0.

Data from Hutchinson, 1963.

Pretest – MA. The former assigns roughly equal effective weight to the two variables; the latter is more or less orthogonal to it in all eight groups. The second composite can be dismissed from consideration; for only one teacher (D) was there any hint of interaction of this difference, and nearly all the regression slopes were quite flat. For the additive composite the regression slopes were rather steep. Figure 10.2 summarizes the results. It will be helpful in interpreting the figure to realize that posttest scores ranged from 3 to 35. The s.d.'s within groups are in the neighborhood of 4 to 7. This adds importance to some differences of around 3 points that appear rather small on the chart.

For Teacher A, very able students did considerably better in the control treatment; very weak students, considerably better in the experimental group. The slope difference for Teacher B was similar but the interaction was ordinal. The control slope for Teacher C was steeper than the experimental slope. In fact, the correlation of posttest with aptitude was exceptionally high (0.77), but Teacher C held down individual differences and his regression slopes were comparatively

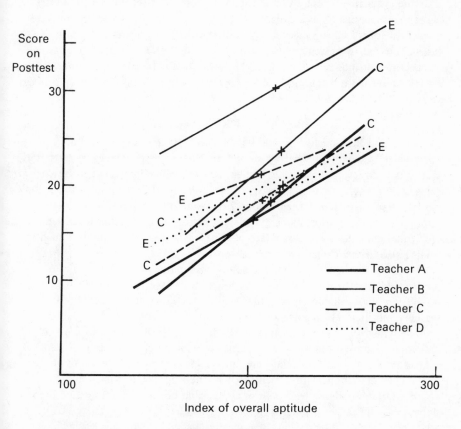

Figure 10.2.

Regression lines in experimental (E) and control (C) classes of four teachers.
Data from Hutchinson, 1963. Each line extends ± 2 s.d. along the aptitude scale.

flat. He was more effective with the experimental method, especially for weak students. Only for Teacher D was the slope steeper in the experimental group, but again there was a low s.d. for outcome and the interaction effect was small. To read the data in another way: B got excellent results from able students under either method, but he got good results from weak students only with the experimental method, succeeded in bringing weak students up to average. These are practically important effects. We doubt that with 32 cases per group the slope differences would prove to be statistically significant. We are inclined nonetheless to see the data as implying *a Teacher effect, a Teacher x Treatment interaction, and an Aptitude x Teacher x Treatment interaction.* It does not appear that one could soundly generalize about a Treatment main effect or a first-order Aptitude x Treatment interaction.

Domino (1974) gave a brief report of four studies, one of which is relevant to this section. (Another appears on our p. 447, while the remaining two we ignore as peripheral to ATI. For earlier work by Domino, see our p. 442.) Extreme groups on a composite of Guilford's tests of divergent thinking were chosen from among Ss in a college poetry course ($N = 40$). These groups were divided to form four homogeneous sections, with two assigned to traditional instruction and two given tutorial instruction. The latter treatment emphasized teacher-student interaction and idea generation. A final exam showed no treatment main effect but significant disordinal interaction; *Highs did best in a tutorial section, while Lows did best in a traditional section.*

Student-teacher match

The notion that teachers should be abler than their students but "not too much abler" is commonplace. We suspect that old research studies we have not come upon do check on whether student general ability interacts with teacher general ability to determine the level of achievement. The hypothesis is a complex one* that suggests that the regression of outcome on the abilities considered jointly has the form a parabolic cylinder. A regression of this form was found with other variables by Majasan (see p. 478). One might see a hint of such a finding also in the Yamamoto study above.

One study was based on the speculation that matching ability profiles of teacher and student would be advantageous. Cleare (see Kropp *et al.*, 1967, pp. 88–97; also available as microfilm UM 67–1303) tested 13 CHEM-Study teachers and their 917 high school students on verbal comprehension, visualization, syllogistic reasoning, semantic redefinition, flexibility of closure, and induction. A pretest-to-midterm gain score was the outcome measure. Cleare's simplest analysis was to calculate the linear regression of the gain score on each of the aptitude scores, within each teacher. The slopes were consistently steep, and the variation among teachers was appreciable but not enormous; the rescaled slopes typically ranged from 1.0 (itself a high value) up to 1.5. There was no relation between the regression slope in a teacher's class and the teacher's own aptitude score.

---

*But not nearly so complex psychologically as Thelen's matching hypothesis which we take up later (p. 480).

Cleare then went on to a complex dyadic analysis that was sensitive to certain of the curvilinear relations a matching hypothesis implies. *S*s were categorized by sex, by ability, and by the similarity of *S*'s ability *pattern* to that of his teacher. *A student whose ability level or ability pattern resembled his teacher's tended to achieve about 2/3 s.d. higher than a student unlike his teacher.* The difference was significant and large enough to be important. Similarity of sex also had a beneficial effect.

Cleare's analysis was sophisticated and convincing, but we doubt that matching on "profile similarity" is the best approach to such inquiries. When dyadic indices are broken up and separate dimensions studied (possibly in a multivariate analysis), the dimensions often are found to have quite different relationships. Moreover, dyadic indices are subject to artifacts and generate unnecessarily complex inter-pretations (Cronbach, 1958).

Another naturalistic study of similarity was that of Shulman, Loupe, and Piper (1968). Student teachers completed an in-basket test before and after the student-teaching experience. The performances were scored to reflect the extent to which the student engaged in inquiry, i.e., sensed problems and resolved them. The change from pretest to posttest was taken as dependent variable. The aptitude measure was a style variable: a composite of six tests which together measured preference for the complex, preference for risk taking, associative fluency, and flexibility or tolerance. This measure was blocked in a 3 x 3 layout. The mean scores for increase in inquiry are given in Table 10.9. There were 46 students, with *N* per cell ranging from 3 to 9. The bottom row shows that the student's change was associated with his "aptitude." Such variations in slope as appear among the rows of the table can be dismissed as a consequence of the small sample.

All in all, matching on abilities as a source of interaction is not well supported. The indications given by Cleare keep the idea alive, but the analysis may not be trustworthy. The Yamamoto finding is equally obscure. It is thought that such surveys as the Coleman report have indicated that student learning is dependent on the teacher's verbal aptitude, and further large-scale research pursuing this and related causal hypotheses is now under way. Such data can be processed to check on the regression slopes within teachers and on the curvilinearity of regression that the matching hypothesis implies. We urge that this be done.

Table 10.9   Increase in inquiry scores among student teachers as a function of their supervisor's inquiry score

Supervisor's level of inquiry	Student level of inquiry at pretest			
	Low	Middle	High	All students
High	-30	-17	16	-10
Middle	- 7	- 2	- 14	- 8
Low	- 5	14	7	4
All	-11	- 2	2	- 4

Data from Shulman *et al.*, 1968.

Ability grouping

The mental testing of this century originated in an ATI hypothesis. Binet believed in special education for children poorly adapted to regular schooling, and his test was intended to identify children who would profit from special treatment. While American testers used mental tests most often to identify students for advanced education where the number of places was limited, they frequently used tests also for assignment to treatments within the school. The 1920's set out to provide universal education through high school, and ability grouping became the principal application of tests. Systematic tracking developed, whereby some students were allocated to special education, others to the slow section in each successive grade, and others to a medium or fast track. In high school, the fast track was college preparatory, whereas the slow track offered more vocational courses. This sorting was sometimes imposed on students and sometimes agreed upon through counseling conferences; either way, students were divided among alternative treatments. Tests were used in Great Britain also, for tracking or "streaming" in the lower grades, and—as secondary schooling was expanded—for allocation of students between grammar schools and other secondary schools.

This is not the place to discuss grouping as social policy, but it is important to look at the empirical findings. Investigators have been asking, since 1920, whether assignment to the slow-paced section is advantageous for the child with low scores and whether assignment to the fast section benefits the able child. These are questions about the interaction of general ability and past achievement with wide-range/narrow-range grouping for instruction.

Considering the importance of the grouping policy and the benefits claimed for it, systematic research has been surprisingly sparse. Investigators endlessly calculated correlations relating ability to outcome within a single treatment—usually the conventional academic one. The studies contrasting outcomes with and without grouping were comparatively few, and not all of them evaluated separately the effects on bright and dull students. Even so, the studies that offer some information on the presence or absence of interactions are too numerous for us to reexamine. Nor is this necessary, as there have been several synoptic reviews of the literature. A review by Ekstrom (1959) gave a detailed critical survey of the work down to the last decade.

The most recent major review (Findley & Bryan, 1971) was more oriented toward policy. It was carried out for the U.S. Office of Education with a distinguished planning committee. The review concentrated on programs assigning students, on the basis of ability, to separate classrooms within a graded school. Grouping within a classroom was left out of account, since that procedure is regarded as advisable when adequately flexible. We cannot do justice to the multi-faceted discussion of Findley and Bryan, but this paragraph (their p. 54) is the distillate of empirical findings on achievement under grouped and nongrouped organizations:

Briefly, we find that ability grouping as defined above shows no consistent positive value for helping students generally, or particular groups of students, to learn better. Taking all studies into account, the balance of findings is chiefly of no strong effect either favorable or unfavorable. Among the studies showing significant effects, the slight preponderance of evidence showing the practice favorable to the learning of high ability students is more than offset by evidence of unfavorable effects of the learning of average and low ability groups, particularly the latter. There is no appreciable difference in these effects at elementary and secondary school levels. Finally, those instances of special benefit under ability grouping have generally involved substantial modification of materials and methods, which may well be the influential factors wholly apart from grouping.

The writers amplified this statement by noting that the children of poor and minority parents go preponderantly into the slow sections, so that grouping may work to the further disadvantage of these sectors of the community and undercuts desegregation policies.

Findley and Bryan went on to condemn ability grouping because it damages the self-concept and adjustment of low-ability students, but this conclusion does not appear to be warranted. We shall review a few major studies on this point whose results conflict radically. Findley and Bryan reported these same studies fairly and covered some other studies also. But the total of this evidence does not sustain their conclusion about adjustment.

Alongside the discouraging evidence regarding the effect of grouping on achievement we can place a summary of the effects of special education. This research is less substantial, in part because the population is small and because control cases had to be sought in those few school districts that kept the retarded in the regular classroom. G. Orville Johnson (1962) concluded from the literature that

there is almost universal agreement that the mentally handicapped children enrolled in special classes achieve, academically, significantly less than similar children who remain in the regular grades.

The Findley-Bryan review and others establish the presence of ATI. In the elementary classroom and in the common subjects of the high school there is *some modest disordinal Aptitude x Treatment interaction.* (This is a technical paraphrase of the paragraph quoted from Findley and Bryan above.)

To avoid overgeneralization, we have referred to the common curriculum. One of the first uses of mass testing, still a prominent one, is to decide which students shall enter Latin and algebra and college-preparatory science. Nothing in the Findley-Bryan review or other such writings argues that equally good results would be obtained if students were enrolled in those subjects without regard to their intellectual development to date. The contrast of algebra with business arithmetic (for example) can scarcely be the subject of direct empirical research, since the two courses have different outcomes and can be compared only by a *tour de force* of value judgment. (But recall the Petersen study, p. 261.)

Some excellent questions could be asked by an historically minded sociologist, however, comparing life histories of graduates of school systems that introduced guidance programs for adolescents in the 1920's with histories of graduates from other systems. The two-track high school has been criticized as perpetuating an hereditary caste system, even though those who introduced it intended to promote social mobility based on merit. The factual question as to the life chances of adolescents with different ability and origins, with and without the guidance program, is an ATI question not yet examined.

The other fundamental caution in generalizing, which Findley and Bryan properly emphasize, is that when schools assume that homogeneous grouping *in itself* will have significant consequences their teaching practices are modified very little. Most interactions we consider in this book carry the germ of a possible assignment policy; one can think of assigning Highs to Treatment A and Lows to Treatment B, or vice versa. But where homogeneous/heterogeneous grouping is by itself the treatment variable, such a proposal is nonsense. Suppose that heterogeneous grouping *is* good for Lows: one cannot assign Lows to a wide-range group unless one also assigns the Highs to the same class in order to contribute to that range. A decision to group has to be based on the belief that when Highs and Lows are separated and instructed in *different* ways, the overall outcome is better than when they are kept together. The policy question requires a comparison of results for grouped Highs under Method A and grouped Lows under Method B against results for comparable students in ungrouped classes using Method A or B or some Method C. Comparatively little research gives information on this, the real question about grouping.

Too often, the sections experience only quantitative differences in instruction: more stipulation and a faster pace in the superior groups vs. a dull, plodding, stripped-down, repetitive treatment in the slow groups. This is not the "mental orthopedics" Binet had in view when advocating a separate education for the dull, and it is the merest start toward the ideal of "alternative treatments." Treatments effective for the below-average child have not been invented or, if invented, have not been recognized amid the flotsam of ineffective innovations. Interaction effects detected so far are faint, but that by no means implies that the best possible treatment for the below-average or the above-average is the same as the treatment adopted for the middle range.

Findley and Bryan found grouping within particular school subjects commendable, so long as the instruction for the student is determined on the basis of a careful appraisal of the relevant profile of skills, habits, and interests. Under this practice, even if a comparatively homogeneous class is formed for teaching one subject, there will be differentiated instruction within the class. Moreover, the student should shift from group to group as he proceeds from subject to subject; this not only is instructionally sound but it avoids segregation of sections of the student body according to some overall index of development.

Some specific studies. To add concreteness to the conclusions above, we shall review a few major studies. We start with two studies that Borg (1964) singled out as of exceptional merit. At the elementary school level he considered Hartill's (1936) study "the best designed work to date." Over 1000 students experienced homogeneous grouping for one semester and heterogeneous grouping for one semester, the order being counterbalanced. Teachers were assigned to both treatments in turn. A major effort was made to modify the course of study to fit ability levels. The statistical conclusion was that grouping benefited the average students and the Lows, while reducing the gains of superior students. These standard-test results, however, have to be interpreted in the light of the instruction. In the high-ability sections, lessons shifted to supplementary topics once the class had normal mastery of fundamentals, so that a full account of the amount learned was not given by the standard test over the basic curriculum. In low-ability sections, much extra time was given to the fundamentals the posttest covered. Although *there was an interaction,* it seems to boil down to the obvious: If groups work on different lessons they learn different things.

Among studies in high school Borg particularly praised that of Drew (1963). Grouped/nongrouped sections in English were compared, with every effort being made to adapt instruction to the individual in either treatment. The sample consisted of 432 ninth-graders, and eight teachers who taught both kinds of classes. In high-ability sections, the emphasis was on enrichment, not acceleration. Grouping had *no appreciable effect,* good or bad, on the achievements Drew tested. As in the Hartill study, the tests were not able to assess the broader content of the enriched curriculum. There was a strong interaction effect on self-concept. As can be seen in Figure 10.3, *grouping enhanced the self-esteem of Lows but reduced that of Highs.* The Self-as-Learner scale seemingly collected information on interest and work habits as well as on self-judged competence. On this scale also, a positive effect of grouping appeared for Lows.

Borg himself (1964) compared two Utah school districts. System A grouped students on the basis of a composite achievement score and System R practiced "random grouping." for the purpose of comparing outcomes Borg and his associates sorted the System R pupils, on paper, into levels matching those of System A. Roughly 100 to 400 students in each system, in each of five grades, were followed for a four-year period. Interpretation was complicated by various other school policies, including the fact that students were regrouped at the start of each year. The most straightforward analysis compared beginning-of-year and end-of-year tests within Grades 4, 5, and 6 for a fixed cohort. In Grade 4, an interaction suggested that grouping helped abler students and did not hurt weaker ones. In Grade 5, System R produced greater gains; if there was an interaction, its character was different in different subjects. In Grade 6, the systems differed negligibly. Borg stated that when initial tests in Grade 4 were compared with tests at the end of Grade 7, the Highs achieved more under grouping and the Lows achieved more in wide-range classes. He did not give data on this comparison and was inclined to dismiss the difference among Highs as a Hawthorne effect present in only the first year of the study. Similar obscurities surrounded comparisons in the other three cohorts. Borg did report data over a four-year span

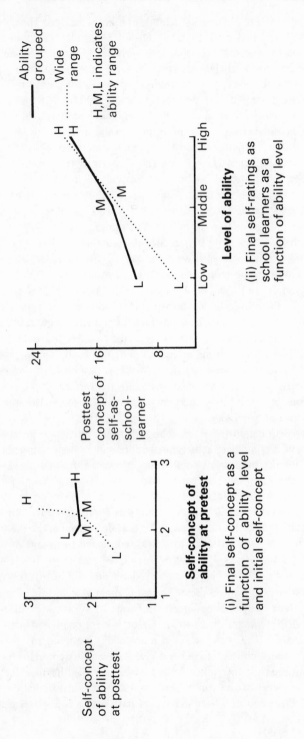

Figure 10.3.

Effect of ability grouping on self-concept. Data from Drews, 1963. Drews did not publish the means for the pretest on self-concept; the values plotted are taken from Borg's secondary account.

for the original Grade-6 cohort, but his analysis was insensitive to interactions. Plotting the data, we perceive interactions in both mathematics and science, but in conflicting directions. In mathematics, the largest difference was at the low end of the scale, where System A got better results. There was a significant but small effect in the opposite direction for Highs. In science, on the other hand, the Highs did significantly better in System A and the difference for Lows was negligible. In higher grades, there was a good deal of *de facto* grouping in System R and we can ignore the comparisons. Borg emphasized significance tests to the point of losing sight of trends in the data, but he was probably right in his final conclusion (p. 105) that the two systems had *much the same net effect on achievement*.

Students in System R developed better self-concepts with *no trace of interaction*. The adverse effect of grouping was consistent over virtually all subsets of the data.

This kind of grand, long-term comparison of school policies over whole school systems is confounded in so many ways that neither generalization nor interpretation is possible. A more intensive study tracing careers of pupils and the effects within classrooms would have been illuminating, but this has probably never been done in a large study. The Thelen study (p. 480) comes closest, but measures of accomplishment were left out of Thelen's design.

We shall not try to describe the complex design used in the 86-class experiment, two years long, conducted by M. Goldberg, Passow, and Justman (1966). Achievement was not affected greatly by variation in the grouping pattern, and the character of differences depended on the school subject considered. A much stronger effect was found on self-concept. Dull students had a more favorable self-concept when assigned to a homogeneous, low-level class. Average and superior students had stronger self-concepts when in broad-range classes. This is *a disordinal ATI*.

The National Foundation for Educational Research in England made an extraordinarily large comparison by survey (Barker Lunn, 1970). The survey paired 50 junior schools that streamed students with 50 schools that did not. Due to loss of data some analyses were based on 42 pairs and some on 36. The investigator's statistical analysis, while sophisticated, placed more emphasis on the significance of differences than we consider wise. The sample was subdivided by sex, social class, initial ability, and test form. The significance test was made between streamed and non-streamed schools within each cell so defined. Students (pooled over schools within type) were the unit of analysis. Because the subdivision of the sample reduced N, the great majority of differences were nonsignificant. A clearer picture of the direction and magnitude of differences can be obtained from an appendix (their pp. 356ff.).

There was no main effect on achievement and *no interaction*. It had been found that the teachers in streamed schools were usually conservative in their philosophy and practice. No effects emerged when the teachers in streamed schools were subdivided into conservatives and nonconservatives. The regressions of English and arithmetic reasoning scores at Age 10 on the pretest at Age 7 were nearly identical in these two groups and in the nonstreamed group.

The combination of nonconservative teachers with nonstreaming seems to have had a favorable effect on anxiety and self-concept. While this effect was about equally strong at all ability levels between Ages 7 and 10, the change from 10 to 12 showed a *strong interaction.* Nonstreaming damaged attitudes of able students, while streaming damaged attitudes of Lows (Ferri, 1971, pp. 98, 100.) This finding is in a direction consistent with the Findley-Bryan summary. Ferri's follow-up report used only a small subsample and did not separate by teacher type. (See also Himmelweit's study of streaming and dropout (our p. 485).

Chapter 11 | Cognitive skills, structures, and styles

Previous chapters emphasized classroom research, including broad curriculum studies. Occasionally, they reviewed more limited experiments on instructional variations that looked at differences in learning processes. The present chapter concentrates on processes, reviewing controlled experiments that collected data on intellectual activities during learning or tested hypotheses about process. Studies of "cognitive style" are also included, for these at their best are attempts to understand aptitude as a process of attacking tasks.

Much that is reviewed here is currently fashionable in instructional psychology. While we cannot survey the entire field, this sample of studies suggests that the contemporary research strategy is not powerful enough to forge generalizations about instruction. Most studies are too brief and unrepresentative of school situations. Most rely on small samples of students. Their value, if any, lies in their suggestions about possible mechanisms in learning that give rise to ATI. We shall try to organize their suggestions into a framework for theory.

Categories of ATI process

If experiments on instructional processes are to contribute to understanding of ATI, we need some kind of framework within which to relate or combine suggestions from separate studies. A good place to start is with taxonomic distinctions already used in analyzing laboratory experiments. Melton (in Gagné, 1967) emphasized three basic categories—stimulus discrimination, associative activities, and response integration—as starting points for research on individual

341

differences in learning. From information processing come such alternative terms
as sensory register, working memory, and long-term storage and retrieval. Theorists
of either bent typically add a category referring to executive plans that govern
processing.

Investigators interested in instruction have adopted roughly similar distinctions
(see e.g., Rothkopf, in Krumboltz, 1965; Gagné, 1974). In simple learning, component processes presumably work in series, with the learner cycling through
the series with each new input. In school learning, the situation is not so
orderly; a cycle may last for hours or days, or be so multifaceted that distinctions
among components are hopelessly blurred. Even in the laboratory, carryover
from early trials or conditions alters the character of later cycles. Thus, the temporal
course and duration of learning must be kept in mind when interpreting results.

For this chapter we have sorted research into four crude, overlapping
categories. Some studies relate to several categories. First are observational and
analytic skills, used in initial processing of instructional presentations. There are
aptitudes—visual or spatial or reading abilities—as well as treatment manipulations
that seem particularly relevant here. Perhaps arousal phenomena should also be
located in this category. Second come the mediational activities that we shall call
"comprehension" of instruction, including verbal coding, induction, and other
elaborative processes. Third, we examine studies concerned with organizing, recalling, and reasoning from stored knowledge. Some other studies related to rule
learning and discovery are included here. We place studies nominally investigating
"processing strategies" and "cognitive styles" in a fourth category. But terms
like "style" or "strategy" pervade the other discussions.

We have opted to concentrate on the instructional studies most directly relevant
to ATI. But laboratory research on individual differences in learning has been
accumulating at a rapid pace since the milestone symposium edited by Gagné
(1967). We hope that someone will soon provide a comprehensive review of this
stream, updating the rare and early chapter by McGeogh and Irion (1952).

Enhancing observation and analysis

The learner presumably begins with skilled observation of instructional
presentations. To improve learning, instruction can be arranged to direct the
learner's attention to aspects of the stimulus material and to enhance initial processing. Sometimes pictorial material is included for this purpose. We reviewed
some evidence in Chapter 9 that pictures serve better than words in some instruction. But we also noted studies where pictures appeared to distract some Ss
(our p. 242 ff.). Nor are pictures preferred to words as stimuli by all Ss. (our p.
291). Presumably preference for pictures is determined by, or helps develop,
skill in pictorial observation. From elsewhere comes the suggestion that films
designed to enhance observation of physics demonstrations are effective primarily
with Ss already experienced in film learning (p. 274). These hints point beyond
many of the routine pictorial or spatial/verbal studies of Chapter 9.

Tuning of observational skill

Salomon (1974) carried out a series of short experiments in contrived situations where S was to learn from visual displays and demonstrations. He sought to show that variations in arousal or tuning procedure interact with person characteristics. The basic idea was that providing a filmed model of an effective process would change behavior, either by eliciting a response already present or by teaching a new one.

In one study, Salomon aimed to heighten the student's ability to single out details in complex visual arrays. Four conditions were compared, one of them a control with only the pretest and posttests. (N = 80 eighth-graders). A "modeling" treatment presented three short films in which the camera zoomed in on details of three paintings; 80 details were thus singled out in each film. A "short circuit" condition displayed only the detail on which each zoom ended; the whole painting and these close-up details were shown on separate slides. A third "activation" group saw only a slide of the painting as a whole. Whatever the treatment, S was asked to write a note on each of the 80 details within each painting during the study period.

The pretest and one posttest were cue-attendance tasks (CA). Viewing a random montage of stimuli (different from the paintings) just once, S was to list all the details he noticed. A second posttest provided a measure of information seeking (IS). A problem with six equally appealing solutions was given. S could ask for additional bits of information, paying a penalty of one point for each request; S then chose a solution and indicated his certainty about it. The score was the number of information requests divided by the reported certainty; a high score was given to the person who requested more information and was less certain about his solution. Thus, CA was a transfer test of ability and IS was a test of style. The two posttests correlated about 0.50.

On both outcome measures, modeling and activation treatments gave the highest average scores. Short-circuiting was better than the control condition. When the CA posttest was regressed onto the CA pretest, an ATI was found. A similar ATI appeared on the IS posttest. Ss initially high in CA did best in the activation condition. They needed no training, and their CA performance declined when they were given the model. *Low-CA students clearly benefited more from the zoom technique than from other treatments.* Zooming evidently redefined the task; Salomon suggests that the film model gave the learner an operation to imitate. This disrupted the performance of the initially skillful S, while compensating those whose initial CA skill was low. Short-circuiting was of no benefit; providing a series of close-ups was sufficient to disrupt Highs but was insufficient, without the zooms, to prompt Lows.

A second experiment sought to replicate and extend these results. A new group of 56 eighth-graders received the modeling/activation treatments (crossed with a verbalization variable which had no important effect and which we ignore). The aptitude scores came from CA, Embedded Figures, and a verbal ability test.

A CA posttest was scored for number of details noticed and for the extent to which details were reported in a spatially organized way. An IS task (different from that used earlier) was scored to take into account the amount and importance of the information requested.

ATI was marked. *Again, modeling was best for Ss initially low on CA and activation was again better for Highs.* This interaction appeared on both the CA outcome score for number of details and the differentiation score, but was significant only with the latter. A similar pattern occurred with the other aptitudes. IS scores did not show an interaction effect of these aptitudes. All three of Salomon's aptitudes were substantially intercorrelated, implying that a general ability accounts for the result.

On the CA organization score, *significant ATIs* were also obtained. Ss low on verbal ability or on Embedded Figures apparently organized their search less after modeling than after activation. Scanning by Highs was more organized after modeling than after activation; the model evidently encouraged Highs to organize at the expense of listing details. Identification of details was related to organization for activation Ss ($r = 0.41$), but there was no correlation in the modeling group ($r = -0.10$).

A third experiment in the series may have trained an ability. Forty-two ninth-graders were asked to visualize how solid objects such as cardboard boxes would look when opened out flat. As a model, a 15-minute film showed five objects being slowly unfolded and refolded. A "short circuit" condition showed slides of just the initial and final stages of the folding process. The presentations for these groups were repeated on each of three days. Aptitudes were Thurstone's Paper Folding Test and GPA in language studies and in mathematics. The posttest was Thurstone's Surface Development Test. A control group received only aptitude tests and the posttest.

The modeling treatment was best on the average. Salomon found an unusual ATI with GPA in previous language courses, but the small sample leaves the finding open to question. Language GPA was strongly related to the Surface Development posttest in the control group. This relation was reversed in the treatment groups, where posttest performance on Surface Development of Lows was good and that of Highs was poor. Salomon suggested that this result could arise from interference between the logical verbal operations characteristic of High-Verbal Ss and the spatial operation displayed by the film model, but he did not have direct data on style of analysis. The other two aptitudes did not give ATI.

Two inferences deserve further study. First, demonstrating a perceptual-cognitive transformation can bring the person to use such a transformation. This seems to echo Flavell's ideas about "production deficiencies" (p. 130). Second, poor performers benefit substantially from such treatments, while Highs may be hindered. Seemingly, Ss who are effective initially ought to continue their present practices; it may be harmful to suggest an alternative set of operations. Such disruption might be no more than transient, however. With time, Highs might recover to perform as well as under other conditions, making the ATI ordinal. Salomon's evaluation study of *Sesame Street* in Israel (p. 44) suggests just this. An 8-hour dose of *Sesame Street* benefited Lows, giving a result for them something like the present one, on a test something like CA. But no decrement for Highs was found.

Laboratory studies of what makes a demonstration effective touch on questions like those of Salomon. These studies may suggest educationally useful ATI. Corsini (1969), for example, asked children to imitate simple acts ("Put the yellow bead in the blue car.") Four conditions, ranging from verbal instructions alone to verbal instructions accompanied by a demonstration, were applied (N = 52). Among second-graders and older preschool children, the four conditions produced almost equal results. Children below Age 4½ found the task very difficult in the verbal-only condition. They did better with demonstration only and with verbal-order-plus-demonstrated-act. They did best, actually outperforming 5-year-olds, in an attention-directing condition; in this, the yellow bead was held up as it was mentioned but the act of putting bead and car together was *not* demonstrated. The *Age* x *Condition interaction* was significant. Demonstration was of little help to the older children (just as demonstration failed to help Salomon's able Ss).

The conclusion was confirmed by Coates and Hartup (1969). In their study (N = 72), the 7-year-old who watched a demonstration passively later imitated it as well as (perhaps better than) the one who had to describe the model's action. For the 4- to 5-year-old, repeating the adult demonstrator's oral description of what he was doing greatly improved imitation.

Earlier, Salomon (1968) had taken style in problem-solving as a dependent variable. Teachers-in-training received treatments designed to arouse either "hypothesis generation" (HG) or "cue attendance" (CA). The scenes of a commercial silent film (5 minutes in length) were cut and spliced into a haphazard sequence. We are concerned wtih 52 Ss who saw either the coherent or the scrambled film repeatedly at individual screenings. The HG S was asked to provide many alternative explanations or hypotheses about the underlying story at the end of each showing. (The coherent version was capable of yielding alternative interpretations.) The film was replayed until S produced at least 12 hypotheses. CA Ss were asked to recall stimulus details; the film was repeated until Ss had listed 150 visual details. The treatment provided practice but gave no "training"; the procedure could do no more than arouse one or another style of attending.

Immediately after the film exercise, S worked on the problem of developing and staffing an English department serving Spanish-speaking students. Each S was to generate questions he would want to have resolved as he worked on the problem; the information-search (IS) score was the number of questions he listed. *Ss with GRE-Verbal above 550 asked more questions after HG treatment; Lows produced more questions after CA treatment.* The disordinal ATI contrasting two approaches to the scrambled film was significant. A similar, nonsignificant pattern appeared in the coherent-film groups. CA apparently induces one to lift restrictions on attention, to report details without evaluating. This may be better for Lows because it promotes attention to detail; but it may bore able Ss. Perhaps HG requires more analysis, overloading the Lows while challenging the Highs.

Teaching a new strategy

Whereas Salomon, Corsini, and Coates-Hartup induced a set to attend, another pair of studies deliberately taught a method for attacking concept-attainment tasks (C. Stern & Keislar, 1967; Keislar & Stern, 1970). It was conjectured that the best strategy for a child would depend on his MA. Pairs of figures differing in color, size, number, and shape were projected; in response to each slide, S indicated which exemplar fitted with a key figure. Each response was called right or wrong. One group of third-graders was taught a multiple-hypothesis strategy in which S attends to both of the exemplars and uses positive as well as negative information. Another group was taught a single-hypothesis strategy. In this, S held one hypothesis in mind as long as the responses it generated were rewarded, and switched to another hypothesis after one wrong result. This is a kind of trial-and-error procedure.

According to an eight-problem posttest, the win-stay-lose-shift method was more effective on the average, presumably because it was mastered thoroughly. ($N = 120$, including control Ss.) MA did correlate with performance more strongly after multiple-hypothesis training ($r = 0.41$) than after a single-hypothesis training ($r = 0.15$). The interaction was not significant, but the analysis was only a weak test for this comparison. This same effect reappeared as a significant interaction in the 1970 comparison of the two strategies on three criteria (posttest, delayed posttest, and transfer). Second- and third-graders ($N = 82$) were divided on MA (three levels) and randomly assigned to training conditions. The interaction appeared on all three criteria, significantly on two of them. *Highs performed better with the multiple-hypothesis method, while Lows performed better with the single-hypothesis method.* The two studies agree: Children can be taught problem-solving strategies, and which strategy should be taught depends on the child's ability.

Arousing attention

One unusual short experiment reported by Hatano (1972, and personal communication) sought to arouse cognitive dissonance as preparation for a science experiment in Grade 4, on the constancy of weight when sugar is dissolved in water. A pretest elicited S's initial prediction as to what would happen; on the basis of this, Ss were classified as conservers or nonconservers. One week later came the principal session. The experimental Ss were then told about the (hypothetical) distribution of predictions in a similar class at another school, along with reasons such children put forward to defend each kind of answer. The experimental S then had a chance to make a new prediction. Controls had no such preparation. The posttest that followed the demonstration included transfer items, including a question about the change in weight of baby plus milk when the baby drinks the milk.

The false norms tended to alter predictions in the direction of conservation, to increase confidence in predictions, and to arouse curiosity. Among conservers on the pretest, the arousal procedure was of no benefit; they actually fell behind conservers in the control sample. Those who gave wrong answers on the pretest profited greatly from the arousal procedure. The regression slope of the far-transfer test on pretest was positive for controls, slightly negative for experimentals. Evidently, *arousing dissonance was helpful for those who started with wrong beliefs and harmful for those who had correct but perhaps shaky ideas to begin with.* Dissonance-arousal is used frequently in Japanese science-teaching. It is premature to extrapolate from Hatano's one-shot experiment to the use of dissonance-arousal as a recurrent procedure in daily classwork.

Segmenting and translating instructional stimuli

Two of the "mathemagenic" events Rothkopf (in Krumboltz, 1965) regarded as important for instructional research were called "segmentation" and "translation." The learner presumably isolates key phrases in sentences and organizes them in chunks for memory. Beyond this segmenting process, he may translate stimuli into other forms, producing new arrangements or images that structure the material in his mental store. Chapter 8's comparisons of verbal, pictorial, and symbolic presentations can be considered to be examples of translations created by the experimenter. We find only two studies where the experimenter introduced alternative kinds of segments.

Cromer (1970) dealt with poor readers in junior-college. He distinguished "deficit problems" (inability to identify words) from "difference problems" (inability to integrate separate meanings in sentences). A vocabulary score was used to divide poor readers into these two classes. Then, each poor reader was matched on IQ with a good reader. All Ss (N = 64) read stories with sentences printed in four formats: conventional sentences/vertical word lists/spaced phrase groupings/fragmented phrases. Order of presentation of these conditions was counterbalanced in a within-S design. Various time and error measures for oral and silent reading were used; we concentrate on the comprehension posttest.

A main effect favored good readers. Treatment had no main effect. Deficit/difference (i.e., vocabulary levels) interacted significantly with sentence format. However, Cromer gave means and interpretation only for a revised analysis in which several "good" and "poor" readers were reclassified *post hoc* as "poor" and "good," respectively, due to reversals in their performance in the regular-sentence condition. We have read mean z values from the author's histogram, transformed them ($100z + 75$) and tabulated results in Table 11.1.

Phrase grouping was by far the best condition for poor readers in the difference

Table 11.1   Mean comprehension score of good and poor
              readers as a function of text format

Printing Format	"Deficit" cases and their matches		"Difference" cases and their matches	
	Poor Readers	Good Readers	Poor Readers	Good Readers
Conventional sentences	4	113	0	145
Spaced phrases	20	135	135	114
Spaced fragments	43	117	33	75
Single-word lists	73	145	14	70

Data from Cromer, 1970.

group (i.e., those with normal Vocabulary but poor Sentence Comprehension). Poor readers of the deficit class (Vocabulary and Sentence Comprehension both poor) did well in no condition. Single-word lists gave them at least a modicum of comprehension. The implication is that segmenting into phrases compensates the "difference" type of poor reader, allowing comprehension of sentence meaning on a par with that obtained by good readers. The author suggested that displaying a phrase reduces the tendency of such Ss to read word-by-word. Word lists are particularly bad for these readers. Sentences printed as word lists are best for low-Vocabulary readers. Apparently they give attention to each word, whereas they might skip words in regular sentences. Fragments and word lists appear to be disruptive for some good readers.

Montgomery (1973) compared two ways of teaching a 9-day unit on measuring area to second- and third-graders ($N = 54$). One method used measuring units congruent with the geometric areas to be measured or compared; the other used noncongruent units. The aptitude measure was unusual, consisting of a pretest, a brief lesson on units of measurement, and a posttest. This procedure allowed Montgomery to classify Ss as having/not having mastery of prerequisite concepts, but it eliminated from the study 29 Ss not fitting the classification criteria. Immediate achievement, transfer, and retention outcomes were used. Main effects favored Highs, and the noncongruent method. The transfer test showed a *faint, ordinal ATI,* favoring use of noncongruent units for Lows. There was no other trace of interaction.

One study may have involved both segmenting and translation skills. Skanes *et al.* (1974) studied the effects of brief explanations and practice with letter/number series on performance on the Thurstone Letter-Series Test. The theory of this task put forth by Simon and Kotovsky (our p. 169) suggests that it requires both pattern analysis and rule-generating processes. Raven and Otis ability tests were given to more than 2000 children, Grades 5 to 9, in 78 class-rooms. Classrooms were then assigned randomly, stratified by grade, to one of five conditions. Two of these included a pretest on one form of the Thurstone problems, training on letter/number series, and a posttest on another Thurstone form; these conditions were termed "direct" and "indirect" transfer, respectively. Two other conditions received parallel training but no pretest. A fifth condition served as control. Multiple regression analyses included grade, sex, and age in addition to the aptitude and treatment variables.

All main effects, except pretest/no pretest, accounted for significant posttest variance. R^2 for the full model approximated 0.50. Direct practice was best on the average, but dropping Otis and Raven main effects from the full model caused the largest reductions in R^2: 0.05 and 0.08, respectively. Two significant ATI were studied further with the Johnson-Neyman-Potthoff technique. *Ss with Otis IQ above 100 (75% of the sample) did better with the pretest than without; those with Otis IQ below 84 (8% of the sample) did better without the pretest.* Thus, the pretest helped Highs and hurt Lows. Both motivational and cognitive interpretations of this seem plausible. A more interesting finding concerned training conditions. *Ss with Raven IQ below 104 (60% of the cases) showed higher performance with direct training on letters, while those with Raven IQ higher than 133 (1% of the cases) benefited more from indirect training using numbers.* To explain this the authors referred to Ferguson's view of ability as transfer, Cattell's fluid/crystallized distinction, and to the idea derived from Jensen that direct training should reduce the native difference between Highs and Lows on transfer tasks. But such interpretations rest heavily on the difference in regressions for Raven and Otis, and this was not studied. Test intercorrelations were not reported, and the regression analysis was not conducted in such a way as to study their combined/special contributions. Nor was the interaction of pretest and transfer conditions tested. Without further analysis, we prefer the more parsimonious conclusion that pretests help Highs, while direct training helps Lows.

Two simple experiments also suggest that spatial ability reflects skill in translating and thus solving verbal problems. Gavurin (1967) presented anagrams under two conditions. The six letters of a word appeared on tiles placed on the desk top. The 14 *S*s in one group were allowed to move the tiles around while searching for the word. The tiles were fixed in an arbitrary order for 13 other *S*s, who could rearrange them only mentally. The correlation of Minnesota Paper Form Board with performance in the first condition (overt manipulation) was essentially zero (-0.18). The correlation was 0.54 in the second condition (covert transformation). Prohibiting manipulation forced *S* back on internal processing; high-spatial *S*s could do this better. Manipulation, then, compensated for an inaptitude.

Frandsen and Holder (1969) pursued this finding with verbal problems: syllogisms, time-rate-distance, and logical deduction. In the week between pretest and posttest, half the *S*s were given an hour of instruction on Venn diagrams and similar methods of visualizing relationships. The 36 *S*s were selected as extreme groups on DAT Spatial Relations, and matched on DAT Verbal Reasoning. High-spatial *S*s were superior to low-spatial *S*s on verbal problem-solving at pretest, but the training overcame the deficit of Lows.

These findings can be used to support the separation of translation from verbal mediation. But it is not certain that these activities should be classed with observational skills, as we have done here. It appears that the act of segmenting or translating instructional stimuli is best classed as an observational skill when it is accomplished by the learner. When the experimenter prearranges stimuli in these ways, his act is best described as augmenting comprehension by compensating for weaknesses in observation or analysis.

Augmenting comprehension

Having observed and analyzed instructional stimuli, the learner must go on to comprehend. Various techniques exist for augmenting comprehension; one can segment, annotate, or elaborate text to highlight the organization. As noted previously, verbal text can be translated into oral or pictorial presentations, and vice versa. Outlines can be added, or learners can be induced to outline for themselves, underline, etc. Few studies evaluating such devices have attended to ATI. Some studies of advance organizers and adjunct questions have checked ATI, with confusing results.

Advance organizers

The century-old notion of the apperceptive mass has always helped educators to think about the way past experience is used to grasp new instructional material. The idea is applied in miniature in Ausubel's suggestion that, when a student is to learn from text, he will benefit from an "organizer" that provides him a context for the new material. We first take up studies by Ausubel and Fitzgerald.

In Study I (Ausubel & Fitzgerald, 1961), three kinds of organizer were added to a 2500-word passage on Buddhism. A "comparative" organizer stated abstract similarities between Buddhism and Christianity. An "expository" organizer listed principles of Buddhism. A control condition provided information on Buddha himself (irrelevant). Ss were 155 undergraduates.

The organizers raised scores on a delayed posttest. The regression onto a pretest on knowledge of Christianity was shallower with the comparative organizer than with the other treatments. The slope onto verbal ability was steep in every treatment, and particularly steep with the expository organizer. The partial correlations lead us to think that the interaction derived from variations in initial knowledge of Christianity, the organizers helping the student with weak background. They presumably made S less dependent on his background knowledge as he interpreted the text, or as he stored it for retrieval.

In Study II (1962), on 143 undergraduates, an expository organizer preceded passages on endocrinology. Control Ss had no organizer. Although only one of several comparisons of correlations reached significance, the trend of results is suggestive. *Again, the organizer tended to facilitate learning by Ss with low verbal* *ability or low prior knowledge.* The partial correlations were not in agreement with those of the 1961 study, however.

In Study III (Fitzgerald & Ausubel, 1963), one group read an "organizer" passage about the Civil War while another group read something irrelevant (N = 264). Both then studied a passage on the Civil War. The group given the organizer was superior on the posttests. Students having higher pretest scores did better, but *no ATI* appeared.

Ausubel and M. Youssef (1963) used comparative/control organizers with passages on Buddhism and Zen Buddhism. ATIs of general verbal ability and prior knowledge of Christianity did not reach significance, but again it appeared that the comparative organizer benefited Lows. In all these studies, we would prefer to examine the multiple regression of outcome onto the two aptitudes jointly within each treatment.

M. D. Merrill (reported in Stolurow, 1965) compared four conditions of PI. One group was given a schema of an imaginary science called "Xenograde Systems" and a preview of the material. Other groups were given the schema plus a review *after* instruction/the preview without the schema/the review without the schema. Linear PI was used to present lessons about the science to high-school students. The report was sketchy, but ATI on an application measure was reported. *Ss with high IQs performed best when provided the schema, while Lows were better off without it.* Presentation without schema or preview produced superior recall at all IQ levels. Merrill's organizer thus seemed to be more harmful than helpful, and the ATI effect was the reverse of Ausubel's.

Merrill and Stolurow (1966) examined the effects of summaries-in-advance and of two kinds of review on CA learning of the same imaginary-science materials. *S*s were 71 college freshmen, selected from a larger group to represent corners of the bivariate distribution of verbal and quantitative aptitudes. *S*s studied the material for three hours or less. ATI was not significant, but descriptive data were not given. Leith (p. 424) did find a nonsignificant interaction using treatment variations rather similar to those of Merrill and Stolurow. *The samples in both studies were too small to warrant a conclusion.*

Proger *et al.* (1970) compared pretest/advance organizers. *S*s were 124 twelfth-graders who had been grouped by the school into classes at five ability levels; classes were randomly split into treatment groups. *S*s spent 15 minutes reading a passage on the Amish. Before reading, subgroups answered true-false questions/completion questions *or* studied an abstract in paragraph form/an outline of the text in numbered sentences. The immediate multiple-choice posttest included items on general topics covered in the pretests or the advance organizers, as well as specific items on topics not previewed.

No significant treatment effects or interactions were obtained on posttest items not seen previously. This extends the typical Ausubel result by showing that arousal *per se* does not produce the organizer effect. Treatment effects and interactions appeared on posttest items that had been previewed. Organizers produced substantially better results than pretests in the three classes of low ability, but in the two abler groups hardly any difference. The most striking finding was an enormous spread of class means for Ss given completion questions to be answered in advance. This greatly impeded the weak students.

Abramson and Kagan (1974a,b) conducted a pair of studies on the effects of constructed response/reading and prior familiarization/no prior familiarization with PI materials. Familiarity was achieved by providing some Ss with selected terms and drawings from the program as an advance organizer. The program concerned myocardial infarction and required a single session for administration. Immediate and delayed posttests, each with verbal and EGC tracing partscores, were used.

The first study (N = 60 graduate students) used sex as the only person variable. Multiple regression analysis showed no consistent main effects. On both verbal scores, males did better with familiarization and reading or no familiarization and constructed response, while females did better with familiarization and constructed response. The tracing score gave no interaction with sex; familiarization-reading was best at posttest, no familiarization-constructed response was best after delay.

The second study used the same instruction, treatments, and posttests, adding a median split on Otis mental ability as aptitude (N = 83 junior high school Ss.) Regression analysis gave significant main effects for sex (favoring females), aptitude, and response mode (on tracing only, favoring constructed response). Several higher-order ATI were also statistically significant. On three of four outcome measures, *Highs were served better by constructed response without familiarization, while Lows were better off with a combination of constructed response and familiarization.* Sex entered two interactions but means were not reported for these.

Koran and Koran (no date) taught 89 fourth-graders about insects by PI. One organizer gave general concepts and examples; a second gave the concepts without examples. A control group had no organizer. No main effects and no ATI of IQ appeared. A significant ATI using errors on program as criterion seems unimportant.

The Proger, Abramson-Kagen, Ausubel-Youssef, and two Ausubel-Fitzgerald studies showed advance organizers benefiting Lows to some extent. This evidence is insufficient to support use of advance organizers in schooling. In most school lessons, the preceding months of the course and other previous courses have already built up an apperceptive mass. A student comes to the Civil War after studying sectionalism, industrialization, abolition, and States' Rights. Perhaps the concept of advance organizers suggests some kind of whole-then-part presentation of each new unit of content, but no research has employed organizers within a regular stream of instruction. Extended studies are made even more necessary by the finding that results on immediate tests and delayed tests often disagree.

Of the studies above, only the Merrill work on science developed a substantial body of instructional material. Merrill's study with Stolurow lacked power. In his other study, the advance organizer seems to have made learning more difficult for Lows and retention more difficult for everyone. This is understandable, if the organizer differed enough from the passage to set up interference. Interference among Lows is not particularly surprising; it was seen in the Orton and Brownell studies (p. 250f.; 248). Interference among Highs seems to have occurred in the Gagné-Gropper study (p. 9.14ff). Interference also appeared in some of the work on learning by observation reviewed earlier, and may be assumed to account for some effects of questions inserted in text, taken up later in this chapter. Organizers cannot be recommended sweepingly if some organizers handicap able students and others handicap the poor ones.

Interference

Concern about interference motivated two studies by Leith and his coworkers. The design and analysis were unusually interesting; we can give only an inadequate summary.

Leith and McHugh (1966) split college freshmen ($N = 80$) at the median on a general mental test, then assigned them to two orders of teaching patrilineal and matrilineal kinship systems, crossed with four conditions of theory presentation: theory first/between the two lessons/last/no theory. There were separate posttests for patrilineal, matrilineal, and theory content. Only *one ATI* was significant; this appeared on the theory test. The High-Low difference, counting all posttests, was greatest with no theory or with theory given between lessons. It was smallest with theory given last.

Leith and Davies (1966) then made a similar study with different content and younger Ss. Engineering drawings of front, side, and plan views of objects may be laid out according to the British (B) or American (A) convention. The latter is more intuitive and easier to teach. Davies' programmed material for teaching each system was given to 119 secondary students. Some were taught B only, some A only, some A then B, some B then A. Also, some Ss were given a "facilitator" (F) between the two sections of the instruction, this being a statement to clarify the contrast between systems. One group, for example, had the sequence BFA. Posttest scores were strongly related to Matrices scores.

On the harder task (B items), the ATI had a p value of .10. If the authors had contrasted treatments systematically instead of throwing them all into an overall significance test, the ATI would likely have been clearly significant. The authors are to be given credit, however, for some elegant multiple-range tests. The B test proved to be quite difficult. Among Lows, on Matrices a mean higher than 2.0 (out of 8 possible) was earned by only those receiving pure B instruction. In other treatment groups Lows did considerably worse. The scores of the Highs varied erratically (but there were as few as seven cases per cell). The High-Low difference was great (ca. 3 points) for the BFA group; i.e., *the mediator helped the Highs avoid the interference* that would otherwise have occurred. The High-Low difference was small for the other five treatments. *On the A posttest, there was no ATI.*

Leith and Davies offered a theoretical interpretation which we shall try to capture in a few sentences. A learner, they said, can assimilate material that fits with his established conceptual systems, but material that fits them badly will tend to be distorted. A mediator that makes differences clear is expected to reduce interference. If one must teach conflicting ideas, it is better to teach the harder one first, then to offer an organizer to contrast the two ideas, and then to elaborate the easier idea. Since learners have to comprehend the contrasts of ideas if the strategy is to work, disordinal interaction is expected. This kind of ATI is of limited interest, since it offers no advice regarding the teaching of Lows. Many kinds of subject-matter have built-in interference (map projections, competing past tenses in a foreign language, monetary vs. fiscal economics); research helpful in teaching substantial bodies of conflicting material to students of limited ability would be a significant undertaking.

Adjunct questions

In the Proger study above, pretests were used as "treatments." Perhaps they stimulated curiosity, or anxiety, or defined questions for study. Others have investigated ATI effects for questions preceding, interspersed in, or following the material to be studied. However, if the results we recounted on the use of advance organizers were somewhat contradictory, those for inserted questions appear to be in open conflict. Although ATI were found here and there, we will be able to draw no general conclusion.

Rothkopf's research (1970), and that of Frase (1970) and others, has concentrated on the effects of adding questions to text. In a typical experiment, questions are inserted before (or after) paragraphs to which they are relevant; students read these but do not answer them. On posttests, students answer these questions (intentional learning) plus questions on other content from the passages (incidental learning). The lessons are invariably of short duration. It is unlikely that adjunct questions or other such devices have similar effects on all learners. The Hershberger study, reviewed earlier, found evidence of this, but the patterning was complicated (see p. 206).

Hollen (1970) compared three conditions of text learning: questions before each paragraph/questions after each paragraph/no questions. Ss were college students; Associative Memory, Chunking Memory, Memory Span, and Vocabulary were assessed before instruction. Hollen found no treatment main effect. Associative Memory was related to performance under the "no question" condition and under the "question before passage" condition. The "question after passage" condition, however, seemed to wipe out the advantage of those who remember well. Conceivably, these questions force Ss to rehearse or consolidate associations, aiding those with low associative ability but interrupting whatever consolidation processes Highs would otherwise adopt. Other aptitudes did not interact.

We turn next to studies by Berliner relating memory abilities to learning from televised lectures at the college level. (Studies I and II were reported together in 1971; Study III in 1972.) In each study there were three basic conditions:

Ss answered questions inserted at intervals in the videotape (Q)/were instructed to take notes on the lecture (N)/were told to pay attention (A). Immediate and delayed (one-week) posttests were given. As aptitudes, Memory Span and Memory for Ideas were tested. In Studies II and III, Memory for Sentences was measured also. In Studies I and II, the content taught was Chinese history; in Study III, Indian history. Other characteristics of the studies are shown below.

Results were inconsistent within Study I and across the three studies. The samples within treatments (ranging from 27 to 86, were too small to provide statistical power.

On the average, Q and N were superior to A in Studies I and II. In Study III, Treatment Q was no better than A, and both were significantly inferior to N. With Memory Span in Study I, ATI was significant in a subsample that took one form of the posttest and nonexistent in the subsample that took an alternate form. After this curious result, Berliner chose to use in Study II only the post-test form that had shown ATI. Here, the ATI was replicated. The slope in N was positive, in Q negative, and in A close to zero. But in Study III, ATI disappeared! N and Q gave slightly negative slopes, and that for A was positive.

The results using Memory for Ideas were also inconsistent. The N condition showed steep positive slopes in all three studies. Those for Q and A were shallower in Study I, significantly so if one looks only at total scores. But Berliner reported analyses for part scores on aptitude as well as outcome, and these slopes varied inconsistently. In Study II, slopes in N, Q, and A were positive and nearly identical. In Study III, slopes for N and Q remained similar and positive, but that for A was significantly shallower, using part-scores. The ATI is thus unlike that found in Study I. The third aptitude, Memory for Sentences, gave positive slopes in all treatments in Studies II and III.

The Berliner research represents a rare attempt to replicate ATI and to generalize across lessons. While one replication might be claimed, the result is mysterious, viewed against the background of the other failures to replicate. *No conclusion is justified.*

DiVesta and Gray (1972) related Memory Span to note-taking/no note-taking during a 30-minute lecture, on immediate and delayed posttests. Other treatment dimensions were designed to vary the thematic relatedness or coherence of the lecture. In one experiment ($N = 90$), ATI results were not reported, so presumably they were not significant. In a second ($N = 240$), some positive correlations were obtained with note-taking and some negative correlations without note-taking; this pattern resembles some of Berliner's data. But ATI was not significant. (See also our p. 427 for another study on note-taking by these authors.)

In another minor study, Peters (1972) measured recall of words from dictated lists and also oral reading rate, as aptitudes. He then provided a 10-minute lecture (via audiotape), with Ss in only one of two listening groups allowed to take notes. Other Ss read the same material. Allowing for two speeds of oral presentation, there were six treatment groups ($N = 82$). An immediate posttest was regressed onto each aptitude separately. On average, note-taking had a deleterious effect, but *one or more significant interactions* occurred. With a lecture at normal speed, or with reading, Lows clearly did better when not taking notes; Highs were slightly better off when taking notes. The results when the lecture was delivered fast were just the opposite. The regression slope was flat with note-taking, and fairly steep without. When the lecture went fast, note-taking impeded Highs and perhaps helped Lows slightly.

A further study of inserted questions came from Shavelson *et al.* (1974b). They inserted questions before/after the passage to which they were relevant. The questions had been classified according to whether they called for knowledge (here labeled F, factual) or for comprehension, application, analysis, etc. (H, "higher-order"). Junior college students (N = 87) were assigned randomly to one of four treatments (e.g., F questions, before) or to a fifth group receiving no questions. A narrative of 1500 words on "The Lisbon Earthquake" served as content. The aptitude tests were Vocabulary, Hidden Figures, Letter Span, Memory for Semantic Implications, and Taylor Manifest Anxiety. The posttest included higher-order and factual questions, some of which had been presented with the passage. It was administered immediately and again one week later.

Only the HA group—"higher-order questions after"—did at all better than the no-question group. Only Vocabulary showed nominally significant ATI, but we cannot be certain about the results; N was small, and, as the authors noted, statistical assumptions were violated. In the HA treatment, the regression onto Vocabulary had a modest negative slope; for three other treatments the slope was positive (Figure 11.1). The controls had a steeper slope with the immediate test than on the posttest. If these findings—regarding one of four abilities, with about 20 Ss per treatment—can be trusted, *"Higher-order questions, after" is the best condition for Ss with Vocabulary score below about 10.* Above a score of 12 the advantage, if any, lies with factual questions, after. Here again, it seems possible that questions after a passage help the Lows, not the Highs.

Letter Span was introduced specifically to check again on Berliner's one replication. It produced correlations about as large as those of Vocabulary, at least on the immediate test (r's ranged from 0.65 to –0.17 for Vocabulary, 0.54 to –0.17 for Letter Span). ATI were not significant, and regression slopes gave a pattern different from any of Berliner's findings. On the immediate test the slopes ranked thus: HB (strongly positive), HA, FA, FB (zero), control (strongly negative). The control treatment was the one most like Berliner's "paying attention, which had given him zero or positive slopes! Berliner's questions were factual, inserted within the lecture after relevant passages; factual questions had produced some negative slopes for him. The FA treatment, the one most like Berliner's, gave nonsignificant slopes, positive with the immediate test and negative with the delayed test. Hidden Figures and Memory for Semantic Implications can be ignored. Only in isolated instances did they relate to outcomes.

Shavelson *et al.* (1974a) then tried again to replicate the earlier findings of Berliner and Shavelson *et al.* They used a 104-page textbook on precision teaching, to be read during six weeks of a college course (N = 231). Ss were divided among four conditions: lower-order questions; after; higher-order questions, after; a

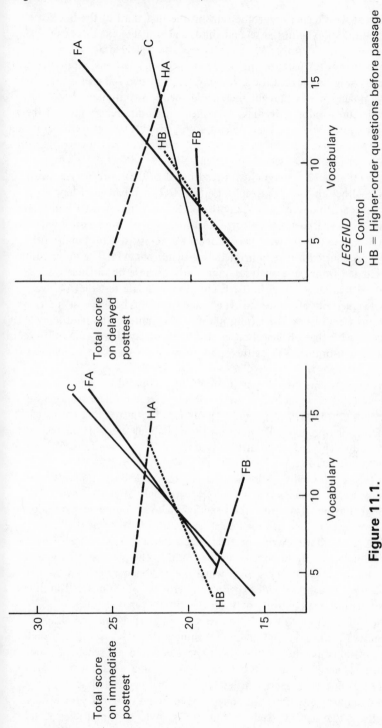

Figure 11.1.

Regression lines with various kinds of adjunct questions after Shavelson et al., 1974b. The length of each line indicates the range of Vocabulary.

LEGEND

C = Control
HB = Higher-order questions before passage
HA = Higher-order questions after passage
FB = Lower-order questions before passage
FA = Lower-order questions after passage

shaping treatment with higher-order questions in the first third of the book, prompts for self-questioning in the second third, and straight text thereafter; straight text-reading as a control. An immediate posttest yielded a total score and various part-scores for parts of the text and types of questions. Aptitudes were Vocabulary, Figure Classification, Letter Span, and two self-report measures reflecting how much time Ss thought they could spend in continuous concentration on lectures and text reading. Treatment mean differences favored the control group (!) on all but one achievement score; five differences were significant. The authors reported that *no ATI were nominally significant,* but their regression and Johnson-Neyman analyses were not shown.

For Sanders (1973), 72 undergraduates read/heard a 2000-word passage with questions inserted before each paragraph/inserted after each paragraph/not inserted. Grade average (blocked) was the aptitude. Some Ss received an immediate posttest, some a delayed posttest. Cell size, then, was three! (We ignore two additional within-S factors.) There were main effects for ability and for aural/written presentation, and assorted interactions including significant ATI. The no-question group was excluded from these analyses, apparently because its variance was heterogeneous—a treatment effect in itself. On the immediate test the ATI was disordinal, with questions-after best for Highs and questions-before best for Lows. As the questions were of low order (multiple-choice comprehension and knowledge) this result agrees with that of Shavelson *et al.* But the delayed test (on a different set of 12 Ss) gave disordinal ATI of the opposite pattern! Again, *no conclusion is warranted.*

Two kinds of questions prior to instruction were compared by Apter, Boorer, and Murgatroyd (1971). Ss (N = 174) were 10–12 years old, taken from classes that had previously been formed by ability grouping. The instruction consisted of a 60-frame, factual program. The posttest showed about the same modest effect from multiple-choice and constructed response pretest questions. *No hint of interaction* appeared.

Rothkopf (1972) inserted questions into a passage on geology, presented in 90 segments by means of slides. The questions began only after the 24th segment of text. Beyond that point, the experimental S encountered a question on each segment just after he had read it; these seem to have been recall questions. The chief criterion was a posttest over segments 25–90; none of the test questions duplicated those inserted in the reading. The posttest on segments 1–24 provided a baseline learning sample which we may view as an aptitude (an index of ability or motivation). All experimental groups (which differed in minor ways) did better than the control groups on the criterion measure.

The relation of criterion to baseline measure was reported only for 18 experimental and 18 control Ss who used contrasting styles of work on segments 1–24. Rothkopf timed reading on the first 12 segments and the second 12 segments then identified as "accelerators" the persons whose reading speed increased. *An apparent ATI* was not significant. Accelerators who had poor baseline scores benefited from adjunct questions. The questions made no difference for others. The implication is that capable students and steady students do not need to be prodded with questions.

Koran and Koran (1972) contributed another study related to the number and spacing of inserted questions. College Ss (N = 93) read a 5,000-word text on marine biology in a single sitting. Randomly, they received one question after every page/four questions after every four pages/no questions. The posttest included intentional items (echoing the inserted questions) and incidental items (new items of comparable difficulty), all factual. Verbal ability and associative memory were tested as aptitudes. The questioned groups averaged higher than the control group on intentional items, but not significantly higher on incidental items. *ATI was significant* for the incidental items on the posttest. The interaction was similar in pattern, but not significant, for items previously encountered. The regressions onto verbal ability had steep positive slopes in the groups receiving spaced or no questions and had a zero slope in the group with frequent questions. The two groups receiving questions had a steep regression slope of outcome on associative memory. The no-question group had a zero slope.

Grover (1966) contrasted two kinds of questions given after each study period. Ninth-graders (N = 101) worked on convergent/divergent questions after reading about the Sixth Amendment to the Constitution. In the former group, the teacher periodically gave correct answers; in the latter, he encouraged all answers, however diverse. A posttest consisted of further divergent questions on the amendment. The inadequate published report mentioned one finding of interest: quantity and quality on this posttest were highly predictable in the divergent group, much less predictable in the convergent group. The predictors in the former group were prior grade average, sex, and the Unusual Uses test. The divergent training (coaching? tuning?) evidently helped the able students to display their full ability.

The experimental treatment of Hiller (1972a) might be regarded as a variant on the "questions after" theme. All Ss read the passage on the Lisbon Earthquake, then half took a 48-item multiple-choice test. A week later all Ss took this test. Hiller inquired whether the immediate test had different effects upon Ss with different abilities (and different personalities—see p. 467). The two ability measures were the student's grade average and his score on a standard test in English usage. Hiller analyzed separately by sex. The men showed no main effect, but for women having the immediate test was advantageous. From the correlations for the 67 men and 78 women, we have estimated regression slopes.

Among women, those with good grade records were helped most by the added test (ATI not significant). The finding was similar to that of Shavelson *et al.* on a delayed posttest after use of factual inserted questions (FA/C in Figure 11.1). Hiller's test score, however, was a mixture of higher-order and factual questions (not separately scored). Women's scores on the English pretest generated a strong pattern like that for grade average. The regression onto men's grade averages also had the same pattern. Low-GPA men were hurt by the immediate test, while Highs were helped. *However, the ATI effect on men's English scores was disordinal in the opposite direction.* Men weak in English skills benefited from the added test.

A post-experiment questionnaire in Hiller's second study (1972b, see our p. 467) raised an issue relevant to this section. Students said that they disliked some experimental conditions (e.g., inserted questions, and, even more, passive reading). They preferred to use their own idiosyncratic study methods: under-lining, notetaking, etc. Thus, some of the experiments reviewed above probably compared unrealistic treatments having disruptive effects. In many such studies, procedures designed to promote mathemagenic behavior were counterproductive for some kinds of learners. These negative effects were sometimes pronounced, and they draw our attention back to the number of other negative effects found in studies earlier in this chapter (e.g., Salomon, Proger *et al.*). Apparently, in-structional stimuli such as advance organizers, inserted questions, and brief quizzes may be "mathemathanic" as well as "mathemagenic." Notetaking too seems to have its detrimental effects. Experiments that manipulate study con-ditions probably need to consider what methods students normally rely on in studying and what methods they actually used in each condition of the ex-periment.

Promoting logical analysis and inference

Learners may attempt to trace out the structure built into the lessons or they may provide a structure of their own. They may even attempt to store information without processing. Which tactic they adopt no doubt influences what they learn. Classroom studies have demonstrated that strong interactions can arise in com-parisons of rote vs. meaningful instruction (Chapter 8) and of inductive vs. deductive teaching (Chapter 9). The studies to be considered in this section pursue the same themes, but they are typically studies of short duration. The emphasis is more on the thought processes than on the outcomes.

Thinking through the meaning of lessons

Goldman (1972) asked students to say how they studied, and then investigated their performance in statistics and in an experimental psychology course they were also taking. Goldman asked each *S* whether his method of studying statistics was formal-logical (trying to learn the rationale behind statistical tech-niques) or mnemonic (trying to learn from the examples, without thinking through the reasons). In the statistics course, there were several criteria. In ex-perimental psychology, the criteria were examination scores and grades. Of 67 *S*s, 35 described their strategy as logical, 32 as mnemonic. This contrast is not a "treatment" difference, but it is reasonable to suppose that such styles could be induced.

The Logical group scored a bit higher on six aptitude tests from the French kit, and had significantly better outcomes. The correlations of aptitude with outcome were generally low in the Logical group and larger in the Mnemonic group. So that we could examine regression slopes, Goldman supplied us the within-group s.d.'s of aptitudes and outcomes. The six aptitudes and eight out-comes gave 48 pairs of regression slopes. To sort out interactions, we counted the number of comparisons where the Mnemonic slope was greater than and at least double that in the Logical group. The 48 comparisons are not independent, and we may be examining a result specific to these small samples. Within the samples, *the regression of outcome on general ability was steeper in the Mnemonic group.*

A concrete sense of typical relationships can be given by considering the mathematics-reasoning pretest. The Logical and Mnemonic means on this were 6.05 and 5.90 respectively, with s.d.'s 2.27, 2.37. Table 11.2 reports results on all criteria; for those criteria where the highest score was 4, all values have been scaled up by a factor of 10. Success of Mnemonic students was more positively related to aptitude; some puzzling negative relations appeared in the experimental-psychology course.

The findings, if replicated, would indicate that the weak student who tries to think through the course content is able to overcome his aptitude limitations. It is hard to understand why the mnemonic approach should have worked better

Table 11.2 Relations of outcomes in two psychology courses to a pretest on mathematical reasoning

Outcome	Style of S	Mean	s.d.	r with aptitude	Regression slope
Sum of weekly quizzes in statistics	L[a]	72.1	11.5	0.13	0.7
	M	64.0	18.4	0.49	3.8[b]
Examination on statistics concepts	L	23.6	8.4	0.19	0.7
	M	18.1	7.9	0.35	1.2
Examination on numerical problems in statistics	L	30.8	13.1	0.27	1.6
	M	25.8	13.5	0.49	2.8[b]
Course grade in statistics	L	31.1	10.0	0.25	1.1
	M	24.3	13.4	0.52	2.9[b]
Total examination score in experimental psychology	L	68.4	8.7	0.04	1.5
	M	64.2	9.0	0.14	5.3[b]
Grade for laboratory reports	L	30.5	10.2	− 0.20	− 0.9
	M	24.3	10.1	0.21	0.9[b]
Grade for a research proposal	L	30.5	11.3	− 0.28	− 1.4
	M	27.8	9.4	− 0.60	− 2.4[c]
Course grade in experimental psychology	L	31.4	9.4	− 0.22	− 0.9
	M	26.8	7.8	0.17	− 0.6

Data from Goldman (1972, and personal communication)

[a] L = Logical; M = Mnemonic

[b] Interaction is disordinal; Mnemonic best for Highs

[c] Interaction is ordinal; Mnemonic worst for Highs.

for students with high aptitude scores. The study needs to be repeated, and then explained.

In correspondence, Goldman suggests that many Logical Ss develop a coherent view of the course content, whereas the Mnemonic S approaches the material item by item. If so, individual differences in the Logical group are likely to be cumulative and to depart from the order of aptitude rankings. By this hypothesis, the aptitudes continue to influence day-by-day success of the Mnemonic student because for him each lesson is a new effort. The Goldman results need to be connected with the research on meaningfulness, sequence in programmed instruction, and deductive teaching that we have reviewed. There is probably little point in offering meaningful instruction to a student who adopts a mnemonic style.

The work of Greeno and Mayer (unpublished; but see Mayer, 1974) is closely related to Goldman's stylistic variable. College students ($N = 44$) learned binomial probability through CAI. A "formula" treatment (mnemonic?) emphasized an algorithm. In a "general concepts" treatment (logical?), the stress was on how concepts combine to make up a formula. (These treatments were crossed with presence/absence of review questions inserted in the instructional sequence; but this variable did not enter into ATI.) Pretests included knowledge of probability concepts, arithmetic concepts, and a test of orderliness of thought (use of formal operations). Also, Ss reported their own SAT-M scores. The six pages of instruction for S's treatment were given in a single session.

ATI were examined by three-level blocking of each aptitude in turn within the main 2 x 2 table. The resulting cell Ns ranged from 1 to 7; hence, the study lacked power. All aptitude main effects on the posttest were positive and significant all treatment effects were nonsignificant. *The interaction of the probability-and-permutations pretest with the formula/general concepts contrast* was disordinal. Highs did better than Lows with concepts and worse with the algorithm. Greeno and Mayer argued that the more meaningful treatment required familiarity with probability concepts and the handling of permutations; hence it was appropriate for Highs. The less meaningful algorithmic approach which did not call upon these structures was better for Lows—but insufficient for Highs. (Math aptitude and arithmetic gave no interactions.) We are left with a puzzle, because the result is superficially in sharp disagreement with that of Goldman. Goldman found a steeper slope among Ss who made *less* use of meaning. The reconciliation may lie in this: Goldman observed performance over a whole course. His aptitudes were quite general. Goldman, like Gagné, argued that such general aptitudes become less pertinent in later stages of a truly hierarchical, integrated course, and that specific mathematical subskills evolve as the main source of individual differences. Greeno's studies (see below for another) used very short training that built upon existing subskills. A specific pretest on probability can generate a steeper slope in a meaningful treatment in the period shortly following the test. But more general tests of the French-kit type may have a steeper slope in the formula treatment, or in a noncumulative course, or among students who fail to make use of connections. The Greeno data for SAT-M and arithmetic did not fit any hypothesis. The results with them were inconsistent. Moreover, N was extremely small.

The Greeno-Mayer posttests were composed of many very short subtests covering diverse content. We cannot give an adequate summary of the complex plan or of the effects of treatment on the various outcomes. The general-concepts condition evidently produced a cognitive structure, with components strongly related to other aspects of S's knowledge and easily applicable in problem solving. The formula condition seemed to produce stronger relations among components of the structure, allowing for easier application of the concept as a whole. But this difference in structural outcome was not a function of aptitude. Structural differences in outcome—between conditions—occurred mainly for Ss in the middle aptitude block, but the study was too small for such a curvilinear regression to be taken seriously.

Although ATI could perhaps be practically useful for assigning Ss to alternative conditions if amount-learned were the only criterion, the authors noted that policy ought to consider qualitative differences in outcome. An assignment designed to increase amount learned—under the Greeno-Mayer conditions—would place Lows in a formula (or rule-learning) condition where they would gain technical facility but poor understanding. This is reminiscent of the observations of Brownell-Moser. (See p. 248 ff.)

A result similar to that of Greeno and Mayer was obtained by Egan and Greeno (1973) when they compared discovery/rule learning. The similarity suggests that concept/formula treatments and induction/rule learning be considered together. The Egan-Greeno Study II is notable for its discussion of processes carried on during learning. The work of the learner presumably called upon one set of abilities in the rule treatment and upon another in the discovery treatment.

The training, carried out in a single period by means of a computer, allowed S to pace himself, review, etc. ($N = 72$). The rule group was taught the formula for combining binomial probabilities, while the discovery group had to infer it from examples. The four aptitude measures were SAT-M, a test of elementary concepts of probability, a test of orderliness of thought, and a test of arithmetic calculation. This last test did not predict, perhaps because S had a calculator at hand during the learning period.

The posttest had a strong relation to aptitude in the discovery group and almost none in the rule group. The following means, read approximately from a chart, show percentages of error on the posttest.

Level of pretest on probability concepts	Low	Medium	High
Rule-group errors	38	31	20
Discovery-group errors	66	33	19

SAT-M and Permutations gave roughly similar trends. Thus, the discovery method was distinctly disadvantageous to students of low ability; it did not harm students of medium and high ability. Discovery produced meaningful, better-integrated knowledge, which would seem more readily transferable to new problems. However, the better original learning in the rule condition (attributable chiefly to its superiority at low ability levels) prevented this qualitative difference from appearing as a main effect on transfer problems.

To capture the Egan-Greeno interpretation, we quote from their discussion:

> These data indicate that the result of learning by discovery is a well-integrated, cognitive structure. Subjects can solve problems that require relating what they knew previously to the principle learned about as well as problems that require direct application of the principle. This feature of cognitive structure has been termed "external connectedness" and was found to be characteristic of subjects who learned about binomial probability under instruction emphasizing general concepts rather than a formula (Mayer & Greeno, 1972). Thus, there is some support for the claim (Gagné, 1965)* that meaningful conceptual learning and the discovery and generalization of a principle result in about the same outcome.
>
> The result of learning by rule is primarily the addition of new components to cognitive structure rather than the reorganization of existing components. These new components include a list of defined variables and the sequence of operations relating them. The new components may in fact have a great degree of internal connectedness as shown by the advantage of subjects learning by rule on familiar problems and problems posed in the context of the formula. However, the fact that the advantage is lost when the problems require more interpretation shows that the new structural components added by rule subjects were not well integrated into existing cognitive structure. A test of long-term retention should, if this explanation is correct, show that the discovery subjects retained more information. The test of relearning after 24 hours used in the present study merely demonstrated that neither group had forgotten much instruction during that time (p. 96).

Egan and Greeno attended also to the number of errors during learning and time spent. But the errors in learning cannot be compared, since the tasks of the two groups were markedly different. The time spent in learning was confounded with treatment, as the discovery group took longer and perhaps received an advantage thereby. It would have been fairer to provide additional exercises for the rule group to make time constant for all. As it is, one knows that the treatments were equal in outcome for the better students but unequal in cost. One suspects that the better-consolidated knowledge of the discovery group would show to advantage in later work with such mathematics.

A further distinctive feature of the study was its use of a multifaceted dependent variable. A transfer test was designed to include some problems stated in words and some in symbols. These were subdivided into familiar problems

---

*Reference is to the first edition of Gagné (1970).

(like those in the lessons), and problems of the Luchins type requiring penetration through noise to a simple insight. Significant interactions were obtained between aptitude and type of problem. A weighted combination of aptitudes predicted performance on all kinds of problems, but was most strongly related to Luchins performance. Overall, slopes were steeper in discovery than in the rule condition.

Having said all this about Egan-Greeno's Study II, any reference to their Study I is anticlimax. Its techniques were less elegant (e.g., printed programmed instruction instead of CAI) and its results more equivocal. N was only 57. An interaction of borderline significance occurred which might be dismissed if it were not consistent with their theory and with Study II. The arithmetic test and a concept test *appeared to interact* with treatment, low ability again being a great handicap in discovery. The test of formal thought and SAT-M *did not interact.*

One other thing needs to be said about this work. The authors treated the four aptitude measures as distinct and rationalized elaborately regarding their separate relevance or irrelevance. But surely the measures intercorrelate, and we may be seeing merely the effect of general ability, modified by sampling errors. Any differential interpretation (e.g., that computation interacts and SAT-M does not) implies that the *difference* between two tests enters into an interaction. This study did not directly evaluate such a differential interpretation.

Reasoning and memory in concept attainment

The concept-attainment experiment has been a favorite technique for analytic studies of inductive processes. The experimenter alters the stimuli or the conditions of learning so as to modify the amount and nature of the induction.

Dunham and Bunderson (1969), in a sense, compared guided discovery/pure discovery, and showed that how the task is structured changes the ability correlates of success. Success in a treatment where meaning was supplied seemed to depend particularly on a reasoning factor, whereas, when no structure was supplied, it was memory that counted. Twelve ability tests were given to 136 high-school students and six orthogonal factors were extracted. Each S worked on nine separate concept-attainment tasks. Verbal ability, Logical Reasoning, and Memory Span had little to do with the number of trials required to attain concepts. Inductive Reasoning had similar correlations with outcome in each treatment.

One group received only minimal instructions. The other group was told of two logical rules which, if followed, would allow S to organize information from successive trials so as to attain the solution rapidly. No significant main effect appeared. Evidently the rules did not "get across" to most Ss in the second group, but their means were superior to those of the first group.

The interesting aptitude relationships came from the Associative Memory and General Reasoning factors. *Success in the more naive group depended heavily on associative memory,* i.e., on ability to store what was learned about one display after another. *Success in the second group depended appreciably on general reasoning* (marked by the test Necessary Arithmetic Operations).

Even though the report gave no information on regression slopes, and even though the "treatment" was deplorably brief and hurt as many Ss as it helped, this is a provocative study. It seems to confirm that which ability determines one's success depends on the way one stores incoming information. When one has no alternative but to tuck isolated bits into memory, he relies on "Level I" abilities. If he can sort out the truly relevant information, he reduces the memory load; then ability to reason makes the difference. (But why did "general reasoning" interact, and not "induction"? In other studies with much the same aptitude tests, French-kit tests supposed to measure induction and general reasoning did not separate out as two factors.)

In effect, the rule group was taught a technique for assembling information. Such skills play an important part in scientific observation and in other intellectual disciplines. Teaching these techniques enables a student to bring abilities to bear that he could not otherwise use, relieving the load on memory. Such an instructional procedure is "compensation" in the sense of Chapter 6; it allows the student to substitute an ability he has, for one he lacks. (Presumably one could in time teach everyone to use information well so that the treatment would be best for everyone.)

A similar finding was obtained in a related study where 68 college Ss were divided between two rule groups (Dunham, 1969). One group practiced on attaining concepts from paired instances of the same category. In the other group, the paired stimuli were instances of different categories. A transfer problem, presenting single instances, tested concept learning by an anticipation method. Reasoning ability correlated with transfer performance only in the like-instances group. The relationship was the reverse for memory: positive correlation among "unlike-instances" Ss, no correlation among like-instances Ss.

A non-manipulative study (Chang, 1974) confirmed the differential roles of reasoning and memory. Chang had each S work on ten concept-attainment tasks of a given type. Type A could be solved by discriminating which two out of three binary dimensions were relevant. Type B could be solved only by learning the correct response to each of the eight stimulus combinations. As predicted, Type-A success depended very much on induction and very little on memory, while Type-B success had the opposite pattern.

Brief mention may be made of two other studies of concept attainment. Blaine and Dunham (1969; $N = 60$) varied memory support. Ss in one of two groups were allowed to see the previous instance and its correct category while responding to the next instance. In the group given no memory support, rote memory was related to learning rate. *With even limited support, the correlation was negative (!).* A factor labeled "classes memory" had the same positive slope in both treatments.

Bunderson and Hansen (1971) gave inductive instruction only to 110 Ss in four treatment conditions: memory support/no memory-support; crossed with simple/complex examples. A delayed posttest and a score representing the number of examples (NOE) needed to bring the student to criterion provided two dependent variables. A low NOE score shows rapid mastery. The aptitudes were

Table 11.3 Regression slopes relating inductive learning to two aptitudes under four experimental conditions

Aptitude	Outcome measure	Slope with memory support			Slope without memory support			Slope for pooled conditions	
		Simple	Complex	Pooled[a]	Simple	Complex	Pooled[a]	Simple displays[a]	Complex displays[a]
Reasoning	NOE[b]	7.5	1.0	4.2	-0.2	2.0	0.9	3.6	1.5
	Posttest	6.0	8.0	7.0	-2.7	3.2	0.2	1.7	5.6
	Transfer	4.5	1.2	2.8	1.2	1.2	1.2	2.8	1.2
Memory	NOE[b]	-2.0	-0.5	-1.2	3.0	2.0	2.5	0.5	0.7
	Transfer	-1.0	1.5	-0.2	2.0	0.0	1.0	0.5	0.7

Data from Bunderson and Hansen, 1971. All slopes are read from charts and are given in raw-score units of the dependent variable, relative to a standard score on the predictor.

[a]Equally weighted average of the two component groups.

[b]Sign reversed, so that a positive slope indicates good performance associated with high aptitude.

associative memory and a reasoning factor that embraced both inductive and general reasoning. The authors displayed charts for certain combinations of regressions, from which we have read the slopes in Table 11.3. Good memory was advantageous in the absence of memory support; the interaction was rather strong—but not significant with this modest sample. The negative slope with memory support again appeared. The interaction effect on the transfer test was weaker but similar. *Reasoning interacted significantly, being more important with memory support.*

Associative Memory also served as aptitude in a brief study by Blaine, Dunham, and Pyle (1968; $N = 56$). They found a small positive correlation in the absence of memory support, a small negative correlation with one kind of support, and a large positive correlation with another type of support that Highs used to good advantage. While memory support is a powerful variable, *no general statement about its interactions can be made.*

Bunderson and his associates carried out studies with computerized lessons on M. D. Merrill's Xenograde Science. Some of this work attempted to generalize the Dunham-Bunderson work on memory. In each study, factor scores for Associative Memory and Reasoning were derived from tests like those in the French kit.

The first pilot studies examined ATI before and after revision of the Xenograde program. The first, with 51 Ss in four treatments, allegedly turned up a significant disordinal interaction. (Only secondary accounts are available; e.g., Bunderson, Merrill, & Olivier, 1971.) Good associative memory reduced NOE in expository instruction. Apparently there was just the opposite slope in the example-only instruction. The program was difficult and was simplified prior to the Bunderson-Merrill-Olivier study.

In their work, a total of 80 Ss were divided between rule and example-only treatments. S was instructed to make a record of every display, but not all Ss used this memory support fully. The example-only group required more examples and scored somewhat lower on all the immediate and delayed tests. *NOE had a negative slope onto reasoning in the example-only treatment and a zero slope in the ruleg treatment.* The same combination of slopes appeared with associative memory; this result is the opposite of that in the pilot study. The investigators attributed this fact to the simplification of the lessons, but the absence of memory support must also have had an effect. It appears that the ruleg structure reduced the load on both aptitudes. The report did not discuss regressions of any of the tests, but we infer that no significant interaction appeared.

Paul Merrill (1970) divided 150 Ss into four groups. Each group saw the Xenograde examples demonstrating one rule after another, after receiving an introductory lecture on the science. Half the Ss saw the rule the example demonstrated at the same time they saw the example. The other half were in an inductive, examples-only mode. These groups were further split, with half the Ss being given a statement of the "subobjective" (e.g., "Given the values of ..., predict the value of . . ."). It was thought that the objective might help to focus attention. A "mastery" procedure was followed. With respect to any rule, S

was given a test following his study of the initial example of tabular data. Only if he met the criterion was he allowed to proceed to the next rule; otherwise, he worked on another example and test. NOE and study time varied greatly. These variations were systematically related to treatment and aptitude, but Merrill took NOE as his principal outcome measure, instead of emphasizing the posttests and controlling statistically for NOE or time.

Merrill concluded that supplying rules and/or objectives speeded up the work. Moreover, the rules treatment produced better results on a transfer test, despite the shorter study time and the smaller use of discovery during learning. Unlike some inductive teaching, Merrill's procedure did not lead S to state a rule in words after he discovered it. The significant interaction effects on NOE and time were summarized in the statement that supplying objectives or rules reduced the demand upon reasoning abilities. I.e., *Lows on reasoning benefited especially from the added structure.* Merrill's regressions for NOE on reasoning replicated those of Bunderson *et al.;* with a weak significance test, the interaction was not significant. In the no-objectives conditions, which matched those of Bunderson *et al.,* Merrill's regressions of NOE were also much like those of the earlier study.

While Merrill said that the posttests displayed no interactions, this seems to be a result of his overemphasis on significance tests of low power. The correlations of outcome with reasoning and memory varied no more than would be expected by chance. On the immediate posttest, however, the s.d.'s were 4.9, 11.7, 12.9, and 12.2; the small value was for the example-only group. Since the same mastery procedure was used with everyone, and since the means were similar, this is a strange result. On the retention and transfer tests the s.d.'s for that group were about half the size of those in the other groups. This difference, accompanied by appreciable correlations of outcome with reasoning, implies an interaction in which unaided inference depended little (!) on reasoning. It seems likely that the effect would have been wiped out by a control on working time.

Loosely related to the Merrill study, but not involving the inductive/deductive variable, was a study by J. Hansen (1972, see p. 418). He tested interactions of reasoning and memory. The Xenograde program presented test questions after each example. Conditions were: feedback on these questions/no feedback/feedback if desired by S ($N = 98$ female undergraduates). The regression slope of posttest score onto reasoning was steeply positive in the feedback condition, moderate positive when feedback was at S's option, and zero with no feedback. *The ATI was significant, but opposite to the prediction.* Memory did not interact.

The studies have a good deal of consistency, but the use of a small sample in any one treatment, the failure to control working time, and the emphasis on the NOE score limit the interpretation of results. All in all, it appears that one can reduce the importance of memory ability by allowing notetaking; but some regression slopes found with memory support need clarification. In most studies, supplying generalizations before examples greatly reduce the load on reasoning and on memory. Sometimes the treatment that called upon reasoning also called upon memory; sometimes one could emphasize reasoning instead of memory or vice versa.

Perhaps the most important contribution of this program of work was Bunderson's (1969) comment on research strategy.

> Our efforts to unravel the role of cognitive factors in concept learning
> have made two points quite clear. First, a very careful analysis of the in-
> formation-processing requirements in each treatment is required. This is
> often incomplete and or inaccurate prior to the first or even the second
> study. Second, minor and often subtle variation in treatments may produce
> major shifts in the relationships of abilities to outcome measures.
> [If, as here, interactions are ordinal,] the instructional designer could
> better spend his time improving the predominantly superior treatment
> and assigning all students to it. . . . Useful ATI's must be sufficiently
> robust to survive a variety of modifications in programs, for revision is
> the instructional designer's principal aim. For ATI research, this under-
> lines the need for more replication, including replication under a series
> of revisions leading to improvements in treatments. . . . Perhaps [how-
> ever] ATI studies should only be conducted on instructional treatments
> which have already saturated their improvement potential through design
> and revision.
> A significant ATI may not imply the need for designing two treatments
> at all. The relationship of an aptitude to an outcome may suggest instead
> that the task should be redesigned to eliminate the demand on that
> aptitude. In the rule group of Study 1 the relationship was probably due
> to the memory requirement posed by the . . . statements of the rules.
> Redesign of these statements completely eliminated the effect of memory
> in Study 2 in the rule group. In this case the aptitude "tested" the program
> and found it wanting [pp. 7, 9, 10].

Miscellaneous studies of inductive/deductive treatments

We use this section for a roundup of varied studies on the inductive/deductive theme, most of them less substantial than the studies covered earlier in this chapter and in Chapter 10. The first two programs of work considered here were concerned with comparatively specialized abilities. Following these, we turn to miscellaneous briefer studies having to do primarily with possible interactions of general abilities. Such positive results as appear in that section confirm the view that regression slopes are steeper in inductive treatments.

Complex hypotheses regarding differential abilities guided a study by the Florida State group. The study crossed inductive/deductive with verbal/figural treatment (Kropp, Nelson, & King, 1967, pp. 69–87; King, Roberts, & Kropp, 1969). We reviewed the verbal/figural contrast earlier (p. 286). Six aptitude measures were available, but three were not expected to interact with the inductive/deductive contrast. The content, regarding mathematical sets, was taught to about 400 fifth- and sixth-graders, in a program requiring about 1½ hours. The deductive treatment explained concepts and then gave examples; the student was a passive reader. The inductive method offered more examples, both positive and negative, but did not directly explain or define concepts. Ss were asked to think of further examples, but induction of a rule was not explicitly required. An immediate posttest contained verbal and figural items. The inductive aptitude

measures were Figure Grouping and Word Grouping from PMA; an Inference test
from CTMM was deductive.

Treatment main effects were negligible. A first ATI analysis used all six
aptitude measures, with the four treatment groups separated. This was difficult
to interpret; hence, the authors collapsed the verbal and figural groups. For the
aptitudes presumed relevant to the inductive/deductive contrast the rescaled
multiple-regression weights were:

$$Y_{Ded} = 0.25 \text{ Inference} + 0.01 \text{ Figure Grouping} + 0.17 \text{ Word Grouping} + \text{constant}$$

$$Y_{Ind} = 0.04 \text{ Inference} + 0.18 \text{ Figure Grouping} + 0.34 \text{ Word Grouping} + \text{constant}$$

Here we see a disordinal interaction in the theoretically plausible direction. The
authors asserted that the differences in regression coefficients for Inference and
Word Grouping were significant. We doubt the appropriateness of the significance
test, which was carried out separately on each pair of regression weights; we believe, however, that an overall test would have shown the interaction to be significant.
This appears to be the rare case where specialized abilities did enter into an interaction. To be educationally important, the findings would have to be confirmed
with treatments of greater duration.

Tallmadge and his associates (Tallmadge & Shearer, 1969, 1971; Beswick &
Tallmadge, 1971) pursued a line of research that included the inductive/deductive
contrast as one main treatment variable. The 1969 report covered two studies,
each with different content (linear programming and aircraft recognition). Instruction
was by guided discovery or didactic and rote. Lessons were presented to Navy
trainees (N = about 115 for each course), in a one-day session with an immediate
posttest. The aptitude measures included the Navy classification battery and 11
short special-ability tests. (Regarding personality measures, see also p. 407.)

On the average, inductive instruction was superior for transportation problems
and deductive instruction for aircraft recognition. Correlations of aptitude with
achievement were calculated under each treatment; the difference of correlations
between treatments was tested. (S.d.'s were not given.) Only three comparisons
were significant, and these were trivial content contrasts rather than method
contrasts. One encompasses an ATI that may be important, however. In the
highly mathematical course on linear programming, *Arithmetic correlated higher
with outcome from inductive rather than from deductive teaching.* Several reasoning
tests positively correlated with learning of this course under either treatment. Associative memory correlated with learning to recognize aircraft under either treatment.

The 1971 study again taught aircraft recognition, with an inductive/deductive
contrast. A celestial-navigation course with four alternative treatments was also
taught, in four conditions: inductive/deductive crossed with "understanding"/
"rote". Navy trainees (N = 353) were divided among those six treatments. Aptitude
scores came from the Navy Classification battery, plus Hidden Figures and Gestalt

Completion. Outcomes showed no treatment main-effects and apparently *no ATI* of abilities.

Yabroff (1963) compared inductive/deductive forms of PI using 272 college students. The program, on statistical topics, had two versions within each treatment. In one, rules and examples alternated frequently (high alternation). In the other, all rules appeared at the start of the unit or at the end (low alternation). The treatment required only a single class period. The Miller Analogies Test was used to form high- and low-ability groups. 2 x 2 x 2 anova was performed on post-tests of knowledge and problem-solving. The two methods were about equally effective overall. A three-way interaction, small in magnitude but significant, appeared on the time score of the problem-solving posttest. Lows solved problems more quickly after deductive, high-alternation PI. Highs finished the test faster after inductive high-alternation, or deductive low-alternation, treatments. *If the inductive treatment benefited anyone, it was the student with high ability.* No ATI effects showed in the accuracy score, but one could be expected on a timed posttest. A significant ATI for errors on the program is to be ignored, as this intermediate variable was not operationally comparable from treatment to treatment.

The Yabroff materials and criterion measures were applied by Koran (1971) to 167 teacher-education students. Several aptitudes were measured. Only simple regression analyses were used, and correlations of aptitude measures with criterion measures were not reported. Of 12 *F* tests for ATI effects on the posttest, at least four were significant. As in the Yabroff study, time to solve criterion problems most often interacted. In general, it appears that *good verbal comprehension and reasoning went with rapid work, to a greater degree in the inductive, high-alternation treatment.* Aptitudes had little relation to speed of solving problems following any other treatment. The finding is roughly like that of Yabroff. The analysis and report shed no light on the possible differential relevance of the several aptitudes measured.

Hermann (1971) compared "ruleg" (rule-then-example) and "egrule" methods of PI. Fifth- and ninth-graders (*N* = 256) were divided for analysis into high IQ and average IQ groups (above and below IQ 110). Two learning tasks supposedly representing concept-learning and principle-learning were crossed with type of PI in a 2 x 2 design. The instruction was completed in a single session. Posttests four weeks later provided retention, near-transfer, and far-transfer scores. Each student also "relearned," using the program variant he had worked from earlier, but the resulting time and error scores cannot be compared, we think, as the groups were performing different tasks. Two significant ordinal ATIs were obtained for IQ, but with 84 statistical tests this was *probably a chance occurrence.*

Three studies in vocational education from the University of Illinois presented about one hour of instruction on one or another technical skill, with immediate and delayed tests of retention and transfer. The sample size in each inquiry was about 120 cases, in didactic/guided-discovery/no-instruction groups. W. E. Ray (1954) taught micrometer skills. Moss (1964) taught a printing-shop task (letterpress imposition). Rowlett (1964) taught orthographic projection. Ray and Moss examined the interactions of general ability while Rowlett used the Minnesota Paper Formboard. *No ATI appeared with any of the posttests in these studies.*

Gagné's instructional programs on number-series formulas were used by Becker (1967). Becker hypothesized that, among high-school students, those high on verbal tests and also low on mathematical reasoning would achieve better in the "didactic" treatment, while low-verbal, high-quantitative students would do better with "discovery." His 68 *S*s were selected to give additional representation to persons whose verbal and quantitative ranks differed markedly. An immediate achievement test and two transfer measures served as dependent variables. Although a pilot study had given seemingly significant support to the hypothesis, in the main study *no ATI appeared.* Both aptitudes were positively related to achievement, regardless of instructional method.

Use of examples in exposition was examined in a study of mathematics instruction at the college level (Rector & Henderson, 1960). Each topic was taught by PI, in a pattern of characterization (C) plus exemplification (E). The duration of instruction was evidently brief. The treatments used various orders: CE/EC/ECE/C alone. Using SAT-M scores, 192 *S*s were blocked for analysis of variance. An attempt was made to assess comprehension at three levels. The significance tests indicated no interactions (*F*'s near 1), but the test was of low power and *the means for Highs and Lows hint at more interesting relations.* The regressions were steep and nearly parallel for the posttest on higher processes (Level III). For Level II (application), the slope in C was very steep and that in ECE was comparatively shallow. The Lows did their best in ECE, which is just what we would expect if extra examples help Lows to apply concepts. On the posttest of straight knowledge (Level I), the C treatment was much superior to the others, among both Highs and Lows. ECE had an exceptionally flat slope; i.e., the treatment was only a little inferior to C among Lows in the sample, but considerably inferior among Highs.

Tanner (1968) programmed principles of mechanics for 389 ninth-graders. His three treatments were:

Expository-deductive. Students read rule-and-principle statements before working the problems that served as examples.
Discovery-inductive. Principles were not stated. Problems appeared in a systematic guiding order.
Unsequenced discovery. Principles were not stated. Problems appeared in random order.

Comprehension, lateral and vertical transfer, retention, and interest scores were Tanner's dependent variables. About 3½ class periods were required for instruction and testing. DAT Mechanical Reasoning correlated about 0.50 with the cognitive criteria, but *did not interact* with treatment. On a subgroup for whom CTMM scores were available, a *nonsignificant ATI appeared;* "discovery" treatments were a bit better for high-IQ *S*s and the "deductive" treatment better for low-

IQ Ss. *Sex interacted significantly,* according to the comprehension and lateral-transfer criteria. "Expository" methods were best for boys, while "discovery" produced better performance among girls, as in the Rizzuto study (p. 313).
ATI could well have been analyzed within sex, though the sample for this purpose was limited.

A 12-minute instructional period was used by Corman (1957) in an elaborate design. Katona's match problems ("Move n matches to make a figure of s squares") were used. Training gave S no/some/much information about a rule for solving these problems. Also, a method variation was used: no guidance/giving complete set of moves to be practiced/hinting that S might shade in certain squares. The treatment variables were crossed, giving nine combinations. Ss were 255 twelfth-graders, split near the median on a speeded Otis test of mental ability. In every cell, Highs did better than Lows. The difference between Highs and Lows on simpler problems almost vanished when no information about the rule was given, hints via shading or answers on the practice problems were given and rule information was not. On a difficult transfer test the interaction was similar. The finding is complexly patterned and *does not support the simple conclusion that more hints or more rule-giving will help Lows to overtake Highs.*
In some treatments (especially the ones with much rule information), the Lows were unable to grasp all they were told. We recall that Bunderson had the same difficulty.

An unusual study by Grote (1960) gave evidence contradictory to that of many other discovery/didactic comparisons; but his instruction lasted only 39 minutes. Eighth-graders (N = 180) were divided into thirds on ability, then assigned to one of five conditions to learn physics. The instructional task had two parts, so Grote created two conditions of straight discovery/didactic instruction and two others that used both methods in opposite order. The fifth group served as control. Outcome measures represented immediate learning on each part of the task, and retention and transfer after one and six weeks. Retention was greatest from the didactic treatment and transfer best from the mixed approach with discovery first. The analysis showed strong main effects for aptitude and disordinal ATI. On retention scores, didactic instruction was clearly best among Highs. Discovery yielded scores among Lows slightly better than those obtained in the didactic treatment. The transfer measure gave ordinal patterns; the order discovery-then-didactic was particularly helpful to Lows.

The inductive method gave comparatively poor results and *no interaction* with ability in a short study by Nelson and Frayer (1972). Seventh-graders (N = 228) studied simple geometric concepts. Groups were given posttests at different times so that the N for any one regression line was about 30. The regressions of immediate and delayed outcomes onto an arithmetic pretest were approximately parallel. The discovery group did somewhat less well than the expository group even though they spent three times as long in study. This investigation was a nearly exact replication of an earlier investigation by Scott (1970) with 256 sixth-graders, which also found *no interaction.*

Another study of a small sample of young children (Peters, 1968) also *left the presence or absence of interactions in doubt.* The children were to learn conservation of number in instructional activities of about 20 minutes' duration, either through pure discovery, through discovery guided by visual cues, or from direct, partly expository teaching. About 30 *S*s were assigned to each treatment or a control group. The aptitude measures were a test of language facility (LCT) and a test of analytic style (AS) derived from Kagan and Sigel. As we explained on p. 38, sampling variations made it impossible to draw conclusions from the regression of the posttest onto LCT and AS alone. Peters therefore added the pretest as a third predictor. Some differences in regression slope were large enough to be important if established on a larger sample and a longer treatment. Analytic style seemed not to interact. Highs on the pretest did about equally well in all treatments, but Lows did much better after the verbal-didactic treatment. There was some indication that language ability made an appreciable difference in learning from perceptually guided discovery and no difference in the pure-discovery treatment.

Cognitive styles

The term "cognitive style" implies an habitual pattern or preferred strategy of information processing. Those who use the term choose to distinguish "styles" from "abilities" and "personality traits," although this separation cannot be defended logically or empirically. Sensory and perceptual functions, and problem-solving, first provided evidence of styles. More recently, attention has turned to styles in learning. For example, Goldman's classification of students as "logical" or "mnemonic" in their study practices (p. 360 ff. above) made a stylistic distinction.

Interest in styles developed in part because traditional research on ability failed to expose the processes generating individual differences. The investigator of a cognitive style often uses correlational and experimental data to sketch networks of relations that characterize it as a construct. The style is typically taken up in isolation, by one investigator and his followers. Correlations of stylistic variables with ability and personality measures have not been assembled systematically to clarify the overlap among stylistic variables.

Two stylistic variables in particular have begun to enter research on interactions: "conceptual level" (CL) and "field-independence" (FI). These styles reflect both ability and personality. Another broad category has to do with miscellaneous tactics of the subject in verbal learning experiments.

Conceptual level

CL is assessed by a sentence-completion test that is essentially projective. *S* is asked to write six essays, on rules, criticism, parents, disagreements, following directions, and uncertainty. Each is scored for level of conceptual complexity. The complex person is said to perceive his environment as differentiated and integrated; the person who perceives diffusely or stereotypically does not. Highs show greater maturity in personal relations and greater tendency to think abstractly. They are flexible and creative, inclined to explore and relatively tolerant of stress. For a discussion of early research and theory on the CL concept, see Hunt and Sullivan (1974).

David Hunt and his associates have actively searched for ATI, hypothesizing that CL will interact with the structure of a task, Lows needing more structure and Highs needing less. Instructional comparisons varying structure might be rule/ example only, didactic/discovery, teacher-centered/student-centered, etc. Perhaps the holist/serialist contrast of Pask and Scott (see p. 389) is a similar hypothesis. And we can expect CL to correlate with verbal ability. Some workers point to the relation of CL to moral maturity, ego development, and future orientation, and imply that this marks it as something other than ability. But personality correlates are to be expected for most ability measures.

Hunt's first ATI study was part of an evaluation of Upward Bound. This program gave intensive summer courses to underprivileged young people preparing to enter college. Hunt and Hardt (1967) examined 1622 Ss in 21 localities (a ten per cent sample of all such activities). They administered a climate questionnaire with items such as "When the students make a suggestion, the program is changed." This enabled them to classify programs as predominantly structured/ predominantly flexible. Secondly, each program was classified according to whether its students were predominantly High or Low in CL. This analysis prorated the local institution as the sampling unit.

Program effectiveness was represented in ten change scores. The authors reported on only the seven variables where the overall change was significant and positive. Two of these showed main effects, favoring structured programs on change in self-esteem and flexible programs on change in perceived possibility of college graduation. Four variables (change in attitude toward summer program, motivation for college, perceived possibility of college graduation, and interpersonal flexibility) gave significant ATI. *The programs served High-CL groups better if flexible, and Low-CL groups better if structured.* Similar interactions, not statistically significant occurred with two other criteria (self-evaluated intelligence, internal control).

A second analysis at the individual level was not reported. In the data so pooled, the authors said, similar ATI appeared but did not reach significance. This study would have been clarified by separating within-program and between-program components of regression. We would of course also like to see academic aptitude analyzed alongside CL, to rule out the obvious alternative explanation. Hunt, Hardt, and Victor (1968) sought to replicate these findings the next year. Most of the programs in the second sample had to be classified as structured treatments, however, and most groups had low CL; no ATI test was possible. Four other experiments have been reported, all of them small.

Tomlinson and Hunt (1971) contrasted rule-example/example-rule/and example-only treatments. These were seen as having high/intermediate/ and low degrees of "structure." No student was left without the rule; at the end of the study period a review stated the rule and related it to the examples. The topic of cognitive dissonance was introduced in texts that required one period of study. On the next day and again one week later, an essay test was given. The delayed test, with general ability partialled out, served as the principal criterion. Ss were 120 eleventh-graders from opposite ends of the CL distribution. Analysis of variance yielded main effects for CL and sex, girls and Highs doing best. Sex, and Sex x CL did not interact with treatment.

The CL x Treatment interaction was significant. *Highs were markedly superior to Lows in two inductive treatments.* In the ruleg condition, Highs did a little worse than Lows. Lows did far better with ruleg instruction than when working from examples; among Highs the treatment differences were small. Hunt's theory had predicted such results. The effects of ability were "removed from the analysis" by linear regression, implying that the effect can be attributed to CL and not to ability. We would prefer a direct demonstration of the functioning of both ability and CL. This is all the more important because many studies find ruleg treatments superior on the average, and because we found earlier that general ability, though not interacting consistently with inductive/deductive treatments, often showed an interaction pattern similar to that reported here.

Noy and Hunt (1972) studied 64 twelfth-graders at the extremes on CL. Their general ability was also tested. Externally directed use of an information bank as a learning condition was contrasted with self-direction. The bank held cards on aspects of Freud's life and work arranged in 34 categories. In the self-direction condition, S was allowed to ask questions, to receive related cards, and to retain and review these until he had no more questions, or until 30 minutes had elapsed. Each S in the other condition received exactly the same cards, in the same order, as a particular S from the other treatment chose. The S with whom he was thus "yoked" was of the same CL. It is doubtful that this treatment contrast did indeed systematically alter "structure." After treatment, each S wrote for 20 minutes giving his impression of Freud, wrote as many adjectives as he could to describe Freud, and answered recall questions pertaining to the information cards he had received during treatment. Scores were derived for recall of knowledge, number of themes and specific impressions noted, categories of adjectives used, and synthesis of material in the essay. In testing interactions for significance, general ability was partialled out of the criterion. Main effects favored self-direction and the High CL's in nearly every comparison. The report gave the correlations in Table 11.4. Lacking standard deviations, we cannot compare regression slopes. As in the Tomlinson-Hunt study, the investigators did not test ATI of general ability; rather, they covaried ability before testing CL interactions for significance. ATI of CL were significant. No conclusion is warranted, in view of the small sample, but it seems *unlikely that CL interacts in the population.* The correlations suggest that general ability did interact ordinally with treatment. The correlations of knowledge and synthesis with ability were notably higher in the external-direction condition. The significance of this comparison was not tested.

A similar investigation was conducted by Fry (1972). Students were classified on scholastic aptitude and a measure of inquiry styles developed by Shulman *et al.* (See p. 333.) Fry regarded the latter as a measure of cognitive complexity and noted that it correlated positively with the ability score. The *S*s were placed within quadrants of the joint distribution of these tests and then 48 cases of each type were divided among three treatments and a control group (uninstructed) that we shall ignore. A file of videotapes on the nature of computers was prepared, with a file of questions that could be answered by each segment of the videotape. The "random" group saw the segments of tape in haphazard order. The self-controlled group called up whatever sections of the tape covered the questions they wished to have answered; while they were free to see some segments twice or to omit some, their control was primarily over sequence. The fourth group had an externally controlled sequence that experts had determined as educationally sound. This sequence was modified so that each *S* in the group failed to see (or saw more than once) whatever segments a self-managing *S* of the same type had omitted (or reviewed).

Fry's anova on gain scores found no significant interaction of the aptitudes singly or jointly, but the design and analysis lacked power. Fry went on to analyze within each student type and to report patterns of interaction. From the published cell means, we reach a somewhat different summary of the data. First we considered the composite of the two aptitudes, by pooling the High-Low and Low-High cells within each treatment and examining the three means (High-High, uneven ability, and Low-Low). The regressions were essentially parallel save that the achievement for the externally controlled, uneven-ability group was above the line. Then we split the mixed groups, contrasting the High-Ability, Low-CL and Low-Ability, High CL cells within each treatment. Among these cases, High-

Table 11.4   Correlations relating outcomes to general ability and CL under student-directed and system-directed treatments

| | Student-directed | | System-directed | |
Outcome measure	General ability	CL	General ability	CL
Knowledge	0.18	0.35*	0.51*	0.41*
Themes	0.29	0.13	0.06	0.18
Adjective categories	0.24	0.29	0.19	0.35*
Impressions	0.38*	0.23	0.49*	0.38*
Synthesis	0.29	0.46*	0.51*	0.38*

After Noy and Hunt, 1972.

*$p < .05$.

Lows did better than the Low-Highs; that is, High CL could not offset poor overall ability. The one potentially important effect is that *persons high in ability and low in CL did considerably better under external direction* than would have been expected from the trend in the other cells in the design. Fry had predicted this effect, apparently on the grounds that Low-CL's are less able to use independence. The data gave little support to the expectation that High-CL's would do better under self-direction. The Fry result is not consistent with that of Noy and Hunt, but the data were presented in such different ways that direct comparison is impossible. If a significant interaction exists in the Fry data, it is associated with CL differences within the high-ability group. Noy and Hunt did not check on the possibility of such a second-order interaction. Fry produced no evidence of an interaction for general ability such as Noy and Hunt found.

McLachlan (1969) made a similarly detailed assessment of outcomes in another small study. Ss learned about Picasso's *Guernica* by lecture/discovery methods. All Ss viewed a projected slide of the picture plus eight slides of its components. Lecture Ss heard a tape-recording that described each component and gave some interpretive comments. Discovery Ss had no lecture; they viewed the slide in their own way. Both groups were urged to figure out the meaning of the whole. Ss were 64 eleventh-graders chosen from the extremes on CL. Treatment groups were matched on sex, status as an art student, and verbal ability. CL and ability correlated 0.15 in the original full-range sample. As a posttest, Ss wrote short answers to questions about the painting's meaning and the relevance of the parts to it. Essays were scored for comprehension, integration, and recall of component meanings.

The anova showed main effects favoring lecture and High CL. Integration was related to CL in the discovery group and very little related in the lecture group. The interaction was ordinal, and the direction supports Hunt's conception of the rigidity of the Low-CL student. Providing him with strong hints regarding interpretation compensated for his handicap. A pretest on attitude showed a weak but significant interaction. Those who preferred unstructured teaching did better than others in the discovery group and were at a disadvantage in the lecture. No report on interactions of verbal ability was given. The authors stated that comprehension and recall did not interact.

McLachlan's appendix allowed us to compute the results in Table 11.5. His own analysis was made within sexes, even though this reduced cell size to 16. It is not unlikely that interest in art is sex-related, but with this cell size statistical tests are of little use. For cognitive aptitudes and outcomes, slopes for boys were close to zero in both treatments, while slopes for girls were more often positive. *The presence of interaction is dubious.* Perhaps the results using art attitude as outcome would be confirmed in another sample: Highs on CL responded positively after the discovery treatment while Lows responded positively after the lecture. Other outcomes gave differences in slope that were small and easily attributable to chance.

Hunt et al. (1974) reported a series of three studies on student CL in relation to teacher behavior, of which one dealt with ATI. Extreme groups of high and

Table 11.5 Correlations and regression slopes relating outcomes to aptitudes in lecture and discovery treatments

Aptitude	Outcome measure	Treatments							
		Lecture				Discovery			
		Males		Females		Males		Females	
		r	b	r	b	r	b	r	b
CL	Total Integration	0.02	0.01	0.53*	0.33	0.21	0.15	0.67*	0.50
	Subj. Integration	0.02	0.01	0.46	0.17	0.47	0.24	0.72*	0.32
	Comprehension	0.07	0.03	0.38	0.23	0.24	0.14	0.07	0.04
	Recall	0.11	0.02	-0.02	0.00	0.40	0.09	-0.01	0.00
	Attitude toward Art	0.17	0.23	-0.33	-0.98	0.32	0.64	0.19	0.58
Verbal Ability	Total Integration	-0.05	-0.04	0.50*	0.13	-0.28	-0.12	0.26	0.12
	Subj. 1ntegration	0.08	0.04	0.20	0.03	-0.10	-0.03	0.19	0.05
	Comprehension	-0.09	-0.04	0.41	0.11	-0.25	-0.09	-0.36	-0.13
	Recall	0.19	0.04	0.18	0.02	0.35	0.05	0.16	0.05
	Attitude toward Art	-0.06	-0.10	-0.18	-0.23	-0.08	-0.10	0.01	0.01
Initial attitude toward art	Total Integration	0.22	0.07	0.06	0.01	0.24	0.08	0.21	0.06
	Subj. Integration	0.14	0.03	-0.31	-0.03	0.50*	0.11	0.28	0.05
	Comprehension	0.21	0.04	0.45	0.07	0.35	0.09	0.54*	0.12
	Recall	0.26	0.02	0.05	0.00	0.52*	0.05	-0.10	-0.02
	Attitude toward Art	0.61*	0.37	0.49*	0.40	0.68*	0.62	0.54*	0.64
Initial attitude toward instructional method	Total Integration	-0.34	-0.11	0.42	0.12	-0.09	-0.04	0.70*	0.20
	Subj. Integration	-0.44	-0.11	0.04	0.01	-0.16	-0.05	0.61*	0.10
	Comprehension	0.18	0.04	0.41	0.12	-0.13	-0.04	0.13	0.03
	Recall	-0.28	-0.03	-0.18	-0.02	-0.33	-0.04	0.01	0.00
	Attitude toward Art	-0.03	-0.02	0.33	0.47	-0.39	-0.45	0.25	0.29

*$p < .05$

low CL Ss (N = 100 ninth-graders) were divided among four treatments such
that each subgroup was homogeneous on CL and matched on sex and general
ability. The treatments contrasted inductive teaching/"synectic" teaching (teacher
behavior characterized as high-level information processing with little evaluative
feedback)/two control groups which we ignore. The instruction was an hour on
Hemingway. Observations of the teachers showed that inductive teaching used
more teacher talk, with higher-level information, more neutral sanctioning, and
fewer opinion and negotiation statements than did synectic teaching. Outcome
measures included attitude about teaching methods, a test of factual recall, and
an essay scored for the number of causal inferences relating Hemingway's life
and work. Anova showed no significant main effects or interactions, but the
causal-inference data displayed a borderline ATI; *inductive teaching was best for
all Ss but synectic teaching gave a steeper positive slope.*

The findings of the Hunt program suggest, though weakly and inconsistently,
that Low-CL students are helped by more directive teaching, whereas Highs do
better when they have more control over the situation. CL and verbal ability may
interact with treatment somewhat differently, but none of the studies was well
calculated to test this possibility. Our earlier conclusion (p. 319, 370)
that didactic instruction suits less-able Ss better than inductive teaching is
superficially similar to the conclusion in this section.

Hunt has also written about other kinds of aptitude-treatment match: between
S's motivation and the form of feedback or reward, between S's values and the
values emphasized in the teaching, and between S's preference for particular
sense modalities and the modality of presentation.

An isolated study by Siegel and Siegel (1965) investigated a style that should
be similar to CL. "Educational set" was represented by a forced-choice inventory
distinguishing factually oriented and conceptually oriented Ss. Two college biology
courses were taught by closed-circuit television. In each course, 128 Ss were
chose from 800 as extreme groups on ability (ACT), pretested knowledge, course-
specific motivation (a Thurstone attitude scale), and educational set. Instructional
conditions were: proctor in room/no proctor; hourly quizzes emphasizing factual/
conceptual objectives; occasional personal contact with TV teacher/no contact.
This design yielded a 2^7 factorial anova, with one S per cell. Outcome measures
were final examinations on both factual and conceptual content.

In one course, aptitude main effects favored high ability, prior knowledge,
attitude, and conceptual set Ss. *No treatment main effects or ATI were statistically
significant.* In the other course, judged by the authors as taught at a lower and
more repetitive level, main effects favoring proctoring, personal contact with
teacher, and high ability appeared. Only the conceptual outcome measure gave
ATI discussed by the authors. These were three-way interactions, where cell
means were based on 16 Ss. From the reported means, it appears that *conceptually oriented Ss who are high in ability and/or prior knowledge are served
best by quizzes emphasizing conceptual objectives; factually oriented Ss are better
off with factual quizzes,* even though the criterion is a conceptual examination.
The interaction apparently faded out among Ss low in ability and/or prior
knowledge. There is evidence also that the presence of a proctor accentuates this

ATI, while personal contact with the teacher confuses it, making factual quizzes best for conceptual Ss. Interpretation would require reanalysis with regression methods.

Field independence

The principal work on field independence (FI) has been directed by Witkin. (See Witkin et al., 1962, for early research, and Witkin, 1973, for a summary relating to education.) FI is usually represented by scores on Embedded Figures tests or performance tests such as Rod and Frame, where Ss must ignore a visual and/or postural context to locate a true vertical. The S who is able to locate a simple figure or a vertical position in a complex context is said to be field-independent or analytic; one who has difficulty in such tasks is said to be field-dependent or global.

There is reason to believe that field independence is, in whole or part, fluid ability. Witkin himself has said (1973, p. 7) that of "the three main factor components" of the Wechsler, the one centered on Block Design, Object Assembly, and Picture Completion ". . . happens to be essentially identical with the field-dependence-independence dimension." This component represents a fluid ability as distinct from the verbal-educational component.

Other variables go by similar names. "Analytic style" in categorizing common objects has been defined by Kagan, Moss, and Sigel (1963). The score depends on whether S groups object according to some function or abstract property, or according to superficial qualities and associations. This is, on its face, a "style" —but it also is related to mental ability. Another variable studied by Kagan is "reflection-impulsivity." On a test such as Matching Familiar Figures, Ss with fast reaction times and many errors are called "impulsive"; those with longer latencies and few errors are called "reflective." Error scores, at least, probably relate to fluid ability.

Perhaps workers such as Witkin and Kagan are only demonstrating what Binet built into his definition of intelligence: the principle that weakness in analysis or self-discipline is a cause of poor intellectual performance. Then "field dependence" is a deficit rather than a style. It is our understanding from personal communication, however, that Witkin regards the field-dependent person as having a positive advantage in dealing with some kinds of complex situations—particularly interpersonal situations—where the analytic person uses his intelligence badly. As matters now stand, we lack evidence that a stylistic construct must be added to the construct "fluid ability" to explain the results of Witkin and Kagan.

Evidence is also insufficient at present to judge the independence of these styles. Although they appear to be conceptually related, occasional reports show little correlation in selected samples. (For example, Stanes and Gordon, 1973, reported $r = -0.01$ between FI and analytic style.)

Only a few studies examine the interactions of FI or related styles with instruction. Some of these treat style as aptitude; others consider it an intellectual attribute to be modified and make it the dependent variable.

Two brief experiments were carried out by J. K. Davis (1967) with negative results (N = 30 and 40 chosen as extremes on Hidden Figures). The studies used concept-identification tasks. FI did have an ordinal interaction with a particular aspect of the difficulty of the tasks used, but it did not interact with the kinds of complexity where Davis had expected "cognitive style" to produce an interaction. Neither the rationale nor the educational relevance of Davis's variables is clear to us.

Grieve and J. K. Davis (1971) compared expository/discovery teaching in ninth-grade geography, using groups randomly chosen from the high and low halves of an FI distribution (N = 117). In the discovery treatment, generalizations were not to be put in words until the end of the work period. In the expository treatment, the generalizations were verbalized by the teacher as a first step in instruction. Instruction took 11 hours. Two outcome measures were used; factual knowledge on Japanese geography and a transfer measure on using similar geographical materials. Data were analyzed separately by sex.

Initial tests of treatment effects and ATI failed of significance in both sexes. The authors then reduced their sample to extremes on FI (N = 74). With boys, ATI was significant and disordinal; expository instruction was best for Highs, discovery was best for Lows, in producing both knowledge and transfer. ATI was still not significant for girls, but means were not given. Grieve and Davis suggested that discovery helped Lows by providing a more intensive, personal, and concrete experience with more teacher-learner exchange. According to Witkin, Lows should prefer a congenial social context.

Beller (1967) examined language training methods for poor (and mostly black) nursery-school children (N = 81). Sigel's test of conceptual styles classified 30 as descriptive-analytic and 29 as contextual-relational. Responses of 22 were too brief to allow classification. These groups were randomly apportioned among three treatments, one emphasizing word and object associations of a descriptive-analytic sort, one emphasizing contextual-relational associations, and a control condition in which children received attention but no language training. Training was given to pairs of children in 13 brief sessions. Although several dependent measures were apparently made, the analysis concentrated on two: change scores on ITPA (the posttest being given seven months after training) and a paired-associate learning task that measured association and recognition memory for objects and pictures using words taught and other words. Trial 1 of this test served as an immediate posttest; Trials 1–4 provided a learning measure using words from the training sessions, and Trials 5–6 gave a transfer score.

The analytic training produced the best recognition of words previously studied (Trial 1), while the contextual-relational method produced the best association score. ATI, not statistically significant, was found on all Trial 1 outcomes. *Ss given training that "matched their own styles" were always superior to Ss given training that did not match.* On the data for Trials 1–4, *no ATI appeared.* The transfer data suggested that the contextual-relational method facilitated transfer to new material, but again *there were no ATI.*

Various pretest differences on ITPA were observed, with "analytic" Ss generally higher. The unclassifiable Ss (i.e., low in initial verbal ability) changed most on ITPA as a whole (including visual sequencing), particularly when given the contextual-relational treatment. Analytic Ss, however, improved on visual sequencing in the analytic treatment and declined when given the contextual-relational treatment. The third group, with a contextual-relational style, declined when given the analytic treatment. *This implies ATI, favoring the matching of treatment and style.* But Beller's report gave no ITPA data, so we cannot study the result in detail.

Coop and Brown (1970) sought to extend Beller's results to college students. They used two treatments, one teacher-structured and factual, the other requiring independent problem-solving. Both factual knowledge and conceptual generalization were measured as outcomes. Extreme groups of 40 analytic and 40 nonanalytic students, classified by Sigel's test, were taught a series of lessons. The structured method was better on the average and *did not interact* with the Sigel measure.

Rennels (1970) trained poor black children (N = 78 eighth graders) in perception of spatial relations. All Ss were at least two years behind in reading. An analytic treatment was designed to emphasize field independence, while a synthetic treatment emphasized field dependence. There was also a control group. Instruction occurred once a week through five weeks. The analysis divided Ss into thirds on FI and also included sex. A pretest served as covariate. *No ATI appeared;* the analytic method was best on the average. FI correlated with achievement. Data were not given so we cannot probe further. The author did report that FI correlated 0.45 and 0.31 with Thurstone Spatial Relations and Perceptual Speed, respectively, in this sample.

Lee, Kagan, and Rabson (1963) reported that analytic Ss have an advantage in learning certain kinds of concepts. Groups with extreme conceptual styles were defined (N = 30). Six concepts were presented in a standard concept-attainment procedure, with trials to criterion as the dependent measure. Two concepts were analytic (e.g., objects with a missing leg), two relational (e.g., wearing apparel), and two inferential (e.g., objects related to school). *Analytic Ss learned analytic concepts faster than inferential or relational concepts, while Low-analytic Ss learned relational concepts rapidly and analytic concepts slowly.* While this is a significant interaction, the contrast is between *kinds* of content learned rather than modes of instruction. The finding might have implications for school learning; the best way to organize lessons might differ for Ss differing in style.

One further study suggests that teacher style might influence some aspects of student style, but it did not examine ATI (Yando & Kagan, 1968). After identifying ten teachers as reflective (analytic?) and ten as impulsive, the investigators randomly selected 160 first-graders from these teachers' classes. Then, the Matching Familiar Figures Test was administered in early fall and again in spring near the end of the school year. Error and response-time scores represented reflection impulsivity. Metropolitan Reading Readiness Test scores were also available.

Response latencies were much higher in the spring. Children with highly experienced, reflective teachers increased their response time much more than did children with other kinds of teachers. This would imply that reflective teachers make some children more reflective; the effect was strongest for boys. However, the frequency of errors did not change. We distrust results based on change scores in this study, since initial differences bias findings. Multiple-regression analysis with teacher score and initial measures on the pupil, and their product, would have been more informative as predictors.

One small study by Grippin (1973) included both the Witkin and Kagan variables, with an astonishingly complex result. The Ss worked through a short program teaching the Russian equivalents of words, and took an immediate and a delayed posttest. The treatment variable was simple. Half of the Ss were given a series of word pairs and, on the same page, one of the English words with a blank in which to copy the Russian equivalent. The contrasting "strong prompt" condition was identical except that the word to be placed in the blank was underlined in the initial presentation. Hence, S in this condition was relieved of the necessity to search through irrelevant material. Ss were 62 sixth-graders. Grippin analyzed within sexes, and even with samples of 15–16 Ss per treatment she found many results significant at the .05 level. Findings were inconsistent, as is to be expected when eight regression weights are assigned in a small sample. The chief result can be described in terms of the four subgroups formed by median splits on the Rod and Frame measure of FI and the MFF measure of impulsiveness. The delayed test showed little difference between subgroups in the "weak" treatment where S had to do more work. In the strong treatment, Ss in two cells continued to score high: the field-independent, careful Ss and the field-dependent, impulsive Ss. Scores dropped markedly in the other two cells. Neither trait, considered alone, interacted to an appreciable degree. *This ordinal interaction is very difficult to rationalize.*

The studies on FI and the related variables called analytic style and reflectiveness are a rather motley collection at this stage of the work. A few findings suggest that it helps to make the treatment similar in style to that of the learner. This is a reasonable hypothesis, fitting our capitalization or preferential model (see p. 169). But there are enough inconsistencies to make generalization impossible for the present. As research on style moves further into instructional studies, it will be essential that a multitrait multimethod approach be used to pin down the meaning of these aptitude measures.

Strategies in verbal learning

We have spoken loosely of "strategy" or "style" in this chapter. While the two terms are often interchanged, "style" seems to imply a degree of stability midway between "ability" and "strategy." Presumably, students differ in the number and kind of strategies they have at their command, as well as in their choice of strategy on a particular task. Having dealt with studies that adopt formal tests as measures of cognitive style, we review here two attempts at diagnosing strategies on the basis of observations made during learning. These kinds of analyses may

Table 11.6   Correlations relating abilities and strategies to recall under three conditions

		Ability measure				Strategy score	
Condition	Trial	Associative Memory	Associative Fluency	Semantic Spontaneous Flexibility	Semantic Mnemonics	Active Sequential Organization	Modification of Strategy
	1	0.47*	0.15	0.08	0.11	0.05	0.09
	2	0.59*	0.24	0.06	0.13	0.00	− 0.28*
	3	0.67*	0.35*	0.17	0.19	− 0.07	0.23
	4	0.69*	0.39*	0.16	0.04	− 0.03	0.32*
	5	0.60*	0.39*	0.12	0.10	− 0.01	0.29*
	6	0.67*	0.33*	0.13	0.07	− 0.02	0.30*
	7	0.62*	0.34*	0.08	0.12	0.01	0.34*
Free	8	0.60*	0.40*	0.19	0.14	0.06	0.26*
recall	9	0.63*	0.29*	0.15	0.12	0.01	0.25
	10	0.60*	0.24	0.08	0.19	0.00	0.33*
	11	0.61*	0.22	0.12	0.12	− 0.02	0.34*
	12	0.58*	0.30*	0.20	0.18	0.07	0.29*
	13	0.55*	0.18	0.12	0.20	0.13	0.32*
	14	0.60*	0.15	0.16	0.19	0.12	0.37*
	15	0.49*	0.21	0.11	0.23	0.15	0.37*
	16	0.56*	0.22	0.24	0.15	0.18	0.25
	17	0.51*	0.35*	0.24	0.16	0.16	0.27*
	18	0.45*	0.20	0.09	0.22	0.16	0.23
	1	0.42*	0.12	0.00	− 0.02	0.11	0.20
	2	0.37*	− 0.02	0.24	0.04	0.00	0.06
	3	0.58*	0.01	− 0.03	0.20	0.33*	0.01
	4	0.60*	− 0.04	− 0.05	0.14	0.36*	0.08
	5	0.58*	0.03	− 0.15	0.15	0.38*	0.03
	6	0.64*	0.12	− 0.20	0.17	0.39*	0.01

Grouped anticipation						
7	0.64*	0.19	−0.26	0.13	0.41*	−0.01
8	0.60*	0.24	−0.27*	0.13	0.38*	−0.07
9	0.59*	0.28*	−0.26*	0.11	0.32*	−0.09
10	0.52*	0.33*	−0.26*	0.10	0.29*	−0.08
11	0.48*	0.32*	−0.27*	0.05	0.35*	−0.08
12	0.48*	0.33*	−0.28*	0.10	0.30*	−0.11
13	0.39*	0.34*	−0.30*	0.12	0.23	−0.06
14	0.46*	0.32*	−0.24	0.07	0.17	−0.11
15	0.35*	0.35*	−0.30*	0.08	0.14	−0.09
16	0.35*	0.36*	−0.30*	−0.07	0.11	−0.06
17	0.29*	0.30*	−0.33*	0.06	0.09	−0.10
18	0.28*	0.32*	−0.33*	0.14	0.11	−0.02
Serial anticipation						
1	0.19	−0.14	0.13	−0.22	−0.02	0.28*
2	0.44*	0.11	0.12	0.10	−0.23	−0.13
3	0.34*	0.18	0.12	0.19	−0.26*	−0.10
4	0.48*	0.12	0.06	0.29*	−0.20	−0.10
5	0.45*	0.13	0.02	0.36*	−0.15	−0.08
6	0.39*	0.12	−0.07	0.37*	−0.10	−0.04
7	0.47*	0.20	0.01	0.40*	−0.09	0.05
8	0.47*	0.20	0.01	0.33*	−0.03	0.00
9	0.49*	0.14	−0.04	0.37*	−0.04	0.07
10	0.46*	0.15	−0.04	0.32*	0.05	0.04
11	0.41*	0.13	−0.10	0.29*	0.13	0.10
12	0.39*	0.03	−0.19	0.27*	0.18	0.06
13	0.38*	0.03	−0.15	0.23	0.20	0.12
14	0.36*	0.06	−0.15	0.26*	0.24	0.11
15	0.39*	0.05	−0.14	0.24	0.21	0.11
16	0.41*	0.03	−0.15	0.22	0.22	0.09
17	0.38*	0.12	−0.08	0.26*	0.22	0.05
18		0.05	−0.08	0.22	0.18	0.06

$*p < .05.$

After Frederiksen, 1967.

ultimately provide connections among concepts of ability, style, strategy, and learning process.

An intricate and technically advanced study by C. Frederiksen (1969) examined both abilities and strategies. Three groups of college students learned 60 miscellaneous words by an anticipation method (N = 120). One group was to anticipate word by word; one was to anticipate words in groups of five (in their original haphazard order), and one (free-recall) was asked to anticipate the whole list of 60 words. The task had 18 trials. A large number of aptitude scores from the French-kit were reduced to seven composites. A follow-up questionnaire asked about the strategies S used.

Five strategy factors were considered: organization by grouping, semantic mnemonics, active sequential organization, active vs. passive (rote) order-preserving mnemonics, and modification of strategies.

The complex results cannot be presented fully here. The most useful source for our summary is the author's Tables 19–21, 29–31, and 35, which gave correlations of ability and strategy indices with success in word recall, along with correlations among abilities and strategies. Our Table 11.6 shows how selected variables correlated with outcome under each condition. Associative Memory was strongly related to performance in all conditions, but particularly in free recall and grouped anticipation. A decline in these values occurred during later trials. Associative Fluency correlated significantly with score on early trials in free recall, with score on late trials in grouped anticipation, and not at all in serial anticipation. The correlations of Semantic Spontaneous Flexibility tests with score differed across treatments in magnitude and sign. This type of divergent thinking and grouped anticipation seemed antithetical. However, with 40 cases per group, this might be fortuitous. The modification-of-strategy index gave similar negative correlations in free-recall, and essentially zero correlations in other conditions. The strategy of active sequential organization related to performance in grouped anticipation, while semantic-mnemonic strategy related to performance in serial anticipation. Not shown are the strong positive correlations of verbal ability and memory span with outcome in the free-recall condition. These variables did not predict performance in the other two conditions.

Abilities correlated only modestly with reported choice of strategy within treatment, and not in ways one might expect from the patterns in Table 11.6. The strategies S used were shown to be largely a function of the experimental condition to which S was assigned. Knowing about S's strategy did improve within-group prediction of performance slightly.

Frederiksen's work demonstrates the value of seeing learning as a process in which S actively applies a strategy. Since the strategy may or may not fit the task requirements and S's abilities, an obvious extension of treatments is to teach strategies and their use.

We insert here a related, small study by Weener and Tzeng (1971). They applied a 2 x 3 design (N = 66) to investigate strategies in organizing word lists for recall. Word lists were high/low in category saliency, presented under conditions which allowed free categorization of words/assigned these same categorizations to yoked controls/assigned categorizations at random. The aptitude measure was the Remote Associates Test (RAT). A main effect favored free categorization. The pronounced ATI was not statistically significant with this sample size. RAT predicted recall in the condition where the category assignments of words were randomly determined (i.e., relatively meaningless) but not when categories had meaning. RAT is thought to represent ability to connect seemingly remote ideas; this might be used in organizing random words for recall.

Pask and Scott (1972, 1973) developed computerized diagnostic procedures to classify S as a "serialist" or a "holist," according to the details of his behavior in learning and in "teachback" tutoring. The authors' description is unusually rich as an aptitude definition:

> Serialists learn, remember and recapitulate a body of information in terms of string-like cognitive structures where items are related by simple data links: formally, by "low order relations." Since serialists habitually assimilate lengthy sequences of data, they are intolerant of irrelevant information unless, as individuals, they are equipped with an unusually large memory capacity. Holists, on the other hand, learn, remember and recapitulate as a whole: formally, in terms of "high order relations."
>
> There are two subcategories of holist called *irredundant holists* and *redundant holists.* Students of both types image an entire system of facts or principles. Though an irredundant holist's image is rightly interconnected, it contains only relevant and essential constituents. In contrast, redundant holists entertain images that contain *logically* irrelevant or overspecific material, commonly derived from data used to "enrich" the curriculum, and these students embed the salient facts and principles in a network of redundant items. Though *logically* irrelevant, the items in question are of great psychological importance to a "redundant holist", since he uses them to access, retain and manipulate whatever he was originally required to learn [p. 218-219, emphasis is authors'.].

Pask and Scott had Ss learn science material by CAI. First, part of a taxonomy on "Martian fauna" was taught to diagnose 16 Ss as holists/serialists. A second part of the taxonomy and a lesson on metabolism were taught by holist/serialist programs to half of each strategy group. An immediate posttest served as the primary dependent variable on each content. ATI were marked. In each case, Ss whose strategy matched that of the instructional program achieved more than Ss mismatched with the programs. The work deserves to be repeated on a grander scale.

Implications for research strategy

Summary of this chapter is impossible. The research has generated hypotheses but no firm conclusions. Inconsistencies abound, when essentially the same queston about the effect of a small variation in instructional treatments is asked in one experiment after another. It seems increasingly dubious that simple generalizations about ATI effects of inserted questions, for example, will be established.

The inconsistencies that appear so dramatically here are similar to the inconsistencies, less thoroughly documented, that appear throughout Chapter 7 and at several places in Chapters 8 and 9. And this is characteristic of the literature of instructional psychology. In the *Journal of Educational Psychology*, for example, most experimental studies try to establish fairly simple generalizations about main effects of alternative treatments and, increasingly, about interactions. The treatments are chosen on the basis of extremely simple theory, or are simply capsule versions of commonplace instructional practices. Traditional studies of learning employ nonsense syllables and tight treatment controls to arrive at replicable generalizations and theoretical propositions. Theory about process has been emerging from such work. But the instructional research is almost impossible to consolidate into theory. And, if it does not lead to generalizations strong enough to override variations in the material taught, the form of the posttest, etc., it is of little use.

This raises serious questions about the strategy of all instructional research, whether or not it is concerned with ATI. This book must summarize the research that exists, and so is heavily weighted with experiments conceived in the traditional mode and carried out on a small scale. If educational psychology is to break away from the fruitless attempt to establish simple generalizations, the experiments of the future will have to be conceived differently from those that have become the "normal science" of the current generation.

Now may be the time in the history of educational research to encourage empirical case studies which take advantage of opportunities for thorough observation of alternative kinds of instruction in naturalistic settings. Probably these can best be thought of as one-group evaluation studies, in which a complex treatment of substantial duration is documented, and in which relations of aptitudes to outcomes is thoroughly and objectively examined. While one will not generalize from one reading program or one science course to instruction generally, he will get ideas far more significant for instructional psychology than he gets from isolated and artificial instructional experiments that do not penetrate beneath the posttest score. Systematic experiments in the tradition of the laboratory do have a place. As Brunswik argued (see Snow, 1974), these serve molecular, reductionistic ends; *possible* mechanisms involved in adaptation to an instructional environment may be identified thereby. As suggested in our Chapter 6, such experimentation provides a powerful means of task analysis. But generalization about molar behavior in adapting to real environments will require research that is representative of instructional complexity and duration, and that concerns itself with what students do in typical situations.

The controlled studies of the future should derive their treatments or hypotheses from complex theoretical models, which combine ideas from representative evaluations with the possibilities suggested from the laboratory. They will not predict generalizations about the effects of "note-taking" or some other treatment described in terms of its externals. An analysis of the natural task to be set before the learner, and of the alternative acts the learner *could* perform on the material, should—when theory is sufficiently matured—allow a prediction of the effect of an experimental intervention such as a particular means of directing attention. The analysis will be specific to a particular instructional treatment (just as a computer simulation is specific to a particular kind of problem). Confirmation of predictions will first confirm not a generalization about a main effect or an ATI, but the validity of the system of analysis. That same system of analysis might predict a different interaction in a somewhat different instructional setting.

We could recast what has been said above as follows: The premise of ATI research to date is that generalizations about main effects are too simple; one can account for more variance by identifying relevant first-order ATI. The inconsistency among first-order ATI persuades us that higher-order ATI, combining aptitudes with many parameters of the instructional situation, are operative. Complex effects cannot possibly be pinned down by empirical stabs in the dark, or by experiments testing only simple generalizations.

As a final implication to be drawn from this chapter, however, we must add another word of caution. Many investigators seem to assume that learning is one directional—from control group up—and theoretical processes are usually always conceptualized as facilitative. Rothkopf coined the term "mathemagenic" to stand for events during instruction that "give birth to learning." This implies that instructional effects, if any, are presumably for the better. But we found it necessary to posit the existence of "mathemathanic" effects (from the Greek word *thanatos*) that "give death to learning." Many of the studies reviewed gave evidence that some instructional variation was distinctly bad for a fraction of the learners. And some instructional treatments seemed to be beneficial to one subgroup while at the same time having negative effects for another subgroup. This dark side of instructional psychology has long been neglected, probably because main effects are so rarely negative, but it is forced upon us by ATI.

Chapter 12 | Personality x Treatment interactions: General issues and studies of anxiety

The literature on the interaction of personality variables with treatments is voluminous, even when we ignore experiments not concerned with learning. The research is far more heterogeneous in its themes than the work on ability, because of the multiplicity of personality measures and the inadequacy of general, over-arching constructs such as "adjustment" or "motivation for schooling." In the face of these problems, we shall force into a common rubric investigations that are not truly comparable, seeking some degree of synthesis.

While the ATI question is formally the same as when an ability measure is used, hypotheses about personality tend to be more complex; hence, special methodological problems arise. This chapter will discuss methodology for research on Personality x Treatment interactions in general terms. It will then review a fraction of the research on anxiety and related traits, with further evidence to appear in Chapter 13.

Anxiety, lack of confidence, dependency, "neuroticism," compulsiveness, etc., will be considered together. For synoptic purposes we can think of a syndrome of self-deprecation, expecting to fail, seeing the environment as threatening, being prone to anxiety states, and so on. To cope with a threat, the fearful person will adopt one or another defensive strategy: withdrawal, impulsive action, or com-pulsive self-control. At the opposite extreme are secure and confident persons who, when motivated, can work with full efficiency. We shall usually write simply the letter A for "anxiety" or "anxious," and refer to persons as Low-A's and High-A's.[1] The Low-A may not be free from anxiety, just as in earlier chapters

---

[1] Anxiety will be written without a capital when the emphasis is on the abstract idea or construct and capitalized when we are emphasizing an Anxiety score determined by some operation.

the person "Low" in ability was not necessarily subnormal. It is also to be recognized that the operational meaning of A shifts from study to study, since investigators employ different instruments (which may or may not differ importantly in their psychological properties).

Formal problems of design and analysis

State Anxiety and other intermediate variables

In the literature of the last five years, it has been common to differentiate trait Anxiety from state Anxiety, the latter being elicited by questions about S's feelings in the immediate setting at the moment of questioning. The two kinds of variables are only modestly correlated. We shall give no more than incidental attention to state A. While states must be brought into theoretical explanations of the consequences of trait A, state measures can rarely be used practically in education. (In the special setting of CAI, a measure of state A could perhaps be used to regulate treatment. It has been suggested that if questions on state A were asked midway in the student's work at the computer, the difficulty of the next lesson segment could be appropriately adjusted. Leherissey, O'Neil, & D. Hansen, 1971b.)

We regard state A as an intermediate variable rather than as an aptitude, since it is assessed in the treatment setting and is in part a consequence of the treatment. (Cf. our earlier remarks on classroom climate, p. 301.) This is apparent when Ss in a stressful treatment and Ss in a nonstressful treatment are classed as Highs if they reach a certain score on state A, say X^*. Persons in one treatment whose state is described by X^* may differ considerably in personality from those who reach the same level of arousal in the other treatment. More can be learned about events during treatment by returning situation-specific, time-specific state A to the role of intermediate variable, keeping trait A in the position of independent variable.

Many studies of the interaction of A with task difficulty have used errors-during-instruction as dependent variable. We argue against this practice. To treat the error count as outcome is to assume that it is bad for the learner to make errors—yet the group that makes more errors may learn more (e.g., in an experiment contrasting overt/covert response). We take the count of errors during learning to be an intermediate variable. The conditions under which it is observed differ from treatment to treatment, but to assess an educational outcome fairly one must test Ss under identical conditions. While comparisons of treatment means on error count are rarely of value in themselves, a path analysis within treatments would be of interest. It would indicate how errors during instruction depend on the person's traits, how they precede or follow state A, and how the whole complex affects the posttest score.

Curvilinearity of relations

The relation of anxiety to learning was the theme of Spence and his colleagues (K. Spence, 1958; J. Spence & K. Spence, 1966). Their theory led them to expect a curvilinear regression. Success in a particular learning task can have an arch-shaped regression on trait or state Anxiety, with performance relatively poor for High-A's and Low-A's and relatively good at some intermediate level. Where along the A scale the arch reaches its highest point depends on the difficulty of the task and other conditions.

Early hints of this interactive relationship appeared in 1908, in the work of Yerkes and Dodson on the influence of electric shock on habit formation. The usual interpretation is, broadly speaking, that when the organism is already aroused, additional stress or stimulation is likely to impair efficiency. But when arousal is low, a treatment that heightens arousal is likely to be beneficial. For any individual, working on a certain task, there is presumably some optimal level of stimulation. For any treatment there is some optimal level of arousal. State A is one element, but not necessarily the only element, in "arousal." The Spencean argument implies ATI, and a good deal of experimental research on anxiety does show interactive effects. The evidence for curvilinear regressions is almost entirely indirect, however.

One can modify analyses of ATI to test for curvilinearity. A suitable formal hypothesis describes the regression in Treatment A as follows:

$$(12.1) \qquad \hat{Y}_A = \beta_{Y_A X}(X - \overline{\overline{X}}) + \beta_{Y_A Q}(X - \overline{\overline{X}})^2 + \text{constant}$$

Q is a convenient symbol referring to the quadratic term. This quadratic equation, a special case of (4.3), defines a parabola. The maximum (or minimum) occurs

at $X = \overline{\overline{X}} - \beta_{Y_A X} / 2\beta_{Y_A Q}$.

An equation of this type is fitted to data by an ordinary multiple-regression

algorithm, with X (or $X - \overline{X}_A$ or $X - \overline{\overline{X}}$) and $(X - \overline{\overline{X}})^2$ [or $(X - \overline{X}_A)^2$]

as the two predictors. While X^2 could be taken as the second predictor, its high correlation with X complicates interpretation.

To test the hypothesis that $\beta_{Y_A Q}$ is zero—i.e., that the regression

is merely linear in the population—one fits both the linear equation (3.5) and the quadratic equation (12.1) and calculates sums of squares. For the difference SS_{Res} (linear) $- SS_{Res}$ (quadratic), there is one degree of freedom. An F ratio

is formed by dividing the difference by the error mean square, which in this case is SS_{Res}(quadratic) $\div$ d.f.$_{Res}$ (quadratic). If F is significant, the quadratic term

presumably does improve prediction in the population, though it may be retained on theoretical grounds.

Suppose that Treatment B is more stressful than Treatment A. A simple hypothesis is that this shifts the parabola toward the low end of the Anxiety scale (because Low-A's can cope with and are stimulated by the added stress). The elevation and curvature remain as before. Then $\beta_{Y_B Q} = \beta_{Y_A Q}$, and

(12.2) $\hat{Y}_B = \beta_{Y_B X}(X - \overline{\overline{X}}) + \beta_{Y_A Q}(X - \overline{\overline{X}})^2 + \text{constant}.$

The regressions are curvilinear. Even so, because they have the same curvature the ATI still rests on a simple difference in slopes:

(12.3) $\hat{Y}_A - \hat{Y}_B = (\beta_{Y_A X} - \beta_{Y_B X})(X - \overline{\overline{X}}) + \text{constant}.$

The interaction effect is still linear.

To test the significance of ATI with β_Q assumed constant over treatments, then, one determines whether the residual mean square from this prediction equation [= (4.2)]

(12.4)
$$\hat{Y}_t = b_{0t}(T) + b_1(X_1 - \overline{\overline{X}}_1) + b_Q(X_1 - \overline{\overline{X}}_1)^2 + b_{1t}(X_1 - \overline{\overline{X}}_1)(T) + \text{constant}$$

is significantly less than the residual from the equation with no interaction term [= (4.3)]:

(12.5) $\hat{Y}_t = b_{0t}(T) + b_1(X_1 - \overline{\overline{X}}_1) + b_Q(X_1 - \overline{\overline{X}}_1)^2 + \text{constant}.$

Consider a numerical example. As in Chapter 2, we write $Y \mid X$ for the expected value of Y among persons with score X, and choose numbers consistent with the hypothesis stated above with B the more stressful or more demanding treatment.

X	11	12	13	14	15	16	17
$\overline{Y}_A \mid X$	18	32	42	48	50	48	42
$\overline{Y}_B \mid X$	42	48	50	48	42	32	18
$(\overline{Y}_A - \overline{Y}_B) \mid X$	- 24	- 16	- 8	0	8	16	24

There is evidently a disordinal interaction.

What happens if an investigator analyzes such data for ATI and ignores the curvilinearity? According to the mathematics, inclusion of the b_Q term in the regression equation has no systematic effect on the magnitude of b_{1t}, as $(X - \overline{\overline{X}})(T)$ has little or no correlation with $(X - \overline{\overline{X}})^2$ in an experiment with random assignment. Hence, the conventional linear analysis will report the same interaction effect as the curvilinear analysis does. When there is appreciable curvilinearity, however, the quadratic term reduces the residual mean square. Consequently, the linear analysis loses power. If curvilinearity is likely, the person using a representative sample should at least fit a value of b_Q—uniform over treatments. On the other hand, a significant ATI found by means of linear regression is not invalidated simply because the possibility of curvilinearity was overlooked.

Let us weaken the assumption, to let the curvature vary with treatment. To keep matters simple, we alter the example to show zero curvature in Treatment B:

X	11	12	13	14	15	16	17
$\overline{Y}_A \mid X$	18	32	42	48	50	48	42
$\overline{Y}_B \mid X$	52	48	44	40	36	32	28
$(\overline{Y}_A - \overline{Y}_B) \mid X$	-34	-16	-2	8	14	16	14

The interaction effect here is a quadratic function of X. But most of the effect is accounted for by a linear trend, and an analysis by means of linear regressions or comparison of extreme groups should bring it to light. If the sample had ranged only from 14 to 18, however, the corresponding segment of the A regression would have been nearly parallel to the B regression. A linear analysis or an analysis assuming uniform b_Q would falsely report no interaction (unless the sample is large).

To test for differences in curvature it is necessary to add a term $b_{Y_tQ} (X - \overline{\overline{X}}) (T)$ to (12.4). Fitting coefficients to quadratic terms increases the number of pseudosignificant results, just as adding a further predictor variable does. If terms are added stepwise, however, and each addition is theoretically plausible, the risks are small.

Ability as a second predictor

The regression of an instructional outcome onto a personality trait can plausibly be expected to vary with ability. Rarely has ATI research considered this possibility. Once the suggestion is made that a regression function for personality within a superior group may differ in location or shape from the same function in a group of low ability, it becomes "obvious" that that is more probable than improbable. (Considerable evidence of such an effect with anxiety was reviewed by Gaudry and Spielberger, 1971, Chapter 8.)

How does this insight color our reading of the literature on interactions of anxiety? The Spencean idea is that trait anxiety provides a base level of arousal, and that the further arousal induced by stress may carry the High-A's to a level above the optimum. But Spence and his followers did not go on to spell out that the stress a person experiences depends on the difficulty he has with the task, and that this depends on his ability as well as on the characteristics of the task. A complex task is likely to stress persons of low ability more than it does able persons. Hence, at any level of trait A, when the task is taken seriously, the less able are presumably more aroused.

We return to the first numerical example above, now assuming that those results are for a high-ability group. (See top lines of Table 12.1.) Then for a low-ability group the maximum in each treatment will shift to the left, we hypothesize. We therefore shift the regression functions to the left in the next two lines of the table. (We suggest that the reader draw a figure.) The functions also have been given lower maxima, since lower ability produces poorer performance. We assume no Ability x Treatment interaction in Table 12.1, and no second-order interaction (Ability x Anxiety x Treatment). Table 12.1 shows the same linear interaction effect regardless of whether the analysis is made within ability groups or from pooled ability groups. Separating ability levels in the analysis does disclose that the crossover point varies with ability.

Table 12.1　Ability as a moderator of the interaction of anxiety with treatment

	Treat-ment	Trait Anxiety score[a]						
		11	12	13	14	15	16	17
High ability	A	18	32	42	48	50	48	42
	B	42	48	50	48	42	32	18
Low ability	A	45	47	45	39	29	15	-3
	B	45	39	29	15	-3	-25	-51
Ability levels combined	A	31.5	39.5	43.5	43.5	39.5	31.5	19
	B	43.5	43.5	39.5	31.5	19.5	3.5	-16

Differences (A–B) describing interaction								
High ability		-24	-16	-8	0	8	16	24
Low ability		0	8	16	24	32	40	48
Ability levels combined		-12	-4	4	12	20	28	36

[a]Each entry is a mean outcome for the group and treatment indicated. The data are hypothetical.

The reader can develop a further example with a second-order interaction by making the first line of the table identical to the second.

Whenever ability is correlated with outcome, power is lost if the analysis of Anxiety x Treatment interaction does not take ability into account. We would prefer that the investigator add an Ability term, an Ability x Treatment term, and an Ability x Anxiety x Treatment term to the generalized regression equation. This will usually increase power and will bring any second-order interaction to light. Some power can be retrieved by the simpler expedient of using ability as a covariate but ignoring its possible interactions.

Handling two or more personality variables

In research on abilities, we have observed the necessity of considering predictors simultaneously. Separate dimensions are not likely to interact so strongly with treatment as some composite dimension. Sometimes investigators advance hypotheses involving two personality measures simultaneously (e.g., Neuroticism and Introversion, or Test Anxiety and Need for Achievement). The variables can then be combined to express the explicit hypothesis. More often, investigators examine the possible interactions of each of the traits they assess, one at a time. But it is most unlikely that interactions will fall out neatly along the lines of the original scores. The location of traits in the personality domain was determined at some time in the past by the theory or the statistical predilections of some test developer. It would be sheer coincidence if he had located axes so that one of them maximizes interaction with the treatments now under investigation.

When an investigator has collected two scores, his analysis should take them into account simultaneously. A multiple-regression analysis will determine values of b_{0t}, b_1, b_2, b_{1T}, and b_{2T}. The last two *together* describe the linear interaction effect in the sample. It is this joint effect that usually should be tested for significance and whose contribution to R^2 should be examined, when the strength of the ATI is at issue. The same recommendation applies when more than two traits have been measured, but as the number of traits increases one must be increasingly cautious. Regression weights will change from sample to sample, and this generates much uncertainty when many weights are fitted (for examples see p. 405 ff.) With multiple predictors, adding quadratic and product terms generates a confusingly large number of weights. One can form composites to reduce the number of weights to be fitted, as was done in the Stallings-Snow reanalysis (p. 237 ff.) This will be advantageous wherever the investigator has measured personality traits that correlate substantially. (E.g., he will probably do better to rest his conclusion on a composite of General Anxiety and Test Anxiety, if he has measured both, than on an analysis that treats each in turn. A supplementary analysis is required to establish that one is more potent than the other.)

Multitrait-multimethod designs are strongly to be recommended in research that attempts to understand the effects of personality variables (D. Campbell & Fiske, 1959). This important counsel has been neglected in ATI studies. The Campbell-Fiske design of Stallings and Snow protected them from attributing an interaction effect specifically to *visual* sequencing ability. The multitrait feature of their design disclosed interactions of both visual and auditory tests, i.e., a general effect. The multimethod feature showed that an apparent effect for the ITPA visual test was of uncertain meaning, since the Stallings visual test did not confirm it.

Each investigator of personality applies his own preferred instrument and trait label, which makes findings hard to integrate. Until it is shown by a multitrait-multimethod design that an effect arising with Test Anxiety scores (say) is not equally strong with indicators of general anxiety, or yea-saying, psychological interpretation at the level of the specific subtrait is unjustified. One cannot go beyond an indefinite interpretation.

Higher-order interactions

Higher-order interactions surely exist. Abilities can combine conjunctively or disjunctively as well as additively. E.g., no amount of mathematical ability would enable a nonreader to learn mathematics from a printed verbal exposition. Hence, in principle, one might add to the conventional linear equation the terms

$$\beta_{12} (X_1 - \overline{\overline{X}}_1) (X_2 - \overline{\overline{X}}_2) \text{ and } \beta_{12t} (X_1 - \overline{\overline{X}}_1) (X_2 - \overline{\overline{X}}_2)(T)$$

The latter term describes a second-order interaction. Such interactions, and even higher ones, must be present at least weakly, since it is inconceivable that test developers have hit upon the particular scales of measurement that make all relations strictly additive. But with ability measures there is little likelihood that nonadditive effects will be established, since error variance swamps such departures from planar regression as occur in practice.

One might take a similarly defeatist attitude in considering personality variables, especially as the attempt to use personality measures as moderator variables in academic prediction has sputtered along with no finding of practical value. We are ambivalent about attempts to fit interaction terms for multiplicative combinations of personality variables with each other or with abilities. There are many possibilities, and much too much chance of perceiving "patterns" in what is really error variance. But, for heuristic purposes, it is well to make crosstabulations or plots that would disclose higher-order relations in the sample. This recommendation is encouraged by the reports of higher-order relations that appear here and there (not crossvalidated). Amaria and Leith (1969), for example, reported that an adolescent's work with a like-sex partner depends on S's ability, extroversion, and sex, and on the partner's ability; this complex interaction is entirely believable.

Demonstration: Quantitative description of a
higher-order interaction

Data made available by Tobias allow us to illustrate some technical points. Tobias (1973) had 59 college Ss work through a simple instructional program on heart disease, and another 58 Ss work through the frames in scrambled order. Here we ignore that part of the study in which more technical content was taught. We shall not draw substantive conclusions, as the dependent variable was errors-made-on-the-program rather than the posttest. Our techniques of analysis will depart from those of Tobias, but his published statistical results are sound. In this and other ATI studies, he has made unusually sophisticated use of regression analysis; but we emphasize description of effects more than he does, and significance less.

Tobias published his chief results in a table showing for each dependent variable the step-by-step increments in R^2 along with corresponding F ratios. Quadratic terms were not included as predictors. (At our instigation Tobias made a further analysis which showed that terms in A^2 would add nothing.) The predictor variables were a measure of trait A (At), state A assessed during work on the program (As), an ability measure (X), and certain of their products. Treatment (T) was coded +1 for the orderly program and -1 for the scrambled program. For a regression analysis with errors-on-program as dependent variable, the report gave these statistics (plus mean and s.d. in each treatment):

T	X	As	At	XxT	AsxT	AtxT	XxAsxT	XxAtxT
18	2		1				4	9
29.7**	2.9	< 1	< 1	1.1	< 1	< 1	6.0*	14.9**

$< .05$ $**p < .001$

Tobias made F tests by a step-down procedure. The residual MS from the nine-variable equation was the denominator of the F ratio (107 d.f.). The numerator for the test on T (for example) was the difference in mean square between the prediction from T, X, At, and As together, and the prediction for the last three alone. Along with the results above, we wish to consider the shape of the regression surfaces.

Tobias carried out his analysis on raw scores. His correlation matrix was therefore ill-conditioned, many r's being above 0.90. (T correlated 0.97 with XxT.) When we applied the BMD regression program, it stopped after eight variables, signaling that the tolerance (partial variance) of the predictor $XxAsxT$, coming late in the set, was too low to satisfy the conventional criterion. When a matrix is ill-conditioned, weights can be erratically affected by rounding and sampling errors. Moreover, with correlated predictors, regression weights are hard to interpret. For our analysis we substituted $X - \overline{\overline{X}}$, $As - \overline{\overline{As}}$, and $At - \overline{\overline{At}}$ into the predictor set. The deviation scores were essentially independent; for example, the correlation of T with $(X - \overline{\overline{X}}) \times T$ was -0.02. The two sets of weights were as follows:

	T	X	As	At	XxT	AsxT	AtxT	XxAsxT	XxA
Deviation score b	2.49	0.0026	−0.037	0.0097	−0.0031	−0.13	0.024	0.0048	−0.0
Raw score b	−23.66	0.0026	−0.035	0.0096	0.0515	−2.59	1.285	0.0048	−0.0

The value of R^2 was the same (0.34), whether the calculation was made from raw or deviation scores. The raw-score equation can be converted to an equation in deviation form by substituting $(X - \overline{\overline{X}}) + 512.2$ for X, and similar terms for At and As. A few of the weights so derived departed appreciably from those calculated directly, but for X, As, and At within the range of ± 3 s.d. from the mean the two equations give estimates of the criterion that differ only trivially. The equation for deviation scores is more interpretable, as no mental allowance needs to be made for intercorrelations.

We prefer to consider $X \times As$ and $X \times At$ as additional predictors. In Tobias' model, the term $X \times At \times T$ combined the $X \times At$ effect with the second-order interaction. This was legitimate, but when this combined effect was significant he could not be sure that the second-order interaction by itself was significant. As a matter of fact, the two second-order interactions were significant by themselves, but the $X \times At$ effect also was nearly significant ($p < .10$).

Before interpreting a generalized equation with a dozen terms, we shall demonstrate procedure with a simple case: the equation calculated within the group given the orderly treatment ($T = +1$), considering X, At, and $X \times At$ as predictors:

(12.6)

$$\hat{Y}_{+1} = 0.00538 (X - \overline{\overline{X}}) + 0.04975 (At - \overline{\overline{At}}) - 0.00308 (X - \overline{\overline{X}})(At - \overline{\overline{At}}) + 96.093.$$

Only the product predicted significantly. An equation in this form is difficult to "read," since X and At are scaled differently. It is profitable to do a sort of standardization of the predictor variables. We calculated the s.d. of each predictor, for all cases pooled and increased the regression coefficient by that factor. We have, then, an equation expressed in terms of quasistandardized predictors. Use of the pooled s.d. maintained comparability between equations for the two treatments. Transformed, the equation became:

(12.7)

$$\hat{Y}_{+1} = 0.456 \frac{(X - \overline{\overline{X}})}{84.7} + 0.431 \frac{(At - \overline{\overline{At}})}{8.67} - 2.26 \frac{(X - \overline{\overline{X}})(At - \overline{\overline{At}})}{734.3} + 96.093.$$

The dependent variable remains in its raw-score metric. Now we can quickly gain an intuitive sense of the shape of the surface for the ordered treatment by making a few substitutions.

If $X = +1$ s.d. and $At = +1$ s.d., $\hat{Y} - 96.1 = 0.46 + 0.43 - 2.26 = -1.37$.

If $\quad = +1 \qquad\qquad = -1 \quad$, $\hat{Y} - 96.1 = 0.46 - 0.43 + 2.26 = +2.29$.

If $\quad = -1 \qquad\qquad = +1 \quad$, $\hat{Y} - 96.1 = -0.46 + 0.43 + 2.26 = +2.23$.

If $\quad = -1 \qquad\qquad = -1 \quad$, $\hat{Y} - 96.1 = -0.46 - 0.43 - 2.26 = -3.15$.

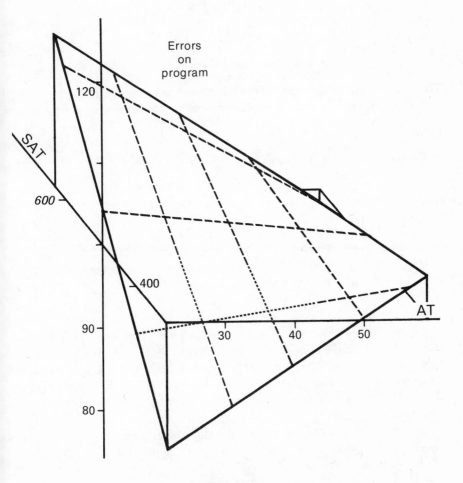

Figure 12.1.

Regression surface relating performance on an orderly program to ability and anxiety.

This is a classic "butterfly" surface. In the ordered treatment, the able Low-A's did better than the able High-A's. The dull High-A's also did better than the able

High-A's (!). (s_y was about 5, so these slopes are not negligible.) Since the dependent variable is a count of correct answers, the means imply that there was a strong ceiling effect; in two quadrants, the means given above exceeded 98 per cent. It does not appear that the interaction could be an artifact resulting from the ceiling, but nonnormality perhaps made the F test undependable.

Calculus can aid in the interpretation. In the orderly treatment,

$$(12.8) \quad \frac{\partial Y}{\partial (X/84.7)} = 0.456 - 2.26\,(At - \overline{\overline{At}})/8.67 = 0.456 - 0.260\,(At - \overline{\overline{At}})$$

This is the regression slope for outcome on X at any level of At. Likewise,

$$(12.9) \quad \frac{\partial Y}{\partial (At/734.3)} = 0.431 - 0.0267\,(X - \overline{\overline{X}}).$$

Setting both equations equal to zero, we get the values $X - \overline{\overline{X}} = 16.1$, $At - \overline{\overline{At}} = 1.$
These locate the "saddle point" above the X mean and close to the At mean.

Now consider the partially standardized equation for the scrambled treatment.

(12.10)

$$\hat{Y}_{-1} = 0.971\,\frac{(X - \overline{\overline{X}})}{84.7} + 0.199\,\frac{(At - \overline{\overline{At}})}{8.67} + 0.426\,\frac{(X - \overline{\overline{X}})(At - \overline{\overline{At}})}{734.3} + 91.68$$

Here no coefficient was statistically significant. The surface for this treatment is comparatively flat; e.g.:

If	X = +1 s.d. and	At = +1 s.d.,	$\hat{Y}$ - 91.7	=	+1.60
If	= +1	= -1	,	=	+0.35
If	= -1	= +1	,	=	-1.20
If	= -1	= -1	,	=	-0.74

The differences between corresponding points on the two surfaces indicate the character of the interactions. Subtracting 1.60 from −1.37, etc., the four differences are −2.97, 1.94, 3.43, and −2.41, respectively. That is, the anxious-and-most-able, and the nonanxious-and-least-able, did better in the scrambled treatment than in the orderly treatment. The other two groups benefited from the ordered sequence.

Finally, let us examine the equation for all variables in the generalized regression model. X, As, and At are in deviation form in the equation below, but for simplicity we do not write the full notation. Asterisks indicate terms that added significantly to prediction in the stepwise analysis.

$$(12.11) \quad \hat{Y} = 2.41\,(T)^* + 0.00185(X)^* + 0.0257(At) - 0.0409(As)$$
$$-0.00108(X)(At)^* - 0.00154(X)(As) - 0.00117(X)(T)$$
$$+0.0218(At)(T) - 0.116\,(As)(T) - 0.00205(X)(As)(T)^*$$
$$+\,0.00492(X)(At)(T)^* + 93.994.$$

In partially standardized form—again with simplified notation—this became:

$$(12.12) \quad \hat{Y} = 2.41\, T + 0.157\, (X) + 0.223\, (At) - 0.132(As) - 0.793(X)\, (At)$$
$$-0.421(X)(As) - 0.099(X)\, (T) + 0.189(At)\, (T) - 0.374(As)\, (T)$$
$$-1.505(X)\, (At)\, (T) + 1.346(X)\, (As)\, (T) + 93.994.$$

We leave it to the reader to explore the within-treatment regressions by substitution or by calculus. He must take care to read these as partially standardized variables. The multiple for standardizing As was 3.23.

The last step in interpretation, now, is to examine the character of the complex interaction. When we subtract the equation for $T = -1$ from the equation for $T = +1$, only the terms that originally contained T remain. Each is doubled in size:

$$\hat{Y}_{+1} - \hat{Y}_{-1} = -0.198(X) - 0.378(At) - 0.748(As) - 3.010(X)\,(At) - 2.692(X)\,(As).$$

Substituting the eight combinations of values of +1 and -1, we find that this difference is large at four points and rather near zero for the other four combinations. We need give detail for only the points where differences are large:

If X = +1 s.d., At = +1 s.d., and As = +1 s.d., the difference is -7.03.
If   = -1   = +1   = +1   ,   +4.77.
If   = +1   = -1   = -1   ,   +6.63.
If   = -1   = -1   = -1   ,   -4.38.

Trait Anxiety and State Anxiety had similar interactions, according to this equation. Able High-A's and dull Low-A's did their best on the scrambled program.

The presence of a strong contribution of $(X)\,(At)\,(T)$ in this analysis implies that the relation of Trait A to the error score was not wholly mediated through the observed State-A score. Possibly this is to be explained by whatever discrepancy there was between the person's true state and his report of his state. Possibly the person with high trait anxiety coped through some tactic (e.g., close attention) that affected his score but that actually held down state anxiety. Still other explanations are possible.

Multitrait exploratory studies

A different methodological issue arises when a great number of scores are treated as predictors in the same study. Some research employs a long and motley list of personality traits, in the hope of detecting interactions not predictable from available theory. Though exploration can be valuable, the blind empiricist runs into difficulty. When one uses dozens of variables, the final statistical results are such a frothy mixture of the real and the ephemeral that it takes an act of faith to pick out any one "significant" interaction as worthy of further research. We therefore cannot encourage an investigator to administer a multiscore instrument such as the California Personality Inventory (CPI) or the Omnibus Personality

Inventory (OPI) and then to score every available scale to "see what enters into interactions." The alternative is nicely pointed up by the Domino studies (p. 442). He picked just two scores from the CPI on the basis of a prototheory and used them as predictors, disregarding all the other scores. His study, with its replication, turns out to be one of the most convincing pieces of work we shall examine.

In research on ability, it is reasonable to boil down data from multiple aptitude tests by examining the interactions of a few principal components. As personality traits are not strongly correlated, the first few components represent relatively little of the useful information. But testing numerous dimensions in turn produces a puzzling set of ATI findings unless there is a very large sample, or a crossvalidatio is carried out, or other precautions are taken to avoid interpreting chance effects. Let us illustrate.

Majer (1970) assessed 22 freshmen who were to take ten weeks of CAI in physics, and 22 others who would take the same course by conventional lecture. At the start, Majer gave Peterson's CSQ questionnaire (13 scores), the Omnibus Personality Inventory (OPI, 14 scores), and two ability tests. He also collected information on background. The CAI treatment seems to have been beneficial. With regard to ATI, Majer reported that the shrunken squared multiple correlation of the nine potent predictors with the final examination was 0.53 in the experimental group and 0.76 in the control group. His report tabulated zero-order r's and identified the nine predictors receiving weight in each group. The two strong predictors in the control group were OPI Masculinity ($r = 0.62$) and a pretest on achievement ($r = 0.45$). Masculinity received the heaviest weight in the experimental group also—but the weight was negative (r with the criterion being -0.44). The achievement measure had an r of 0.22 in this group, but entered only as the ninth predictor. Only four variables appeared in both equations.

This study provided no usable knowledge about ATI. Starting with 30 or more predictors and only 22 Ss per treatment guarantees that chance will determine which variables predict the criterion within a treatment. A "shrinkage" formula can give a more credible estimate of the population value for R, but it cannot correct the weights nor identify the variables relevant in the population.

Our first recommendation for this kind of study is to use more cases. Even 100 Ss-per-treatment—our rule of thumb for simple ATI studies—is much too limited when a dozen predictors are to be considered. (See p. 55 ff.)

Second, the same predictor dimensions must enter the equation fitted to each treatment group. These may be original scores or composites. Stepwise methods may be used to select the active set of predictors (at whatever risk of capitalizing on chance). But the regression equations to evaluate ATI must calculate weights for the same predictor set in every treatment group.

It is important to apply the regression equation from one treatment in the opposite treatment. The cross-correlation of the A equation in the B group must be less than the shrunken A-in-A correlation to justify a report of ATI.

Likewise for B-in-A vs. B-in-B. Otherwise, there is *prima facie* evidence of no interaction even when the regression weights in the equations "look different."

Shaver and Oliver (1968; also Oliver & Shaver, 1966) contrasted Socratic-discussion/recitation regarding public-policy issues, in junior-high-school social studies. Students in the discussion mode were encouraged to take personal positions on issues and to defend these against the teacher's critique. In the recitation mode, the same issues were analyzed and possible decisions were discussed, but the student was not pressed to "take a position." The former approach was more "personal" to the learner, and presumably more stressful. There seems to have been *no interaction with mental ability* (1966, p. 303).

The main study on personality was reported in 1966 (their pp. 312ff.) and in 1968 (their pp. 245–326). Scores on 35 personality traits (Cattell, Guilford-Zimmerman, and other instruments) were available for about 90 students who were taught for two years. There were 12 outcome measures. No multiple regressions were examined. Several scores including Anxiety were discarded when they did not interact. The variables that did show some hint of relationship in the preliminary analysis were carried through 91 analyses of covariance (13 traits, 7 outcomes). A pretest and a general-ability score were partialed out of each outcome. Twelve ATI, out of the 91 formally tested, seemed to be significant. Shaver and Oliver took this finding seriously because they believed 5 (out of 91) to be chance expectancy. But 420 candidate ATI were tested directly or indirectly, making the chance expectation closer to 20, even assuming independence; *the 12 apparent ATI have to be dismissed as chance results.* The sample size was inadequate from the outset. A bad decision was made to block on each trait to form a 3 x 2 design, and to obtain equal cell frequencies by discarding cases. In many significance tests, half the cases were discarded. Hence, the negative evidence on ATI is not definitive.

Harvey (1970) taught science to college students by a "gaming" procedure that required role-playing (see p. 324). Having established that the regression slope of achievement onto a science pretest was near zero in the experimental group, and steep in a group taught conventionally, Harvey went on to correlate 15 variables with the outcome. Skimming off the best six out of the 15 predictors, he carried out stepwise multiple-regression analyses. Perhaps students with a High score on Practical Outlook from the OPI did better in the conventional course and those high in Complexity had a comparative advantage in the novel procedure. But one cannot have confidence in the finding. Due to a decision to subdivide the group on ability, Harvey had only about 20 Ss for each analysis. Consequently, the correlations and *regression weights cannot be taken seriously.* Even worse, different variables entered the equations for different subsamples, making a comparison of regression slopes impossible.

Tallmadge, Shearer, and Greenberg (1968; see also Tallmadge & Shearer, 1969) compared "inductive" and "deductive" instruction. Two one-day training courses (Transportation Technique and Aircraft Recognition) were offered to Navy enlisted men. These were the basis for two experiments, each with N about 115. One method of instruction used an example-then-rule (egrule) form. The instructor gave examples, questions, and partial information about rules for problem-solving. The other method (ruleg) provided straight exposition of rules and their application to problems. The men took the Gordon Personal Profile and the Kuder Preference Record, along with ability tests from the ETS Kit (see p. 371). The authors reported no s.d.'s, so interpretation must rest on correlations (which may falsify the ATI picture.)

In the Transportation course, the correlation of outcome with Arithmetic was much higher in the inductive treatment. *This was presumably a significant ATI.* Interactions of other abilities were negligible in both courses (as we reported on p. 371).

Correlations of Kuder and Gordon scores differed with the treatment. The following differences in *r* exceeded 0.30:

Transportation course (which had mathematical content)
   r was higher in the egrule treatment for Kuder Computational and Scientific scores.
   r was higher in the ruleg treatment for Kuder Musical and for Gordon Ascendancy.

Aircraft course
   r was higher in the egrule treatment for Kuder Social Service, Gordon Ascendancy, and Gordon Sociability.
   r was higher in the ruleg treatment for Kuder Computational, Scientific, and Clerical.

Many of these differences, considered singly, were statistically significant. The reversal of relationships from course to course is interesting, but it could be simply a reflection of sampling error.

The Transportation course, demonstrating alogrithms for solving complex equations, probably had little intrinsic interest for the average man. The Aircraft course called for recognition of pictured planes. For mysterious reasons, the inductive treatment gave superior results in the first course and the deductive treatment in the second. Beswick and Tallmadge (1971) have since "scaled" these and other treatments in terms of the extent to which they appear to arouse curiosity. Their analysis suggests that the treatments cannot be simply described as inductive/deductive. (See p. 166 for further discussion.)

The study could not be expected to yield definitive conclusion with so modest a sample and a dozen personality dimensions. The personality effects and ability effects should have been analyzed together. Even so, it appears that *personality variables interacted in each of two courses, with dissimilar results.* A one-course study could have led to a generalization that persons of a certain type should be taught inductively. This would have been contrary to the finding in the second course. (Cf. p. 22.)

Our fourth example is the mammoth investigation of L. Goldberg (1972). Because previous ATI research had examined the personality domain piecemeal, Goldberg opted for a broad-band exploration of existing personality scales. He felt that this might narrow the list of traits in further research and that it could provide leads for constructing new scales expressly for work on interactions. The study ranged over a lengthy array of measures. Each instrument was scored on all its available scales to produce 428 scores. SAT Verbal and Quantitative scores, year in college, and grade-point averages were also taken into account.

*S*s were 806 undergraduates in two psychology courses. Within each course, *S*s were randomly assigned to one of four treatments: traditional lecture/self-study instruction, crossed with periodic multiple-choice quizzes/writing of integrative papers. These treatments were applied during two class periods each week. All *S*s met in small discussion sections during a third hour. Treatments were maintained for an academic quarter.

A battery of dependent variables yielded orthogonal factor scores for achievement, satisfaction, and amount of supplementary reading done. (The latter did not count in the course grade.) Two scores from end-of-term multiple-choice and essay examinations brought the number of criterion measures to five. For testing the significance of differences between correlations, the two course were combined into a single analysis.* Correlations of each trait, paired with each dependent measure,—about 1700 *r*'s in all—were compared for lecture-plus-quiz (the most structured treatment)/self-study-plus-paper-writing (least structured). Goldberg also compared lecture/self-study (pooling quizzed and paper-writing sections within each), and quizzed sections/paper-writing sections (pooling lecture and self-study conditions). Apparently, more than 19,000 comparisons were made. If these were independent one could expect more than 900 to reach significance ($p < .05$) by chance. Actually, only around 300 reached this level; hence, interpretation is unwarranted. *It is most unlikely that there was appreciable interaction for any of these variables with Goldberg's treatment contrast.*

Only GPA and SAT correlated substantially with outcome. The relations were stronger in the less-structured treatment than in the structured condition (an interaction whose significance is hard to judge).

As a last-chance gambit, Goldberg selected items that seemed to contribute to interaction in one course, then crossvalidated the resulting scales in the second course. In 80 attempts, the size of the correlations supporting the hypotheses did not rise above chance expectation. But as we understand matters, the dynamics of the two courses were not similar.

Conceptual problems

Conceptualization and measurement of anxiety

Even those investigators who concern themselves solely with "anxiety" use diverse measures. These scales are not interchangeable, although they tend to be correlated. Conversely, scales that allegedly measure somewhat different variables (e.g., test anxiety/general anxiety) are correlated, so that one cannot take the distinction seriously in the absence of the proper multitrait-multimethod analysis.

---

*A conversation with Goldberg leads us to wonder whether pooling eliminated important information. The two series of instructional events evidently were far from similar.

Nor is it certain that the instruments labeled as measures of anxiety are psychologically distinct from other aspects of personality. It has been suggested that high scores on the Taylor Manifest Anxiety Scale reflect a yea-saying tendency. Self-concept, dependency, and other self-reported traits may likewise overlap substantially with Anxiety scales. Overlap is especially troublesome when we try to integrate American and British results. The Taylor scale and its successors in the United States correlate only moderately with the Neuroticism scales of Eysenck (Maudsley Personality Inventory and its successors). Eysenck deliberately made his N scale orthogonal to his Introversion scale, whereas Americans tend to leave the analogous dimensions correlated. American Anxiety is a composite of British Neuroticism and Introversion.

In our description of results we shall identify scores coming from the Taylor Manifest Anxiety Scale (or Spielberger State Anxiety or a closely related variable) as Anxiety or A scores. The Sarason scale measures Test Anxiety, TA. The Eysenck, Maudsley, and Hallworth scales will be referred to as measuring Neuroticism (N) even though the British writers often refer to "anxiety." Some investigators measure the Debilitating Anxiety and Facilitating Anxiety of Alpert and Haber—which we abbreviate DA and FA. Our interpretation cannot make use of the distinctions among these traits; almost never does a study carry alternative anxiety measures through the same analysis, allowing their effects to be compared (see Spence & Spence, 1966, pp. 311–312).

To aggregate results we shall employ the concept of "defensive motivation." We conceive of the anxious person as alert to threats. He may have a ready coping style that handles a particular threat effectively (e.g., conformity, dependency) or he may become emotionally disorganized. By backing off to this prescientific concept we renounce any attempt at this time to use such refined theory as Spence's treatment of anxiety as drive. There is insufficient evidence to justify such a particular interpretation of the ATIs we shall encounter. As a contrast to defensive motivation, we shall speak of "constructive motivation." This encompasses Need for Achievement (n Ach, interpreted by J. W. Atkinson as "motive to seek success"), the Gough index of Achievement-through-Independence, and some other measure.

The place of traits in an interactional psychology

Psychologists have various ends in view when they study personality. There is a practical concern for the patient seeking psychological help; the better the psychologist's concepts and instruments, the better he can intervene. There is, at the other extreme, a desire to establish psychological laws that describe and forecast responses to a defined class of situations. Allport long ago made us mindful of the contrast between the idiographic approach of the biographer and the nomothetic approach of the general psychologist. There is no need to argue the relative merits of the two extremes. The biographer or psychologist concentrating on a single individual will try to understand that person's world through his eyes. Yet the psychologist's questions and interpretations will inevitably employ concepts derived from other individuals; hence, he does not construct a purely idiographic interpretation. Conversely, the person who states laws has to accept limits on the universality of his laws. He must introduce parameters to represent features of the person and of the situation. He can at best expect his laws to work on the average, not for each person and each situation.

The problem is to find a promising middle ground. Research has to build up understandings that can apply to persons and situations encountered in the future. There is, as it were, a Persons x Situations matrix. The task of personality research is to group rows and columns to define relatively homogeneous blocks. Then, knowing that a person belongs in Class i and is confronted with a situation of Class j, one can hope to predict such-and-such a response as likely. When one must know *both* i and j to predict the response, the generalization describes an interaction. The older trait psychology was criticized for seeking to account for behavior by person main-effects only—expecting, for example, that a "dominant" person will seek to exert his will in every group. A situational psychology similarly places too large a bet on situation main-effects.

The research worker faces the bandwidth-fidelity dilemma. If he describes persons in terms of finely subdivided traits, he is unable to collect a substantial body of data to verify each sentence of his theory. If he restricts himself to a manageable number of categories and collects solid evidence on the sentences in his coarse-grained theory, he cannot hope to account for the fine texture of behavior. There is some limit to the resolving power of objective psychological research, and no hope of substantiating highly detailed theories of personality by direct observation. One can, of course, make fine-grained studies of a particular individual who is under treatment, but nomothetic propositions do not flow from case studies cast in terms of dissimilar constructs.

Unless we are to abandon entirely the search for theory of personality, it is necessary to construct propositions that are valid on the average over some class of persons and some class of situations, however much variance such a proposition leaves unexplained.

We argued in Chapter 6 that learning is an activity. The learner brings abilities, information-processing habits or styles, and mental sets to the scene. These prove to be well or badly aligned with the task he is set by the instructor. Personality variables enter into this process—indeed, only arbitrarily can one assign such a characteristic as "flexibility" to the ability or personality domain. The predispositions of the learner determine what threats and potential rewards he perceives, and so determine how energetically he addresses the task, what interfering thoughts enter his mind, how alert he is to monitor his own performance, how ready to try a risky response—in general, how he works at learning. There are clear parallels between Mischel's discussion of "social learning person variables" (1973) and the analysis of learning activities in our Chapter 6.

The trait/state distinction properly emphasizes that the events during learning determine success. The trait is significant only to the extent that it forecasts some state. Predicting the person's state is difficult. The working hypothesis of many investigators (notably of Mischel) is that the state of the person depends on his perception of the situation, and that the meaning of the situation varies with the person.

Evidence supporting this mediational view is to be found in many places (e.g., Weiner, 1966). We shall later (p. 446) review the finding of Dowaliby and Schumer. They found that an experimental manipulation of teacher directiveness interacted with trait Anxiety, but they also found the same interaction pattern when there was no variation of treatment. Whether or not students *said* that their teacher was directive seemed to interact with trait A in the same way that the experimental manipulation had interacted.

To come to understand interactions it will be necessary ultimately to study events as they unfold in time. There is, first, the set of entering characteristics of the learner (ability, and trait-A, and stereotypes of teachers, for example). There is, second, the objectively observable treatment. This refers not to the "treatment variable" in the experimenter's mind, but to the signals actually delivered to Ss. (Very likely it takes an observer blind to the hypothesis to report what the treatment actually is.) Third, there is the learner's perception (of the teacher, of his likelihood of succeeding, of the rewards and penalties in prospect, etc.) , and his concomitant emotional states. Fourth come the acts of the learner as he engages with his task, some of them directly observable and some internal events that can at best be inferred. The final set of events is represented in the "dependent variables" of the experiment. Research to date has not tried to depict this panorama of events. Where some of the pertinent immediate responses to the treatment have been recorded (e.g., measures of State-A, reports on the Learning Environment Inventory), they have not been set into their proper position as intermediate variables. Moreover, interpreters have tended to regard student reports as veridical accounts of treatment conditions, rather than as consequences of Person x Situation interactions. All in all, despite the fascinating research to be recounted in this chapter and the next, we have not yet truly begun to investigate the relations of personality to instruction.

Design of treatments and interpretation of treatment variables

High trait-A presumably triggers a response to events during instruction. After a threat, the High-A is likely to be aroused to high state-A. This prediction, however, is not a secure one. If the learner does not perceive the situation as stressful, his response provides no test of the theoretical proposition. If stress is considered to be a pertinent variable, it is advisable to assess S's state in the treatment situation Mysterious, contradictory results in stress studies would be fewer if the states created could be sorted out.

Predictions are often made as if effects were constant over time. But state A decreases as instruction is continued, even under ostensibly stressful conditions. That is, the High-A's are likely to react at early stages of a difficult task with high state-A, and with moderate state-A after a period of adaptation. Errors are frequently made by those high in State-A, early in instruction. After adaptation, their error rate drops to that of others (see, for example, Spielberger, O'Neil, & D. Hansen, 1972). Moreover, work from the laboratory argues that effects of anxiety depend on the person's stage of learning (Spence & Spence, 1966; Spielberger & L. H. Smith, 1966).

This adds to our conviction (pp. 44 ff.) that ATI studies should be of considerable duration if the conclusions are to be applicable to schooling. Most experiments on anxiety, however, have been limited to short treatments. (For these studies, see reviews by Wine, 1971, and I. Sarason, 1972. A review by Phillips, 1972, discusses suggestions for school practice.) Our discontent is especially great regarding the experiments on treatments that dispense praise or blame. These, even though carried out in classrooms, are highly artificial, since Ss are exposed to the experimental treatment only a few days at most. Whatever power praise/blame may have when it is novel, will it remain the same when students become habituated to the teacher's patter? Such a change did appear in the exceptional 11-week study of Leith and Davis (p. 438).

Most studies of anxiety in its relation to treatments have been miniature experiments, carried out on the plan of single-variable laboratory research. Only rarely has a long-continued experiment contrasted one realistic instructional condition with another. Many studies seek to induce a short-term motivational state (e.g., by ego-involving instructions). Other studies manipulate the difficulty of the task, or its "structure."

Even in laboratory research, the operationalization and testing of constructs about situational influences is unsatisfactory. Far too rarely do alternative manipulations represent contrasting explanatory hypotheses. For example: The effects of "difficulty" may be cognitive, in the sense that what S cannot understand "lacks structure," or they may be affective, since the risk of failure is perceived to be higher. No one has designed treatments to represent these two alternative hypotheses and so to pin down just what the operative variable is. To apply the "multivariable-multimethod" concept to treatments will be difficult, but it will be indispensable in reaching interpretations.

The Spences themselves (1966) protested against simple characterization of treatment variables and against attempts to account for complex learning by the drive hypothesis developed in the conditioning laboratory. Their comments on the proposition that anxiety interacts with "difficulty" or "complexity" are especially worthy of note here. After seeking to reconcile the positive and negative findings of research in laboratory learning, they concluded (p. 322):

> As has been illustrated by the present chapter, psychological phenomena tend to be extremely complex, performance even in relatively simple situations being determined by a host of interacting stimulus and individual difference variables. Thus, attempts to develop hypotheses about the behavor of anxiety groups even within a limited type of experimental setting is a major undertaking . . . . The search for more satisfactory experimental arrangements in which to test hypotheses about personality variables has always been a major part of personality research and probably will continue to be so for some time. To repeat. . ., the development of even limited theories is a difficult undertaking in which progress is likely to be slow.

We concur.

Trying to interpret studies even more diverse than those the Spences examined, we cannot hope to reach genuinely theoretical propositions. We shall catalog studies according to the variable in the investigator's mind (inductive/deductive, or structured/unstructured, etc.). When we come to aggregate the findings, we shall again employ a prescientific construct. Effects seem often to be related to the demands the treatment makes. Some instruction allows S to be passively receptive; other instruction requires him to attend actively, to process and reorganize information, to initiate his own responses instead of imitating a model, etc. We shall, therefore, contrast demanding/undemanding instruction. Another set of studies have to do with a threatening/supportive dimension. We by no means contend that the treatment variables we consider together are interchangeable.

Interactions of Anxiety with task characteristics

The student who is characteristically fearful or dependent may find himself uncomfortable in an ambiguous situation, where he is not given clear directions and is left on his own resources. It is often suggested that such a student will respond more effectively when the steps he is to take at each moment in learning are laid out clearly, so that less responsibility rests upon him. It has been thought for example, that a look-and-say method of teaching reading is comparatively demanding, and likely to stimulate High-A's while leaving Low-A's uncomfortable, defensive, and hence ineffective. The mixed findings from the few studies on this theme will be examined first. The ensuing section takes up PI. It has been thought that the orderly program, along with the reassurance offered by feedback or the "covert" mode of responding, may work to the advantage of the High-A. The third section returns to the contrast between inductive/deductive instruction. Several studies started with the thought that didactic presentations place less burden on the learner and so serve the Low-A. One-of-a-kind studies fill the miscellaneous section. Finally, a table assembles the results to that point. A look ahead to the table (p. 422) will help the reader when he loses his bearings among the contradictory findings. We omit virtually all studies of PA learning and studies where errors during practice were taken as the dependent variable.

Structured vs. unstructured instruction in reading

Grimes and Allinsmith (1961) reported that a more structured approach to initial reading serves compulsive and anxious children better than a whole-word procedure. We are able to augment that report with information from Grimes' dissertation (1958) and with unpublished information supplied by Grimes. The school systems of Phonicsville and Sightville differed in their approach to reading during Grades 1 and 2, Phonicsville having a more structured program and more authoritarian teachers. In Grade 3, where the data were collected, both systems were giving considerable weight to phonics. The analysis was confined to children who had been in the system for all three years (72 cases in Phonicsville and 156 in Sightville). The index of pupil accomplishment was a reading test in Grade 3, residualized by partialing out IQ (assessed in Grade 2 or 3). Phonicsville children did better than those in Sightville, on the average.

In Grade 3, the children's version of the Taylor Anxiety Scale was given. Interviews of parents regarding the child's behavior at home gave data for a Compulsivity rating. Anxiety had no relation to the adjusted reading score in Phonicsville (r = -0.02) but the correlation was -0.23 in Sightville; *a significant ordinal interaction.* For Compulsivity the respective correlations were 0.23 and 0.14. The interaction for Compulsivity was significant, according to extreme-groups anova (one-tailed, $p < .05$). This may have been a fortuitous consequence of blocking, since the slopes differed rather little.

Grimes and Allinsmith examined the three-way interaction. They discarded Ss near the median on either personality variable, and then contrasted Ss in the outer quadrants of the Anxiety-Compulsivity space. Compulsives did somewhat better under either treatment than noncompulsives at the same level of Anxiety. The interaction effect of Compulsivity found by Grimes disappeared when Anxiety was held constant. Grimes' ordinal interaction relating Anxiety to treatment reappeared in the more elaborate analysis.

The study is open to some question because of its *post hoc* character. The treatment groups were not necessarily comparable at the outset, although some effort at matching on socioeconomic status was made. The Anxiety score may have reflected reaction to school experience; no data were available on personality at school entrance. The IQs also were a consequence of schooling to some degree. To this point, all analyses have been based on pooled classes. The collapse of the Anderson ATI when class effects were seined off (p. 247) will be recalled.

Grimes gave us the following additional information in a letter (October, 1972). Six years after the original measurement, in Grade 9, the STEP achievement test was administered to the Ss.

> The picture was quite blurred. The children with high ratings on compulsivity lost ground generally, but seemed to divide into two groups, those who degenerated dramatically, and those who continued to make relatively good progress.
>
> Highly anxious children declined comparatively in both communities. Even so, there was still a significant difference in achievement favoring those anxious children whose earlier school years were in the more structured setting. Many of the highly anxious children in the suburban setting (Sightville) had been taken out of the public schools. Tracing their histories revealed that they had continued to fail throughout elementary school, and their affluent parents had searched for more desirable placements in private schools.

A second study with genuine pretests was initiated in 1963 by Grimes but never formally analyzed. We have made a limited analysis of data he provided. Three schools provided 38-55 cases each. Each school had a tightly controlled reading program, at least in Grade 1. Two schools had relatively unstructured basal-reader, whole-word programs. The third school had a highly structured program with a linguistic base during Grade 1 and an unstructured program thereafter. Grimes judged that all schools had excellent individualized, warm teaching. Anxiety, reading readiness, and WISC IQ were assessed at the end of kindergarten. (The readiness scores were not available for our analysis.) At the end of Grade 1 a reading test was given; this can be taken either as a dependent variable or an intervening variable. In Grade 2, a group mental test was given, and Mental Age was calculated from a combination of this with the earlier WISC. Two standard achievement tests in reading at the end of Grade 3 provided the dependent variable.

We carried out a regression analysis within treatments, making no attempt to separate schools or classes. When terms were entered in a stepwise manner, neither the product term for MAxA nor the quadratic term in A accounted for appreciable variance (beyond that accounted for by linear terms). In a linear equation, MA was a useful predictor; in each treatment, the small negative weight for A did not approach significance. *This result is inconsistent with that in the Grimes-Allinsmith sample.* There A generated a negative slope in the unstructured treatment and a small positive slope in the structured treatment. (By way of technical detail: We made a log transformation of Anxiety. We expressed the predictors and criteria as z scores, standardizing on all cases pooled; this standardization lost no generality, and simplified inspection of results. The equation for predicting Grade-1 reading was $0.68\,z_{MA} - 0.08\,z_A$ + constant in the unstructured group, and $0.71 z_{MA} - 0.17\,z_A$ + constant in the structured group. The Grade-1 test scores were superior in the structured treatment.)

In a stepwise prediction of Grade-3 scores, giving primacy to the Grade-1 reading test, anxiety made no contribution. In the structured treatment, MA also added nothing to the prediction, which indicates that its relevant information was entirely captured by the Grade-1 score. To put it differently, any strengths or deficits built up in one year of structured teaching were likely to determine the child's rank after two more years of structured teaching, regardless of his MA. In the unstructured course, however, though the regression of Grade-3 reading onto Grade-1 reading was the same as in the structured treatment, MA was a significant second predictor. This implies a *weak but significant ATI* with ability. Among children with the same Grade-1 achievement, MA predicted which would do better in Grade 3 after an unstructured program. The shift in mode of instruction perhaps allowed bright pupils who had made a poor start to capitalize on their general ability.

An even older reading study (D.E.P. Smith *et al.,* 1956) has some resemblance to the Grimes-Allinsmith work. It was essentially a study of teacher style. University students entering 16 small class sections of a seven-week course to improve their reading were given a questionnaire derived from the 16PF. This could be scored for Anxiety and "Permeability," the main variable in this study. Synonyms suggested for "permeable" are schizoid and disorganized; it thus seems to resemble the low compulsivity of the Grimes study. The study was confined to anxious Ss. Within the group of High-A's, markedly permeable/rigid Ss (69 in all) were chosen for investigation. After teaching his section for a few weeks in a highly structured, directive fashion, the teacher shifted to a nondirective style. The student was left to determine how, and how much, he would work. For half the sections, the order of treatments was reversed. The dependent variable was gain, expressed as a percentage of the person's initial score. This method of analysis is open to criticism.

The mean "comparative increase in reading efficiency" was as follows in each group:

	Compulsive or rigid	Permeable or noncompulsive
Directive, structured treatment	56	91
Permissive, unstructured treatment	95	46

The difference within each column was significant. Groups had been equated in scholastic aptitude and initial rate of reading, but initial differences in comprehension may account for the final superiority of the compulsives. The structured treatment benefited noncompulsives—which seems plausible.

Whitehill and Jipson (1970) found an interaction of Introversion with forced/self-controlled reading practice. This interaction was not significant (so what—in a 3 x 2 anova with 66 Ss). Posttest reading speed had a flat slope onto Introversion among college students trained "traditionally," and a *steep slope (extroverts high) in an experimental treatment.* The traditional group practiced reading with an apparatus that forced them to move through the material at a prescribed rate, presumably set just a bit faster than the student's habitual rate. The training consisted of at least six hour-long sessions. The experimental treatment was similar save that the pace was not forced. The student read as he chose; a signal light indicated that he did/did not meet a prescribed standard of speed. These authors accepted Eysenck's view—"extroverts condition less rapidly"—reasoning that the experimental program with its "aversive reinforcement" would accelerate the learning of extroverts. The experimental treatment leaves more responsibility to the learner.

Work on personality variables in reading should tie in with studies of reading reviewed in Chapter 8, but unfortunately it does not. Only the Grimes-Allinsmith study includes ability data. We urge that future research on reading take ability and personality into account simultaneously.

Active response and confirmation in programmed instruction

Techniques of presenting PI have been manipulated, to test the hypothesis that more stressful or more demanding treatments handicap the anxious. Some studies contrast covert/overt responding. Others ask for overt response, supplying one group of Ss the correct answer while withholding feedback from the others. Reducing feedback throws the learner more upon his own resources.

Campeau (1968) had fifth-graders work on a three-hour instructional program. Half the Ss received feedback after each response (which should have improved learning). The others had to detect errors for themselves by noting contradiction between their conceptions and the content of subsequent frames. Campeau analyzed within sexes and confined attention to extreme groups on the Sarason TA scale; she thus discarded a large part of the data. Her dependent variables were the immediate and delayed posttests with IQ partialed out. There was no main effect for treatment. For girls ($N = 44$), the interaction was significant. *High-A's did distinctly better than others when given feedback,* and distinctly worse with no feedback. For boys ($N = 36$), essentially no effect appeared on the immediate test. On the delayed test, the result for boys moved more into line with that for girls, but the interaction was significant only for girls. This analysis was insufficient to establish that sex moderated the effect.

J. Hansen said that he had findings contrary to Campeau's in his short CAI study (see p. 369). In fact, however, he failed to make use of a measure of trait A he had collected. He did not relate State-A scores to posttest scores within treatments. The relations reported with errors-on-program—an intermediate variable—are not pertinent.

In the Lublin study (p. 194), the Edwards questionnaire score on Need for Autonomy was used as one predictor. Low scores on this variable (dependency?) went with poor performance in PI, in every condition from having no feedback to feedback on every frame. There was *no interaction.*

Schultz and Dangel (1972) treated recitation as a stress situation. We locate the study here, since the manipulation of active response as a variable has some resemblance to the variables used with PI. The aptitude measure distinguished facilitating anxiety (FA) and debilitating anxiety (DA). Ss were 24 extreme "facilitators" (FA $\gg$ DA) and 24 extreme "debilitators" (FA $\ll$ DA). The students viewed a series of 36 slides, and then had the opportunity to review the information in a printed booklet. Next, Ss participated in a group recitation, in sets of six. Twenty questions were set forth; each S knew that he would have to respond to three of them/or to seven of them/or to none of them. With only 12 cases of each type at each rate of recitation, the failure of interactions to reach significance is not conclusive. The important dependent variable is a posttest on items regarding which there had been no recitation. This measure was equally fair to all groups. The two types of students earned the same score in the absence of recitation, and the facilitators *did appreciably better under the recitation condition.* (For a related study see p. 434.)

The Taylor scale was used in a study of the overt/covert response contrast in PI with 110 undergraduates (Tobias & Williamson, 1968). One of two overt-response groups proceeded through a nine-page booklet on binary numbers with no feedback or correction. The others received correct-answer feedback. *Among A's, overt response was disadvantageous when there was no feedback. Among Low-*

A's, either overt-response condition was bad. Reading was a good treatment at both levels of A:

	Low-Anxious	Anxious
Reading	15.6	15.5
Overt response with feedback	12.2	15.5
Overt response, no feedback	12.9	12.3

The slopes in the two overt-response treatments agree with those of Campeau. One could not, however, have predicted good results for Low-A's in the undemanding, unstressful reading treatment.

Tobias and Abramson (1971) applied the same treatments in a further study. This is one of several studies that employ an instructional program on heart disease developed by Tobias. The program requires an hour or more, and has two sections. One section covers relatively simple content with which laymen are likely to be somewhat familiar. The second section covers more technical content. Tobias suspected that effects of anxiety and other variables are altered by changes in difficulty.

In the Tobias data we analyzed earlier in this chapter (presumably typical of the college samples with which the program is used), the correlation of the post-test scores on the two programs was about 0.40. This is not a reliability coefficient, since the programs are not equivalent. Even so, it suggests strongly that learning from such a short instructional program depends to a large degree on non-recurring affective and cognitive events. Strong predictions and strong interactions are not to be expected.

The Tobias-Abramson study found some significant ATI, but these proved difficult to interpret; Tobias regarded the results as essentially negative. The investigators divided 144 college students among six treatments in a factorial design. The three response modes of the Tobias-Williamson study were crossed with ego-involving/non-ego-involving instructions (EI/NEI). Alpert-Haber DA and FA scores were the center of attention. A posttest on each of the two sections of the program was a dependent variable.

The generalized regression analysis carried out by Tobias and Abramson produced an equation of 23 terms. We made relationships more perceptible by rescaling in the manner described in Chapter 2 (p. 28ff.). In order to examine the effects of DA, we set FA equal to $\overline{\overline{FA}}$ in the equations and then pooled sexes with equal weight. The simplified equation had terms in DA, EI, and DA x EI.

The equations for the familiar and technical posttests were quite similar. In the constructed-response and reading conditions, learning had little relation to anxiety with NEI instructions. High A's did distinctly better with EI motivation, whereas Low-A's were not affected by EI/NEI. In the condition of overt response with no feedback, the best scores were those of High-A's under EI instructions and the worst were those of Low-A's receiving NEI instructions. The ATI for Debilitating Anxiety were not significant, but slopes differed greatly with response mode, under EI instructions. The advantage of High-A's, particularly under the more stressful condition, is not what theory would have led us to expect.

Facilitating anxiety is a rather mysterious variable; a high score does not mean "I am tense" but "I do well under pressure." Tobias and Abramson found a third-order interaction of borderline significance on the technical posttest. But the patterning is so strange that *the effect is worth little thought unless confirmed* in other studies. Among women, on both programs, better performance was associated with higher FA and greater EI. Among men with low FA, scores on the familiar posttest were higher under EI conditions; men with high FA earned intermediate scores regardless of EI/NEI. The technical posttest showed better performance of Low-FA's under NEI instructions and better performance of High-FA's under EI instructions. Under NEI instructions FA had a strong negative relation to outcome among men. The three response modes produced much the same regression surfaces.

Leherissey *et al.* (1971a) reported two studies with the easy and difficult heart-disease programs of Tobias. Data were available from a pretest and a trait-A measure. In the first study, treatments were: (1) reading the text with responses filled in ("covert" response); (2) reading the frames, thinking of an answer, and then being told the correct response; (3) choice-response with feedback; and (4) constructed response with feedback. This list proceeds from least demanding to most demanding. In Study I (148 college Ss), on the difficult technical program, the state-A means for the treatment groups displayed this same order. Study II (128 Ss) retained only Treatments (1) and (4). Whereas Study I Ss had the familiar program, then the full technical program, then the posttest, in Study II half the Ss had a much shorter technical program. Thus, for the long-program groups many additional frames intervened before the tests were given.

These two studies are subject to technical criticism. Study time varied from group to group, and posttest scores could not be adjusted for this. The blocked anova provided a relatively weak analysis. By chance, large pretest differences occurred between the groups in the several cells of the design.* And the published charts for Study II were mislabeled. We have reexamined the detailed project reports (1971 a, b).

We adjusted scores for initial differences in the pretest, using the mean (over both studies) of the within-groups regression slopes. Considering both sets of data together, our calculations support the authors' conclusion. The delay of the posttest (in those groups given the longer technical program) was detrimental, but it did not affect the regression slope onto Anxiety. The three reading groups had almost precisely the same V-shaped regression, as shown by these blocked means after our adjustment:

---

*Leherissey *et al.* did not collect SAT data. The Tobias research showing SATxAT and SATxATxT interactions had not yet been done at the time.

	Low-A	Medium-A	High-A
Study I—delayed	21.4	17.1	18.7
Study II—delayed	17.5	14.8	16.2
Study II	24.1	19.1	22.4

An *inverted* arch is nowhere suggested in anxiety theory, yet here the same result appeared in three groups of about 30–40 cases each. Can it be dismissed as a coincidence?

The constructed-response groups did quite badly, and the regression slope in this demanding treatment was nearly flat in each study. The multiple-choice overt group of Study I performed fairly well, and the regression onto Anxiety was steeply positive. I.e., High-A's did very well. Finally, the group following procedure (2) (making silent responses to fill in blanks) did about average. Their regression slope was negative, Low-A's doing comparatively well. We did not have sufficient information to test the significance of these results.

All in all, we are uncertain about this study in view of the inadequate controls and weak analysis. The absence of consistency between the Leherissey Study I and the Tobias-Abamson study raises substantial question about the generalizability of results. Tobias (1972a) has traced the changes of the program from study to study, arguing that these modifications (particularly those made in going from booklet PI to CAI) probably account for the inconsistent results. But insofar as such discrepancies arise, they argue against the usefulness of research that tests generalized hypotheses on a single bit of instructional material.

Inductive/deductive instruction

Leith and others have examined how scores on one of the British personality questionnaires relate to the inductive/deductive variable (pp. 311 ff., 370 ff.). It is not obvious how drive level should be expected to relate to inductive/deductive instruction. Perhaps deductive, didactic PI allows greater passivity and so can be advantageous for Ss with comparatively high drive.

Leith and Wisdom (1970) divided 78 college women among four short PI treatments of a discovery/rule-and-example character. Apparently, the programs consisted of a multiple-choice figure-classification task in which it was possible to solve a problem by calling upon one of five principles. This principle could be given at the start of a set of problems to all of which it applied (ruleg), or could be left for S to infer from successive, similar problems. A third treatment scrambled the problems, rather than blocking those related to one principle. A fourth group had the ruleg information with each answer marked in advance; they could respond to problems passively. The posttest included items to which none of the principles applied. No interaction effect on the posttest was significant.

Table 12.2 Mean gain on a transfer test as a function of instructional program and personality

	Results within personality category[a]				Results for cases pooled across one trait			
	Low drive	Intermediate drive	Intermediate drive	High drive	Low I	High I	Low N	High N
	Low I Low N	Low I High N	High I Low N	High I High N	--	--	--	--
	Results among college women[b]							
A. Passive use of rule with worked examples	2.8	-1.8	4.4[d]	2.0	0.5	3.2	3.6	0.1
B. Rule followed by examples to work	3.0	3.6	3.7[d]	1.5	3.3	2.6	3.4	2.6
C. Examples to work, sequenced	3.2[d]	3.0	3.0	2.2	3.1	2.6	3.1	2.6
D. Examples to work, scrambled	4.0[d]	2.8	3.7	1.0	3.4	2.4	3.8	1.9
	Results among 10-year-olds[c]							
A. Passive use of rule with worked examples	2.5	16.0[d]	0.0	11.5	9.2	5.8	1.2	13.8
B. Rule followed by examples to work	9.0	-4.0	11.0[d]	8.5	2.5	9.8	10.0	2.2
C. Examples to work, sequenced	10.7	8.0	0.5	17.0[d]	9.4	8.8	5.6	12.5
D. Examples to work, scrambled	7.4	4.0	8.3[d]	7.5	5.7	7.9	7.8	5.8

[a] I, introversion; N, neuroticism.
[b] After Leith & Wisdom, 1970.
[c] After Leith & Bosett; data given by Leith, 1969.
[d] Largest entry in the row of four.

The results in Section a of Table 12.2 came from a transfer (problem-solving) test. The data do not support the notion of a "drive" continuum from stable extrovert to unstable introvert. *The neurotic extroverts did conspicuously badly in the condition that allowed them to be passive,* but the variation of the remaining cell means was not large.

This one finding was reversed in a replication on 64 ten-year-olds (Leith & Bosett; see Leith, 1969). The results appear in Table 12.2. By the authors' analysis, the Treatment x Neuroticism interaction was significant. *These effects are highly irregular* and do not resemble those of Leith and Wisdom.

Shadbolt & Leith (see Leith, 1969) had college students ($N = 211$) study an instructional program on genetics that required about three hours. There were alternative didactic/discovery programs, the difference being primarily in the sequencing of content. *Interactions of Neuroticism (N) were not significant* (and were not described). There was a *significant interaction for Extroversion* (Table 12.3), extroverts doing better under guided discovery and introverts better in the didactic treatment.

Trown related N, Extroversion, and general-ability measures to mathematics learning of 11- to 13-year-olds ($N = 128$). Ss worked on PI in vector algebra

Table 12.3   Posttest means in three studies as a function of instructional program and Introversion

Investigator	Subjects	Program	Mean scores of	
			Extroverts	Introverts
Shadbolt[a]	College students	Didactic, whole-then-part	21.4	24.7
		Guided discovery, part-then-whole	24.3	21.0
Trown[b]	Preadolescents	Ruleg	25.1	39.8
		Egrule	42.9	36.8
Leith[c]	Preadolescents	Small-step only	19.4	24.4
		Large step (overview) only	19.9	17.3
		Small-step, then review	22.3	18.1
		Overview and test, then small-step as needed	20.5	21.2

[a] After Leith, 1969.

[b] After Leith and Trown, 1970.

[c] After Leith, 1973.

twice a week for four weeks. They encountered rules either before or after examples. Three outcomes were considered: immediate, delayed, and transfer performance. Trown (1969) did not report numerical results. The somewhat more adequate report of Leith and Trown (1970) used simple analyses and discussed the effects of extroversion only (Table 12.3). *On the ruleg (deductive) sequence the introverts did better.* On the egrule (inductive) sequence the extroverts did better. Trown mentioned that this relation was moderated by ability or N. But she did not report evidence in any detail and the Leith-Trown account dismissed the relations as very weak.

Four kinds of PI were used by Leith (1973) to teach several elementary topics in meteorology to children near Age 12 ($N = 105$). There were small-step and large-step programs. For two additional groups these were combined in two orders. In one, the large-step presentation served as an advance organizer and pretest; if the student did well on the large-step program, he could skip to the next unit ("skip-branching"). In the other order, the small-step version was followed by the large-step version to provide review on that topic; nothing was skipped. The several lessons were spread over a five-week period. Ability correlated with outcome in only two treatments. The difference between Highs and Lows nearly vanished when both programs were provided (in review or in branching order)—a nonsignificant interaction. There was a highly significant interaction for Introversion (lower section of Table 12.3), and no hint of Ability x Introversion x Treatment interaction. *Introverts did much better than extroverts with the small-step version. Extroverts had an advantage when a review was added to the small-step version,* and a modest advantage ($p < .10$) on the large-step program. The data, on their face, suggest that the review impeded test performance of introverts and of able students. It is hard to accept this.

These several studies do not cohere. The data were limited, no common scheme of analysis was adopted, and the treatments varied along several dimensions. Still we may ask, does a deductive, didactic procedure give an advantage to neurotic and/or introverted Ss? Such a tendency appeared among introverts in the following sets of data: Leith-Wisdom passive ruleg, Leith-Bosett active ruleg, Shadbolt whole-then-part, Trown ruleg, and Leith small-step. The effect was reversed for the Leith-Wisdom active ruleg, the Leith-Bosett passive ruleg, and the Leith small-step-then-review procedures. Neuroticism, where considered, had no consistent interaction.

Effects of task difficulty

We mentioned earlier that Eysenck has equated high drive with a combination of Neuroticism and Introversion, has predicted that performance measures will have an arch-shaped regression on drive. We know just one report of such a relation. McLaughlin and Eysenck (1967) selected 64 adults to represent the four combinations of Neuroticism and Introversion, omitting persons close to the median. These Ss learned two paired-associate lists of CVC syllables, one meaningless and one having high association value. The dependent variables were trials-to-criterion and errors-to-criterion. On the easy list the expected arch was found, the best performance being that of the neurotic extroverts ("intermediate drive"), and the second-best that of the stable introverts. On the difficult list the best performance was that of the stable extroverts ("low drive"), as predicted. The scores of the other groups were low. Apart from the educator's lack of interest in rote verbal learning, there is another reason for ignoring studies with this design. Howarth & Eysenck (1968) demonstrated (on a list of medium association value) that the advantage of extroverts in a reproduction test immediately after acquisition vanished within a few minutes and was reversed on a test a day later. Educators are interested in retainable learning, not trials-to-criterion.

A considerable American literature has been motivated by the view that the disadvantage of High-A's becomes greater as task difficulty increases. We shall not review this older literature, which is now covered in many secondary sources. Even though these studies did rather consistently find interactions, most of them are of only tangential value for us. Often, as in the Eysenck-McLaughlin study above, the treatment groups were taught different things and the outcome measures were not comparable. Even where the same material was to be learned in all treatments, the dependent variable was performance during the instruction rather than outcome. None of the studies of difficulty considered second-order interactions (Ability x Anxiety). We have already quoted the Spences (our p. 413) on the theoretical equivocality of much of the work.

When outcome measures are not comparable, a direct significance test for ATI is not possible. At most, one can compare the signs of the within-treatment regression slopes. (Magnitudes are expressed in operationally different units.) In view of such problems, we shall cover only a few representative studies, as succinctly as possible.

Katahn and Lyda (1966) put 40 college students, at the extremes on the Taylor scale, through paired-associates training. *The anxious S did well when the reponse terms were high in his personal repertoire of responses, not otherwise.* Low-A's were negligibly affected by the change in response availability. The importance of response availability in the Burton-Goldbeck study (p. 192) will be recalled.

Irwin Sarason has carried out many laboratory studies of effects of anxiety, one of which (1958) seems especially worthy of our attention. College students ($N = 64$), split at the median on Test Anxiety (TA), learned a serial list of meaningless/meaningful disyllables. Half the Ss were given standard instructions and half were given reassurance ("Don't worry if you make mistakes"). *Many interactions were significant.* With the nonsense list, Low-TA's surpassed Highs under the standard instructions and did worse with reassurance. With the meaningful list, Highs did equally well under both types of instructions and outscored Lows—but reassurance was quite advantageous for Lows (!). The increase in difficulty of list had little overall effect on the score of Lows, but it greatly reduced the scores of High-TA's. When the cases were divided on general A rather than TA, the interactions of that variable were not significant. Without descriptive data we are not certain that the measures had appreciably different regressions.

It will be recalled that the Tobias study used earlier in the chapter for mathematical demonstrations (p. 401 ff.) contrasted orderly/scrambled sequences in PI. There were some evidence of a second-order interaction of SAT, trait A, and treatment, with errors-on-program as dependent variable. But *this effect did not appear* in Tobias' more technical program nor *on the posttests.*

A concept-attainment task performed under ego-involving (EI)/non-ego-involving (NEI) instructions was the center of the Meyers-Dunham (1971) experiment with 180 undergraduates. After learning one concept, S worked on a second problem. As we understand the experiment, if red was the cue for identifying examples in the first task, on the second task green was the cue for "nonshift" Ss, whereas for "shift" Ss squareness (or the like) was the cue. The shift condition is typically more difficult because the mental set to attend to color must be reversed. The dependent variable was the change in trials-to-criterion between first and second problems. *An ability interaction was said to be highly significant.* Ss low in memory span showed appreciable negative transfer under "nonshift" conditions and some positive transfer under "shift" conditions. Ss high in memory span showed no transfer. The report suggested that this relation was not moderated by the EI/NEI treatment. (The "Results" section made no mention of three reasoning tests that had been given. Presumably, reasoning did not interact.)

The interaction of Anxiety was with the combined treatment variables. *High-A's showed positive transfer only in the NEI, nonshift combination of conditions* (least stressful?). For Low-A's, positive transfer was great for EI-nonshift, and moderate for NEI-shift. This finding appears to be consistent with the classical hypothesis of an arch-shaped regression of outcome onto drive.

Miscellany

Whether High-A's are helped when PI replaces conventional instruction has received some attention. The large study by Ripple *et al.* (see p. 185) included measures of test anxiety, compulsivity, exhibitionism, and "convergent-minus-divergent thinking style." Anxiety significantly reduced scores. According to the data in the full ERIC report, there was *no simple interaction* of treatment with any one of these traits. Data on ability-anxiety combinations were not reported.

High-school students ($N = 150$) were split between programmed and conventional teaching of vector geometry by Flynn (1968). Intelligence and a pretest were covaried out of the posttest. (Presumably, they did not interact with outcome, but no statement is made). The regression of the adjusted posttest on Test Anxiety had a zero slope in the conventional group and a positive but shallow slope in the programmed group. Three-level blocking in the analysis of variance reduced the power of the significance test, but the observed advantage of PI for the high-A's is small enough that *the null hypothesis can be accepted.*

F. L. Ryan (1968), teaching the geography of Japan to 86 California fourth-graders, directed attention in advance to pertinent and familiar facts about California geography. For all four groups there were programmed lessons on Japan on five consecutive days. One group had an advance organizer on each day, followed by PI. A second group had one comprehensive organizer on the first day prior to any instruction, and then had PI each day. A third group had both the initial and daily organizers, and the fourth group had no organizer. The organizers were helpful. There was a strong main effect for Test Anxiety (Lows best), but this effect disappeared when ability was covaried out. Posttest scores did not show an interaction of treatment with anxiety. There was a significant interaction effect on time-on-program even after ability was extracted as a covariate. The results are strange: flat regressions and fast times for controls and for those given both the initial and daily organizers; steep regressions (Low TA's faster) for those given the initial organizer only. If outcome had been examined by a path-analytic scheme with time-on-program as intermediate variable, *interactions might have been found.* But the study was a tiny one.

Before summing up the foregoing studies, we shall give a sketchy account of research from the program of F. J. Di Vesta and his colleagues. The duration of treatments and other characteristics leave us unable to make use of the results and we shall omit them from the summary. The studies deal with the possibility that personality variables interact with mathemagenic variables. The Leith study with previews and reviews (our p. 424) might be classified as giving such evidence. On the other hand, A failed to interact in Berliner's (1971) study of mathemagenic variables (our p. 354), Peters and C. Harris (in Di Vesta *et al.,* 1970, pp. 109–124) experimented on 120 high-school juniors who listened to a one-hour lecture. Ss were told to take notes or to use notes given to them or were allowed no notes. The design was 3 x 2, the first variable being crossed with intstructions to review/no opportunity to review. Five personality scores were obtained: DA, FA, internal-external control, dogmatism, and intolerance for ambiguity. Review/no review did not interact significantly with any of these dimensions; hence, the data were collapsed to test interactions of note-taking. Interaction was significant only for Intolerance of Ambiguity. *Tolerant Ss were superior in two treatments but inferior under the no-notes condition.* Persons with high DA were inferior under all three conditions, but the Lows did nearly as badly in the no-notes condition.

Peters and Messier (in Di Vesta *et al.,* 1970, pp. 127–156) carried out a 3 x 2 design in a graduate class of 41 students. Small though this sample was, interactions were significant for various of the traits discussed above.

Giving a quiz with questions in random order hurt the performance of Highs on DA on the second quiz in the course. Making comments on the returned paper also generated some inconsistent interactions.

Di Vesta and Gray (1972) conducted a one-hour experiment, but only five minutes was actually used for study of the passage on which the posttest was based. The remainder of the time was used in an attempt to test hypotheses about the order of experiences; this produced no interesting result. A complex factorial design allowed eight treatment combinations. The authors presented correlations, each based on 15 Ss, for six personality variables. Some differences appeared. For example, persons more tolerant of ambiguity succeeded better ($r = 0.54$) when in a treatment combination of no notetaking, encouragement to rehearse after reading the text, followed by a short test over the passage—followed by the posttest. With no notetaking, no rehearsal, and an unrelated intervening test, the

Table 12.4 Interactions of treatment demand: Summary

Name of one investigator and our page number	Ss per treatment (approx.)[a]	Treatments judged most/least "demanding"	Trait representing defensive motivation[b]	Slope comparison[c]	Remarks
Ripple, p. 426	500	Conventional/PI	A (TA?)	0	For introversion.
Shadbolt, p. 423	100	Discovery sequence PI/didactic PI	N, I/E	± 0	No interaction for N.
Flynn, p. 426	75	Conventional/PI	TA	+	Weak; dubious effect.
Tobias, 401 ff. 421	60	Scrambled PI/ordered PI	A	± 0	Flat slope in demanding program. Able Low-A's much impeded by scrambling. Dull High-A's much impeded by scrambling. Then ATI for errors on program; no ATI for posttest or on second program with technical content.
Trown, p. 423	60	Egrule/ruleg	N,I/E	+ 0	Extroverts superior on demanding treatment. Relations of N very weak.
Leherissey studies, p. 420	35 30 (60)	Constructed-response PI/reading	A	0 ±	Flat slope in most demanding treatment. Lows disadvantaged in next most demanding treatment. V-shaped regression on anxiety in least demanding treatment.
Grimes, p. 415	55–70	Whole-word reading/phonics	A	0	Low-A's slightly superior in both treatments.
Grimes, p. 414	72, 156	Whole-word reading/phonics	A, compulsivity	+	High-A's disadvantaged in unstructured treatment. Compulsivity had no additional interaction.
Meyers, p. 426	45(90)	Dimensional shift in concept attainment/nonshift	A	+	Effect moderated by ego-involvement. High-A's superior in least demanding condition. Results for Low-A's complex.
Tobias-Williamson, p. 418	40	PI without feedback/reading	A	±	Low-A's did their best in least demanding treatment. High-A's helped by feedback in PI.
Campeau, p. 418	40	PI without feedback/PI with feedback	TA	+	Low-A's superior in demanding treatment. Sex may moderate effect.
Tobias-Abramson, p. 419	25(50)	PI with or without feedback/reading	DA	±	High-A's superior with conditions of weak and medium demand under EI instructions. No ATI under NEI instructions.

Study	N[a]	Treatment contrast	Personality variable[b] (16 PF)	Code[c]	Result
Whitehill, p. 417	30	Forced pace/self-pacing with monitor	I/E	+	Extroverts superior in self-paced treatment.
Sarason, p. 425	15(30)	Meaningless syllables/meaningful	TA	+	Low-A's superior in demanding condition with standard instructions. Effect altered by reassurance.
Schultz, p. 418	24	Recitation/no recitation	DA > FA	+	
Leith, p. 422	25	Large step/small-step-plus-review	I/E	+, ±	Extroverts superior in small-step-plus-review condition. Extroverts inferior in small-step condition.
Katahn, p. 425	20	Response terms strange/familiar	A	+	Low-A's superior in demanding treatment.
Ryan, p. 426	20	No advance organizer/initial plus daily organizers	TA	0	
Leith-Wisdom, p. 421	20	Scrambled examples/rule with worked examples	N, I/E	?	Very poor performance of neurotic extroverts in least demanding condition.
Leith-Bosett, p. 422	15	Scrambled examples/rule with worked examples	N, I/E	?	Relations of N and I/E irregular.

[a] N in parentheses pools Ss within an instructional mode in a 2 x 2 or 2 x 3 array of treatments.

[b] I/E indicates Introversion (contrasted with Extroversion). A refers to versions of the Taylor scale or the trait score of the State-Trait Anxiety Inventory.

[c] Code.   + if there was a greater regression slope of performance vs. A or other measure of defensive motivation in the less-demanding treatment.

- if there was a greater slope in the more-demanding treatment.

± if results were mixed.

0 if slopes were similar.

? not classifiable.

persons tolerant of ambiguity were at a disadvantage ($r = -0.47$). The analysis was inadequate, no attention having been paid to regression slopes. For mysterious reasons the authors discussed the possible interactions of only two of the five variables, even though one of these had nearly uniform correlations from treatment to treatment. The fact that tolerance for ambiguity was not generally associated with good performance in the four note-taking conditions contradicts the Peters-Harris result.

There is one more of these miniature, complicated studies to consider. College *S*s ($N = 94$) saw a 22-minute film, and then either studied their notes/made (and heard) three-minute oral summaries/or both (Weener in Di Vesta *et al.*, 1970, pp. 233–248). The authors dismissed the possibility of interactions when they found that the correlations of outcome with FA and DA did not differ significantly across conditions. The differences between s.d.'s of some outcomes seem likely to have produced sizable differences in regression slopes for FA, but the study is small and the effects seem too variable to justify attention. All in all, we conclude that *the studies in this series cannot be taken as evidence for or against interaction,* in view of the brief treatments, spotty analysis, and tiny samples.

Summary and interpretation

Table 12.4 assembles salient facts about the diverse studies of interactions of A with instructional mode. In not one of these studies was information about the possible curvilinearity of regressions extracted from the data (excepting the check Tobias made for us; see p. 401). Only in rare instances was ability taken into account. Moreover, it requires a daring speculation to identify certain treatments as more stressful or more demanding. Even so, an attempt at a synoptic conclusion is called for.

The large number of interactions turned up in these studies is remarkable, especially in view of the low power of most analyses. We have classified the studies, insofar as possible, according to the contrast of the within-treatment slopes. We expected the slope of the outcome-on-A regression to be greater (more strongly positive or less strongly negative) in whichever treatment was least demanding. We expected the nondefensives to do their best when under some pressure and the defensives to do their best when less responsibility was placed on them. The one firm statement warranted by the table is that no unequivocal finding in the opposite direction appeared, whereas several studies of moderate size had results consistent with the hypothesis. In several instances, interaction failed to appear, and *N* in those studies was fairly large. What is perhaps most important is the large number of ± entries, where there were sizable effects in each direction. It does not seem to us that these contradictions ought to be attributed to chance. Rather, the data imply that interactive effects of anxiety and instruction are complex and that no single generalization about the treatment contrasts accounts for them. Describing treatments as "unstructured," or "demanding," or "inductive" accounts for only a fraction of the interactions—such an hypothesis is no more than a first approximation.

There is a comparable difficulty with respect to the trait measures. The results are much too scattered to support a judgment that TA or DA or Introversion is more potent than general Anxiety or Neuroticism. To speak of defensive motivation serves only as a delaying tactic to emphasize that it is premature to state what construct(s) generate interactions.

As we have aggregated studies that originated from a great variety of hunches, with many of the studies employing treatment variables about which little is known, confusion is not surprising. There is clearly need for more substantial experiments that deliberately pit alternative explanations against each other. The experiments will have to be based on an articulated set of ideas about the processes by which the learner responds to the instructional material, including such acts as rehearsal and persistence, and also his perceptions and emotional processes. These will be checked and solidified into theory only if data are systematically collected on intermediate variables. It will be necessary to recognize the multidimensional character of the treatment variables. While any one experiment may be capable of "holding constant" over treatments all aspects save one or two specifically manipulated as variables, these constants become variables as we go from study to study; and it is in such variations that the explanation of inconsistent significant results lies. To put it more directly: It is evidently hopeless to seek to generalize powerfully about such simply conceived contrasts as inductive/deductive or easy/hard or feedback/no-feedback, each taken up independently. Imagination and arduous empirical work will be required before even the beginnings of an adequate theory for this intriguing set of phenomena take form.

Interactions of Anxiety with motivational conditions

Anxious persons are generally expected to respond more strongly to threats to self-esteem. The resultant stress may impair or enhance efficiency. We shall concentrate on the studies of motivation that seem relevant to learning in the classroom, ignoring most studies of test performance under stress. The research falls into three categories: studies of arousal, usually by ego-involving instructions; studies that contrast conditions of evaluation (e.g., more or less supportive evaluation); and studies of teacher style. As studies of teacher style look at a natural rather than a controlled variable, they will be left to Chapter 13. The other findings will be recapitulated in a table at the end of this section (p. 436).

Arousal of ego

In school, tasks are almost always presented as important and the learner almost always thinks he is being judged. Hence, it is hard to visualize a school—even a "progressive" school—that would not stimulate concern to do well. The school does retain the option of intensifying evaluation and competition or of making evaluation less intrusive. In numerous small studies in social psychology, one group of Ss is made to feel that a task is important, whereas the other group is put in a relaxed frame of mind (for example, being told that the investigator is merely trying out the test, not studying S himself). We have already interpreted EI conditions as increasing the drive level of Low-A's (in the Meyers-Dunham study, p. 426). But High-A's responded well to EI conditions in the Tobias-Abramson study (p. 419), so there is conflicting evidence.

Recall and comprehension of a short printed passage (requiring 15 minutes to read) were the dependent variables in Caron's (1963) study based on J. W. Atkinson's theory (see p. 448). Ss were 241 high-school boys with IQs between 109 and 125. IQ was partialed out of the outcome. Reading was done under a condition that aroused the desire to achieve or under a curiosity-only condition. There was a test of factual recall and a test requiring S to apply the theory. For analysis, Ss were blocked on TA, nAch, and prior grades. The results have to be radically simplified here. According to the recall test, the arousal condition was markedly better for those with low prior grades, no matter what their personality scores. The transfer findings confirmed this result in three of four cells. Among those with good prior grades, the largest increase in recall, as a consequence of arousal, appeared among those with High TA and Low nAch (low "resultant motive to succeed," in Atkinson's present terminology). But arousal led to markedly *worse* results on the transfer test among such students. This is a second- or third-order interaction. Various other main effects and interactions were significant, including some interactions of treatment with S's intrinsic interest in the topic studied. *The study supports the view that Personality x Ability patterns interact with motivational conditions.* Much of the evidence could be accounted for as a simple main effect favoring arousal, but such a conclusion does not do justice to the author's theoretical argument.

The Caron study was followed up by Sinclair (1969). He allowed 25 minutes for instruction under EI/NEI conditions, the subject-matter being life among the Trobrianders. Ss were 173 high-school boys. Scores averaged higher under EI conditions, as in Caron's study. Using a factual posttest, there was a significant ordinal ATI. Low-A's did quite well under EI conditions. Under NEI conditions, both extreme groups did rather badly. This is a classical "arch" result, *mild stress being especially beneficial to Low-A's.* (But Caron's data showed a greater benefit of stress to the High-A's.) On a test requiring inference rather than recall, there was no interaction; if anything, the stress condition benefited the High-A's. The fact that Caron had also found contrasting results for recall and transfer makes this noteworthy.

In a study of PI in geometry, Silberman *et al.* (1962) employed TA as an aptitude variable and used EI instructions with some Ss. A shorter study was carried out with 48 Ss. *Conditions intended to arouse/reduce A did not alter the mean outcome from a difficult program. With an easy program there was a disordinal interaction, stress benefiting Low-A's.*

In an even shorter study (Blatt, 1963), 60 Ss selected for high or low Test Anxiety worked on the John-Rimoldi reasoning task under three conditions: evaluative/neutral/play. For High-A's, the neutral, nonevaluative condition was rather unproductive; Highs did best under the play condition. Lows did well under nonevaluative and evaluative conditions and equalled the High-A's under the play condition. The effects were not significant, but the treatment was probably too brief for performance to reach a stable state.

A behavioral test of persistence in the tedious making of tally marks was used by Kipnis and Wagner (1965) as a measure of motivation. Enlisted men ($N = 106$) worked on two anagrams tasks with minimal incentive and minimal ego-involvement. A second group of 108 worked under incentive conditions: cash prizes to high scorers and an assurance that the test was significant to the Navy. (Note that these are not the usual EI instructions.) Surprisingly, there was no main effect for conditions. The Persistence x Incentive interaction was significant. With incentive, the regression of anagrams performance onto Persistence had a positive slope. Without incentive, the regression was **V** shaped. *There was no treatment difference among persistent Ss, a positive effect of incentives on the middle group, and a significant negative effect on Lows.* IQ did not moderate the effect. The authors apparently viewed the low-persistent Ss as having a defensive motivation, such that inducement to strive impaired productivity. The strange results in the other two groups were not explained.

Anxiety seemingly did not interact with arousal in the study of Pagano (1970). Definitions of esoteric psychological terms, chosen to be mutually interfering, were studied under conditions of controlled exposure. The 132 Ss were divided between EI/NEI instructions for original learning. Prior to a retention test two days later, these groups were split again between stress-reduction/EI treatments. Test Anxiety had a near-significant main effect on original learning, with a *negligible interaction.* The loss score on the retention test showed no significant main effect or interaction. While gain scores may be used in interaction studies (p. 73), the loss scores here gave misleading results, as the initial effect subtracted out was a fallible *dependent* variable. Our guess is that the score on the delayed test would have shown a main effect of anxiety and no interaction.

Evaluative conditions

Evaluation by an instructor and evaluation by computer were contrasted by Gallagher (1970). A graduate-level course on the subject of PI was adapted for teaching by computer. One treatment variable was the sequence of tasks, which was predetermined or else left to the student's own preferences. Interactions of this variable were not studied. Instructor evaluation and computer evaluation were applied in each sequence condition. In instructor evaluation, such student products as list of behavioral objectives were judged by a teaching assistant; in computer evaluation, the products "were evaluated by the students themselves via an interactive dialogue with the computer. Upon completion of the interaction, the students passed or failed themselves on the particular product." The 59 students were tested after they completed the prescribed units. Examination means in the four treatments differed little. The information relevant to ATI was presented in the form of zero-order correlations of personality measures with outcome, within treatments. *Trait-A had a strong negative relation to outcome in the "instructor-evaluated" group and a near-zero relation in the self-evaluation group.* It appears that the instructor evaluation (possibly stressful) promoted learning of the Low-A's and that the computer-cum-self-evaluation procedure promoted learning of High-A's.

Schultz and Dangel (in Di Vesta *et al.,* 1971, pp. 225–243; see also p. 418 above) classified students as extreme facilitators/debilitators and required them to study a text. *S*s were told that they would later recite on three out of a set of 18 questions provided to guide their study. The climate during the recitation was made threatening/sustaining by the emphasis placed on evaluation and by withholding/giving praise after each response. Finally, half the *S*s in each cell were asked for verbatim recall, while half were free to paraphrase the text. As there were only 12 *S*s per condition, the study was not powerful. The students for whom FA $\gg$ DA did better under all conditions, save that the difference nearly vanished in the sustaining climate where students were free to paraphrase; this was, of course, the least stressful condition. And *the largest regression slope appeared in the most stressful condition.*

Others have also demonstrated interactions for supportive comments/neutral (or disparaging) comments. The traditional studies have serious faults both as research and as guides to school practice, and we shall give them little space. But the group of studies takes on added interest because of its prominence in Bracht's survey. Bracht (1969) attempted to sift out of the entire literature the investigations that had demonstrated unmistakable disordinal ATI. He located only five studies that met his debatable standards (see our p. 93, 495). Two of the five —Thompson and Hunnicutt, van de Riet—are praise/blame studies.

False reports are given to *S* in these experiments. For purposes of the experiment *S* is led to believe, perhaps over a period of days or weeks, that he is doing badly —whether he actually is or not. One could not defend this procedure as an educational tactic even if it "works well," and one cannot defend the ethics of such experimentation.

The ethical difficulty is especially apparent in the study of Means and Means (1971), which happens to have dealt with ability rather than anxiety. They administered an aptitude test to 72 undergraduates at the start of a course in adolescent psychology, then fed back false information. Certain randomly chosen *S*s were told individually that they had high aptitude for the course; others were told that they had low aptitude, and still another subset were told nothing. On the first course examination, eight weeks later, there was a significant ATI. Groups high and low on previous GPA were contrasted. *The high GPA student did best when told that he lacked aptitude.* This same discouraging information depressed results for Lows. Another study on ability rather than anxiety is that of van de Riet (1964). *S* received praise/reproof/no comment (regardless of his score) following one PA task. A subsequent task of the same sort provided the criterion. *S*s were 90 preadolescent boys who had been classified as normal achievers and underachievers. The underachievers did much worse than normals on the baseline task. There was no change on the second task if no comment had been made.

Following praise, the normals improved whereas the underachievers did much worse than before. Reproof caused underachievers to improve whereas normal achievers declined. After reproof, the underachievers outperformed the normals, but not significantly. The effects were large and contradictory to those of Means and Means.

Perhaps most famous is the praise/blame study of Thompson and Hunnicutt (1944). Sixth-graders (N = 124) were classified as introvert/extrovert. (Persons scored as introvert on a questionnaire of that period probably would also score as comparatively anxious.) Ss worked on a cancellation task; any learning was of a trivial nature, and the treatment may chiefly have affected effort. In one class, the teacher put G ("good") each day on the cancellation paper of each introvert and P ("poor") on that of each extrovert. In a second class, this was reversed. After three days, the scores began to show a significant differential effect. *Discouragement stimulated extroverts and held back introverts (High-A's?). Encouragement had the opposite effect.* But we must note also the even briefer study of Forlano and Axelrod (1937). Their discouraging feedback stimulated both extroverts and introverts.

Rim (1965) adopted the same technique: six trials of a cancellation task, each trial followed by praise for each individual in some groups, by criticism in other groups. Interactions of Neuroticism and Extroversion were examined. Out of 143 Ss Rim gave data for only 113, including 24 controls. *Results were strikingly better for criticized* extroverts. There was no difference for introverts. Performance following praise tended to correlate negatively with N, the Highs doing much better in the "blame" condition than the "praise" condition. Again we note that the Eysenck scale used by Rim defines Introversion to be independent of N.

Readers interested in the praise-blame problem will want to examine the complex findings of Grace (1948). She had only 54 Ss, assessed on nine personality measures, in a short and artificial treatment. She put each S through each condition, with counterbalanced order. Some evidence indicates that the *well-adjusted responded to praise* and the ill-adjusted to reproof.

The next four studies to be considered avoided ethical difficulties either by restricting any evaluation to signals legitimate in the classroom or by leaving negative evaluation out of the design.

The study of Morris *et al.* (1970), was handsomely planned, analyzed, and reported, and extensively discussed; unfortunately, it used a microminiature treatment. PI on English coinage was prepared (for Canadian students) in large-step/small-step versions. Because lack of motivation is troublesome in PI, the investigators sought to arouse motivation by giving students a 20-item pretest and telling them that they had done well. A second group took the pretest but were told that their papers had not yet been scored. A third group filled the pretest time with irrelevant work. N = 252 sixth-graders. The analysis was a 2 x 3 x 3 anova for each program and test. There was an A x Treatment effect—*absence of pretest served High-A's best; pretest with encouragement served Low-A's best.* This result was obtained only with the small-step program. The IQ x A x Treatment interaction was negligible.

Table 12.5   Interactions of variation in incentives or evaluation: Summary

Name of one investigator and our page number	Ss per treatment (approx.)[a]	Treatments judged most/least stressful or arousing	Trait representing defensive motivation[b]	Slope comparison[c]	Remarks
Meyers (p. 426)	45(90)	EI, "shift"/NEI nonshift	A	±	Can be seen as classical arch result.
Tobias-Abramson, (p. 419)	25(75)	EI/NEI	DA	–	This result on easy program only, for reading and for response with feedback only.
Caron (p. 432)	120	Arousal of desire to achieve/curiosity only	TA-nAch	?	ATI present but complexly patterned.
Sinclair (p. 432)	85	EI/NEI	?	+ 0	Classical "arch" for recall. No ATI on transfer test.
Silberman (p. 432)	24	EI/NEI	TA	+	Found on easy program only.
Blatt (p. 432)	20	Evaluative/play	TA	+	
Kipnis (p. 433)	100	Incentive/minimal EI	Persistence	+	
Pagano (p. 436)	35(70)	EI/NEI with stress reduction	TA	0	Unexplained V-shaped regression.

Study	N	Treatment	Variable	Code	Comment
Gallagher (p. 433)	15	Teacher evaluation/computer-aided self-judgment	A	+	
Schultz (p. 434)	12	Threat, no comment/sustaining climate plus praise, freedom to paraphrase	DA > FA	+	
Thompson (p. 435)	60	Criticism/praise	I/E	+	
Forlano (p. 435)	?	Criticism/praise	I/E	0	
Rim (p. 435)	60	Criticism/praise	I/E N	+ -	Criticism advantageous to neurotic extrovert.
Grace (p. 435)	50	Criticism/praise	Various	-	
Morris (p. 435)	40	Pretest not scored/no pretest	A	+	This result for easy program only.
Leith (p. 438)	40	Reproof/praise	I/E, N	0	Treatment continued for 11 weeks.
Clifford (p. 438)	15	Various	?	?	ATI may have been present.
Frederiksen (p. 438)	130	Reference standard/no standard	TA	0	Effect weak and inconsistent.

[a] N in parentheses pools Ss within an instructional mode, in a 2 x 2 or 2 x 3 array of treatments.

[b] I/E indicates Introversion (contrasted with Extroversion). A refers to versions of the Taylor scale or the trait score of the State-Trait Anxiety Inventory

[c] Code
+ if there was a greater slope of performance vs. A or other measure of defensive motivation in the less-stressful treatment.
− if there was a greater slope of performance vs. A or other measure of defensive motivation in the more-stressful treatment.
± if results were mixed.
0 if slopes were similar.
? not classifiable.

Leith and T. Davis (1969; see also Davis & Leith, 1969) taught logarithms over an 11-week period to 127 boys by means of PI. Imbedded in the program were about two comments per lesson carrying a message of praise following a sequence of answers, or implicit reproof ("You should have got them all right.") These comments were standard, not contingent on what responses the student made. There were, then, positive/negative/neutral groups. Extroversion and Neuroticism as measured by Hallworth's questionnaire showed *no hint of ATI*. The main effect (positive comments advantageous) did not emerge until the second month of the instruction.

It is especially appropriate to vary the extent to which actual errors are pointed out by the teacher. This calls for veridical reports to *S*, and if ATI were found with this variable one could suggest a practicable, ethical classroom policy. The only such study we have located (Clifford, 1971) administered the noninstructional digit-symbol task under neutral conditions and later readministered it under one of seven experimental conditions. (E.g., *S* competed with three others and was to receive a reward—genuinely earned—if he outdid them.) The aptitude score came from a pretest on the task, blocked into four levels. Outcome was measured by gain. *It seems likely that interactions were present.* But the analysis had weak data (*N* = 112, divided over seven groups) and Clifford's null hypotheses were complex.

Hypotheses about A, and surprising results in a pilot study, led N. Frederiksen and F. Evans (1972) to make an experimental contrast between an implicitly evaluative condition and a nonevaluative condition. *S*'s task was to formulate hypotheses to explain a chart or other data. In the modeling condition, *S* wrote his list, read a list of answers others had given, and revised his list; by this means he was implicitly reassured that he was free to offer far-out ideas, or was implicitly given a standard against which his own responses appeared weak. There were three experimental treatments: quality model/quantity model/no model. A previous study (Klein, Frederiksen, & Evans, 1969; *N* = 127) had employed only the quantity model. The regression of outcome (judged by the response before revision, but influenced by models encountered on previous subtasks) had the shape of an inverted arch. In the main study with 395 *S*s, vocabulary, ideational fluency, and TA were tested. Nearly all the correlations of these aptitudes with outcome measures were low. An unusual and sophisticated application of multivariate analysis of covariance demonstrated a significant main effect (quantity model beneficial) and a weak tendency for the Low-anxious to do better (all treatments pooled). The interaction of TA was significant for only one of several indices of performance, a quality measure. *Both kinds of model helped the Low-A's* and gave poorer results for the Middle- and High-A's. There was also a Sex x Vocabulary interaction.

Summary and interpretation

Again we summarize in a table some salient features of the loosely related studies. It is especially difficult here to classify treatments. It is reasonable to think of the threatening treatments as arousing the motive to avoid failure. But are treatments that induce positive emotional tone more arousing than neutral conditions, or less arousing?

We checked, as best we could, the results on the hypothesis that added incentive or pressure is advantageous (or less disadvantageous) for the defensive person. In the first section of the table, where the treatment variable is some form of ego-involving injunction, the results are mixed. There are V-shaped and arch-shaped regressions and interactions that vary from one part of a study to another. Our impression, based on the original reports rather than our necessarily brief accounts, is that EI/NEI and Anxiety probably do interact. But it seems critically important to continue in the theoretically sophisticated vein of of the Caron and Sinclair studies, and to check for curvilinear interactions and for joint effects of Anxiety, nAch, and ability. Our recurrent appeal for educationally realistic experiments applies here with special force.

Results on praise, criticism, and similar variables are not impressive. The scattered findings of interaction amount to little; nearly all studies are small and the questions addressed appear to be superficial. Though several studies had interesting features, we perceive few leads for ATI research.

All in all it appears that two decades of thinking about anxiety and arousal have not yet brought the phenomena under control so that effects can be predicted and replicated. We do not conclude that anxiety, introversion, and the like fail to interact with motivational conditions. Rather, the conclusion seems to be that the effects are conditioned by many other aspects of the experimental situation and possibly by additional characteristics of the person.

The only proper last word on the rich but diverse findings of this chapter is a remark made by the old master a long time ago. Said Kenneth Spence (1958, p. 137):

> In order to derive implications concerning the effects of drive variation [i.e., of A and treatment] in any type of complex learning task, it is necessary to have, in addition to the drive theory, a further theoretical network concerning the variables and their interaction that are involved in the particular learning activity.

Chapter 13 | Student personality and the environment for learning

Chapter 10 examined interactions of ability with instructor style. The present chapter considers instructor style as it interacts with personality variables. We again encounter conflicting results, both because of the diversity of measuring instruments and treatments and because of variations from classroom to classroom. As in Chapter 12, we shall find that personality variables interact with remarkable frequency, but the findings are hard to integrate.

This chapter has been peculiarly difficult to organize; studies in one rubric frequently shed light on studies whose operational aspects were quite different. Approximately half the chapter will deal with constructive/defensive motivation. Studies in that section are arranged according to the age of the student group. (Perhaps the pattern of results shifts from level to level, though the evidence on that is not persuasive.) The second major section has to do with student sociability or need for affiliation. Effects associated with student attitudes, beliefs, and preferences are examined in the third section. The fourth section considers demographic variables (sex, socioeconomic status). Whereas the sections so far mentioned consider effects at the classroom level, interactions at the institutional level also arise. The last section of the chapter takes up research on institutional differences.

As prelude to our grand survey of results, we present two investigations. Domino describes as convincing and important a pattern of interaction as occurs anywhere in this book. The McKeachie study will display the technique of an important group and will report a suggestive result. While the replications yield inconsistent results, this equivocality is itself typical of the chapter as a whole.

Two exemplary investigations

Domino's work on Achievement through Independence

A pair of studies by Domino, one naturalistic and one experimental, produced consistent evidence of a powerful interaction: Achievement was better when the instructor encouraged the student's natural style. The instructors were differentiated with respect to their directiveness, i.e., the extent to which they set out work for the student and expected him to comply with external demands. Domino's aptitude variable was the contrast between Achievement through Conformity and Achievement through Independence. In both studies, Domino administered the California Personality Inventory (CPI) and scored it for just two scales: Achievement through Independence (Ai), and Achievement through Conformity (Ac). The High-Ai describes himself as mature, foresighted, demanding, and self-reliant. The High-Ac describes himself as capable, efficient, organized, responsible, and sincere. These are favorable self-concepts, different in kind. The student who conforms dutifully but cannot claim to be effective will score high on neither scale.

Domino's first study (1968) was nonexperimental. Domino interviewed the instructor of every course one of his Ss had taken, assessing how much that instructor emphasized memorization, attendance, objective examination, etc. Instructor tactics favorable to independent acts were also noted. Some 73 courses were classified as encouraging conformity, and 32 as encouraging independence. The grades the student had received were sorted according to the style of the course in which each grade was earned. This gave each student two grade averages.

In the end, Domino had four groups of 22 Ss each, matched on sex and on a nonverbal mental test. The four groups were chosen from the extreme corners of the Ac, Ai distribution. The grade averages were as shown in Table 13.1. The scale of grade averages being limited, the numerical differences did not appear to be great. But some effects were sizable. The High-High students received appreciably better grades than the Low-Lows. Those Low on Ai and High on Ac earned a higher average in structured courses; those with the High, Low pattern

Table 13.1   Student grades as a
               function of independence/conformity and instructor style

Student pattern on personality inventory	Average grade in courses where		
	Instructor encouraged independence	Instructor required conformity	Difference
High Ai, High Ac	3.3	3.0	0.3
High Ai, Low Ac	2.7	2.5	0.2
Low Ai, High Ac	2.4	2.7	− 0.3
Low Ai, Low Ac	2.1	2.3	− 0.2

After Domino, 1968.

did better where they could be independent. It is to be regretted that only the 88 cases at the corners of the Ai, Ac distribution (out of 348) were treated.

Domino's 1971 experiment again used extreme groups. Among sophomores enrolling in introductory psychology, Domino identified 50 High on Ai and Low on Ac, and 50 with the opposite pattern. These groups were divided in half, so that 25 students with a common pattern could be assigned to a section of the course—making four sections, two of each type. An instructor (who did not know the basis for assigning students) agreed to teach two sections in the style that encourages independence, and two in the formal, structured style that demands conformity. Six outcome measures were available. Because it is difficult to hold several distinct numerical scales in mind, we have converted the outcome means given by Domino. We express each as a percentage of the mean in whichever section did best. Table 13.2 gives these rescaled means.

Measures a through d of achievement are probably the most important. The results in Section 1 were definitely best. Section 3 was a close runner-up (except on measure c, where conforming students were unable to show good original

Table 13.2   Six outcomes of a psychology course under four combinations of Personality x Treatment

	Independent students (High Ai, Low Ac)		Conforming students (Low Ai, High Ac)	
	Section 1		Section 4	
Instructor encourages independence	a	95	a	82
	b	100	b	75
	c	99	c	65
	d	100	d	66
	e	100	e	81
	f	100	f	84
	Section 2		Section 3	
Instructor requires conformity	a	89	a	100
	b	85	b	100
	c	100	c	59
	d	83	d	89
	e	93	e	96
	f	82	f	94

Data from Domino, 1971. For each outcome, 100 was assigned arbitrarily to the group with the highest mean, and other means were scaled proportionately.
List of outcomes:
  a. Score on multiple-choice, factual final examination.
  b. Rated quality of knowledge shown in essay final examination.
  c. Rated quality of original thinking in essay final examination.
  d. Grade in psychology course (assigned by instructor without reference to final examination).
  e. Student rating of effectiveness of teacher.
  f. Student rating of excellence of course.

thinking no matter how they were taught). While not all the differences between groups were large, there was a significant interaction effect on every outcome except c. *High-Ai's did best when the instructor's style favored independence; High-Ac's when he favored conformity.*

McKeachie's work on Need for Power

McKeachie's naturalistic study of Need for Power is midway between the two Domino studies in technique (see McKeachie, Isaacson, & Milholland, 1964, Sec. VI-A-3; secondary account in McKeachie, 1961, p. 129f.). Most of the data were collected within sections of a single psychology course. Instructors were observed and then classified as encouraging/not-encouraging students to volunteer questions and comments in class. Need for Power was measured by a projective technique.

The work is fairly typical of the program of McKeachie and his associates which will receive much attention in this chapter. The reports have appeared in a strangely fragmented form, data collected on the same *S*s being distributed over several independent papers. Only secondary accounts of most of this work (McKeachie,

---

Table 13.3   Success of male students as a function of
***n* Power and opportunity for voluntary remarks in class**

Study	Course	Criterion	Need for Power	Per cent who did well when teacher style		Support ATI?
				did "fit"	did not "fit"	
I	French,	Grades	High	45% (55)[a]	31% (39)	Yes
	mathematics,		Low	46% (41)	30% (56)	Yes
	psychology;					
	pooled					
II	Psychology	Grades	High	50% (58)	47% (66)	No?
			Low	51% (69)	45% (69)	Yes
	Psychology	Objective	High	61% (51)	51% (56)	Yes
		test	Low	58% (59)	48% (54)	Yes
		Higher-order	High	47% (62)	49% (71)	No
		test	Low	52% (73)	47% (76)	No?

Data from McKeachie *et al.*, 1964, VI-A-3.

[a]Read: 45 per cent of 55 men with high *n* Power earned good grades when in a class where student comments were encouraged.

1958, 1961, 1963) have reached a large audience; the few published primary reports are by no means comprehensive. We rely chiefly on two ERIC reports which give hundreds of pages of detailed information (McKeachie *et al.*, 1964; McKeachie, Milholland, *et al.*, 1968). In 1958, for what came to be called Study I, data were collected from large classes in French, mathematics, and psychology. Study II collected data in 16 large psychology classes in 1961. We shall discuss in other contexts a companion Study III conducted in 1963, also on psychology classes.

The grade distribution in each class was divided near the median, and the proportion of students earning good grades was determined within groups classified on Need for Power. The first row of Table 13.3 indicates that, among Highs whose instructors encouraged comments or questions, 45 per cent earned superior grades, compared to 31 per cent among Highs having more dominant instructors. McKeachie's statistical analysis, though weak, indicated that some of the differences were significant. The general trend of the findings was in the hypothesized direction: better achievement of Highs when the instructor allowed self-assertion, and of Lows when he did not. But the effect does not seem to have been large or consistent.

It will be noted that these data are for males only. The reports gave no data on women, saying that no interaction was found among them. In another instance where the Michigan group concluded that there was interaction in one sex only (see p. 473), we judge that the effect was present in both sexes. We therefore reserve judgment as to whether sex moderated the effect of Need for Power.*

Interactions of constructive and defensive motivation

Motivational variables to be examined

It is necessary to aggregate findings about somewhat distinct personality characteristics, if we are not to abandon all effort at synopsis. Thus, we are prepared to emphasize the parallelism of the Domino and McKeachie studies; in both, students who were more ready to take initiative benefited from an opportunity to take that initiative. But to assert that the two studies confirmed each other would be rash, in view of the differences in technique. This problem of comprehending results from unlike variables will be with us throughout this chapter.

---

*A report (which ignored instructor style) reported the within-sex correlations for Ai and Ac with grades in Study I (see McKeachie, Milholland, *et al.*, 1968, p. II-10-5). The respective r's for men in psychology were 0.20 and 0.37, compared to 0.03 and 0.10 for women. In mathematics, the r's for men were 0.21 and 0.03. These and other correlations call into question the pooling of three courses.

The pages to come will again deal with the measures of trait anxiety in the Taylor tradition and with other "defensive" traits. We suspect that the A scale has much in common with Ac and with a questionnaire measure of Dependency used by Flanders, though we know of no correlational evidence. Perhaps Need for Order, measured on the Edwards questionnaire by Bar-Yam, can also be interpreted as a defensive coping mechanism. We regard the Ac scale as defensive in a certain sense, though it identifies only the subset of conformers who get good results with that defense. Finally, we can regard unfavorable self-concepts as having something in common with anxiety.

In contrast to the defensive syndrome are measures such as Ai which bespeak a "constructive," confident, assertive, self-directing style. Need for Achievement (nAch) can be given this interpretation, but it may be necessary to distinguish the projective measure of it from the usual questionnaires. The Facilitating Anxiety (FA) score may or may not fit in this category; the high scorer is one who says that pressure stimulates him to do his best in academic settings. Some questionnaires provide a Responsibility score; this could be a cousin of either Achievement through Conformity or Achievement through Independence. The "opposers" identified as a type by Heil (p. 459) seem to represent another dimension, and his "strivers" may be functioning out of anxiety or out of enthusiasm for schoolwork. This roll-call of variables warns of the kaleidoscopic character of the findings to follow.

A third distinct category of variable encompasses Sociability, Need for Affiliation, and the like.

Studies of college instruction

As noted above, the Domino study of Ai/Ac and the McKeachie study of Need for Power gave somewhat similar results. The less defensive or more self-directing students seemed to do better under a less directive instructor. We now bring together a number of studies of college instruction which on the whole support the same conclusion. The results, however, are sometimes inconsistent within a single program of investigation, and a few studies bear on issues tangential to the generalization above. The studies in this section deal with the correspondence between outcomes and student personality under various kinds of instructor. Then we examine studies where the focus is on the student's perception of the instructor rather than the instructor's style. After that, we revert to direct tests of Personality x Style interactions, but in the elementary or secondary school. Studies at lower levels sometimes support and sometimes contradict the generalization suggested by the college studies.

Before turning to the Michigan program, we review experiments much like Domino's. Dowaliby (1971; see Dowaliby & Schumer, 1973) taught two sections of junior-college psychology (N = 68). In one section, he asked questions, encouraged students to question him, and had them participate in experimental demonstrations. In the other section, Dowaliby kept himself in the spotlight and allowed little student participation. The outcome measure consisted of two examinations based on the classwork. There was no treatment main-effect. Taylor A scores generated significant disordinal interactions. In the teacher-dominated class, the slope was flat or positive (with more A, more achievement). In the participative class, the slope was negative. On the whole, *the greater structure of the teacher-dominated class helped the High-A's.*

Domino (1974; see also p. 332) later replicated the Dowaliby-Schumer finding. College Ss in a literature course ($N = 83$) were divided into teacher-centered/student-centered sections, taught by the same instructor. Taylor Anxiety scores related to a composite of four examination scores as predicted: *High A Ss did better with teacher-centered instruction, while Low A Ss did better with student-centered instruction.* There was no average effect for treatment.

In another limited study, Bigelow and Egbert (1968) divided 89 Ss between conventional instruction in a "basic teacher-education course" and an independent-study procedure. In the latter, students came to the instructor only for tutorial help or tests. The criterion was a novel measure of change: Was the student's course grade higher than his prior GPA? Those who, studying independently, did better than they normally did tended to have high scores on CPI scales for Responsibility and Intellectual Efficiency. No mention was made of Ac or Ai or other CPI scales, in relation to achievement; presumably, this means that there was no significant relation for these scales. The sample was much too small for acceptance of any such null hypothesis, however.

Among the successful students in the experimental group, satisfaction with the technique went with low Sociability and low Socialization scores ("opposers"?). Bigelow and Egbert said that no significant personality differences appeared between successful students in traditional and successful students in independent study; but they gave no descriptive data on the comparison and no within-group data for the traditional group. The low power of the study leaves *the ATI question unanswered.*

Koenig and McKeachie (1959) compared a two-week period of independent study vs. two weeks of small-group discussion, both periods being embedded in a psychology course as a supplement to lectures. Each of the 124 Ss participated in both treatments, order being counterbalanced. The criterion was a rating of performance within each two-week segment. The main hypothesis was that independent students (as identified by the California Psychological Inventory) would do better when learning by independent study, while affiliative students (as identified by a modified TAT) would do better with discussion. There was, however, *no interaction*—or at least no significant relation of personality to course grades or to satisfaction. Personality scores other than Need for Affiliation had some relation to participation in discussion and to preferences regarding technique.

Pascal (see p. 477) also found that students preferring independent study differed on several personality variables from those who preferred to learn in a group.

Work of college psychology students in small teams was contrasted with conventional teaching by H. C. Smith (1955). Though he placed 48 Ss in each of the treatments, only 60 cases were available for examining interactions. The report was sketchy, and the significance test lacked power. Pretest-to-posttest gains in achievement showed *no ATI*. The Low-anxious were well satisfied with the lecture method and the High-anxious were dissatisfied; there was a shallower slope of the same kind with the team method. Those who (in advance) expressed strong interest in the team approach evidently learned less from that method than similar Ss did from the lecture. This finding of poor performance in a preferred method is based on data from only a single intact team.

Work at the University of Michigan

Many reports from McKeachie and his colleagues refer to measures of anxiety and motivation to achieve. McKeachie's 1961 paper (his p. 138) made brief reference to a finding on explicitness of standards without giving numerical data. Where the instructor made requirements clear, announced tests in advance, and corrected students' comments, performance of High-n Ach, Low-A students (constructives) declined. Low-low students (unmotivated?) apparently did well with highly structured demands. The High-High and Low-High groups seemingly showed little difference between treatments. Another secondary account (McKeachie, 1958, regarding a dissertation by Patton; also in McKeachie, 1963, pp. 1138, 1158) deals with a comparison of traditional teaching in two psychology classes with experimental teaching in two classes where there were no assessments, lectures, or tests. The experimental teacher left many decisions about course procedures and requirements to the students. The students who took the greatest responsibility learned the most and had the most favorable attitude; such students tended to be independent of authority and high in Need for Achievement. The superior performance of these students in less structured teaching and the inferior performance of the 1961 constructives with "direct" teaching is *consistent with the results of Dowaliby and Domino.*

Elsewhere, nAch and A were related to students' choices of curricula (Isaacson in McKeachie *et al.* 1964, Sec. V-C-1 and V-D-1; Isaacson, 1964). There was a *complex interactive relation* for men, generally supporting the prediction that men low in nAch and high in A will avoid courses of intermediate difficulty, whereas High-Low men will seek out such courses. (See also Helland & Isaacson, in McKeachie, Milholland, *et al.*, 1968, Sec. II-2.) There was no such patterning for women, a fact Isaacson attributed to the dubious validity of projective measures of nAch for women. As we are concerned with achievement rather than preference as a dependent variable, we shall not consider this finding further.

The interaction of nAch with treatment conditions in artificial experiments has been the theme of J. W. Atkinson's work at Michigan. A great volume of work at Michigan and elsewhere, much of it summarized by Atkinson and Feather (1966) or by Heckhausen (1967), has shown interactions, usually with manipulated risk as the treatment variable. A considerable theory has emerged that emphasizes the combination of nAch with A as a predictor. Out of this one might formulate hypotheses about educational treatments. The classroom studies of interactions of nAch, however, have generally not been closely linked to that theory, with the exception of the O'Connor-Atkinson-Horner study (p. 458).

The major reports of the McKeachie program strangely failed to examine how achievement relates to the combined nAch and A measures. All the studies covered by McKeachie in 1961 were included in later primary reports, *except* the contrast of constructives/defensives discussed above. In the larger reports and in a later journal article (McKeachie, Isaacson, Milholland, & Lin, 1968), nAch was treated by itself, never in conjunction with A.

In Study I (1968 data), the instructors were classed in three levels on the basis of student reports that the instructors did/did not set "very high standards" and that the students competed and felt challenged. Obviously, this "treatment variable" confounds student perception and student response with what the instructor did, but McKeachie *et al.* referred to the variable as "achievement cues." In Studies II and III, the variable was defined by student reports on only one item: "He maintained very definite standards of student performance." This sounds more like clarity of requirements than arousal of achievement motives.

The authors stated definite hypotheses about an expected contrast between the high and middle levels on nAch. They made no prediction for women because of the dubious meaning of nAch for them, nor did they predict regarding Low men. We consider it unwise to have stated the hypothesis in terms of thirds of the nAch distribution, since there was no *a priori* basis for expecting the effect to be associated with the 67th percentile rather than the 50th or 80th. Examination of the curvilinear regression, treating nAch as a continuum, would have better reflected the authors' theoretical speculations. Data were given for only 87 men in Mathematics and 65 in Psychology. (The N's were 145 and 85 when the same projective test data were scored on Need for Affiliation [p. 473]; data were discarded here for no visible reason.) There were only 35 men in French (and only 5 of those in the middle group). In mathematics, the grades were higher in low-achievement-cue sections; there was no interaction.

Among the 65 male psychology students in Study I and the 273 in Study II, no trend can be discerned in the 3 x 3 matrix. Among women also, no pattern can be perceived in the data. We concur with the 1964 report: *there was no interaction of nAch* with the rather different treatment variables of the two studies.

We are left with some puzzles. If we throw all courses in Study I and both sexes into a single 3 x 3 table ($N = 514$), there is a strong pattern, not of interaction, but of linear trends: higher grades with higher nAch and with lower degrees of achievement cueing. (There was no such trend in Study II.) McKeachie (1961, p. 136) had reported a significant interaction in a 2 x 2 table pooling all Study I data ($N = 583$); the good grades appeared in the cell where nAch was low and achievement cueing high. But this is the corner where grades were lowest in the 3 x 3 table! We cannot explain the contradiction, but we are inclined to regard it as further evidence that blocking a continuous trait measure can give utterly misleading results even with a large sample.

Another report on achievement cueing (McKeachie, in McKeachie, Milholland, *et al.*, 1968, Sec. II-8) considered the questionnaire measure of FA as a potentially interacting variable. This was interpreted as an indicator of response to pressure rather than of anxiety. The data came from Studies I, II, and III. Among women students in psychology (Studies II and III), High-FA's and Low-FA's did equally well (53 per cent A's and B's) under the so-called achievement-cueing condition. When instructor demand was low, the gain in achievement was very small for Highs (to 58 per cent) and the drop in achievement was large for Lows (to 37 per cent). *This near-ordinal ATI indicates that structure or challenge is valuable to those women who see themselves as poor in handling challenges.* McKeachie suggested that these Lows tended to lack motivation and so needed stimulation. In Study I, for three courses pooled, High-FA's did better regardless of cueing and there was no interaction. The report said that there was no ATI for men in any sample, but gave no data. We reserve judgment on the implied second-order interaction involving sex.

Achievement arousal also figured in an analysis of the DA score (McKeachie & Lin, 1969), using women's data from Studies I–III. The consistency of the three sets of data was impressive to the investigators. It will be recalled that the treatment variable changed from Study I to Studies II and III. For the purpose of publication, however, the data for 572 women were pooled. In Figure 13.1, we have combined High-A's and Low-A's whose instructors did little to arouse concern for achievement, as A had little to do with outcome in this condition. Low-ability, low-A students (who may need to be aroused by task difficulty) were not at their best with low cueing. We have no explanation for the disparity between able and average Ss with strong cueing. *The results, then, are difficult to reconcile with theory.* No mention was made of data for men.

Anxiety data from Study I also figured in a comparison of instructors who did/did not provide a clear organization for their courses. McKeachie (1961, p. 139) gave a secondary account of results for a subset of 108 men and women out of the 825 for whom at least partial data were collected (courses pooled). In a 3 x 3 x 2 analysis considering A, sex, and course organization, there was a "significant interaction." The cell means were highly irregular, and since each was based on about six cases, not worth interpreting. The study gave *no persuasive evidence for interaction,* but neither was it powerful enough to deny interaction.

Instructors were also classified with respect to their giving "anxiety cues." Student responses to two items—"emphasized grades," "made students feel afraid of him"—defined this treatment variable. Stakenas and Milholland (in McKeachie, Milholland, *et al.,* 1968, Sec. II-9) had data from 71 psychology classes, but they discarded about one-third of the sections where the level of anxiety cueing was moderate. There were clearly no ATI for FA, or DA, or for Ability x DA.

Stakenas (*ibid.,* Sec. II-14) surveyed nearly 1,000 students in 39 sections of introductory psychology in 1964 and nearly 500 students in 26 sections of

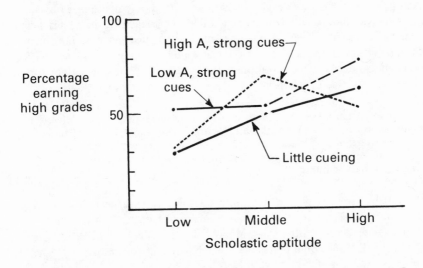

Figure 13.1.
**Grades of women in psychology as a function of anxiety,
ability, and instructor cueing for achievement.**
Data from McKeachie and Lin, 1969.

economics. He measured DA, ability, and study habits. Teachers were characterized
with respect to emphasis on grades, use of unannounced quizzes, and other
evidence of stress on evaluation. This was evidently seen as a combination of
achievement cueing and anxiety cueing. The sample was severely reduced (to 120
Ss) before an analysis of variance was made to test for interactions.

It is difficult to appraise this body of work. The data were extraordinary extensive, but the methods of analysis were weak and they changed from study to
study. The possibility that effects depend on nAch and DA jointly, or on ability
as well as personality, was not systematically pursued. Hints of Sex x Ability x
Personality x Treatment interactions appeared, yet this kind of hypothesis was
not formally examined. Constructive and defensive motivation may have interacted with achievement cueing, but the positive findings reported in 1961 were
not backed up by the later work. Student traits did not interact with the instructor's anxiety cueing. Stakenas and Milholland suggested that the semester-long
duration of a student's interaction with an instructor allows initial reactions
triggered by anxiety to adapt out.

Milholland (see McKeachie et al., 1964, Sec. VII) had done an inconclusive
pilot study on whether students do better under instructors they "match" in
personality. He was sufficiently encouraged to carry out a second, more elaborate
study with 190 Ss (Milholland & Swaminathan, in McKeachie, Milholland, et al.,

1968, Sec. II-13). Student responses to a Thematic Apperception Test were scored on nAch, n Aff, and nPower. Teachers were judged on several dimensions from ratings given by their previous classes, then arranged into pairs similar on four dimensions and moderately dissimilar on a fifth. Only eight of the 11 teachers could be paired by this rule. The outcome measure was a course grade or an achievement test with SAT partialed out. How many students entered any one test for interaction is not clear. We quote the author's reading of the interactions significant in at least one comparison:

> High nAch students do better with the teacher rated high on Culture whereas low nAch students do better with the medium-rated teacher.
> Men students . . . [with] medium n Aff did better with a teacher rated low on Overload whereas medium nAff women did better with a teacher rated medium.

Many variables were in play in this study, and only two teachers represented any one contrast in teacher style. No doubt teachers who differed on one dimension had other unrecognized differences. Milholland found the results discouraging to the thought that one could profitably "match" student personality to teacher personality. We have reviewed evidence (p. 332 ff.) suggesting that matching on ability may have value, and Milholland's evidence is too indirect to assess the value of matching on an ability-personality combination. But the multidimensionality of personality makes "matching" a slippery idea.

Studies of Instructional Media

Whereas the foregoing studies took teacher personality or style of teacher-student interaction as the treatment variable, another set of studies looked at teaching materials. In these studies, the style of individual teachers was not regarded as a systematic variable.

Oosthoek and Ackers (1973) compared the usual lecture instruction in microeconomics with instruction by audiotape. In the tape condition, the student could review any lecture or any part of a lecture as he wished, after first hearing the whole tape in a group session. As we see it, the taped instruction was less demanding, both because of its flexibility and because the tapes were organized more logically. The aptitude variables were DA, nAch, and attainment in a prior course in macroeconomics. Data on nAch and DA were available for about 120 Ss. The system of the University left the student free to appear for examination or to waive credit and not appear. Students learning from the tape were more likely to appear; this offsets the finding that the average examination mark was higher in the lecture treatment. Such differential loss of Ss makes it hard to use the examination data as evidence of interactions.

The self-reported class attendance of students was positively related to nAch in the tape group, negatively related in the conventional treatment. But *no inter-*

Table 13.4   **Examination means for law students receiving taped and live lectures**

Ability	Debilitating anxiety	N's	Medium of lecture		Difference
			Tape	Live	
High	High	34, 33	12.26	9.85	2.41
	Low	19, 31	11.58	11.35	0.23
Low	High	20, 22	9.25	9.41	- 0.16
	Low	24, 30	9.96	8.30	1.66
Combined	High	54, 55	11.14	9.67	1.47
	Low	43, 61	10.68	9.85	0.83
High	Combined	53, 64	12.02	10.58	1.44
Low		44, 52	9.64	8.77	0.87

After Oosthoek and Ackers, 1973.

action between nAch and treatment appeared, with examination mark as dependent variable. There was some hint of a second-order interaction involving ability. Students high on DA did a little better when taught by tape; they had been more inclined than others to listen to the tape repeatedly. The slope of the regression of outcome on ability (judged from earlier work in macroeconomics) was positive, and about the same in both treatments. By the original analysis the Ability x DA x Treatment interaction was significant. The examination means appear in Table 13.4.

The tape method was especially beneficial to the able High-A's and the dull Low-A's. The reader may recall that these are the groups who seemed to benefit from Tobias' scrambled program (p. 403). Insofar as the two very different kinds of demand can be compared, the findings are directly contradictory.

Oosthoek and Ackers next adopted a suggestion from an earlier report by us, and differentiated students with "constructive motivation" (high *nAch*, low DA) from "defensives" who had the opposite pattern. Although the simple comparison of these groups showed no appreciable interaction, significant interaction appeared when ability was also taken into account. *Among able students, the defensives benefited when the lectures were on tape, whereas constructives did equally well in both treatments. Among low-ability students the tape method helped constructives* and there was no difference for defensives. This analysis of extreme groups was based on a small sample. Our methodological preference would be to test the Ability x DA x nAch x Treatment interaction by stepwise regression, using all cases.

In Snow's study (1963; see p. 274), 437 undergraduates studied filmed/live demonstrations in a semester-long physics course and took immediate and delayed achievement tests. Snow had predicted that scores on Responsibility (which may be much the same psychologically as Gough's Ac) would interact with treatment. In fact, disordinal interactions appeared for Ascendancy as well as for Responsibility. The more ascendant, assertive students (high Ai?), and those describing themselves as least responsible (low Ac?), profited more from live demonstrations. The more submissive, responsible students (High Ac's?) seem to have been somewhat better off with film. This suggests that filmed instruction requires some degree of self-disciplined attention, whereas in live instruction social stimulation can control attention.

A college biology course was taught by an "audiotutorial" system in which students worked independently, at their own pace, with quasiprogrammed exercises, audiovisual presentations, and miniature research projects (Szabo, 1969). In this system, as in that of Oosthoek, the student was free to spend more or less time on the course. There was no control group, but grades in a second biology course taken by many of these same students provided data for a contrasting treatment. That second course was taught by traditional lecture-cum-laboratory methods.

Szabo saw his study as primarily an attempt to improve prediction by using multiple predictors. He and J. W. Asher had previously carried out an unpublished evaluation in high-school physics. According to Szabo (his p. 25), six cognitive tests predicted course grade with R 0.22 in the audiotutorial course and with R 0.78 in conventional physics. (The two criteria may not have been comparable.) Instead of perceiving an ATI issue in this result, Szabo argued that the audiotutorial course might be a setting where personality measures would enhance prediction.

For over 600 students in the audiotutorial biology course Szabo had data on abilities, prior grades, ratings by high-school counselors, and Guilford-Zimmerman personality dimensions. The sample was split for purposes of crossvalidation. Szabo reduced his original set of 31 predictors, discarding those whose zero-order r's were not at least weakly significant. His Table 21 reports standardized regression weights as follows in the conventional ("second") course:

0.135 Restraint (GZ) + 0.185 SAT-V + 0.169 CEEB-Science
+ 0.103 Counselor Rating + 0.259 Math Grade (h.s.).

($R = 0.54$). No crossvalidation was carried out in the conventional course. In the audiotutorial course, the corresponding equation was:

0.170 Restraint + 0.161 SAT-V + 0.185 CEEB-Mathematics
+ 0.180 Social Studies Grade (h.s.) + 0.176 Prior Grade Average
− 0.120 Ascendance (GZ) + 0.104 Counselor Rating

($R = 0.63$. We did not include here one weight, for a second-order variable, that is surely a chance finding). In the crossvalidation for the audiotutorial course, only the first five variables had significant weights.

The regressions in the two courses differed little. To be sure, the variables in

the two equations are not identical, but many of the predictors were highly correlated and hence the substitutions mean little. We conclude that there was *no
evidence of interaction* in this study.

Student perception of the teacher as an interacting variable

The person investigating classroom climate or teacher style ordinarily looks
upon that variable as an objective property of the instructional situation, even
when he uses student reports as his source of evidence. Such information, aggregated at the group level, may be as much an indicator of group morale as it is
a veridical report on what the instructor did. Although the studies in Chapter 10
and those reviewed above considered only the aggregated student ratings, one can
also consider the report of the student individually, as a phenomenal description
of the treatment as he experienced it. His perceptions may directly reflect his
personality or may themselves be products of a Personality x Treatment interaction. Thus, J. Goldberg (1968) found that more compulsive students typically
perceived their teacher to be less authoritarian than low compulsives did.
Presumably the Highs found such teaching compatible and so gave more positive
ratings. Moreover, such students have reported that they do more work for
teachers perceived as authoritarian, while low-compulsives said they work harder
for teachers they call nonauthoritarian. Unfortunately, the analysis did not
separate one classroom from another, so the meaning of the results is obscure.
In the limited study of Weiss, Sales, and Bode (1970; 36 students, 2 teachers),
"authoritarian" students gave comparatively unfavorable ratings to the less
"authoritarian" teacher and received poorer grades from that teacher.

Several substantial studies suggest that variation in students' perceptions of
teachers account for at least as much variance as actual differences between
teachers. The clearest demonstration is a study of Dowaliby and Schumer (1973).
We described above (p. 446) their experimental study in which a teacher taught
in two styles. In their second study, the treatment was held constant, the
teacher conducting the class in a style that blended the dominant and participative
techniques of the experimental study.

Midway in the term, anxiety was assessed and the students ($N = 51$) also
responded on a seven-point scale of agreement/disagreement to "I would rate this
as a lecture-type class." Discarding cases who gave responses in the middle of this
scale reduced N to 30. Hard though it is to believe, *this "treatment variable"
produced essentially the same interaction* as the true manipulation of the first
study. Tested achievement was the outcome. Even with the tiny sample, some
of the results reached statistical significance. Cause-effect relations are hard to
disentangle here, but the pair of findings is fascinating. All that was neglected was
to determine, in the true experiment, whether those anxious Ss who did badly
in the teacher-dominated class *thought* they were in an interactive class.

This finding has to be weighed when interpreting studies where teachers were
categorized as—for example—cueing for achievement on the basis of student

perception. Most of the Michigan studies, and that of Bar-Yam, used the perceptual data as if they were veridical accounts of the treatment variable.

A small experiment with PA learning (76 college Ss, up to 30 trials on a list of 45 pairs) was conducted by Karabenick and Z. Youssef (1968). Three sublists of equal difficulty were prepared. But Ss were told by a color code that some pairs were easy to learn, some hard, and some intermediate. In accord with the Atkinson theory, it was predicted that persons with strong defensive motivation (High A, along with Low nAch) would avoid items of intermediate difficulty. Number of pairs correct, on the first ten runs through the composite list, showed little difference between lists for Low-Low or Low-High personality patterns. The L-H and H-L groups did not depart reliably from the overall mean on the "easy" and "hard" lists. But on the supposedly intermediate list there was *a significant interaction in the predicted direction:* better performance for constructives. This, like the Dowaliby-Schumer study, argues that student perception of a treatment is as important as the treatment *per se.*

An elaborate study of 33 teachers and 987 grade-school students was made by Cogan (1954). The student rated the teacher on a number of items which were scored in three categories: inclusive, that is to say nurturant and integrative; preclusive, that is to say hostile and dominating; and conjunctive, which has to do with orderliness, clarity, and level of demand. The chief dependent variables were the student's own report as to how much required work he did, and how much self-initiated work relevant to the classwork. The student gave all this information at the same time, which allowed his response set to raise the correlation between his description of his teacher and his description of himself. The simultaneous measurement of both variables precluded any inference regarding the direction of causation. Cogan did an unusually thorough analysis, presenting a composite chart that included the within-class regression slope for every class—e.g., relating pupil's report of self-initiated work to the degree of inclusiveness he attributed to his teacher. There were *appreciable differences in slope from class to class.* On the whole, pupils who perceived the teacher as inclusive and conjunctive did more work for that teacher, but this correlation ranged above 0.60 in some classes and was close to zero under other teachers.

An equally large investigation by H. B. Reed, Jr. (1959), in much the same pattern, also found large differences in slope. Here again, student descriptions of the teacher were collected late in the year, simultaneously with the information on interest in science that was the dependent variable. The student description of his teacher was scored for warmth, demand, and reliance on intrinsic motivation. The aggregate rating for warmth and motivating technique did correlate (over classes) with mean student interest. The hypothesis that an intermediate level of demand would elicit greatest interest was not confirmed. Reed accepted the hypothesis that within-class slopes did not differ significantly, and it is true that in the majority of classes the slope (e.g., of pupil interest on teacher warmth) was much the same as the average within-class slope. But in several classes there was a steep positive slope, much larger than the average slope; and in several classes the slope was close to zero. The failure of these *conspicuous differences in slope* to reach significance is inevitable, given the limited number of students in any one class.

The Cogan and Reed studies pioneered some techniques of analysis potentially important for ATI work. The findings strongly suggest that, with a fixed teacher style, students react differently, and that these differences influence effort and possibly amount learned. To check such an hypothesis one would need to collect objective data on teacher style, assess the pupil's perception, assess the pupil's performance as independently as possible—and repeat the study the following year on those teachers who show markedly large and small slopes. Year-to-year consistency of the slopes would support the hypothesis and would warrant an attempt to characterize the teacher differences that produced the slopes.

A confusing but imaginative study by Rosenwein combined the theme of student perception of the instructor with the notion of "matching" student and instructor (in McKeachie, Milholland, *et al.*, 1968, Sec. II-5). Rosenwein had working hypotheses a good deal more subtle than either a recommendation to place like persons together or a recommendation to let the student pick the instructor whose style he admires. The following hypothesis is representative: *If* a student wants a warm instructor, and *if* his IQ is high, and *if* he has an instructor whom he perceives as lacking warmth, then he will earn higher grades than a similar student who perceives his instructor as warm (i.e., who is "satisfied"). Rosenwein used data on over 500 psychology students that had been collected in the McKeachie investigations. Each student had been asked to describe characteristics desired in an instructor and, at the end of the course, to describe his section leader.

When he finished tabulating the data, Rosenwein had made a total of 64 significance tests. Reportedly, 11 interactions were significant ($p < .05$). The results had no resemblance to the hypotheses, however; effects varied with sex, with the instructor characteristic rated, etc. The nearest to consistent results were for persons high on A and persons low on n Affiliation. The results were as follows for the High-A's:

If they wanted a warm instructor, *and* perceived their instructor as warm,	men did better (than those who perceived their instructor as cold); women showed no difference.
If they cared little about warmth, *and* perceived their instructor as warm,	both sexes did better; significant for women.
If they wanted clarity of structure, *and* perceived their instructor as giving structure,	men did worse; women showed no difference.
If they cared little about structure, *and* perceived their instructor as giving structure,	both sexes did better; significant for women.

The picture for Low n Aff was much the same (see p. 472). It is hard to know what to make of these results, but *we are inclined to think that genuine, complex ATI were present.* Rosenwein's significance test was very weak, which means that he gave long odds to the null hypothesis. There were in all about 28 instructors and 300 Ss; even this does not give satisfactory power for testing these relations, especially as the sign test was the final arbiter. All in all, it does not appear that the student benefits when given the kind of instructor he says he wants.

Evidence at the elementary level

Most of the studies of instruction of children have employed techniques and variables unlike those at the college level. The study most nearly akin to the college studies is that of O'Connor, J. W. Atkinson, and Horner (see Atkinson & Feather, 1966). They hypothesized on the basis of Atkinson's theory that ability grouping of classes would increase the interest and perhaps the achievement of students high in nAch and low in TA.

Initially, a retrospective pseudoexperiment in a secondary school (J. W. Atkinson & O'Connor, 1963) produced little positive evidence on the main hypothesis. Students who had spent three years in ability-grouped instruction in mathematics were studied as ninth-graders, and later at the end of high school where the superior ones had taken advanced-placement courses. The control group consisted of students finishing high school when the experimentals were in Grade 9; this group had not been subjected to full-scale ability grouping. There were about 250 students in the study.

Among boys of high ability, those with positive motivation (high on nAch-minus-TA) in the control cohort earned better high-school grades than those in the experimental cohort. Those with defensive motivation did better if in the experimental cohort. There was no interaction among low-ability Ss. *Grouping was disadvantageous for able, constructive boys*—contrary to hypothesis. This finding was not statistically significant, as only 74 Ss entered the calculation.

Since the projective measure of nAch was unstable on a retest of girls, it was dropped from the analysis of achievement. The relation of TA to achievement was the same (slightly negative) in grouped and ungrouped classes. There was *no interaction effect* on high-school girls.

The second study was again an uncontrolled experiment contrasting cohorts in different years. This work, covered both in the 1963 and 1966 reports, used data from sixth-grade classes whose members ($N = 436$) had been in undifferentiated groups during Grade 5. Grouping seemed to bring no net benefit or loss for defensive and intermediate Ss. The "regular" stratum of the grouping system included students of all IQs up to 125 in the same class. The middle-ability students (high within their "homogeneous" class) did better than similar ungrouped controls at all levels of motivation. Finally, among the limited number of low-ability Ss, those with constructive motivation benefited from grouping; there was no clear benefit or loss for the others. This is an *ordinal Ability* x *Motivation* x *Grouping interaction reasonably consistent with the Atkinson theory.*

This ordinal effect was possibly contaminated by ceiling effects and other artifacts.

As for the effect on interest, there seems to have been a disordinal interaction. *In homogeneous classes, reported interest in school was much higher among constructives than among defensives.* In heterogeneous classes, there was no relation. This analysis too would have been improved by bringing in additional pretests, by not residualizing, and by examining within-class regressions. To interpret these findings one would need to know how the teachers handled classes—particularly, to what extent competition was stressed in each class.

The contrast between constructive and defensive motivation was exploited brilliantly in an early large-scale study by Heil, Powell, and Feifer (1960). Fifty teachers and their fourth- to sixth-grade classes were studied. On the basis of a questionnaire whose interpretation verged on the psychoanalytic, teacher personalities were classed as "turbulent," "self-controlling," and "fearful." The first group seems to be characterized better as spontaneous—at least in behavior—than as turbulent; in the classroom, they were rated high on all counts: responsive, effective, stimulating (but not particularly consistent). The second group were submissive, ambitious, keeping their impulses in check; in the classroom, they were consistent and devoted, but dull. The fearful teachers were responsible and tended to be child-centered, but they were not responsive to events in the classroom. Heil's typology does not match that of the college studies, but it appears that the spontaneous teachers were both more stimulating and more supportive. In order to reach consistent results, Heil found it necessary to divide teachers using each style into superior and inferior subgroups; the superior teachers were observed to be warmer and more democratic.

The children were sorted on the basis of another questionnaire. There were 203 conformers, 133 strivers, 109 opposers, and 75 waverers (plus 189 unclassified). The conformers evidently had a repressed but effective style reminiscent of Achievement through Conformity. The strivers had an Ai pattern: confident, motivated, exhibitionist. The opposers feared failure, tending to be rigid. The waverers were also anxious, but dependent and indecisive rather than stubborn.

Average achievement for students of each type under each teacher was calculated and adjusted for IQ. A detailed table in the report shows the mean gain for pupils of each type within each class. The dramatic differences are hard to interpret, since the means were generally based on very few pupils. The averages in Table 13.5 are for classes pooled.

The results were complex, and only tentative, with as few as six teachers in some cells. But even six teachers in a narrowly defined cell makes this study more generalizable than other studies of class instruction.

Anxious students had a great advantage with superior, orderly teachers. The opposers even did well with inferior orderly teachers. This is consistent with the long-standing idea that structure helps the anxious. This impression is strengthened by the fact that these students did badly under the generally excellent superior-spontaneous teachers.

As for what appears to be an Ai/Ac contrast, the conformers seemed to benefit most from the stimulation provided by superior spontaneous teachers. The other

Table 13.5　Achievement as a function of student personality and teacher personality

Teacher type	Number of teachers	Mean achievement of students of each type				All students
		Strivers	Conformers	Anxious opposers	Anxious waverers	
Spontaneous, superior	6	130	161	75	82	101
Spontaneous, inferior	6	105	84	53	99	85
Orderly, superior	7	118	146	135	117	125
Orderly, inferior	7	126	91	123	87	106
Fearful, superior	11	115	95	69	77	92
Fearful, inferior	11	99	105	81	73	100
All teachers	48	113	111	87	83	100

Data from Heil, Powell, and Feifer, 1960, p. 51. All group means are expressed relative to the grand mean.

large contrasts in means are irregular and difficult to explain. On the whole the constructively motivated strivers were least affected by teacher differences. One can scarcely raise questions of statistical significance of these results, when teachers are the unit of sampling. Nonetheless, *this appears to be a provocative finding of ATI.* While we see some aspects of these conclusions as consistent with the college-level findings of Domino and Dowaliby, the techniques and concepts of the studies cannot be collated in a convincing manner.

The Heil evidence does argue strongly that research intended to identify "what kind of person makes the best teacher" is futile. The 14 orderly teachers got better results, all students considered. The fearful teachers got rather poor results. The spontaneous teachers were as low on the average as the fearful teachers, but their variation over kinds of students was spectacularly large. The resistant student and the waverer in the spontaneous classroom are evidently cut adrift and go onto the rocks. The dutiful students are evidently swept to unusual peaks of achievement, when the teacher's spontaneity is accompanied by warmth. It may be provocative to recall at this point the tentative findings of Yamamoto (p. 328) based on the Torrance tests. If one assumes that Heil's fearful teachers and perhaps his orderly teachers, and the waverers, conformers, and perhaps the anxious opposers among students would score low on Torrance tests, nothing in Table 13.5 resembles the Yamamoto results.

The Heil study had a strong influence on the work of Wallen (1964, 1966; with Wodtke, 1963). That work was, in the most literal sense, lamentable. Two unusually large bodies of well-conceived data, analyzed with subtle statistical techniques and sophisticated reasoning, yielded next to nothing. The authors ruefully concluded that their data disconfirmed their ATI hypotheses. We can join them in lamenting this, but we are burdened with the even sadder thought that their preoccupation with inferential statistics and neat analyses of variance led them to discard much in their data that was of positive value. The analysis employed the teacher as the sampling unit, though there is almost no hope of achieving adequate statistical power for testing ATI generalizations over teachers.

Informed by a thorough reading of the previous literature, Wallen and Wodtke set out to investigate the interaction of teacher style and student personality. Data on teachers consisted of personality tests and classroom observations. For the students there were pretests on achievement, general ability, creativity, several personality dimensions, and other variables. The study has some resemblance to the exploratory studies discussed in Chapter 12, but its questions were far better specified. The first phase of the work used data on about 65 teachers and their classes. Posttests on achievement and creativity were given at the end of the year and converted to residual-gain measures.

Instead of using all the data, the investigators selected extreme groups to fit into balanced anova. Thus, the 1963 report contrasted two extreme groups of students, those high in general ability and low in dependency/those low in general ability and high in dependency. We of course regret the information lost from the other two corners of this distribution, and also the statistical power lost when the sample was cut to a few students from each class. Even more serious, the analysis was restricted to four teachers at each grade, the ones chosen being at the extremes with respect to warm, permissive style/cold, controlling style.

The Student x Teacher interaction fell short of significance in the analysis for all grades pooled. The authors, however, had already become convinced from correlational analyses within grades that the processes connecting teacher and student characteristics are quite different from Grade 1 to Grade 5. They therefore proceeded to analyze grade by grade. The sample of teachers within a grade was extremely small. Even with very low power, the interaction sometimes reached a *p* value of 0.06. The authors described the effects only for the particular posttests and grade levels where this kind of near-significance appeared, telling nothing about the means of subgroups in adjacent grades (which might enable us to evaluate trends). *The dull, dependent primary children seemed to learn most when their teachers were cold and controlled, while the able, independent children did better with permissive teachers.* This is highly reminiscent of the good performance of Heil's waverers under good orderly teachers and of Heil's strivers under good spontaneous teachers. The only other effect mentioned by Wallen and Wodtke was one in Grade 5 that "suggests" that able independent students in that grade did better with *less* permissive teaching. The pertinent data were not given.

In the second body of data (1966 report), a similar approach was taken. Only Grades 1 and 3 were studied. Again, extreme groups were isolated so that data on nearly 40 teachers per grade and over a thousand children were reduced to analyses of ten teachers (five in each block) and ten children for each teacher. Wallen applied a strict standard of statistical significance, since he was making a vast number of *F*-tests within Grade x Sex groups on several dependent variables. He concluded that *for girls only, in Grade 3 only, on the Vocabulary gain score only, was there significant confirmation* of the trend suggested by the first study. There seems to have been no attempt to look at the consistency of the non-significant differences. We would like very much to see—for each of the nearly 80 teachers—the regression equation relating the posttest to an ability composite, to Dependency, and to their product. This set of equations would either confirm the plausible hypothesis (including the possibility that the relationship varies with the grade level) in a way that the miniature analyses of variance could not, or it would give an unambiguous disconfirmation. The interpretation could safely rest on the psychological consistency of the results even if their pattern falls short of significance.

In another analysis, Wallen (1964) set out to check directly on Heil's conclusion. The teachers were sorted as turbulent, self-controlling, or fearful, the categories named by Heil. Among the pupils, opposers and waverers were sorted out, on the basis of Anxiety and three "need" scores. A third group pooled strivers and conformers. For the sake of balance in anova the sample was reduced to four pupils of each type per teacher.

Of 15 tests of interaction effects on achievement posttests only one reached significance. In this one analysis (Grade-5 reading), the highest cell means were for conformers-strivers (defensives) having spontaneous teachers and for opposers with fearful teachers. But the differences in residual gains were very small and the significance test is hard to credit.

In analyses with Torrance scores as outcome measures, three out of 15 F-ratios for interaction were significant. Insofar as any consistency can be perceived in the 3x3 layout of means (Teacher type x Student type), spontaneous teachers released superior divergent-thinking performance in constructive pupils. The means are so similar, however, that one suspects that the significance test was inaccurately computed.

If one takes Wallen's reading of the data at face value, the lack of significance of most results stands as a failure to replicate the Heil findings. But there are *many reasons for distrusting the replication,* starting with the low power of Wallen's analysis and the unreliability of his criterion scores. Further, one can doubt that Heil's "orderly" *self*-controlling teachers were like the "controlling" teachers of the Wallen study. Worse, Wallen did not distinguish between superior and inferior "turbulent" teachers even though that distinction was crucial in Heil's results. A full report of descriptive statistics on Wallen's cases would have put us in a position to decide whether interactions were lacking.

Studies in the secondary school

There has been surprisingly little work with personality variables other than anxiety in the junior or senior high school. We mentioned above the loosely controlled study on grouping by O'Connor and Atkinson. There is evidence also in two investigations in physics classes.

Bar-Yam (1969; see our p. 301) assessed teacher style by means of the Learning Environment Inventory and measured the student's Need for Achievement and Need for Order by a questionnaire derived from Edwards. Her design allowed her to test 12 ATI effects on two outcomes (effects of two personality measures crossed with three LEI scales). Three of the 12 effects were significant. Achievement motivation did not interact with the Goal-Direction, Formality, or Organization of the physics class.

The regression slope for the final HPP achievement test onto Need for Order was negligible in less directed, less formal classes, but negative in more structured classes. The following means for achievement show a *marked disadvantage of structure for Highs (defensives?):*

	Need for Order		
	Low	Middle	High
Teaching more goal-directed	25.5	22.8	21.7
Teaching less goal-directed	25.8	26.1	25.1

(The within-cell s.d. was about 6 points.) This somewhat paradoxical result seems to parallel that of Amidon below. In a nonsignificant ordinal interaction, Highs reported about the same satisfaction in either type of class, while Lows were much better satisfied when assigned to a more direct course. The other two significant interactions related Need for Order to achievement as a function of Formality and to satisfaction as a function of Organization. An analysis combining personality data with ability data would have been desirable.

When PSSC physics was introduced in the State of Victoria (Australia), Gardner (1974) carried out an evaluation of affective changes. His methods for studying ATI were ingenious and sophisticated. While we doubt that they reached a correct picture of the relationships, the study is nonetheless among the best in the ATI literature. Eight measures of student "need" were assessed by questionnaires derived from the work of George Stern, and eight measures of classroom climate or "press" specific to the physics classroom were developed, in a vein reminiscent of the LEI. Data were available for 1014 students in 58 classes. Some teachers in the study taught two of the classes. The dependent variable was the student's rating of his enjoyment of physics as a field of study, reported at the end of the course. In this sample, there was a sharp drop in interest from the beginning to the end of the course. It was found that seven out of eight need scores related significantly to the change in enjoyment, and five out of eight of the dimensions describing classrooms. Gardner's article does not give full descriptive data on these main effects, but it appears that enjoyment held up best when students described themselves as high on the following needs: achievement, understanding, conjunctivity, energy, play, nurturance, and deference. The press scales that went with greater enjoyment were competitiveness, intellectualization, organization, stimulation, and compulsiveness.

Gardner tested only eight interactions, considering the obvious pairings of need and press scales. Just two of the eight reached significance at the .05 level. His procedure may be described as applied to Ach (need, assessed by questionnaire rather than by the projective methods used by Atkinson) and Comp (press for Competition). Classes were divided into quartiles on Comp. Students were divided into quartiles on Ach. There were, then, 16 cells; a student was located according to his individual score on Ach and the score of his class on Comp. The posttest on enjoyment was analyzed with the pretest on enjoyment as covariate, tests being made of the main effect for need (3 d.f.), press (3 d.f.), and interaction (9 d.f.). The d.f. for the error term was based on the number of individuals. This analysis is open to question because within-class and between-class effects of need are mingled, because the number of classes limits the number of degrees of freedom for effects involving press, because blocking lost much information, and because many Need x Press combinations were ignored. Moreover, the possibility that the pretest itself interacted was suppressed.

A table of cell means was provided for the Ach/Comp interaction, and we have prepared Figure 13.2 from it. As Gardner read the data, "very high achievement-oriented students best maintain their positive attitudes with teachers in the highest quartile on Competitiveness; very low achievement-oriented students fare best in an environment which is very low on Competitiveness. In simple language, the high achiever likes to be prodded, whereas the low achiever enjoys the subject more if he is not." (pp. 191-193). We found, however, that the data points for

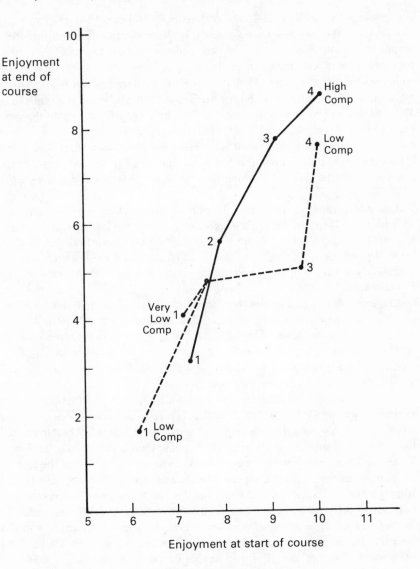

Figure 13.2.

Enjoyment early and late in a physics course, as a function of teacher style and student personality.

Data from Gardner, 1974, p. 192.

Class scores on Press for Competition (Comp) were assigned to quartiles. Numerals in the figure represent the students' individual standings on Need for Achievement, 1 indicating the lowest quartile.

the very-high-Comp and high-Comp treatments formed parallel tracks (with greater enjoyment in the very-high-Comp classes). We have averaged the data for these groups to simplify Figure 13.2. The two groups of low-Comp classes gave means that agreed fairly well except in the lowest quartile of Ach, and we have therefore combined their tracks except in that last cell. If we have lost information by this aggregation, it is information about zigzags that probably would not replicate. The only large effect is that students medium high on Ach drop more than expected in low-Comp classes. The data points for those lowest on Ach are consistent with each other and do not warrant Gardner's interpretation. Just a few classes may have pulled down the one point that seems to produce most of the interaction. We are inclined to think that the reported *interaction was an artifact of the analysis.*

Less information was given regarding the significant interaction of need for Play with press for Pleasure. Among students low on Play, the less playful teacher generated somewhat more enjoyment than the teacher who introduced a light spirit. Among the pupils high on need for Play, the slope was negative; comparatively great enjoyment with the more playful teacher. *This interaction seems to make sense.*

The research program of Flanders began in a dissertation study by Amidon (Amidon & Flanders, 1961). A single teacher adopted a "direct" or an "indirect" style in eighth-grade classes. The instruction, plus all tests, required no more than two hours in any group. A "direct pattern of influence" is one in which the teacher restricts the student's options and makes him more dependent; it is rather like the directive style of Dowaliby and Domino.

Amidon concentrated his statistical work on students in the top quarter on a Dependency score ($N = 140$); we regard this score as another indicator of defensive motivation. Achievement in this restricted group was appreciably better under the indirect method of instruction. Instead of testing interaction directly by comparing Lows and Highs, Amidon drew a conclusion about interaction from the fact that no main effect for treatment appeared in the intact group of 560 students. Although the analysis was sketchy and the descriptive statistics incomplete, the evidence of ATI was clear. *The indirect approach was superior for dependents and inferior for those low in Dependency.* The advantage of the indirect method for dependents had been anticipated by Flanders and Amidon. They argued that the student who tries to conform to teacher demands will be distracted from using his full powers of thought. But they might equally well have speculated that the clear demands in the direct method put the conformer more at ease. That would have been in line with the thinking of most other investigators.

A subsequent study (Flanders, 1965) considered the natural variation among teachers. Teachers were chosen to represent extremes in style and in rapport with students, as judged from a questionnaire filled out by the class members. Teachers were then observed as they taught a two-week experimental unit, and their methods classified as "direct"/"indirect". One two-week unit was taught in 15 social-studies classes (Grade 7), and another in 16 mathematics classes (Grade 8). The achievement posttest, with pretest covaried out, was used as dependent variable.

The pretest over the mathematics unit had a high correlation with the post-test. With little variance left to be explained, *no interaction* or main effect was found. Among social-studies classes the adjusted outcome was significantly better in the classes with the most indirect teaching. There was *no interaction* with IQ or Dependency. At this point Flanders said that he was not prepared to discard the hypothesis of ATI for these variables. Though he said that "a series of experiments" had shown positive results. we could find no trace of any prior study save Amidon's.

Minor studies of mathemagenic variables

The attempts to demonstrate interactions of ability with inserted questions and similar devices have been extended by Clodfelter and by Hiller to the personality domain. Like the work reviewed in Chapter 10, the studies were of short duration.

A three-week physics course (two hours per day) for enlisted men was the subject of Clodfelter's (1969) experiment. There were seven treatment conditions ($N = 294$ in all): a quiz immediately after each lesson/a quiz the next day/no quiz; and, among the quizzed groups, feedback of a score the next day/feedback of correct answers the next day/feedback of correct answers the same day. On the final examination the delayed-quiz groups did best. The author tested interactions by evaluating partial correlations of CPI scales for Ac and Ai after pooling various cells of the design. Such correlations are hard to evaluate, especially as sampling fluctuations alter the definition of the partial variate from one group to another. Evidently the presence or placement of a quiz made little difference in regression slopes. *The regression slope of examination scores onto Ai, with Ac held constant, was zero with immediate feedback of answers, and positive with delayed feedback of answers or none.* That is, High Ai's tolerated absence of feedback. The reverse was true for Ac with Ai constant, the only large correlation being for immediate feedback. High Ac's then, needed feedback. The interaction appears to have been disordinal. The implication of the rather large slope differences seems to be that defensives are somewhat impeded by immediate feedback, and are at their best when withholding of feedback increases their responsibility. The constructives, on the contrary, are at their best when supported by feedback.

Hiller (1972a; see p. 359) also considered a quiz as a treatment. Responsibility, Self-confidence (with respect to intellectual achievement), Locus of Control, Dogmatism, GPA, and ACT English scores were correlated with learning from prose. Hiller's study was not designed to examine ATI, but his report included the information needed for an ATI analysis.

College Ss read a passage, then half of them were tested on it (48 items, multiple choice). A week later, without warning, all Ss were given the same test. The immediate posttest, then, was a limited experimental "treatment," probably stimulating covert review and consolidation. There were *no important relations among the 78 women. In the data for 67 men, all personality measures were strongly related to retention in the experimental group,* but not at all related to score in the control group. From Hiller's report we estimated regression slopes and *F*-ratios; see Table 13.6. The great instability of statistics based on small samples should be borne in mind. Since the treatments did not differ on the average, it is likely that the slopes crossed in the middle of the range on each personality measure. As can be seen, the ability measures were positively related to performance in both conditions, but GPA was more strongly related in the text-test treatment. The ACT test, a measure of competence in conventional English usage, was more strongly related in the text-only condition; perhaps it is a surrogate for reading ability.

The test after study benefited male high achievers who had constructive motivation responsible, confident, undogmatic. Performance of women apparently was predictable from ability measures alone, with no interactions. The interpretation of these findings is not clear, nor is the study substantial enough to represent real instructional conditions.

In another study (Hiller, 1972b), a difficult 1687-word text introducing a mathematical topic was revised to form moderately difficult and relatively easy versions. About 700 educational psychology students were divided among the three versions, and further divided among conditions: difficult inserted questions/

Table 13.6   Regression slopes and correlations relating delayed test scores to characteristics of male students

Aptitude measure	Ss receiving immediate test (N = 35)		Ss receiving no immediate test (N = 32)	
	r	b	r	b
Responsibility for intellectual achievement	0.33	0.54*	0.06	0.08
Internal vs. external locus of control	0.44	0.78*	0.09	0.12
Intellectual self-confidence	0.67	1.19*	0.26	0.35
Dogmatism	− 0.49	− 0.17*	− 0.19	− 0.05
Grade-point average	0.45	6.96*	0.34	4.04
ACT	0.22	0.44	0.46	0.71*

Data from Hiller, 1972a. Asterisks refer to statistical comparisons of regression slopes, the asterisk being placed alongside the steeper slope (positive or negative).

*$p < .05$

easy inserted questions/instructions to study the text "as you do typically"/instructions to read passively. Aptitudes were ACT-English, FA, DA, Locus of Control, Dogmatism, Social Desirability, and Self-confidence. Missing data reduced the sample for ATI analyses to about 450.

There were main effects on the immediate posttest. Hiller reported AT correlations. Table 13.7 gives the correlations for the immediate posttest. As he did not give means and s.d.'s for aptitude variables, we cannot examine regression slopes. Many of the marked differences among correlations remain after differences in s.d.'s for outcome are considered.

Though Hiller did not report anything specific about regressions, he had inspected them and reported that all the interactions were ordinal. DA was most detrimental to performance with hard inserted questions. *The student low in Self-confidence and the anxious student were particularly well off when allowed to study in their own way,* especially on more difficult texts. ACT-E evidently was more related to performance in some conditions than in others, but we cannot judge the reliability of these differences.

Summary

When we look back upon the studies so far encountered, we are first struck by the frequent appearance of ATI. A number of studies showed no interaction, and some of these were large-scale studies; but the majority of studies did find interactions. The studies are by no means perfectly consistent; indeed, results could scarcely be more contradictory than those of Amidon and Dowaliby. Only weak generalizations can be advanced. Treatments are loosely specified. Teachers described as using the same style no doubt varied a good deal. Moreover, class dynamics may produce inconsistent results where the same teacher teaches the same subject to successive classes. Different patterns of interaction may appear at different grade levels, at different ability levels, and with different types of subject matter.

Several investigations find that students with constructive motivation tend to benefit from treatment conditions that provide more freedom and more challenge, i.e., treatments that look to the learner himself to supply a good deal of the "structure" and specification of the task. Consider the treatment variables that produced such an interaction:

Teacher encouraged independence and participation	Domino (two studies) McKeachie (study of Need for Power; for men only);
Independent study Audiovisual media	Bigelow (but not Koenig) Snow; Oosthoek (for students of limited ability)
Spontaneous teachers	Heil (for superior teachers only)

Table 13.7 Immediate test results following various study procedures, as a function of five traits

Study aids or conditions	Approx. N	Outcome		Correlation with outcome of[a]			
		Mean	s.d.	SC	FA	DA	ACT-E
Difficult text							
Passive responding	63[b]	13.0	3.4	0.30	0.32	− 0.25	0.46
Idiosyncratic	44	13.6	1.9	− 0.02	0.32	− 0.10	0.33
Easy questions	61	12.0	3.3	0.31	− 0.04	− 0.21	0.60
Hard questions	51	11.0	3.0	0.43	0.33	− 0.43	0.35
Moderately difficult text							
Passive responding	51	14.5	4.3	0.21	0.10	− 0.20	0.43
Idiosyncratic	30	14.3	4.0	0.13	0.22	− 0.23	0.33
Easy questions	38	12.3	3.5	0.12	− 0.11	0.07	0.18
Hard questions	44	13.1	4.1	0.41	0.11	− 0.45	0.29
Less difficult text							
Passive responding	25	13.8	3.2	0.09	0.13	0.07	0.41
Idiosyncratic	34	14.4	3.0	0.12	0.12	− 0.25	0.22
Easy questions	22	13.5	3.2	0.26	0.06	− 0.14	0.50
Hard questions	21	12.9	2.7	0.28	0.05	− 0.29	− 0.12

Data from Hiller, 1972b.

[a] SC, self-confidence; FA, facilitating anxiety; DA, debilitating anxiety; ACT-E, English test.

[b] This N applies eo the means and standard deviations. For the correlations N was usually 10–20 per cent lower.

More complex interactions of constructive motivation appeared in the study of O'Connor *et al.* on ability grouping; by and large, the authors felt that the interaction was in line with the theoretical expectation. There is also a problem of interpreting Heil's finding of constructives superior with "orderly" teachers, and Clodfelter's finding that constructives did better when given immediate feedback. Not to be overlooked is the failure of McKeachie *et al.* to find interactions of Need for Achievement with extent of "achievement cueing" by instructors, and their failure to find a relation of facilitating anxiety (a form of constructive motivation?) with anxiety cueing. Bar-Yam got negative results with Need for Achievement. Milholland's attempt at matching students with instructors also failed to turn up any important effect of constructive motivation.

(This brief summary has not included several equivocal findings, nor the complex departures of particular results from the main conclusions of a study.)

On the whole, the consistency among the relations listed above warrants the use of the constructive-motivation hypothesis as the armature in further, more subtle classroom research. Both teaching style and student personality are multivariate, and future studies will have to go beyond testing relations of variables taken singly. Moreover, the studies will have to reckon with the evidence that the student's perception mediates the interaction and generates personality-dependent ATI effects even where the teacher is "constant."

The evidence on defensive motivation is clouded. In Chapter 12, we encountered baffling inconsistencies among small-scale studies with limited treatments, but we found some tendency for defensives to do better when the instruction placed less demand on them. Several findings in this chapter have the same flavor; among the treatments that seemed to help the defensives were these:

Structured, directive instruction	Domino, Dowaliby
Orderly, superior teachers	Heil
Achievement cueing	McKeachie (FA; women only)

There is the mysterious finding of Oosthoek and Ackers that comparatively unstructured instruction by tape was advantageous to *able* defensives, and the very complex results on Ability x Anxiety of McKeachie and Lin. Interactions of the general kind under discussion here failed to appear in some of the McKeachie studies and in the large study of Flanders.

Considering together the results of Chapters 12 and 13, then, it appears that no confident assertion is to be made about effects of anxiety and other defensive motivation. There is ample evidence that at times it has powerful effects in conditioning the student's response to a teacher. We suspect that anxiety, once aroused, causes the student to adopt one or another defensive maneuver; his maneuver may reduce State A or it may not, and it may promote or impede effective learning. Until more research is focused on the process by which the anxious student engages the instructional stimuli, little can be learned; prediction directly from trait scores can do no more than turn up fluctuating and inexplicable results.

Interactions of affiliative motives

Hypotheses come readily to mind about possible relations between the student's sociability or desire for warm personal relations and the instructor's warmth or the student's opportunity to communicate with peers during instruction. Among the studies of the preceding section, Sociability or Need for Affiliation entered the studies of Bigelow, Koenig, Milholland, and Rosenwein. Bigelow (p. 447) found that students low in Socialization tended to like an independent-student procedure. Although Koenig and McKeachie (p. 447) found that women with strong Need for Achievement preferred small-group work or independent work to lecture instruction, they found no relation of preference to Need for Affiliation. Students who "thought the instructor should be authoritarian" did badly in independent study. There was a relationship of doubtful significance in Milholland's study of "matching" (p. 452). Rosenwein's findings about students low in Need for Affiliation were complex; they did not, in general, confirm his predictions. For example, among High-Affs who wanted a warm instructor *and* perceived their instructor as warm, women did better and men did worse (than those who perceived their instructor of the same sex as cold).

Doty and Doty (1964) reported that *sociable students in college psychology did worse in PI than others.* (N = 100; there was no contrasting conventional group.) Lublin (p. 418) had a similar finding.

B. A. Doty (1970) did a fully experimental contrast, teaching a topic in physiology to 300 college students by six short, taped lectures with opportunity for questioning/a lecture-discussion/or a small-group discussion without a teacher. Judging from the correlations reported, interactions occurred; at times the correlations were opposite in sign in different treatments, and significant. It appears that the *sociable Ss responded to the live treatments* better than to the tape. Also, students high on a test of divergent thinking responded better to the small-group procedure. There may be other interactions in the data that the analysis failed to make evident.

A study of eight teachers (Christensen, 1960) failed to demonstrate ATI. The teachers were of four types—warm permissive/cold permissive/etc.; within each cell of the fourfold pattern Christensen examined the learning of just ten fourth-graders high on "affect-need" and ten Lows (N = 80). The dependent variable was a measure of residual gain in achievement during the year. The report gave no descriptive statistics on outcome, and the absence of significant F ratios is *not convincing evidence* that interaction was absent.

A small sample and an idiosyncratic analysis make it difficult for us to evaluate Beach's (1960) finding that a lecture method and a class-discussion method of teaching child psychology were best for unsociable Ss, and a small-group method best for sociable Ss. There were 98 Ss in four treatments, applied in different sections of a semester-long course. The overall mean was highest with the lecture, next highest with independent study. In the lecture group, achievement had a steep negative slope of regression onto Sociability. Independent study served equally well for Ss high and low in Sociability. In the sample, at least, there was a *strong disordinal interaction.*

Baron and Bass (1969) asked disadvantaged young adults to work on problems of three types: scale reading, angle reading, and block design. After a baseline measurement, trials were conducted under verbal reinforcement ("Good" on nine trials, "not so good" on three randomly selected trials)/material reinforcement (poker chips redeemable for prizes, again on a 75 per cent, noncontingent schedule). The dependent variable seems to reflect effort more than learning, as there was no informative feedback. On two of the three tasks, *verbal reward elicited stronger effort than material reward among persons with strong (self-reported) need for social approval.* Material reward worked better with most other Ss.

The Michigan program (McKeachie, 1961, p. 128; McKeachie *et al.,* 1964, Sec. VI-A-1; McKeachie, Lin, Milholland, & Isaacson, 1966) considered Need for Affiliation (nAff) as measured by a projective technique. Minor inconsistencies appear among reports on the same study, as cases were added and regrouped. We shall rely on the 1964 account. In Study I (Table 13.8), women psychology students low in nAff tended to earn poor grades when the instructor was rated as warm (by the class as a whole). In our table, this enters as a case where the warm style "did not fit" the Low-affiliative student.

Among the High-affiliative, there was no treatment effect. Among men in psychology the same tendency of Lows to do badly was found, and furthermore the Highs did their best with a warm instructor. In mathematics (not in our table), where there were data for 145 men, both Highs and Lows earned better grades with warm instructors. (This is not the reading of the data given by McKeachie *et al.*) There were too few women to provide data in mathematics; mysteriously, nothing was said about the French classes of Study I. When a test was used in place of grades as the criterion in the psychology course, the evidence was quite mixed. Moreover, Study II (1964, 1966) and data for males in Study III (1966) gave only weak support to the hypothesis. In Study III, no data for women were reported; the report said that Highs performed as predicted but that Lows gave results contrary to the hypothesis.

Table 13.8 summarizes the data from psychology courses. There are some inconsistencies, and the categories in the last column are crude. But if we simply count entries we have

	No	?	Yes
Men	6	3	7
Women	4	2	6

Since we have placed null effects as well as reversed effects in the No column, and weak positive relations in the ? column, this constitutes evidence that *student n Aff and instructor warmth interacted.* We cannot concur with the investigators'

Table 13.8 Percentage of psychology students doing relatively well, as a function of n Aff, and warmth of instructor

Sex	Study	Criterion	n Aff	Per cent who did well when teacher style		Supports expected ATI?
				did "fit"	did not "fit"	
M	I	Grades	High	50% (16)[a]	38% (21)	Yes
			Low	55% (20)	32% (28)	Yes
		Objective test	High	50% (14)	53% (21)	No
			Low	55% (20)	50% (28)	?
		Essay test	High	50% (14)	47% (21)	?
			Low	40% (20)	53% (28)	No
	II	Grades	High	63% (57)	44% (59)	Yes
			Low	45% (56)	45% (45)	No
		Objective test	High	64% (33)	61% (31)	?
			Low	59% (95)	43% (75)	Yes
		Higher-order test[b]	High	65% (40)	50% (78)	Yes
			Low	55% (118)	54% (100)	No
	III	Grades	High	55% (47)	48% (33)	Yes
			Low	60% (43)	60% (35)	No

F	I	Essay test	High	55% (29)	38% (26)	Yes
			Low	39% (28)	41% (22)	No
		Grades	High	53% (36)	50% (34)	?
			Low	52% (42)	36% (36)	Yes
		Objective test	High	33% (36)	53% (34)	No
			Low	51% (41)	45% (34)	Yes
	II	Essay test	High	50% (36)	38% (34)	Yes
			Low	61% (41)	44% (34)	Yes
		Grades	High	50% (87)	46% (108)	?
			Low	43% (93)	55% (85)	No
		Objective test	High	56% (82)	49% (93)	Yes
			Low	59% (53)	52% (48)	Yes
		Higher-order test	High	48% (111)	49% (126)	No
			Low	37% (73)	49% (61)	No

Data from McKeachie et al., 1964, VI-A-1; and McKeachie et all, 1966.

[a]Read: With warm instructor, among 16 students with high n Aff, 50 per cent earned superior grades.
With not-warm instructor, among 20 students with low n Aff, 55 per cent earned superior grades.

[b]Total N for each group given in 1964 report, p. VI-A-1-10, is not the sum of the Ns for the H and L subgroups. We used that sum as our N.

view that the relationship differed for men and women. Nor are we convinced that the effect on grades was stronger than the effect on objectively measured learning.

Nothing much needs to be said by way of summary of the studies on affiliative motives. Positive relations in the anticipated direction appear rather often, but they are not often strong. Relationships with satisfaction may be stronger than the relationships with learning itself.

We have chosen this point, where we have just examined a major study in detail, to make a general comment about the McKeachie program of research. The Michigan work was a serious, large-scale inquiry. It collected extensive data, replicating many analyses. It based some of its questions on hypotheses derived from laboratory work. It made an exceptional effort to apply sound statistics. And the empirical reports include perceptive discussions of theory and methodology. The work, however, has become available in a trickle of primary publications carrying fragments of the results, in secondary accounts such as lectures and hand-book chapters that give nonrepresentative data, and in two little-known assemblages —one of 300 pages and one of 800—of reprints and file memoranda. The reports display the data that yielded significant results and say little about the relations that fell short of significance. Sometimes the latter are the larger part of the data. In the case of the data on affiliation, we were able to see a consistent result where the authors saw only inconsistency. The Michigan group adopted analytic techniques that tended to obscure results. E.g., they blocked cases for analysis of variance, they neglected to use ability as a covariate or moderator variable, they failed to study instructors or classes individually, they failed to examine traits simultaneously. All that is entirely understandable, given the state of the art during the 1960's. Although we are sure that more could have been learned from the data with more powerful analyses, we are not at all confident that any analysis would dispel the inconsistencies that troubled McKeachie *et al.*

Student preferences and beliefs

Educational philosophies often assign a large role to student choice in determining what a person shall study and perhaps how he shall study. The arguments seem to embody the empirical assumption that he will learn more if he studies by a method consistent with his preferences. The same theme of congeniality is to be found in the belief that one can learn most easily from a teacher whose ideas or beliefs are like one's own.

Only a few investigators have tried to produce ATI by capitalizing on student preferences. In one early study (James, 1962), technical content was presented in a lecture mode or a reading mode to 368 Air Force trainees. *S*s had a chance to express a preference for either of these, or no preference. The design was carefully counterbalanced, so that within each choice group and each ability level (Armed Forces Qualifying Test) an equal number of men were taught by each mode. In both treatments, a test question followed each paragraph of the material. There were two significant interactions. Reading produced higher scores, and this advantage was greater for students of high ability. Scores differed among choice groups, but matching instruction to preference conferred no advantage. The highest scores were earned by the trainees who had no preference between methods. It is hard to understand the interaction from the published results, and both the measure of preference and the instructional treatment were limited.

Tobias (1972b) reported two experiments. In the first study, third- and fourth-graders chose between visual/aural spelling instruction. Four sessions of drill and practice were conducted by CAI in each condition. Ss (N = 13) chose their method for each session, after receiving a sample of both methods. Each control-group S was matched to a preference-group S on sex, grade, and prior spelling achievement; on each day he received whichever method his match chose. There were two other control groups, one assigned always to visual, one always to aural. There was a pretest, an immediate posttest after each session, a delayed posttest, and an attitude measure. There were no differences among methods and apparently no ATI. The sample size and duration of treatment make the study worthless save as a suggestion about design of research.

Tobias' second study used 89 college students who chose between constructed-response PI/PI-with-blanks-filled-in. Roughly 40 Ss tried short programs of the overt and covert types and then made a choice for the main study. Other Ss were randomly assigned to one or the other treatment. On a posttest, constructed response gave better results on the average, but there was no advantage for those given a choice. Unlike the first study, this one did nothing to ensure that those choosing Method A were like those assigned to Method B in the pertinent aptitudes.

Atkinson (1972) has pursued the question of optimum design in CAI, concerning himself with such detailed decisions as whether at a given moment more trials should be given on the associations S has almost mastered or on those where he is still very weak. He reports that the S allowed to judge such matters for himself learns less rapidly than the S trained according to rules developed out of theory and experimental trial.

Pascal (1971) allowed 185 college students to state their choice among independent study (with a reading log and term paper)/lecture/lecture with group discussion. S was then assigned by a random process. On the course examination, a scale of attitude toward the subject-matter, and other measures, being taught by one's preferred method conferred no advantage. It did appear that those receiving their first choice of method ended with a more favorable attitude toward the subject-matter.

Pascal (1973) later sought to identify the personality correlates of preferences in this group of Ss. Ss choosing independent study scored higher on autonomy, thinking introversion, complexity, theoretic orientation, and practical outlook than did those who chose lecture. In addition, they reported more previous experience with independent study and more extracurricular reading. We do not know whether such personal characteristics relate differently to performance under preferred/less preferred methods. Possibly some Ss do particularly well when given their choice, and some gain nothing. Until ATI conceptions of this sort are examined, the study of preference as a means of individualization is likely not to be rewarding.

These studies cast doubts upon the appropriateness of assigning students to their preferred instructional method. Other studies reinforce the doubts. Rosenwein's results (p. 457 ff.) could at most be called mixed: sometimes matching treatment to preference gave better results, sometimes worse; sometimes they had no effect. Yelvington (p. 260) and Smith (p. 448) likewise had evidence of students doing worse in the treatment they said they preferred. An exception might be the use of self-pacing; Kress and Gropper (p. 204) found an advantage in matching instructional pace to the preferred tempos of Ss. Another might be the McLachlan finding (p. 379) that Ss preferring unstructured teaching did better with discovery methods. All in all, however, the evidence discourages the romantic view that self-selection of the instructional diet pays off.

Whereas we judge that student preference does not generally interact with method, benefit does seem to result when instructor beliefs and student beliefs are congenial. A good deal of research on communication or persuasion argues that one is more receptive to a message when one agrees with the communicator in other ideas or loyalties. In particular, attention may be drawn to the brief but thoughtful statement of ATI hypotheses about response to various kinds of persuasion, by Hovland, Janis, and Kelley (1953, pp. 199–202). As evidence they cited only the well-known Janis-Feshback study, in which a communication emphasizing the dangers of decay if teeth are neglected was ineffective with anxious persons. The noneducational literature on persuasion has been reviewed by McGuire (1968).

Dramatic evidence for the interaction of teacher and student beliefs was offered by Majasan (1972). Twelve college psychology teachers indicated their views about the aims, content, and methods of work of scientific psychology. The questionnaire was scored on a scale from radical behaviorism (low BQ score) to a phenomenologist-humanist view (high BQ score). Students in the introductory psychology classes of these teachers filled out the same scale, at the very beginning and at the end of the course. The number of cases ranged from 20 to 62 per class. Ability measures were collected from school files; these, and also the instruments used to assess achievement, varied from class to class.

Majasan had predicted from social-psychological theory that the best achievers would be those whose initial view of psychology was like the instructor's. To test this, he plotted the residualized achievement score against the student's belief. In several classes there was a curvilinear regression. The student BQ associated with peak achievement, given in Table 13.9, was determined by the trimmed-mean technique. In classes where the instructor's BQ score was toward one or the other extreme, the regression was linear. The location of peak achievement was also toward that extreme and hence consistent with the prediction. The evidence in

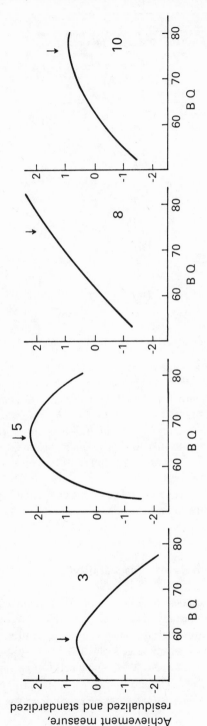

Figure 13.3.

Course achievement in four psychology classes as a function of congruence of the student's and instructor's beliefs. Data from Majasan, 1972. Arrow indicates instructor's BQ score.

Copyright © 1975 by the American Psychological Association. Reprinted by permission.

Table 13.9   Instructor's BQ score and characteristics of the regression
               relating outcome to student BQ scores in his class

Instructor and class number	Instructor's BQ score	BQ score yielding best outcome	Regression coefficients[a] for	
			BQ	$(BQ-\overline{BQ})^2$
1	55.5	56.7	1.23	-0.0108
2	57.0	58.7	0.17	-0.0017
3	59.0	61.4	0.92	-0.0079
4	59.5	63.8	0.86	-0.0068
5	68.0	67.6	1.77	-0.0129
6	71.0	69.7	0.46	-0.0027
7[b]	72.5	71.0	-0.04	0.0012
8	74.0	73.3	0.29	-0.0012
9	74.5	73.1	0.31	-0.0019
10	76.0	72.0	0.62	-0.0041
11	77.0	71.4	-0.21	0.0021
12	82.0	71.8	-0.13	0.0023

After Majasan, 1972.

[a]To predict a standardized criterion with zero mean and unit s.d. in each class. BQ is left in
raw-score units.
[b]Criterion based on student project, not test scores.

every class* was compatible with the prediction that *a student is more likely to
do well when his initial basic beliefs resemble those of his instructor.* There were
discrepancies between the instructor BQ and the peak student BQ in Classes
10–12 where instructors ranged farther toward the humanistic extreme. The impressive overall correspondence cannot be attributed to bias in marking—objective
tests were the basis for the outcome measure in most classes. The tests, however,
were assembled by the instructor, so the test content or scoring key might have
been biased toward his preconceptions.

A study of "teachability"

Among the most original studies we review, and one pregnant with ideas for
future ATI research, is Thelen's study (1966) of "teachability" grouping. The
work has that intensive, anthropological character we have so often urged, and
still was carried out on an impressively large scale. Thelen chose to make his
report an impressionistic overview rather than a detailed, formal, and complete

*In Class 7, the regression was quite flat, but this statement nonetheless holds true.

account. While there is sufficient documentation to make his conclusions credible, the reader cannot dig into matters as he might like.

Thelen asked 13 teachers of various subjects in Grades 8-11 to identify a dozen or so "S" students in their present classes who were "successful, getting a lot out of my class" and a number of "U" students who were less successful. These students responded to a total of 405 questionnaire items. The same questions were asked of the pool of 60-200 students who could be assigned to that teacher next year. A scoring key, made up of the responses that differentiated a certain teacher's S's from his U's, was applied to his pool during the summer. Enough high scorers were drawn from the pool to fill an experimental class presumed to be "teachable"—i.e., to fit this teacher's preferred pattern. From the residue of the pool a control class was selected. Thus each teacher taught two classes, one (E) selected to fit an ideal inferred from his evaluations of students he knew, the other (C) run-of-the-student-body.

The 13 teachers' keys generally included items in which the student reported himself as adjusted and ambitious, and as responsive to external direction, task-setting, and evaluation. But these core items made up only 20-40 per cent of the key; in each teacher's key, a large number of items appeared in the keys of only a few other teachers. The thrust of Thelen's argument is that aptitude for profiting from a teacher is defined by each teacher's characteristics, so that there is likely to be a suitable teacher for every kind of student. We need data on such crucial questions as these: How reliable is the keying for any teacher? (I.e., if he named two dozen S and U students, would keying from the responses of half of them agree with the key derived from the second half?) If students are scored by the keys of different teachers, how high do the scores correlate? What fraction of a school population is below the median on *every* teacher's key? If general teachability is defined by a modal key, and several students with the same general teachability are assigned to a teacher, do the ones higher on that teacher's specific teachability key really do better? (Thelen's design confounded general and specific teachability.) Does Thelen's indirect method of establishing a key elicit a different "ideal" from the teacher than transparent, direct questioning would elicit? All such questions may have been rejected by Thelen's group as unduly pedantic in a first exploration, but the positive results of the study warranted a meticulous tidying-up operation.

Thelen's team observed the E and C classes sufficiently to conclude that the teacher used much the same style in both, but that his E class resonated better to his style so that, with more solidarity, the teacher was free to be himself. On the whole, both group morale and teacher satisfaction were higher in the E class.

The teacher's own final examination was given as a pretest and again at the end of the year. A gain score showed no net E/C difference. This analysis is inadequate. The E and C students of any teacher (or all teachers) may have differed radically in sex, social class, general ability, and pretest achievement; no information on such matters is presented, in part because "teachability grouping" is held up as a radical alternative to ability grouping. Comparison of gain scores is treacherous unless groups are alike at pretest. *Eleven out of 13 teachers gave higher grades in the E class, and to the "more teachable" students within the E and the C class.* This can be interpreted as valid evidence of ATI, if the marks represented the students' attainment of goals that the gain scores on a test failed to reflect. It can also be interpreted as evidence of teacher bias.

Much of the report is given to case studies of five teachers. The summaries make it clear that the teachers were seeking different things, both in their educational aims and in their classroom relationships. Teachability meant ability to accept the teacher's initiatives and to provide him the stimulation (or absence of it) he needed. Some teachers are far more eager than others to have students who are bent on learning. One teacher got poor results with his E class. His idiosyncratic key had pulled into the E class students who sought security, who disliked to take initiative, and disliked being judged on merit. The teacher himself was passive, and the absence of leadership was frustrating.

Students' experience in the classroom is a social-psychological phenomenon. The spirit and style of the group emerges as the teacher's manner and tactics and those of the student members play on each other. The experience may be satisfying without being educative. In one of Thelen's classes where the teacher and students rather disliked each other, the experience was educative because both parties found gratification in a challenging relationship. The "teachable" student, in Thelen's operational definition, is not the one who learns most, he is the student the teacher most enjoys teaching at. One can scarcely expect the same resonance to develop each time a teacher draws a class that scores high on his "teachability" scale.

Interactions indicated by demographic classifications of students

Persons who differ in sex, age, and social status tend to differ psychologically. They respond differently to this or that social stimulus, and they may respond differently to the intellectual demands of a particular kind of instruction. Developmental psychology is primarily concerned with the main effects associated with age. But these main effects have less psychological interest than the comparative question: Do the same psychological laws hold for persons of different ages? And this, obviously, is an inquiry about interactions of age with experimental conditions. Similar comparative questions arise in the study of sex differences and in the study of social-class effects on development.

A proposed generalization from educational psychology or other behavioral science may be culture-specific. One can even doubt the generality of a finding across decades "within the same culture," and so can take seriously the possibility of Cohort x Treatment interactions (Cronbach, 1975). Changes in views of authority or in the prevailing philosophy of life among college students may indeed make invalid in the 1970's a "law" about teaching that was valid in the

1950's. As of now, we cannot point to evidence documenting any such interaction, however.

Age, sex, class, culture, and cohort probably should not be regarded by the psychologist as central variables (Ghiselli, 1974). The variability within any demographic subgroup is enormous. Presumably, most of the effects associated with, say, age, are caused (mediated) by age-correlated variables such as strength and mental age. Therefore, one can hope that demographic findings will in time be translated into findings about *psychological* qualities of the individual, and so reduce to aptitude-treatment interactions.

We cannot undertake to review the literature on demographic variables. The reader will learn much about the interactions of sex from Maccoby and Jacklin (1975). Interactions with age are implicit in nearly every page of the Mussen *Manual of Child Psychology*, which of course also considers sex and social class. We shall do no more here than review a few scattered studies that relate to themes already considered.

Sex

Many investigators carry out analyses within sexes, and then suggest that sex moderates a treatment effect or an ATI when a relation found in one sex is not

Table 13.10 Mean grades of psychology students whose teachers differed in sex and style

Teacher cues for achievement and affiliation	Teacher sex	Student ability		
		Low	High	Difference
High-High	Male	2.67	2.79	0.12
	Female	2.35	3.07	0.72[c]
Low-Low	Male	1.96[a]	3.21[b]	1.25[c]
	Female	2.64[a]	2.73[b]	0.09

Data from House and McKeachie (in McKeachie, Milholland, *et al.*, 1968).
N of students 11–27 per cell; total *N* is 147.

[a]Difference for this pair of values significant by *t*-test.

[b]Difference for this pair of values significant by *t*-test. The value of 2.73 combines disparate means of 2.33 for male students and 3.00 for female students. Sex of student did not much affect results in other cells.

[c]Difference across this row significant by *t*-test.

significant in the other. Recall, for example, the reading studies of Chapter 9. Although we would not disregard such a disparity, the interpretations may be overcomplicated. The fact that the Aptitude x Treatment interaction is significant in one sex and not in the other is not strong evidence of Sex x Aptitude x Treatment interaction. That interaction would have to be established by a direct test. Yet, sample sizes are rarely sufficient to make a powerful test of such a second-order interaction.

Male/female college teachers were taken by House and McKeachie as a "treatment" contrast that might interact with ability (McKeachie, Milholland, *et al.*, 1968, Sec. III-10). Within the data of Study II, seven women teaching sections of introductory psychology were paired with men for purposes of the analyses. Within a pair both teachers were High-High with regard to use of affiliation cues and achievement cues, or both Low-Low. The students of each teacher were blocked on SAT, then their grades were examined. Student nAch, nAff, and n Power did not interact significantly with sex of instructor. Ability of student and type of instructor did interact (significantly, when students were taken as the unit of analysis). The means in Table 13.10 show *some disordinal interactions of impressive size.* If further work of this kind is to be undertaken, investigators should not remain content with pooling data for like-sex teachers. In the High-High category, not all male teachers would produce flat within-class regressions, nor would all female teachers produce a steep one. "Clinical" observations of the classes would be needed to give information on the origins of such differences.

The relation of sex of teacher to sex of student was taken up in a short paper by McKeachie and Lin (1971), but we are unable to reconcile their data with the conclusions. Learning was greater with warm female instructors, for students of either sex. As we read the data there was *no interaction of instructor sex with student sex.*

A number of studies in the lower grades have provided convincing evidence that sex of student does not interact systematically with sex of teacher (e.g., Waetjen & Fisher, 1966; Farrall, 1968; Ellis & Peterson, 1971; Asher & Gottman, 1973). We do not find this surprising, in view of the psychological heterogeneity to be found in same-sex groups.

Social class

We have not searched for studies on interactions of social class with instructional method. If such interactions exist, they are of the utmost importance for educational practice, particularly since certain minority groups fall economically in the lower social strata.

As long ago as 1948, Allison Davis, Tyler, and others were urging schools to develop new instructional styles suited to the lower class (Eells *et al.*, 1951). The thrust of their argument was deflected by their attempt to develop a "culture fair intelligence test." The validity of this test was judged adversely when the test failed to predict achievement in conventional schooling. The original logic calling for new kinds of instruction in which a new kind of test could be predictive was lost from view.

What is formally a very similar argument appears in Jensen's insistence on the social-class linkages of "Level I" (rote learning) and "Level II" (analytic) abilities. Level I ability, according to his data, is unrelated to social class, whereas there is an association for Level II (g, v:ed). Some educational objectives could perhaps be better attained, for the student averaging high in Level I and low in Level II, by making more use of rote methods in the classroom. No evidence regarding the relevance of memory tests to school learning under alternative procedures is now available, however, Any attempt to evaluate instruction that *is* related to memory abilities will have to give as much attention to transfer outcomes (including the growth of Level-II abilities) as to the responses directly taught.

If the heuristic ideas of Davis or Jensen were ultimately to be validated by the invention of teaching methods under which the lower-class student does comparatively well, the conclusion should not be left in that form. It would be wrong to assign students to a kind of instruction explicitly on the basis of their SES. (The extent to which schools have done this inadvertently has been a justified source of complaint.) SES is no more than an indicator of certain motivational patterns, thinking styles, or skills. Not all lower-class students have these modal patterns and surely many students of higher SES do have them. Hence, the question must be pursued to the point of identifying and measuring the interacting qualities of the individual (*or the classroom group!*) that SES indexes.

Reports from the University of Texas indicate that there are substantial and meaningful interactions of SES with the variables most commonly considered in research on teaching. As we understand matters from informal communications (Peck, Brophy, and others) the teaching techniques advanced by modern educational theory (particularly, opportunity for student self-direction, supportive-spontaneous teaching) *appear to produce superior results for children from well-to-do homes and inferior results with poor children.* The data leading to this conclusion come from extensive investigations of dozens of teachers, and the report will thus be a major contribution to the ATI literature. But it will need to be understood in relation to other studies such as Featherstone's (p. 324). Any further comment now would be premature.

We insert here an isolated but suggestive study that has SES as one variable. As part of a larger project, Himmelweit (1966) made a rather unusual study of the interaction of social class and ability with school environment in predicting school dropout. Four grammar schools in England were studied. Schools A and B served working-class or mixed (working- and middle-class) populations. Though both used ability grouping (streaming), School A continually emphasized ability as a symbol of excellence, while School B deemphasized it. Schools C and D were predominantly middle-class. School D emphasized an elitist track system based on the *effort* the student had displayed rather than his tested ability, whereas School C reduced stratification as much as possible. Individual measures of stream (assigned level), self-assessed class position (perceived success), and father's occupation were cor-

Table 13.11 Correlations of school-leaving age with student's
            stream, self-assessed position, and father's occupation

| Variable | Correlation of variable with age at which student left school | | | |
| | More stratified schools | | Less stratified schools | |
	A (N = 86)	D (N = 41)	B (N = 70)	C (N = 66)
Stream (assigned success)	0.58*	0.42*	0.22	0.14
Self-assessed position (perceived success)	0.04	0.22	0.38*	0.36*
Father's occupation	0.04	0.43*	0.17	0.23

After Himmelweit, 1966.

*$p < .01$.

related with age of leaving school, with the result shown in Table 13.11 ($N = 263$).

The conclusion seems to be that, in the schools with clear status hierarchies, the status initially assigned to a student predicts his likelihood of remaining in school. In schools where this assignment was not an important status symbol, dropout was predicted by the student's own image of his success. But other factors varied within and between the four schools, IQ being one of them. This study could be repeated with adequate samples in a number of schools and with a more illuminating stepwise regression analysis. Better yet, an effort could be made to assess actual intellectual performance as the student entered the school and a year or so later.

The institutional environment as a "treatment"

Just as the single classroom has an atmosphere that brings out the best in some students and retards others, so an entire institution has a style or climate. A novel climate is deliberately created in the "alternative school" that seeks to appeal to young people who are not attuned to the conventional school. An attempt to alter climate is implicit in the policy of differentiating collegiate institutions.

College characteristics

It is appropriate to study interactions of student characteristics with college environments. Astin (1970) pointed out that findings about main effects of environments are not of much use, unless an existing institution is to be drastically modified or a new one designed. But interactions are directly useful even when major institutional change is unlikely. Interactions permit distribution of prospective students among existing institutions, facilitating mutual choice by student and college so that each student body is made up of the persons most likely to benefit from that college's instructional and community style. Indeed, the basic purpose of establishing schools of different types, or independent colleges within a university campus, is to provide options for students of different temperaments. Such person-situation matching ought to benefit personal growth in ways tests and grades do not reflect.

Even so, regressions of grades or standard tests on personal characteristics are worth examining. Romine, J. Davis, and Gehman (1970) chose two colleges that differed markedly in their feeling of "community" as evaluated by the CUES instrument. A total of about 600 women were sorted into three levels on degree of independence from family, determined by questionnaire.

The analysis was novel. First, grades were regressed on ability, using a weighted combination of two SAT scores and high school rank. The R of 0.55 for the supportive campus was sufficiently above the 0.38 for the impersonal campus that it may indicate ATI for ability. Next, the regression of actual grade onto grade predicted by the equation was determined, within the college, within each level of dependency. Dependent students (ability held constant) did better at both schools, except that at low ability levels, at the impersonal schools, the highly independent outdid equally able dependents.

The analysis and reporting of the study was idiosyncratic and in our opinion inefficient. The hypothesis was that within each college there is a regression function of the form

$$b_{1t}X_1 + b_{2t}X_2 + b_{3t}X_3 + d_t (X_4 - \overline{X_4}) (b_{1t}X_1 + b_{2t}X_2 + b_{3t}X_3) + e_t X_4$$

$-X_1$ being SAT-V; X_2 being SAT-M; X_3, high school rank; and X_4, the moderator variable, being the measure of student independence. A straightforward regression study would tell whether X_4 served as a moderator variable and would assess its influence. The regression functions for two schools could be compared, though with the understanding that the GPA scale shifts from place to place. Unfortunately, the published analysis used successive fragments of the data, chopping up 250 students in one college and 344 in the other into sets as small as 50. Moreover, after running significance tests, the authors reported t values rather than the descriptive statistics. This loses power and may lead to wrong conclusions.

Where present student bodies have different regressions of achievement on aptitude, two interpretations are possible. It may be that institutions now draw from different populations, such that the AT regressions would differ even if the treatments were uniform. The differences may instead result because the environments have differential effects.

Astin (1970) has discussed pertinent methodological and logical issues. Many of his recommendations are similar to ours. Studies from ETS have also examined methodology. Rock in particular has tried to modify the routine multiple-regression methods that Astin advocates. He and his colleagues usually take, as outcome data, the GRE area examinations given near graduation. These they residualize, partialing out scores from SAT four years earlier by means of a uniform regression equation for all colleges. The mean residual outcome within the college is then assessed. A regression equation across colleges is set up to forecast this residual from college characteristics. A particular college can be examined "clinically" if it falls far from the regression line.

One can also study the possibility that, in a certain college, the regression of the GRE posttests on SAT pretests is unusual. Centra, Linn, and Parey (1970) selected and matched seven white colleges with seven black colleges. Data from the senior class of each college (N = 733) were used to compute a separate regression line for each college. *The slopes were significantly heterogeneous;* some colleges seemed better suited to low-ability Ss, while others got better results from Highs. Slope seemed not to depend upon ethnicity.

Rock, Centra, and Linn (1970) showed that college characteristics discriminate between more/less effective colleges (positive/negative residual GRE means). These results imply *main effects for college characteristics,* and do not bear on the question of interactions. The authors did not report on regression slopes within their 95 colleges (N = 6855). A later analysis of data for 100 students from each college by Rock, Baird, and Linn (1972) identified groups of colleges that were similar on mean SAT score, and on slope and intercept for AT regressions. They first formed hierarchical clusters; then applied discriminant analysis to find college characteristics that distinguished among clusters. Regressions onto either SAT-V or SAT-M were then calculated within each cluster; dependent variables were the GRE Humanities, Social Sciences, and Natural Sciences Area Tests. With Humanities as outcome, five clusters of colleges were identified, two of which had especially shallow within-college slopes onto SAT-V. The cluster with the highest effectiveness at the mean turned out also to have the steepest slope. Natural Sciences had a shallow slope onto SAT-M in one of three clusters; again, the interaction was ordinal. With regard to Social Sciences, as outcome, slopes within clusters appeared to be parallel.

Pervin (1967) used a Semantic Differential to examine student-college interaction. Students evaluated on 52 bipolar scales, the concepts College, Self, Students, Faculty, Administration, and Ideal College. "Distances" within pairs of concepts can be computed for each student. Pervin correlated these distance scores with the dissatisfaction the student reported about various aspects of his college (N = 3016, 21 colleges). A substantial number of significant positive correlations of this sort were obtained. When the self-vs.-administration distance (say) correlated highest with statements of dissatisfaction with the administration, Pervin interpreted this as indicating validity for the instrument. It was demonstrated for two particular schools that

. . . dissatisfied students at one school saw the college as more conservative, less equalitarian, and less scholarly, and the self as more liberal, more equalitarian, and more scholarly than did satisfied students. On each of these scales the relationship was reversed for dissatisfied students at the second school; that is, at the second school dissatisfied students saw the college as more liberal, more equalitarian, and more scholarly, and the self as less liberal, less equalitarian, and far less scholarly than did satisfied students. (Pervin, 1967, p. 299).

A three-mode factor analysis convinced Pervin that similar contrasts existed throughout his mass of data. The data were not reported in detail for all colleges and Pervin's report does not lend itself to summary. But Pervin's approach does seem to hold promise for ATI studies, especially if the analysis were extended. Regression analyses using the concept ratings separately should be more informative than the distance scores. Achievement criteria should come into the picture also.

The most elaborate analysis on the college environment is that of George Stern (1969). He sees the institution's "press" (Henry Murray's term) setting conditions in which persons with certain "needs" can thrive and others cannot. He evaluates press by having students identify which statements are true of their institution (e.g., "Students try in all sorts of ways to be friendly, especially to newcomers "). Needs are measured by a self-description index. Stern's conceptualization implies that learning will be affected by the interaction of student's needs and institutional press; but he does not offer evidence on interactive effects. His empirical reports to date stop with evidence on the prevalence of various need-press combinations.

The earliest stage of this research used the clinical perspectives and research methods of the early 1950's. Stern, Stein, and Bloom (1956) argued that the press of the College of the University of Chicago would be suited to the "non-stereopath" and unsuited to the "stereopath" (who is fearful, submissive, rigid, lacking in constructive motivation). It is demonstrated (their pp. 106ff.) that extremes of these two types differ radically in their response to the College. Most notably, within the first year, 23 percent of stereopaths had left the College, compared to only one per cent of the nonstereopaths. ($N = 162$.) *The case for ATI was left unfinished,* for the theoretical argument implied that there are colleges where the stereopaths would have been satisfied and would have done well. No data on such a "second treatment" were collected.

Stern's position has been, from the outset, an ATI position. It is understandable that, in laying out his methods and concepts for the first time, he should deal with the dimensionality of his instruments, and then document the existence of main effects in press (across campuses or divisions of campuses) and main effects in need (across student bodies). Next he demonstrated that students in one college are likely to have a need pattern different from those in colleges with other patterns of press, and many of these differences seem to make psychological sense. One other type of study did bring in genuine criteria; but the analysis did not compare the case where the school press fits the modal individual need with the campus where these do not match. We are, then, disappointed in the incompleteness of this program of work. But the base has been laid for testing the ATI hypothesis that, given a certain college press, incoming students with one need pattern thrive, while others do badly.

It will probably be less expensive and more natural, as a next step in this area, to do longitudinal studies to see who survives for two or four years in various environments. The style of thinking and analysis exemplified by Domino and McKeachie (pp. 442, 444, 448) could be usefully applied in cross-college work. But comprehensive studies relating need and press to achievement and "personal growth" criteria may be a long way off.

Chapter 14 | What do we know about ATI? What should we learn?

In education, dozens of drastic reforms, from alternative schools to computer-regulated systems, now bid for attention. In nearly all of them, adaptation to individual differences (or group differences) is the theme. Human resources are badly used when society puts everyone into one-track schooling and periodically culls out the unsuccessful. The need is for multiple, interbridging pathways. Social planners must accept "optimal diversity of opportunity" as their ruling principle. (The phrase is Arthur Jensen's.) The search for interactions is an idea whose time has come.

Planners are already prepared to place large bets on proposals to fit treatments to individuals, as is evident in this statement by then-Secretary of Health, Education, and Welfare Elliot Richardson, before a Congressional committee in 1972. He started by quoting Mosteller and Moynihan:

'It is absurd to reject the possibility of compensatory educational programs' doing what they set out to do. . .'

But I [said the Secretary] would go further and assert that the data more recently available suggest that well-managed, adequately financed compensatory programs which focus on the basic cognitive learning skills can crack through the educational barriers of the past.

With careful diagnosis of present skill levels, adequately defined program objectives, and learning from mistakes, it can be done. The learning styles, including the incentive motivational style and communication styles, of children vary from individual to individual within a group and from group to group on ethnic, socio-economic, and regional bases. The approach that will work is the approach that carefully assesses the learning styles of children on a classroom by classroom basis and then adapts the teaching styles, curriculum, and instructional materials to take advantage of the learning styles of the children.

The ideals expressed in this paragraph are ideals that all educational psychologists can endorse, and indeed are ideals that they have endorsed for at least two generations. But when political leaders seize upon a speculative idea, it is time for those closer to the research to take sober thought. Do we really know anything generalizable about "basic cognitive learning skills"? If that phrase refers only to the size of the child's vocabulary, we do. We also know a good deal about the child's readiness to invent mediating connections when asked to hold a pair of words in mind. But we know precious little about the numerous mental activities of a child working on cumulative lessons in school. Similarly, the psychologist can say little about "incentive motivational style" or "communication style." He is not ready to put forward viable recommendations about tailoring year-long instructional procedures to fit different kinds of pupils.

Psychologists do know some things, and so do the educators who have been conscientiously testing schemes for compensatory education. Between them, they know some good questions to ask, they know some procedures that don't work, and they know some procedures that have worked well in hot-house situations. Judging from the reports they make to the profession, far more is unknown than known. Richardson's words express a hope whose full realization will be far in the future.

The present book offers an interim consolidation of ideas about "learning style," "aptitude," and the like. We have reviewed findings on the hunches of a decade or more ago. No Aptitude x Treatment interactions are so well confirmed that they can be used directly as guides to instruction. Some of the research has been fruitless because questions about individual differences in learning have been phrased incorrectly; but much has been learned. This chapter considers where we stand and where educational psychologists should direct their next efforts. It does not reiterate all the findings from previous chapters, nor all the specialized methodological and theoretical points.

Do ATI exist?

Aptitude x Treatment interactions exist. To assert the opposite is to assert that whichever educational procedure is best for Johnny is best for everyone else in Johnny's school. Even the most commonplace adaptation of instruction, such as choosing different books for more and less capable readers of a given age, rests on an assumption of ATI that it seems foolish to challenge.

Do positive findings replicate and generalize?

The isolated report of a single study does not found a Gibraltar-like conclusion. Effects can occur "by chance" or they can be real, one-time-only effects that do not warrant a generalization. Consider Domino's finding (p. 442) that students with constructive motivation do best when allowed autonomy, and that defensive students do best when the instructor imposes a firm structure on the course.

Domino's report gains solidity from the fact that much the same result was found by his two investigations with different techniques. Yet Amidon found what seems to have been the opposite result (p. 466). Does the discrepancy merely reflect the difference between college and junior-high-school Ss?

The problem of replication or generalization is ubiquitous in social research (Cronbach, 1975). The natural-science model requires one to propose a broad hypothesis that, bolstered by evidence in a number of settings, becomes the assertion of a truth. But the natural scientist is able to include in his truths the phrase "other conditions being equal" and to arrange that nearly all conditions in his test tubes *are* equal. A science of social institutions cannot be a test-tube science.

The substantive problem before us is to learn which characteristics of the person interact dependably with which features of instructional methods. This is a question of awesome breadth. In principle, it calls for a survey of all the ways in which people differ. It requires that individuality be abstracted into categories or dimensions. Likewise, it calls for abstractions that describe instructional events in one classroom after another. The constructs descriptive of persons and instructional treatments pair up to form literally innumerable ATI hypotheses. It is impossible to search systematically for ATI when the swarm of hypotheses is without order. The present summary only starts toward the high ground from which perspective may be gained.

Among ATI hypotheses that might be tested, it is to be expected that the majority will be false. That is to say, when a person variable and a treatment variable are paired speculatively, the interaction effect is likely to be negligible. Even if a speculation is sound, fine-tuning of the treatment conditions is needed to bring the relation squarely under the investigator's eyepiece. Until then, the phenomenon is sure to wander in and out of view, as relevant uncontrolled conditions vary haphazardly from one "replication" to the next.

Nor can we hope to establish generalizations that will hold up in every similar educational setting. The inconsistencies among studies that purport to study "the same treatment" are not simply signs of poor technique, which will abate when educational research "becomes fully scientific." Real effects vary from one setting to another because of unanticipated interactions. The classroom dynamics, the personality of the teacher, and the specific instructional materials have their effect even when the blueprint for a "treatment" is being followed meticulously. A generalization will almost never prove to be true in more than, say, 75 per cent of classrooms of a type (e.g., first-grade classrooms in urban settings). Such a probabilistic truth is informative, as a source of practical policies and as a basis for insight. But we cannot be content to set policy for the individual classroom in terms of an Iron Law that has a 25 per cent chance of working out badly for that class. School practice will have to be flexible, and sensitive to here-and-now data, simply because so many conditions moderate the effects of any educational plan in the instance. While results in ATI studies have often been negative, this does not deny the hypothesis. Most studies used samples so small that a predominance of "chance results" was rendered inevitable. What the results deny is the hope that a few years of research on a limited scale will produce both a solid theory and a set of practically useful generalizations about instruction. Learner x Treatment interaction is an essentially new scientific problem, and reaching consolidated understanding in such matters often requires decades.

The preceding chapters have summarized much evidence for ATI, and we are about to list illustrative positive findings. The optimistic outlook of this chapter will be qualified by our awareness that ATI cannot be pinned down as generalizations. But *any* optimistic statement about ATI research on instruction may surprise some readers of the recent literature. Several large-scale research efforts have reported either no ATI findings or an uninterpretable mixture of conflicting results—the Bond-Dykstra, McKeachie, and Wallen programs may be recalled as examples. The impression that ATI are illusory rather than merely elusive has spread, as a by-product of two illdigested reports. An early compilation of our notes on ATI studies was given limited distribution (see preface); since we did not at that time discount studies having inadequate statistical power, the predominant impression was negative. At about the same time, Glenn Bracht reviewed much the same literature. His tally of positive and negative findings, relayed by others through secondary sources, cast a pall over the prospects of work on interactions.

Comments on Bracht's review. Bracht (1969, 1970) did not set out to determine whether ATI exist. Rather, he started out with a belief in individualizing instruction along ATI lines. That faith was shaken by "the paucity of experimental findings showing disordinal interactions between alternative treatments and personological variables." Bracht endeavored to sort out ATI studies on the basis of their parameters. His aim was to locate types of studies where the payoff rate was relatively high, so that the next research worker could then concentrate where he was likely to strike it rich. Bracht's chief conclusion was that payoff was associated with firm control of treatment conditions and with "factorially simple" aptitude measures.

What seemed to stick in the mind of Bracht's readers was the infrequency of ATI findings. Bracht's mentor, Gene Glass, insisted:

> 'There is no evidence for an interaction of curriculum treatments and personological variables.' I don't know of another statement that has been confirmed so many times by so many people . . . [I]f these interactions exist, they exist with respect to very narrow and specific variables, not to the general, factorially complex IQ's and abilities that we typically measure. (Glass, 1970, pp. 210–211).

There is a need to reassess Bracht's discouraging survey. Bracht had located 90 studies where ATI were examined. As some considered more than one aptitude, Bracht tallied 108 comparisons of regression slopes. He concluded that just five of the comparisons gave adequate evidence of ATI.* With the usual choice of .05

---

*Of these five studies, we have not included those of H. Marshall; J. W. Atkinson and W. Reitman; and C. I. Hovland, A. Lumsdaine, and S. Stouffer. Only the Hovland study was close to an educational issue, and it dealt with a rather specialized question. The two remaining studies, by van de Reit and by Thompson and Hunnicutt, are discussed on page 434 ff. Because of their artificiality, we do not consider them particularly important examples of ATI.

as the α risk, five "significant" results will appear merely as a result of sampling variation. Hence, it is easy for Bracht's reader to conclude that the whole ATI literature is amply described by the null hypothesis, and that the effort to find interaction is futile. Our survey, which leads us to a more positive conclusion, covers the educationally significant studies among Bracht's set of 90—except those for which we had only an abstract. We reason differently from Bracht, and consequently reach a different conclusion.

We take ordinal interactions seriously (see p. 33 f.), whereas Bracht lumped "ordinal or no interaction" together as if the two were equally lacking in interest. Moreover, where the sample regression lines were disordinal, Bracht dismissed the interaction as "ordinal" unless the data satisfied an unreasonably stringent test for disordinality in the population (see p. 93). Bracht arbitrarily discounted some positive results. The Snow study (see p. 274, 453) reported five disordinal inter-actions in the sample data on immediate recall; Bracht reported these to be ordinal, by his usual rule of inference. More important here are the two ATI for delayed recall that Bracht found to be disordinal by his test—and then dismissed! Said he (his p. 120): "Since the delayed recall scores were subject to other factors than the experimental treatments, the extent to which the treatment differences at each ability level can be attributed to the treatment tasks is unknown." Consequently, Bracht listed the study as an instance of "ordinal or no interaction." Presumably "other factors" refers to the uncontrolled activities students pursued between the end of each experimental lesson and the pertinent course examination a week or so later. We, however, advocate using delayed measures to test educational effects, and see no bias in the Snow design that warrants ignoring the result. In general, retention of educational learning must be assessed under ecologically representative, uncontrolled conditions.

Bracht often worked from an abstract. We chose to work only from full reports, finding that the full report often leads us to a conclusion unlike that suggested by the abstract. Moreover, if Bracht found an abstract obscure, the study went into his category of ordinal-or-no-interaction. This maneuver could not but contribute to a "paucity" of disordinal interactions in Bracht's summary.

Bracht usually took any author's statement of findings at face value, save for imposing his special test for disordinality. We have sought to apply consistent logic to all studies. We have interpreted related studies cumulatively, where neces-sary reorganizing the data. We sometimes dismiss an interaction the author found significant, or vice versa. One example of our departure from Bracht is seen in the studies of Calvin *et al.* (above, pp. 322 ff.) Bracht reported each Calvin study accurately, but after saying that the three replications reported similar non-significant differences, Bracht tallied all three as "ordinal or no interaction." We see the studies, as a group, as solid evidence for an interaction that is probably disordinal.

Our final difference from Bracht is that we recognize the β risk as well as the α risk. When a strong and genuine effect is present in the population, chance will dictate acceptance of the null hypothesis in some fraction of the samples. With the samples typical in past ATI research, that fraction is very high—perhaps in the neighborhood of 95 per cent. That is to say, if Bracht found 95 nonsignificant results in a set of 100 typical studies, this was entirely consistent with the view that, in the population, practically important ATI effects occur for most (!) of the treatments and aptitudes studied. Bracht's reasoning was penurious rather than merely parsimonious.

Effects associated with general abilities

After the first enthusiasm for mental tests wore off about 1930, the concept of a general ability has been under recurrent challenge. In the 1930's, Thurstone made a case for differentiated ability factors as being far more suited to both research and practical decision making. Guilford has kept that view alive and has extended it. The work on decision theory out of which our concern with ATI developed led to similar doubts about the general test as a predictor. Cronbach and Gleser (1957, esp. pp. 124ff.; pp. 139ff. in 1965 edition) indicated that tests of broad, general abilities are likely to contribute less to educational decisions about individuals than more specialized tests. "A general test is, by its very nature, positively correlated with success in a great variety of treatments, and its value for placement is limited by that fact." They went on to use the allocation policies of British schools as an example, suggesting that the 11+ examination, while a valid predictor of grammar-school success, probably applied equally well to the secondary school and therefore had little or no differential validity for assisting in that placement decision. "There must be attributes (methods of problem solving? preference for abstract thought? character traits? interests?) which are more relevant to one mode of instruction than the other."

It has become fashionable to decry the use of measures of general ability, and sometimes their use has been prohibited in school systems. The attackers usually insist that the tests do not assess ability to learn, and it is often proposed to substitute measures of achievement or "learning styles." Along with the objections to student classification comes increasing talk of "mastery learning." This kind of instruction can, it is said, eliminate individual differences in educational outcomes. One can bring all students to achieve mastery of the same lessons, by a combination of close monitoring, adequate time for the individual on each unit, and diagnosis to guide the choice of instructional and remedial methods.

As we reviewed the literature on instructional learning, we were forced to reconsider some of the suppositions behind these various arguments. While we see merit in a hierarchical conception of mental abilities, with abilities differentiated at both coarse and fine levels, we have not found Guilford's subdivision a powerful hypothesis (see pp. 155 ff.). Instead of finding general abilities irrelevant to school learning, we find nearly ubiquitous evidence that general measures predict amount learned or rate of learning or both. And, whereas we had expected specialized abilities rather than general abilities to account for interactions, the abilities that most frequently enter into interactions are general. Even in those programs of research that started with specialized ability measures and found interactions with treatment, the data seem to warrant attributing most effects to a general ability. (For examples, see the work of the Florida research group, particularly Davis, p. 257 f., and Behr, p. 286 f; our reanalysis of data from Dunham, Guilford and Hoepfner, p. 134; and the study of Stallings and Snow, p. 237 ff. For the rare exceptions, see Kropp-Nelson-King, p. 370 f.; Edgerton, p. 316.) We have found that tests of general ability relate to subsequent performance in just about the way achievement tests at the start of the course do. Consequently, we doubt that supplanting the general test will appreciably reduce the disadvantage some social groups now have in the educational system.

It is reasonable to expect that the relations of outcome in a particular educational setting to pretests should be somewhat different for (a) tests of abstract, adaptive problem solving with minimal verbal loading, (b) tests of general intellectual development including measures of information, verbal reasoning, arithmetic reasoning, etc., (c) tests of educational development (whether limited to reading and study skills or more comprehensive), (d) pretests that cover specifically the content of the lessons to be taught or the particular skills and concepts the lessons will build upon. The first three are all general measures, the fourth specific. Unfortunately, comparable results for these types of tests are lacking. Only rarely have investigators carried two kinds of measures side by side through a study. Even more rarely have the investigators tested directly whether the pair of regression slopes for a measure in one category differs from the pair for a measure in a second category, or provided data that allowed us to make such a comparison. Even such evidence as we could extract on this issue was rendered equivocal by the fact that sample sizes almost never afford a powerful test of the difference between two differences in regression slope.

Unable to make fine distinctions, we have chosen to aggregate the findings over broad categories of "general" tests. In this section, when we speak of "general ability," we shall mean measures of intelligence, scholastic aptitude, nonverbal reasoning, etc., including the variables often represented by the symbols g and $v{:}ed$. We shall consider reading tests, general aptitude batteries, and prior grade-point average within this rubric along with "mental tests." We shall consider Block Design and Hidden Figures and a few other narrower tests as giving evidence on general ability, even though those tests could be interpreted as measures of spatial reasoning or some more exotic construct such as field independence. Where we wish to speak also of measures of school achievement, we shall speak of "general abilities"—plural. We do not include pretests on elements of a lesson within the general category; but since they probably correlate substantially with the general measures, we may reasonably expect their gross relationships to learning over a long period of instruction to be much the same. It is an open question whether divergent thinking ("creativity"), cognitive complexity, impulsiveness, and other constructs proposed as distinct from general ability actually can be measured so as to give information independent of general abilities.

Power of general abilities to predict success in learning

Measures of general mental ability or scholastic aptitude or academic achievement do predict learning of new material. The correlation is often in the range 0.40 to 0.60, about equal to that found when grade averages are the criterion. This is true even in brief learning experiments, where the outcome measures very likely have low task-to-task reliability.

It is time to lay to rest the idea that "ability to learn" is distinct from what mental tests or measures of past learning reflect. Herbert Woodrow, in pressing this point in the 1940's, no doubt adhered to the hypothesis that biological properties of the nervous system account for better or worse ability to learn. Tests very likely are remote from such basic neurophysiological characteristics. Today we are inclined to emphasize the functioning of the developed nervous system as a whole, and to include within that whole the codes and strategies for processing information that the person has constructed through the interplay of biology and experience. Tests reflect these systems. Woodrow made the mistake of relying on gain scores for much of his supporting evidence. Moreover, he overgeneralized from rather meaningless laboratory tasks to all learning.

Learning rate could be evidenced, presumably, by performance on a series of lessons that "start from scratch." Many of the instructional experiments we reviewed have presented lessons whose content was wholly divorced from the remainder of the curriculum. Some of the small mathematical experiments with the teaching of directed line graphs or the like, for example, have presented a fresh topic. Insofar as the general abilities predicted performance in such courses—and they did—the effect cannot be attributed merely to the inclusion within the new lessons of mathematical responses previously mastered by a fraction of the Ss. Rather, the effect has to be attributed to work habits, word-processing skills, analytic and critical skills, and attitudes. It is still meaningful for ATI research to postulate that a different mix of processes may be needed to respond to a different mode of instruction (or a different kind of content).

Can individual differences in achievement be caused to vanish? We can expect individual differences in educational accomplishment. Adaptation of instruction in the light of ATI is expected to reduce differences below those a lockstep curriculum would produce; but if learning is independent of general abilities only under exceptional conditions, our expectations must be kept modest.

Some enthusiasts take the position that a sound educational technology will reduce or eliminate individual differences in performance. This is seen in a definition of educational effectiveness put forth by Davies (1972, pp. 51-52). He adopts a slogan associated with programmed instruction and mastery approaches, that when sound teaching procedures are used 90 per cent of the students will attain 90 per cent of the intended outcomes. More generally, says Davies, education can be seen as effective only when the normal curve of distribution of outcomes disappears, and the relation of outcomes to general ability approaches the vanishing point. Similar views on "mastery learning" (e.g., Bloom in Block, 1971, p.

49) come from writers who are interested also in ATI. Our disagreement is more a matter of rhetoric than of facts, but it does seem important to contrast the positions.

Bloom has espoused the Overlap Hypothesis of John Anderson (p. 110), which implies that intellectual growth is a process of random increments. This is the very opposite of the proposition that, when all Ss share common opportunities to learn, general abilities forecast the amount to be gained in the next period of time. Since we do not regard differences in growth as random, we found it necessary to review this issue. Our final conclusion (p. 150) was to echo Robert Thorndike, that the issue is a false one. There is no need for us to discuss here the pros and cons of mastery learning. The "mastery" strategy is to keep the student working on a unit until he passes a test at a high level, the teacher giving such help as he can. This infinitely elastic time schedule clearly makes sense in training where the learner has real need to finish the training, where objectives of instruction are circumscribed, and where there is little concern for transfer of the learning to situations not covered by the lessons. The discussions of mastery learning to date have nothing to say about any educational program that has more "liberal" aims, and that has to make use of a fixed number of years of the child's life.

The propaganda about breaking the link between aptitude and achievement can be illustrated by quoting Block (his p. 11). He recommended diagnosis of student performance so that "corrective" exercises can be prescribed to fit the individual; we concur. Then he said:

> As progressively better correction procedures are developed, the relationship between individual differences and student learning suggests that the relationship may be largely an artifact of present instructional practices. The findings demonstrate that if no attempt is made to optimize the quality of each student's classroom instruction, then individual differences in student entry resources (e.g., IQ, aptitudes, and previous learning) are reflected in their achievement. However, if the quality is made optimal . . . then the differences are not reflected in student achievement.

There are two ways to read such a statement. It might imply that students of low general ability can be brought to the same level of school accomplishment as students of high general ability, in the same overall period of schooling. This appears improbable, and we are not persuaded by the evidence Block cites—see our p. 139. The alternative reading is a credible one; the school can use a fixed number of years either to give each student a broad program in which many will fall short of mastery, or to bring everyone to mastery on a limited program while allowing only the fast learners a broader educational diet. This is by no means to eliminate individual differences.

The arguments for mastery learning date from about 1963, when Bloom had just completed his studies of growth in mental ability, and when enthusiasm for programmed instruction was high. John B. Carroll, reflecting on his own experiments with PI, put forward a "model of school learning" that has been a principal inspiration to Bloom and other writers on "mastery." But Carroll did not hold that ability differences can be made irrelevant, as is shown in a passage from his paper (1963b) that applied his model to PI. He referred to

> the argument or claim that programed instruction can virtually guarantee learning for nearly everybody to any specified criterion and thus "wash out" individual differences in terminal ability. But even if these arguments are valid . . . it is probable that programed instruction will simply trade off individual differences in final achievement for individual differences in learning time.

Now insofar as learning time is correlated with the aptitudes that tests measure—and our evidence argues for such a correlation—general abilities are going to correlate with any broad index of later achievement.

One can mask individual differences only by restricting the supplementary instruction of the faster student to off-the-line topics that are not counted in the final evaluation. Myopic as such evaluation appears to be, it is not uncommon. An example is the extensive Hartill study on ability grouping (our p. 337), which applied something rather like mastery procedures in the "fundamental" portion of the curriculum and ignored the "enrichment"—i.e., the broader education—the abler pupils received.

We once hoped that instructional methods might be found whose outcomes correlate very little with general ability. This does not appear to be a viable hope. Outcomes from extended instruction almost always correlate with pretested ability, unless a ceiling is artificially imposed.

The pervasive correlations of general ability with learning rate or outcomes in education limits the power of ATI findings to reduce individual differences.

Interactive effects

AT regression slopes that differ from treatment to treatment are more probable for general abilities than for any other aptitude considered in the ATI literature. Typically, a fairly steep slope is observed in one treatment. Sometimes the second slope is moderately strong, sometimes close to zero, and sometimes negative. Significant interactions are more likely in experiments that continue over several weeks than in short experiments. We can list succinctly the treatment variations that tended to produce steeper slopes for the regression of outcome onto general abilities. Later we shall list those variations that rather consistently produced no slope difference, or entirely irregular differences. We shall not, however, try to catalogue all the treatment variables on which some bit of evidence is available.

When one treatment is fully elaborated, whereas the other leaves much of the burden of organization and interpretation to the learner, the regression slope in the former tends to be less steep. That is, Highs profit from the opportunity to process the information in their own way; Lows tend to be handicapped. This is not a universal rule, but it encompasses a wide range of results.

In teaching military plotting, the slope was steep in a conventional treatment and shallower when a TV presentation broke the task down for the learner (Taylor,[*] p. 180). A terse instructional program stripped to minimum essentials gave a flatter slope than a redundant text (Hershberger, p. 206); but possible evidence in the opposite direction came from Valverde, p. 206, and Leith, pp. 207, 424. The regression was flatter for students who studied a redundant text than among those who had a stripped version (Kropp, p. 207). Preliminary preparation to overcome gaps in background reduced the AT regression slope in the Gagné-Gropper study (p. 266).

Short, preliminary, stage-setting or "organizers" sometimes have an advantage for Lows, and may be useless or detrimental for Highs. Steeper regression slopes in groups without organizers—i.e., ATI showing that organizers help persons Low in general ability—appeared in some studies (Ausubel, p. 350; Proger, p. 351). Results were not consistent; even within a single study one often finds an interaction effect on an immediate measure and not on a delayed or transfer measure, or vice versa. At times a preliminary statement of main ideas may help the Highs (M. Merrill, p. 351). *Highs* were helped, at least to a modest degree, when supplementary organizers preceded very difficult content in the Leith and Merrill studies. Highs could make some use of the organizer, whereas the Lows could not. In the other studies, the organizer appears to have been sufficiently simple that Lows could take advantage of it. One can only speculate as to why the added background lesson was detrimental to performance of Highs in some of the studies. Once in a while (e.g., Salomon, p. 343 ff.) one suspects that the new organizer conflicted with schemata Highs already had available.

Instructional treatments have sometimes been augmented by demonstrations or other devices that help the learner to comprehend more clearly just what he is to do. A clarifying device can reduce the slope of the AT regression, helping the Lows without hindering the Highs. The support for this generalization was gathered under artificial conditions. Lows were helped in searching for visual information by a film demonstration of effective search and of the visual transformations needed in solving spatial problems (Salomon, pp. 343 ff). In the child-development laboratory, a similar effect appeared when alternative forms of live demonstration were compared (Corsini, p. 345; Coates, p. 345).

Elaboration that takes the form of systematic explanations places a burden of comprehension on the learner, which tends to help Highs. An attempt to develop arithmetic through coherent generalizations helped abler students in the studies of Thiele (p. 248) and Orton (p. 249). The finding of steeper slopes in a "modern" algebra course (Sabers, p. 288) may have the same origin. On the other hand, we cannot read the G. L. Anderson (p. 245), Edgerton (p. 253) or McConnell (p. 248) data as fitting this conclusion.

A videotaped demonstration of complex teaching style was more effective for Lows and less effective for Highs than study of a transcript of the same scene

---

[*]In this section, our cross-references cite only the first author of a multiple-author study.

(Koran, p. 276). This evidence is clouded by the fact that the result appeared
for just one ability test and not for others that should also measure general ability.
Some later work (Marantz, p. 277), however, found a similar anomalous result
with this same instrument.

Some studies have compared straightforward verbal instruction ("semantic"
treatments) with treatments that substitute symbols or diagrams wherever possible.
In teaching modulus-seven arithmetic and in teaching of advanced mathematics,
the regression slope onto general ability was steeper for the more verbal treatment
(Behr, p. 286; J. Davis, p. 383). In two studies where grammar was taught by
a purely verbal and by a partly figural method (King, Fredrick, p. 263 ff.), we
judge that interaction was absent. There is a vast difference between the mathematical
content where the interaction appeared, and the grammatical content in the
studies where the interaction is dubious.

Some studies consider a verbal/spatial contrast. General (or verbal) ability related
more to outcome from the verbal treatment, in about half of these studies (Allison,
Bracht, Behr, pp. 280-291 *passim,;* Gropper, p. 273). Evidently, for some instructional content, using other forms of communication to supplement or replace
part of the verbal content will help Lows. The change may, however, be disadvantageous to Highs.

Variables yielding inconsistent interactions with general ability. Advocates of
programmed instruction anticipated that developing the content in an orderly
manner, by small steps, with continual overt response and correction, would help
Lows. To counter the criticism that such an elaborate program would extend the
working time of Highs and cause them to be bored, the concept of branching
was added. In a branched program, a concept is elaborately developed only for the
student who has difficulty with it. The evidence on all these treatment variables
is so inconsistent that one must reject the suggested generalization, as a whole and
in each of its parts.

The conclusion is not that such treatment variations never interact. When two
programs are compared that vary in one or more of these respects, one may find
the interaction envisioned by the hypothesis, or a main effect with little or no
interaction, or—on rare occasions—an interaction in the direction opposite to that
anticipated. While ATI are more in the expected direction than in the opposite
direction, the interactions appear only fitfully. No one has been able to describe
the conditions that make such an interaction likely.

Great inconsistency arises also in the investigation of adjunct questions. Supplementary questions, presented before, or after, or at intermediate points in a
text selection or lecture, often improve learning for students generally. Recent
studies have looked for interactions of such treatments with broad ability variables
(Hershberger, p. 206 ; Hollen, Berliner, Shavelson, Hiller, p. 356 ff.). While some
kind of ATI appears in nearly every study, contradictions abound. No generalization
has emerged, and it may be that the microexperiments typically used in this level
of work are incapable of producing replicable results.

More heavily verbal treatments frequently have an advantage for students with comparatively more advanced mental development or greater verbal ability (Thiele, p. 248; Allison, p. 280; Behr, p. 286; J. B. Davis, Jr., p. 257; Gropper, p. 273 but not Gagné-Gropper, p. 266; Koran, p. 276). In the DePauli study (p. 253), a technical training device that reduced the verbal loading generated a comparatively flat slope even in a course that had considerable theoretical content.

The attempt to contrast inductive with didactic instruction is rendered difficult by the diversity of treatments and the brevity and artificiality of many of the studies. There is a general tendency (pp. 311-320; 370-375) for the regression of outcomes onto general abilities to be somewhat steeper under discovery or guided-discovery conditions. A good many studies, however, showed no interaction.

Instruction at a more rapid pace can generate a steep regression slope (Petersen, p. 261). Such interactive effects are frequently rendered equivocal, however, by the experimenter's decision to exclude from the posttest the added material the accelerated group has studied. Studies of homogeneous grouping do not demonstrate strong ATI effects on achievement, in part because of this limited measurement (pp. 334 ff.). There was some tendency for grouping to raise the self-concepts of Lows and to reduce those of Highs in Drews' study (p. 337).

General ability does not interact strongly with classroom climate, or teacher style, but there are some indications of steeper regression slopes with more permissive instruction (Wispé; McKeachie, Flanders; Ward; Calvin, pp. 320-326.).

More latitude for self-direction is also welcomed by Highs working individually. Allowing Ss to study items from cards, choosing the items for attention, benefited the Highs (Taylor, p. 180). Self-direction in using an instructional program generated a steeper slope than the usual procedure in a few studies (pp. 207 ff.), but no interaction was found by Tagatz (p. 187). Hunt's (p. 376 ff.) work on conceptual style yields a similar implication.

In nearly all these relationships, we see the Highs doing better when given greater freedom to proceed in their own manner, when thrown more upon their own resources. And we see regression slopes becoming flatter when more of the intellectual work is done for the learner. In this respect, findings here are consistent with those summarized in the previous section.

Despite this, the idea that conventional instruction has a steeper slope than programmed instruction or similar procedures was not supported. Interactions were fairly common, but as likely to be in one direction as in the other. What causes PI to give a flat slope in one study and a steep slope in another cannot be determined from the reports to date, but it is clear that the simple PI format has different consequences in different groups or with different subject matter. The need to study effects class-by-class was especially evident in the study of performance contracting (p. 188); an overall result, consistent with the null hypothesis, masked effects running in opposite directions in different communities. The Maier study (p. 182) showed that the teacher's attitude could make a difference in the effectiveness even of PI.

Within the style broadly identified as PI, experiments have contrasted small steps with large steps, overt reponse with covert response, regular order with scrambled order. None of these contrasts generated consistent interactions (pp. 190–215).

Discussion. The ATI described to this point all echo the theme that the person with superior intellectual development learns better than others, when intellectual adaptation is required during learning. Adaptation comes about through many processes: self-confidence, analytic attitude, stored aids to mediation (e.g., vocabulary, logical schemata, overlearned elementary content on which the new lessons can be built), effective tactics (e.g., chunking, labeling, identifying main points), biological reactions (e.g., brain metabolism), and so on. If these were to be separately appraised an association among them would be found, not because they are "the same thing" but because each of them facilitates the development of the others. Intellectual development is cumulative; the person who succeeds in early intellectual adaptations lays down skills and attitudes that help him a year later in learning new lessons. Development does not proceed along a uniform front. The preadolescents with high IQs who do badly on tests of divergent thinking are a striking example. On the whole, however, among American middle-class students, the variations within the profile of adaptive processes are probably small compared to the gross variations across persons.

This amounts to a statement that a single rank order does predict success in most meaningful learning. But it predicts more strongly under some conditions than others. It is in those ATI that we can escape the inevitability of "them as has, gets." Learning depends on general intellectual development to a greater degree when active intellectual work is required of the learner. Procedures that reduce the intellectual demand often reduce the differences between Highs and Lows. When such tactics are brought under control and applied to instruction of Lows over a long period, many Lows will overtake many of the Highs, at least in their mastery of the subject matter of the lessons. It stands to reason that some other facets of development will also benefit; for example, confidence surely grows as a byproduct of success.

Attributing interactions to diverse measures of ability, ranging from the artificial Hidden Figures test to previous school marks in the subject to be taught, is unsatisfying. No doubt some dimension within the domain of general abilities accounts more strongly for the kinds of interaction we describe than other sub-dimensions do. The present literature does not permit us to compare the importance of such subdimensions.

The issue of general/special aptitudes can be resolved by making routine use of multitrait-multimethod design in ATI studies. Ultimately, however, we need a process theory of aptitude. This theory will come from ATI research, supported by process analyses of aptitude tests as well as instructional tasks. We emphasize test analyses here, because such studies are a rarity relative to analyses of learning tasks. Those who call for research on "the new aptitudes" or "intrinsic individual differences" point frequently to laboratory studies of information processing in learning as examples. Experimental psychologists are showing renewed interest in the analysis of intellectual processes and, increasingly, in the relation of these to individual differences displayed by tests. (See, e.g., E. Hunt, Frost, & Lunneborg, 1973.) Whether these efforts will define new aptitude constructs, as opposed to elaborations of existing aptitude constructs, remains to be seen. To distinguish general/special or new/old aptitudes will require close coordination of test and task analysis.

Mental tests are samples of the facility, efficiency, and to some extent the strategy and effort with which learners process intellectual problems. To say that mental tests are not concerned with psychological processes is absurd, even though it is true that the mental testing tradition has been more concerned with practical correlates than with process theories of tests. We believe aptitude tests and learning tasks differ in the form with which they are used to represent cognitive processes, rather than in the content of the processes so represented. More precise analyses of tests and tasks should lead to identification of the cognitive processes common to each. When these commonalities are known, aptitude measures can be redesigned or built anew to represent them with increased clarity. These may take the form of work samples or miniature laboratory experiments, or they may resemble conventional tests. ATI research in natural settings may be able to use these instruments to obtain clearer understanding of cognitive functioning in instruction. But the data reviewed in this book offer little to sustain the view that such "new" measures will define "new" aptitudes. We rather think they will allow a more detailed process description of the aptitude constructs presently in hand. A number of research efforts reported in earlier chapters, and particularly in Chapter 11, step in this direction. So far, however, no research program has adopted this as a primary goal, and we cannot realistically assess its potential for understanding ATI in instruction.

Interactive effects of specialized abilities

Spatial and mathematical abilities

It was once thought that specialized aptitude measures in the Thurstone or Guilford systems would help to fit instructional styles to the student, but the findings to date are unpromising. Thus, it was supposed that spatial ability would generate a steeper regression slope in a treatment that was more "spatial." In retrospect, the hypothesis was badly stated. A training program that uses diagrams or symbols is not necessarily spatial. Spatial abilities are probably required if, in the course of training, the person must visualize changes in shape under rotation and other operations. No such treatments have been clearly specified. At times, the function of diagrams in a "spatial" treatment is to reduce the load on S's spatial abilities. Preponderantly, spatial abilities have failed to interact with more/less emphasis on diagrams in the treatment (Allison, p. 280; Markle, p. 281; Bracht, p. 283; Behr, p. 286; Kropp, p. 286). A more visual presentation did interact with spatial ability in a study of Gagné (p. 266). In a few studies, strange interactions of spatial ability turned up (Osburn, p. 288; Hills, p. 288; Edgerton, p. 316).

A few studies have given indications that interactions of mathematical abilities differ from those of general ability. Thus, Wasik (p. 309) may have found a steeper slope onto mathematical abilities for students who took PSSC physics, and Cain (p. 310) found such a steeper slope for "yellow-version" BSCS biology. Since both of these experimental courses were comparatively technical, the finding is plausible.

Prior learning experience

The findings that most clearly suggest a possible matching of special aptitudes to special instructional techniques are the interactions that depend upon prior learning experience. A treatment serves best those students who have already learned how to take advantage of that kind of treatment. Brownell and Moser (p. 248) reported that children for whom meanings were carefully developed during two years of arithmetic instruction profited from similar explanation of borrowing in subtraction. The same explanations only confused children whose previous instruction had relied on demonstration and drill. Experience in viewing instructional films interacts similarly with film/nonfilm instruction (Snow, Vandermeer, p. 274 ff.; see also Nagel, p. 210, on PI).

The residue of experience is a heightened ability to make use of more such experience. That aptitude can presumably be measured by learning samples. A Film Memory Test of this kind interacted with a videotape/text contrast (Koran, p. 276). The Pre-Ach measure of the Gagné-Gropper study was another learning sample presenting visual displays, and it interacted in an understandable manner with a visual/verbal contrast. Perhaps work samples assessing learning from various kinds of approach (e.g., guided discovery, linear programmed text, etc.) will enter into ATI. Inferior performance on a work sample must not be looked upon as a fixed inaptitude. This kind of ability to learn presumably arises out of experience with the pertinent kind of instruction. Hence, the person who does poorly on the learning sample will presumably develop the required aptitude if he is given proper experience with the instruction for which he was initially unprepared.

Memory

Conventional memory tests have been used in several ATI studies, though we find no study that checks on the Jensen hypothesis that such tests will interact with rote/meaningful instruction. In fact, no studies have investigated ATI for memory tests with any kind of extended instruction.

The Berliner work (p. 354) provided a partial replication of an interaction for memory. Memory for sentences and memory for ideas did not interact with treatments intended to alter study method. A test of short-term memory (STM) interacted in the same way in two studies. Among *S*s directed to take notes, the ones with good STM did well and the others did not. The Lows did well when embedded questions directed the learner's attention, and Highs did badly. Simple "pay attention" instructions generated a flat AT regression. The possible meaning of this result and the mysterious failure of replication in Berliner's further study and that with Shavelson were discussed in Chapter 11.

Hollen (p. 354) found an interaction of associative memory with adjunct questions. Learning of text was related to this aptitude when there were no questions or when questions preceded the text, but the regression slope was flat when questions were placed at the end of the passage. This is another of the scattered studies hinting that prosthetic devices may impair the learning of Highs.

Interactive effects of traits and styles

In the personality domain, interactions were found with considerable frequency, and some combinations of variables and treatments appear more promising than others. But the evidence is too scattered to permit confident conclusions.

Teacher characteristics interact with various characteristics of the student. Hypotheses may be stated at a high level of generalization, notably in the suggestion (p. 485, 326) that traditional teaching styles produce a flatter regression of outcomes on social class than styles that are more progressive. At the other extreme is the study that lacks constructs but displays teacher differences—for example, Thelen's procedure for creating an idiosyncratic scoring key to identify students who will respond well to a certain teacher (p. 480). There are studies in between that isolate a single dimension or characteristic of the teacher and find an interaction. The Majasan use of a belief scale (p. 478) is an example, as are several of the studies in the McKeachie program (Ch. 13, passim.).

It has probably been a mistake to restrict a given study to one of these levels of discourse. After analyzing a study such as Thelen's at the case level, it should be possible to characterize the teachers and their scoring keys along some of the traditional dimensions. It would also be possible, of course, to apply traditional instruments along with the novel Thelen instrument, in order to learn whether traditional constructs can account for the results.

The strong but simple generalization such as Majasan's ought to be broken down to indicate what kind of transactions in the classroom, or what reactions by the student, seem to cause the effect. The single-trait studies have identified some significant variables, but no single trait will account for much of the student's response to instruction. Much could have been added to trait studies by compiling case studies of the several instructors and class sections. Perhaps the report that came nearest to making full sense of personality data was that of Heil *et al.* (p. 459). If it is true that teacher variables and student traits come together in complex configurations, and if it is true that student sex and student ability may further condition the interaction, hypotheses about one variable at a time are somewhat off the mark, and bound to have limited validity.

A good deal of evidence does point to the significance of constructive motivation (p. 469). The Domino study (p. 442) is accompanied by a dozen others scattered through Chapter 13, indicating that the constructively motivated student responds better to teaching that throws responsibility upon him—that is, to less directive, more spontaneous teaching. It is not yet clear whether the questionnaire measure of Achievement through Independence and the projective measure of Need for Achievement give the same result; both enter into several interactions. Nor is it clear whether the combination of nAch with low Anxiety gives firmer results than nAch alone; but several findings (p. 432, 448) confirm predictions from J. W. Atkinson's theory that uses the two together.

The student's perception of his teacher may be just as significant a source of interaction as the teacher's actual style. The most direct evidence on this point comes from Dowaliby and Schumer (p. 446). The LEI technique in which students characterize the climate of the institution or classroom lends itself well to comparisons of students within the same classroom who describe it differently.

There has been more inquiry into the interactions of defensive motivation (anxiety, introversion, etc.) than of any other variable. The treatment has rarely continued long enough for the student to make an adaptation to the experimental instruction. For this and other reasons, the findings have been quite inconsistent. Nonetheless, interactions did appear with considerable frequency. Often (p. 424, 469), the defensive student tended to do better than the Low-defensive when the treatment made less demand for self-direction or independent thinking. But many a study that considered two outcome measures found both this effect and the opposite.

Interactions of defensive motivation with the stressfulness of treatments were not consistent. The final conclusion (p. 439; see also 469) has to be that these variables do interact, but that the nature of the interaction is far from simple. The most sophisticated work (a study by Caron and a successor study by Sinclair, p. 432) profitably measured both transfer and recall. Caron found able High-defensive students doing well on recall under arousal conditions and badly on a test of transfer. Sinclair did not find inferior weakened transfer, however. The importance of this work does not lie in its empirical conclusions as such. Even if the two studies were entirely consistent the educator should ask for evidence on instruction of appreciable duration. What is important is that Caron was able to derive inferences about complex interactions from a personality theory and to align his findings with that theory.

Studies in which praise, criticism, or the like formed the treatment variable produced no useful information.

Scattered studies on Need for Affiliation and similar traits produced evidence of interaction (p. 472 ff.). Personality seemed to be reflected in student satisfaction more than in achievement. All in all, however, methods providing considerable opportunity for face-to-face interaction in a supportive atmosphere seemed to be advantageous for the sociable students and superior to such alternatives as independent study, programmed instruction, and impersonal live teaching. The interactions may or may not have been disordinal.

Recommendations regarding research strategy and procedure

The research methods in common use are inefficient and produce misleading results. Precisely the same evaluation was made by McKeachie (1963, pp. 1122ff.) in his review of research on instruction in colleges. Even though his first concern was with main effects rather than interactions, the criticisms he made supplement ours, and should be considered alonside this section.

In recapitulating our chief suggestions, we do not set forth a prescription for every investigator to follow. To elaborate a research plan in one direction is to sacrifice something else. The wisest choice of plan will differ with the situation and the hypothesis under test.

Hypothesis formation and choice of variables

Treatments. Catch-as-catch-can approaches will rarely produce useful findings about ATI. True, one can obtain information inexpensively by comparing instructional treatments that have already been installed, perhaps in different schools. Aptitude measures can be collected and the within-treatment regressions studied. One who does this may hit on an interesting finding—as Osburn and Melton (p. 288) did—but interpreting such a result is difficult. Introducing treatments based on an hypothesis asks a more pointed question.

The treatments used in past experiments have generally suffered from brevity and artificiality. The question before us is how students respond to instructional treatments. We are not going to learn this from studies that, mimicking laboratory experiments, present a single brief lesson repetitively until it is mastered, or confine instruction to a drill-and-practice mode with no explanation, or introduce utterly artificial motivating procedures. We will need to collect data from instructional procedures that realistically progress through a body of material. The procedures should be good instruction, insofar as one can judge *a priori* or by tryouts. The instruction should be continued long enough that the student is thoroughly familiar with the style of the instruction; educational policy cannot be based on what the student does in his first encounter with an instructional style.

A remarkably large fraction of the studies have chosen mathematical subject matter. Other skill subjects—science, foreign language, reading, and formal English usage—are heavily represented in the research literature. Subject matter that seeks to communicate generalizations about human affairs (literature, social studies, philosophy, ecology, even psychology) is very little represented—the Austin Bond study stands almost alone. There is virtually no research on productive kinds of thought (written expression as distinct from grammar, planning of scientific inquiry, etc.). It is far easier to design and appraise experimental instruction to cover well-defined facts and skills, than it is to study the higher forms of learning. Moreover, to develop a sense of history or a true concept of cause and effect takes a long time.

It is not profitable to contrast techniques defined only by gross labels (e.g., TV/live, or PI/conventional). Any treatment has many specific characteristics that determine the outcome; hence, in successive studies of the same gross contrast conflicting findings are not surprising.

The choice of treatment variables will need to be deliberate and judicious. Such elementary hypotheses—dull students should have small-step programs, spatially bright students should be given much spatial material—are evidently not worth much. Rational choice of treatments can perhaps be achieved through process analysis. On a small scale, the Burton-Goldbeck study (p. 192) and the Greeno work (p. 362) illustrate what we have in mind. Such research will need to pursue a taxonomy of instructional situations, with a level of detail comparable to that worked out by Fleishman (p. 165) for psychomotor tasks.

If teachers have working hypotheses as to the processes the student can and should use in a particular kind of instruction, the student should be coached to use those methods. Research workers should not be interested in the effectiveness of the student's naive strategies. It follows that the ATI problem becomes one of identifying aptitudes that make it possible for some students to adopt a desirable strategy. Given contrasting treatments, a comparison of processes should guide the choice of aptitude measures; but the process analysis will also suggest ways in which the effectiveness of each treatment can be enhanced. It is time to take seriously Hawkins' remark (p. 130) about the "prepared" subject of an experiment; education deals, most of the time, with subjects who are fully habituated—for better or worse—to the traditional mode of instruction.

We wish also to encourage the search for ATI in the context of evaluation. There is no point in assessing whether performance contracting or yellow-version biology is superior to or the same as a contrasting treatment, if the effects differ radically from school to school and from student to student within the class.

The evaluator takes treatments as found. Even though he does not manipulate them, he can take pains to determine just what transpires in each classroom, so that he can interpret his final results in terms of the actual treatment variables rather than the nominal ones.

Aptitudes. The investigator may start with an aptitude variable he would like to study. To keep discussion simple, we suppose that he would like to locate treatments such that Highs on the aptitude do better in one treatment and Lows do their best in the other. Highs are expected to make progress if the instruction demands the skills they displayed on the aptitude test. And Lows are expected to progress if the treatment makes little demand on the skills they lack. Hence, the investigator needs to form a theory about what kinds of intellectual activity make for good performance on the aptitude measure, and what deficiencies are most responsible for low scores. It is on this basis that he shapes instructional treatments, one to employ this ability and one to sidestep the deficiency.

The psychological relation of aptitude to treatment was not spelled out when it was hypothesized that spatial ability forecasts success in learning from diagrams. Now we know better. There must be ways to increase the demand for spatial analysis when a treatment uses figural presentations, so as to capitalize on the skills of Highs. There must also be ways to make figures easy to comprehend, so that poor spatial processors learn more about essentially spatial content than they would without the figures.

As there is no point in studying ATI of an aptitude that can be quickly changed, we suggest that Ss be familiarized with any aptitude measure before the predictor score is collected. We admit, though, that there is no empirical support for the hunch that scores collected under these circumstances will have more relation to outcomes and be more significant as a basis for theory.

Even when especially interested in one characteristic of the learner, the investigator should measure additional aptitudes. If chiefly concerned with a specialized ability, he nonetheless should include one or more general measures. This will allow him to reject (or support) the hypothesis that general ability explains the AT regressions he finds for his narrower test. It is almost always advisable to give a pretest over the content to be taught or over the relevant background information.

The foregoing paragraph is in line with the first of two recommendations of Campbell and Fiske: that indicators reflecting promising counterhypotheses should be included in any validation study. The second recommendation, that the construct entering the main hypothesis be appraised by two or more methods, also has been unwisely neglected in ATI work. When the investigator designs a treatment to fit (say) the Raven Matrices as an aptitude, he surely is not concerned with abstract symbols in a matrix layout. Rather, he expects the successful learner to call on broad processes: abstracting from perceived similarity, self-critical checking of hypotheses, etc. If the investigator tests these processes in several ways, his findings will not be swayed by the specifics of Raven's test. Any consistent finding over the two or three aptitude measures will strongly support his true hypothesis. Suitable tests might be Figure Series, or Block Design, or Verbal Analogies made from familiar words.

In view of the cost of an instructional experiment, and in view of the fact that an ATI conclusion rests just as much on the initial tests as on the much more costly treatment, a substantial investment in initial measurement is warranted. Not only tests, but academic and personal history data may be recorded. The possible enrichment of findings repays the modest increase in effort. To be sure, this has some flavor of the shotgun attack, but no detrimental consequences result when the statistical analysis emphasizes central hypotheses first, leaving other measures to exploratory analyses from which no conclusions are drawn.

Because true-score regressions are more illuminating than observed regressions, reliability information on the aptitude measures is needed. If an aptitude construct has been measured by multiple methods, as recommended above, this provides data that can take the place of more usual reliability analyses. Such a design presumes that the several methods are representative of a universe of methods, and the intraclass correlation across methods provides a properly conservative kind of coefficient of generalizability. This leads in the direction of calculating regressions of outcomes on the factor-score representing a construct, rather than onto any one true score. Pilot testing of such methods of analysis is needed.

Design

Trade-offs are possible in experimental design. One can measure more aptitudes with shorter tests, sacrificing reliability of any one test in order to introduce more methods or more dimensions. One can offset low reliability by treating more Ss. One can treat so many Ss that results give precise figures for a population, or one can conduct a study half as large, and save enough resources for a second run redesigned in the light of the first experience.

Sample sizes will need to be considerably larger than in the past, if ATI experiments are to have a good probability of detecting strong, practically significant effects. In a study using a representative sample, 100 or more Ss per treatment are required (see p. 45). A smaller sample may be acceptable if the design uses extreme groups or uses systematic sampling. A still larger sample is needed to examine more subtle questions such as curvilinearity of regressions or differences between interactions of multiple variables.

The extreme-groups design has been considered advantageous in previous research on ATI. When one wishes to test a specific ATI hypothesis about one aptitude, it is economical to assign only persons in the tails of the aptitude distribution to the treatments, since persons near the mean give little information on regression slopes. The extreme-groups design can be extended to two aptitudes, but a prohibitively large subject pool is required if one proposes to select on the basis of three or more aptitudes. If, as we have recommended, one carries several aptitudes into an ATI analysis even when one's hypothesis focuses on just one of them, it is still possible to select extreme groups on that central aptitude. But the advantage of the extreme-groups design is much reduced as one begins to entertain relatively complex hypotheses.

If one can control assignment to treatment, it is highly desirable to stratify on one or more aptitudes in order to make random assignments within strata. Several studies (e.g., Peters, p. 38, Hutchinson, p. 329) found troublesome differences in pretest distributions when subgroups were formed at random. We do not favor discarding cases after treatment is finished, in an effort to achieve strict orthogonali or control. If loss of cases is correlated with treatment conditions (as in Block's study, p. 139), this is an outcome to be taken seriously.

It is possible to learn about ATI from treatment groups that are not all alike— e.g., groups that the school has separated on the basis of ability and then treated differently. The true-score regressions within High and Low groups are obtainable without the trouble of arranging an "experiment." Dissimilar sections may be used in a deliberate quasiexperiment. Where an experimental treatment is expected to be advantageous for students of low ability, it may be entirely appropriate to split a class and teach the Highs by the old method and the Lows by the new one. The comparison of true-score regressions tells a great deal about the interaction (p. 33).

The design in which Ss are trained to criterion, allowing time to vary, seems unlikely to be appropriate for typical questions about instruction (see p. 44). In school subjects, there are always further lessons beyond the experimental criterion; hence, the main question is how much can be taught in a fixed period of time.

Multistage experiments with branching treatments will sooner or later be needed. ATI studies have asked about effects at the end of a uniform treatment period. It has been supposed that ultimately persons can be assigned to treatments on the basis of their initial characteristics. But, as was seen in the Sullivan study (p. 23, 162), the proper initial instruction can alter the very aptitudes that warranted the initial assignment. Hence, the question arises: How quickly does aptitude information become obsolete? The answer will depend on both the nature of the aptitude and the treatment. Even now, some studies of CAI provide for nearly continual adaptation of the details of the treatment, if not of its style. Broader adaptations of instruction must also face the time question. A sequential experiment may apply two treatments for a fixed initial period, after which Ss are reassigned for a second period of uniform length. More difficult to manage, but more informative, is the design in which periodic tests are given and students are reassigned as soon as their aptitude characteristics change.

Data on the process of instruction and learning

The planned instructional treatment is not the treatment delivered, either because of accidental departures from plan or because the group as a social unit begins to shape events (Mann, p. 44; Thelen, p. 480). Relatively inexpensive devices can give a picture of what actually happened. Most simply, one can debrief the teacher at the end of the experimental period, or obtain a log from the teacher, or administer the LEI (p. 298). Unstructured observations are valuable in studies with just a few classes, since the unique events in each class may contribute a good deal to the effects one wishes to ascribe to the treatment.

It should be informative to collect process data on individuals within the class. Observation of individuals will rarely be practical, but questionnaires have sometimes given evidence of significant individual reactions (e.g., p. 455, 456). Instead of using LEI as an index of classroom climate, differences among members of the same class can be taken as indices of individual morale. Debriefing interviews of a sample of the Ss would not be an expensive step, relative to the other costs of an ATI study.

When Ss work individually on a lesson or a paired-associate list, information on process ought to be equally profitable. Aptitudes influence response to treatment, because learners act differently upon the material. They direct their attention differently, they try different kinds of encoding and retrieval, and they develop a sense of competence or incompetence. Debriefing interviews or observations should be useful in many contexts, but to extract rich information on the process of learning will require expert psychological technique.

Appraisal of outcomes

Those studies that measured multiple outcomes have commonly found rather different interaction effects on different outcomes (e.g., Brownell-Moser, p. 248, Edgerton, p. 317, Babikian, p. 314, Caron, p. 432). Even when diverse outcomes point in the same direction (e.g., Domino, p. 442), the effort to collect that evidence has been well rewarded. The rather different findings for recall and transfer, for higher and lower cognitive outcomes, and for immediate and delayed posttests have so far been too inconsistent for any large conclusion to be built upon them. Yet there are good theoretical reasons for expecting treatments to have complexly patterned outcomes. And some of the patterns are so dramatic (e.g., Babikian) as to demonstrate that the study that appraises only immediate recall is likely to reach an unsound educational or psychological conclusion.

Analysis

Most of our recommendations regarding analysis have been worked out as if only one outcome was to be considered at a time. We shall review them here as if there were a single outcome measure, and then recall briefly some of the ways to consider outcomes simultaneously.

Raw outcome scores should be the dependent variable. Under no circumstances should scores be standardized within treatments (p. 27). We recommend against using gain scores or residual gain scores; the pretest scores ought to be treated as one of the potentially interacting variables. There is justification for converting the raw-score scale if some transformation more adequately represents the utility of outcomes in a certain context. It may rarely be advisable to transform scores so as to correct a gross departure from normality; but such a transformation is pertinent to inferential, and not descriptive, statistics.

To describe fully and soundly effects in the sample is the proper goal of data reduction. Inferential statistics qualify the interpretation of descriptive statistics; this makes them important, but subordinate. We emphasize this because the person who reports "no significant interaction" and reports no descriptive statistics makes it impossible for the profession to accumulate weak findings. This process of accumulation is more important in studies of interaction than in studies of main effects, because the power of ATI studies is limited. Practically important effects at the group level are most unlikely to be established as statistically significant in any one study. Bayesian statistics may be of particular service in ATI research, since prior findings are weighed alongside present findings, with due weight on the sampling errors in each. We have not attempted to develop this possibility.

Regression analysis is always the method of choice. Past studies have often relied on analysis of variance and have clouded their results in so doing. Even in the extreme-groups design to which it is logically appropriate, anova has no advantage.

Several variants of regression analysis are suitable; indeed more than one can profitably be applied to the same study. For the moment, let us speak as if there were just one aptitude variable. Then a sensible first step is to plot, for each class, the joint distribution of aptitude and outcome. This enables one to recognize not only the general trend of the results but also any curvilinearity, ceiling effect, outliers, etc. The first steps in compiling the data may well be to calculate the AT slope within each class and to plot the regression lines together, as we did for Hutchinson's data (p. 329). The plot helps one to distinguish between-class and within-class effects. This technique was pioneered in Cogan's dissertation, but seemingly no example has previously been published. We favor estimating regression equations relating outcome to *true* score (p. 33), particularly when intact groups have been assigned to treatments.

If the plot of within-class regressions does not show radically different results in different classes, the investigator will probably wish to pool classes within treatments for a synoptic analysis. (This step entails strong assumptions.) The investigator can calculate the within-treatment regression lines and establish confidence limits for each of them (p. 85).

Confidence limits appear to us to be the appropriate method for bringing statistical inference to bear. The chief fault of the technique is that results are difficult to display.

Generalized regression analysis (pp. 65, 94, 395) provides F ratios for assessing the significance of treatment main effects, aptitude main effects, and ATI. It can be extended to multiple aptitudes, to curvilinear regressions, and to higher-order interactions. Moreover, the regression equations within treatments and the corresponding multiple correlations can be obtained as by-products. We believe, then, that generalized regression analysis will be very widely used in ATI studies. Its chief limitation is that it does not carry on its face an indication of the power of an analysis to reject a null hypothesis, as the confidence limits do.

Regression analysis ought, in large studies, to separate between-class and within-class interactions (p. 99 ff.).

It is hard to give general advice about the handling of multiple aptitude measures. The alternatives are to treat them singly, to carry out a multiple-regression within treatments, to enter them in a generalized regression analysis, to form composites or principal components and then apply one of the preceding methods, or to make a full multivariate analysis. Analyzing the aptitudes one at a time draws attention to patterns of possible interest. On the other hand, when the interaction of X_1 reaches significance and that for X_2 falls short, it by no means follows that the difference in the interactions is significant. In another sample that difference might be reversed. The investigator has to choose between extracting relatively complex information and relatively simple information; the latter is more dependable, but less "rich." We are inclined not to favor multivariate analysis as demonstrated by Lo (p. 219); it places significance testing ahead of descriptive analysis.

It is critically important to examine the regressions of the same combination of variables in each treatment. The conventional within-treatment multiple-regression analysis is likely to generate equations that look different, as the correlations between aptitudes vary somewhat from sample to sample. The particular weighting of variables that interacts most strongly is likely not to be best in the next sample. Confidence limits, however, take such variation into account.

For most purposes, a few *a priori* composites seem likely to represent the reasonable hypotheses adequately. Combining aptitudes of the Guilford type into a single score often accounts for all effects that rise above the noise level (e.g., pp. 134, 240). Similarly, Bunderson and Dunham have made good use of composites for reasoning and memory (p. 365). It may be advisable to reduce rank by forming principal components, where *a priori* hypotheses are lacking.

Reducing the number of aptitude measures is particularly important if one wants to explore higher-order interactions. And there are sufficient hints of interactions arising from ability and personality together, or personality and sex together, that any large study ought to check on higher-order effects.

Multiple outcomes can similarly be reduced to composites. If one supposes that a test of knowledge and a test of application are affected differently, for example, one requires two composites. The first is a suitably weighted sum which represents the overall achievement, the second would be a component orthogonal to the first. Only if both composites interact is it worthwhile to interpret two separate effects. The handling of dependent variables in previous work has been crude, and has left the reader uncertain whether the effects on different variables truly differ. The most satisfactory example of procedure is Lo's extraction of two principal components from diverse reading achievements.

Structural regression analysis is probably advantageous for outcomes (and aptitudes) that follow each other in time or for which there is a clear causal relation. An example is the finding of an exceptional dependence of delayed performance upon immediate performance in one of the Gagné-Gropper treatment groups (p. 266).

Reporting

ATI research has been plagued by inadequate reporting. Investigators searching for main effects collect data that seem to demonstrate or to deny ATI, but fail to test fully or to describe those effects. Investigators searching for ATI dramatize whatever relations reach conventional significance levels and say very little about results that do not. The entire literature suffers from the tradition of reporting significance tests without descriptive data.

With full descriptive reports, the reader can think about relations in the sample and compare them with others in the literature. For each aptitude variable (or for each composite) we should have treatment-group means and s.d.'s. We should have AT regression slopes, means, and s.d.'s within treatments for all outcomes or outcome composites. In an extreme-groups design, one might report means for Highs and Lows in place of slopes.

We have mixed feelings about the advisability of publishing reports of exploratory studies, studies with modest samples, and studies whose results contradict reasonable expectations. The ideal obviously is for an investigator to cumulate studies with essentially the same variables until he has a well-established, reproducible phenomenon to report. This is not a demand for replication in the narrowest sense. Successive modifications of a treatment or of a measuring technique can be good scientific practice. (But we are not content when a person carries forward to his next study the measure that seemed to "give results" in a first, limited study. Replicating absence of an effect is often important, especially when both interacting and noninteracting measures seem to embody similar constructs.

Can placement policies be derived from ATI generalizations?

The dominant perspective in ATI research has been a search for generalizations that could be the basis for placement policies. It was assumed that alternative treatments could be installed, and that information collected in a short period of time could indicate which treatment each student should receive. The assignment would ordinarily be for a period of something like a semester. Decisions difficult to reverse, such as the choice of a college, would hold for several years.

Nearly all investigations of ATI have been cast as a search for generalizations. Research on main effects sought generalizations such as "Learning by discovery is superior to learning from text presentations." The ATI research tests the generalization, "Students superior in general ability profit more from the discovery method; Lows profit more from the didactic method." The evidence does often point in that direction, but the inconsistencies are more impressive than the trend. Some time ago these were apparent enough to warrant the advice (Cronbach, in Shulman & Keislar, 1966, p. 77):

. . . that we search for limited generalizations of the following form:

With subject matter of this nature,
inductive experience of this type,
in this amount,
produces this pattern of responses,
in pupils at this level of development.

That is, investigators were advised to look for a fourth-order interaction: Ability x Age x Subject-matter x Treatment x Outcome. After reviewing a much larger body of research in this book, we are convinced that the relationships are at least this complicated (Cronbach, 1975).

The implications of this insight for ATI research are formidable. A program of research to track down the fourth-order interactions of any aptitude would require prohibitively large amounts of investigator and subject time. Furthermore, even if a fourth-order generalization were established, it would have so narrow a field of application that it could play little part in school policy. Furthermore, any real treatment is multidimensional and more than one ATI may be relevant. If we accept Majasan's finding that the student does better when his beliefs match the instructor's, and accept Domino's finding that the student's willingness to conform should match the instructor's pressure to conform, six or more alternative treatments are required to accommodate these two dimensions—even before we begin to consider abilities, sex, etc.

Instead of generalizing and then deriving a decision rule from the generalization rules for placement will have to be developed *ad hoc.* It is impossible to determine what kinds of student should attend College X, from abstract principles about the "dimensions" of college experiences. A study in which the regressions of outcomes within College X are contrasted with regressions in other schools appears to be required. For years authorities on validating tests for selection have insisted on local validation, since the combination of variables best for one institution fits a sister institution poorly. The same strategy is evidently needed to justify classifying students. The attempt to evaluate performance contracting as a national policy led to a negative conclusion because it sought a universal rule. But in a particular community, the program of a particular contractor sometimes had positive effects; with another combination of specific treatment and setting variables the "contracting treatment" was detrimental. Hence, only local evidence could justify continuing the contract. In Harvard Project Physics, effects apparently differed according to the climate that developed in a particular classroom. The evaluation left us uncertain as to whether these effects were due to reproducible aspects of the situation or were nonrecurring phenomena of a certain time and place and set of persons. The studies of Thelen and Mann made it evident that the dynamics of a particular group have powerful consequences.

The practical value of a study in a field setting—whether an evaluation study or a conclusion-oriented study—is to tell the next community the promising variables to take into account. Perhaps more important, the generalizations add to the insight with which individual teachers and curriculum developers approach their task. Even if they make no formal assessments, their everyday decisions will be influenced by the awareness that a certain variable has had significant consequences in many places. Probabilistic generalizations contribute to the understanding of the educational process.

Majasan's finding, for example, is pregnant with questions regarding communicati processes in the classroom. Work to elucidate those processes probably will lead to larger practical benefits in the long run than an attempt merely to place the student with an instructor who shares his beliefs.

It will be evident in what we have said throughout this book that we have serious reservations about the dominant style of research in instructional psychology. Insofar as educational reality is shaped by multiple parameters of student and treatment, traditional experiments cannot be powerful enough to support adequately complex conclusions. Insofar as variance arises out of the history of a particular class, it will be impossible to catch important causes, in the net of statistical inference. Without minimizing the value of statistical inference as a discipline, we would reverse priorities in instructional research. Finding out what happened in the course of an educational experience and reporting it is the prime duty of the investigator. In instructional research, hypothesis-testing turns us toward sterility.

Criticisms made of the ATI approach

Throughout modern times, educators and those concerned with school policy have pressed for matching instruction to the individual. The need to capitalize on individual differences is obvious—yet counterarguments are heard.

In this section, we pay no attention to the sheer substantive question as to whether sufficiently strong and dependable ATI have been discovered. If the judgment were negative, research could continue. There should be agreement that schooling will not be adapted on any large scale until the basis for the adaptation is validated. Likewise, we put aside criticisms that arise out of antagonism toward assessment of individual differences. Critics of this stamp object to testing for selection; but the whole point of ATI research is to reduce selectivity.

The challenge of pluralism

One group of critics, antagonistic to a dominant social philosophy, deny that educational goals should be the same for all learners. Communities, it is said, differ in life styles, hence in the aims proper for their schools, and individuals within communities ought to be free to choose their personal goals. Judging everyone's education by the same standards denies both individual self-determination and community selection of educational goals, it is said. Educational pluralism could be advocated or criticized on many grounds; but for our purposes the central question is whether a concern for ATI is incompatible with pluralism. A search for ATI is committed to a pluralism of method, but it compares all methods on the same outcomes. Can ATI findings serve a pluralism of goals?

To make the issue concrete, let us consider two treatments: a computer-scheduled program for teaching mathematical skills and a plan to develop mathematical competence in the course of self-selected projects. If those interested in one program place zero value on the outcomes toward which the other program aims, no comparison can be made and no ATI question arises. But that surely is not the case. At the lesson level, there can be total disagreement about desired outcomes. One segment of the community may not care at all that the student learn about intersections of sets; another segment may not care at all about shop calculations. An objective stated at a more comprehensive level has positive value in the eyes of virtually everyone: e.g., ability to calculate accurately and facilely, understanding that enables one to make rough estimates, confidence in numerical work, ability to restate practical problems so that they can be solved. The difference between subcommunities or individuals is not that each regards some of these goals as contrary to the child's best interests. They differ only in the extent to which they are willing to reduce attainment of one goal to attain another more fully. ATI research will not, of itself, indicate what treatment a student with certain aptitudes should be assigned to. Nothing but the cost of research prevents a statement to him in this form:

> With your aptitudes, it is most likely that if you enter the conventional program you will at the end of the year be around level 13 on outcome A, around level 8 on outcome B, and around level 16 on outcome C. If you enter the alternative program instead, the corresponding levels are likely to be 8, 13, and 16.

Now the student or the parent or the school itself can select the treatment in the light of his (their) values. To be specific, if outcome A is manipulation of algebraic abstractions and B is enthusiasm for school, parents who value higher learning may strongly prefer the conventional treatment.

Undesirability of permanent classifications

A second objection is that an assignment system labels children and tends to predetermine their futures.

The proposal to choose instructional plans on the basis of the learner's measured characteristics, i.e., to capitalize on ATI, is merely one of many forms of classification. Schools offer options now and will offer more options in the future, so some kind of classification is inescapable. Classification cannot be condemned in all its forms; it is important to perceive *what* is hazardous in classification schemes, and to circumvent the dangers. There are two objections: classification can become a system of social segregation; and it can embody—however unintentionally—irreversible decisions about the student's educational career and life chances.

Conceivably, ATI findings could give new credibility to the long-established practice of tracking or streaming. Insofar as these policies tend to place the children of the poor in one corner of the school where they associate only with one another, and to place the advantaged children in an entirely different social environment, they do contribute to a caste system. But it is no remedy to make each class a crosssection of economic levels and offer the same instructional program to all. The dramatic report of Rist (1971) on the discriminatory practices of black primary teachers dealing with poor, black children shows that the real problem is not one of middle-class bias, or racism, or the malign influence of tests. The problem is one of inadequate, inflexible adaptation to pupil differences. The research suggests that the treatment for the student low in general ability should differ from that for the able students; this, considered alone, does lead toward the same division of students across much or all of the school program. There are good reasons for this finding: a person with poor verbal development is handicapped in every field until the verbal load is consciously reduced. On the other hand, there are course-to-course variations even with conventional teaching; the weakest fraction of the class in science is not identical with the weakest fraction in mathematics or foreign language. The risk of segregation is greatly reduced if classification is carried out separately in each school subject.

To prevent classification from having permanent detrimental effects, assignments have to be reassessed at intervals.

ATI research moves the school further away from segregation when many kinds of ability are shown to interact. There should be a strong effort to pin down the distinctive ATI of fluid ability and of learning-sample tests. Finding just how these imply a different response to treatment than is implied by school-record-to-date will undermine the tendency to form one class for "generally able" students and another for "the intermediate level." Consolidation of findings about the impact of personality on response to instruction offers even greater promise of improving effectiveness without establishing classes at different "levels."

The most important safeguard against rigidity of streaming is to make the development of aptitude a deliberate goal of instruction. In fact, if this is not done, there is a serious risk of narrowing the learner's development. Consider the proposal to teach Chicano children with Spanish as primary medium of instruction. Insofar as this gets them off to a better start, it is likely to be profitable; but since sooner or later their schooling will continue in the English language, reliance on Spanish perpetuates a significant disadvantage. Hence, English has to be phased into the program to develop aptitude for instruction in English.

Another example is the recommendation that basic skills be taught by rote or drill to those who are comparatively weak in reasoning. This suggestion is not to be rejected out of hand merely because the word "rote" is distasteful. Better that primary pupils attain literacy and numeracy by whatever means than that they should fail; perhaps a similar case can be made at later grades. But the Brownell work reminds us that if beginners are not shown meaningful connections, they will not learn to learn from logically coherent instruction. Hence, purely rote teaching leaves them permanently unfit for meaningful instruction. Assuming that the ATI for rote vs. meaningful instruction does become solidly established in some subject at some grade level, it would then be defensible to make rote the main vehicle for teaching that subject to certain students. But alongside this teaching there must be an effort to promote skill in the kind of learning at which these students are deficient. A coordinated attack could capitalize on strengths while repairing weaknesses.

Ways to adapt instruction

Educators can cope with individual differences in a number of ways. They range from Procrustean methods that involve little adaptation, through intuitive and little tested rules for adaptation, up to, in principle, tested rules derived from theory.

The least responsible solution is to fix the curriculum and method of instruction and to "adjust" the student body to the method, selecting at the outset and making it easy for the discouraged student to drop out.

We may distinguish between two broad kinds of adaptation. One is to choose different educational goals for different persons, and the other is to choose different educational means toward the same goals. The former serves to develop the person's capacity for self-expression in work and leisure. It cannot be the only policy, however. The easy escape of shunting some students into a "non-academic" curriculum cannot be tolerated, so long as proficiencies formerly considered "academic" are necessary for most kinds of success and participation in society. Educators have to invent methods to open opportunity to persons who would not attain traditional goals in traditional ways. Teachers have adapted methods by various tactics: diversifying reading materials to suit children with different skills and interests, setting out a range of projects calculated to appeal to different pupils, providing individualized remedial work, and so on.

Adaptations differ with respect to their scale, and with respect to their tactics. The most far-reaching choice is that between institutions run along different lines, as between a Montessori preschool and a permissive one. This preselects the child's total school experience during a period of a year or more. At a second level are choices of "stream" within a single school. Differentiation of students into fast, slow, and intermediate tracks affects the rate at which material is introduced, the standards upheld, and to some extent the content introduced.

Some plans set up alternative series of lessons or projects, or alternative curricula, to which a student can be "assigned" or self-assigned for a period of time. Another possibility is microadaptation where the path of instruction is modified minute by minute as the instruction proceeds. It takes one form in the computer, where very small units of instruction are available in considerable variety and capable of being assembled in myriad sequences. It takes a different form in clinical work, where an experienced instructor who has a highly developed theory of individual differences analyzes closely the moment-by-moment performance and shapes his interactions with the learner accordingly. While classroom teachers are similarly in a position to use this form of microadaptation, they usually can do this only to a much lesser degree.

The adaptations a teacher or clinician makes in the course of instruction are based on continually updated observations rather than on standard tests given once a year. The variables taken into account are numerous and may be unique to a particular course of study or a particular student. ATI research can aid in this highly differentiated adaptation by supplementing the "professional common sense" with which the teacher otherwise operates. For instance, the hints we have found that supplementary explanations or questions may impair the learning of Highs becomes a significant warning to the teacher even though we do not know when and why these interventions hurt.

Our way of formulating questions about individual differences contrasts with the method in which R. C. Atkinson (1972) and many other users of the computer proceed. We try to locate traits that come into the person's work on most of his lessons in one school subject and perhaps many subjects; even if concerned with the teaching of third-grade arithmetic, we are unlikely to consider any trait narrower than "can (or cannot) use explanations of algorithms." The computer, however, can tally the errors a student makes on different types of items within a single lesson and use this count to determine the exercises or explanations to present next. It is impractical to develop unique rules for every lesson sequence by means of research on it. Instead, a process of generalization is developed, in such a form as, "If the student reaches a score of 80%, move on to the next lesson of the sequence, i.e., to elaboration of the content." Such a rule allows for review and consolidation in the context of the later lessons, while sending weaker students into more intensive review or clarification at once.

There is no intellectual antagonism between the two approaches. It might ultimately be possible to measure relatively stable parameters of the individual (preference for risk, perhaps?) that would suggest how the branching rules could be modified (shift from 80% to 70% in the rule above?) to enhance his attentiveness and mastery. For the present, however, it seems appropriate for the trait approach of ATI and the response-sensitive approach of CAI to develop independently.

In another kind of adaptation, weekly or monthly assignments are individualized. Variants of this are found in Individually Prescribed Instruction, Project PLAN, and other schemes reminiscent of the Dalton and Winnetka plans of a generation ago. Decisions are based largely on detailed measures of the student's achievement to this point. The basic concept is that each unit of instruction lays a base of proficiency on which the next unit can build. Conversely, one can specify the proficiencies needed to master a new unit, and then, after taking inventory of what the student can do, put him through remedial work. Mapping hierarchies of subskills and elementary concepts in the subject matter has undoubted value. It is best suited when the goal is to train in well-specified subject matter; it clearly can be made to work to teach manipulation of decimals, for example. It is much less applicable to the broad concomitant outcomes of instruction: development of mathematical intuition, comprehension of mathematics as a system of thought, and the like. Teachers can make rough guesses as to the sorts of activities that will best promote mathematical thinking for a particular student using general concepts about ability and motivation that they have distilled from past experience. System designers can to some degree formalize such wisdom and supply materials to help students of various types. But plans to teach higher outcomes are much more speculative.

The long-range requirement is for understanding of the factors that cause a student to respond to one instructional plan rather than another. These plans should differ in more than the amount of time devoted to specific drills. The range of instructional procedures open to the educator is enormous—individual projects, workbooks, teacher-monitored problem-solving, group projects, discussion, etc. New media extend the range of methods and also extend the capability of the school to administer flexible and diversified programs. There is no reason to assume that an eclectic mixture of all methods will serve every kind of student. There must be some kinds of students who respond best to group discussions, and others who do much better by themselves. The same is to be said of all the parameters of instruction: level of comprehension required by the presentation, rigor of supervision, presence of competition, etc.

ATI has come of age. Research on instruction will need to incorporate its implications in theory and in practice, regardless of how one ultimately proceeds with instructional adaptation. ATI methods and ideas have a fundamental role to play in educational evaluation as well as in educational design, and in psychological science generally. As this role continues to unfold, we can expect new lines of research to reopen old questions, as well as to define issues not considered by the traditional experimental and correlational investigators working separately. This handbook will have served its purpose if it helps guide these new efforts to productive advance.

References

Abramson, T., & Kagen, E. (1974a) Familiarization of content and different response modes in programmed instruction. *Paper presented to American Educational Research Association.*

Abramson, T., & Kagen, E. (1974b) Achievement from programmed instruction for junior high school students resulting from experimentally induced familiarization of content and different response modes. *Paper presented to Eastern Psychological Association.*

Aitken, M.A. (1973) Fixed-width confidence intervals in linear regression with applications to the Johnson-Neyman technique. *British Journal of Mathematical and Statistical Psychology,* **26**, 261–269.

Allen, W.H., Filep, R.T., & Cooney, S.M. (1967) Visual and audio presentation in machine programmed instruction. Unpublished report. Dept. of Cinema, University of Southern California. ED 016 400[1].

Allison, R.B. (1960) Learning parameters and human abilities. Unpublished report, Educational Testing Service. UM 60-4958.

Alvord, R.W. (1967) Learning and transfer in a concept-attainment task: A study in individual differences. Unpublished doctoral dissertation, Stanford University. UM 68-11, 263.

Amaria, R.P., Biran, L.A., & Leith, G.O.M. (1969) Individual versus co-operative learning. I. Influence of intelligence and sex. *Educational Research,* **11**, 95-103.

Amaria, R.P., & Leith, G.O.M. (1969) Individual versus co-operative learning. II. The influence of personality. *Educational Research,* **11**, 193–199.

Amidon, E., & Flanders, N.A. (1961) The effect of direct and indirect teacher influence on dependent-prone students learning geometry. *Journal of Educational Psychology,* **52**, 286–291. Longer version: UM 59-6014.

---

[1]ED indicates ERIC document number. UM indicates University Microfilms identification.

Anastasiow, N.J., Sibley, S.A., Leonard, T.M. & Borich, G. (1970) A comparison of guided discovery, discovery, and didactic teaching of mathematics to kindergarten poverty children. *American Educational Research Journal,* **7,** 493–510.

Anderson, G.J. (1968) Effects of classroom social climate on individual learning. Unpublished doctoral dissertation, Harvard University. UM 69-11,506. Shorter version: *American Educational Research Journal,* 1970, 7,135–152.

Anderson, G.L. (1941) A comparison of the outcomes of instruction under two theories of learning. Unpublished doctoral dissertation, University of Minnesota. Shorter version in E.J. Swenson *et al., Learning Theory in school situations.* Minneapolis: University of Minnesota Press, 1949.

Anderson, J.E. (1939) The limitations of infant and pre-school tests in the measurement of intelligence. *Journal of Psychology,* **8,** 351–379.

Anderson, J.S. (1964) A comparative study of CHEM and traditional chemistry in terms of students' ability to use selected cognitive processes. Unpublished doctoral dissertation, Florida State University. UM 65-309.

Anderson, R.C. (1959) Learning in discussion: A resumé of the authoritarian-democratic studies. *Harvard Educational Review,* **29,** 201–215.

Anderson, R.C., & Kulhavy, R.W. (1972) Imagery and prose. *Journal of Educational Psychology,* **63,** 242–243.

Anderson, R.C., Kulhavy, R.W., & Andre, T. (1971) Feedback procedures in programmed instruction. *Journal of Educational Psychology,* **62,** 148–156.

Apter, M.J. Boorer, D., & Murgatroyd, S. (1971) A comparison of the effects of multiple-choice and constructed response pretests in programmed instruction. *Programmed Learning and Educational Technology,* **8,** 251–156.

Ashbaugh, W.H. (1964) Effects on achievement of written responses to programmed learning materials for students of differing academic ability. *Psychological Reports,* **14,** 780–782.

Asher, S.R., & Gottman, J.M. (1973) Sex of teacher and student reading achievement. *Journal of Educational Psychology,* **65,** 168–171.

Astin, A.W. (1970) The methodology of research on college input. Part One. *Sociology of Education,* **43,** 223–254.

Atkinson, J.W., & Feather, N. (Eds.) (1966) *A theory of achievement motivation.* New York: Wiley.

Atkinson, J.W., & O'Connor, P. (1963) Effects of ability grouping in schools related to individual differences in achievement-related motivation. Unpublished report, University of Michigan. ED 003 249.

Atkinson, R.C. (1972) Ingredients for a theory of instruction. *American Psychologist,* **27,** 921–931.

Ausubel, D.P., & Fitzgerald, D. (1961) The role of discriminability in meaningful verbal learning and retention. *Journal of Educational Psychology,* **52,** 266–274.

Ausubel, D.P., & Fitzgerald, D. (1962) Organizer, general background and antecedent learning variables in sequential verbal learning. *Journal of Educational Psychology,* **53,** 243–249.

Ausubel, D.P., & Youssef, M. (1963) Role of discriminability in meaningful parallel learning. *Journal of Educational Psychology,* **54,** 331–336.

Babikian, Y. (1971) An empirical exposition to determine the relative effectiveness of discovery, laboratory, and expository methods of teaching science concepts. *Journal of Research in Science Teaching,* **8,** 201–210.

Baker, K.D., & Snow, R.E. (1972) Teacher differences as reflected in student : aptitude-achievement relationships. Unpublished report, Center for Research and Development in Teaching, Stanford University. ED 062311.

Barker Lunn, J.C. (1970) *Streaming in the primary school.* London: National Foundation for Educational Research.

Baron, R.M., & Bass, A.R. (1969) The role of social reinforcement parameters in improving trainee task performance and self-image. Unpublished report, Department of Psychology, Wayne State University.

Barrish, B. (1970) Inductive versus deductive teaching strategies with high and low divergent thinkers. Unpublished doctoral dissertation, Stanford University, UM 71-2857.

Bar-Yam, M. (1969) The interaction of student characteristics with instructional strategies: A study of students' performance and attitude in a high school innovative course. Unpublished doctoral dissertation, Harvard University.

Bashaw, W.L., & Findley, W.G. (Eds.) (1968) Symposium on general linear model approach to the analysis of experimental data in educational research. Unpublished report. University of Georgia. ED 026 737.

Bateman, B.D. The efficiency of an auditory and a visual method of first grade reading instruction with auditory and visual learners. *Curriculum Bulletin,* University of Oregon, **23**, No. 278, 1–14.

Bayley, N. (1949) Consistency and variability in the growth of intelligence from birth to eighteen years. *Journal of Genetic Psychology,* **75**, 165–196.

Bayley, N. (1954) Some increasing parent-child similarities during the growth of children. *Journal of Educational Psychology,* **45**, 1–21.

Beach, L.R. (1960) Sociability and academic achievement in various types of learning situations. *Journal of Educational Psychology,* **51**, 208–212.

Beane, D. (1965) A comparison of linear and branching techniques of programmed instruction in plane geometry. *Journal of Educational Psychology,* **58**, 319–326. Longer version: ED 020677; UM 3204.

Becker, J.P. (1967) An attempt to design instructional techniques in mathematics to accommodate different patterns on mental ability. Unpublished doctoral dissertation, Stanford University. UM 67-11,016.

Behr, M.J. (1967) A study of interactions between "structure-of-intellect" factors and two methods of presenting concepts of modulus seven arithmetic. Unpublished doctoral dissertation, Florida State University. UM 67-14,440. Shorter version: *Journal for Research in Mathematics Education,* **1**, 29–42.

Bell, N.T. (1966) Teacher characteristics and method in adjunct instruction. Unpublished doctoral dissertation, Purdue University. UM 66-13, 172.

Beller, E.K. (1967) Methods of language training and cognitive styles in lower-class children. Paper presented to the American Educational Research Association.

Berger, E.J., & Horowitz, T.A. (1967) Evaluation of experiments in mathematical discovery. In J. M. Scandura (Ed.), *Research in Mathematics Education,* Washington: National Council of Teachers of Mathematics.

Berkun, M.M., Swanson, L.W., & Sawyer, D.M. (1966) An experiment on homogeneous grouping for reading in elementary classes. *Journal of Educational Research,* **59**, 413–414.

Berliner, D.C. (1971) Aptitude-treatment interaction in two studies of learning from lecture instruction. Paper presented to American Educational Research Association. ED 046 249.

Berliner, D.C. (1972) The generalizability of aptitude-treatment interaction across subject matter. Paper presented to the American Educational Research Association. ED 062642.

Berliner, D.C., & Melanson, L. (1971). Interaction of aptitude with conventional and computer-assisted instruction in a decoding task. Unpublished. Far West Laboratory for Educational Research and Development.

Beswick, D.G., & Tallmadge, G.K. (1970) Study of training equipment and individual differences: An analytical reconstruction of two learning style experiments in terms of curiosity theory. Unpublished report, American Institutes for Research, Palo Alto. Shorter version: *Journal of Educational Psychology*, 1971, **62**, 456–462.

Bhushan, V. (1971) "An exploratory study of the effects of socio-economic status on learning". *Programmed Learning and Educational Technology*, **8**, 219–224.

Bigelow, G.S., & Egbert, R.L. (1968) Personality factors and independent study. *Journal of Educational Research*, **62**, 37–39.

Bissell, J.S. (1970) The cognitive effects of pre-school programs for disadvantaged children. Unpublished doctoral dissertation, Harvard University. UM not available.

Blaine, D.D., & Dunham, J.L. (1969) The effect of available instances on the relationship of memory abilities to performance in a concept learning task. Paper presented to American Educational Research Association ED 041 724.

Blaine, D.D., Dunham, J.L., & Pyle, T.W. (1968) Type and amount of available past instances in concept learning. Paper presented to American Educational Research Association. ED 041 724.

Blalock, H.M., Jr., & Blalock, A.B. (Eds.) (1968) *Methodology in Social Research*. New York: McGraw-Hill.

Blatt, S.J. (1963) Effects of test anxiety and instructional context on problem solving. Unpublished report, Yale University. ED 001 123.

Block, J.H. (1970) The effects of various levels of performance on selected cognitive, affective, and time variables. Unpublished doctoral dissertation, University of Chicago. Shorter version in Block, 1971.

Block, J.H. (Ed.) (1971) *Mastery learning: theory and practice.* New York: Holt, Rinehart & Winston.

Bloom, B.S. (1964) *Stability and change in human characteristics.* New York: Wiley.

Bloom, B.S., Hastings, J.T., & Madaus, G.F. (1971) *Handbook of formative and summative evaluation of student learning.* New York: McGraw-Hill.

Bock, R.D., & Wiley, D.E. (1967) Quasi-experimentation in educational settings. *School Review*, **75**, 353–366.

Bogartz, R.S. (1965) The criterion method: Some analyses and remarks. *Psychological Bulletin*, **64**, 1–14.

Bond, A.D. (1940) An experiment in the teaching of genetics. *Teachers College Contributions to Education*, No. 797. New York: Teachers College, Columbia University.

Bond, G.L. (1935) The auditory and speech characteristics of poor readers. Teachers College Contributions to Education, No. 657. New York: Teachers College, Columbia University.

Bond, G.L., & Dykstra, R. (1967) The cooperative research program in first-grade reading instruction. *Reading Research Quarterly*, **2**, 5–142.

Bordeaux, E.A., & Shope, N.H. (1966) An evaluation of three approaches to teaching reading in first grade. Unpublished report, Goldsboro City Schools, Goldsboro, N.C. (ED 010062)

Borg, W.R. (1964) An evaluation of ability grouping. Unpublished report, Utah State University, Logan. Briefer account: *Journal of Experimental Education*, 1965, No. 2.

Borgatta, E.F., & Bohrnstedt, G.W. (Eds.) (1969) *Sociological methodology 1969*, Washington, D.C.: American Sociological Association.

Borgatta, E.F., & Bornstedt, G.W. (Eds.) (1970) *Sociological methodology 1970*. Washington, D.C.: American Sociological Association.

Borich, G.D. (1971) Interactions among group regressions: Testing homogeneity of group regressions and plotting regions of significance. *Educational and Psychological Measurement, 31,* 251–253.

Borich, G.D., & Wunderlich, K.W. (1973) Johnson-Meyman revisited: Determining interactions among group regressions and plotting regions of significance in the case of two groups, two predictors, and one criterion. *Educational and Psychological Measurement, 33,* 155–159.

Bottenberg, P.A., & Ward, J.H., Jr. (1963) Applied multiple linear regression analysis. Technical Documentary Report PRL-TDR-63-6. 6570th Personnel Research Laboratory, Lackland Air Force Base, Texas.

Bracht, G.H. (1969) The relationship of treatment tasks, personological variables and dependent variables to aptitude-treatment interactions. Unpublished doctoral dissertation, University of Colorado. UM 70-5820. Shorter version: *Review of Educational Research,* 1970, **40,** 627–745.

Bracht, G.H., & Glass, G.V. (1968) The external validity of experiment. *American Educational Research Journal, 5,* 437–474.

Brady, E.B. (1970) Achievement of first- and second-year pupils in graded and nongraded classrooms. *Elementary School Journal, 70,* 391–394.

Brakken, E. (1965) Intellectual factors in PSSC and conventional high school physics. *Journal of Research in Science Teaching, 3,* 19–25.

Brewer, J.K. (1972) On the power of statistical tests. *American Educational Research Journal, 9,* 391–401.

Briggs, L.J. (1967) Sequencing of instruction in relation to hierarchies of competence. Unpublished report, American Institutes for Research, Palo Alto. ED 018975.

Brogden, H.E. (1951) Increased efficiency of selection resulting from replacement of a single predictor with several differential predictors. *Educational and Psychological Measurement, 11,* 173–196.

Brown, G.I. (1958) A study of the relationship between classroom climate and learning, as demonstrated by competency in reading and arithmetic of third grade pupils. Unpublished doctoral dissertation, Harvard University.

Brown, J.L. (1970) Effects of logical and scrambled sequences in mathematical materials on learning with programmed instruction materials. *Journal of Educational Psychology, 61,* 41–45.

Brown, W.F. (1963) An evaluation of the Madison Project method of teaching in arithmetic situations. Unpublished report, Syracuse, N.Y., City School District. ED 003 053.

Browne, M.W. (1970) A critical evaluation of some reduced-rank regression procedures. *Research Bulletin* 70-21, Educational Testing Service.

Brownell, W.A., & Moser, A.G. (1949) Meaningful versus mechanical learning: A study in grade three subtraction. *Duke University Research Studies in Education,* No. 8. Durham, N.C.: Duke University Press.

Buckland, P.R. (1967) The response in a linear program: Its mode and importance. *Programmed Learning and Educational Technology, 4,* 47–51.

Buckland, P.R. (1968) The ordering of frames in a linear program. *Programmed Learning and Educational Technology, 5,* 197-205.

Buckler, W.I. (1958) A college English teacher looks at television: Composition. *Journal of Educational Sociology, 31,* 346–352.

Budoff, M., & Quinlan, D. (1964) Reading progress as related to efficiency of visual and aural learning in the primary grades. *Journal of Educational Psychology*, **55**, 247–252.

Bunch, M.E. (1936) The amount of transfer in rational learning as a function of time. *Journal of Comparative Psychology*, **22**, 325–337.

Bunch, M.E., & McCraven, V.G. (1938) The temporal course of transfer in the learning of memory material. *Journal of Comparative Psychology*, **25**, 481–496.

Bunderson, C.V. (1967) Transfer of mental abilities at different stages of practice in the solution of concept problems. *Research Bulletin* 67-20, Educational Testing Service. UM 66-4986.

Bunderson, C.V. (1969) Ability by treatment interactions in designing instruction for a hierarchical learning task. Paper presented to American Educational Research Association.

Bunderson, C.V., & Hansen, J.B. (1971) The interaction of associative memory and general reasoning with availability and complexity of examples in a computer-assisted instruction task. Unpublished report, University of Texas, Austin.
(See also ED 047513)

Bunderson, C.V., Merrill, P.F., & Olivier, W.P. (1971) The interaction of reasoning and memory abilities with rule-example vs. discovery instruction in learning an imaginary science. Unpublished report, University of Texas, Austin, Computer-Assisted Instruction Laboratory.

Burket, G.R. (1964) A study of reduced rank models for multiple prediction. *Psychometric Monographs*, No. 12.

Burnkrant, E.G., & Lambert, P. (1965) A comparison of the effects of various learning procedures upon punctuation and content in a free writing situation. *Programmed Learning*, **2**, 158–169.

Burton, B.B. & Goldbeck, R.A. (1962) The effect of response characteristics and multiple-choice alternatives on learning during programmed instruction. Unpublished report, American Institutes for Research, Pittsburgh, Pa.

Bush, R.R., & Lovejoy, E.P. (1965) Learning to criterion: A study of individual differences. Unpublished paper delivered at Stanford University.

Cain, R.W. (1964) An analysis of the achievement of students in selected high school biology programs in relation to their mathematical aptitude and achievement. Unpublished doctoral dissertation, University of Texas. UM 65-4297.

Callahan, R.E. (1962) *Education and the cult of efficiency*. Chicago: University of Chicago Press.

Calvin, A.D., Hoffman, F.K., & Harden, E.L. (1957) The effect of intelligence and social atmosphere on group problem solving behavior. *Journal of Social Psychology*, **45**, 61–74.

Campbell, D.T. (1969) Reforms as experiments. *American Psychologis*, **24**, 409–429.

Campbell, D.T., & Fiske, D.W. (1959) Convergent and discriminant validation by the multitrait-multimethod matrix. *Psychological Bulletin*, **56**, 81–105.

Campbell, D.T., & Stanley, J.C. (1963) Experimental and quasi-experimental designs for research on teaching. In Gage, N.L., (Ed.), *Handbook of research on teaching*. Chicago: Rand McNally.

Campbell, V.N. (1964) Self-direction and programmed instruction for five different types of learning objectives. *Psychology in the Schools*, **1**, 348–359.

Campbell, V.N., & Briggs, L.J. (1962) Studies of bypassing as a way of adapting self-instruction programs to individual differences. Unpublished report. American Institute for Research, Palo Alto. ED 003 660.

Campeau, P.L. (1967) Selective review of literature on audiovisual media of instruction. In L.J. Briggs, *et al*. *Instructional media*. Palo Alto: American Institutes for Research. ED 003172.

Campeau, P.L. (1968) Test anxiety and feedback in programmed instruction. *Journal of Educational Psychology*, **59**, 159–163. ED 003225.

Caron, A.J. (1963) Curiosity, achievement, and avoidant motivation as determinants of epistemic behavior. *Journal of Abnormal and Social Psychology*, **67**, 535–549.

Carroll, J.B. (1960) Vectors of prose style. In T.A. Sebeok (Ed.), *Style in language*. Cambridge, Mass.: The M.I.T. Press.

Carroll, J.B. (1963a) A model of school learning. *Teachers College Record*, **64**, 723–733.

Carroll, J.B. (1963b) Programmed instruction and student ability. *Journal of Programmed Instruction*, **2**, No. 4, 7–11.

Carroll, J.B. (1971) Learning from verbal discourse in educational media: A review of the literature. *Research Bulletin* 71-61, Educational Testing Service.

Carroll, J.B. (1972) Review of Guilford, J.P. & Hoepfner, R. *The analysis of intelligence*. *Contemporary Psychology*, 17, 321–324.

Carroll, J.B. (1974) Psychometric tests as cognitive tasks: A new "structure of intellect". *Research Bulletin* 74-16, Educational Testing Service.

Carroll, J.B., & Leonard, G. (1963) The effectiveness of programmed "Grafdrills" in teaching the Arabic writing system. Unpublished report, Graduate School of Education, Harvard University. ED 015450.

Carroll, J.B., & Spearritt, D. (1967) A study of a "model of school learning". Unpublished report, Graduate School of Education, Harvard University. ED 045477.

Carry, L.R. (1967) Interaction of visualization and general reasoning abilities in curriculum treatment in algebra. Unpublished doctoral dissertation, Stanford University. UM 68-11,280.

Cartwright, G.P. (1962) Two types of programmed instruction for mentally retarded adolescents. Unpublished masters' thesis, University of Illinois. Shorter version: *American Educational Research Journal*, 1971, **8**, 143–150.

Cattell, R.B. (1971) *Abilities: Their structure, growth, and action*. Boston: Houghton Mifflin.

Cavanagh, P., Thornton, C., & Morgan, R.G.T. (1965) The Autotutor and classroom instruction. Three comparative studies. 3. The British European Airways Study. *Programmed Learning*, **2**, 118–125.

Centra, J.A., Linn, R.L., & Parey, M.E. (1970) Academic growth in predominantly Negro and predominantly white colleges. *American Educational Research Journal*, **7**, 83–98.

Chall, J.S. (1967) *Learning to read: The great debate*. New York: McGraw-Hill.

Chall, J.S., & Feldman, S.C. (1966) A study in depth of first-grade reading. Unpublished report, City College of the City University of New York. ED 010036. Shorter version: *Reading Teacher*, 19, 569–575.

Chang, S.H. (1974) Individual differences in information processing during classification learning at varying levels of task complexity. Unpublished doctoral dissertation, Stanford University [no UM #]

Christensen, C.M. (1960) Relationships between pupil achievement, pupil affect-need, teacher warmth, and teacher permissiveness. *Journal of Educational Psychology*, 51, 169–174.

Clark, H.H. (1973) The language-as-fixed-effect fallacy: A critique of language statistics in psychological research. *Journal of Verbal Learning and Verbal Behavior*, **12**, 335–359.

Clifford, M. (1971) Motivational effects of competition and goal setting in reward and non-reward conditions. *Journal of Experimental Education,* **39,** No. 3, 11-16.

Clodfelter, D.L. (1969) The quiz, knowledge of results, and individual differences in achievement orientation. ED 038856. Unpublished report, Washington University, St. Louis.

Coan, R.W. (1964) Facts, factors, and artifacts: The quest for psychological meaning. *Psychological Review,* **71,** 123-140.

Coates, B., & Hartup, W.W. (1969) Age and verbalization in observational learning. *Developmental Psychology,* **1,** 556-562.

Coffing, D.G. (1971) Eye movement preferences as individual differences in learning. Unpublished doctoral dissertation, Stanford University. ED 063757; UM 71-23, 527.

Coga, M.L. (1954) The relation of the behavior of teachers to the productive behavior of their pupils. Unpublished doctoral dissertation, Harvard University.

Cohen, J. (1968) Multiple regression as a general data-analytic system. *Psychological Bulletin,* **70,** 426-443.

Cohen, J. (1969) *Statistical power analysis for the behavioral sciences.* New York: Academic Press.

Cohen, J. (1973) Statistical power analysis and research results. *American Educational Research Journal,* **10,** 225-230.

Cole, M., Gay, J., Glick, J.A., & Sharp, D.W. (1971) *The cultural context of learning and thinking.* New York: Basic Books.

Compton, C.L. (1970) The relationship between intersensory integration skills and multisensory approaches in remedial readers. Unpublished doctoral dissertation, Stanford University. UM 71-2747.

Conger, A.J. & Lipshitz, R. (1973) Measures of reliability for profiles and test batteries, *Psychometrika,* **38,** 411-427.

Cooley, W.W., & Lohnes, P.R. (1975) *Evaluative inquiry in education.* New York: Irvington Press.

Coop, R.H., & Brown, L.D. (1970) Effects of cognitive style and teaching method on categories of achievement. *Journal of Educational Psychology,* **61,** 400-405.

Cooper, R.M., & Zubek, J.P. (1958) Effects of enriched and restricted environments on the learning ability of bright and dull rats. *Canadian Journal of Psychology,* **12,** 159-164.

Corman, B.R. (1957) The effect of varying amounts and kinds of information as guidance in problem solving. *Psychological Monographs,* **71,** No. 2.

Corsini, D.A. (1969) The effect of nonverbal cues on the retention of kindergarten children. *Child Development,* **40,** 599-607.

Costello, R.J., & Runham, J.L. (1971) Inductive reasoning processes in concept learning. Paper presented to the American Educational Research Association. ED 050162.

Costner, H.L. (Ed.) (1973) *Sociological methodology 1973.* Jossey-Bass, 1973. Probably 1971 and 1972 also.

Cowan, P.J. (1967) Autoinstructional materials in teaching physics in small high schools. *Journal of Experimental Education,* No. 1, **36,** 46-50.

Cromer, W. (1970) The difference model: A new explanation for some reading difficulties. *Journal of Educational Psychology,* **61,** 471-483.

Cronbach, L.J. (1953) Correlation between persons as a research tool. In O.H. Mowrer (Ed.), *Psychotherapy: Theory and research.* New York: Ronald.

Cronbach, L.J. (1957) The two disciplines of scientific psychology. *American Psychologist,* **12,** 671-684.

Cronbach, L.J. (1958) Proposals leading toward an analytic treatment of social perception scores. In R. Taguiri & L. Petrullo (Eds.), *Person perception and interpersonal behavior*. Stanford: Stanford University Press.

Cronbach, L.J. (1963) *Educational psychology* (2nd ed.). New York: Harcourt, Brace, & World.

Cronbach, L.J. (1975) Beyond the two disciplines of scientific psychology. *American Psychologist*, **30**, 116–127.

Cronbach, L.J., & Drenth, P.J.D. (1972) *Mental tests and cultural adaptation*. The Hague: Mouton.

Cronbach, L.J., & Furby, L. (1970) How we should measure "change" — or should we?*Psychological Bulletin*, **74**, 68–80. Errata, *ibid.*, 218.

Cronbach, L.J., & Gleser, G.C. (1957) *Psychological tests and personnel decisions*. Urbana: University of Illinois Press. (2nd ed., 1965)

Cronbach, L.J., Gleser, G. C., Nanda, H., & Rajaratnam, N. (1972) *The dependability of behavioral measurements: Theory of generalizability for scores and profiles*. New York: Wiley.

Cronbach, L.J., & Snow, R. (1969) Individual differences in learning ability as a function of instructional variables. Unpublished report, School of Education, Stanford University. ED 029021.

Cronbach, L.J., & Webb, N. (1975) Between-class and within-class effects in a reported aptitude X treatment interaction: Reanalysis of a study by G.L. Anderson. *Journal of Educational Psychology*, **67**, 717–724.

Crowley, R.J. & Rudy, D.J. (1969) Student aptitude and the instructional function of videotape. Unpublished report, Colgate University.

Curry, R.P. (1959) Report of three experiments on the use of television in instruction. Unpublished report, Cincinnati Public Schools.

Curry, R.P. (1960) Report of four experiments in the use of television in instruction. Unpublished report, Cincinnati Public Schools.

Darlington, R.B., & Rom, J.F. (1972) Assessing the importance of independent variables in nonlinear causal laws. *American Educational Research Journal*, **9**, 449–462.

Davies, I. K. (1972) Style and effectiveness in education and training: A model for organizing teaching and learning. *Instructional Science*, **1**, 45–88.

Davis, J.K. (1967) Concept identification as a function of cognitive style, complexity, and training procedures. Unpublished report, Research and Development Center for Cognitive Learning, University of Wisconsin.ED 024167.

Davis, R.H., Marzocco, F.N., & Denny, M.R. (1967) Interaction of individual differences with methods of presenting materials by teaching machine and computer. Unpublished report, Michigan State University. ED 017 190. Shorter version, *Journal of Educational Psychology*, **61**, 198–204.

Davis, T.N., & Leith, G.O.M. (1969) Some determinants of attitude and achievement in a programmed learning task. In W.R. Dunn, & C. Holroyd (Eds.) *Aspects of educational technology. II*. London: Methuen.

Dayton, C.M., Schafer, W.D., & Rogers, B.G. (1973) On appropriate uses and interpretations of power analysis: A comment. *American Educational Research Journal*, **10**, 231–234.

Deep, D. (1966) The effect of an individually prescribed instruction program in arthmetic on pupils at different ability levels. Unpublished doctoral dissertation, University of Pittsburgh. ED 010210, UM 66-13, 483.

Della-Piana, G. (1961) An experimental evaluation of programmed learning: Motivational characteristics of the learner, his responses, and certain learning outcomes. Unpublished report, University of Utah. ED 002953. Shorter version: *Journal of Educational Research*, 1962, **55**, 495–501.

Della-Piana, G.M., Eldredge, G.M., & Worthen, B.R. (1965) Sequence characteristics of text materials and transfer of learning. Unpublished report, University
of Utah. ED 003346.

DePauli, J.R., & Parker, E.L. (1969) The introduction of the generalized Sonar
Maintenance Trainer into Navy training for an evaluation of its effectiveness.
Technical report 68-C-0005-1, Naval Training Devices Center, Orlando, Fla.

Di Vesta, F.J., & Gray, G.S. (1972) Listening and note taking. *Journal of
Educational Psychology*, **63**, 8–14.

Di Vesta, F.J., Peters, D.R., Sanders, N.M., Schultz, C.B., & Weener, P.D. (1970)
Instructional strategies: Multivariable studies of psychological processes related
to instruction. Annual report. Unpublished report. Pennsylvania State University. ED 044022.

Di Vesta, F.J., Sanders, N.M., Schultz, C.B., & Weener, P.D. (1971). Instructional
strategies: Multivariable studies of psychological processes related to instruction. Annual report, Part II. Unpublished report. Pennsylvania State University. ED 055448.

Dixon, W.J. (Ed.) (1973) *BMD Biomedical computer programs*, 3rd ed. Berkeley:
University of California Press.

Dixon, W.J., & Massey, F.J., Jr. (1969) *Introduction to statistical analysis* (3rd
ed.). New York: McGraw-Hill.

Dockrell, W.B. (Ed.) *On intelligence.* Toronto: Ontario Institute for Studies in
Education.

Dolch, E.W., & Bloomster, M. (1937) Phonic readiness. *Elementary School
Journal*, **38**, 201–205.

Domino, G. (1968) Differential predictions of academic achievement in conforming and independent settings. *Journal of Educational Psychology*,
59, 256–260.

Domino, G. (1971) Interactive effects of achievement orientation and teaching
style on academic achievement. *Journal of Educational Psychology*, **62**, 427–
431. ED 046353.

Domino, G. (1974) Aptitude by treatment interaction effects in college instruction. Paper presented to American Psychological Association.

Doty, B.A. (1970) Teaching method effectiveness in relation to certain student
characteristics. *Journal of Educational Research*, **60**, 363–365.

Doty, B.A., & Doty, L.A. (1964) Programmed instructional effectiveness in
relation to certain student characteristics. *Journal of Educational Psychology*,
55, 334–338.

Dowaliby, F.J. (1971) Teacher-centered vs. student-centered mode of college
classroom instruction as related to individual differences. Unpublished masters
thesis, University of Massachusetts.

Dowaliby, F.J. & Schumer, H. (1973) Teacher-centered vs. student-centered
mode of college classroom instruction as related to manifest anxiety. *Journal
of Educational Psychology*, **64**, 125–132.

Drews, E.M. (1963) Student abilities, grouping patterns, and classroom interaction. Unpublished report, Michigan State University.

Dreyer, R.E., & Beatty, W.H. (1958) Instructional television research. Project
number one: An experimental study of college instruction using broadcast
television. Unpublished report, San Francisco State College.

Dubin, R., & Taveggia, T.C. (1968) The teaching-learning paradox. Eugene:
Unputlished report, Center of the Advanced Study of Educational Administration, University of Oregon.

Duncan, K.D. (1966) A further note on the card index and key system. *Programmed Learning*, **3**, 78–87.

Duncanson, J.P. (1964) Intelligence and the ability to learn. *Research Bulletin* 64-29, Educational Testing Service. UM 65-4908. Shorter version: *Journal of Educational Psychology,* 1966, **57**, 220-229.

Dunham, J.L. (1969) Investigations of the role of intellectual abilities in concept learning. Paper presented to American Educational Research Association.

Dunham, J.L., & Bunderson, C.V. (1969) The effect of decision-rule instruction upon the relationship of cognitive abilities to performance in multiple-category concept problems. *Journal of Educational Psychology,* **60**, 121-125.

Dunham, J.L., Guilford, J.P. and Hoepfner, R. (1968) Abilities pertaining to classes and the learning of concepts. Report 39, Psychological Laboratory, University of Southern California. Shorter version: *Psychological Review,* 1968, **75**, 206-221.

Dunkin, M., & Biddle, B. (1974) *The study of teaching.* N.Y.: Holt, Rinehart, & Winston.

Dykstra, R. (1968) Summary of the second-grade phase of the Cooperative Research Program in primary reading instruction. *Reading Research Quarterly,* **4**, 49-70.

Eastman, P.M. (1972) The interaction of spatial visualization and general reasoning abilities with instructional treatment in quadratic inequalities: A follow-up study. Unpublished doctoral dissertation, University of Texas. UM 73-7, 544.

Edgerton, H.A. (1956) Should theory precede or follow a "How-to-do-it" phase of training. Unpublished report, Richardson, Bellows, Henry, & Co., New York.

Edgerton, H.A. (1958) The relationship of method of instruction to trainee aptitude pattern. Unpublished. Richardson, Bellows, Henry & Co., New York.

Edward, S.M. (1964) A modified linguistic versus a composite basal reading program. *Reading Teacher,* **17**, 511-527.

Edwards, A. L., & Cronbach, L.J. (1952) Experimental design for research in psychotherapy. *Journal of Clinical Psychology,* **8**, 51-59.

Eells, K., *et al.* (1951) *Intelligence and cultural differences.* Chicago: University of Chicago Press.

Egan, D.E., & Greeno, J.G. (1973) Acquiring cognitive structure by discovery and rule learning. *Journal of Educational Psychology,* **64**, 85-97.

Eigen, L.D. (1962) A comparison of three modes of presenting a programmed instruction sequance. *Journal of Educational Research,* **55**, 453-460.

Eimas, P.D. (1966) Effects of overtraining and age on intradimensional and extra-dimensional shifts in children. *Journal of Experimental Child Psychology,* **3**, 348-355.

Ekstrom, R.B. (1959) Experimental studies of homogeneous grouping: A review of the literature. Princeton, N.J.: Educational Testing Service.

Ellis, J.R., & Peterson, J.L. (1971) Effects of same sex class organization on junior high school students' academic achievement, self-discipline, self concept, sex role identification, and attitude toward school. *The Journal of Educational Research,* **64**, 455-464.

Entweistle, D.R., Huggins, W.H., & Phelps, F.W., Jr. (1968) Response mode in technical programs. *American Educational Research Journal,* **5**, 403-411.

Eysenck, H.J. (1957) *Dynamics of anxiety and hysteria.* London: Routledge & Kegan Paul.

Eysenck, H.J. (1967) Intelligence assessment: A theoretical and experimental approach. *British Journal of Educational Psychology,* **37**, 81-98.

Farrall, C. (1968) Pupil adjustment as related to sex of pupil and sex of teacher. *Psychology in the Schools,* **5**, 371-374.

Featherstone, H.J. (1973) Cognitive effects of preschool programs on different types of children. Cambridge, Mass.: Huron Institute. ED 082838.

Federico, P.A., (1971) Evaluating an experimental audio-visual module programmed to teach a basic anatomical and physiological system. Unpublished report, Technical Training Division, Air Force Human Resources Laboratory, Lowry AFB, Colo.

Feldman, M.E. (1965) Learning by programmed and text format at three levels of difficulty. *Journal of Educational Psychology*, **56**, 133–139.

Ferguson, G.A. (1954) On learning and human ability. *Canadian Journal of Psychology*, **8**, 95–112.

Ferguson, G.A. (1956) On transfer and the abilities of man. *Canadian Journal of Psychology*, **10**, 121–131.

Ferri, E. (1971) *Streaming: Two years later.* London, National Foundation for Educational Research.

Ferris, F.L., Jr. (1962) Testing in the new curriculums: numerology, "tyranny", or common sense? *School Review*, **70**, 112–131.

Ferster, Fred (1971) The generalized Johnson-Neyman procedures: An approach to covariate adjustment and interaction analysis. Paper presented to the American Educational Research Association.

Fiedler, F.E. (1973) The effects of leadership training and experience: A contingency model interpretation. *Administrative Science Quarterly*, **18**. 453–460.

Filep, R.T. (1967) The relationship of learner characteristics to media stimuli and programming sequences. Unpublished doctoral dissertation, University of Southern California.
ED 013541; UM 67-402.

Findley, W.G., & Bryan, M.W. (1971) *Ability grouping: 1970. Status, impact, and alternatives.* Athens, Ga.: Center for Educational Improvement.
ED 048381-384.

Fitzgerald, D., & Ausubel, D.P. (1963) Cognitive versus affective factors in the learning and retention of controversial material. *Journal of Educational Psychology*, **54**, 73–84.

Flanders, N.A. (1965) Teacher influence, pupil attitudes, and achievement. *Cooperative Research Monograph* No. 12, Washington, D.C.: Government Printing Office.

Fleishman, E.A. (1966) Human abilities and the acquisition of skill. In E.A. Bilodeau (Ed.) *Acquisitions of Skill.* New York: Academic Press.

Fleishmann, E.A. (1972) On the relation between abilities, learning, and human performance. *American Psychologist*, **11**, 1017–1032.

Fleishmann, E.A. (1974) Toward a taxonomy of human performance. Paper presented to American Psychological Association.

Fleishman, E.A., & Hempel, W.E., Jr. (1954) Changes in factor structure of a complex psychomotor test as a function of practice. *Psychometrika*, **19**, 239–252.

Fletcher, J.D., & Atkinson, R.C. (1972) An evaluation of the Stanford CAI program in initial reading. *Journal of Educational Psychology*, **63**, 597–602.

Flynn, J.T. (1968) Contribution of a non-cognitive variable to geometry achievement using an auto-instructional procedure. *Journal of Educational Research*, **62**, 449–452.

Forlano, G., & Axelrod, H.C. (1937) The effect of repeated praise or blame on the performance of introverts and extroverts. *Journal of Educational Psychology*, **28**, 92–100.

Frandsen, A.N., & Holder, J.R. (1969) Spatial visualization in solving complex problems. *Journal of Psychology*, **73**, 229–233.

Frase, L.T. (1970a) Boundary conditions for mathemagenic behaviors. *Review of Educational Research*, **40**, 337–348.

Frederiksen, C.H. (1969) Abilities, transfer, and information retrieval in verbal learning. *Multivariate Behavioral Research Monographs*, No. 2.

Frederiksen, N. (1972) Toward a taxonomy of situations. *American Psychologist*, **27**, 114–123.

Frederiksen, N., & Evans, F.R. (1972) Effects of models of creative performance on ability to formulate hypotheses. *Research Bulletin* 72–54, Educational Testing Service.

Frederiksen, N., Jensen, O., & Beaton, A.E. (1972) *Rediction of organizational behavior.* Elmsford, N.Y.: Pergamon.

Fredrick, W.C. (1971) A comparison of verbal statement, symbolic notation, and figure representation of grammar concepts. *Research in the Teaching of English*, **5**, 46–59.

Fredrick, W.C., Blount, N.S., & Johnson, S.L. (1968) A comparison of verbal statement, symbolic notation and figural representation of grammar concepts. Unpublished report, Center for Cognitive Learning. University of Wisconsin. ED 029892.

Freedman, D.G. (1958) Constitutional and environmental interactions in rearing of four breeds of dogs. *Science*, **127**, 585–586.

Freibergs, V., & Tulving, E. (1961) The effect of practice on utilization of information from positive and negative instances in concept identification. *Canadian Journal of Psychology*, **15**, 101–106.

Fry, E.B. (1965) First grade reading instruction using a diacritical marking system, the initial teaching alphabet, and a basal reading system. Unpublished report, Rutgers University. Shorter version: *Reading Teacher*, 1967, **20**, 687–693. See also ED 013176 and 015846.

Fry, J.P. (1972) Interactive relationship between inquisitiveness and student control of instruction. *Journal of Educational Psychology*, **63**, 459–465.

Funkhouser, G.R., & Maccoby, N. (1970) Communicating science to non-scientists, Phase I: A correlational study of textual variables and audience effects. Unpublished report. Institute for Communication Research, Stanford University.

Furukawa, J.M. (1970) Chunking method of determining size of step in programmed instruction. *Journal of Educational Psychology*, **51**, 247–254.

Gagné, R.M. (1960) Ability differences in the learning of concepts governing directed numbers. In R. Feuerabend (Ed.), Research problems in mathematics education. *Cooperative Research Monographs*, No. 3, 112–113. Washington, D.C.: Government Printing Office.

Gagné, R.M. (Ed.) (1967) *Learning and individual differences.* Columbus, Ohio: Merrill.

Gagné, R.M. (1970) *The conditions of learning.* (2nd ed.) New York: Holt, Rinehart and Winston.

Gagné, R.M. (1974) Task analysis—its relation to content analysis. *Educational Psychologist*, 11, 11–18.

Gagné, R.M., & Gropper, G.L. (1965) Individual differences in learning from visual and verbal presentations. Unpublished report, American Institutes for Research, Pittsburgh, Pa. ED 010377.

Gagné, R.M., & Paradise, N.E. (1961) Abilities and learning sets in knowledge acquisition. *Psychological Monographs*, **75**, No. 14.

Gallagher, P.D. (1970) An investigation of instructional treatments and learner characteristics in a computer-managed instruction course. Unpublished report, CAI Center, Florida State University. ED 011269.

Gallegos, A.M. (1968) A study and comparison of experimenter pacing and student pacing of programmed instruction. *Journal of Educational Research*, **61**, 339–342.

Galton, F. (1869) *Hereditary Genius*. London: Macmillan.

Gardner, P.L. (1974) Pupil personality, teacher behavior and attitudes to a physics course. In P.L. Musgrave (Ed.). *Contemporary studies in the curriculum* Sydney: Angus and Robertson, 1974, pp. 173–199. Longer version: Attitudes to physics. Unpublished doctoral dissertation, Monash University, 1972. Shorter version: *British Journal of Educational Psychology*, 1974, **44**, 123–130.

Gaudry, E., & Spielberger, C.D. (1971) *Anxiety and educational achievement*. New York: Wiley.

Gavurin, E.I. (1967) Anagram solving and spatial aptitude. *Journal of Psychology*, **65**, 65–68.

Ghiselli, E.E. (1974) Some perspectives for industrial psychology, *American Psychologist*, **29**, 80–87.

Gibson, J.J. (Ed.) (1947) *Motion picture testing and research*. Washington, D.C.: Government Printing Office.

Glaser, R. (1972) Individuals and learning: The new aptitudes. *Educational Researcher*, **1**, 5–12.

Glaser, R., & Resnick, L. (1972) Instructional psychology. *Annual Review of Psychology*, **23**, 207–276.

Glass, G. (1970) Discussion In M.C. Wittrock & D.C. Wiley, (Eds.) *The evaluation of instruction*. New York: Holt, Rinehart, & Winston.

Goldberg, J.B. (1968) Influence of pupil attitudes on perception of teachers' behaviors and consequent school work. *Journal of Educational Psychology*, **59**, 1–5.

Goldberg, L.R. (1972) Student personality characteristics and optimal college learning conditions: An extensive search for trait-by-treatment interaction effects. *Instructional Science*, **1**, 153–210. ED 045049.

Goldberg, M.H., Dawson, R.I., & Barrett, R.S. (1964) Comparison of programmed and conventional instruction methods. *Journal of Applied Psychology*, **48**, 110–114.

Goldberg, M.L., Passow, A.H., & Justman, J. (1966) *The effects of ability grouping*. New York: Teachers College Press.

Goldberger, A.S., & Duncan, O.D. (Eds.) (1973) *Structural equation models in the social sciences*. New York: Seminar Press.

Goldman, R.D. (1972) Effects of a logical versus a mnemonic strategy on performance in two undergraduate psychology classes. *Journal of Educational Psychology*, **63**, 347–352.

Grace, G.L. (1948) The relation of personality characteristics and response to verbal approach in a learning task. *Genetic Psychology Monographs*, **37**,73–103.

Green, D.R., & Riley, M.W. (1963) Interclass grouping for reading instruction in the middle grades. *Journal of Experimental Education*, **31**, 273–278.

Greeno, J.G., & Mayer, R.E. (1975) Structural and quantitative interaction among aptitudes and instructional treatments. *Journal of Educational Psychology*, in press.

Grieve, T.D., & Davis, J.K. (1971) The relationship of cognitive style and method of instruction to performance in ninth grade geography. *Journal of Educational Research*, **65**, 137–141.

Grimes, J.W. (1958) The interaction of certain pupil personality characteristics with methods of teaching reading in determining first-grade achievement. Unpublished doctoral dissertation, Harvard University.

Grimes, J.W., & Allinsmith, A.W. (1961) Compulsivity, anxiety, and school achievement. *Merrill-Palmer Quarterly*, **7**, 247–271.

Grippin, P.C. (1973) Field independence and reflection-impulsivity as mediators of performance on a programmed learning task with and without strong prompts. Paper presented to American Psychological Association. Longer version: UM 73-19, 674.

Gropper, G.L. (1965) Controlling student responses during visual presentations. Unpublished report, American Institutes for Research, Pittsburgh, Pa. ED 003212.

Gropper, G.L., & Lumsdaine, A.A. (1961) An experimental comparison of a conventional TV lesson with a programmed TV lesson requiring active student response. Unpublished report. American Institutes for Research, Pittsburgh, Pa. ED 003640.

Gross, A.L. (1973) Prediction in future samples studied in terms of the gain from selection. *Psychometrika*, **38**, 151–172.

Grote, C.N. (1960) A comparison of the relative effectiveness of direct-detailed and directed discovery methods of teaching selected principles of mechanics in the area of physics. Unpublished doctoral dissertation, University of Illinois. UM 61-00132.

Grover, B.L. (1966) Prediction of achievement in divergent and convergent learning situations. *Journal of Educational Research*, **59**, 402–405.

Guetzkow, H., Kelly, E.L., & McKeachie, W.J. (1954). An experimental comparison of recitation, discussion, and tutorial methods in college teaching. *Journal of Educational Psychology*, **45**, 193–209.

Guilford, J.P. (1967) *The nature of human intelligence*. New York: McGraw-Hill.

Guilford, J.P. (1972) Some misconceptions of factors. *Psychological Bulletin*, **77**, 392–396.

Guilford, J.P. (1974) Rotation problems in factor analysis. *Psychological Bulletin*, **81**, 498–501.

Guilford, J.P., & Hoepfner, R. (1971) *The analysis of intelligence*. New York: McGraw-Hill.

Gulliksen, H. (1968) Louis Leon Thurstone, experimental and mathematical psychologist. *American Psychologist*, **23**, 786–802.

Guttman, L. (1965) The structure of relations among intelligence tests. *Proceedings, 1964 Invitational Conference on Testing Problems*. Princeton, N.J.: Educational Testing Service.

Guttman, L. (1966) Order analysis of correlation matrices. In R.B. Cattell, (Ed.) *Handbook of multivariate experimental psychology*. Chicago: Rand McNally.

Hahn, H.T. (1965) A study of the relative effectiveness of three methods of teaching reading in grade one. Unpublished report, Oakland County Schools, Pontiac, Mich. ED 010644. Shorter version: *Reading Teacher*, 1966, **19**, 590–594. See also ED 022645 and *Reading Teacher*, 1967, **20**, 687–755.

Hancock, R.R. (1972) A study of the interaction between sex difference, structure-of-intellect factors and modes of teaching a mathematical relation. Unpublished doctoral dissertation, University of Illinois, Urbana. UM 73-17, 227.

Hansen, J.B. (1971) An investigation of cognitive abilities, state anxiety, and performance in a C.A.I. task under conditions of no feedback and learner control. Unpublished doctoral dissertation, University of Texas. UM 73-449.

Harlow, H.F. (1949) The formation of learning sets. *Psychological Review*, **56**, 51–56.

Härnqvist, K. (n.d.) Canonical analyses of mental test profiles. Unpublished report, University of Göteburg, Sweden.

Harris, C.W. (1967) On factors and factor scores. *Psychometrika,* **32**, 363–379.

Harris, M.L., & Harris, C.W. (1971) A factor analytic interpretation strategy. *Educational and Psychological Measurement,* **31**, 589–606.

Harter, S. (1965) Discrimination learning set in children as a function of IQ and MA. *Journal of Experimental Child Psychology,* **2**, 31–43.

Harter, S. (1967) Mental age, IQ, and motivational factors in the distribution discrimination learning set performance of normal and retarded children. *Journal of Experimental Child Psychology,* **5**, 123–141.

Hartill, R.W. (1936) Homogeneous grouping. Teachers College Contributions to Education, No. 690. New York: Teachers College, Columbia University.

Hartley, J. Linear and skip-branching programmes: A comparative study. *British Journal of Educational Psychology,* 1965, **35**, 320–329.

Hartley, R.N. (1968) An investigation of list types and cues to facilitate initial reading vocabulary acquisition. Unpublished report, Institute for Mathematical Studies in the Social Science, Stanford University.

Harvey, W.L. (1970) A study of the cognitive and affective outcomes of a collegiate science learning game. Unpublished report, CAI Center, Florida State University. ED 050552.

Hassinger, D.E. (1965) An experimental study of density ratio in programmed instruction. *Journal of Programmed Instruction,* **3**, No. 2, 1–8.

Hatano, G. (1972) Effects of cognitive motivation on epistemic observation. Paper presented to International Congress of Psychology.

Hayes, R.B., & Nemeth, J.S. (1965) An attempt to secure additional evidence concerning factors affecting learning to read. Unpublished report, Pennsylvania State Department of Public Instruction. ED 003360. See also ED 015846 and *Reading Teacher,* 1967, **20**, 694-697, 703.

Haynes, J.R. (1970) Hierarchical analysis of factors in cognition. *American Educational Research Journal,* **7**, 55–68.

Heckhausen, H. (1967) *The anatomy of achievement motivation.* New York: Academic Press.

Heckman, R.W. (1967) Aptitude-treatment interactions in learning from printed instruction: A correlational study. Unpublished doctoral dissertation, Purdue University. UM 67-10, 202.

Heil, L.M., Powell, M., & Feifer, I. (1960) Characteristics of teacher behavior related to the achievement of children in several elementary grades. Unpublished report, Brooklyn College. ED 002843.

Heilman, A.W. (1965) Effects of an intensive inservice program on teacher's classroom behavior and pupil reading achievement. Unpublished report, Pennsylvania State University, ED 003359.

Herman, W.L., Jr., Potterfield, J.E., Dayton, C.M., & Amershek, K.G. (1969) The relationship of teacher-centered activities and pupil-centered activities to pupil achievement and interest in 18 fifth-grade social studies classes. *American Educational Research Journal,* **6**, 227–239.

Hermann, G.D. (1971) Egrule vs. ruleg teaching methods: Grade, intelligence, and category of learning. *Journal of Experimental Education,* **39**, No. 3, 22–33.

Herron, J.D. (1966) Evaluation of the new curricula. *Journal of Research on Science Teaching,* **4**, 159–170.

Hershberger, W. (1964) Self-evaluation responding and typographical cueing. *Journal of Educational Psychology,* **55**, 288–296.

Hiller, J.H. (1972a) Relationship between learning from prose text and attitude measures; dogmatism, internal-external, intellectual achievement responsibility, and intellectual self-confidence. Unpublished report. Southern Illinois University.

Hiller, J.H. (1972b) Effectiveness of various strategies for studying lessons, as a function of text difficulty. Paper presented to American Psychological Association.

Hills, J.R. (1957) Factor-analyzed abilities and success in college mathematics. *Educational and Psychological Measurement*, **17**, 615–622.

Himmelweit, H.T. (1966) Social background, intelligence and school structure: An interaction analysis. In J.E. Meade and A.S. Parkes (Eds.) *Genetic and environmental factors in human ability*. London: Oliver & Boyd.

Hittle, D.R. (1969) Directed discovery, form of presentation, and laboratory schedule for nonscience students in the freshman chemistry laboratory. Unpublished doctoral dissertation, University of Indiana. UM 70-7990.

Hoepfner, R., & Guilford, J.P. (1965) Figural, symbolic, and semantic factors of creative potential in ninth-grade students. Report No. 35, Psychological Laboratory, University of Southern California.

Hoepfner, R., Guilford, J.P., & Bradley, P.A. (1970) Transformation of information in learning. *Journal of Educational Psychology*, **61**, 316–323.

Hoepfner, R., Guilford, J.P., & Merrifield, P.R. (1964) A factor analysis of the symbolic-evaluation abilities. Report No. 33, Psychological Laboratory, University of Southern California.

Hollen, T.T., Jr. (1970) Interaction of individual abilities with the presence and position of adjunct questions in learning from prose materials. Unpublished doctoral dissertation, University of Texas. UM 71-11, 554.

Hopkins, K.D., Oldridge, D.A., & Williamson, M.L. (1965) An empirical comparison of pupil achievement and other variables in graded and ungraded classes. *American Educational Research Journal*, **2**, 207–215.

Horn, J.L., & Knapp, J.R. (1973) On the subjective character of the empirical base of Guilford's structure-of-intellect model. *Psychological Bulletin*, **80**, 33–43.

Horn, T.D. (1966) A study of the effects of intensive oral-aural English language instruction, oral-aural Spanish language instruction and non-oral-aural instruction on reading readiness in grade one. Unpublished report, University of Texas. ED 010048. Shorter version: *Reading Teacher*, 1966, **20**, 38–42.

Horst, P.R. (1974) Generalized reduced rank prediction systems. *ORI Technical Report*, 14, No. 3. Eugene: Oregon Research Institute.

Hovland, C.I., Janis, I.L., & Kelley, H.H. (1963) *Communication and persuasion*. New Haven: Yale.

Howarth, E., & Eysenck, H.J. (1968) Extraversion, arousal, and paired-associate recall. *Journal of Experimental Research in Personality*, **3**, 114–116.

Hull, C.L. (1945) The place of innate individual and species differences in a natural-science theory of behavior. *Psychological Review*, **52**, 55–60.

Humphreys, L.G. (1968) The fleeting nature of the prediction of college academic success. *Journal of Educational Psychology*, **59**, 375–380.

Hunt, D.E. (1971) *Matching models in education. The coordination of teaching methods with student characteristics*. Toronto, Canada: Ontario Institute for Studies in Education.

Hunt, D.E., & Hardt, R.H. (1967) The role of conceptual level and program structure in summer Upward Bound programs. Paper presented to the Eastern Psychological Association.

Hunt, D.E., Hardt, R.H., & Victor, J.B. (1968) Characterization of Upward Bound, 1968-1968. Unpublished report. Syracuse University. [No ED #]

Hunt, D.E., Joyce, B.R., Greenwood, J., Noy, J.E., & Weil, M. (1974) Student conceptual level and models of teaching: Theoretical and empirical coordination of two models, Paper presented to the American Educational Research Association.

Hunt, D.E., & Sullivan, E.V. *Between psychology and education.* Hinsdale, Ill.: Dryden, 1974.

Husband, R.W. (1947) Positive transfer as a factor in memory. *Proceedings of Iowa Academy of Sciences,* **54**, 235–238.

Hutchinson, W.L. (1963) Creative and productive thinking in the classroom. Unpublished doctoral dissertation, University of Utah. UM 63-6, 278.

Insel, P.M., & Moos, R.H. (1974) Psychological environments: Expanding the scope of human ecology. *American Psychologist,* 29, 179–188.

Isaacson, R.L. (1964) Relation between n Achievement, test anxiety and curricular choices. *Journal of Abnormal and Social Psychology,* 68, 447–452.

Jacobs, J.N., & Bollenbacher, J.K. (1959) An experimental study of the effectiveness of television versus classroom instruction in sixth-grade science in the Cincinnati Public Schools, 1956–1957. *Journal of Educational Research,* 52, 184–189.

Jacobs, J.N., Bollenbacher, J.K. & Keeffer, M. (1961) Teaching seventh-grade mathematics by television to homogeneously grouped below average students. *The Mathematics Teacher,* **54**, 551–555.

Jacobs, J.N., Yeager, H. & Tilford, E.J. (1966) An evaluation of programmed instruction for the teaching of facts and concepts. *Journal of Programmed Instruction,* 3, No. 4, 29–38.

Jacobs, P.I., Maier, M.H., & Stolurow, L.M. (1966) *A guide to evaluating self-instructional programs.* New York: Holt, Rinehart, & Winston. ED 033587.

Jacobs, P.I., & Vandeventer, M. (1971) The learning and transfer of double-classification skills: A replication and extension. *Journal of Experimental Child Psychology,* 12, 240–257.

Jacobs, P.I., & Vandeventer, M. (1972) Evaluating the teaching of intelligence. *Educational and Psychological Measurement,* 32, 235–248.

James, N.E. (1962) Personal preference for method as a factor in learning. *Journal of Educational Psychology,* 53, 43–47.

Jeffrey, W.E. & Samuels, S.J. (1967) Effects of method of reading training on initial learning and transfer. *Journal of Verbal Learning and Verbal Behavior,* **6**, 354–358.

Jensen, A.R. (1969) Can we boost intelligence and academic achievement? *Harvard Educational Review,* **39**, 1–123.

Jensen, A.R. (1971) Individual differences in visual and auditory memory. *Journal of Educational Psychology,* 62, 123–131.

Jensen, A.R. (1973) *Educability and group differences.* New York: Harper and Row.

Jensen, A.R., & Rohwer, W.D., Jr. (1965) Syntactical mediation of serial and paired-associate learning as a function of age. *Child Development,* **36**, 601–608.

Johnson, G.O. (1962) Special education for the mentally handicapped: A paradox. *Exceptional Children,* 29, 62–69.

Johnson, L.W. (1966) The effect of grouping by sex and reading method on reading achievement. Unpublished doctoral dissertation, Stanford University, UM 67-4, 307.

Johnson, M. & Posner, G. (1971) Testing the effect of verbal-quantitative aptitude discrepancy on the learning of deductive reasoning through programmed instruction. Unpublished report. Research Foundation, State of New York. ED 052633.

Johnson, N. & Kotz, S. (1970) *Continuous univariate distributions,* Vol. 2. Boston: Houghton-Mifflin.

Judd, W.A., Bunderson, C.V., & Bessent, E.W. (1970) An investigation of the effects of learner control in computer-assisted instruction prerequisite mathematics. Unpublished report, Computer-assisted instruction laboratory, University of Texas. ED 053 532.

Kagan, J., Moss, H.A., & Sigel, I.E. (1963) Psychological significance of styles of conceptualization. *Monographs of the Society for Research in Child Development*, **28**, 73-112.

Kapel, David E. (1965) An analysis of the effectiveness of two modes . . . in programmed instruction. *Journal of Programmed Instruction*, **3**, No. 2, 21-34.

Karabenick, S.A., & Youssef, Z.I. (1968) Performance as a function of achievement level and perceived difficulty. *Journal of Personality and Social Psychology*, **10**, 414-419.

Karraker, R.J. (1967) Knowledge of results and incorrect recall of plausible multiple choice alternatives. *Journal of Educational Psychology*, **58**, 11-14.

Katahn, M., & Lyda, L.L. (1966) Anxiety and the learning of responses varying in initial rank in the response hierarchy. *Journal of Personality*, **34**, 287-299.

Katz, Phyllis A. (1967) Acquisition and retention of discrimination learning sets in lower-class preschool children. *Journal of Educational Psychology*, **58**, 253-258.

Keislar, E.R., & Stern, C. (1970) Differentiated instruction in problem solving for children of different mental ability levels. *Journal of Educational Psychology*, **61**, 445-450.

Kelley, M.L., & Chen, M.K. (1967) An experimental study of formal reading instruction at the kindergarten level. *Journal of Educational Research*, **60**, 224-229. ED 022533.

Kendrick, W.M. (1966) A comparative study of two first grade language arts programs. Unpublished report, Department of Education, San Diego County, Calif. ED 010032. Shorter version: *Reading Teacher*, 1966, **19**, 590-594. See also ED 013253 and *Reading Teacher*, 1967, **20**, 687-755.

Keppel, G.P. (1965) Problems of method in the study of short-term memory. *Psychological Bulletin*, **63**, 1-13.

Ketcham, C.H., & Heath, R.W. (1963) The effectiveness of an educational film without direct visual presentation of content. *AV Communication Review*, **11**, 114-123.

Kierstead, R. (1963) A comparison and evaluation of two methods of organization for the teaching of reading. *Journal of Educational Research*, **56**, 317-321.

King, F.J., Kropp, R.P., O'Donnell, R.C., Ojala, W.T., & Vitale, M.R. (1969) Effectiveness of two ways of teaching grammar to students of different ability patterns. Unpublished report, Florida State University. ED 041896.

King, F.J., Roberts, D., & Kropp, R.P. (1969) Relationship between ability measures and achievement under four methods of teaching elementary set concepts. *Journal of Educational Psychology*, **60**, 244-247.

Kipnis, D., & Resnick, J.H. (1969) Experimental prevention of underachievement among intelligent impulsive college students. Unpublished report, Temple University.

Klauer, K.J. (1969) Schülerselektion durch Lehrmethoden? *Zeitschrift für Erziehung Swissenschaftlichen Forschung*, **3**, 86-97.

Klein, S.P., Frederiksen, N., & Evans, F.R. (1969) Anxiety and learning to formulate hypotheses. *Journal of Educational Psychology*, **60**, 465-475.

Knight, M.A.G. (1964) The Autotutor and classroom instruction. Three comparative studies. 2. The Royal Air Force Study. *Programmed Instruction*, **1**, 89-96.

Koenig, K., & McKeachie, W.J. (1959) Personality and independent study. *Journal of Educational Psychology*, **50**, 132-134.

Koran, J.J., Jr., & Koran, M.L. (n.d.) Differential response to structure of advance organizers in science instruction. Unpublished report, University of Florida.

Koran, M.L. (1969) The effect of individual differences on observational learning in the acquisition of a teaching skill. Unpublished doctoral dissertation, Stanford University. UM 69-17, 435. Shorter version: *Journal of Educational Psychology*, **62**, 219-228.

Koran, M.L. (1971) Differential response to inductive and deductive instructional procedures. *Journal of Educational Psychology*, **62**, 300-307.

Koran, M.L., & Koran, J.J., Jr. (1972) Differential response to question pacing in learning from prose. Paper presented to American Educational Research Association. ED 062096.

Kotovsky, K., & Simon, H.A. (1973) Empirical tests of a theory of human acquisition of concepts for sequential patterns. *Cognitive Psychology*, **4**, 399-424.

Kress, G.C., Jr., & Gropper, G.L. (1966) A comparison of two strategies for individualizing fixed-paced programmed instruction. *American Educational Research Journal*, **3**, 273-280.

Kropp, R.P., Nelson, W.H., & King, F.J. (1967) Identification and definition of subject-matter content variables related to human aptitudes. Unpublished report, Florida State University. ED 010627, 010628.

Krumboltz, J.D. (Ed.), *Learning and the educational process.* Chicago: Rand McNally.

Kruskal, J.B. (1964) Multidimensional scaling by optimizing goodness of fit to a nonmetric hypothesis. *Psychometrika*, **29**, 1-27.

Kuhlman, C.K. (1960) Visual imagery in children. Unpublished doctoral dissertation, Radcliffe College. (See also Hollenberg, C.K. Functions of visual imagery in the learning and concept formation of children, *Child Development*, 1970, **41**, 1003-1015.)

Kulm, G., Lewis, J., Omara, I., & Cook, H. (1974) The effectiveness of textbook, student-generated, and pictorial versions of presenting mathematical problems in ninth-grade algebra. *Journal for Research in Mathematics Education*, **5**, 28-35.

Lambert, P., Miller, D.M., & Wiley, D.E. (1962). Experimental folklore and experimentation: The study of programmed learning in the Wauwatosa Public Schools. *Journal of Educational Research*, **55**, 485-494.

Larkin, T.C., & Leith, G.O.M. (1964) The effects of linear and branched methods of programmed instruction on learning and retention of a topic in elementary science. *Programmed Learning*, **1**, 12-16.

Lee, L.C., Kagan, J., & Rabson, A. (1963) Influence of a preference for analytic categorization upon concept acquisition. *Child Development*, **34**, 433-442.

Leherissey, B.L., O'Neil, H.F., Jr., & Hansen, D.H. (1971) Effect of anxiety, response mode, and subject matter familiarity in computer assisted learning. Unpublished report, CAI Center, Florida State University. ED 053574, 060650. Shorter version: *Journal of Educational Psychology*, 1973, **64**, 310-324.

Leherissey, B.L., O'Neil, H.F., Jr., & Hansen, D.N. (1971b) Effects of memory support on state anxiety and performance in computer-assisted learning. ED 042206. Shorter version: *Journal of Educational Psychology*, 1972, **62**, 413-420.

Leith, G.O.M. (1969) Learning and personality. In W.R. Dunn, & C. Holroyd, (Eds.) *Aspects of Educational Technology. II.* London: Methuen.

Leith, G.O.M. (1973) The effects of extroversion and methods of programmed instruction on achievement. *Educational Research,* **15**, 150–153.

Leith, G.O.M., & Bosett, R. (1967) Mode of learning and personality. Unpublished report, School of Education, University of Birmingham, England. Shorter version in Leith, 1969.

Leith, G.O.M., & Davies, D.F. (1966) Interference and facilitation in a programmed learning task. *Programmed Learning,* **3**, 154–162.

Leith, G.O.M., & Davis, T.N. (1969) The influence of social reinforcement on achievement. *Educational Research,* **11**, 132–137.

Leith, G.O.M., & Eastment, D.E. (1970) A study of prompting versus confirmation in machine and text presented programmed learning under two conditions of responding. *Programmed Learning,* **7**, 13–20.

Leith, G.O.M., & McHugh, G.A.R. (1966) The place of theory in learning consecutive conceptual tasks. *Education Review,* **19**, 110–117.

Leith, G.O.M., & Trown, E.A. (1970) The influence of personality and task conditions on learning and transfer. *Programmed Learning and Educational Technology,* **7**, 181–188.

Leith, G.O.M., & Wisdom, B. (1970) An investigation of the effects of error making and personality on learning. *Programmed Learning and Educational Technology,* **7**, 120–126.

Levin, G.R., & Baker, B.C. (1963) Item scrambling in a self-instructional program. *Journal of Educational Psychology,* **54**, 138–143.

Levin, J.R. (1972) Comprehending what we read: An outsider looks in *Journal of Reading Behavior,* **4**, No. 4, 18–28.

Levin, J.R., Horvitz, J.W., & Kaplan, S.A. (1971) Verbal facilitation of paired-associate learning: A limited generalization. *Journal of Educational Psychology,* **62**, 439–444.

Lewis, D.G., & Gregson, A. (1965) The effects of frame size and intelligence on learning from a linear program. *Programmed Learning,* **2**, 170–175.

Li, J.C.R. (1964) *Statistical inference.* Vol. 2. *The multiple regression and its ramifications.* Ann Arbor: Edwards.

Lindahl, L.G. (1945) Movement analysis as an industrial training method. *Journal of Applied Psychology,* **29**, 420–446.

Linn, R.L., & Werts, C.E. (1973) Errors of inference due to errors of measurement. *Educational and Psychological Measurement,* **33**, 531–543.

Little, J.K. (1934) Results of use of machines for testing and for drill upon learning in educational psychology. *Journal of Experimental Education,* **3**, 45–59.

Lo, M.-Y. (1973) Statistical analysis of interaction and its application to data from the Cooperative Research Program in primary reading instruction. Unpublished doctoral dissertation, State University of New York at Buffalo. UM 73-29, 111.

Lord, F.M. (1956) The measurement of growth. *Educational and Psychological Measurement,* **16**, 421–437.

Lord, F.M. (1958) Further problems in the measurement of growth. *Educational and Psychological Measurement,* **18**, 437–454.

Lord, F.M. (1963) Elementary models for measuring change. In C.W. Harris (Ed.) *Problems in measuring change.* Madison: University of Wisconsin Press.

Lord, F.M. (1974) Significance test for a partial correlation corrected for attenuation. *Educational and Psychological Measurement,* 34, 211–220.

Lott, A.J., & Lott, B.E. (1969) Group cohesiveness and individual learning. *Journal of Educational Psychology,* **60**, 75–78.

Love, W.D., & Tucker, L.R. (1970) A three-mode factor analysis of serial learning, Unpublished report, University of Illinois, Urbana.

Lublin, S.C. (1965) Reinforcement schedules, scholastic aptitude, autonomy, need, and achievement in a programmed course. *Journal of Educational Psychology*, **56**, 295–302.

Lucow, W.H. (1954) Estimating components of variation in an experimental study of learning. *Journal of Experimental Education*, **22**, 265–271.

Lucow, W. (1964) An experiment with the Cuisenaire method in grade three. *American Educational Research Journal*, **1**, 159–167.

Maccoby, E.E., & Jacklin, C.N. *The psychology of sex differences.* Stanford: Stanford University Press.

Macdonald, J.B., Harris, T.L., & Rarick, G.L. (1966) An experimental study of the group versus the one-to-one instructional relationship in first grade basal reading programs. Unpublished report, University of Wisconsin. ED 010330, Shorter version: *Reading Teacher*, 1966, 19, 643–646, 652.

Magnusson, D. (1969) An analysis of situational dimensions. Reports from the Psychological Laboratories, the University of Stockholm, No. 279.

Maier, M.H., & Jacobs, P.I. (1964) Programmed learning—some recommendations and results. *Bulletin of the National Association of Secondary School Principals*, **48**, 242–255.

Maier, M.H. & Jacobs, P.I. (1966) The effects of variations in a self-instructional program on instructional outcomes. *Psychological Reports*, **18**, 539–546.

Majasan, J.K. (1972) College students' achievement as a function of the congruence between their beliefs and their instructor's beliefs. Unpublished doctoral dissertation, Stanford University. UM 73-4548.

Majer, K.S. (1969) A study of computer assisted multi-media instruction augmented by recitation sessions. Unpublished doctoral dissertation, Florida State University. UM 70-3825. Shorter version: *AV Communication Review*, 1970, 18, 169–179.

Manley, M.B. (1965) A factor analytic study of three types of concept attainment tasks. *Research Bulletin* 65-31, Educational Testing Service UM 66-7, 171.

Mann, R.D., *et al*. (1970) *The college classroom: Conflict, change, and learning.* New York: Wiley.

Manning, J.C. (1966) Evaluation of levels-designed visual-auditory and related writing methods of reading instruction in grade one. Unpublished report, University of Minnesota. ED 010030.

Marantz, S., & Dowaliby, F.J. (1973a) Film versus lecture methods of instruction as related to imageability. Paper presented to American Educational Research Association.

Marantz, S., & Dowaliby, F.J. (1973b) Individual differences in learning from pictorial and verbal instruction. Unpublished report, University of Massachusetts.

Marita, M. (1965) A comparative study of beginning reading achievement under three classroom organizational patterns: Modified individualized, three-to-five groups, and whole-class, language-experience. Unpublished report, Marquette University. ED 003477. Shorter version: *Reading Teacher*, 1966, 20, 12–17.

Markle, N.H. (1970) Differential response to instruction designed to call upon spatial and verbal aptitudes. Unpublished doctoral dissertation, Stanford University. UM 70-18, 443.

Marr, J.N., Plath, D.W., Wakeley, J.H. & Wilkins, D.M. (1960) The contribution of the lecture to college teaching. *Journal of Educational Psychology*, **51**, 277–284.

Marshall, H.H. (1969) Learning as a function of task interest, reinforcement, and social class variables. *Journal of Educational Psychology*, **60**, 133–139.

Mayer, R.E. (1974) Acquisition processes and resilience under varying testing conditions for structurally different problem-solving processes. *Journal of Educational Psychology*, **66**, 644–656.

Mayer, R., & Greeno, J.G. (1972) Structural differences between learning outcomes produced by different instructional methods. *Journal of Educational Psychology*, **63**, 165–173.

Maynard, F.J., & Strickland, J.F., Jr. (1969) A comparison of three methods of teaching selected mathematical content in eighth and ninth grade general mathematics courses. Unpublished report, University of Georgia, Athens, Georgia. ED 041763.

Mazurkiewicz, A.J. (1965) First grade reading using modified co-basal versus the initial teaching alphabet. Unpublished report, Lehigh University. ED 003361.

McConnell, T.R. (1934) Discovery vs. authoritative identification in the learning of children. *University of Iowar Studies in Education*, **9**, No. 5, pp. 3–62.

McGeogh, J.A., & Irion, A.L. (1952) *The psychology of human learning*. Toronto: Longmans Green.

McGuire, W.J. (1968) Personality and susceptibility to social influence. In E.F. Borgatta & W.W. Lambert (Eds.), *Handbook of personality theory and research*. Chicago: Rand McNally.

McKeachie, W.J. (1958) Students, groups, and teaching methods. *American Psychologist*, **13**, 580–584.

McKeachie, W.J. (1961) Motivation, teaching methods, and college learning. In M.R. Jones (Ed.), *Nebraska symposium on motivation*, Lincoln: University of Nebraska.

McKeachie, W.J. (1963) Research on teaching at the college and university level. In N.L. Gage (Ed.) *Handbook of research on teaching*. Chicago: Rand McNally.

McKeachie, W.J. (1969) Interaction of achievement cues and facilitating anxiety in the achievement of women. *Journal of Applied Psychology*, **53**, 147–148.

McKeachie, W.J., Isaacson, R.L., & Milholland, J.E. (1964) Research on the characteristics of effective college teaching. Unpublished report, University of Michigan. ED 002948.

McKeachie, W.J., Isaacson, R.L., Milholland, J.E., & Lin, Y.-G. (1968a) Student achievement motives, achievement cues, and academic achievement. *Journal of Consulting and Clinical Psychology*, **32**, 26–29. Also in McKeachie *et al.*, 1964.

McKeachie, W.J., and Lin, Y.G. (1966) Achievement standards, debilitating anxiety, intelligence and college achievement. *Psychological Record*, **19**, 457–459.

McKeachie, W.J., & Lin, Y.G. (1971) Sex differences in student response to college teachers: Teacher warmth and teacher sex. *American Educational Research Journal*, **8**, 221–226.

McKeachie, W.J., Lin, Y.-G., Milholland, J.E., & Isaacson, R.L. (1966) Student affiliation motives, teacher warmth, and academic achievement. *Journal of Personality and Social Psychology*, **4**, 457–461. Also in McKeachie, Milholland, *et al.*, 1968.

McKeachie, W.J., Milholland, J.E., Mann, R. & Isaacson, R.L. (1968) Research on the characteristics of effective teaching. Unpublished report, University of Michigan, ED 024347.

McLachlan, J.F.C. (1969) Individual differences and teaching methods in student interpretation of modern art. Unpublished master's thesis, University of Toronto. Shorter version: Differential effects of discovery learning as a function of conceptual level. *Canadian Journal of Behavioral Science*, 1973, **5**, 152–160.

McLaughlin, R.J., & Eysenck, H.J. (1967) Extraversion, neuroticism and paired-associate learning. *Journal of Experimental Research in Personality*, 2, 128–132.

McNeil, J.D. (1962) Programmed instruction as a research tool in reading: An annotated case. *Journal of Programmed Instruction*, 1, 37–42.

McNeil, J.D. (1964) Programmed instruction vs. usual classroom procedures in teaching boys to read. *American Educational Research Journal*, 1, 113–119.

McNeil, J.D., & Keislar, E.R. (1963) Value of the oral response in beginning reading: An experimental study using PI. *British Journal of Educational Psychology*, 33, 162–168.

McNemar, Q. (1958) On growth measurement. *Educational and Psychological Measurement*, 18, 47–55.

Means, R.S., & Means, G.H. (1971) Achievement as a function of the presence of prior information concerning aptitude. *Journal of Educational Psychology*, 62, 185–187.

Meddis, R., & Bowditch, E. (1966) Program validation and the use of matched controls. *Programmed Learning*, 3, 101–106.

Melton, A.W. (Ed.) (1964) *Categories of human learning.* New York: Academic Press.

Merrill, M.D., & Stolurow, L.M. (1966) Hierarchical preview vs. problem-oriented review in learning an imaginary science. *American Educational Research Journal*, 3, 251–261.

Merrill, P.F. (1970) Interaction of cognitive abilities with availability of behavioral objectives in learning a hierarchical task by computer-assisted instruction. Unpublished doctoral dissertation, University of Texas. ED 051668; UM 71-164. Shorter version: *Journal of Educational Psychology*, 1974, 66, 534–539.

Meyer, D.L. (1974) Statistical tests and surveys of power: A critique. *American Educational Research Journal*, 11, 179–188.

Meyers, J., & Dunham, J.L. (1971) Effects of anxiety on aptitude by treatment interactions in concept learning. Paper presented to American Educational Research Association.

Miller, J. (1964) An experimental comparison of two approaches to teaching multiplication of fractions. *Journal of Educational Research*, 57, 468–471.

Miller, R.B. (1962) Task description and analysis. In R.M. Gagné (Ed.) *Psychological principles in system development.* New York: Holt, Rinehart and Winston.

Mischel, W. (1973) Towards a cognitive social learning reconceptualization of personality. *Psychological Review*, 80, 252–283.

Moely, B.E., Olson, F.A., Halwes, T.G., & Flavell, J.H. (1969) Production deficiency in young children's clustered recall. *Developmental Psychology*, 1, 26–34.

Montgomery, M.E. (1973) The interaction of three levels of aptitude determined by a teach-test procedure with two treatments related to area. *Journal for Research in Mathematics Education*, 4, 271–178.

Moore, J.R. (1964) An experiment in programmed instruction: Voting in Iowa, ninth grade civics. Unpublished doctoral dissertation, State University of Iowa. UM 65-490.

Morgan, E.F., & Light, M. (1963) Statistical evaluation of two programs of reading instruction. *Journal of Educational Research*, 57, 99–101.

Morris, V.A., Blank, S.S., McKie, D., & Rankine, F.C. (1970) Motivation, step-size and selected learner variable in relation to performance with programmed instruction. *Programmed Learning and Educational Technology*, 7, 257–267.

Moss, J., Jr. (1964) The relative effectiveness of the direct-detailed and the directed discovery methods of teaching letterpress imposition. *Journal of Educational Research, 58*, 51–55.

Murphy, H.A. (1965) Reading achievement in relation to growth in perception of word elements in three types of beginning reading instruction. Unpublished report, Boston University. ED 003478.

Nagel, T.S. (1968) Effects on achievement and attitudes of two writing styles used with programmed material. Paper presented to American Educational Research Association.

Nelson, B.A., & Frayer, D.A. (1972) The effects of short- and long-term retention of presenting selected geometry concepts: a replication. Unpublished report, Research and Development Center for Cognitive Learning, University of Wisconsin. ED 065314.

Newman, A.P., & Lohnes, P.R. (1976) In W.W. Cooley & P.R. Lohnes (Eds.) *Evaluative inquiry in education.* New York: Irvington Press.

Niedermeyer, F., Brown, J., & Sulzen, B. (1969) Learning and varying sequences of ninth-grade mathematics materials. *Journal of Experimental Education, 37*, No. 3, 61–67.

NLSMA Reports. E.G. Begle, and others (Eds.) (1972 and earlier) 26 volumes. Stanford University: School Mathematics Study Group.

Novick, M.R., Jackson, P.H., Thayer, D.T., & Cole, N.S. (1972) Estimating multiple regressions in *m* groups: A cross-validation study. *British Journal of Mathematical and Statistical Psychology, 25*, 33–50.

Noy, J.E., & Hunt, D.E. (1972) Student-directed learning from biographical information systems. *Canadian Journal of Behavioral Science, 4*, 54–63.

Nuthall, G. (1968) An experimental comparison of alternative strategies for teaching concepts. *American Educational Research Journal, 5*, 561–584.

Oakan, R., Wiener, M., & Cromer, W. (1971) Identification, organization and comprehension for good and poor readers. *Journal of Educational Psychology, 62*, 71–78.

O'Connor, V.J. (1950) An examination of instructional films for characteristics of an effective teaching presentation. *Harvard Educational Review, 20*, 270–284.

Olander, H.T., & Robertson, H.C. (1973) The effectiveness of discovery and expository methods in the teaching of fourth-grade mathematics. *Journal for Research in Mathematics Education, 4*, 33–44.

Oliver, D.W., & Shaver, J.P. (1966) *Teaching public issues in high school.* Boston: Houghton Mifflin.

Olivier, W.P. (1971) Program sequence by ability interaction in learning a hierarchical task by computer assisted instruction. Unpublished report, University of Texas, Austin. ED 051670.

Olson, G.M., Miller, L.K., Hale, G.A., & Stevenson, H.W. (1968) Long-term correlates of children's learning and problem-solving behavior. *Journal of Educational Psychology, 59*, 227–232.

Oosthoek, H., & Ackers, G. (1973) The evaluation of an audio-tape mediated course. II. *British Journal of Educational Technology, 4*, 54–73.

Orton, K., McKay, E., & Rainey, D. (1964) The effect of method of instruction on retention and transfer for different levels of ability. *School Review, 72*, 451–461.

Osburn, H.G., & Melton, R.F. (1963) Prediction of proficiency in a modern and traditional course in beginning algebra. *Educational and Psychological Measurement, 23*, 277–288.

Ott, M.D., & Macklin, D.B. (1974) A trait-treatment interaction in a college physcis course. *Journal of Research in Science Teaching,* in press.

Owen, S.G., Hall, R., Anderson, J. & Smert, G.A. (1965) A comparison of programmed instruction and lectures in the teaching of electrocardiography.
Programmed Learning, **2**, 2-13.

Pace, C.R., & Stern, G.G. (1958) An approach to the measurement of psychological characteristics of college environments. *Journal of Educational Psychology*, **49**, 269-277.

Pagano, D.F. (1970) Effects of test anxiety on acquisition and retention of
material resembling the content of college courses. *Journal of Experimental
Research in Personality*, **4**, 213-22.

Paivio, A. (1971) *Imagery and verbal process.* New York: Holt, Rinehart &
Winston.

Pascal, C.E. (1971) Instructional options, option preference, and course outcomes. *Alberta Journal of Educational Research*, **17**, 1-11.

Pascal, C.E. (1973) Individual differences and preference for instructional
method. *Canadian Journal of Behavioural Science*, **5**, 272-279.

Pask, G., & Scott, B.C.E. (1972) Learning strategies and individual competence.
International Journal of Man-Machine Studies, **4**, 217-253.

Pask, G., & Scott, B.C.E (1973) CASTE: A system for exhibiting learning
strategies and regulating uncertainties. *International Journal of Man-
Machine Studies*, **5**, 17-52.

Payne, D.A., Krathwohl, D.R., & Gordon, J. (1967) The effect of sequence
in programmed instruction. *American Educational Research Journal*, **4**,
123-132.

Persons, S. (Ed.) (1950) *Evolutionary Thought in America.* New Haven: Yale
University Press.

Pervin, L.A. (1967) A twenty-college study of Student x College interaction
using TAPE (transactional analysis of personality and environment): Rationale, reliability, and validity. *Journal of Educational Psychology*, **58**, 290-302.

Pervin, L.A. (1968) Performance and satisfaction as a function of individual
environment fit. *Psychological Bulletin*, **69**, 56-68.

Peters, D.L. (1968) Piaget's conservation of number: The interaction of language
comprehension and analytic style with three methods of training. Unpublished doctoral dissertation, Stanford University. UM 69-8, 239. Shorter version:
Journal for Research in Mathematics Education, 1970, **1**, 76-87.

Peters, D.L. (1972) Effects of note taking and rate of presentation on short-term
objective test performance. *Journal of Educational Psychology*, **63**, 276-280.

Petersen, H., Guilford, J.P., Hoepfner, R., & Merrifield, P.R. (1963) Determination of 'structure-of-intellect' abilities involved in ninth-grade algebra and
general mathematics. Report No. 31, Psychological Laboratory, University
of Southern California. (Shorter version: *Educational and Psychological Measurement*, 1965, **25**, 659-682.) ED 003257.

Peterson, J.C., & Hancock, R.R. (1974) Developing mathematical materials for
aptitude-treatment interaction. Paper presented to the American Educational
Research Association.

Phillips, B.N., Martin, R.P., & Mayers, J. (1972) Interventions in relation to
anxiety in school. In C.D. Spielberger (Ed.), *Anxiety: Current trends in theory
and research.* New York: Academic Press. (For an extended version, see
ED 053401.)

Porter, A.C., & Chibucos, T.R. (1974) Selecting analysis strategy. In G. Borich
(Ed.) *Evaluating educational programs and products.* Englewood Cliffs, N.J.:
Educational Technology Press.

Porter, D.A. (1961) An application of reinforcement principles to classroom
teaching. Unpublished report, Laboratory for Research in Instruction,
Harvard University.

Potthoff, R.F. (1964) On the Johnson-Neyman technique and some extensions thereof. *Psychometrika,* **29**, 241–256.

Proger, B.B., Taylor, R.G., Jr., Mann, L., Coulson, J.M., & Bayuk, R.J. (1970) Conceptual pre-structuring for detailed verbal passages. *Journal of Educational Research,* **64**, 28–34.

Pyatt, J.A. (1969) Some effects of unit structure on achievement and transfer. *American Educational Research Journal,* **6**, 241–260. ED 017008.

Rathbone, C., & Harootunian, B. (1971) Teachers' information handling when grouped with students by conceptual level. Paper presented to American Educational Research Association.

Ray, H.W. (1972) Final report on the Office of Economic Opportunity experiment in educational performance contracting. Unpublished report, Battelle Laboratories, Columbus, O.

Ray, W.E. (1957) An experimental comparison of direct-detailed and directed discovery methods of teaching micrometer principles and skills. Unpublished doctoral dissertation, University of Illinois. UM 25270. Shorter version: *Journal of Experimental Education,* No. 3, 1961, **29**, 271–280.

Rector, R.E., & Henderson, K.B. (1970) The relative effectiveness of four strategies for teaching mathematical concepts. *Journal for Research in Mathematics Education,* **1**, 69–75.

Reed, H.B., Jr. (1959) Pupils' interest in science as a function of the teacher behavior variables of warmth, demand, and utilization of intrinsic motivation. Unpublished doctoral dissertation, Harvard University. (Shorter version: *Journal of Experimental Education,* 1961, **29**, No. 3, 205–229.)

Reed, J.E., & Hayman, J.L., Jr. (1962) An experiment involving use of *English 2600,* an automated instructional text. *Journal of Educational Research,* **55**, 476–484.

Reese, H.W. (1964) Discrimination learning set in children. In L. Lipsitt & C. Spiker (Eds.) *Advances in child development and behavior.* Vol. 1. New York: Academic Press,

Reid, H.C., & Beltramo, L. (1965) The effect of different approaches of initial instruction on the reading achievement of a selected group of first grade children. Unpublished report, Cedar Rapids (Ia.) Community School District, ED 003488. Shorter version: *Reading Teacher,* 1966, **19**, 601–605.

Rennels, M.R. (1970) The effects of instructional methodology in art education upon achievement on spatial tasks by disadvantaged Negro youths. *Journal of Negro Education,* **39**, 116–123.

Richardson, E.L. (1972) Statement. Education subcommittee, Committee on Labor and Public Welfare, U.S. Senate. March 24, 1972.

Rim, Y. (1965) Extraversion, neuroticism and the effect of praise or blame. *British Hournal of Educational Psychology,* **35**, 381–384.

Ripple, R.E., Millman, J., & Glock, M.D. (1969) Learner characteristics and instructional mode: A search for disordinal interactions. *Journal of Educational Psychology,* **60**, 113–120. Longer version: ED 016380.

Rist, R.C. (1970) Student social class and teacher expectation. *Harvard Educational Review,* **40**, 411–451.

Rizzuto, M. (1970) Experimental comparison of inductive and deductive methods of teaching concepts of language structure. *Journal of Educational Research,* **63**, 269–273.

Robinson, H.M. (1972) Visual and auditory modalities related to methods for beginning reading. *Reading Research Quarterly,* **8**, 7–39.

Rock, D.A., Baird, L.L., & Linn, R.L. (1971) Interaction between college effects and students' aptitudes. *American Educational Research Journal,* **9**, 149–161. ED 053163.

Rock, D.A., Centra, J.A., & Linn, R.L. (1970) Relationships between college characteristics and student achievement. *American Educational Research Journal*, 7, 109-121.

Roebuck, M. (1970) A definite conclusion in a comparison between conventional and programmed instruction. *Programmed Learning and Educational Technology*, 7, 21-23.

Roff, M.E. (1941) A statistical study of the development of intelligence test performance. *Journal of Psychology*, 11, 371-386.

Rogers, R.L., & Quartermain, D. (1964) Effects of item sequence, step size and intelligence on a teaching machine program. *Perceptual and motor skills*, 19, 946.

Rohwer, W.D., Jr. (1971) Learning, race, and school success. *Review of Educational Research*, 41, 191-210.

Rohwer, W.D., Jr., & Matz, R.D. (n.d.) Improving aural comprehension in white and in black children: Pictures versus print. Unpublished report. University of California, Berkeley.

Romine, B.H., Davis, J.A., & Gehman, W.S. (1970) The interaction of learning, personality traits, ability, and environment: A preliminary study. *Educational and Psychological Measurement*, 30, 337-347.

Rosenshine, B. (1971) *Teaching behaviours and student achievement*. London: National Foundation for Educational Research in England and Wales.

Rothkopf, E.Z. (1970) The concept of mathemagenic activities. *Review of Educational Research*, 40, 325-336.

Rothkopf, E.Z. (1972) Variable adjunct question schedules, interpersonal interaction, and incidental learning from written material. *Journal of Educational Psychology*, 63, 87-92.

Rowlett, J.D. (1960) An experimental comparison of direct-detailed and directed discovery methods of presenting tape-recorded instruction. Unpublished doctoral dissertation, University of Illinois, ED 003183; UM 60-1684.

Ruddell, R.B. (1965) The effect of four programs of reading instruction with varying emphasis on the regularity of grapheme-phoneme correspondences and the relation of language structure to meaning on achievement in first grade reading. Unpublished report, University of California, Berkeley. ED 003820; see also ED 021701.

Ryan, F.L. (1968) Advance organizers and test anxiety in programmed social studies instruction. *California Journal of Educational Research*, 19, 67-76.

Ryan, J.J. (1968) Effects of modern and conventional mathematics curricula on pupil attitudes, interests, and perception of proficiency. Unpublished report, Minnesota National Liboratory. ED 022673.

Sabaroff, R. (1963) A comparative investigation of two methods of teaching phonics in a modern reading program: A pilot study. *Journal of Experimental Education*, 31, 249-256.

Sabers, D.L. (1967) A study of the predictive validity of the Iowa Algebra Aptitude Test for prognosis in ninth grade modern mathematics and traditional algebra. Unpublished doctoral dissertation, University of Iowa. UM 67-16, 832.

Salomon, G. (1968) Interaction of communication-medium and two procedures of training for subjective response uncertainty of teachers. Unpublished doctoral dissertation, Stanford University. UM 69-8, 258.

Salomon, G. (1972) Heuristic models for the generation of aptitude-treatment interaction hypotheses. *Review of Educational Research*, 42, 327-343.

Salomon, G. (1974) Internalization of filmic operations in relation to individual differences. *Journal of Educational Psychology*, 66, 499-511.

Salomon, G., Eglstein, S., Finkelstein, R., Finkelstein, I., Mintzberg, E., Malve, D., & Velner, L. (1972) Educational effects of "Sesame Street" on Israeli children. Unpublished report, School of Education, Hebrew University of Jerusalem, Israel.

Samuels, S.J. (1967) Attentional process in reading: The effect of pictures on the acquisition of reading responses. *Journal of Educational Psychology*, **58**, 337–342.

Samuels, [S.] J. (1971) Is a picture worth a thousand words? *Reading Newsreport*, **5**, 19–22.

Sanders, J.R. (1973) Retention effects of adjunct questions in written and aural discourse. *Journal of Educational Psychology*, **65**, 181–186.

Sarason, I.G. (1958) Effects on verbal learning on anxiety, reassurance, and meaningfulness of material. *Journal of Experimental Psychology*, **56**, 472–477.

Sarason, I.G. (1972) Experimental approaches to test anxiety: Attention and the uses of information. In C.D. Spielberger (Ed.) *Anxiety and behavior*, Vol. II. New York: Academic Press.

Scharf, E.S. (1961) A study of the effects of partial reinforcement on a behavior in a programmed learning situation. In R. Glaser & J.I. Taber (Eds.), *Investigations of the characteristics of programmed learning sequences*. Pittsburgh: University of Pittsburgh.

Schneyer, J.W., Schultz, C.B., & Cowen, S. (1966) Comparison of reading achievement of first-grade children taught by a linguistic approach and a basal reader approach. Unpublished report, University of Pennsylvania. ED 010051. See also ED 022661 and *Reading Teacher*, 1967, **20**, 704–710.

Schramm, W. Learning from instructional television. *Review of Educational Research*, 1962, **32**, 156–157.

Schultz, C.B., & Dangel, T.R. (1972) The effects of recitation on the retention of two personality types. *American Educational Research Journal*, **9**, 421–430. See also ED 055448.

Schurdak, J.J. (1967) An approach to the use of computers in the instructional process and an evaluation. *American Educational Research Journal*, **4**, 59–73. ED 013539.

Scott, J.A. (1970) The effects on short- and long-term retention and on transfer of two methods of presenting selected geometry concepts. Research and Development Center for Cognitive Learning, University of Wisconsin. ED 044314.

Sederberg, C. (1966) A comparison of mathematics teaching methods for average and below-average ninth grade pupils. *Journal of Educational Research*, **59**, 435–440.

Seibert, W.F., Reid, J.C., & Snow, R.E. (1967) Studies in cine-psychometry II: Continued factoring of audio and visual cognition and memory. Unpublished report, Audio Visual Center, Purdue University, ED 019877.

Seibert, W.F., & Snow, R.E. (1965) Studies in cine-psychometry I: preliminary factor analysis of visual cognition and memory. Unpublished report, Audio Visual Center, Purdue University.

Seidel, R.T., & Rotberg, T.E. (1966) Effects of written verbalization and timing of information on problem solving in programmed learning. *Journal of Educational Psychology*, **57**, 151–158.

Sells, S.B. (Ed.) (1963) *Stimulus determinants of behavior*. New York: Ronald Press.

Senter, R.J., Neiberg, A., Abama, J.S., & Morgan, R.L. (1964) An evaluation of branching and motivational phrases in a scrambled book. *Programmed Learning*, **1**, 124–133.

Shavelson, R.J., Berliner, D.C., Loeding, D., Porteus, A.W., & Stanton, G.C. (1974a) Adjunct questions, mathemagenics, and mathemathanics. Paper presented to American Psychological Association.

Shavelson, R.J., Berliner, D.C., Ravitch, M.M., & Loeding, D. (1974b) The effects of position and type of question on learning from prose material: Interaction of treatment with individual differences. *Journal of Educational Psychology*, **66**, 40–48.

Shaver, J.P., & Oliver, D.W. (1968) The effect of student characteristic-teaching method interactions on learning to think critically. Paper presented to the American Educational Research Association.

Shay, C.B. (1961) Relationship of intelligence to step size on a teaching machine program. *Journal of Educational Psychology*, **52**, 98–103.

Sheldon, W.D., & Lashinger, D.R. (1966) Effect of first grade instruction using basal readers, modified linguistic materials and linguistic readers. Unpublished report, Syracuse University. ED 010031.

Sheldon, W.D., Nichols, N.J., & Lashinger, D.R. (1967) Comparison of three methods of teaching reading in the second grade. Unpublished report, Syracuse University. ED 013713. See also ED 024524.

Shepart, R.N., Romney, A.K. & Nerlove, S.B. (Eds.) (1972) *Multidimensional scaling: Theory and applications in the behavioral sciences*. Vol. I. New York: Seminar Press.

Shoemaker, D.M. (1973) *Principles and procedures of multiple matrix sampling*. Cambridge, Mass.: Ballinger.

Showel, M. (1968) Development of two automated programs for teaching military justice to men of various aptitude levels. Unpublished report, Human Resources Research Office, George Washington University. ED 028314.

Shuell, T.J., & De Angelo, L. (1971) Learning ability, study time, and learning-to-learn. Paper presented to American Educational Research Association.

Shulman, L.S., & Keislar, E. (Eds.) (1966) *Learning by discovery*. Chicago: Rand-McNally. ED 015504.

Shulman, L.S., & Keislar, E.R. (Eds.) (1972) Application of a learning hierarchy to sequence an instructional program, and comparison of this program with reverse and random sequences. Unpublished report, Florida State University, Tallahassee: Department of Educational Research. ED 063807.

Shulman, L.S., Loupe, M.J., & Piper, R.M. (1968) *Studies of the inquiry process*. East Lansing: Michigan State University. ED 028157.

Siegel, L., & Siegel, L.C. (1965) Educational set: A determinant of acquisition. *Journal of Educational Psychology*, **56**, 1–12.

Silberman, H.F.; et al. (1962) Development and evaluation of self-instructional materials for underachieving and overachieving students. *Technical Memorandum 727*. System Development Corporation, Santa Monica, Calif.

Simon, B. (1970) Classification and streaming: A study of groupin in English schools, 1860–1960. In P. Nash (Ed.), *Education as history*. New York: Random House, 1970. Pp. 115–159.

Simon, H.A., & Kotovsky, K. (1963) Human acquisition of concepts for sequential patterns. *Psychological Review*, **70**, 534–546.

Sinclair, K.E. (1969) The influence of anxiety on several measures of classroom performance. *Australian Journal of Education*, **13**, 296–307.

Skanes, G.R., Sullivan, A.M., Rowe, E.J., & Shannon, E. (1974) Intelligence and transfer: Aptitude by treatment interactions. *Journal of Educational Psychology*, **66**, 563–568.

Skapski, M.K. (1961) Ungraded primary reading program: An objective evaluation. *Elementary School Journal*, **61**, 41–45.

Smith, D.E.P., Wood, R.L., Downer, J.W., & Raygor, A.L. (1956) Reading improvement as a function of student personality and teaching method. *Journal of Educational Psychology*, **47**, 47–59.

Smith, H.C. Team work in the college class. *Journal of Educational Psychology*, **46**, 274–286.

Smith, L.M. (1962) Programmed learning in elementary school: An experimental study of relationships between mental abilities and performance. Unpublished doctoral dissertation, University of Illinois. UM 63-3,337.

Smith, M.E., & Seibert, W.F. (1966) Prediction of effects with selected characteristics of linear programmed instruction. Unpublished report, Audio Visual Center, Purdue University, ED 014912.

Smith, N. (1962) The teaching of elementary statistics by the conventional classroom method versus the method of programmed instruction. *Journal of Educational Research*, **55**, 417–420.

Snow, R.E. (1963) The importance of selected audience and film characteristics as determiners of the effectiveness of instructional films. Unpublished report, Purdue University. Shorter version: *Journal of Educational Psychology*, 1965, **56**, 315–326.

Snow, R.E. (1970) Research on media and aptitudes. In G. Salomon & R. Snow (Eds.) Commentaries on research in instructional media: An examination of conceptual schemes. *Viewpoints. Bulletin of the School of Education, Indiana University*, **46** (5), 63–89.

Snow, R.E. (1974) Representative and quasi-representative designs for research on teaching. *Review of Educational Research*, **44**, 265–292.

Snow, R.E., & Salomon, G. (1968) Aptitudes and instructional media. *AV Communication Review*, **16**, 341–356. ED 023295.

Sobel, M.A. (1956) Concept learning in algebra. *The Mathematics Teacher*, **49**, 425–430. Longer version: UM 8835.

Spache, G.D., Andres, M.C., Curtis, H.A., Rowland, M.L., & Fields, M.H. (1966) A study of a longitudinal first grade reading readiness program. Unpublished report, Florida State Department of Education, Tallahassee. ED 003355. Shorter version: *Reading Teacher*, 1966, **19**, 580–584.

Spence, J.A., & Spence, K.W. (1966) The motivational components of manifest anxiety: Drive and drive stimuli. In C.D. Spielberger (Ed.), *Anxiety and behavior*. New York: Academic Press.

Spence, K.W. (1958) A theory of emotionally based drive (D) and its relation to performance in simple learning situations. *American Psychologist*, **13**, 131–141.

Spencer, D.U., & Moquin, L.D. (1965, 1966) Individualized reading versus a basal reader program at first grade level in rural communities. Unpublished report, Johnson State College, Vt. ED 003486 and 012686.

Spielberger, C.D. Conceptual and methodological issues in anxiety research. In C.D. Spielberger (Ed.), *Anxiety: Current Trends in Theory and Research*. New York: Academic Press, 1972.

Spielberger, C.D., O'Neil, H.F., & Hansen, D.N. (1972) Anxiety, drive theory, and computer-assisted learning. In Maher, B.A. (Ed.), *Progress in experimental personality research*, Vol. 6. New York: Academic Press, 1972.

Spielberger, C.D., & Smith, L.H. (1966) Anxiety (drive), stress, and serial-position effects in serial-verbal learning. *Journal of Experimental Psychology*, **72**, 589–595.

Stake, R.E. (1961) Learning parameters, aptitudes, and achievement. *Psychometric Monographs*, No. 9.

Stallings, J.A. (1970)Reading methods and sequencing abilities: An interaction study in beginning reading. Unpublished doctoral dissertation, Stanford University.

Stanes, D., & Gordon, A. (1973) Relationships between Conceptual Style Test and Children's Embedded Figure Test. *Journal of Personality*, **41**, 185-191.

Stauffer, R.G., & Hammond, W.D. (1965) Effectiveness of a language arts and basic reader approach to first grade reading instruction. Unpublished report, Delaware University, Newark. ED 003484. Shorter version: *Reading Teacher*, 1966, **20**, 18-24. See also ED 027163.

Stern, C., & Keislar, E.R. (1967) Acquisition of problem solving strategies by young children and its relation to mental age. *American Educational Research Journal*, **4**, 1-12.

Stern, G.G. (1969) *People in context.* New York: Wiley.

Stern, G.G., Stein, M., & Bloom, B.S. (1956) *Methods in personality assessment.* Glencoe, Ill.: Free Press.

Stevenson, H.W. (1971) *Children's Learning.* New York: Appleton-Century-Crofts.

Stevenson, H.W., Hale, G.A., Klein, R.E., & Miller, L.K. (1968) Interrelations and correlates in children's learning and problem solving. *Monographs of the Society for Research in Child Development,* **33**, No. 7.

Stewart, J.C. (1965) An experimental investigation of imagery. Unpublished doctoral dissertation, University of Toronto.

Sticht, T.G. (1971) Failure to increase learning using the time saved by the time compression of speech. *Journal of Educational Psychology,* **62**, 55-59.

Stolurow, L.M. (1964) Social impact of programmed instruction: Aptitudes and abilities revisited. In J.P. DeCecco, (Ed.) *Educational technology.* New York: Holt, Rinehart & Winston.

Stolurow, L.M. (1965) Psychological and educational factors in transfer of training. Unpublished report, Training Research Laboratory, University of Illinois, Urbana. ED 010526, 012821.

Stolurow, L.M. (1966) Programmed instruction and teaching machines. In P.H. Rossi & B.J. Biddle (Eds.) *The impact of new media on education.* Chicago: Aldine.

Stuck, D., & Manatt, R. (1970) A comparison of audio-tutorial and lecture methids if teaching. *Journal of Educational Research,* **63**, 414-418.

Stukat, K.-G. (1965) Construction and field testing of a grammar program. *Programmed Learning,* **2**, 14-30.

Sullivan, H.J., Okada, M., & Nidermeyer, F.C. (1971) Learning and transfer under two methods of word-attack instruction. *American Educational Research Journal,* **8**, 227-239.

Szabo, M. (1969) The relationship of intellective, personality, and biographical variables to success and its prediction in an independent study science course at the college level. Unpublished doctoral dissertation, Purdue University. (UM 70-8979) Briefer account: *Journal of Research in Science Teaching,* 1971, **8**, 225-229.

Szetala, W. (1973) The effects of text anxiety and success/failure on mathematics performance in Grade Eight. *Journal for Research in Mathematics Education,* **46**, 152-160.

Tagatz, G.E., Otto, W., Klausmeier, H.J., Goodwin, W.L., & Cook, D.M. (1968) Effects of three methods of instruction upon the handwriting performance of third and fourth graders. *American Educational Research Journal,* **5**, 81-90.

Tallmadge, G.K., & Shearer, J.W. (1969) Relationships among learning styles, instructional methods, and the nature of learning experiences. *Journal of Educational Psychology,* **60**, 223-230. Longer version: NAVTRADEVCEN 67-C-0114-1 and 67-C-0114-2.

Tallmadge, G.K., & Shearer, J.W. (1971) Interactive relationships among learner characteristics, types of learning, instructional methods, and subject matter variables. *Journal of Educational Psychology*, **62**, 31–38. Longer version: NAVTRADEVCEN 68-C-0271-1.

Tallmadge, G.K., Shearer, J.W., & Greenberg, A. (1968) Study of training equipment and individual differences: The effects of subject matter variances. Unpublished report, American Institutes for Research, Palo Alto, ED 034020.

Tanaka, M.N. (1968) Classification skills in first grade children: The effects of different instructional methods. Paper read to American Educational Research Association.

Tanner, R.T. (1968) Expository-deductive *vs.* discovery-inductive programming of physical science principles. Unpublished doctoral dissertation, Stanford University. UM 68-15, 102.

Tanyzer, J.J., & Alpert, H. (1965) Effectiveness of three different basal reading systems on first grade reading achievement. Unpublished report, Hofstra University. (ED 003485). Shorter version: *Reading Teacher*, 1966, **19**, 636–642.

Taylor, J.E., & Fox, W.L. (1967) Differential approaches to training. Unpublished report, Human Resources Research Office, Alexandria, Va. ED 019624.

Thelen, H.A. (1967) *Classroom grouping for teachability.* New York: Wiley.

Thiele, C.L. (1938) *The contribution of generalization to the learning of the addition facts.* Teachers College Contributions to Education, No. 763. New York: Teachers College, Columbia University.

Thistlethwaite, D.L., & Campbell, D.T. (1960) Regression-discontinuity analysis: An alternative to the ex post facto argument. *Journal of Educational Psychology*, **51**, 309–317.

Thomas, B. & Snider, B. (1969) The effects of instructional method upon the acquisition of inquiry skills. *Journal of Research in Science Teaching*, **6**, 377–386.

Thompson, G.G., & Hunnicutt, C.W. (1944) The effect of praise on the work achievement of "introverts" and "extroverts". *Journal of Educational Psychology*, **35**, 257–266.

Thorndike, R.L. (1966) Intellectual status and intellectual growth. *Journal of Educational Psychology*, **51**, 121–127.

Thorndike, R.L. (Ed.) (1971) *Educational measurement.* Washington, D.C.: American Council on Education.

Tobias, S. (1969) The effect of creativity, response mode, and subject matter familiarity on achievement from programmed instruction. *Journal of Educational Psychology*, **60**, 453–460.

Tobias, S. (1972) A history of an individualized instructional program of varying familiarity to college students. Unpublished report, CAI Center, Florida State University.

Tobias, S. (1972b) Preference for instructional method and achievement. Paper presented to Eastern Psychological Association.

Tobias, S. (1973) Sequence, familiarity, and attribute by treatment interactions in programmed instruction. *Journal of Educational Psychology*, **64**, 133–141. ED 052631.

Tobias, S., & Abramson, T. (1971) Interaction among anxiety, stress, response mode, and familiarity of subject matter on achievement from programmed instruction. *Journal of Educational Psychology*, **62**, 357–364. Longer version: ED 040603.

Tobias, S., & Williamson, J.H. (1968) Anxiety and response mode in programmed instruction. Paper presented to American Educational Research Association.

Todd, W.B., & Kessler, C.C. IV. (1971) Influence of response mode, sex, reading ability, and level of difficulty on four measures of recall of meaningful written material. *Journal of Educational Psychology*, **62**, 229–234.

Tomlinson, P.D., & Hunt, D.E. (1971) Differential effects of rule-example order as a function of learner Conceptual Level. *Canadian Journal of Behavioral Science*, **3**, 237–245.

Traub, R.E. (1964) The importance of problem heterogeneiety in programmed learning. *Research Bulletin* 64–26, Educational Testing Service. UM 65-2, 160. Shorter account: *Journal of Educational Psychology*, 1964, **57**, 54–60.

Travers, R.M.W. (Ed.) (1964) Research and theory related to audiovisual information transmission. Unpublished report, Bureau of Educational Research, University of Utah. ED 003625.

Trown, E.A. (1970) Some evidence on the interaction between teaching strategy and personality. *British Journal of Educational Psychology*, **40**, 209–211.

Tucker, L.R. (1958) An inter-battery method of factor analysis. *Psychometrika*, **23**, 111–136.

Tucker, L.R. (1971) Relation of factor score estimates to their use. *Psychometrika*, **36**, 427–436.

Tucker, L.R., Damarin, F., & Messick, S. (1966) A base-free measure of change. *Psychometrika*, **31**, 457–473.

Tuckman, B.W., & Orefice, D.S. (1973) Personality structure, instructional outcomes, and instructional preferences. *Interchange*, 4, 43–48.

Twedt, D. (1952) A multiple factor analysis of advertising readership. *Journal of Applied Psychology*, **36**, 207–215.

Twelker, P.A. (1967) Two types of teacher-learner interaction in learning by discovery. Unpublished report, Teaching Research, Monmouth, Oregon. ED 018117.

Underwood, B.J. Degree of learning and the measurement of forgetting. *Journal of Verbal Learning and Verbal Behavior*, 1964, **3**, 112–129.

Unwin, D. (1966) An 'organizational' explanation for certain retention and correlation factors in a comparison between two teaching methods. *Programmed Learning*, **3**, 35–39.

Valverde, H.H., & Morgan, R.L. (1970) Influence on student achievement of redundancy in self-instructional materials. *Programmed Learning and Educational Technology*, **7**, 194–199.

van de Riet, H. (1964) Effects of praise and reproof on paired-associate learning in educationally retarded children. *Journal of educational Psychology*, **55**, 139–143.

Vandermeer, A.W. (1950) Effect of film viewing practice on learning from instructional films. Unpublished report, Pennsylvania State University.

Vernon, P.E. (1969) *Intelligence and cultural environment*. London: Methuen.

Vilscek, E.C., & Cleland, D.L. (1964–1968) Comparison of the basal and the co-ordinated language experience approaches in first grade reading instruction. Unpublished report, University of Pittsburgh. ED 012687 and 022647. Shorter version: *Reading Teacher*, 1966, **20**, 31–37.

Waetjen, W., & Fisher, J. (1966) English achievement and separation by sex for instruction. *Psychology in the Schools*, **3**, 55–58.

Walberg, H.J. (1969) Class size and the social environment of learning. *Human Relations*, **22**, 465–475.

Walberg, H.J. (1970) A model for research on instruction. *School Review*, **78**, 185–200.

Walberg, H.J. (1971) Generalized regression models in educational research. *American Educational Research Journal*, **8**, 71–91.

Walberg, H.J. (1972) Social environment and individual learning: A test of the Bloom model. *Journal of Educational Psychology*, **63**, 69–73.

Walker, H.M., & Lev, J. (1953) *Statistical inference*. New York: Holt.

Wallen, N.E., & Wodtke, K.H. (1963) Realtionship between teacher characteristics and student behavior. Part I. Unpublished report, University of Utah. ED 001250.

Wallen, N.E., & Wodtke, K.H. (1964) Relationship between teacher characteristics and student behavior. Part II. Unpublished report. University of Utah. ED 001257.

Wallen, N.E. (1966) Relationship between teacher characteristics and student behavior. Part III. Unpublished report, University of Utah. ED 010390.

Wallis, D., & Wicks, R.P. (1964) The Autotutor and classroom instruction. Three comparative studies. 1. The Royal Navy Study. *Programmed Learning*, **1**, 31–47.

Ward, J.N. (1956) Group-study versus lecture-demonstration method in physical science instruction for general education college students. *Journal of Experimental Education*, **24**, 197–210.

Ward, L.F. (1883) *Dynamic Sociology*. New York: Appleton.

Ward, L.F. (1906) *Applied sociology*. New York: Macmillan.

Wasik, J.L. (1971) A comparison of cognitive performance of PSSC and non-PSSC physics students. *Journal of Research in Science Teaching*, **8**, 85–90.

Webb, L.F. (1971) Interaction effects between selected cognitive abilities and instructional treatment in algebra. Unpublished doctoral dissertation, University of Texas. UM 72-11, 432.

Weener, P., & Treng, O (1971) The effects of subjective organization instructions and verbal creativity on the recall of random and organized lists. In F.J. DiVesta *et al.*, Instructional strategies: Multivariable studies of psychological processes related to instruction. Annual report, Part II. Unpublished report. Pennsylvania State University. ED 055448.

Weiner, B. (1966) The role of success and failure in the learning of easy and complex tasks. *Journal of Personality and Social Psychology*, **3**, 339–344.

Weiss, R., Sales, S., & Bode, S. (1970) Student authoritarianism and teacher authoritarianism as factors in the determination of student performance and attitudes. *Journal of Experimental Education*, **38**, No. 4, 83–87.

Weitzman, R.A. (1963) A factor analytic method for investigating differences between groups of individual learning curves. *Psychometrika*, **28**, 69–80.

Welch, W., & Walberg, H.J. (1972) A national experiment in curriculum evaluation. *American Educational Research Journal*, **9**, 373–383.

Welch, W., Walberg, H.J., & Watson, F.G. Curriculum evaluation: Strategy, implementation, and results. Manuscript in preparation.

Whitehill, R., & Jipson, I. (1970) Differential reading program performance of extraverts and introverts. *Journal of Experimental Education*, **38**, No. 3, 93–96.

Williams, J.P. (1965) Effectiveness of constructed response and multiple-choice programming modes as a function of test mode. *Journal of Educational Psychology*, **45**, 111–117.

William, J.P. (1963) Comparison of several response modes in a review program. *Journal of Educational Psychology*, **54**, 253–260.

Williams, J.P., & Levy, E.I. (1964) Retention of introductory and review programs as a function of response mode. *American Educational Research Journal*, **1**, 211–218.

Wine, J. (1971) Test anxiety and direction of attention. *Psychological Bulletin*, **76**, 92–104.

Winer, B.W. (1971) *Experimental design.* (2d ed.) New York: McGraw-Hill.

Wispé, L.G. (1951) Evaluating section teaching methods in the introductory course. *Journal of Educational Research,* 45, 161–186.

Witkin, H.A. (1973) The role of cognitive style in academic performance and in teacher-student relations. Unpublished report, Educational Testing Service, Princeton, New Jersey.

Witkin, H.A., Dyk, R.B., Faterson, H.F., Goodenough, D.R., & Karp, S.A. (1962) *Psychological differentiation.* New York: Wiley.

Wittrock, M.C. (1963) Response mode in the programming of kinetic molecular-theory concepts. *Journal of Educational Psychology,* 54, 89–93.

Wodtke, K.H., Brown, B.R., Sands, H.R., & Fredericks, P. (1967) Scrambled versus ordered sequencing in computer-assisted instruction. Unpublished report, Pennsylvania State University, 1967. ED015678.

Woodrow, H. (1938a) The relation between abilities and improvement with practice. *Journal of Educational Psychology,* 29, 215–230.

Woodrow, H. (1938b) The effect of practice on test intercorrelations, *Journal of Educational Psychology,* 29, 561–572.

Woodrow, H. (1940) Interrelations of measures of learning. *Journal of Psychology,* 10, 49–73.

Woodrow, H. (1946) The ability to learn. *Psychological Review,* 53, 147–158.

Woodruff, A.B., & Shimabukuro, S. (1967) Studies of individual differences related to performance on programmed instruction. Unpublished report. Northern Illinois University, De Kalb. ED 006009.

Woodruff, A.B., Shimabukuro, S., & Frey, S.H. (1965) Methods of programmed instruction related to student characteristics. Unpublished report, Northern Illinois University, De Kalb. ED 0033 35.

Wunderlich, K.W., & Borich, G.D. (1973) Determining interactions and regions of significance for curvilinear regressions. *Educational and Psychological Measurement,*

Wyatt, N.M. (1965) Reading achievements of first grade boys versus first grade girls using two approaches: A linguistic approach and a basal reader approach with boys and girls grouped separately. Unpublished report, University of Kansas, Lawrence. ED 003358.

Yabroff, W.W. (1963) The comparative effects of inductive and deductive sequences in programmed instruction. Unpublished doctoral dissertation, Stanford University. UM 64-1, 662. Shorter version: *American Educational Research Journal,* 1965, 2, 223–235.

Yamamoto, K. (1963) Relationships between creative thinking abilities of teachers and achievement and adjustment of pupils. *Journal of Experimental Education,* 32, No. 1, 3–27.

Yando, R.M., & Kagan, J. (1968) The effect of teacher tempo on the child. *Child Development,* 39, 27–34.

Yeager, J.L., & Kissel, M.A. (1969) An investigation of the relationship between selected student entering characteristics and time required to achieve unit mastery. Unpublished report. Learning Research and Development Center, University of Pittsburgh. ED 031938.

Yelvington, J.A. (1968) An exploratory study of the effects of interaction between cognitive abilities and instructional treatments upon attitudes, achievement, and retention. Unpublished doctoral dissertation, Florida State University. UM 68-16, 393.

Subject Index

Author Index

$770414670